THE TAPESTRY
OF CULTURE

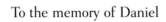

To the memory of Daniel

THE TAPESTRY OF CULTURE

An Introduction to Cultural Anthropology

Ninth Edition

**Abraham Rosman,
Paula G. Rubel, and Maxine Weisgrau**

ALTAMIRA
PRESS

A Division of

ROWMAN & LITTLEFIELD PUBLISHERS, INC.
Lanham-•-Boulder-•-New York-•-Toronto-•-Oxford

AltaMira Press
A division of Rowman & Littlefield Publishers, Inc.
A wholly owned subsidiary of The Rowman & Littlefield Publishing Group, Inc.
4501 Forbes Boulevard, Suite 200
Lanham, MD 20706
www.altamirapress.com

Estover Road
Plymouth PL6 7PY
United Kingdom

British Library Cataloguing in Publication Information Available

Library of Congress Cataloguing-in-Publication Data

Rosman, Abraham.
  The tapestry of culture : an introduction to cultural anthropology / Abraham Rosman, Paula G. Rubel, and Maxine Weisgrau. — 9th ed.
       p. cm.
  Includes bibliographical references.
  ISBN-13: 978-0-7591-1140-0 (cloth : alk. paper)
  ISBN-10: 0-7591-1140-5 (cloth : alk. paper)
  ISBN-13: 978-0-7591-1139-4 (pbk. : alk. paper)
  ISBN-10: 0-7591-1139-1 (pbk. : alk. paper)
  eISBN-13: 978-0-7591-1158-5
  eISBN-10: 0-7591-1158-8
  1. Ethnology. I. Rubel, Paula G. II. Weisgrau, Maxine K. III. Title.

GN316.R67 2009
306—dc22   2008045391

Printed in the United States of America

♾™ The paper used in this publication meets the minimum requirements of American National Standard for Information Sciences—Permanence of Paper for Printed Library Materials, ANSI/NISO Z39.48–1992.

Contents

Preface

THE STORY OF THE BOOK

The Tapestry of Culture had its genesis in teaching introductory anthropology courses at Barnard College, Columbia University, to several generations of undergraduate students of different ages. The first edition of *The Tapestry of Culture* was published almost thirty years ago. Since that time, the theoretical frameworks of anthropology have changed greatly, as have our theoretical perspectives; the successive editions of the book have reflected these changes.

In the past decade, the lives of people scattered over the world have undergone enormous changes. At this point in time, there is a necessity for Americans to understand that there are still parts of the world that are organized in very different ways than is our own country. Anthropology offers a way of understanding the nature of such societies and their values. At the same time American anthropology has also changed drastically, responding to scholarly and political influences as well as the changing generations. The influence of postmodernism has created a much more contested and fragmented anthropology than that of thirty years ago. It has generated new debates over theory and practice in anthropology. The content of *The Tapestry of Culture* explains these debates, as well as what is still generally accepted and agreed upon by most anthropologists.

HALLMARK FEATURES

The Tapestry of Culture adopts a distinctive approach to anthropology, which attempts to accommodate the history of anthropological thought as well as the various viewpoints in the field today. It examines contemporary cultural differences but also seeks to point out similarities that emerge as a result of comparative study. The approach emphasizes the interpretation of symbols and the meaning of things in everyday life. Using anthropological tools, the task of the book is to translate the concepts, ideas, and behavior of other cultures into a language recognizable to contemporary students. Today the trend is to see every ethnography as a description of a unique setting; however, beyond each society's uniqueness, the presence of cultural similarities is apparent and compelling. From its inception, anthropology has always been comparative, enabling generalizations to be made about human behavior. Formerly, anthropologists generalized about the nature of rules regarding residence and kinship terminology, but, at present, generalizations may deal, for example, with the nature of ethnic group behavior and the role religion plays in many instances of ethnic conflict.

Contemporary anthropologists pay particular attention to the nature of ethnographic texts, and most still consider ethnography based on field research the heart of the discipline. One of the best ways for students to be introduced to anthropology is by reading ethnographies so that they can feel the excitement of a first-rate fieldworker engaged in his or her work. Seeing the Trobriand Islands through Bronislaw Malinowski's eyes as he describes them in *Argonauts of the Western Pacific* conveys to students his feeling of being a castaway on a strange shore and his sense of adventure and discovery, in addition to informing them about Trobriand culture as it was at the turn of the twentieth century. However, students must be provided with the concepts and theories that anthropologists use in order to understand and appreciate such ethnographies and to comprehend the differences between a society like the Trobriands and our own.

The Tapestry of Culture provides a concise and up-to-date conceptual framework with which to understand not only classic ethnographies but also the ethnographies about complex societies being written today. In teaching introductory anthropology, we have used classic ethnographies of the early and mid-twentieth century as well as those describing aspects of industrialized societies, such as the multiethnic neighborhoods of urban settings. *The Tapestry of Culture* is organized so that it can be used with the particular ethnographies that suit the instructor's interests.

The title of our book refers to culture metaphorically as a tapestry, composed of many interconnected threads, in which the whole is more than the sum of its parts. Standing back from the tapestry, one no longer sees the individual threads, but an overall design. The anthropologist does not see "culture," the overall design of the tapestry, while doing fieldwork. Rather, he or she converses with individuals and observes their actions—this is the equivalent of the threads. From this, the anthropologist, collaborating with members of the culture, creates a picture of an aspect of that culture which he or she describes in ethnography. Therefore, culture is an analytical concept, an abstraction from reality. Like a tapestry, each culture has an overall design, even though we, as anthropologists, do take it apart, study the components (by employing categories such as kinship, economics, and religion), and then examine the interconnections between them. However, the fit between the parts in reality is always far from perfect and there are always disjunctions and contradictions. In today's globally connected world, the disjunctions and contradictions often dominate the picture of a particular culture, including our own.

Anthropology, as the study of humans and their ways of life, has the task of understanding the ways in which people bring about changes in their cultures, deal with these changes, and try to understand them. During the past century, the world changed more than it had in the previous 5,000 years. Ethnicity and ethnic identity are crucial issues in the world today. Nation-states and empires have fractured and reformulated. People of different ethnic groups who lived together in one state and even intermarried are now fiercely at war with one another. Technological advances in many fields have brought about great changes in industrial societies like our own. Outsourcing and remote technologies have made many earlier types of employment obsolete, but not everyone has access to the new century's employment skills or technologies. These changes in production require the rethinking of the economic organization of modern industrial societies. Technology has even overtaken and transformed aspects of human reproduction and ideas about the human body; we now require new ways of thinking about motherhood, fatherhood, and parenting. Ideas about gender and sexuality are being reformulated, with significant consequences for family organization.

The authors have all traveled a great deal in distant parts of the globe, providing a firsthand look at the momentous changes that are taking place. We have observed how Pushtuns respond to religious fundamentalism in the Swat region of Pakistan. We have watched the way in which many Mongolian families have returned to nomadic pastoralism as their nation detached itself from the former Soviet empire and its industrial collapse. We have seen how globalization affects market towns in Myanmar (formerly Burma) where tribal people still maintain their own identities vis-à-vis the majority Burmese. We have observed the expansion of the Indian economy as a consequence of outsourcing from America and expanding globalization. We have observed rural agriculturalists as they plant new crops that will be exported and sold in the United States, Europe, and Japan. And, we have observed community activism that challenges the social and political status quo in multiple settings around the world.

NEW TO THE NINTH EDITION

In this new edition, as is our usual practice, we have added a great deal of new material and made discussions and examples in every chapter more current, in accord with present-day thinking in the anthropological literature. Our new coauthor, Maxine Weisgrau, brings her field experience in northern India, as well as her background in teaching anthropology, development, and gender, to this edition of *Tapestry*. We highlight below the major changes to the text to be found in the ninth edition. Although some issues have been with us since the beginnings of the discipline, contemporary commentators and critics within and outside anthropology have compelled us to confront them anew.

Chapter 1, "Anthropological Perspectives," contains updated definitions of terms like culture, cultural rules and universals, social structure, and agency. There is an expanded discussion of the evolution of culture and the development of language using recent archeological and paleontological information. The current state of postmodernist theory, historical anthropology, neo-Marxism, and evolutionary psychology is discussed, as well as the effects of globalization as a subject of anthropological inquiry.

Chapter 2, "The Anthropological Method," includes an expanded discussion of the experiential and reflexive aspects of fieldwork. In addition, we consider the role of multisited fieldwork in the study of complex societies. This chapter also illustrates the uses of multiple sources in comparing and analyzing marriage rituals in two different times and places.

Chapter 3, "Language and Culture," discusses the evolution and structure of language. There is greater emphasis on the role language plays in power and policy decisions. Newer research on male and female speech in the workplace is explored. The current research on the global spread of English and world Englishes as a consequence of the development of a world market is explored.

Chapter 4, "Learning Language and Learning Culture," includes new theoretical ideas about how children learn language, such as when vowels and word order begin, and the role this plays in cognitive development. There is an expanded discussion of learning culture, specifically, how moral socialization of Chinese children contrasts with Quechua children, who learn within a permissive society. The construction of person and self in multiple situations is also examined.

Chapter 5, "Symbolic Meanings," explores the relationship between the Indian caste system and food symbolism. The symbolism of the human is examined through discussions about the way in which some societies prefer plumpness in women and other societies, such as our own, prefer women who are thin. There is also an expanded section on how body symbolism plays out in organ transplantation.

In Chapter 6, "Ties That Connect," we deal with the present-day role of kinship in Uzbekistan, Kazakstan, and Turkmenia, and how kinship dominates the politics of the Gulf States of Kuwait and Oman. We discuss the return of family and its significance in China today. A new subsection, "The Impact of Biological Technologies on Kinship," deals with the role reproductive technologies plays in kinship in the United States and the new issues families now confront. For example, are male medical students related to the many children born from their donated sperm? And if they are, what are their parental obligations? Do their biological offspring have the right to know their genetic parents? The growing importance of gay and lesbian families and the new forms of family being created are also investigated.

Chapter 7, "Gender and Age," includes an expanded discussion of masculine perspectives in gender studies and feminist anthropology. Sexualities and gay, lesbian, bisexual, and transgendered perspectives in theory and practice cross-culturally are discussed. There is also an exploration of the lives of transgendered Indian Hijras as described in ethnography. The politics of gender and aging in the contemporary United States are brought up to date.

Chapter 8, "The Economic Organization of Societies: Production, Distribution, and Consumption," includes several new sections in light of the enormous economic changes that have taken place on a global level. We consider how former hunter-gathers like the Australian Aborigines are beginning to receive financial benefits from companies who are exploiting their traditional knowledge. The issue of land rights and changes in the indigenous position on "ecotourism" are also discussed. The modern exploitation of reindeer pastoralism by Siberians is described. The phenomenon of the globalization of work, as exemplified by Indian call centers and the labor exploitation that occurs is examined. The transnational clothing market and the way in which this clothing is reconceptualized and recommodified is another example of globalization. Food is an another important expression of cultural values explored in this chapter. This is illustrated by the way in which the Yapese food repertoire pits local foods against pizza.

Maxine Weisgrau has a Ph.D. in anthropology from Columbia University. She has conducted field research in Rajasthan, India, since 1988, documenting local nongovernmental organizations and their interaction with rural communities. Her book *Interpreting Development: Local Histories, Local Strategies* (1997) explores multiple perspectives and often conflicting interpretations of development, and the impact of shifting strategies of local and global organizations. She is the coeditor (with Morton Klass) of *Across the Boundaries of Belief: Contemporary Issues in the Anthropology of Religion* (1999). She is also coeditor of (with Carol E. Henderson) and contributor to *Raj Rhapsodies: Tourism, Heritage and the Seduction of History* (2007), an interdisciplinary analysis of the impact of Rajasthan's colonial histories on contemporary tourism encounters. She is the author of the forthcoming *Experiencing Life and Death Before Birth: Anthropology and the Unborn*. She has taught anthropology, development, and women's studies courses at many colleges and universities, including Barnard College and Columbia University, and is currently Associate Adjunct Professor at Barnard College and Columbia University's School of International and Political Affairs (SIPA).

Maxine Weisgrau writing up field notes.

Chapter 1
Anthropological Perspectives

HUMANS POSSESS CULTURE that makes them significantly different from other members of the animal kingdom. Culture refers to the human behavior, symbols, beliefs, ideas, and the material objects humans make. It is also referred to as the "way of life" of a people. Though humans have culture, they are still primates and share 99 percent of their genes with other members of this biological order. Other animals have systems of communication such as calls, but no other animal has the equivalent of human language. The behavior of humans is governed by cultural rules, while all other animals have patterns of behavior that are determined by their genetic makeup. No other animal cooks its food and eats meals according to cultural rules the way humans do.

Some anthropologists argue that one must constantly consider man within this larger biological context since only then will we be able to understand how language and culture evolved in humans. What were the biological and ecological conditions that permitted or encouraged these evolutionary developments? In contrast, other theorists have argued that knowing the biological and evolutionary background of humans tells us nothing when we set out to study cultural behavior and languages. To them, the fact that humans are animals is simply irrelevant in the study of human cultural behavior. We intend to deal with this subject below.

What are the premises with which anthropologists today investigate the culture or way of life of a people, with all its variations and permutations? Each culture has an underlying logic of its own. For people from another culture, it is like looking through the looking glass at a world very different from one's own where people behave in strange ways. People's behavior makes sense once we understand the premises by which they live. The anthropologist's task has been to "translate" cultures and their premises to make them understandable to us, but also to categorize cultures in terms of the analytical concepts developed in anthropology that permit comparison to reveal cross-cultural differences and similarities.

The task of anthropology historically has been to focus on societies other than our own. Though people are becoming more aware of different cultures today, as a consequence of the spread of ideas through globalization, anthropology still has a mission to perform. It is to learn more about other cultures to permit better intercultural communication so we can better understand other peoples. For example, the term *tribal societies* is mentioned frequently by the media. What specifically does it mean? Its meaning has consequence for the foreign policy of the United States. Another consequence of learning more about other cultures is that we learn more about ourselves. The anthropologist's methods are different from those of other social scientists, and that difference influences the nature of the discipline—its concepts, procedures, and theories.

Anthropological investigation of a way of life other than one's own is like a trip into another universe where people behave in very different ways, and the rules may be turned on their heads. Anthropological research involves a journey—a journey in space, a journey through time, a psychological journey into an alien world. The anthropologist must abandon the prejudices of his or her own society and suspend its cultural rules, learn the way of life of the society he or she has entered, and then return to tell "its story." By doing this, the anthropologist seems to put himself or herself in the position of being the "authority" about that society. Some of the literate members of many societies that anthropologists have studied disagree. Some have called the gathering, analysis, and publication of information about the society that the anthropologist has studied an "appropriation" of their culture. Though, over the years, novelists and science fiction writers have been drawn to such journeys into different worlds, the anthropologist's journey is different. Fiction writers usually never leave home and merely imagine the far-off place about which they are writing. They have a variety of points of view, which are very personal. They may look at people from other cultures as "cruel savages" or as living in a kind of Eden that is close to nature.

Cultures were never separate bounded entities. From the beginning, human beings have always moved or traveled beyond the borders of the area they called home. This was the means by which *Homo sapiens* eventually peopled most of the earth. The characteristics of one culture have always spread from one culture to another. The process of globalization has brought American culture in the form of Pepsi-Cola and McDonald's menus to the most remote parts of the world, but a traveler to distant places is still impressed with the differences between cultures. Many Chinese people eat sea cucumbers and dogs. Roast dog is served in the restaurants of Guandong. Americans do not consider such creatures to be food. People in every culture think that what they eat is "the right stuff." Veiling is another cultural feature increasingly shared by many societies but not our own. In societies in the Middle East, women veil, but in Tuareg society, it is the men who veil.

The belief that one's own culture represents the best way to do things is known as **ethnocentrism**. Ethnocentrism emphasizes the pride a group has in its cultural accomplishments, its historical achievements, the supremacy of its religious beliefs, and the "god-given" virtues of its sexual and culinary practices. Ethnocentrism also includes the idea that other people's (often one's closest neighbors') beliefs, customs, and practices are like those of "animals." Ethnocentrism is at the root of ethnic conflict, and the **ethnonationalism** so prevalent in the world today.

Anthropology examines the world of cultural differences. It examines cultural practices within their own larger cultural contexts. **Cultural relativism** is the idea that each culture is unique and distinctive but that no one culture is superior. This is in sharp contrast to the ethno-

Among the Tuareg of the central Sahara it is the men who wear the veil.

centric point of view. Cultural relativism is also in opposition to the concept of cultural universals. Given cultural relativism, how does one deal with the question of morality, that is, good and evil? On the one hand, there are those who believe that killing another human being should be universally condemned. On the other hand, there are cultural relativists who argue that killing within ceremonial or ritual contexts like head-hunting and cannibalism in the past was a core feature of societies in which it occurred. For instance, the Marquesans were cannibals and took trophy heads, as described by Melville in *Typee*. A doctrine of **universal human rights**, which emphasizes the rights of the individual over those of the community, would condemn such killings. Those supporting universal human rights say community-supported genital mutilation and arranged marriages, which are found in many parts of the world, are violations of the rights of the individual. Many citizens of the United States feel that the death penalty as practiced here, but renounced by practically all Western countries, is a violation of the universal moral principle that no one except God has the right to take the life of another human being. This conflict over the death penalty becomes an international issue when the United States attempts to extradite an alleged criminal from a country that has renounced the death penalty to face the death penalty here. Today there is an ongoing debate between supporters of a universal morality and supporters of moral relativism. Subjects like the death penalty or abortion are widely discussed in our own society. Many who object to abortion as the taking of human life support the death penalty and this represents a basic contradiction. As we shall see, such contradictions and contested views of one's culture are not uncommon in many cultures.

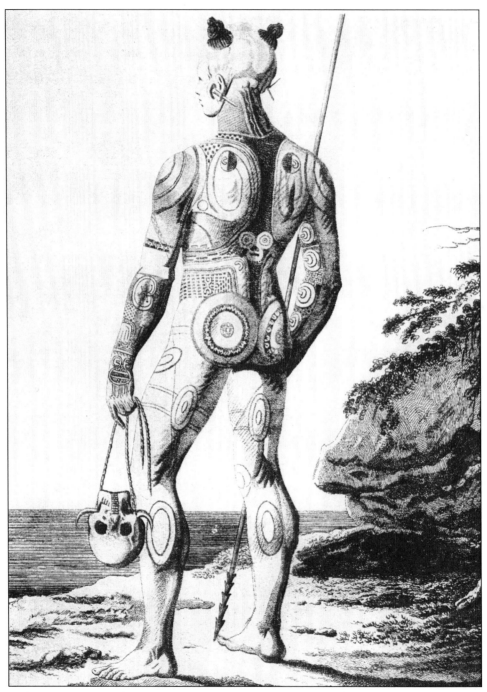

Tattooed Marquesan youth holding a trophy head taken from an enemy depicted in the account of Langsdorff's voyages published in 1804.

In addition to cultural differences, anthropologists are also concerned with what cultures have in common, that is, cultural universals. Anthropologists can utilize the **comparative approach** to compare and contrast cultures, which identifies fundamental similarities of cultural patterning as well as differences. For example, until World War II, the Rwala Bedouin of the Saudi Arabian desert depended primarily on their camel herds for subsistence. Up to the Russian Revolution, the Kazaks, in what is now Kazakhstan, relied on their herds of horses in the grassland steppe environment where they lived. Despite the fact that the environments they inhabited were totally different (desert as compared to grasslands) as well as the animals they herded, the Rwala Bedouin and the Kazaks shared a number of cultural features. They both moved with their animals over fixed migration routes during the year to provide pasture. They lived in similar nomadic encampments consisting of several groups of people, related by kinship, each with its own tent. They depended on exchanging the products of their herds (such as milk, butter, cheese, and hides) with townspeople for commodities they could not provide for themselves, such as flour and tea. Because of these basic similarities, anthropologists characterize them both as a type of society called nomadic pastoralist. But important cultural differences existed between the Rwala and the Kazak. They spoke totally different languages belonging to unrelated language families and had different beliefs and practices. Societies in other parts of the world who shared many characteristics but tended different kinds of animals fall into the same larger category of nomadic pastoralists.

CULTURE

The central concept in anthropology is **culture**. It consists of the things people make, their behavior, their symbols, beliefs, and ideas. In their definitions of what constitutes culture, anthropologists have emphasized different aspects of culture, and in that sense, it could be said that the concept is "contested." Some have focused upon culture as a set of ideas and meanings that people use, derived from the past and reshaped in the present. In this view, historically transmitted patterns of meaning, embodied in symbols, are the means by which humans communicate, perpetuate, and develop their knowledge about and attitudes toward life. The role of the anthropologist, then, is to grasp, comprehend, and translate those ideas and meanings so people of other groups may understand them. Other anthropologists, influenced by evolutionary psychology, see culture as the means by which human beings have adapted to their environment. They argue that the repertoire of cultural traits of a particular group must have been the result of evolutionary selection. This repertoire of cultural traits is characterized as adaptive; otherwise, it would not have been perpetuated. But many traits present in cultures are not adaptive. According to the central tenet of evolutionary theory, natural selection, individuals with adaptive cultural traits are reproductively successful, produce more offspring, and flourish, while those with cultural traits that are not adaptive do not pass on their genes. This perspective emphasizes what humans have in common with other animal species, each of which is adapted to its environment.

Other disciplines study the various types of human activities; but each studies a specific sector of this activity as if it was largely autonomous. Thus, economists study aspects of the economy like the gross national product or the stock exchange. Political scientists study how laws are enacted.

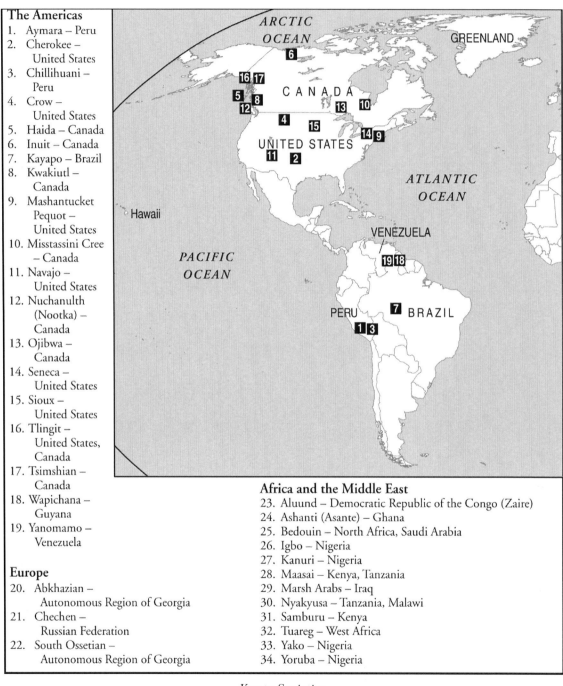

The Americas
1. Aymara – Peru
2. Cherokee – United States
3. Chillihuani – Peru
4. Crow – United States
5. Haida – Canada
6. Inuit – Canada
7. Kayapo – Brazil
8. Kwakiutl – Canada
9. Mashantucket Pequot – United States
10. Misstassini Cree – Canada
11. Navajo – United States
12. Nuchanulth (Nootka) – Canada
13. Ojibwa – Canada
14. Seneca – United States
15. Sioux – United States
16. Tlingit – United States, Canada
17. Tsimshian – Canada
18. Wapichana – Guyana
19. Yanomamo – Venezuela

Europe
20. Abkhazian – Autonomous Region of Georgia
21. Chechen – Russian Federation
22. South Ossetian – Autonomous Region of Georgia

Africa and the Middle East
23. Aluund – Democratic Republic of the Congo (Zaire)
24. Ashanti (Asante) – Ghana
25. Bedouin – North Africa, Saudi Arabia
26. Igbo – Nigeria
27. Kanuri – Nigeria
28. Maasai – Kenya, Tanzania
29. Marsh Arabs – Iraq
30. Nyakyusa – Tanzania, Malawi
31. Samburu – Kenya
32. Tuareg – West Africa
33. Yako – Nigeria
34. Yoruba – Nigeria

Key to Societies

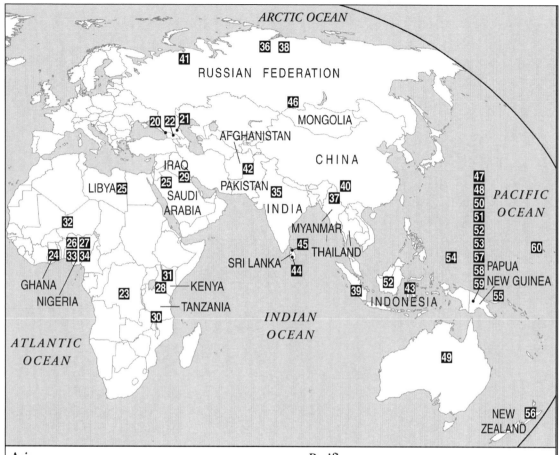

Asia

35. Bhil – Nortern India
36. Evenki (Tungus) – Siberia (Russian Federation)
37. Kachin – Myanmar
38. Mansi – Siberia (Russian Federation)
39. Minangkabau – Sumatra, Indonesia
40. Na – Yunan Province, China
41. Nentsy – Western Siberia (Russian Federation)
42. Pashtun (Pathans) – Afghanistan, Pakistan
43. Sa'dan Toraja – Sulawesi, Indonesia
44. Sinhalese – Sri Lanka
45. Tamil – Sri Lanka
46. Tuva – Siberia (Russian Federation)

Pacific

47. Abelam – Papua New Guinea
48. Arapesh – Papua New Guinea
49. Australian Aborigines -- Australia
50. Enga – Papua New Guinea
51. Gimi – Papua New Guinea
52. Iban – Borneo
53. Karam – Papua New Guinea
54. Ko'a – Palu'e Eastern Indonesia
55. Lesu – New Ireland, Papua New Guinea
56. Maori – New Zealand
57. Maring – Papua New Guinea
58. Trobriand – Papua New Guinea
59. Wogeo – Papua New Guinea
60. Yap – Micronesia

Art historians study the works of Rembrandt. Musicologists study Mozart's symphonies. Religious specialists study Luther's role in the Reformation. The anthropologist also investigates these fields, but the emphasis is on their interrelationship. Anthropology's approach is holistic and uses culture as an organizing concept and stresses the relationship between these fields. The emphasis is on the way in which economics may affect politics as well as art. In turn, religion and economics may be examined in terms of how they affect one another and so on. Earlier, anthropologists focused on small-scale societies and the focus of these other fields was primarily upon Western industrialized societies. Today, anthropologists focus on the impact of economic and political change in what were small-scale societies but are now part of nation-states, while economists may do their research in Asia and Africa where Westernization and modernization are having an impact. As we shall see later, the concept of culture is now utilized by other disciplines like cultural studies.

The concept of culture also unites cultural anthropology with anthropology's other subdisciplines. **Archaeology** examines the past history of cultures through their material remains. **Physical anthropology** investigates human evolution and the relationship between the culture of humans and their physical nature. **Linguistics** is the study of language and the relationship between language and culture. The research that anthropologists may do often crosses these subdisciplinary boundaries. For example, an investigation into the peopling of the Pacific, that is, the migration of humans into Australia, New Guinea, and the Oceanic islands, demonstrates how all four subdisciplines may play a role in a research endeavor. The physical and linguistic differences of the people would be of significance in investigating how the different cultures of the areas were transformed through time. Archaeology would show when people moved into these areas and how their cultures changed through time. Cultural anthropology examines the way in which migration and relative isolation brings about changes and cultural diversification.

Professionals from other disciplines are now paying attention to the concept of culture. The World Bank employs anthropologists to do research because its leaders recognize that cultural ideas and meanings provide the important context that must be understood in order to solve economic problems (Shweder 2001: 438). Cultural studies, which has appeared on the academic stage in recent years, uses a concept of culture that is primarily oriented toward literary concerns and is really remote from the anthropological concept of culture.

Today, individuals live their lives in a world of overlapping cultures. The Navajo, who have been studied by generations of anthropologists, still retain their Navajo identity even though they are part of a much larger complex culture, American culture, participating in the larger American economy and political system. Most Navajo are bilingual, speaking the Navajo language and English. They retain elements of their Navajo belief system and practice many Navajo rituals. Within the Navajo population, there is considerable cultural variation among individuals, between communities, and between regions. Navajo people have always been very receptive to new cultural ideas. The practice of herding sheep, the weaving of blankets, and the manufacture of silver jewelry, so central to Navajo culture today, were introduced by the Spanish centuries ago, at the time of their conquest of the New World. Although the Navajo adopted these arts from the Spanish, the styles they use are distinctively Navajo. But earlier, the Navajo chose not to adopt the horticultural practices of their neighbors, the Hopi and Zuni. What emerges from the Navajo example is an awareness that culture as a concept exists at many levels—the individual, the community, and the larger society or political entity.

Up to one hundred years ago, the boundaries of cultures were much more "fixed." One hundred years ago, when professional anthropology was in its earliest phase, field workers treated the cultures that they studied as if they were so isolated that their cultural boundaries were impenetrable. Some selected islands for study because of their relative isolation. For example, Raymond Firth studied the island of Tikopia, treating it as an isolate with fixed boundaries, even though Tikopians did have some contact with the outside world. Cultures today do not exist within fixed boundaries; they blend into one another. At cultural boundaries, individuals are bilingual, frequently intermarry, and often join together in rituals. Since cultural boundaries are no longer fixed, changes are constantly taking place in culture, often as a consequence of globalization. Because boundaries are fluid, individuals are active participants involved in reworking their cultures and their traditions in terms of influences from the outside.

All cultures have a certain degree of internal consistency. We have called this book *The Tapestry of Culture* because the imagery of a tapestry aptly conveys a picture of culture as integrated. Many strands, many colors, many patterns contribute to the overall design of a tapestry, just as many items of behavior and many customs form patterns that, in turn, compose a culture. Culture is integrated only to a degree. There are very frequently internal inconsistencies and contradictions, as will be illustrated in later chapters. Cultures are not single, monolithic entities. In most societies like American society, there are subcultures based on regional, class, ethnic, or religious differences, and the like. Feminist studies have made us much more aware that men and women have differing views of their culture. In other societies, because of power differentials between masters and slaves, workers and bosses, or Brahmans and Untouchables, each side will have a differing perspective on the culture that they share. From each of these categories one will get only "partial truths" about the culture. One could say that bosses and workers do not share the same set of ideas, beliefs, and values and each constitutes a separate subculture. This may still be true in some American industries; however, today, in the corporate world, at least. the distinction between workers and bosses is not so clear-cut from a definitional point of view. Patterns and regularities of culture do not remain eternally the same but, rather, change through time. Every significant new invention—such as the electric light bulb, the telephone, the automobile, and the computer—has resulted in major changes in different parts of American culture.

Culture is learned and acquired by infants through a process referred to by anthropologists as **enculturation**. Mental structures or schema are created in the individual as a result of the process of enculturation. People who share a culture have reoccurring common experiences, which lead them to develop similar mental schema. Individuals are enculturated not as passive recipients, but as active agents. They internalize cultural practices but may change and transform those practices as a result of their experiences. Individuals learn another culture when they migrate to a new country, but the degree to which they learn this new culture may vary, and some may learn very little of the new culture.

Culture is transgenerational; that is, it continues beyond the lifetimes of individuals. There is a stability and consistency of cultural patterning through time, despite the fact that culture is continually being reworked and re-created. Culture is always a dialogue between past and present. Changes occur, some of which are the result of internal developments, innovations, and inventions, while others represent introductions from outside. Anthropologists study the process of culture change through time by examining historical, archival, and, sometimes, archaeological data deriving from the excavation of prehistoric sites. Tradition can be seen as the "past" as it is recollected in the present. Innovators and rebels, who try to transform their societies, have a view of the society that is different from that of other members. It is a dream of a different future, of a "brave new world," which demands that present ways of doing things be changed.

HUMAN EVOLUTION AND CULTURE

It is the possession of culture that distinguishes humans from all other animal species. In all other animal species, except for primates, social behavior and communication are determined primarily by instinct and are essentially uniform throughout each species. Though it was originally thought that only humans possessed culture, recent research has revealed that some primates exhibit behavior that seems to resemble culture. Gombe chimpanzees in Zambia like to eat termites. During the termite season, they spend a long time at termite mounds, and carry "termite-fishing wands," grasses, vines, or twigs, which are inserted into the termite mounds to extract the termites. They also bring extra "tools" with them (Lieberman 1998: 24). Chimpanzees in the Tai area of West Africa use stone and wood hammers and anvils to crack open nuts. McGrew earlier described thirty-four different populations of chimpanzees that had been observed making and using different tools. They use the same tool to solve different problems, and different tools to solve the same problem; hence, they have what can be described as a tool kit (McGrew 1993: 158, 159). This behavior is transmitted intergenerationally and would seem to be proto-cultural behavior.

The cultural behavior of humans, *Homo sapiens*, is not only learned and transmitted from one generation to the next, but is also based on language and the capacity to create symbols, in contrast to what we have described above for other primates. Human cultural behavior is not limited, as is chimpanzee learned behavior, but is infinitely expandable. Ape-human comparisons, as Tattersall notes, only provide a background for understanding the way in which human mental capacities for culture evolve (1998: 49).

The evolution of the human species from proto-human and early human forms involved a number of significant physical changes, including the development of bipedal erect locomotion, increase in brain size, and especially neurological reorganization. Not only fossil evidence, information from comparisons of molecular, genetic, and DNA evidence from contemporary forms, but also analysis of ancient DNA and archeological remains are used to provide information about the nature of the evolutionary tree leading up to modern humans. Earlier hominid forms, most of which belong to the genus *Australopithecus*, emerged about 4.2 million years ago, were small, lightly built, and upright but with small brain size. About 2.5 million years ago, the oldest recognized stone tools, Oldowan, were manufactured from pebbles, and seem to be associated with *Australopithecus*. The first *Homo* species was *Homo erectus*, "which appeared around 1.9 MYA (million years ago) in Africa, and exhibited a height and weight similar to modern humans, but with a smaller brain. H. erectus, associated with Acheulean technology in some places, spread rapidly over much of the old world including Georgia, Indonesia, and China" (Jobling et al. 2004: 262). There are two theories about the emergence of *Homo sapiens*, anatomically modern humans. One sees the development of this species in Africa probably from 130 to 180 thousand years ago, with migration later to other parts of the world, 50,000 or 60,000 years ago. In contrast, the "multiregional evolutionary model" sees the evolution of *Homo sapiens* from *Homo erectus* forms as occurring in different regions of the world with genetic interchange between populations in continued contact and natural selection operating as factors in the transformation. Neanderthal forms are usually seen as a distinct and separate species, *Homo neanderthalensis*, though they seem to have continued to exist for a time after the development of *Homo sapiens*. The DNA that has been extracted from Neanderthal bones is distinct from that of present-day humans. Their exact relationship to *Homo sapiens* has been the subject of much debate.

Language is the vehicle for cultural expression, hence its origin has been the subject of much interest. Some see bipedalism as setting the stage for the eventual development of vocal language. Recently a more detailed theory has been propounded that views bipedalism as giving rise to body language and visual gesture, which are seen not only as the dominant features of human interaction, but as the primary means of communication for our early hominid ancestors (Turner 2000). With the use of visually based language (gestures), the brain expanded, and this resulted in a pre-adaptation for verbal language. Verbal language could only appear after the anatomical features necessary for its production were in place. The vocal tract of *Homo erectus*, the hominid from which *Homo sapiens* is descended, was not yet organized in the form necessary for vocal communication.

Although Neanderthals had larger brains and some of the same features that made human language possible, since the pharynx was still not in the same place as in *Homo sapiens* and other parts of the vocal tract were different, they could not produce vowels and were not considered capable of producing fully human language (Lieberman and McCarthy 1999). A newer hypothesis has now emerged, which holds that changes in facial characteristics, vocal tract, and breathing apparatus from *Homo erectus* to Neanderthal would have enabled the latter to speak (Buckley and Steele 2002). In terms of the latter theory, the evolution of language must have occurred between the time of *Homo erectus* (1.9 million years) and that of Neanderthal.

It is clear that language and the use, creation, and manipulation of symbols, which are central to culture, evolved as did brain size and tool use. However, at this point there is no definitive information about the way in which language evolved, since there are no "linguistic fossils" representing intermediate forms of language, which would be equivalent to the tools from the Paleolithic period. The central role of language in culture will be explored more fully in chapter 3. Art and music, which employ symbols, make their first appearance in the Upper Paleolithic with the people called Cro-Magnon, who were *Homo sapiens* like us.

The marked development of cerebral asymmetry noted above is connected to right- and left-handedness. The earliest stone tools were made by right-handed individuals (Tattersall 1998: 76). The increase in sophistication and complexity of the tools manufactured by early human beings occurred with expansion in brain size and intelligence. The early archaeological record shows the widespread geographical distribution of the same pattern or style of tool type. This indicates the presence of the features that characterize culture.

Recent research has pointed to another significant development in the evolution of culture—cooking. Many animal species eat raw meat, but none cooks its food. In contrast, no human society relies on raw meat for significant parts of their diet, but all cook their food. Cooking transformed vegetation into "food," making it much more digestible. In examining the archeological traces of cooking, Wrangham et al. see vegetable food, particularly tubers, which they argue were collected and brought back by females, as the basis for cooking. They assume that females also did the cooking (1999). Once cooked, such food became a valuable resource, which had to be protected by males, since it was easily subject to marauding and theft. These features, together with the formation of an extended period of female sexual receptivity, probably led to strong male-female bonds, a pattern not found among nonhuman primates. These researchers argued that the important transformations that resulted from cooking occurred when the first hominids or humans appeared some 1.9 million years ago before the appearance of big game hunters.

Later forms of hominids became efficient hunters of large game animals as well. Meat, too, is more digestible when cooked. The cooked tuber hypothesis is downplayed by later researchers who claim that "increased meat-eating was influential in the early *Homo* clade . . . [and there is] abundant documented evidence of carcass acquisition, transport, butchery, and increased meat-eating by early *Homo*" (Bunn and Stanford 2001: 355). Early humans like *Homo erectus* show the important fossil changes that one would expect to be associated with eating cooked food. The size of their molars, used to grind food, is much reduced. Cooking of food, of course, presupposes the control of fire. However, the search for definite proof of controlled use of fire by human presents many problems. It is difficult to distinguish between naturally occurring fires and controlled use for cooking or warming. However, many of the sites where *Homo erectus* was found show evidence of fire and are presumed to be occupation sites. According to Goren-Inbar, "firemaking probably started more than 1 million years ago among groups of *Homo erectus* in Africa and Asia" (2005). The *Homo erectus* site at Zhoukoutien shows definite evidence of fire. The ability to use fire and cooking are universally found in all human cultures. Claude Lévi-Strauss (1990) sees cooking as a defining feature of humanity. He has pointed out that the ideas about the discovery of cooking are present in human myths throughout the world.

Still another feature distinguishes human cultural behavior from animal behavior. Human behavior is governed primarily by cultural rules, not by the need for immediate gratification. The capacity to defer gratification was increasingly built into human physiology as humans evolved. Lions and wolves eat immediately after a successful hunt, often gorging on raw meat. Human beings do not eat the minute they become hungry. With the introduction of cooking, humans deferred eating until long after the hunt, until cooking was completed. Everything about human eating is controlled by rules. Sex is similarly subject to cultural rules. Unlike other animals, humans do not have a period of estrus during which they need to have sexual intercourse and not during any other time. Instead, human beings usually follow their culture's set of rules as to when and where to have sex and the various positions to use.

CULTURAL UNIVERSALS

The biological nature of the human species requires that all cultures solve the basic problems of human existence such as providing themselves with food and reproducing. As a consequence, though cultural differences do exist, all cultures share certain fundamental similarities, which are referred to as **cultural universals**. Though languages differ, they are all characterized by certain universal features, such as the presence of nouns, possessive forms, and verbs that distinguish between the past, present, and future. Chomsky's theory of universal grammar postulates that infants have an innate cognitive structure that enables them to learn the grammatical complexities of any language (1998, 1999, 2000). Though languages are different from one another, they all have these universal features. Human consumption of food follows cultural rules regarding what is eaten, when, with whom, and how—with which utensils you eat, with the right hand, and not the left. All cultures have some kind of incest taboo, though the relatives with whom they must not have sexual intercourse vary, as we will describe in chapter 6. Rites of passage, such as birth, reaching adulthood, marriage, and death, are celebrated ceremonially by societies, though not all of them celebrate each of these rites of passage. Some anthropologists have pointed out that all cultures have law, government, religion, conceptions of self, marriage, family, and kinship (Brown 1991, Kluckhohn 1953). These universal cultural categories are present in all human societies since each must deal with the problems and concerns that all humans face (Goodenough 1970: 120). Ultimately, it is the characteristics of the human species and the human mind that form the basis for cultural universals. Languages and cultures are structured in a particular manner as a consequence of the fact that the mind of *Homo sapiens* is organized in a certain way. According to recent evolutionary psychologists, there is a "neurocognitive specialization for social exchange reliably developed across striking variations in cultural experience. It is one component of a complex and universal human nature" (Cosmides and Toobey 2005: 623). This means that social exchange is universal in all cultures, based on innate characteristics of human cognitive structure, though the rules of social exchange vary from one culture to another.

CULTURAL RULES

Cultural rules dictate the way in which basic biological drives are expressed. What is learned and internalized by human infants during the process of enculturation in different cultures are **cultural rules**. The enormous variations between cultures are due to differences in cultural rules. Defining these cultural rules is like trying to identify the rules that govern a language. All languages operate according to sets of rules, and people follow these in their speech. It is the linguist's job to determine the rules of grammar that the speakers of languages use automatically and are usually not aware of. Frequently, people can tell the anthropologist what the cultural rules are. At other times, they may behave according to rules that they themselves cannot verbalize. The anthropologist's job is to uncover those cultural rules of which people may be unaware. The existence of rules does not imply that speakers of a language or members of a culture are robots who speak and act in identical fashion. Each infant learns cultural rules in a distinctive manner, and every speaker of a language has his or her distinctive pronunciation and linguistic mannerisms. Individual variation is considerable in spoken language, and it is equally present in cultural practice. Rules are meant to be flouted, and often individuals respond to rules that way. Lawyers and accountants in our society advise people on how to get as close as possible to the limit of the law. If they cross over the line and the government becomes aware of it, they will be in trouble with the IRS or the attorney general. Lastly, individuals are not simply recipients of culture; they are active participants in reworking their cultures and their traditions. As a consequence, there is variation in observing the rules.

Rules governing sexual behavior in terms of with whom it is allowed, as well as when, where, and how, are highly variable. For example, when Powdermaker studied the village of Lesu, in Papua New Guinea, it was acceptable for sexual intercourse to take place before marriage (1933). The marriage relationship was symbolized by eating together. When a couple publicly shared a meal, this signified that they were married and could henceforth eat only with one another. Even though husband and wife could have sexual relations with other individuals, they could not eat with them. In our society, in contrast, until the beginning of the sexual revolution about 60 years ago, couples engaged to be married could eat together, but sexual intercourse could not take place until after marriage. The act of sexual intercourse symbolized marriage. At that time, if either spouse had intercourse with another individual after marriage, that constituted the criminal act of adultery. However, either spouse could have dinner with someone of the opposite sex. From the perspective of someone in our society, the rules governing marriage in Lesu appear to be like our rules from 60 years ago "stood on their heads."

We noted earlier that workers and bosses have differing cultural perspectives. Their repertoire of cultural rules likewise may vary. Similarly, subcultures also exhibit variability in their cultural rules. This is referred to as **intracultural variation**.

On occasion, as we noted above, individuals may violate cultural rules. All cultures have some provision for sanctioning the violation of cultural rules as well as rewards for obeying them. In the same way that the sets of cultural rules differ, both rewards and punishments also differ from one culture to another. Cultural rules also change over time. When many individuals consistently interpret a rule differently than it had been interpreted before, the result will be a change in the rule itself. An example of this sort is the fact that sexual intercourse in our society is no longer solely a symbol of marriage, as we have noted.

SOCIETY

Another concept paralleling culture is that of **society**. Culture deals with meanings and symbolic patterning, while society has been used to deal with the organization of social relationships within groups. Culture is distinctive of humans alone, although there are some primates that have what we have characterized as proto-culture. However, all animals that live in groups, humans among them, can be said to have societies. Thus a bee hive, a wolf pack, a deer herd, and a baboon troop all constitute societies. As in a human society, the individual members of a wolf pack are differentiated as males and females, as immature individuals and adults, and as mothers, fathers, and offspring. Individual wolves in each of these social categories behave in particular ways. That there are resemblances between wolf and human societies should not be surprising, since both wolves and humans are social animals. Today, there are no absolutely bounded social entities of the type that were labeled societies in the past. Nation-states that are independent political entities are connected to other nation-states. Many nation-states are multiethnic, containing groups with somewhat different cultural repertoires. Though anthropologists might begin their research with such groups as if they were separate entities like societies, in the final analysis, their social and cultural connection to other such groups and to the nation-state must be considered. These groups share cultural ideas, and still other ideas are contested, but they have some ideas in common as part of the nation-state.

SOCIAL STRUCTURE

The particular patterns of social relationships that characterize a society or social group are referred to as its **social structure**. Patterns of social structure are based on cultural rules. Societies or social groups may be organized on the basis of family, kinship, residential propinquity, common interest, friendship, or class. These groupings have continuity through time. Social structure may be distinguished from **social organization** (Firth 1951). While structure emphasizes continuity and stability, organization refers to the way in which individuals perceive the structure and context of any situation and make decisions and choices from among alternative courses of behavior. Organization emphasizes flux and change and refers to variations in individual behavior. This emphasis on individual choices and decisions is also defined as **practice** (Bourdieu 1977). **Agency** refers to the point of view of the individual making the choices. The range of choices people can choose from is always shaped by the social structure. The action they take as "agents" may serve to reconfigure the social structure (Ahearn 2001: 115).

In societies or social groups, individuals usually occupy more than one position or **social status** at the same time. An individual may be a father and a chief at the same time. Societies, of course, vary in the number and kinds of social statuses. The behavior associated with a particular social status in a society is known as a **social role**. Social roles involve behavior toward other people. For example, in Papua New Guinea, a headman will lead his followers to attend a ceremony sponsored by another headman and his followers. When the headman orates on such an occasion, he speaks for his group, and he is carrying out the social role of headman. Interaction of people in their social roles and interaction between groups define two kinds of social relationships. These social relationships can be analyzed in terms of differentials in power, prestige, and access to resources. The headman has more power, prestige, and resources than his followers. Inequality characterizes many social roles, so that a father has power over his children, a manager has power over workers, and a sergeant has power over his squad. The social structure contains a network of social roles, that is, the behavior associated with a particular position or status, and a distribution of power through that network.

ANTHROPOLOGICAL THEORIES

The discipline of anthropology has been professionalized for more than 130 years. To more clearly understand the work that anthropologists are doing today, as well as the results of their past research, it is necessary to briefly survey the significant theoretical and methodological approaches that have informed, shaped, and focused this research. When anthropology was developing during the nineteenth century, it was envisioned as a science, patterned after the natural sciences. This image was dominant until the early part of the twentieth century. In the decades that followed, anthropology oscillated between humanistic and scientific approaches. One must also keep in mind that the framework within which anthropologists worked during the nineteenth and much of the twentieth century was one of colonial empires.

Cultural Evolution

The nineteenth century was a period of colonial expansion and the development of great empires by European powers. Darwinian evolutionary theory was dominant. Social Darwinism, which proclaimed the survival of the fittest, was used to justify the domination of native peoples, as well as the exploitation of the underclass in industrial societies. During this period the discipline of anthropology, which focused on the study of indigenous peoples of the colonies that had been established, came into being. The significant theory of the time was **cultural evolution**. Sir Edward Tylor's (1871) contribution was to define culture, the central concept in anthropology, in a broad, all-encompassing manner that included language and all the customs characteristic of a social group.

Generally, the anthropologists of that time remained in their armchairs and utilized the accounts of missionaries, explorers such as Captain Cook, travelers such as Prince Maximilian who explored the area of the Louisiana Purchase, and others who described the native peoples they encountered in their travels. Many of these descriptions were ethnocentric and biased. Lewis Henry Morgan and Tylor, the major nineteenth-century theorists, conceptualized cultural evolution in terms of stages through which all societies had progressed, with the simple societies developing into increasingly more complex forms, culminating in their own Victorian society. In their view, some societies, namely those of the "savages" being encountered by missionaries and others, represented cases of contemporary examples of earlier stages, that is, cases of arrested development or survivals.

The evolutionists organized their data and utilized the comparative approach, which we discussed earlier. They looked for similarities and differences in cultures, classified them into cultural types, and ordered the types from simple to complex. They were ethnocentric in their evaluation of other societies. Western religion, family life, and so on, were all assumed to be the apogee of evolutionary development. Morgan's emphasis on the economic base of society as the determining factor of stages of cultural evolution caught the attention of Friedrich Engels. Engels's *The Origin of the Family, Private Property and the State* (1884) includes a reinterpretation of Morgan's *Ancient Society* (1877). Both Marx and Engels were very taken with the work of

Morgan because, like Morgan, they saw the evolution of culture as determined by the technology and the subsistence base.

At the beginning of the twentieth century, anthropologists recognized the weaknesses of the nineteenth-century evolutionary approach, since the data on which the theories were based were found wanting. The characteristics of Western societies, such as monogamy and monotheism, were arbitrarily selected to represent the highest forms of societal development. As data were collected, based on fieldwork by trained anthropologists, it was clear that not *all* societies had passed through the same evolutionary stages. Fieldwork revealed that monogamy and monotheism were found in societies other than the most evolved. At that point, nineteenth-century evolutionary theory based on universal stages was discarded.

In the 1940s, a new form of evolutionary theory was proposed by Leslie White (1943, 1949, 1959). He saw culture as a whole, over the world, evolving and becoming more complex as human beings in different places developed increasingly more efficient ways of capturing energy from the environment. In contrast to White and his universal evolutionary scheme, Julian Steward (1955) was interested in how particular societies in similar environments evolved.

All anthropologists today would agree that complex forms of society have evolved from simpler ones. However, contemporary cultural anthropological theory, by and large, is not concerned with evolutionary questions. Most anthropologists feel that evolutionary theory does not take into account the unique aspects of culture on which they choose to focus. Evolutionary questions remain important to archaeologists. Anthropologists like Ingold, for example, are interested in the role human consciousness plays in cultural evolution and in whether there is a cultural analogue of natural selection (1996). Evolutionary psychology and neo-Marxism, which we shall discuss below, are contemporary forms of evolutionary theorizing.

Cultural Relativism

Though Franz Boas started out as a supporter of the evolutionary point of view, his fieldwork with Eskimos (known today as Inuit) of Baffin Island in the late nineteenth century, and somewhat later with a variety of Northwest Coast societies, especially the Kwakiutl, soon led him to abandon the evolutionary approach. After learning the Kwakiutl language, he came to respect the significant differences between the way the Kwakiutl viewed the world and the way other people viewed it. He moved away from an evolutionary perspective, considering all cultures and languages equally distinctive and complex in different ways. This emphasis on uniqueness came to be referred to as **cultural relativism** or **cultural particularism**. Boas saw cultures as symbolic systems of ideas. His work stressed the gathering of texts in the native language concerning all the aspects of the life of the people, especially art, mythology, and language. Boas felt that anthropologists should first concentrate on learning about the history of the development of particular societies, such as the Kwakiutl and other Native American Indian societies. This became known as **historical particularism**. His emphasis on cultural relativism came to be associated with the humanistic approach that characterized the work of his students Benedict, Sapir, and Kroeber.

Functionalism

The British reaction against nineteenth-century evolutionary theory took a somewhat different form. British anthropologists at the beginning of the twentieth century supplanted evolutionary theory with a model, derived from biology, of society as a living organism. The basic organizing principles they used were the linked concepts of structure and function. **Structure** is a description of form and the relationship of parts to one another, while **function** refers to how the structure works. They spurned speculation and substituted fieldwork for it, that is, the empirical field observations by academically trained anthropologists who had spent a year or more working with a group of people, learning their language and observing and participating in their culture. This fieldwork was conducted with tribal people living as subjects within a colonial empire.

Bronislaw Malinowski, a major functionalist, was one of the founders of modern anthropological fieldwork. He spent an extended period of time doing fieldwork in the Trobriand Islands off New Guinea. He identified the institutions that made up the "skeleton" of society (i.e., their structure) and then described in detail how those institutions functioned. Malinowski saw cultural institutions functioning in response to basic human biological needs, as well as to what he called culturally derived needs. In his two-volume work *Coral Gardens and Their Magic* (1935), he described that part of the economic institution of the Trobrianders concerned with horticulture. He described planting and cultivating yams, but also magic spells involved in yam cultivation, and how yams are used in the exchange system of fulfilling obligations to kin and chiefs.

The other British functionalist, A. R. Radcliffe-Brown, moved in a somewhat different direction. Using a comparative approach, he tried to develop typologies to sort and categorize different kinds of societies (1952). He was concerned with the "anatomy" of societies, with social structure, which he defined as "this network of actually existing social relationships" (1952: 190). To Radcliffe-Brown the function of a part of the social structure, such as a clan, meant the contribution made by the clan to the ongoing life processes of the society. He strongly opposed what he referred to as "conjectural history," which had been characteristic of evolutionary theory. Real history, he argued, existed only where there were written records kept by the people themselves. Unfortunately, the effect of Radcliffe-Brown's position was to inhibit all kinds of historical research by British anthropologists for one or two generations.

With the breakdown of colonial empires after World War II, the functionalist theoretical framework, which emphasized unchanging societies existing in a state of equilibrium, came under attack. British anthropologists, such as A. L. Epstein and Philip Mayer, began to follow the tribal people whom they had studied earlier as they moved into the cities and went to work in the mines, documenting the economic and political changes that were occurring in their lives. Others, rejecting Radcliffe-Brown's injunction against conjectural history, such as E. E. Evans-Pritchard and M. G. Smith, turned to archival research to document the histories of societies with which they were doing ethnographic research. A much more processual model, which emphasized not social structure but social organization concepts and the way in which structures change, eventually came into play.

Structuralism

Structuralism as a theoretical approach is closely associated with the work of the French anthropologist Claude Lévi-Strauss. He used the linguistic method to analyze culture. Sounds in a language by themselves have no meaning but are part of a larger structure that conveys meaning. In the same way, the elements of a culture must be seen in their relationship to one another as they form a structure that conveys cultural meanings. The structural anthropologist attempted to determine the underlying structure of a culture, which corresponds to the grammar of a language in the linguist's analysis, and may not be in the consciousness of the speaker. Lévi-Strauss saw Boas as his intellectual ancestor. It was Boas who first pointed out that the grammar of a language was not part of the consciousness of the speaker and, in a parallel fashion, that culture also had an underlying structure that operated in the same way. Structuralists analyzed cognitive systems, kinship structure, art, mythology, ritual, and ceremony, among other things. Structural anthropologists were comparative in that they attempted to determine whether there were similarities in underlying structures in different cultures. Thus, this approach may group together societies that seem to be very different at first glance. Lévi-Straussian structuralism has been strongly rejected by postmodernists and poststructuralists because its models were too abstract and its approach was basically ahistorical.

Symbolic Anthropology

Symbolic anthropology, which had its efflorescence in the 1970s, is concerned with the interpretation of culture and the search for meaning. This emphasis relates to the centrality of meaning in the structuralism of Lévi-Strauss, which is one of its intellectual antecedents. Culture is seen as a system of symbols, and the task of the anthropologist is to decipher its meanings. In the 1970s, anthropologists such as David Schneider and Clifford Geertz began to focus on the tangle of interrelated meanings that cultures encode. The task of the anthropologist then became one of translating the layers of meaning of a particular cultural phenomenon into our concepts and our language. Clifford Geertz (1972), in his attempt to understand the meaning of the Balinese cockfight, called this type of translation a "thick description." Thick description means that culture is viewed as a text to be read and interpreted. This emphasis on deciphering meaning has been associated in anthropology with particularism and cultural relativism, both of which are basically anticomparative.

If anthropologists who wrote ethnographies were collecting ethnographic information in the form of texts, then anthropological analysis was the analysis of texts. During the past years, Geertz's approach has increasingly become akin to literary criticism. In the mid-1980s, in *Works and Lives*, Geertz (1988) analyzed the ethnographic accounts of four anthropologists. He argued that understanding these writings is similar to understanding a fictional body of work by Melville or Mark Twain. The meaning of a text is found in the author's voice, and the anthropological material contained therein must be interpreted in that light. In contrast, Schneider continued to see each ethnography as representing the symbolic system of a particular and uniquely different culture. There was no room for a comparative approach in the anthropology of both Geertz and

Schneider. In the tension between anthropology as a science seeking to make generalizations through the use of the comparative approach, and as an aspect of the humanities seeking understanding, the symbolic approach came down squarely on the side of the humanities.

Historical Anthropology

Anthropologists have always been concerned with the temporal or historical dimension of culture. The arm-chair anthropologists of the 19th century constructed a schema that attempted to describe the evolution of human culture. The Boasians, especially A. L. Kroeber, and others during the early twentieth century, attempted to reconstruct the history of particular cultures by looking at the spread of culture traits. They were dealing with cultures without written histories that they could consult, and further, they were interested in what was called "traditional culture" in those days. This was all later condemned by Radcliffe-Brown as "conjectural history." But from the time of Western contact, these cultures were embedded within a historical framework of conquest and colonialism, which many anthropologists at that time did not consider relevant. Clearly what was being described from the conquerors' point of view, in the archival and other historical sources, was significant and important to any understanding of these cultures. As British anthropologists began to pay more and more attention to the effects of colonialism on the people they were studying, they recognized that history was a technique to help explain the consequences of European influence, and that they needed to acquaint themselves with the tools of the historian.

Only then could anthropologists understand the nature of the interaction between the colonizers and those they had colonized, and how each had reconstructed their world as a consequence of the other. Clearly, control, white domination, and the difference in the power differential were central in such an intellectual enterprise. The regional, nation-state, and emerging global contexts with their political and economic dimensions are also significant. One must consider how the local and global interpenetrate each other over time. What is also relevant in this endeavor was how the relationship of archival research and ethnography was to be constituted. As Cohen noted, the anthropologist was to "treat the materials the way an anthropologist treats his field notes" (Axel 2002:9 [1987:2]). It is clear that the methodologies of both history and anthropology are relevant to any investigation. Even earlier, decades ago, anthropologists such as two of the authors of this book (Rubel and Rosman) had to pay attention to the changing historical context of the society or social group, with its picture of colonialism and domination, which they were studying. These were to be found in archives, which in the case of Rubel's study of the Kalmyk Mongols (1967) meant going back to material three centuries old to ferret out information. Weisgrau's work in Rajastahan (1997; Henderson and Weisgrau 2007) traces continuities between British colonial documents and contemporary ideas about tourism and Bhil identity.

Those who do what is referred to as **ethnohistory** work with not only archival but also archeological and oral history materials to trace the history of cultures that have no written record. The local peoples' narratives of their own history are important. This includes not only oral history but tradition and myth (Donham 2001: 143). In his version of historical anthropology, Wolf was interested in the colonial discourse that developed between colonizers and colonized, and how non-

European populations reacted to the introduction of capitalism and the way, in turn, these reactions determined the direction of capitalism in Europe (Wolf 1982). Sahlins' theoretical approach, which combines history and structuralism, shows how the Hawaiians perceived Captain Cook, after his arrival on the island, as the god Lono, in terms of their own cultural categories. Since each year they ritually killed the god Lono, they killed Cook, and this killing not only affected subsequent events involving Hawaiian-European relations (i.e., history) but also resulted in changes in Hawaiian cultural rules (structure) (Sahlins 1985). As Dirks, Eley, and Ortner observe, "[Anthropology] has been moving in a historical direction. Only slightly less obviously, history has become increasingly anthropological" (1994: 5). Anthropology cannot be the historical context alone, meaning only a temporal sequence of events and transformations; it must still pay attention to cultural meanings, their interpretations, and how individuals act in terms of those cultural meanings.

Postmodernism in Anthropology

Beginning in the 1980s and 1990s, anthropology, along with the other human sciences, underwent a reassessment, which was labeled **postmodernism**. Anthropologists' analyses and translations of the cultures of others were deemed insufficient and inadequate. Postmodernism in anthropology found fault with generalization and a more scientific approach. They challenged "the assertion that science and rationalism can lead to full and accurate knowledge of the world . . . arguing that these are specific historically constructed ways of knowing" (McGee and Warms 2008:532). Anthropology has always straddled both the humanities and the social sciences. Postmodernists thought that anthropology should totally embrace humanism, emphasizing cultural relativism and striving to capture the uniqueness of each cultural situation, which postmodernists saw as lost when one generalizes. The ethnographer brings along his or her own cultural categories and therefore cannot be a detached, objective observer of another culture. The anthropologist must be aware of those cultural categories since they frame the research. The idea that the anthropologist could also encompass the totality of another culture was abandoned for James Clifford's position that we can only achieve "partial truths" (1986).

Clifford and other postmodernists saw the ethnographic texts, which have been produced as Western representations of the culture being examined, as being reconceptualized in our Western categories. Since the ethnographer and his or her informants, the people within the culture who provide information, are to be seen as part of the same social time and space, the ethnographer's task becomes that of an interpreter or translator. Often the ethnographer's understanding of the culture is presented in the ethnography along with the understandings of the informants for the reading public to make its own conclusions.

Some have seen the ethnography, the product of the dialogue between informant and fieldworker, as not sufficiently representative of the variety of points of view or ideas held by individuals in the culture. They have argued that different segments of a society may have contesting views regarding cultural meanings and that opposing views should be represented in the ethnography in the informants' own words. In order to pay more attention to these views, some anthropologists have presented their analyses to their informants for comment. Some postmodernists prefer that the informants' voices take center stage in telling their story, utilizing the life history approach, which has traditionally been part of anthropological methodology. This is in response to the feeling that in the past the voices of ethnographic subjects have been marginalized or displaced by the sole authoritative voice of the ethnographer, the voice which had told "the story."

The role of the native ethnographer, that is, the individual who is a member of the culture who has received training as an anthropologist, is also related to the matter of representation. Such individuals are seen as having intuitive understanding of the culture and greater ability to empathize with the people and interpret their culture than an anthropologist who is a member of another culture. However, there are those who argue that greater empathy comes at the expense of the perspective and understanding that an outsider can bring. It is said that anthropologists studying their own culture cannot be objective, tend to justify behavior in an ethnocentric way, and often have their own political agendas.

When anthropology is seen as a science, observation plays an essential role. However, to postmodernists who emphasize the humanistic view of anthropology, observation plays a secondary role to dialogues with informants and the recording of the information that informants present as an ethnographic text. In the ethnographic accounts that postmodernists applaud, analytic conceptual frameworks are completely absent because it is felt that in each society, which is considered a unique entity, the categories must be understood in their own terms and cannot be equated with categories in other societies, as is done in comparative cross-cultural research.

Postmodernist anthropologists have considered the writing of ethnographic descriptions to be so central that one of them defines anthropology as "a discursive category, a type or group of types of writing that have important filiations to other modern cultural and academic fields" (Manganaro 1990: 5). They are interested in learning what rhetorical devices are being used to convince the reader that the fieldworker was "there" and that his or her observations and conclusions are accurate representations of the lives of the "others" whom anthropologists have studied. When culture is seen as a text, as in Geertz's view, and ethnography becomes a type of writing, then anthropology moves much closer to literary theory. Anthropology, in the postmodernist point of view, becomes part of a new humanistic interdisciplinary approach, which also includes philosophy, history, art history, and architecture. Postmodernists have forced anthropologists to rethink the nature of fieldwork. They have put the emphasis in ethnography upon knowing how the ethnographer felt as a person in the fieldwork situation and was perceived by the community, the experiential aspects of the field. This focus upon the ethnographer is a recent reflective turn in anthropology, as exemplified by the work of Barbara Tedlock.

CONTEMPORARY TRENDS

Anthropologists today do their research with a variety of perspectives. Since contemporary approaches are so varied, no single set of assumptions is shared today, in comparison to the theoretical points of view we have discussed up to this point. To paraphrase Mao Tse-tung, "a thousand blossoms have bloomed." Because of the dismissal of scientific approaches by postmodernists, most present-day anthropological approaches used in research do not constitute theories in the formal sense.

Postmodernism had forced anthropologists to rethink the basic concepts, premises, and goals of the discipline. To many postmodernist anthropologists the self-critical aspects of anthropology, in which writers of ethnographies reflected on their own culture, continued to be important in research, as exemplified by Behar's "returning to Jewish Cuba" (2007). Other anthropologists have been quite interested in "subaltern," or underclass, cultures in America as well as other nations, focusing for example on the way of life of drug dealers in East Harlem and welfare families in Brooklyn. This focus on the life of everyday people is to show that they are not the passive instruments of elite domination, but rather actors making decisions and choices within the structure of constraints. They are able, if they desire, to modify their behavior and patterns of relationships, and in this way effect change.

Globalization

The radical political agenda of many postmodernists that is more or less evident frequently highlights how the global affects the local and vice versa. Anthropological research since the 1950s clearly reveals what a potent force globalization has become. Africans have cell phones and Papua New Guineans have transistor radios. Globalization and its local effects are therefore forces with which anthropologists must deal. For example, in Highland New Guinea, what are the local effects of growing coffee as a cash crop and selling it to traders who come along the Highlands highway? This represents an incorporation into a worldwide network of coffee moving from villagers to, ultimately, your morning cup of coffee. What is the power relationship between the traders and growers, what are the ideas associated with this relationship, and how do these affect other parts of the way of life of these people and their relationship with the several levels of politics and ultimately the Papua New Guinea state? Are those on the local scene relatively powerless, as one might expect? Some who use the globalization framework are interested in the way ideas and perceptions are formed and manipulated by the elites of capitalist systems in order to hold subalterns in their places, disguising what is in reality class exploitation (Ong 1999).

With globalization has come the idea of a "**world culture**," that is, the universality of particular cultural traits, whose spread is a consequence of globalization. Cultural universalism refers to cultural elements such as the Internet, McDonald's, and Nike sneakers. Technological objects such as "Blackberries" are known over the world although many people do not possess them. Scientific ideas have the same status. This parallels the idea of a "world polity," that is, the world as a single social system exemplified by multinational corporations and the United Nations (Lechner and Boli 2005). (See also Berger and Huntington who talk about an emerging global culture [2002: 2].) World culture operates alongside and interpenetrates the more particularistic aspects of local culture. For example, the McDonald's in Moscow serves a local variation of the McDonald's menu. The relationship between the local and the global has become a significant focus, no matter the topic of one's research.

Neo-Marxism

With regard to Marxist thinking in anthropology, many talk about the demise of the older version of this theoretical framework and its rebirth in several different forms. Berger points out how the campaign by French farmers against McDonald's represented a transformation of the economic concerns of the farmers and became "a defense of French civilization against American barbarity" (2002: 2). "Neo-Marxists" are interested in the nature of the power relations present in the "symbolic production of culture . . . [which sees culture as] 'politicized' [and] as a 'site of contestation'" (Barnard and Spencer in Baldwin et al. 2006). The traditional focus of Marxism on power relations has continued in a new form. A particular culture is a consequence of a particular power structure. Rejecting an "essentialist" definition of culture, culture becomes ideology that is a consequence of economic and political forces operating in a processual manner (Baldwin, Faulkner, and Hecht 2006: 48). Hall's definition of culture (1980) with its focus on the "unconscious forms and categories which produce consciousness" still continues to have relevance (as cited in Faulkner et al. 2006). This would seem to be a return to Lévi-Straussian structuralism, the structural Marxian version. The older version of "Marxist world system theory" emphasized the "penetration" of the capitalist system with the coercion of the less powerful by the more powerful. More recently, the focus for understanding globalization has become the idea of "circulation" and exchange, though it is recognized that this circulation of goods and ideas takes place in an assymetrical space (Dissanayake 2006: 29).

Evolutionary Psychology

Evolutionary psychology is another approach that impinges on anthropology. The significant focus of this approach is the application of Darwinian natural selection to the study of the human mind, which becomes a product of evolution like any other part of the human body. Brain and mind "evolved to solve problems encountered . . . during the Upper Pleistocene . . . [it] is equipped with species-specific 'instincts' that enabled our ancestors to survive and reproduce and which give rise to a universal human nature" (Workman and Reader 2004: 1). Evolutionary psychology is based upon the concept of universals we introduced earlier. Following Noam Chomsky, who argued that all languages exhibit a number of universal features, the evolutionary psychologists argue that not only languages but also cultures are all based on common underlying patterns. This is because the human brain is organized in a certain way. Thus the structure of the mind, including human cognition, results in or produces both the universal structures of language and of culture. Evolutionary psychologists argue that there is a gene for reciprocity or social exchange. This results in the universal characteristic that everywhere humans exhibit behavior demanding reciprocity in exchange (Cosmides and Toobey in Buss 2005). The cooperative behavior of humans and other species, more specifically "reciprocal altruism" in which one gives and does not get an immediate return, which is basically delayed reciprocation, is also a universal. If this is a universal principle based on the genetic structure of humans, then why do we see so many varieties of types of exchange? That is because cultures everywhere elaborate different aspects of social exchange, just as universal features of "language" are shaped so that each language is unique. Evolutionary psychologists also argue that there is a fundamental underlying structure for morality. Pinker thinks that there is most likely a gene for morality (*New York Times Magazine*, January 13, 2008). A good person is one who is generous and fulfills obligations in social exchange; a bad person is one who lies, cheats, and defrauds and does not uphold obligations. As in social exchange, however, every culture elaborates its own aspect of morality—for some it involves laws about food, for others respect for authority or fairness in business, and so on. Xenophobia, or fear of strangers, is also seen as having played significant roles in the evolution of human behavior.

The postmodern emphasis on uniqueness meant that the comparative aspect of anthropology, which pays attention to what cultures have in common as well as how they differ, was left by the wayside. The postmodernist argument has been that even the physical world is not characterized by deterministic regularities—so why should we expect such regularities to characterize human social behavior? However, this viewpoint ignores the fact that because of the constraints of culture, there is no absolute freedom of action or complete randomness in human behavior. People do behave in ways that demonstrate cultural regularities. The emphasis now is on substantive ethnographic materials and questions, and the comparative dimension is reemerging as relevant and important in anthropology.

＊＊＊

The journey to another place or another time, which we defined at the beginning of this chapter as the hallmark of anthropology, is recapitulated by each fledgling anthropologist as she or he embarks on fieldwork. Lévi-Strauss, in his personal memoir, *Tristes Tropiques* (1961), saw his own fieldwork in terms of just such a journey. His journey to the field took him from the Old World to the New World, from the cold North to the tropical South, to a world that contrasted in every respect with his own. His goal was to find what he characterized as a simple form of society, since he felt that to understand how societies work, it is best to study one that is elementary in its organization. As in all fieldwork situations, he was first struck by great cultural differences. However, in time, Lévi-Strauss, the sophisticated French student of philosophy, saw behind the painted faces of the Nambikwara a humanity he shared with them. He wrote, "I had been looking for a society reduced to its simplest expression. The society of the Nambikwara had been reduced to the point at which I found nothing but human beings" (Lévi-Strauss 1961: 310). The pages that follow represent a journey into the world of anthropology.

SUMMARY

- The central concept of anthropology is culture. Culture consists of the things people make, their behavior, their beliefs and ideas.
- The belief that one's own culture represents the best way to do things is known as ethnocentrism.
- Cultural relativism is the idea that each culture is unique and distinctive, but that no one culture is superior.

- Some anthropologists utilize the comparative approach to compare cultures. This method identifies fundamental similarities of cultural patterning as well as differences.
- Anthropology's holistic perspective uses culture as an organizing concept and stresses the relationship among economics, politics, art, religion, and other activities.
- Cultures should not be conceived of as separate, bounded entities. Individuals usually live their lives in a world of overlapping cultures.
- Changes are constantly taking place in culture. Individuals are not simply recipients of culture; they are active participants involved in reworking their cultures. Their activity is referred to as agency.
- Culture is integrated, but only to a degree. Contradictions are frequently found within a culture.
- Culture is learned and acquired by infants through a process referred to by anthropologists as enculturation.
- As cultures reproduce themselves, changes occur.
- Culture deals with meanings and symbolic patterning, while society deals with the organization of social relationships within groups.
- Chimpanzees use tools and this constitutes a type of proto-culture.
- The evolution of culture was dependent on the prior development of bipedalism and increased brain size.
- Verbal language could only appear after the anatomical features necessary for its production were in place.
- The development of cooking some 1.9 million years ago led to changes in the evolution of culture.
- Though cultural differences do exist, all cultures share certain fundamental similarities, which are referred to as cultural universals.
- The variations between cultures are due to differences in cultural rules.
- When individuals interpret cultural rules, they are acting as agents. As a consequence, there is variation within a culture in observing the rules.
- Social structure, which is constituted of particular patterns of social relationship, includes social groupings that may be organized on the basis of family, kinship, residential propinquity, common interest, or class.
- Nineteenth-century anthropology, conceived of as a science, was dominated by evolutionary theory.
- Evolutionary theory then was succeeded by cultural relativism, as propounded by American anthropologists. Each society was seen as unique and different.
- British anthropology rejected evolutionary theory and adopted functionalism, which stressed the concepts of structure and function.
- Structuralism sees the elements of a culture in relationship to one another as they form a structure that conveys cultural meanings.
- Contemporary analytical approaches are much less unified and do not share a single set of assumptions, as did the theoretical points of view. Many contemporary anthropologists work within historical or symbolic frameworks that do not constitute theories in the formal sense.

- Postmodernism in anthropology has found fault with the scientific approach and with generalization, arguing that anthropology should totally embrace humanism and strive to capture the uniqueness of each cultural situation.

SUGGESTED READINGS

Cerroni-Long, E. L., ed. *Anthropological Theory in North America*. Westport, CT: Bergin & Garvey, 1999. An overview of contemporary anthropological theory at the end of the century.

Erickson, Paul A. and Liam Donat Murphy, eds. *Reading for a History of Anthropological Theory*. Peterbourgh, Ontario: Broadview Press, 2001. A selection of historical readings from Karl Marx and Edward Tylor to Michael Taussig and Marilyn Strathem.

Kuper, Adam. *Culture: The Anthropologists' Account*. Cambridge: Harvard University Press, 1999. A historical examination of the culture concept, along with an evaluation of its usefulness.

Layton, Robert. *An Introduction to Theory in Anthropology*. New York: Cambridge University Press, 1997. A general introduction to anthropological theory, which takes into consideration the fragmentation of the subject over the past two decades.

Manganaro, Marc, ed. *Modernist Anthropology: From Fieldwork to Text*. Princeton, N.J.: Princeton University Press, 1990. A collection of papers dealing with modernism and postmodernism.

SUGGESTED WEBSITES

www/discoverchimpanzees.org. Look at the site to compare chimpanzee behavior and communication with human culture and human language.

www.morris.umn.edu/academic/anthropology/chollett/anth4901/links.html. A list of websites giving biographies and theoretical positions of some fifty eminent anthropologists from the nineteenth century to the present.

http://lilt.ilstu.edu/rtdirks. A series of sites having to do with the anthropology of food and food habits around the world.

Chapter 2

The Anthropological Method

THE METHODOLOGY USED BY nineteenth-century anthropologists, who focused on the evolution of culture, involved examining the information collected by travelers, explorers, missionaries, and colonial officials who visited or lived for a time in the parts of the world where societies of interest to anthropologists were located. After the turn of the century, fieldwork by professionally trained anthropologists who lived among the people, observing them firsthand, learning their language, and participating in their ceremonies, became the defining ethnographic methodology for anthropology, and still is today.

FIELDWORK

Franz Boas was the first person to carry out what we would call fieldwork. In 1883–1884, he worked with the Eskimos, now called Inuit, of Baffin Island in Labrador. He first familiarized himself with the literature on the area, including accounts of voyages of discovery and missionary descriptions of Inuit ways of life. He learned the Inuit language from missionary word books and grammars. His research problem was to examine the way in which the Baffin Islanders migrated over the terrain and exploited the region economically. He traveled by dogsled from village to village, and lived in people's igloos. Shortly after this, Bronislaw Malinowski was the first Englishman to carry out extended fieldwork in the Trobriand Islands.

How does one gain perspective on another society? The answer for the anthropologist has always been to step outside the web of his or her own cultural world to closely examine another, often vastly different, way of life. But before entering that "other cultural world," anthropologists today must develop a set of research questions to be posed, and consider the methods to be used to answer them. This set of questions is referred to by some as a research design. However, these questions are not cast in stone, and are frequently transformed as the field research proceeds. The anthropologist must also apply for funds to do the research, sometimes from private foundations or from government agencies such as the National Science Foundation. Before leaving for the field, the present-day anthropologist, like Boas, must become acquainted with the area in which the research is to be done by doing a literature search, reading whatever has been published on the area of the research, as well as on the research questions. He or she also consults unpublished archives, census data, colonial records, and the like before the fieldwork commences, as well as during and after leaving the field to gain a historical perspective.

The heart of fieldwork is **participant observation**—living with other people, learning their language, and coming to understand their behavior and the ideas that are important to them. It usually includes living in their kind of house, be it the black goat-hair tent or a mud-brick house; donning their dress on ceremonial occasions (see Rosman in Kanuri garb in the illustration on page xvii); and eating their food. This is how one learns about the everyday life of the people. Fieldworkers celebrate the happiness of birth rites and mourn at funerals. If possible the field language is learned before the anthropologist goes to the field. Otherwise, the anthropologist learns the language in the field while learning the culture at the same time. Very often, going to the field involves negotiations with various authorities and making connections with individuals who are part of the research setting one has selected. When first immersed in a different culture, the fieldworker experiences **culture shock** on recognizing that his or her own culture is not "natural," because other people do things differently. At first, as the anthropologist learns this new culture, he or she is in the position of a child in that culture.

Participant observation involves an inherent contradiction. A participant operates inside a culture, while an observer is like a stranger, looking in from the outside. On the other hand, an observer is expected to remain detached and to report objectively what he or she sees and hears. As Hume and Mulcock note, "[T]he practice of ethnography also assumes the importance of maintaining enough intellectual distance to ensure that researchers are able to undertake a critical analysis of the events in which they are participating" (2004: xi). Learning another culture is very different from objectively analyzing and interpreting it. Since the anthropologist is interacting and participating with other people, it is impossible for him or her to be completely objective. Participant observation is difficult to carry out because it involves this basic paradox. It remains an ideal that is never completely realized.

Participation in another culture means learning how to view things from the "insider's" point of view, that is, from another culture's point of view. This means investigating the concepts and ideas that order that world. When anthropologists do fieldwork, they bring with them their own cultural categories, ways of seeing things, and personal values. They try to avoid allowing these to color their perceptions. Paying attention to one's own cognitive framework as one operates in another culture is categorized as **reflexivity**. As O'Reilly notes, "Contemporary ethnography . . . attempts to be reflexive, that is to say it is conducted in full awareness of the myriad limitations associated with humans studying other human lives" (2005: 14). This means being aware of the fieldwork context, the nature of the power relationship between "researcher and researched," the possible effects of colonialism, the question of whose voice or voices are to be represented in the research, and finally, how the ethnographic text is to be produced. Reflexivity means constructing the ethnographic text not only in terms of one's own authorial style, but also in terms of historical, political, and economic factors and relevant global and technological developments.

In addition to observations, anthropologists gain information by interviewing individuals in the culture, who are referred to as **informants** (or consultants). These interviews were usually open-ended, meaning that when the informant was stimulated by the anthropologist's questions to go beyond them following different "information paths," the anthropologist followed along. These contrast with interviews based solely on questionnaires, which have fixed boundaries. To the anthropologist today, the informant is a fieldworker-colleague. In the interaction between informant and anthropologist, the informant increasingly learns what her or his fieldworker-colleague is interested in finding out and also gains a certain amount of knowledge about anthropology. In trying to explain their culture to the questioning anthropologist, informants often begin to understand their own culture in a way they did not before. When informants attempt to explain their culture to anthropologists, the informants are objectifying their own cultural experiences. They may become conscious of cultural rules in their own society that they had not previously been aware of. In their interactions, informants and anthropologists are, in a sense, operating in an area between their two cultures. This process is repeated with other informants, and a pattern begins to emerge. The data are checked against the anthropologist's own observations.

The personal relationship between anthropologist and informant is a complex one. Individuals who become mentors and sources of much information for the anthropologist are referred to as **key informants**. The key informant for Rosman while he was doing fieldwork among the Kanuri was the District Head, a titled aristocrat (pictured in the illustration on page xvii) much older than the fledgling anthropologist, whom he adopted. This relationship was crucial for the fieldwork, since many people trusted the anthropologist and were willing to talk to him as a consequence of it. However, given this connection, other sources of information were closed to the anthropologist because those who had such information were in opposition to or belonged to another faction of the community.

Fieldwork involves reciprocity on the part of the anthropologist. However, the nature of what the anthropologist returns to his or her informants is highly varied. In rural as well as urban areas, the anthropologist with a vehicle often reciprocates by becoming chauffeur for the entire community, as Rubel did for the Kalmyk Mongols with whom she worked in New Jersey. Frequently, anthropologists become partisans, taking on the causes of the community as advocates in the media or becoming expert witnesses for them in the courts. When legal conflicts between the Hopi and the Navajo arose concerning land ownership, anthropologists who had done research with the Navajo advocated their side of the case, while those who had worked with the Hopi looked at the case from the Hopi point of view.

Anthropological fieldwork involves a whole series of ethical considerations. As O'Reilly has noted, "The extent to which we are, or can be, open and honest about our research, gain fully informed consent from participants, disclose what we are studying and producing, respect confidentiality and avoid exploitations raises dilemmas for every ethnographer" (2005: 81–82). Fieldwork involves the anthropologist in a moral dilemma. It could be said that anthropologists use informants for their own ends, since the anthropologists return home with the information gathered. The analysis and publication of this information in a dissertation or book helps the career of the anthropologist, but in what way does it help the people whose way of life has been recorded? Often, research done by anthropologists in the past may be of use to the subjects of that research today. For example, the Kwakiutl as well as other Native American peoples have found that ethnographies written at the turn of the century like those of Boas are of value as written records of traditions, the knowledge of which by this time is being lost. Such information often proves important for Native Americans in pursuing claims regarding fishing and land rights. The product of the anthropologist's work also makes a scholarly contribution to the wider understanding of human behavior.

The anthropologist performs two kinds of **translation**. First, there is the translation from the language of the informants to the anthropologist's native tongue. Problems usually arise because the terms in the indigenous language are never exactly equivalent to the concepts in English. For example, when property passes from one generation to the next before the death of the members of the senior generation, as among the Kwakiutl, this is sometimes translated as inheritance in the ethnographic literature. However, the definition of inheritance in English presupposes the death of the member of the senior generation, so this is not a correct translation. The second type of translation is to translate the cultural categories of the society being studied into the language of anthropology, that is, the conceptual framework being set forth in *The Tapestry of Culture*. The basic assumption of this kind of translation is that cultures have characteristics in common, above and beyond those aspects that are unique. Comparative research, using anthropological concepts, reveals this.

"Writing down" as O'Reilly observes, is the beginning of fieldwork. The researcher writes down (transcribes) discussions with informants along with his or her observations. "Writing up" involves pulling together everything he or she knows about a category (marriage, households, betel-nut chewing, cockfighting, inheritance, etc.). These are overlapping categories. For example, cockfighting in Bali involves religion as well as politics. This is still description. Some prefer to use the term "fine description" (Frake 2007: x); others "thick description." But anthropology is more than description. The interpretation of the material is just as important. This is supplied by the anthropologist who begins with what the informants have told him or her. Interpretation involves moving beyond the meaning of symbols given by the informant. In the Kwakiutl marriage described below, some of the participants blackened their faces as they would for warfare; the anthropologist interprets this to mean that warfare symbolizes marriage. The two sides were in an antagonistic relationship to one another and in the future they would compete for the children of the marriage to become members of their respective groups. The analysis attempts to illuminate the structure and meaning of a culture.

In the past, anthropological fieldworkers investigated societies that were small both in scale and in population size, where all the spheres of human activity could be explored by a single investigator. Some anthropologists selected islands for study, while others went off to Africa and elsewhere, selecting a village or a camp on which to concentrate and from which they generalized about the culture. This unit had its own name and was sometimes referred to as a **community**. The community was bounded in the sense that its members concentrated their interactions within it, and it had an internal social structure. The interaction of the community with other communities was always of concern to the anthropologist.

ANTHROPOLOGY MOVES TO THE STUDY
OF COMPLEX SOCIETIES

In the study of small-scale societies, the community had been taken to represent the culture as a whole. When anthropologists began to study complex societies in the 1930s, it was clear that a single community could not be considered representative of, for example, India, France, or Japan. Such complex societies could not be encompassed in their totality at the level of detail at which the anthropologist worked. **Complex societies** are very heterogeneous and culturally diverse with regional, class, occupational, religious, and ethnic differences. Such diverse groups have subcultures of their own that may become units of analysis for the anthropologist. He or she must keep in mind that what is happening locally is always related to what is happening on a broader national or international level.

Anthropologists working in complex societies may also focus on particular problems, such as rural-urban migration or the effects of the closing of a mine or factory in a company town. They may even study nuclear weapons scientists at Livermore and Los Alamos National Laboratories (Gusterson, 1996). The unit of analysis here is dictated by the problem. It may be a farming community, a labor union, a corporation, or a social movement. In the United States, for example, an anthropologist might focus on some aspect of American culture, like the debate over abortion, or choose to examine cultural aspects or particular problems among the different racial and ethnic populations that are the sub-groupings of our society.

Earlier, anthropologists tended to work in areas where their own nations had established colonial empires. American anthropologists worked with American Indians, and British and French anthropologists worked in British and French colonies. Some of the entities that anthropologists in the past assumed were indigenous groupings were, in reality, colonial constructs. After first contact with Europeans, small-scale societies and even indigenous states were increasingly brought under the jurisdiction of larger political entities, typically European colonial empires. Colonial administrations imposed a structure consisting of tribes and districts replacing indigenous units in order to govern more easily. At first, anthropologists paid little attention to the nature of the articulation of "tribes" to the colonial empires of which they were a part. Today they are interested in the historical process of how these societies were incorporated into newly formed nation-states. These groups have been transformed into ethnic groups, often in conflict with one another, and with the nation-state. Modernization, industrialization, and globalization have made small-scale societies part of a world system, and anthropologists now investigate how they have responded to these changes.

In recent years, postmodernist anthropologists have become concerned with being more reflexive, that is, informing the readers of the ethnography about the experiential aspects of the fieldwork, not just the anthropological conclusions of the field research. In "confessional" ethnography, the fieldworker is at the center of the stage, and the focus is on how he or she came to know a particular social world, not on that world itself. The way of life of the people being studied becomes secondary to the fieldworker's feelings and experiences. These new ideas about the ethnographic enterprise have had an impact on the field, if only to make anthropologists more explicit about what they are doing when they do fieldwork. The anthropologist also reveals how the various aspects of fieldwork, and other types of research related to the project at hand, are translated into conclusions in the form of an ethnography that accurately reflects the social world that the anthropologist has chosen as a subject of research.

It is typically the case that anthropologists come from powerful industrialized nations to conduct research in Third World countries, and the initial relationship in the field may be perceived in terms of dominance and subordination, or power differentials, between anthropologists and informants. Often, anthropologist and informant use one another. The anthropologist may be at the mercy of the informant's desires, sometimes being used to further his or her political ambitions. Informants may see the anthropologist as exploiting them in that he or she is "taking away" their myths, rituals, and traditions, and erroneously representing and portraying them as violent people or helpless victims to the outside world. All these factors, which are involved in the interaction, influence the nature of the information that is obtained and must be taken into account when the data are being analyzed.

As noted earlier, in addition to fieldwork, anthropologists utilize other techniques to collect data, such as historical and archival information, as well as data from archaeological and linguistic investigations and census materials. Research on a culture's past, sometimes referred to as the ethnohistorical approach or historical anthropology, has become particularly significant as anthropology has moved to a processual model.

Increasingly, the social reality that an anthropologist chooses to study is "deterritorialized," meaning that it is what is now referred to as **multi-sited ethnography**. As Marcus has noted, "Multi-sited ethnography is designed around chains, paths, threads, conjunctions or juxtapositions of locations in which the ethnographer establishes some form of literal, physical presence" (Marcus 1995: 205). Multi-sited ethnography takes many forms. Strauss (2005) focuses on yoga and the way it has moved West, and then back to India again, and Werbner (1996) has focused on Pakistanis living in Britain and their transnational contacts with their Pakistani homeland.

A KWAKIUTL MARRIAGE

Marriage is both a cultural category as well as an event, or series of events. In the following pages we will analyze marriages from two different societies: a Kwakiutl marriage at the turn of the twentieth century as described by Boas (1966) and the American wedding of Maria Schriver and Arnold Schwarzenegger in the 1980s. In examining marriage in these two very different societies, we will demonstrate how weddings illustrate very different themes in Kwakiutl society and in American society. Nevertheless, as shall be seen, there are also fundamental similarities. In both societies, extravagant spending and showering guests with opulent gifts is a way of showing high status and acquiring great prestige.

The groom's party arrives by canoe at an early stage of a Kwakiutl marriage. A crest belonging to the groom's *numaym* decorates the front of the canoe. Edward L. Curtis took this picture before 1914.

In addition to short visits, Boas did three months of participant observation during the Kwakiutl Winter Ceremonial of 1894–1895. The rest of the enormous bulk of ethnographic material on the Kwakiutl was collected by means of informant interviews by Boas or most frequently by George Hunt. Boas trained him to be a field researcher and to record texts in phonetic transcription in Kwak'wala, the language of the Kwakiutl. Though Hunt's mother was Tlingit, another tribe on the Northwest Coast, and his father was Scottish, he grew up at Fort Rupert, British Columbia, the home of a number of Kwakiutl tribes, and was a native speaker of Kwakw'ala.

In Boas's time, the aim of the anthropologist was "**salvage anthropolgy**"—that is, to record as much of the traditional culture as possible before it disappeared. As a consequence, his description did not note that the Kwakiutl at that time were part of the larger Canadian economic and political systems. The blankets they distributed in the ceremonies described below were purchased from the Hudson Bay Company trade store. Enormous amounts of material goods involved in the ceremonies were obtained with money earned from working locally in canneries and from employment in Victoria, British Columbia, and elsewhere. This description of a Kwakiutl marriage was based on informants' accounts collected primarily by George Hunt as well as some participant observation by Hunt. Boas organized the data into a description of the marriage rite, which remained unpublished until after his death. It describes the marriage rites of the children of chiefs that occurred in the nineteenth century. It combines a general description of the rites with events from actual marriages. To the reader, this may appear to be more a description of several elaborate exchanges of property, primarily the Hudson Bay blankets (as can been seen in the illustration of a distribution), rather than an account of the marriage of two people. The advance in social rank of the participants and their groups, which derived from the **potlatch** (a large-scale ceremonial distribution), often entirely overshadowed the marriage's primary purpose—the coming together of a man and a woman to establish a family.

There were three stages to a Kwakiutl marriage. The first stage was the beginning of negotiations between the parents of the young people, sometimes even without their knowledge. First messengers and the chiefs were sent by the groom's side to the bride's father requesting the bride in marriage. They were rewarded with blankets, and returned to the groom, who also gave them blankets. That night, the groom went to eat in the bride's house, sitting next to her. The bride's father told the groom that he expected to receive five hundred blankets as the bride-wealth payment. After the groom's father assembled the five hundred blankets, they were piled in front of the door of the bride's father's house. The groom's father, accompanied by several chiefs, then went to the house of the bride. The blankets were handed over to the bride's father, and he expressed his thanks.

Several months later, at the next ceremony, the men of the groom's **numaym** (the Kwakiutl term for kin group) and those of other *numaym* blackened their faces and dressed like warriors as they went to the house of the bride with the final payment of blankets. These would "move" the bride. Her doorway was protected against the "invading warriors," who often had to run a gauntlet of flaming torches or go through a ring of burning cedar bark soaked in oil. At one wedding, after the groom's men proved they were not afraid of fire, the bride's father "called forth the Devourer of Tribes [a mythical monster], who had devoured all those who had tried to woo his daughter. It was a large mask of a sea bear attached to a bear skin (worn by a man). Seven skulls and a number of long bones were hidden under the bear skin. As soon as the man wearing this masked dress came forth, the bride's father poked its stomach with a pole and it vomited skulls and bones."

Then the chiefs from the groom's side made their traditional wedding speeches. In these speeches, the chiefs called upon their supernatural powers, which had come from ancient mythological times inherited down through their families. These powers were said to be used to "move the bride." Each received a payment of blankets for, as the Kwakiutl say, "the weight of his breath," referring to the speech that was delivered at the wedding. Their combined breath acted as a weight upon an imaginary scale used to move the bride. The greater the names of the bride, the more speeches, or "breath," were needed to move her to the groom.

After the last of the chiefs had spoken, the ceremony of giving out the blankets brought by the groom's side for the bride's side took place. After the bride's side piled up two hundred blankets alongside the bride, a chief from the bride's side said, "Come to your wife and take her into your house with these two hundred blankets as her mat." The bride then walked to the groom's side and was led to the seat she was to occupy. In the evening, distinguished young men from the

Kwakiutl tribes sang love songs and led the bride and groom back to his father's house. The groom sat alongside his new wife, and this part of the marriage ceremony came to an end.

Some time later, usually after a child was born to the couple, the wife's side prepared to make a large return of goods to the husband's side, which Boas refers to as the "repurchase of the wife" by her own *numaym*. The Kwakiutl refer to this as payment of the marriage debt. Since the wife's group was the "receiver" of the marriage potlatch from the groom's group, it was under an obligation to make a return. This return at another potlatch did not consist of Hudson Bay Company blankets but of objects referred to in Kwakiutl as "trifles" or "bad things." From the list of items included, trifles and bad things meant just the opposite. The return was far in excess of what the wife's father had received. In an example of a repurchase, the items included the following traditional Kwakiutl valuables—120 box covers set with sea otter teeth, 100 abalone shells, copper bracelets, horn bracelets covered with dentalia shells, miniature coppers, 1,000 strings of dentalia one fathom long, 200 dressed deerskins, 500 cedar bark blankets, 200 mats, an equal number of wooden boxes, two neck rings of twisted copper, and hammered copper objects of great value, "as mast of the marriage debt canoe." Names or titles and privileges were also given to the son-in-law as part of the repurchase payment.

The speaker for the chief distributes blankets at a Kwakiutl wedding potlatch held in 1894.

When everything was ready, the wife's father announced that he was going to hold a potlatch to repay the marriage debt. The song leader of the *numaym* wrote a new song to commemorate the occasion, describing the privileges and the copper that were to be given to the groom. Coppers were ceremonial objects in the form of a shield, made of beaten local copper, which attained increased value in terms of the number of blankets paid for them as they passed from chief to chief at potlatches. At the ceremony, after breakfast, the men of the father-in-law's *numaym* carried the goods to the son-in-law's house. There they arranged the box covers, which were part of the distribution, in a square or rectangle (a catamaran) because it was supposed to represent the boat upon which the father-in-law came to repay the debt. All the other goods were piled on top, and the father-in-law's *numaym* "went on board," and sang the song of repayment of the marriage debt. In keeping with the symbolism of warfare, the younger brother of the son-in-law, his face blackened as a warrior, rushed out and split one of the box covers with an ax, thereby "sinking the catamaran." The box containing symbols of the privileges to be given to the son-in-law was carried out from the father-in-law's house, and the wife emerged from the house bearing the copper that was to be transferred. The father-in-law's speaker presented the box of privileges and the copper to the son-in-law. Then the wife's father's speaker arose and bestowed names that traditionally belonged to her family upon the husband and his two sisters. These names constituted the final part of the marriage repayment.

Marriage for the Kwakiutl was a series of events that extended for years, since the repurchase of a wife was normally not held until after the birth of a child. When the wife had been repurchased by her father, she was free to return to him unless her husband purchased her for the second time. This would be followed by a second repurchase by her own group. These exchanges of property via potlatches could take place up to four times, after which the wife's rank was so high, because of the goods expended in successive repurchases, that she could "stay for nothing." The families of both groom and bride respectively increased their rank and prestige with each potlatch and its transfer of goods.

Boas's English translation of the Kwakw'ala texts that describe Kwakiutl marriage includes terms such as *property, debt, privileges, inheritance, rank, seats, names,* and *titles.* These English terms do not easily map onto Kwak'wala terms that have no precise equivalents in English. We would not consider rights to use a personal name as "property," but Kwakiutl "names" are the "property" of a *numaym.* In our culture, an individual possesses a personal name, which is not inherited after death in the same manner as property. These points all illustrate problems of translation encountered in describing another culture. Another problem for Boas in the translation of the description of a Kwakiutl wedding was that Boas never could find a satisfactory English translation for the Kwakiutl term *numaym,* which refers to a kind of kin group. He therefore left the Kwakiutl term untranslated in his description. When there are too many such native terms, the reader's ability to comprehend is seriously hindered.

Analysis of the ritual of marriage among the Kwakiutl reveals that it embodies many of the central themes in Kwakiutl culture. The Kwakiutl emphasis on rank was reiterated again and again throughout the course of the marriage potlatch. The high rank of the bride demanded that there be large payments for her. At the same time, such payments enhanced the rank of the giver, the groom. The importance of making a return for what one has received was reflected in the repurchase payment made by the bride's side. Seating of guests at the potlatch and the order in which they received gifts revealed their ranking with respect to one another. The claim to rightfully own a title or name was made by a chief at a potlatch when he recited the line of ancestors through whom the title was passed until it reached him.

In the Kwakiutl marriage, we see that marriage is a symbolic form of warfare. Warriors from the groom's side come to "capture" the bride. Marriage and warfare are similar in that the two sets of affines are in opposition to one other, and in competition. Since one's wife comes from what is in the marriage symbolically the "enemy" side, there may be implications for husband/wife relations, and for gender relations generally. The groom's side recompenses the bride's side, when they take her, by paying "bride-wealth." Just as the payment of "blood money" recompenses the side in a feud that has suffered a loss, bride-wealth payment pays for the "capture" of the bride. The symbolism of warfare continues when the bride's *numaym* repurchases her, using a symbolic war canoe.

AN AMERICAN MARRAIGE

American weddings are differentiated according to religion, ethnic background, occupation, and social class. The factor of personal preference, absent in the Kwakiutl wedding rituals, plays an important role in the wide range of American weddings that occur each year. Each Sunday, the *New York Times* has a column describing interesting weddings, which illustrates their wide diversity. Weddings are conducted by male and female rabbis, priests, and ministers, Wiccan ritualists, swamis, and so on. They often meld different traditions such, as Jewish and Korean, and Native American, African-American, African, Christian, and Egyptian Kemetic rituals.

Kwakiutl marriage rituals had kinship, economic, religious, political, aesthetic, and performative dimensions, which led Marcel Mauss, the French anthropologist of the early twentieth century, to refer to such rituals as **total social phenomena** (1925). In complex societies, in addition to the variegated nature of social groupings, there are complex political economies and institutional specializations. As a consequence, when one examines weddings in America, one finds that there is a wedding industry: wedding magazines, wedding boutiques, wedding planners, individuals who specialize in providing distinctive commodities and specialized services, and even a TV channel devoted to the different aspects of weddings. Just as the Kwakiutl wedding informed us about Kwakiutl culture, an analysis of an American wedding provides insights into the particular American subculture of the individuals who are marrying.

Books on etiquette, such as *Good Housekeeping's Book of Today's Etiquette*, provide guidelines on how to conduct an American wedding. They are statements of the ideal pattern. We have chosen to describe the wedding of two well-known celebrities in American society because of its similarities to the Kwakiutl marriage of the children of high-ranking chiefs. We will describe the wedding of Maria Shriver and Arnold Schwarzenegger, which was held on April 26, 1986. Since it took place 23 years ago, it is necessary to examine it as a historical event, in much the same way we did for the Kwakiutl wedding.

The materials, or "cultural documents," used to assemble the description of this wedding are today considered media material, or texts, or representations, the subject matter of the Anthropology of Mass Media. As Coman notes, "[W]hen mass media cover a public ceremony or event involving ritual behavior . . . they alter it . . . [by imposing] a new configuration . . . the media [making] a change of emphasis: They place the center of interest . . . at the emotional level (of the actors and officiating agents) leaving the ritual structure in the shadow" (2005: 47). This means that we must be very clear about our sources of information, and their particular perspective. The media then become a rich source for research on the culture of weddings among the elite of American society—the Kennedys.

The following description is not based on participant observation and fieldwork. Instead, it is based upon the public information provided in *Time* magazine, the *New York Times*, and the *Cape Cod Times*. Because Shriver and Schwarzenegger were celebrities, there was sufficient information to construct a description we could analyze.

Just as the daughter of a Kwakiutl chief belongs to the highest ranks of her society, Maria Shriver, a member of the Kennedy clan, belongs to the moneyed American elite. Her mother, Eunice, was a sister of the late president John F. Kennedy. Her father, Sargent Shriver, was the first director of the Peace Corps, a former ambassador to France, and the Democratic nominee for vice president in 1972. At the time of her marriage, the bride was co-anchor of the *CBS Television Morning News*. The Austrian-born Schwarzenegger is the son of a local Austrian police chief, now deceased. The two first met eight years earlier, a year after her graduation from Georgetown University, at a tennis tournament sponsored by the Kennedy family. At that time she was working for a small television station. She interrupted her own career in 1980 to work on the presidential campaign of her uncle, Ted Kennedy. In 1981, she moved to Los Angeles to continue her career in television, and to be near her boyfriend, Arnold Schwarzenegger. He has a degree in business and marketing from the University of Wisconsin, but became famous as a bodybuilder, and then as a movie star.

Arnold proposed to Maria during a trip to Austria in August 1985, and they subsequently purchased a $3 million house in Pacific Palisades. They did not marry until she was thirty and he was thirty-eight, eight years after they first met. This may have been due to the demands of their two careers. Women with careers now tend to marry when they are in their thirties, though this was not the case in American society at an earlier time.

The wedding was held at the summer residence of the Kennedys in Hyannis, Massachusetts. At the rehearsal dinner, which was held at the Hyannisport Country Club, Arnold's mother hosted an "Austrian clambake" and served lobster and wiener schnitzel, and Arnold dressed in traditional Tyrolean lederhosen. A bachelor party for Arnold had been held a month earlier in Santa Monica. The Roman Catholic wedding mass, performed by the Reverend John Baptist Riordan, was held at St. Francis Xavier Roman Catholic Church, the Kennedy family's parish church in Hyannis. Since the couple wanted their wedding to be a "private" affair, details of the wedding were kept from the media. The flow of information about the wedding was controlled by a publicist hired to handle wedding press coverage. Kennedy influence was used to maintain tight security and keep gossip columnists and journalists away. Provincetown Boston Airline, which flies to Hyannis, was persuaded to lock up its computer a day before the wedding so that the guest list would not be revealed. The bride, ever career-oriented, told her viewers she would be off for several days, without mentioning her forthcoming wedding, and the groom arrived the day before the wedding from Puerta Vallarta, where he had been filming a new movie, *Predator*, the film that subsequently launched him as a superstar.

The bride wore a white muslin, silk, and lace gown with an eleven-foot train made by Christian Dior, who had designed the wedding dress of the bride's mother in 1953. The groom wore a classic gray cutaway coat, pleated white shirt, gray vest, and gray-striped ascot, what Emily Post deems appropriate for afternoon weddings. A fellow bodybuilder, Franco Columbu, served as best man. The thirteen ushers included the bride's four brothers, the bridegroom's cousin and nephew, and bodybuilder friends of the groom. The maid of honor was the bride's cousin Caroline Bouvier Kennedy, daughter of the late President Kennedy. Among the bridesmaids were several other Kennedy cousins. Some sixty women, guests, and members of the bridal party had their hair coiffed at the local beauty salon on the morning of the wedding, but the bride's hair was done by her own hairdresser, who came from Los Angeles. Besides members of the Kennedy family, the more than 450 guests included television celebrities Diane Sawyer, Tom Brokaw, and Barbara Walters; advice columnist Abigail Van Buren; pop artist Andy Warhol (wearing a black leather jacket over a black tuxedo, and black Reebok sneakers); and singer/actress Grace Jones. Wearing the most recent fashions of that time, female guests were attired in dresses sporting geometric designs from the art deco period and from pop art. Since reporters were barred from the church itself, a viewing stand was erected across the street for them.

The bride and her father walked up the aisle to the familiar wedding march, Wagner's "Bridal March" from the opera Lohengrin ("Here comes the bride"). In the religious ceremony that had been planned by the bride and groom, the couple exchanged traditional Roman Catholic vows, rewritten to remove sexist language, replacing "man and wife" with "husband and wife." Short selections from the New Testament were then read by Senator Ted Kennedy and by a friend of Schwarzenegger. Intercessions, which are included in a Roman Catholic wedding, written by the wedding couple and read by the bride's parents and brother, called for an end to terrorism and war, proclaimed the bride and groom as a model couple, honored deceased Kennedys, and discussed the meaning of Passover. These topics were a reflection of themes important in America at the time. Discussing the meaning of Passover, which was taking place that month, demonstrated the ecumenical feelings of the bride and groom. Oprah Winfrey, the television host, then read Elizabeth Barrett Browning's poem "How Do I Love Thee?" a choice of the bride. After a series of musical selections, the ceremony concluded with the bridal couple's walking together down the aisle to Rodgers and Hammerstein's "Bridal March" from *The Sound of Music*.

After the ceremony, limousines and buses took the guests to the Kennedy compound for the reception. All air traffic within a two-mile radius of the compound was prohibited from cruising below 2,000 feet for the entire day. The reception was held in two huge white tents, with heaters to keep out the chill winds. Fruit trees in pink and white blossoms decorated the tents. The guests danced to music played by Peter Duchin's band, which often plays at society occasions. An elaborate lunch (including cold lobster in the shell and chicken breast with champagne sauce) was concluded with the cutting of an eight-tier, 425-pound wedding cake, topped by traditional figures of a bride and

Maria Shriver and Arnold Schwarzenegger leaving the church after their wedding.

groom, baked by the Shriver family chef and modeled after Maria Shriver's parents' wedding cake. The couple took a brief honeymoon before returning to work. Today, Arnold is now governor of California, and Maria is not only First Lady of California, but a contributing editor for *Dateline NBC* and an author of several books. The couple has four children, two boys and two girls.

Many events that occurred in connection with the wedding were not reported by the press. There is usually a formal meeting of the two sets of parents before the wedding, if they have not met before. There is no information on whether or how the Shrivers met Mrs. Schwarzenegger. Often, the bride receives an engagement ring, and an engagement party is held. Wedding gifts may be publicly displayed at the bride's home. According to *Good Housekeeping's Book of Today's Etiquette*, "The expenses of the wedding are divided in a time-honored way." The bride's family pays for the following: invitations; reception cards and announcements; rental of the place for the ceremony; fees for the organist, choir, and sexton; transportation of the bridal party from house to church or temple and from there to the reception; bridesmaids' bouquets; the bride's gifts to the bridesmaids; the bride's wedding dress and trousseau; and all the expenses of the reception. The groom pays for the engagement and wedding rings, marriage license, contribution to the clergyman, flowers for the bride's mother and groom's mother, and the bachelor dinner. No information was provided regarding the financial arrangements of the Shriver-Schwarzenegger wedding. Today, couples often live together, sometimes for several years, before getting married. Despite this, they may elect to go through some or all of the ceremonies associated with an American wedding. The bride still wears a white gown, a symbol of virginity.

Just as a Kwakiutl wedding reveals themes and patterns central to Kwakiutl culture, so does an American wedding illuminate symbolic themes in American culture. The bride in her white gown symbolizes purity and virginity, though given today's sexual mores, she probably does not possess these attributes. Nevertheless, the bride is not likely to wear a purple gown. The hall bedecked with blossoms and the wedding march with its all-too-familiar lyrics echo the same themes. In American society, the powerful, moneyed elite frequently reiterate their familial connections at ritual occasions. Thus we are reminded in various ways of Maria Shriver's connection to her mother, Joseph Kennedy's daughter, to the late President Kennedy, and to the rest of the Kennedy clan. Like her mother's gown, her gown was designed by Dior; and her wedding cake was a replica of her mother's. This extravagant wedding with 450 guests was characterized by the couple as a "private" affair. However, though they called it a private affair, Maria and Arnold meant just the opposite, just as in a Kwakiutl wedding reference to "trifles" meant just the opposite. The fact that there was a publicist controlling information dispensed about the wedding attests to its public nature. Though the press was kept out of the church during the wedding ceremony, a stand was erected for them to assure that they witnessed and publicized the wedding.

THE COMPARATIVE APPROACH

Earlier we noted that fieldwork and participant observation were the hallmarks of anthropological methodology. In the same manner, the comparative approach has been important to the discipline. What does a comparison of the Kwakiutl and American weddings reveal? In comparison to the Kwakiutl wedding, in an American wedding the focus is almost exclusively on the bride and groom, even when one of them is a member of an important family, The Shriver-Schwarzenegger wedding more or less conformed to the ideal pattern of an American wedding, though much grander in scale. American weddings are less a matter of two kin groups establishing a relationship, as was the case in a Kwakiutl wedding, and more a matter of bringing together and displaying the groom's and bride's personal networks of friends and colleagues. At the Kwakiutl wedding, marriage is a matter of relationships between kin groups. It is symbolized by the witnessing by an enormous audience of the capture of the bride by warriors of her husband's *numaym*, who "move" her to her husband's group.

In the American wedding, the emphasis is on the bride and groom. Both had established careers and were such well-known celebrities that the audience in attendance, comprising their personal networks, was large and studded with famous personalities, making this wedding different from other American weddings. Celebrities such as Oprah Winfrey and Andy Warhol used the occasion of the wedding to draw attention to themselves by their dress and behavior. The bride and groom planned the wedding, acting as the centers of all activity, though other individuals from their respective families as well as friends and relatives played some part. This emphasis on the couple themselves echoes the importance in American culture of the newly formed family as autonomous and separate from other families. The Kwakiutl wedding, on the other hand, was a total social phenomenon in which the entire community was involved and in which elements of economics, politics, and political maneuvering concerning transfer of a whole series of privileges as well as property were at issue. In fact, Boas, the observer, noted that these things overshadowed the purpose of the wedding—to establish a new family. In the American wedding, economics were involved, in that goods were purchased, and there were many expenditures. The Kwakiutl marriage itself was an institution for transfers of large amounts of property. Religion was involved in the American wedding, in that a priest officiated and Roman Catholic vows were exchanged. Similarly, in the Kwakiutl marriage the rights and privileges exhibited demanded the recitation of myths linking people to their ancestors, a cornerstone of Kwakiutl religious belief. In a Kwakiutl marriage the whole underlying structure of Kwakiutl society is played out. In contrast, in America, where there has been more institutional separation, an entire wedding industry exists. A wedding really focuses on the couple who is establishing the new family, and other aspects are only tangentially related.

In addition to the differences, there are some interesting similarities that should not go unnoticed. In both Kwakiutl and American societies, all weddings are public ceremonies witnessed by guests. In both instances, the guests who attend the ceremony and communally eat the food perform the function of publicly witnessing a rite of passage. In the American wedding described, an attempt was made to keep it "a private affair," limited to just 450 witnesses. However, as celebrities, the bride and groom also wanted the entire society to witness their wedding, but they wanted to control the information that was made available. In both societies, prestige is determined by the size of the outlay, which, in turn, relates to the social status of the families involved. The more lavish the display, the greater the standing and renown of the participants and their families. Potlatches have been described as boastful displays of "conspicuous consumption." Wealthy Americans have been accused of using such displays at weddings to promote themselves, and promoting one's self can help in name recognition, especially in politics. In this respect the extravagant display of the Shriver-Schwarzenegger wedding was very much like a potlatch.

SUMMARY

- The defining methodology of anthropology is fieldwork conducted through participant observation, which involves an inherent contradiction because one is at the same time an observer outside the culture as well as a participant within it. Cultural shock is the realization that other people do things differently and one's own culture is not "natural."
- The fieldworker must learn how to view things from the native's point of view, that is, according to the concepts and ideas that order their world. The anthropologist talks to informants, but also makes his or her own observations.
- The anthropologist gains information from people referred to as informants, who eventually become fieldworker-colleagues.
- Fieldwork involves reciprocity in the sense that informants provide information and the anthropologist gives various forms of assistance, including acting as a partisan for the group in legal matters.
- The anthropologist does two kinds of translations. The first is from the indigenous language to the anthropologist's own language and the second is into the analytical concepts of anthropology.
- The unit of analysis for anthropology in small-scale societies was the community. As anthropology has shifted to complex societies, the unit of analysis is now dictated by the particular problem selected.
- Postmodernists have forced us to make our fieldwork procedures more explicit, including informing readers about the experiential aspects of fieldwork and how the data are translated into conclusions in the form of ethnography.
- In addition to fieldwork, anthropologists utilize other techniques to collect data, such as historical and archival information, as well as data from archaeological and linguistic investigations and census materials.
- Rich, detailed ethnographic descriptions, applied in the comparative approach, reveal certain basic similarities between American and Kwakiutl weddings, along with the differences in symbolic meanings.

SUGGESTED READINGS

Codere, Helen. "Kwakiutl," in *Perspectives in American Indian Culture Change*, edited by Edward Spicer. Chicago: University of Chicago Press, 1961. An account of Kwakiutl culture change from the time of the Indians' original initial contact with white society to the contemporary period.

DeWalt, Billy R. *Participant Observation: A Guide for Fieldworkers.*Walnut Creek, CA: Altamira Press, 2002. A detailed account of how to do participant observation, a central aspect of anthropological fieldwork.

Robben, Antonius and Jeffrey A. Sluka. *Ethnographic Fieldwork: An Anthropological Reader.* Malden, MA: Blackwell Publishers, 2007. A collection of articles, both historical and contemporary, regarding how fieldwork is conducted.

SUGGESTED WEBSITES

www.schwarzenegger.com. Governor Arnold Schwarzenegger's official website with information on his life, photos, and memorabilia.

www.native-languages.org/kwakiutl.htm. Information on the Kwak'wala language and an introduction to Kwakiutl culture.

www.alanmacfarlane.com/DO/filmshow/film30.htm. *Reflections on Fieldwork.* This film takes the viewer through the whole fieldwork experience.

Chaper 3
Language and Culture

LANGUAGE AND CULTURE ARE like two sides of a coin. Language is a part of culture, yet it is more than that since language is the means through which culture is communicated, expressed, and learned. As human culture developed, some means of communication—a language—also developed. Only humans have the capacity for language, grammar, syntax, and speech. In any language, a limitless number of possible sentences can be constructed and used to convey an infinite number of cultural ideas. This allows humans to communicate cultural ideas and symbolic meanings from one generation to the next in a cumulative fashion, and to constantly create new cultural ideas. Because of this, human language is significantly different from any other system of animal communication. Language classifies the world around us. It classifies things; it classifies actions; it classifies our experiences. Objects and events are ordered by language into categories of time and space. This is what "grammar" does in addition to performing many other functions. Each language has its own grammar. The "logic" of a culture is also the "logic" of its language, how it orders the world. As we shall see, the concepts and the methods used for analysis are the same for language and culture.

THE EVOLUTION OF LANGUAGE

There is no doubt that animals have the capacity to communicate with one another, from honey bees that use an elaborate dance to communicate the presence of a new food source, to monkeys, chimpanzees, and other primates who have developed call systems to communicate the presence of predators. Some primates have been taught sign language to communicate, to answer questions, and to perform other limited tasks. However, human communication in contrast to animal communication is verbal, uses arbitrary symbols, has words with meanings, can transmit cultural ideas, involves spontaneous usage, turn-taking, the double layering of sounds and words, reference to objects not present, and the presence of structure and creativity (Workman and Reader 2004: 229–30). In no animal communication system are all these criteria present, nor do communication structures of any primate involve grammar of any sort.

How did this ability of humans to acquire language evolve? According to Pinker and Bloom, the presence of language gives humans a selective advantage, since information can be more efficiently conveyed (1990). In other words, natural selection favored forms among whom the capacity for language had developed. A number of hypotheses have been offered regarding the "why" of language evolution, that is, why did the capacity for language develop. Bickerton, for example, sees the evolution of a proto-language with single words and minimal syntactic organization that evolved in order to label objects in the environment, followed by the development of syntax and abstract categories that evolved with "reciprocal altruism" (1995). No example of either stage of what Bickerton has hypothesized has ever been found.

Chomsky has argued that there is an innate cognitive basis for human language, that babies are predisposed to language learning and child language acquisition (which we shall discuss in detail in the next chapter). However, Chomsky does not propose that these mechanisms are the result of natural selection but that "the language organ evolved for some other purpose and was co-opted, or exapted for its current purpose" (Workman and Reader 2004: 259).

The genetic basis for this "innate disposition" has not yet been ascertained, although researchers working with the language disorder known as "specific language impairment," which is the result of a damaged gene, see this as a demonstration of the presence of a series of genes relating to this innate capacity (Workman and Reader 2004: 263, See also MacNeilage and Davis 2005: 711). Regarding when the capacity for language began to evolve, some have argued that *Homo erectus*, which appeared in Africa some 2 million years ago, had the capacity for some form of language on the basis of the presence of two areas of the brain related to language. Neanderthals are also seen as capable of speech and the possession of some form of language. Other specialists disagree, claiming that language only appeared with *Homo sapiens* (Lieberman 1998).

THE STRUCTURE OF LANGUAGE

Like culture, language is patterned. As the Swiss linguist Ferdinand de Saussure (1915) pointed out, the units of language that carry meaning are two-sided. One side is the physical characteristics that make up the word. These characteristics consist of sounds, or vibrations of the vocal chords, transmitted through the air, which emanate from one person and are received by the ear of another. The other side consists of the word's meaning or what it stands for. For example, the word *tree* is made up of a particular series of sounds—t/r/e—and it stands for:

The same object is referred to as *arbre* in French and *Baum* in German. Thus the connection between any combination of sounds that make up a word and its meaning is mostly arbitrary—that is, there is no intrinsic and natural connection between the sounds of a word and its meaning. The same meaning—tree—is conveyed by a different combination of sounds in each language. Occasionally, there is some natural connection between sound and meaning, as occurs in words that imitate natural phenomena, such as *buzz* and *hiss*. Language is therefore not completely arbitrary.

Phonemic Structure

We have mentioned that language is patterned. Let us begin at the level of sound, the building blocks of language. Every language has a small number of basic sounds, usually between twenty and forty, which are used in various combinations to make up the units of meaning. These basic sound units are called **phonemes**. All languages are constructed in the same way. From a small number of phonemes, arranged in different ways, an infinite number of words can be produced. For example, the English word *pin* differs in meaning from *pan* since /i/ is a different phoneme from /a/. Add /s/ to *pin* and you get the plural form of *pin*, that is, *pins*. But if the /s/ is added to the beginning of the word, rather than the end, the result is *spin*, a word with a totally different meaning. Thus, the same phonemes in a different order produce a word with a different meaning.

If the reader has been paying close attention, he or she will have noted that the /p/ in *pin* is different from the /p/ in spin. If you hold a sheet of paper in front of your mouth and pronounce pin loudly, the paper will flutter because the /p/ in *pin* is aspirated (air blows out of the mouth). Pronounce *spin* and the sheet of paper remains still, because the /p/ in *spin* is not aspirated. The two /p/'s are said to be **allophones** of the same phoneme. They are variant forms of the single English phoneme /p/. They vary because of the different contexts in which they are found.

The phonemes of a language form a structure or system. The phonemes of English can be divided into vowels and consonants. For a native speaker, English consonants seem independent

and unrelated to one another. However, let us examine the following list of some English consonants:

t	d
p	b
f	v
s	z
k	g

When one makes the sounds /t/ and /d/, the tongue, teeth, and lips, which are called the points of articulation, are in the same position for both. This is also true for the other paired sounds on the two lists—/p/ and /b/, /f/ and /v/, /s/ and /z/, and /k/ and /g/. There is a relationship between the group of consonants in the left-hand column and the group of consonants in the right-hand column. The consonants in the column on the left are all pronounced without vibrations of the vocal cords. They are voiceless consonants. The vocal cords vibrate when those in the right-hand column are pronounced. These are called voiced consonants. The distinction between voiced and voiceless consonants is one of the several kinds of distinctions characterizing English phonemes. All these features organize the set of English phonemes into a structure and serve to differentiate each phoneme from every other. If the phonemes of a language are structured, then what is their function? Phonemes serve to differentiate words like *pin* and *pan*. Though phonemes themselves do not carry meaning, their function is to differentiate words in terms of their meanings.

Morphemic Structure

The units of language that carry meaning are called **morphemes**. Morphemes are not equivalent to words, because some words may be broken into smaller units that themselves carry meaning. For example, the word *shoemaker* may be subdivided into three separate morphemes: shoe, make, and -er, each with its own meaning. Each of these morphemes is in turn made up of phonemes. Some morphemes, like shoe, can stand independently. These are called free morphemes. Others, like -er, meaning "one who has to do with," are always found bound to other morphemes (as in speaker, singer, and leader) and are referred to as bound morphemes. Sometimes two or more forms, that is, combinations of phonemes, have the same meaning. The form -er has the same meaning in English as -ist in the word pianist. These two forms, -er and -ist, are known as **allomorphs** of the same morpheme. Every language has its own morphemic structure.

Syntax and Grammar

The rules by which larger speech units, such as phrases and sentences, are formed compose the **syntax** of a language. English, like all other languages, has rules about the order of words in a sentence. Word order conveys meaning. Thus, "man bites dog" has a meaning different from "dog bites man." The ways in which a language indicates singular and plural are also part of its syntax.

The complete description of a language is known as its **grammar**. This would include the phonology (a description of its phonemic system), the morphology (a description of its morphemic system), and the syntax. In addition, a complete description of a language would also include a **lexicon**, or dictionary, that lists all the morphemes and their meanings.

LINGUISTIC RELATIVITY

When linguists began to encounter languages unrelated to Indo-European, a language family whose languages were spoken in Europe, they thought (incorrectly) that the newly discovered languages like those spoken by Native North Americans could be analyzed in terms of Latin grammatical categories. These linguists were ethnocentric in their approach and termed languages "advanced" if they were spoken by people who were "civilized." Hunters and gatherers, who were considered at a lower cultural level, were said to speak "primitive" languages. It became evident to Boas, and later to others, that there is no one-to-one relationship between technological complexity or cultural complexity, and linguistic complexity. All languages known to linguists, regardless of whether the society had writing, are equally complex. This is known as **linguistic relativity**. It parallels the concept of cultural relativity. Furthermore, Boas convincingly demonstrated that it was necessary to analyze each language in terms of its own structure.

LINGUISTIC UNIVERSALS

Earlier, we pointed out that anthropology uses the comparative method to investigate cultural similarities and cultural differences. Linguistics adopts the same approach. The differences between languages are immediately apparent and the similarities point to the universals in language. There are two approaches to language universals. In the first approach developed by Greenberg, he compared languages to see what they had in common (Greenberg 1966). For example, by examining word-order patterns, he demonstrated that subject precedes object in declarative sentences. Among the broad conclusions of this approach are that all languages have vowels and consonants, nouns and verbs, and some form of negative construction (Bybee 2006: 180). The second is based on Noam Chomsky's approach to a universal grammar, a "language faculty," which is based on the underlying cognitive structure of the human mind (Cook and Newson 2007: 45–50). While the first approach is empirical and inductive, the second, which we discussed earlier, is highly theoretical and deductive.

LANGUAGE AND COGNITION

There is a close and intimate relationship between language and experience. Boas's study of the Kwakiutl language, which led him to his concept of linguistic relativity, includes a discussion of how, in Kwak'wala, the speaker must indicate how she or he knows about an action other individuals are performing. For example, in the sentence:

"The lady was washing clothes."

it is necessary in Kwak'wala to make the following distinctions: Did the speaker actually see the lady washing clothes? Did the speaker infer that she was washing clothes from the sound that was heard? Did a third party tell the speaker that she was washing clothes? In our language distinctions in tense must be made, however in Kwakiutl the distinctions which indicate how the speaker knows the information must also be made, and are part of the grammar of the language. In some languages the grammar includes forms by means of which speakers must specify how they acquired the information they are imparting. English does not have this feature as part of its grammar, though the information can be provided by the speakers, if they wish to give it, with additional words. Boas made the general point that in all languages, grammatical rules, such as the one in this example, are obligatory. The speakers of a language are not usually aware of these grammatical rules, though they guide all utterances. Boas pointed out that such grammatical rules remain unconscious.

People speaking different languages have a different way of organizing what they experience. Thus a Kwakiutl person always attends to how he or she receives information, because this is necessary in conveying information to others. Since a vital issue is how you know what you know, one can imagine the comparison between the precision of a Kwakiutl speaker as a witness at a court trial and the lack of specificity of the equivalent English-speaking witness at the same trial. The relationship between language and how society organizes experience was also explored by Boas's student Edward Sapir. He argued that language was a guide to social reality. Conceptualizations of the real world are seen, to a great extent, to be based unconsciously upon the language usage of a society. This line of argument was carried to what many people considered an extreme position by Benjamin Lee Whorf. He proposed that the conception of the world by a member of a particular society was determined by the language or "fashion of speaking" of that society.

ETHNOSEMANTICS

There is a close connection between the way language is organized and the way culture is organized. This can be seen most clearly by examination of a specific cultural domain, such as the organization and classification of the world of animals, the world of plants, or the system of colors. In all languages, there is a set of terms used to refer to animals. The world of animals is separable from other domains in the world. It is distinct from the domain of plants, though they both are alive in contrast to the inanimate world of rocks and soils. People using different languages will sort the world of animals in ways different from our own. For example, the Linnaean system of classification, which we use, groups human beings, bats, and whales as mammals on the basis of such criteria as being warm-blooded, suckling their young, and having hair. Whether these animals fly, live on the land, or swim in the sea is not important. Other peoples use different criteria for their animal classifications. The Karam of Papua New Guinea, studied by Ralph Bulmer, distinguish birds from other animals in their language. However, the cassowary, a flightless bird like an ostrich, which stands over five feet tall, is not placed in the category of birds (where we place it). Rather, the Karam place it in an anomalous category. Unlike birds, it does not fly. It walks on two legs and is seen as related to humans. We have noted above that our category of mammals is distinguished by a series of criteria, distinctive features, or components, which differentiate this category from that of reptiles. Though this classification was developed by Linnaeus in the eighteenth century, it is for the most part in accord with the classification based upon Darwin's theory of evolution, later scientifically confirmed. The categories are hierarchically organized into successively more inclusive groupings, from species to genus to class. When anthropologists like Bulmer study Karam language and Karam culture, they not only collect the meanings of all animal terms and the categories in which the Karam place them but must then determine the reasons why the Karam sort and classify animals in this way. They ascertain the distinctive features the Karam employ when they classify forms such as the cassowary. Each language employs its own cultural logic in making classifications. The anthropological investigation of this topic is known as **ethnosemantics**.

Another cultural domain that has been studied in this manner is the set of linguistic terms used for colors. Every language has a set of terms for colors, though the number of these terms varies from one language to another. Viewers looking at a rainbow see an undivided series of colors, one color grading into another, while as speakers of different languages they will divide this spectrum differently. Brent Berlin and Paul Kay did a comparative study of basic color categories in many different languages throughout the world that shows that the classification of colors in different languages is not completely arbitrary (1969). What Berlin and Kay have demonstrated is that the color spectrum is not randomly divided. There is order and regularity in the way in which languages add to the number of color terms. This does not mean that people over the world, who lack terms for particular colors, cannot in a descriptive fashion express in their language the colors they see (without a term for blue they might say "it is the color of a robin's egg"). What it does mean is that the color categories their language possesses will organize their experience in a particular way.

In this general discussion of ethnosemantics, we have shown the way in which the concept of distinctive features is used. A common way of distinguishing two categories from one another is for one of the categories to possess an attribute that the other category lacks. In the Linnaean classification, mammals are warm-blooded animals while reptiles are not. Thus, one might say that the category of mammals is the "plus" category. This is a distinction biologists make. The linguist Roman Jakobson makes a similar classificatory distinction, which he called **markedness**. The category in which the attribute was present he called the marked category, and the category in which it was absent, the unmarked category. Jakobson pointed out that in linguistics, the unmarked category is the more general and inclusive of the two. For example, in English, we have the words *lion* and *lioness*. The marked category is the word *lioness* (-ess is added to lion, thus marking it). *Lion* includes *lioness*, as in the sentence "Christians were thrown to the lions." The presence of marked and unmarked categories is a universal (Greenberg, 1966).

SOCIOLINGUISTICS

Saussure made a distinction between **langue** and **parole,** that is, between language and speech. To obtain information about a language, the fieldworker observes and records many examples of speech. These examples are analyzed in order to obtain a picture of the grammar, or underlying structure, the "langue" of that language. **Sociolinguistics** deals with the analysis of parole, or speech, and its social functions. Recently, anthropological linguists have been interested in a more integrative way of understanding how language organizes social life. Language is an integral part of the construction of social life; it also provides a window on the social process. Language forges shared cultural understandings and acts as a medium of social exchange and connection between people (Mertz, 1994: 441). In chapter 1, we discussed the concepts of social structure, social organization, and agency. Agency emphasizes individual choices and parallels parole (or speech) in that each individual has his or her own idiosyncratic speech patterns. Nevertheless, just as the behavioral choices (or agency) of each individual are constrained by the rules of his or her social structure, so too, are speech patterns constrained by the grammar of the language (Ahearn, 2001). The speech pattern used by individuals provides the initial force for language change.

Male and Female Speech

In many societies, there are distinctions between male and female speech, though, of course, men and women speak to one another as members of the same speech community. As infants and young children learn their language and their culture, they are simultaneously learning female- and male-specific behavior, as well as appropriate gender-related forms of speech. Recently, this simple binary opposition between masculine and feminine has been replaced by "[g]ender . . . conceptualized as plural, with a range of femininities and masculinities available to speakers at any point in time" (Coates 2004: 4). In a survey of differences between male and female communicative competence (meaning grammar and appropriateness of usage) in a range of linguistic settings in Great Britain, Coates noted that men dominate the conversation in a variety of different environments, though not all, by interrupting women, by controlling the topics of the conversation, and by becoming silent. Men talk more, swear more, and use imperative forms to get things done. In contrast, women use more tentative speech, use more linguistic forms associated with politeness, and make greater use of minimal responses (like "uh-huh") to indicate support for the speaker. In single-sex conversations, a different pattern emerges. Whereas men disagree with or ignore each other's utterances, women's style in conversations with other women is collaborative, melding or blending their talk. They tend to talk about people and feelings, rather than about things. In contrast, men pursue a style of competitiveness, individual assertion and power, and discuss current affairs, travel, and sport (Coates 2004: 128). These different styles sometimes result in miscommunication between the sexes.

In another approach to the examination of "men's talk," Coates focused on the stories men told as a means of understanding British masculine cultural ideas (2003). Her analysis revealed that most men are oriented toward and constrained by "the hegemonic norms of masculinity," although some in her sample were prepared to challenge these norms (Coates 2003: 196ff). More recently, the relationship between language and sexuality in the linguistic tactics of gay men has also been the subject of research. As Droschel notes, "[H]ow do a sample of British and American gay men negotiate and construct their sexual identities through their knowledge and use of gay slang?" (2007: 118). She demonstrates the way in which the growth of heterogeneity in the gay community has resulted in a diversification of vocabulary use with the development of different linguistic subsets. She focuses on the way in which "gay individuals explore and constantly recreate the lexical system in order to construct their identities" (Droschel 2007: 137).

Gender and language in the workplace has also been the subject of research for some time. Early research showed that for professional-lay interaction such as that between doctors and patients, gender was a significant factor. Male patients often controlled conversations with female doctors, and male doctors "used more aggressive power-asserting strategies, compared to the female doctors' co-operative and mitigated approaches" (Holmes 2006: 145). More recent approaches have focused on how males and females using discourse in the workplace construct positions of equality or authority depending on context. As women moved into positions of authority, the nature of the workplace and the discursive styles used became more complex. Mullany's study of managerial business interaction in United Kingdom corporations, particularly evident at business meetings, revealed that the language and speech strategies managers used to status equals and subordinates depended more on their institutional position rather than on their gender (Litosseliti 2006: 130). Litosseliti notes, for example, that "[w]ar and sport metaphors in business are examples of language use that arguably reinforces masculine discourses and social practices while marginalizing feminine behavior" (2006: 147). Holmes suggests that "women with aspirations to leadership are faced with a dilemma—unless they learn to operate in the masculine styles which dominate so many workplaces, they will not be taken seriously. On the other hand, more feminine ways of interacting at work, although often paid lip-service and apparently valued when men adopt them as aspects of their management style, are, it is claimed, regarded negatively when adopted by women in many organizations" (Holmes 2006: 210).

Women do not always assume a subordinate role using polite forms of speech, in contrast to the assertive style of men's speech. In a study of a Malagasy-speaking community of Madagascar, Keenan (1974) has observed that men tend not to express their sentiments openly, are not confrontational, do not show anger, and behave with discretion, especially on ceremonial occasions. In contrast, women tend to speak in a straightforward manner, directly expressing anger and criticism that may insult the person being addressed. Women do much of the bargaining, buying, and selling in this society and, therefore, direct speech is characteristic of the marketplace.

African-American Speech

Differences in language usage in the United States parallel regional and class, as well as racial, differences. The speech of the African-American community, referred to in the past as Black English but now referred to as **African-American Vernacular English (AAVE)**, in contrast to Standard English (SE), is the subject of much scholarly research and debate (Morgan 1994,

Mufwene et al. 1998, Kautzsch 2002, Rickford 2006). AAVE was originally viewed by some as a collection of mistakes and deviations from Standard English, which reflected deficits in the cultural behavior of its speakers. What are the roots of AAVE? As Rickford points out, there are two schools of thought, "The Anglicist or dialectological position is that AAVE's features come primarily or entirely from regional dialects spoken by white indentured servants and other English settlers . . . . The opposed, creolist position is that AAVE reflects substrate African influences and the simplifying, restructuring processes associated with pidginization" (2006: 27; see also Dillard 2005). Kautzsch uses written sources such as ex-slave narratives to construct the sociohistorical background for the development of AAVE (2002). Though AAVE is also seen as having creole affinities and creole roots, it is not viewed as a full-fledged creole. However, Gullah, the language spoken on the Sea Islands off the coast of Georgia, is considered by some to be a creole, structurally related to the creole languages that developed on the islands in the Caribbean where English was the colonial language (Rickford 1998: 191, Rickford 2006: 28).

Originally, it was believed that African languages and cultures were completely destroyed by the experience of slavery. However, today scholars have challenged this opinion and have come to the conclusion that the African heritage continues to exist in both African-American language and culture. According to Smitherman, the uniqueness of AAVE is to be found in the following three areas: "(1) patterns of grammar and pronunciation; (2) verbal rituals from the oral tradition and the continued importance of the word as in African cultures; and (3) the lexicon, developed by giving special meaning to English words, a practice that goes back to enslavement and to the need for a system of communication that only those in the slave community could understand" (1998: 207). Many studies have analyzed the African-American male style of speech referred to as signifying, sounding, or playing the dozens. This kind of verbal skill, which is an echo of the verbal rituals of the African language tradition, is most frequently associated with adolescent males and involves taking a serious topic that is culturally significant and playing with it in an ironic, sarcastic, and humorous fashion (Morgan, 1994: 333).

Labov and others concluded that AAVE should be viewed as a system, with an invariant core, that should be analyzed without reference to other dialects (Labov 1972, 1998). Many studies of AAVE were carried out in the 1960s in northern cities. Labov's findings from his Harlem research project and his later research received much prominence. His work demonstrated that phonological, syntactic, and lexical features mark African-American English as different from American English, though some of these differences were also present in other American English dialects. Most recently, Labov has proposed that AAVE represents the coexistence of General English grammar (syntax, morphology, phonology) (GE), which is similar to the grammar of Other American Dialects (OAD) and the African-American (AA) component (1998: 117ff.). According to Labov, the General English system of AAVE provides the grammatical component, permitting a semantic efflorescence in the AA component. Others like Alim have identified "many aspects of the BL syntactic (grammar) and phonological (pronunciation) systems that mark it distinct from . . . [White Mainstream English WME]" (2004: 233).

In his recent work, Labov regards the continuing divergence of AAVE from OAD and the fact that "many important features of the modern dialect are creations of the twentieth century and not an inheritance of the nineteenth" (Labov, 1998: 119). However, Vaughn-Cooke disputes Labov's prediction about the continuing divergence of AAVE from Standard English, noting that Labov has not presented "adequate evidence to support his claim, and that through extensive press coverage, he has disseminated erroneous information about a group of speakers to millions of people" (2003: 108). The claim about divergence is "contrary to expectations" (Stevens 1985).

Language is an important aspect of the construction of cultural identity. African-American Vernacular English is seen by some as a symbol of slave mentality, in particular by members of the Nation of Islam, but by others as a symbol of resistance to slavery and oppression (Morgan 1994: 338–39). More significantly, today African-American Vernacular English plays a role in the construction of African-American identity in a multicultural America. However, as Mitchell-Kernan points out, both African-American Vernacular English and Standard English are necessary to improve one's life chances, since lack of Standard English harms one in school and in the workplace while absence of African-American Vernacular English deprives one of status within one's ethnic group (Mitchell-Kernan 1972, cited in Morgan 1994). In recent years, there has been an increase in the size of the African-American middle class. Studies have noted that for African Americans, the higher the class, the greater the consciousness of racial identity (Morgan 1994: 337–38). This is illustrated by African-American students in elite college campuses who employ African-American lexical, phonological, and grammatical features of African-American Vernacular English in both formal and informal contexts in order to reinforce their ethnic identity (Baugh 1987, 1992, cited in Morgan 1994: 338). DeBose describes a middle-class informant who was bilingual in Black English as well as Standard English and used "**code-switching**" depending on whether she was in an in-group or out-group context (2005: 139).

LANGUAGE CHANGE AND HISTORICAL LINGUISTICS

As noted in chapter 1, cultures are continually undergoing some degree of change. Since language is a part of culture, it too is always changing. Of course, during one's lifetime, one is not aware of linguistic change, except for changes in vocabulary, particularly slang words and expressions. If we compare our language usage today with that of the language of Chaucer's tales, the extent to which English has changed over the past centuries is obvious. It is apparent that present-day **dialect** differences represent developments, or language changes, from a single earlier form of the language. How do such dialect differences arise in the first place? **Speech communities** are made up of members of a group within a society who interact and speak frequently with one another. One speech community that is very similar to a neighboring speech community will develop slight differences in pronunciation or vocabulary, differentiating it from its neighbor. As these differences increase, they become the basis for greater dialect differentiation. Dialect differentiation, over time, leads to further divergence and eventually to the development of two separate languages.

If one examines French, Spanish, Portuguese, and Italian, one can immediately recognize many similarities. Some languages, such as Spanish and Portuguese, are more closely related than others, such as French and Portuguese. Because of the high degree of mutual intelligibility between Spanish and Portuguese, one could argue that these two languages are more like different dialects of a single language. All these languages, along with other languages, such as Rumanian, are daughter languages, descendants of the vernacular Latin spoken by the common people during the time of Julius Caesar. It differs from the literary Latin familiar to us from the scholarly works of that time. Dialects of the Latin language spread over large parts of Europe and the Mediterranean world as a result of Roman conquest. These dialects of Latin later developed into separate languages. The vernacular Latin of the Roman period is referred to as the **proto-language**. In parallel fashion, English, Dutch, German, and the Scandinavian languages compose the Germanic language family—all descended from a common proto-language called Proto-Germanic. The European languages we have just mentioned, along with other European and Asian languages, such as Persian, Hindi, and Bengali, form a large family of related languages called the Indo-European language family. All these languages are descended from a common ancestor, Proto-Indo-European. Where was this ancestral language located geographically? Recent research that combines linguistics with archaeology locates the original ancestral language in Anatolia (present-day Turkey) about 8,700 years ago. The earliest branches, Hittite and Tocharian, split off from Proto-Indo-European at this time. According to Renfrew, Indo-European languages were spread by the earliest farmers who migrated from Anatolia into Greece and the Balkans bringing with them agriculture and the Indo-European language (Atkinson and Gray 2006: 102).

A second large migration, referred to as the Kurgan expansion, occurred around five thousand years ago from the Ukrainian area, leading to the divergence of the Slavic, Germanic, Italic, and Celtic sub-families. Since the Proto-Indo-European speakers had words for beaver, otter, birch, and aspen, and used euphemisms for the ritually important bear, they must have lived in a temperate climate—that of the Ukraine. Other Indo-European speakers moved south into Iran and southeast into India, resulting in the diversification that produced other branches of Indo-European. Not all languages spoken in Europe are part of this family. Finnish and Hungarian belong to the Finno-Ugric family, while Basque, which is completely unrelated to any other language, is called a language isolate.

For the languages of Europe where written records have existed for millennia, the historical sequence of language development is known. Languages thought to be related are studied using the **comparative approach**. This can be illustrated with an example from the Germanic languages. The English word *dance* has as its equivalent the German word *Tanz*, and the English word *door* has as its equivalent the German *Tur*. These forms have the same meaning, and their phonemic structures are similar but not identical. These pairs are referred to as **cognates**. The initial d in English regularly corresponds to the initial t in German. These two forms represent modern divergences from the original phoneme in Proto-Germanic. This is just a single example of the many sound correspondences to be found between German and English.

As a result of their earlier association with small-scale societies, anthropologists have studied the languages of the indigenous people of North and South America, Africa, and Oceania. These languages had not been recorded in written form. In the same fashion as the European languages, these languages are organized in terms of language families, utilizing the concept of cognates and the comparative method. Some of these language families are very large, encompassing many languages, whereas others may be very small or may even be isolates, like Basque. Recently, linguists have shown the relationship between language families like Indo-European and Uralic, Altaic, Eskimo-Aleut, and Chukchi-Kamchatka, placing them in a single super-family, Eurasitic. The objective of this research is to try to show the hierarchical relationship between language families and the way in which different language groups developed as *Homo sapiens* spread out from Africa. The aim is to create a model of the Proto-Language from which all other languages developed (Cavalli-Sforza 2000: 169).

Languages also change as a result of **diffusion**, or borrowing from speakers of one language by speakers of another language. This may be the borrowing of words, sounds, or grammatical forms. Contact and borrowing come about in a number of different ways, some of them peaceful, others not. An excellent example of language change as a consequence of military conquest occurred after the Norman conquest of England (A.D. 1066). The Norman invaders, the conquering class, were speakers of an earlier version of French, while the subjugated English spoke Anglo-Saxon, a Germanic language that was the precursor of English. The English borrowed a series of terms referring to different kinds of cooked meat from the language of the French. The cow (Saxon), when cooked, became beef (*boeuf* in French); calf (Saxon) became veal (*veau* in French); sheep (Saxon) became mutton (*mouton* in French); and swine (Saxon) became pork (*porc* in French). The French words for the cooked versions have been incorporated into English.

Contact Languages—Pidgins and Creoles

One consequence of the European exploration and colonization of many parts of the world was to bring indigenous languages into contact with European ones. The result was the development of new languages known as contact languages, or **pidgins** and **creoles**. Pidgins are created by social conditions, like trade, that require the development of a "makeshift" language to enable communication between two or more language communities (McWhorter 2005: 11). The most important characteristic of pidgins is that for all speakers, they are second languages. Governed by rules, they have vocabularies and grammars that are simpler than their source languages. They are sufficiently different from their source languages so as not to be mutually intelligible with them (Sebba 1997: 15).

Several varieties of Pidgin English developed in the Far East and the Pacific out of nautical jargons during the nineteenth century. These have since become national languages. Tok Pisin is the Melanesian variety of pidgin. It originated among workers in the German colony of New Guinea, especially those from the islands of New Ireland and New Britain, who were recruited to work on German-owned plantations in Samoa. They brought the pidgin back with them on their return. Fifteen percent of the vocabulary of Tok Pisin derives from Tolai, spoken in the area around Rabaul, on New Britain, the early headquarters of the German colonial government (Lynch, 1998: 223–24).

When a pidgin language is no longer a second language, it is called a creole (Baker and Muhlhausler 2007: 92). For over 100 years, Tok Pisin remained a second language for its speakers,

A sign telling customers that they must order in English at a Philadelphia take-out restaurant is an example of language imperialism in the United States. The English-only ordering policy resulted in a discrimination complaint against the restaurant.

second to their native language. However, in the twentieth century, during the postwar period, Tok Pisin began to become the primary language for families in the urban areas of Papua New Guinea, where the adults came from different language areas, as a consequence of increasing rural urban migration and social mobility (Sebba 1997: 107). Tok Pisin is in the process of becoming a creole. Since the independence of Papua New Guinea in 1975, Tok Pisin has been the official language of the nation. Harrison notes that upon revisiting the village of Avatip, on the Sepik River, where he had done fieldwork in the late 1970s, the children no longer spoke their vernacular language; "Papua New Guinea Pidgin" (Tok Pisin) was their first language (Harrison 2001: 4).

Language Imperialism versus Language Renewal

One type of linguistic change is what Muhlhausler has called **linguistic imperialism** (1996). Before the arrival of Europeans in the late fifteenth century, the Pacific area was one of marked linguistic diversity. Up to 4,000 languages were spoken there, most of them in Melanesia, where 2 million people speak (or spoke) one quarter of the world's languages (Muhlhausler 1996: 10). This intensive language diversity existed side by side with bi- and multilingualism. As a consequence of European colonization and language imperialism, English, French, or German, or one of the pidgins we have discussed earlier became the dominant language in the respective colonial areas, and a trend from linguistic diversity to monolingualism and language death began. There were many changes in the indigenous languages that persisted, including losses of lexical items and changes in grammatical forms. The question of indigenous language maintenance in a new nation-state like Papua New Guinea pits multilingualism against the need of the nation-state to build a national culture and to have a single national language, in this case, Tok Pisin (or Neo-Melanesian, its more formal name), as a matter of policy. In urban areas of Papua New Guinea intermarriage is more common, and Tok Pisin is the language of the household as well as of the public arena. In rural areas, however, older people often speak only the indigenous language, while others are bilingual, speaking the indigenous language and Tok Pisin.

In some states in the United States, there have been attempts at legislation to make English, and only English, the official language. The argument advanced for doing so is, as in the case of Papua New Guinea, that the use of English alone would reinforce the notion of a single American culture and nation and have a unifying effect. This represents a kind of linguistic imperialism in the face of the current multilingual nature of education in our school system and the use of a multiplicity of languages in the courtrooms and the voting booths of the United States.

When a language dies, does that mean that the culture has died along with it? Language is often used as an important marker of cultural or ethnic identity, as we have pointed out for African Americans. When a community is bilingual in their indigenous language and in the dominant language of the nation-state, we find that each language may have its own functions and that switching from one language to another follows predictable patterns. Even when the trend toward monolingualism progresses, and only the grandparental generation speaks the indigenous language fluently, underlying patterns may be perpetuated. Woodbury cites a fascinating example of this in an Alaskan community. College students from Inupiaq and Yupik (Eskimo) communities use a variety of devices as qualifiers in written English essays to avoid sounding assertive. Circumspection is part of the way an individual should behave in their native culture (Kwachka and Basham 1990, cited in Woodbury 1993). This way of nativizing a replacement language is fragile and tentative since it is likely to disappear under pressure from the mainstream community. Woodbury concludes that while we cannot assume that a culture has died when a language has died, a fundamental way of organizing the surrounding world eventually disappears when a language dies, because it simply cannot be translated into the words and phrases of the dominant language. According to Woodbury, "Loss of a language leads to an unraveling, or restructuring, or reevaluation of cultural tradition" (1993: 14). Harrison notes, "Many linguists now predict that by the end of our twenty-first century—the year 2101—only half of . . . [the 6,912 languages spoken in 2001] may still be spoken" (2007: 3).

A large erosion of indigenous languages took place after the conquest of North America by the English, French, and Spanish. The recent response of many American Indian groups, like the Navajo, was to attempt to maintain and rejuvenate their language by developing Navajo language materials using the phonetic alphabet to teach the language to their children in a school setting. There is even a college at Rimrock in New Mexico that provides Navajo language instruction.

LANGUAGE, POWER, AND POLICY

Language is always politically important. The way in which speech is used to express power varies from culture to culture. For example, among the Kanuri, speaking in a low and unexcited tone demonstrates control and exercise of power. In contrast, in Western cultures, demonstration of power is often achieved by cursing, screaming, and ignoring the personhood of others present, as was characteristic of the speeches of Hitler and former President Nixon.

Governments and institutions in power make policy decisions about language usage. These policies often govern the use of languages in schools. For example, Ricento notes that "in Somalia, a country which lacks a functioning government, the only functioning schooling is financed by Arabs, which means that Arabic has replaced Somali—the national language—in school curricula" (2006: 6). Policies of language usage also relate to national identity. Blommaert describes how postcolonial Tanzania declared an indigenous language, Swahili, the official language of the country, along with "the former colonial language English" (2006: 238ff).

Political policy and power are involved when a government selects a particular language as a national language from a number of options. Political leaders in newly independent India faced the need to establish language policy that reconciled India's linguistic plurality with widespread official use of English. The language diversity of India is widely acknowledged by linguists and politicians alike; the enumeration of this diversity also depends on political policy. Dasgupta notes that the 1961 census mentions 1,642 languages; the 1971 census reported 221, and the 1981 census 106 languages (2003: 25–26). There were a number of different language hierarchies depending on political, economic, and social factors. Prior to independence from Great Britain, the primary language issues on the subcontinent were linguistic diversity, and the relative statuses of Urdu, Hindi, Sanskrit, and English. Urdu use is associated with Muslims in South Asia, but spoken Urdu is generally understood by Hindi speakers. Hindi written in Devanagari script is the language associated with the northern part of India (often referred to as the Hindi belt) and followers of Hinduism. In South India, unrelated languages such as Tamil, Kanada, and Telegu were also spoken. With the simultaneous partition of India, Pakistan, and East Pakistan the new Indian government focused on a national language policy that favored Hindi and Hindustani (the spoken form of Hindi associated with many northern Indian states) using Devanagari script and English, already widely in use in legal and administrative systems.

The challenges faced by the Indian government in 1947 were similar to those of other newly independent states: debates around a national language and the use of the colonial language; the status and official uses of minority languages (Brown and Ganguly 2003: 3–5). The status of English in India was debated widely in the postindependence period; there were practical considerations for its retention, in that it provided, unlike any of the Indian languages, an internationally recognized language of science, technology, and business. The counter argument was that a newly independent state could not establish its own identity until it abandoned a foreign colonial language and adopted one of its own (Brass 1994: 161).

The use of Hindi as a national language was supported by its numerical domination; however, these claims were challenged by its limited regional distribution in the northern half of India. Se-

English is widely understood in Malaysia, so advertisements in Kuala Lumpur, the capital, are usually in multiple languages.

lection of Hindi would have hampered non-Hindi speakers' access to civil service positions, education, and many other economic and social benefits of citizenship. The Tamil-speaking states of the south of India were strongly opposed to this. However, compromises were instituted in the 1950s and 1960s. The final one included "the joint use of Hindi and English in Parliament, for the use of Hindi as the language of communication between the Center and the Hindi-speaking states and for the use of English for communications between the Center and non-Hindi-speaking states. However, the Act and the overall compromise also contained multilingual elements, particularly on the matter of the languages of examinations for entry into the Indian Administrative Service and other Union services" (Brass 1994: 167).

WORLD ENGLISHES AND THE SPREAD OF ENGLISH

The English language was spread over the world in two waves. It was first carried by English-speaking immigrants to what are today the United States, Canada, South Africa, Australia, and New Zealand. Different versions of the English language are spoken in all these countries. These differences were brought about through the process of dialect formation. The second spread of English was the consequence of England's colonial expansion to parts of Africa, South and Southeast Asia, and the Caribbean. English is spoken today in countries such as Nigeria, Ghana, Kenya, Tanzania, South Africa, India, Pakistan, Bangladesh, Malaysia, and Singapore. According to Bhatt, English is so widespread that it has far exceeded the spread of Latin during the expansion of the Roman Empire, as cited earlier in this chapter (Bhatt 2001: 529).

Linguists have emphasized two somewhat contradictory processes. On the one hand, in the context of Britain's colonial empire, the spread of English is an example of linguistic imperialism, which produces a hierarchical ordering of the speech of colonial "masters" and that of indigenous speakers. As Pennycook points out, "There are . . . continuing relations of global inequality . . . of economic, political, military, communicative (communication and transport), cultural and social imperialism—and the global spread of English" (2001: 61). The second process stresses English as the language of a world market, that is, the language of global commerce. Peoples in the new nations, which emerged in the postcolonial period, learned the language for practical economic reasons, rather than having been forced to learn English by their colonial masters. English, the former colonial language, was selected by the African National Congress for use in its struggle against apartheid in South Africa (Ricento 2006: 4). In postcolonial South Asia, learning English served several different functions. The knowledge of English has enabled Indians to be in the forefront in writing software programs for the computer industry, which is closely tied to the United States as a consequence of outsourcing. English was also useful in other areas. Like pidgin, English served as a medium of communication when people spoke mutually unintelligible indigenous languages; it was a method of gaining further education; it helped in legal and administrative areas; it enabled entry into English literary genres such as English literary journals, newspapers, and political journals (Bhatt, 2001: 531–32). The last point, however, is a source of controversy. Is it better for writers from what formerly were colonial areas to write in the colonial language (English or French) or in their indigenous language or dialect? Writers such as Salmon Rushdie, Chinua Achebe, or V. S.

Naipul have chosen English as their medium of expression. The language of hip-hop/rap, a part of American urban youth culture, has also spread to other parts of the world (Pennycook 2003).

Many linguists have adopted a point of view that stresses that the context in which English is learned and spoken, in each particular colonial setting, is uniquely different. The context in which English is learned in India is different from that of Nigeria or South Africa, so that in each of these areas a different variant of English is spoken. Instead of speaking about the spread of the same form of English throughout the world, linguists speak about many World Englishes. Bhatt states that "nonnative English speakers thus created new, culture-sensitive and socially appropriate meanings—expressions of the bilingual's creativity—by altering and manipulating the structure and function of English in its new ecology" (2001: 534). He provides an interesting example from the English that is spoken in India. There is a device in English known as "the tag question" to turn a statement into a question, such as: "He said he would come home early, didn't he?" In Indian English, such tag questions are transformed into: "You are going home soon, isn't it?" Politeness in verbal expression demands that the "you" and "he" forms be replaced by what is called an undifferentiated tag—"isn't it?" In the tag question example above, the way in which English is used by Indians is shaped and modified by Indian social structure.

Linguists who have adopted a World English perspective—meaning that there are many forms of English, and not a single correct one with incorrect subservient variants—are aware that their view carries a political agenda with it. The external threat to indigenous languages that is posed by the spread of English and World Englishes is countered by the idea of "language rights," that is, "the right to identify with, to maintain and to fully develop one's mother tongue(s)" (Pennycook, 2001: 63). This linguistic right, which the Navajo are implementing, is seen as a fundamental human right.

The *New York Times* of August 26, 2002 announced that a new university that is being formed with branches in several Central Asian countries—Tajikistan, Kyrgyzstan, and Kazakhstan—requires that students learn computer science and English before they begin their matriculation toward their bachelors' degrees. English is seen as "the language that people in the region believe will best connect them to the outside world" (Crosette 2002). They will be learning standard English. Whether it will be modified in the manner we have described above is an interesting question.

SUMMARY

- Language allows humans to communicate cultural ideas and symbolic meanings from one generation to the next in a cumulative fashion and to constantly create new cultural ideas.
- Every language has a small number of basic sounds, called phonemes, usually between twenty and forty, which are used in various combinations to make up the units of meaning. The phonemes of a language form a structure or system. They themselves do not carry meaning but function to differentiate words in terms of their meanings.
- The units of language that carry meaning are called morphemes.
- The rules by which larger speech units, such as phrases and sentences, are formed compose the syntax of a language.

- There is a close connection between the way language is organized and the way culture is organized, as seen in the systems of classification of the world of animals, the world of plants, or the system of colors.
- Men and women play different though usually complementary gender roles in society, and differences in male and female speech reflect this.
- The speech of African Americans, referred to as African-American Vernacular English (AAVE), has its own distinct phonology, morphology, and syntax and is not an incorrect or incomplete version of English. It constitutes an important marker of ethnic identity.
- Dialect differentiation over time leads to further divergence and eventually to the development of two separate languages.
- Using the comparative method, languages thought to be related are compared to derive the proto-language from which they are descended. The original homeland of the speakers is determined from the words for plants, trees, and animals in the proto-language.
- Aspects of language are borrowed by speakers of one language from another through a process of diffusion.
- New languages known as pidgins and creoles developed when colonization brought European languages into contact with indigenous ones.
- English has spread over the world as a result of emigration, conquest, and the dominance of the language in world commerce. The result is that there are many forms of English subsumed under World English, not a single correct one.

SUGGESTED READINGS

Bonvillain, Nancy. *Language, Culture, and Communication: The Meaning of Messages.* Upper Saddle River, NJ: Pearson Prentice Hall, 2008. General discussion about the relationship between language and culture.

Duranti, Alessandro, ed. *Linguistic Anthropology: A Reader.* Malden, MA: Blackwell Publishers, 2001. A comprehensive reader that covers a wide diversity of contemporary topics in linguistic anthropology. The major contemporary anthropological linguists discuss their current research.

Riley, Philip. *Language, Culture and Identity: An Ethnolinguistic Perspective.* New York: Continuum, 2007. A discussion of how language relates to ethnic identity.

SUGGESTED WEBSITES

www.sil.org. A list of the known languages of the world, the locations of the speakers of these languages, and their groupings into language families. Also includes information on language isolates such as Burushaski and Basque.

http://eleaston.com/world-eng.html. Lists of varieties of English spoken around the world, which, taken together, form World English.

www.brainconnection.com/topics/?main=fa/evolution-language. A discussion of the evolution of language with particular reference to brain development.

Chapter 4

Learning Language
and Learning Culture
Culture and the Individual

WHAT ARE THE WAYS IN which individuals born into a particular society learn its language and its culture, and the behaviors that individuals in that culture consider appropriate? What is the relationship of the individual to his or her culture, the range of personality variation within cultures, and the ways of dealing with individuals whose behavior is outside the norms of their culture? This relates to how mental illness is defined in particular cultures, and how innovators and rebels, whose societies sometimes consider them mentally ill, are viewed.

HOW CHILDREN LEARN LANGUAGE

Language learning begins even before the child is born. Recent advances in research techniques have shown that the fetus can hear and differentiate its mother's voice from other sounds, such as music or white noise as they are filtered through the amniotic fluid, as early as the last trimester before birth. Auditory stimuli elicit changes in fetal heart rate and in motor responses such as kicking. Since it has been shown that the newborn immediately identifies his or her mother's voice, it is clear that this recognition is learned prenatally, when the fetus learns to recognize its mother's intonation and stress patterns (Karmiloff and Karmiloff-Smith 2001: 43–44). Studies of the speech perception of infants have shown that "infants are born to perceive most if not all of the speech contrasts used by natural languages . . . [and are] able to . . . learn any natural language" (Tomasello and Bates 2001: 16). There are major changes in the development of the newborn infant's vocal tract shape with the descent of the larynx and a sharpening of the angle between oral and pharyngeal cavities (Polka et al. 2007). At four days or earlier, newborns can discriminate phonemes and perceive well-formed syllables as units. They can distinguish the difference between the rhythmic characteristics of mother's language and other languages. French

A five-month-old infant responds to her father's use of "motherese" or "baby-talk."

babies suck harder when they hear French and less hard when they hear Russian (Karmiloff and Karmiloff-Smith 2001: 44, 45). Between six and twelve months, infants lose the ability to perceive nonnative speech contrasts as they move to master the sound structure of their own speech community.

"Motherese" is a special language in our society that mothers use in their interactions with their infants. In some cultures, mothers may speak to the fetus. Stress patterns within words and sentences are exaggerated in motherese. Repetitions and questions with rising intonation are used to attract the infant's attention. Gathercole and Hoff note that the "high pitch and exaggerated intonation contour of motherese [make] it especially interesting to infants" (2007: 110). It is the rhythm pattern, not word meaning, that attracts the attention of the infant. This serves to demonstrate that "the dynamics of social interaction play a role in encouraging the infant's attention to language" (Karmiloff and Karmiloff-Smith 2001: 47). However, Schieffelin has shown that in some cultures parents barely speak to their infants until the latter produce speech. At that point they converse with the child in adult language (1985). There is considerable variation cross-culturally in the extent to which parents and other adults modify their speech for children or even speak directly to children, yet children still learn language, hence language development cannot depend on the existence of motherese (Gathercole and Hoff 2007).

Infants initially respond to phonetic differences in a "language neutral manner but their perception becomes more language specific by the end of the first year of life" (Polka et al. 2007: 156). At about six months, the ability of infants to discriminate non-native vowel sound begins to decline (Gerken 2007: 175). Interestingly, for English infants, recognition of the clicks in Zulu or lexical tone contrasts in Chinese persisted though the "native language filter" was already operating. The infant also becomes familiar with word pattern and stress pattern, often through motherese. Where motherese is absent, information on segmentation comes from adult speech where it may not be so easy to detect.

So far, we have been concerned with the infant's perception of speech, but what about speech production by infants? Between two and three months of age, during which time the baby is learning to create sounds, the infant produces cooing sounds that are nonlinguistic; between four and six months, its marginal babbling consists of vowel- and consonant-like sounds (these sounds may go beyond his or her native language, but when not heard often, they are dropped); from seven months onward, other vowel and consonant transitions like da-da are produced; by ten months the infant's native tongue begins to affect the types of sounds produced; just past the first year word production usually begins (Karmiloff and Karmiloff-Smith 2001: 56, 57).

The building of infant vocabulary relates to external factors such as sex—girls tend to produce language earlier than boys because girls' brains mature somewhat faster. Mothers' linguistic competence and intelligence, maternal socioeconomic status, parental education, social competence, and attitudes toward child-rearing are also factors that relate to the way parents interact with the child (Karmiloff and Karmiloff-Smith 2001: 60). Though infants do not produce comprehensible words until between twelve and twenty months, they can understand words before that point. It has recently been shown that children as young as fourteen months can also learn word-object pairings (Disendruck 2007: 271). As Saffran and Thiessen note, "One process which is critical to word learning is the ability to detect correspondence between words and objects and to form an association between them" (2007: 74). By twenty-four months, toddlers can produce fifty different words. At first, single words are used to designate whole concepts and categories—the use of the word *dog* for all four-legged animals, the so-called "taxonomic bias" (Markman and Hutchinson 1984 in Saffran and Thiessen 2007: 75).

Learning the meanings of words does not occur in a vacuum. Cognitive development and social constraints (i.e., aspects of the child's social environment) all play a role in language learning. As Baldwin and Meyer note, "[F]rom as early as 12 months of age, children themselves actively monitor meaning—relevant social clues that others exhibit, and put these clues to work to guide inferences about reference and meaning" (2007: 100).

According to the evidence, the age at which infants begin to detect precursors of syntax varies from seven months to the middle to the second year (Gerken 2007: 184–85). A study by Shady et al. (1995), focusing on word order, presented 10.5-month-olds with normal English sentences and those in which determiners and nouns were reversed. The children listened longer to the unmodified sentences, suggesting that they were able to tell the difference between the two (Gerken 2007: 180–81). English-speaking children soon learn the importance of word order in their language. Though sentence production at two years is rudimentary, the child has already become sensitive to complex grammatical forms and the nature of word order. It is clear, however, that sensitivity to grammar is greater than production of grammatical form. Grammatical speech, in the form of word combination, can begin with as few as fifty to one hundred fifty words.

Word order is an integral part of syntax. Nouns, either as subject or object, refer to things; verbs refer to actions. Children at age three or so begin using sentences, and position in the sentence (i.e., grammar) determines meaning (semantics). Pinker argues that children pick up this relationship between position and meaning, and use it (Pinker 2004a, b; see also Cattell 2007: 227–29). Sometimes, through the process of overgeneralization, they make mistakes. These mistakes are themselves interesting. Having learned that "verbs" connote actions, they extend the verb incorrectly, as in, "I'm going to cover a screen over me," spoken by a child (Pinker 2007: 38). As grammar is learned, the precise meaning and use of different verbs are learned, and mistakes are made less and less frequently. Some studies have revealed cross-linguistic differences in the development of the use of nouns and verbs. Children usually learn nouns first, except when learning non-Western languages such as Chinese, Korean, Tzotzil, and Tzeltzal, in which verbs are more salient (Tomasello and Bates, 2001: 59).

LEARNING ONE'S CULTURE

Scholars such as Schieffelin and Ochs see learning of linguistic forms as closely interrelated to the cultural setting within which learning takes place (1996). Sociocultural information is encoded in the organization of conversation, and from earliest infancy, children acquire cultural knowledge as they are involved in such interactions. As children learn language from those surrounding them, those who care for them, and those with whom they interact, they also learn social roles, politeness and deference toward elders, autonomy, assertiveness, and initiative. Children learn the appropriate request forms in order to operate successfully in the all-important reciprocity and exchange activities that organize Kaluli society, for example (Schieffelin and Ochs 1996: 255, 256). They are learning cultural values and what is appropriate behavior for a child in their culture. While Kaluli children learn that autonomy and assertiveness are valued in their culture, Samoan children learn that assertiveness toward elders is bad, and Japanese children learn that indirectness and circumscribed behavior are valued over directness. Particular forms of language as they relate to correct forms of behavior in each society are taught to children.

Shaming is part of moral socialization for Chinese children. It is recognized, under the influence of Confucianism, as "an underscored moral virtue in Chinese culture" (Fung 2006: 181). In fact, there are 113 hierarchically ordered core terms in Chinese for shame. Chinese parents tend to be highly lenient and indulgent in their attitudes towards infants and young children in sharp contrast to the strict discipline imposed on older children. At around four to six years of age disciplinary techniques "like threatening, scolding, shaming and physical punishment will become acceptable and are frequently applied" (Ho 1986 in Fung 2006: 184–85). A variety of linguistic devices were used to communicate that a transgression had occurred. However, Fung notes, "[T]he Chinese indigenous concept of strict discipline or training takes place in a supportive, involved, and devoted context of parent-child relationship (Chao 1994 in Fung 2006: 186).

Children raised in Chillihuani, a Quecha-speaking village in the highlands of Peru, grow up in very marginal living conditions where "specific behavioral norms centering on respect are necessary to make society work and assure survival" (Bolin 2006: 151). This is an egalitarian society in which children at an early age are " introduced to a culture of respect . . . to other people and the deities but [also] . . . to all forms of life" (Bolin 2006: 33). Children are raised in a permissive atmosphere and at a young age are "introduced to the unwritten law of reciprocity, the hallmark of Andean life" (Bolin 2006: 152). They grow up within an extended family and participate in adult activities, learning through observation in an environment where children are treated with respect and take on work tasks when they feel ready for them. Although the norm of reciprocity is found in a great many other societies as well, there is little information as to when it is introduced in the life cycle.

Self-reliance is a characteristic that is more valued in some societies than in others. It is inculcated in the young infant through the process of **enculturation.** Before World War II, self-reliance was encouraged and fostered in both American infants and German infants, but after World War II, in America, an ideology of love and trust replaced this. American mothers never leave infants alone and rush to pick them up when they cry, believing that if they were to do otherwise, the child would feel abandoned and not develop a secure sense of attachment. In contrast, German mothers may leave an infant alone while they go out shopping, and will pick up a crying child only if they think he or she is hurting. They want the infant to be enculturated into a sense of independent self-reliance and are concerned lest the child become "spoiled." At ten months of age, German infants expect less attention from their mothers than do American infants. According to Levine and Norman, these differences in child-rearing practices between Germans and Americans begin during the first year of life and are part of each culture's concepts of moral virtue (2001: 91). German moral concepts of "love of order" and "self-reliance" contrast with the American moral precept of parental love given freely.

Brown has described the way in which Tzeltal-speaking Mayan farmers in southern Mexico have socialized their children from babyhood to "lie" in culturally appropriate ways (2002: 243). Since lying is routine in Tzeltal, children must begin to learn it early in life in order to become effective in their lying. By the age of four or even earlier, Tzeltal children become aware that people can hold false beliefs and lie. They learn how to tell when others are lying to them as well as how to lie themselves. Children learn to manage social lies "with fair competence by the age of five or so, when they are called to perform them as they are sent around to different households on errands" (Brown, 2002: 268–69). It is interesting to compare American culture to Tzeltal culture with regard to lying. Though American values denigrate lying, it occurs frequently among politicians, baseball players, and corporate executives. However, it is wrong to lie to one's young children.

Different cultures emphasize different values in their child-rearing practices. While some emphasize assertiveness and self-reliance, others emphasize just the opposite—that the child must learn its appropriate subordinate position in relation to its elders. Some cultures stress the need to foster the close attachment between parent and child, and others teach the child to lie to keep one's true feelings from others. It is apparent that each culture favors a certain kind of person. To achieve this, children are brought up to behave in culturally desirable ways.

Learning Gender Roles

Gender roles and the kinds of persons men and women are expected to be are also acquired during the socialization and language acquisition processes. If boys are expected to be more assertive than girls in a particular culture, they are taught by the individuals around them to be that way. Their assertive use of language reflects this gender difference. However, though in preadolescent years American girls become less confident and more deferential, African-American girls become more assertive and self-sufficient (Gilligan et al. 1990 and Eckert 1994 in Rogoff 2003: 192)

In the Middle East and North Africa, differentials in gender treatment begin at birth when there is greater celebration of a boy's birth, and he is subject to more intensive and prolonged nurturing than is a girl (Gregg 2005: 195). By the age of five to seven, "parents increasingly instruct their children about the behaviors appropriate for boys and girls and begin rewarding compliance and punishing deviance more seriously" (Gregg 2005: 204). By this time, girls spend much of the day helping their mothers, taking care of younger children, while boys are less supervised and often teased into competition to facilitate assertiveness. Male and female circumcision in this area marks the end of early childhood. In most parts of the world, since young children are more often in the company of women, young boys and girls usually help with female activities (Rogoff 2003: 183). After early childhood, boys move away from the home to be in the company of other boys, while the gender role of girls begins to parallel that of women. Interestingly, Rogoff notes that coeducational school "clearly subverts traditional forms of gender differentiation" (2005: 204).

For Australian parents and children, male and female gender roles are mutually exclusive. The chores performed at home were primarily complementary, with fathers and boys concerned with tidying the yard, washing the car, and working on the periphery of meal preparation, and mothers and girls concerned with domestic tasks. Further, in play situations at school, "girls felt at home in home corner setting, where they were familiar with the rituals and positions involved. The boys, on the other hand, were more comfortable exploring the boundaries of socially acceptable behavior and developing the skills they felt they would need as adults to work outdoors and outside the home" (Lowe 1998: 209). It is apparent that children enter school with gender roles already clearly defined, being aware of the complementarity of roles. Observation of the interaction of children in play settings in school reveals that in their behavior they also enact male domination of space and language and female submissiveness (Lowe 1998: 214). In the United States and Australia, some educators have made deliberate efforts, in their organization of the classroom and class activities, to make children aware of the possibility of roles that are more egalitarian in nature, rather than those roles that suggest male dominance and female subordination.

Currently, anthropological theories "following Chodorow, trace the development of gender identities to earlier patterns of attachment and separation . . . boys start out 'as if girls . . . there is yet no duality. . . . Then the developmental tasks of boys and girls diverge" (Gregg 2005: 205–206). Girls retain the core feminine sense of self and identification with their mothers while boys must achieve a masculine self. The machismo image or the "hypermasculine" warriors of New Guinea are ways of solidifying masculine identity, suppressing the earlier "feminine" self and separating boys from their mothers. In some societies this separation is achieved by male

By teaching her daughter how to bake, an American mother communicates symbolic information about both food and gender roles.

circumcision or male initiation rituals. Male initiation rites, which may include circumcision, are more common and more prominent than rites for females.

CULTURE AND PERSONALITY

Not only do individuals in a society learn a language and a culture, but they acquire the personality structure, and the idea of personhood and self, that are characteristic of their culture. In all societies, people exhibit individual personality differences as a result of genetic differences, upbringing, and particular life experiences. Each individual has a certain personality that is more or less stable over his or her lifetime. This is not to say that individuals never change. An individual's personality can change, sometimes through his or her own efforts and sometimes with the assistance of a therapist. The stability of individual personality is the result of the interaction of genetic, biological predispositions and the individual's life experience from birth on. They act consistently in different kinds of situations.

Although there is a range of personality types in every society, in any one society there is a preponderance of individuals with a particular kind of personality. Personality types differ from one society to the next. The attempt to characterize the personality types that are dominant in different societies and tribes goes back to ancient times. Tacitus, the Roman historian, of the first century A.D., in his work *Germania: On the Origin, Geography, Institutions, and Tribes of the Germans*, characterized the Germans as "a race without either natural or acquired cunning, they disclose their hidden thoughts in the freedom of the festivity." He also noted that they represent a strange combination of idleness and sloth and readiness to go to war. Tacitus tried to capture what was distinctive about the personality characteristics of the Germans as a people. Throughout history, such characterizations of different peoples have been made. One must always be wary of stereotypes based on prejudice, as distinguished from accurate characterizations based on data and observations. The anthropologists Mead and Benedict explored the relationship between culture and personality in the 1930s.

Child-Rearing and Personality

We have discussed how children acquire language and learn the rules of their own culture. In the process, the particular personality characteristics favored in that culture are also inculcated in them. Through the process of enculturation, children learn not only the rules of their culture, but also, as noted earlier, the values of their society. In addition, they increasingly become motivated to act according to those values. The motivations that have been built in during the enculturation process are what lead most people to conform to those rules. To act otherwise—to violate rules—produces guilt in the individual. As the psychoanalyst Erich Fromm (1944) long ago noted, stable individuals in a well-integrated culture will want to do the things that they have to do.

Erik Erikson, a psychoanalyst strongly influenced by anthropologists, broadened Freud's stages of psychosexual development in order to make them applicable to non-Western cultures (1963). He saw differences in culture and in child-rearing as being related to differences in the adult personality. Among the Sioux of South Dakota, children were freely breast-fed up to age three, and there was no systematic weaning. The Sioux child was toilet trained by imitating older children, and the matter of toilet training was treated in a very relaxed fashion. Erikson saw a clear relationship between the way in which the Sioux handled these two developmental stages and the value that the Sioux placed on the generous adult individual, as expressed, for example, in the economic institution of the "giveaway." In contrast, among the Yurok of California, a child was breast-fed for only six months, and weaning, which was called "forgetting the mother," could be brought about by the mother's leaving the house for a few days. Autonomy was encouraged very early. In Erikson's view, these aspects of child-rearing were tied to an adult Yurok personality characterized by retentive hoarding, suspicious miserliness, and compulsive ritualization. It was Erikson's view that the Yurok, who had their own shell money, adapted well to American economic institutions since their personalities and their own economic system were already very similar to those of American culture. Sioux culture and Sioux personality were quite different: thus the Sioux did not adapt well to American culture.

The Relationship of Social Structure to Personality

In all societies, people are minimally differentiated according to age and sex. Individuals who make up a society occupy different social positions, different statuses in the society. Beyond this, there are many other bases for differentiation. Individuals who occupy different statuses within the same society are likely to have different personality characteristics. For example, shamans in a society will have somewhat different personalities from nonshamans in the same society. The Big Man, a type of political leader, which we discuss in chapter 9, had a somewhat different personality from his followers. These differences in personality characteristics result from individual differences in socialization. There are two ways to view this relationship between social status and personality. In the first view, individuals with certain kinds of personality characteristics will gravitate toward those social roles or occupations that suit their personalities. For example, in our own society, individuals who are self-confident, assertive, and willing to take risks often gravitate toward entrepreneurial positions in the business world. Others, with personality traits such as a tendency to intellectualize and a curiosity about the world but a sense of uneasiness in dealing with other people, are more likely to become scientists and to do research.

In the second view, people moving into particular social roles will undergo personality changes brought about by the demands of the role. A classic example of this is Thomas à Becket, who, as chancellor of the exchequer in the twelfth century, was a free spirit, who caroused and drank with King Henry II. When Becket was appointed archbishop of Canterbury, he proceeded to behave according to that role. He changed from a frivolous, pleasure-seeking individual to the committed defender of a moral cause who chose martyrdom at the command of his former friend, the king, rather than betray his principles.

CULTURE AND MENTAL ILLNESS

If, in our society, a man said one day that a guardian spirit had come to him and told him that it would protect and watch over him throughout his life as long as he followed certain commands and obeyed certain taboos, we would consider him mentally ill. If he reported that he had actually seen and spoken to the spirit, we would say that he was having hallucinations. However, adolescent boys among the Crow Indians were expected to go on a vision quest to seek such a spirit. Earlier, seeing visions was very common among the Crow, as well as among many other Native American societies that also had the vision quest. What is regarded as a symptom of mental illness in one society may be merely one aspect of normal, healthy life in another.

The anthropological definition of **mental illness** takes the normal, expected, and acceptable behavior in a culture as a baseline and views deviance from this baseline as abnormal behavior or mental illness. Seeking a vision was normal and expected behavior for Crow boys, and they might torture themselves and undergo deprivation until the vision came to them. But visions of spirits are not considered normal behavior in our society. Someone who sees them and hears them is said to be exhibiting abnormal behavior. Another instance of exhibiting signs of abnormal behavior is the belief in witchcraft. Among the Navajo and the Basseri, individuals who believed that someone was practicing witchcraft on them would not be considered abnormal. However, in most segments of our society, individuals who came into the emergency room of a hospital complaining of internal pains and saying that they had been bewitched would be considered mentally ill.

This approach to abnormal behavior and mental illness is essentially a relativistic one. Nevertheless, anthropologists who cross-culturally study forms of mental illness use certain general categories. They distinguish between disorders caused by brain damage and behavioral disorders, in which there is no apparent brain damage. The latter category is subdivided into psychoses, such as schizophrenia, depression, and paranoia, and neuroses of a variety of types. Depressive illness has been examined cross-culturally (Kleinman and Good, 1985). Grief is the emotion that accompanies bereavement, which is experienced in all societies. In many different cultures, depression as an emotion or affect seems to be experienced in a similar fashion. However, the boundary line between a depressed state as normal behavior and abnormal depressive disorder has not yet been established. Depressive illness has a psycho-physiological syndrome of behaviors that can be recognized by clinicians cross-culturally. At the same time, the cultural meanings of depressive illness and the cultural expression of the symptoms differ from one culture to another. Universal aspects of other mental illnesses, such as schizophrenia, neuroses, and personality disturbances, have also been recognized (Draguns 1980). However, these illnesses are also culturally shaped. Variations in their manifestations are related to social, economic, technological, religious, and other features of the societies in which they are found.

Some kinds of symptoms seem to be specific to a particular culture. These symptoms have been viewed in two quite different ways. One view is that there are universal psychopathological disease categories (such as schizophrenia and depression) that are manifested in different kinds of behavior from one culture to another. The opposing view is that universally stressful situations produce different kinds of diseases in different cultures.

Amok is a form of mental illness found in Malaysia and Indonesia. The central feature of *amok* is that the victim kills people while in a temporarily deranged state, experiencing complete amnesia of the attack afterward. Some researchers consider *amok* a disease specific to these particular cultures, while others consider it a form of depression psychosis produced by extreme stress, which is culturally determined. We get our expression "to run amok" from this mental illness of Southeast Asia. It has been pointed out that *amok* occurs in societies in which individuals may go into a trance. While in a trance they perform "stereotyped behavior, which allows the release of repressed feelings" (Azhar and Varma 2000: 171–72). A suggested explanation for *amok* in Malaysia is that it may be an extreme expression of aggression in a society that strictly prohibits such expression. Symptoms similar to *amok* have also been reported in the United States (Azhar and Varma 2000: 173). The same explanation for the occurrence of *amok* in Southeast Asia may also account for students "running amok" and slaughtering classmates and teachers in American schools and then killing themselves.

Latah is another disease found in Malaysia. Found predominantly in females, its symptoms are a startle reaction, after which the individual falls to the ground and performs compulsive imitation of words, gestures, and acts. The person may also utter obscenities. In a recent survey of *latah*, Winzeler (1995) indicates that it occurs in association with societies in which there is familiarity with trance states and that practice shamanism. Both *latah* and *amok* were much more common in the past than they are today. They have been replaced by depression, hypochondriasis, and anxiety, which are now treated with therapies that include the use of the Quran (Azhar and Varma 2000: 184). These forms of behavior are recognized as abnormal by the peoples of the cultures themselves, and native terms are used to describe them. Good has pointed out the profound role that culture plays not only in the expression of symptoms but also in the course the illness takes (1992).

The belief in witchcraft and sorcery in some societies is not an indication of mental illness, as would be the case in our own society. However, in Algeria, a sick person is believed to be possessed by *jinn* (spirits), and this is considered to be a form of "madness" (Al-Issa 2000: 103). This condition is often considered to be the result of sorcery. People believe that someone, motivated by envy, will use the "evil eye," so that the victim's behavior and desires come under the control of supernatural beings. The *marabout*, a saint and healer, is one type of traditional therapist who treats such patients. According to Al-Issa, "Exorcism consists of conversing with the evil spirit through the patient" to convince him to leave (2000: 104). The use of traditional therapists such as the *marabout* are not only legal but on the increase in Algeria. In countries such as Iraq, Kuwait, and Tunisia, such therapies are illegal because they are associated with underdevelopment and backwardness in contrast to modernization (Al-Issa 2000: 104).

Mental illness has been defined as abnormal behavior, that is, behavior that is different from the cultural norm in a particular society. It is important to differentiate deviant behavior that represents mental illness from deviant behavior that does not. Not all those who violate the rules of a society are, by definition, mentally ill. Some are criminals; some are rebels; some are innovators.

In Russian culture, political extremists were characterized as mad (Miller 2007: 115). According to Brown, "After 1905 the police began to place politically dangerous individuals in mental hospitals" (2007: 291). After "glasnost" this practice of punitive psychiatry became a subject of debate. People within an authoritarian culture may consider all rebels (opposed to the government or to the church) as "out of their minds."

Rebels and Innovators

From time to time, individuals appear who renounce important aspects of their own culture and propose that a radically different way of doing things be substituted for the old way. They are frequently considered mentally ill by the members of their society, but when they are successful in attracting followers and in overthrowing the old order, they are called innovators and revolutionaries. These individuals are often central in bringing about changes that result in significant transformations. Their conceptualization, which may come to them in the form of a vision or a dream, is often a new organization for society.

The typical personality type of the well-adjusted individual in all cultures incorporates the motivations and values of the culture. Such an individual will want to do the things considered desirable in the society and will not think of changing them, and is very different from the rebel and innovator. The rebel, therefore, should differ in personality in some significant way from the typical person. Erik Erikson (1969) explored the relationship between successful rebels, their early life experiences, and their cultures in a series of biographical case studies of individuals such as Martin Luther and Gandhi. His emphasis is on the psychological characteristics of innovators as these relate to the cultural setting within which these individuals lived and their effect on history. Erikson has stressed the significance of these individuals to the historical process of cultural change. This approach might be seen as ancestral to psychohistories being done by some historians today.

PERSON, SELF, AND THE STRUCTURE OF EMOTION

The socially constituted person, as distinguished from the individual self, is a concept with a long history in anthropology. Individuals learn to perform a repertoire of social roles, and those roles constitute a major component of the social person. The notion of the self is a human universal, though the conception of the person may vary from one society to the next. Each society has its own conception of what emotions persons can appropriately express and when they can be expressed, as well as its own ideas about what characterizes the good person and the bad person. A distinction can be made between the "poles of biological and existential universals on the one hand and cultural particulars [regarding the nature of the self] on the other" (Sax 2000: 7).

While the person may be conceived of in different ways in various cultures, there are certain universal characteristics of the person. These universal features are present in the early stages of the process of development of the person. Developmental psychologists are of the opinion that the boundedness of self and self-motivation are found in children in all societies. During the enculturation process in some societies, such as Java and Bali, a different notion of self is inculcated. All infants share boundedness and act as autonomous entities who are in contrast with others. However, as the child develops in some non-Western cultures, he or she learns to suppress this autonomous self.

Clifford Geertz examined differences in personhood in Java, Bali, and Western societies (1974). Rather than putting himself in the place of the Other or conducting psychological tests, as did earlier psychological anthropologists, Geertz preferred to analyze the series of symbolic forms that people in a culture use to represent themselves to themselves and to others. Like Margaret Mead, he began his analysis with the Western conception of the person, which he described as "a bounded, unique, more or less integrated motivational and cognitive universe, a dynamic center of awareness, emotion, judgment, and action organized into a distinctive whole and set contrastively both against other such wholes and against its social and natural background" (1974: 126).

The Balinese view of the person is as an appropriate representative of a category, rather than a unique individual. People attempt to mute individual personal characteristics and to emphasize, in contrast, features of status. Geertz, who frequently used the dramatic or theatrical metaphor to describe Balinese culture, likened Balinese persons to a cast of characters. In Bali, the face itself is considered a mask. Geertz's point is that the Western concept of the person as an autonomous, bounded entity operating in his or her own way vis-a-vis other like entities is not shared by other cultures. Since Geertz is a cultural relativist, who emphasizes the unique features that differentiate cultures, he also views personhood as being distinctive for each culture.

The Hindu vision of the self is that there is an eternal self and an ephemeral self whose caste, class, gender, personality, and subjectivity are transient. The conception of the self in Western cultures, in which the self is seen as the locus of creativity and moral value, is viewed very negatively among Hindus (Sax 2000: 10–11). Marriot, in his model of the Hindu self, sees it as an entity composed of shifting and inherently unstable substance. Interestingly, this seems to parallel the postmodern view of the deconstruction of the self/person in which the self/person has no status except as the transient effect of a variety of causes. Sax examines a series of public ritual performances, which he sees as "an especially powerful means for creating (and sometimes undermining) selves, relationships, and communities, because they inscribe cultural concepts on the whole person, the body as well as the mind" (Sax 2000: 14). What he demonstrates through his analysis of the series of *Pandav lila* public rituals, which are part of the village tradition of the Garhwalis of North India, is that the "empirical 'selves' of Garhwalis are multiple" (Sax 2000: 161). The public performance and all that it entails plays out the nature of the multiple selves of this population.

Differences in the conceptualization of the self in the United States, India, Java, Bali, and Japan are expressed in language. In order to use the proper linguistic forms in Javanese or in Japanese, the speaker must know his or her relationship to the listener (or receiver). Misperceiving the relationship and using the wrong or impolite form is a disgraceful act. Thus, the speaker must know certain information—for example, whether the person being addressed is a professor, is of a higher social class, or is older than the speaker. Relative age is always a factor—one is either a younger brother or an older brother. One must always use the appropriate form of address. In discussing the Japanese concept of the self, Brown suggests that it is basically relational—the self constantly viewed in relation to others (higher or lower, more respectful or less respectful, older or younger). In contrast, the American self is bounded (rather than relational), autonomous, and individualistic (Brown 1996: 47–48). As the anthropologist Dorinne Kondo observed, when she conducted her research in Japan, "I was always defined by my obligations and links to others" (Kondo, cited in Brown 1996: 47). Kitayama et al. echo this point, noting that East Asians show a predominantly interdependent mode of being while middle-class North Americans primarily exhibit an independent mode of being (2007). The self exists only in relation to others. Because it is necessary for the Japanese child to learn the complexities of the social structure and his or her place in relation to all others within that structure, learning the proper forms of linguistic expression may take hard work and years of training.

Ewing deals with how the self is constructed in a transnational situation. A Turkish woman, though born in the Netherlands, Ewing moves between the culture of her Turkish homeland and the culture of the Netherlands. She is the daughter of a Turkish guest-worker whose family has established permanent residence in the Netherlands yet maintains close ties with Turkey (Ewing 2000: 97). It is no longer a matter of giving up "old ways" and an old identity and becoming modern, but something more complicated. Even though young people born in the Netherlands, where their parents are guest-workers, live in encapsulated communities and go to schools that exclusively serve immigrant populations, these young people are nevertheless influenced by Dutch and

European media, and a very different vision of the self and gender relations than is operative in the communities of their homeland, Turkey. Ewing describes a young Turkish woman, a professional with a business school education and a career, who had been in an arranged marriage with her mother's sister's son who was an uneducated assembly line worker in a pillow factory. She had lived a compartmentalized existence, part of a professional cosmopolitan world, on the one hand, while on the other hand she had been engaged at the age of eleven and married at eighteen within her Turkish world, which she had visited every summer as a child. Her self in these two worlds was significantly different, though as she got older she resisted the arranged marriage and being more and more engulfed in Turkish culture and identity, in which girls and women are subservient to the will of their parents and the dictates of Turkish culture. Her parents eventually won out, though a factor was her desire to be identified as a "good girl" within Turkish culture (Ewing 2000: 107). Eventually, however, she ran away from her husband and finally was able to get a divorce and make a settlement with him and her parents, giving her the independence and professional identity she so vigorously sought (Ewing 2000).

The concept of the individual "caught between two worlds" and properly belonging to neither is an old one. It has also often been explored in novels. Dr. Aziz, in *A Passage to India*, memorably captures the dilemma of the educated Indian who is unable to cross the cultural boundary of colonialism and establish a friendship with Mr. Fielding. Dr. Aziz finds that he cannot change his Indian identity to assume another identity that will allow him to establish a true friendship. Individuals often feel that they cannot simultaneously live in two worlds. Novelists frequently succeed in capturing this dilemma more effectively than social scientists.

Though the form in which emotion is expressed varies from one culture to another, certain aspects of emotional states, such as happiness and grief, are universal and largely innate. However, the way in which emotion is expressed and interpreted is culturally determined (Wierzbiecka 1999: 249).

The structure of emotion begins to be inculcated during early childhood. As Holodynski et al. note, "In a cultural context with an individualistic orientation like Germany, caregivers tend to view themselves and their children as independent and autonomous . . . and a child has the right to display such a negative feeling in the relationship if the cause of the emotion justifies such a reaction. . . . In a cultural context with a collectivist orientation like Japan, an interdependent self-construal is held in high esteem . . . and the expression of negative emotions . . . is undesirable" (2006: 209–210).

Emotion is expressed through gestures such as facial expressions and bodily movements. It is also asserted through various levels of language (i.e., intonation, nouns, and phrases). Wierzbiecka presents an interesting series of contrasts between Anglo American and Polish attitudes toward emotions and their expression (1999: 240ff.). For example, Polish culture values the truthful expression of one's feelings, saying and showing what one really feels, in contrast to Anglo-American culture, in which a display of good feelings is valued even if one does not necessarily feel that way. For Americans, this is coupled with the suppression of bad feelings, which may damage one's image and be unpleasant for other people. Americans are seen as smiling all the time even if that is not how they feel. Wierzbiecka argues that Americans are being deceptive when they hide their true feelings behind polite language ("Have a nice day"), while Poles are simply honest. One might also conclude that for Americans it is not appropriate to present a picture of bad or insincere feelings about another person or his or her ideas, but this is not a matter of "lying." Among the Swat Pathans (and also the Mafia), to allow one's enemies to know one's true feelings is to show one's weakness, so one must therefore always hide feelings and emotions and present oneself as even-tempered and not show anger. These examples raise the question of whether there is a universal recognition of what constitutes lying. From the evidence on the Poles, Americans, and Swat Pathans, it is clear that there is cultural variability regarding whether or not lying is culturally valued. Earlier we saw that lying was a cultural requirement for the Tzeltzal Mayans, which they inculcated in their children during child-rearing.

Our examples illustrate how societies vary in the nature of personhood, the self, and the structure of emotion. We saw that Americans view each individual as an autonomous entity who operates in opposition to other similar entities. In contrast, the Japanese self constantly operates in relation to others, and his or her position is not autonomous, but relational. This is consistent with the general distinction made between individualism and collectivism. As Mascolo and Li note, "[I]ndividualist (most Western) cultures are those that emphasize individuals as separate, autonomous self-contained entities. In contrast, collectivist cultures (most non-Western cultures) place primary value on group orientation, the goals and needs of others, and readiness to cooperate" (2004: 1). Though they fall within the collectivist category, Balinese selves are different in still another way—they are always playing a part, a role, in a drama. Faces are like masks used to portray emotion of the role rather than the person's true emotions. The Poles and Germans are straightforward regarding their emotions in that they show what they feel, while one can say that Americans, along with Pathans and members of the mafia, are insincere and do not reveal their true feelings to others. In these various ways the self in different cultures is expressed in dissimilar ways.

SUMMARY

- At birth, the infant can already distinguish the sounds of his mother's language from those of other languages.
- The infant gradually learns which sound combinations most frequently occur in mother tongue, which are correct and which incorrect, as these are related to speech segmentation and word boundaries.
- By 24 months, toddlers can produce fifty different words.
- At the age of two, grammatical speech, in the form of word combination can begin with as few as fifty to one hundred fifty words.
- Sociocultural information is encoded in the organization of conversation, and from earliest infancy, children acquire knowledge as they are involved in such interactions.
- Self-reliance, a characteristic that is valued more in some societies than in others, is inculcated in the infant through the process of enculturation.
- Gender roles and the kinds of persons men and women are expected to be are also acquired during the socialization and language acquisition processes.

- Not only do individuals in a society learn a language and a culture, but they acquire the personality structure and the idea of personhood and self that are characteristic of their culture.
- In the process of acquiring language and learning the rules of their culture, individuals are inculcated with the particular personality characteristics favored in that culture.
- What is regarded as a symptom of mental illness in one society may be merely one aspect of normal, healthy life in another.
- One view is that universal psychopathological disease categories (such as schizophrenia and depression) are manifested in different kinds of behavior from one culture to another. The opposing view is that universally stressful situations produce different kinds of diseases in different cultures.
- The emotional endowment of humans is universal and largely innate. However, the way in which emotion is expressed and interpreted is determined culturally.
- The notion of the self is a human universal, though the conception of the person varies from one society to the next.

SUGGESTED READINGS

Casey, Conerly and Robert B. Edgerton, eds. *A Companion to Psychological Anthropology: Modernity and Psychocultural Change.* Malden, MA: Blackwell Publishers, 2005. A collection of articles dealing with psychological changes brought about by culture change and modernization.

Levine, Robert. *Culture, Behavior, and Personality: An Introduction to the Comparative Study of Psychosocial adaptation.* 2nd edition. New Brunswick, NJ: Aldine Transaction, 2007. A general study of the development of personality as it relates to culture using the comparative approach.

Lindholm, Charles. *Culture and Identity: The History, Theory and Practice of Psychological Anthropology.* Boston: McGraw-Hill, 2001. Overall coverage of psychological anthropology and the dialectic between the self and the other.

SUGGESTED WEBSITES

www.chinasprout.com/html/column3.html. A bilingual speech therapist points out the universals in the process of language acquisition.

www.as.ua.edu/an/lFaculty/murphy/cult&per.htm. A historical survey of the culture and personality school in anthropology, presenting its basic premises, information about key figures, and recent critiques of this approach.

www.linguistics.unimelb.edu.au/research/projects/ACLA/. Case studies of three Aboriginal communities addressing the question of Aboriginal child language acquisition.

Chapter 5
Symbolic Meanings

IN THE FIRST SCENE OF CITIZEN KANE, one of the most famous films ever made, a powerful old man who is dying utters the mysterious word *Rosebud*. The symbolic meaning of this word is an important clue to his character and to the unfolding narrative. *Rosebud*, whose meaning is not revealed until the conclusion of the film, is an important personal symbol to Kane. It has meaning only for Kane and not for the culture as a whole. The behavior of people in a culture is framed according to a set of **symbols** or cultural ideas. This constitutes the overall design of the tapestry of their culture. To understand people's economic behavior, political behavior, and social behavior, one must understand the system of cultural meanings that permeate these institutions. In their day-to-day actions, people create and convey cultural meaning as they re-create their culture. How they walk, how they dress, and how they talk all convey cultural meaning. When people change their behavior, the meaning also changes. One must "read" culture like a text to understand the meaning of cultural behavior.

The analysis of symbols deals with the meanings of words, the meanings of actions, and the meanings of objects in a culture. In addition to involving meaning, symbols are also expressive, and convey emotion. This is especially true with regard to symbols in art and in religion. As noted in chapter 3, language itself is a system made up entirely of symbols. All symbols, like the morphemes of language, operate as if they are two-sided coins. On one side are the physical characteristics, and on the other side are the meanings, or what the symbols stand for. Symbols and their meanings guide people's actions and also motivate such actions. Further, people's behavior itself has symbolic meaning to those who observe it.

Metaphor, a kind of symbol, is an important analytical concept used by anthropologists in the study of symbolic systems. A metaphor is an idea that stands for another set of ideas. The meaning of the metaphor is the recognition of the connection between the metaphor itself and the "something else" it represents. In the Kwakiutl marriage ceremony, discussed in chapter 2, many of the activities described were also characteristic of warfare, such as blackening faces, dressing like warriors, and running through a gauntlet of fire in order to demonstrate courage. Among the Kwakiutl, marriage is metaphorically a form of warfare. Warfare is an apt metaphor for marriage among the Kwakiutl, because in both, two sides compete with each other. The competitive aspect in the marriage ceremony is also seen in the potlatch, which pits one side against the other.

In our society, games are often used as metaphors for life. Games involve struggle and competition. Sometimes you win and sometimes you lose, but games must be played according to a set of rules. Games demand from the players strategic ability, risk taking, stamina, and courage—virtues in our culture. During Nixon's presidency, White House officials talked about "playing hardball" and used the expression from baseball, "When the going gets tough, the tough get going." Baseball was being used to stand for something else—politics—because both include competition, struggle, and some element of danger, though they may differ in other respects.

The chessboard is a miniature world peopled with a feudal society. In the classic movie *The Seventh Seal*, the White Knight plays against Death, represented by the black pieces. The White Knight plays for his life against Death, which represents the Black Death—the plague sweeping Europe. In this film, the moviemaker, Ingmar Bergman, talks about life and death using the chess game as a metaphor.

Lakoff and Johnson, who have written extensively about metaphor, argue that human thought processes are largely metaphorical, that metaphors are not solely a matter of symbolic relationship. They claim that "[o]ur ordinary conceptual system, in terms of which we both think and act, is fundamentally metaphoric in nature" (2003: 3). They extend this argument to claim that we express our experiences of the world through metaphors. Lakoff provides a typology of different kinds of metaphors. "Structural metaphors" are "cases where one concept is metaphorically structured in terms of another" (Lakoff and Johnson 2003: 14). Their example is that arguments between two persons are like warfare between two countries (i.e., "His criticisms were right on target."). Here are some other examples:

Marriage is like warfare.
Football is like warfare.
Chess is like warfare.

In all these metaphors, the two sides involved form the structure A:B as C:D, which is why Lakoff and Johnson call them "structural metaphors." Other metaphors they present are "orientational metaphors," for example, "wake up," "get up," or "he sank into a coma." Pinker, the evolutionary psychologist, has also accepted the argument that metaphoric thinking characterizes the human species.

Another type of symbol is a **metonym**. Like a metaphor, a metonym is also based upon a substitution of one thing for another, but in this case the symbol standing for the something else is one of the several things that constitute the something else. Thus the monarch can be referred to as the head of state, and the crown or throne can stand as a metonymic symbol for the monarchy. The capital of any type of government can be referred to as the seat of government. In each case, a part has been taken and used to stand as a symbol for the whole.

One category of symbols, **public symbols**, constitutes the cultural system for society. Many of these cultural symbols are known, understood, and shared by all members of the society. However, some symbols, often the most important ones, are more esoteric and may be known only by religious practitioners. Individuals also create symbols out of their own experiences, which are not commonly shared by others. These are known as **private symbols**, and are the symbols of our dream life and fantasies. In the creative process, the artist, novelist, or filmmaker uses private symbols. The process of interpretation of artistic works by the public and the critics involves trying to decipher what the private symbols of the artist mean. We will discuss how the creative artist uses private and public symbols in chapter 12.

There are two ways in which the study of symbolism can be approached. The first is to examine a particular symbol and the different meanings that are attached to it in various cultures. The second is to begin with the other side of the coin—to study the thing symbolized and the different symbols used for it.

THE SYMBOLISM OF FOOD

We will examine the symbolism of food to show how a symbol may have various meanings attached to it in different cultures. From the utilitarian or materialist perspective, food is ingested by humans to sustain life. It is made up of calories, protein, fats, minerals, and carbohydrates and is introduced into humans by eating. This aspect of food is equivalent to the physical manifestations or sounds that make up a word. Not to go beyond this aspect of food in terms of one's investigation would be like analyzing words without considering their meanings.

Eating is a metaphor for sexual intercourse in a great many societies, including our own. Why is one a metaphor for the other? What do the two actions have in common? These two acts are completely different physiologically; nevertheless, they are tied together in their symbolic significance. In many societies, "eating" can be used figuratively for sexual intercourse. "To hunger for" is a metaphor for sexual desire. Among the Mehinaku of the Amazon region, having sex is defined as "to eat to the fullest extent. . . . The essential idea is that the genitals of one sex are the 'food' of the others" (Gregor 1985: 70). In a different part of the world, among the Lardil of Mornington Island, Australia, "there is a strong identification between food and sex, sexual intercourse and eating" (McKnight 1999: 23). In discussing eating practices among Americans, Lukanuski has pointed out the same equation and intertwining of eating and sex (1998: 114).

Eating is a metaphor that is sometimes used to signify marriage. In many New Guinea societies, like that of Lesu on the island of New Ireland in the Pacific, and that of the Trobriand Islanders, marriage is symbolized by the couple's eating together for the first time. Adolescent boys and girls freely engage in sexual intercourse without commitment to marriage and without any gossip or criticism from the community. But eating together constitutes a public announcement that they are now married. Eating symbolizes their new status as a married couple.

Earlier, in our society, it was just the reverse. One could take a date to dinner, but engaging in sexual intercourse was a sign of marriage. This is no longer the case.

In other New Guinea societies such as Wogeo, if a man eats with a woman, then she is like his sister and he can't marry her. Here, eating is equally symbolic but has the reverse meaning. Instead of marriage, eating symbolizes a brother-sister relationship—those who cannot marry. Among the Na of China, sexual intercourse is forbidden among close consanguineous relatives. The Na say, "Those who eat from the same bowl and the same plate must not mate" (Cai Hua 2001: 125).

In some New Guinea societies, the nuclear family is not the unit that eats together, as is the case in American society. The men take their meals in the men's house, separately from their wives and children. Women prepare and eat their food in their own houses, and take the husbands' portions of food to the men's house. This pattern is also widespread among Near Eastern societies, where men usually eat with other men and women with other women, and husbands and wives do not eat together. This is the case among the Marri Baluch of western Pakistan where the family arranges marriage between close relatives, and husbands never eat with their wives. But in adulterous relationships between a Marri Baluch man and woman, illicit eating together symbolizes their love for one another. In Lesu, the symbolic meaning of eating is exactly opposite

In many societies men prepare food and eat with other men in public, as in this inter-village gathering in rural Rajasthan.

from its meaning among the Marri Baluch. In Lesu, marriage is symbolized by a man and woman sitting down and eating together, but a woman never eats with her lover.

Recognition of the metaphoric connection between eating and sexual intercourse can also help to explain some other cultural rules that have to do with taboos against eating certain things. In some societies, members of a clan, a type of kin group, are not allowed to eat the animal or bird that is their totemic ancestor. Since they believe themselves to be descended from that ancestor, it would be like eating that ancestor or eating themselves. Eating the totemic animal or ancestor is equivalent to sexual intercourse within the group, which is incest. For example, among the Si-uai of Bougainville in the Solomon Islands, eating the totemic animal is seen as a form of incest, having intercourse with a person from one's own clan. There is another incest-like prohibition involving food among the Abelam and the Arapesh of Papua New Guinea. The Arapesh express it in the form of an aphorism:

Other people's mothers
Other people's sisters
Other people's pigs
Other people's yams which they have piled up
You may eat,
Your own mother
Your own sister
Your own pigs
Your own yams which you have piled up
You may not eat.

The pigs that a person raises are considered his children, and the owner of a pig is referred to as its father. The Arapesh explicitly recognize the symbolic connection between eating and sexual intercourse, as evidenced in the prohibition against eating one's own pigs and yams and the prohibition against incest with one's sister and mother. In Abelam and Arapesh, the taboo against eating one's own pigs and yams compels social groups to exchange their pigs and yams with other groups, resulting in ongoing exchange relationships with those groups.

It would be unthinkable to eat with one's enemies. Even in our own society, one may be compelled to say a polite good morning to one's enemy, but the line is drawn at breaking bread together. This is generally true in societies around the world. Eating together, or commensality, symbolizes goodwill and peaceful relations. What happens when enemies accidentally find themselves together for one reason or another? The Pathans of Swat, Pakistan, place great stress on hospitality, which is symbolized by giving food. Even if the host learns his guests are enemies, with whom he would normally not share food, the rules of hospitality dictate that as guests they must be fed. When the guests are ready to leave, the host escorts them to the border of his territory where his obligations of hospitality end, and he is free to treat them like enemies and kill them.

The association between food prohibitions and rank is found in its most extreme form in the caste system of India. A caste system consists of ranked groups, each with a different economic specialization. In India there is an association between caste and the idea of pollution. Because of the fear of pollution, Brahmans and other high-ranked individuals will not share food with, eat from the same plate as, or even accept food from an individual from a low-ranking caste. Members of highly ranked groups can be polluted by coming into contact with the bodily secretions, particularly saliva, of individuals of lower-ranked castes.

Food has a great many meanings in present-day American society. For example, regions are symbolized by different foods. Grits, fried chicken, barbecue, black-eyed peas, collards, and mustard greens represent the South. Some foods, like the Big Mac and Classic Coke, which symbolize America, have become international and can be found in almost every part of the globe. The multiethnic nature of America today is symbolized by ethnic foods and ingredients, such as bagels, pita bread, and oriental condiments, which are on the shelves of supermarkets in small towns and large cities. This reflects the fact that ethnic identity has become increasingly important as a component of American identity. Particular dishes distinctive of a national cuisine are used to create an ethnic identity. For example, the principal characters in the *Godfather* films are constantly signaling their Italian-American identities by what they cook and eat ("Take the cannoli; leave the gun"). Americans of other ethnicities also eat cannolis.

Social Groups, Social Categories, and Their Symbols

In the previous section, we selected something tangible, food, and then discussed the various meanings attached to it in different cultures. Group identity may be symbolized in a number of other ways in addition to cuisine. For example, a social group such as a clan may be represented by a **totemic animal**, with pictorial representations of the animal being used to signify that clan. The Kwakiutl, as well as other tribes of the Pacific Coast of Canada, painted the specific totemic animals of their groups on the facades of their houses and carved these animals on the totem poles standing before their houses. These tribes were like many other societies of the world in that personal names given to members of the group were the property of the entire group. When a person died, his or her name returned to the pool of names, to be used again when a child was born. There was also the belief that a name carried an identity, and that identity was perpetuated through the names handed down from generation to generation. In this way, individual identity was linked to clan identity, since, to the outside world, the name symbolized membership in the group.

In general, the clan as a social group may be associated with particular spirits, including spirits of the clan ancestors, who are said to dwell in specific locations in the clan territory. The spirits and the territory represent the clan. Strangers crossing the territory or hunting in it are in danger from the spirits that protect it. In such a situation, in which the land symbolizes the continuity of the social group (the clan) from mythical times to the present, the land could not be sold by clan members for money without destroying the identity of the group itself. Thus, an animal, a painting, a carving, a name, or a territory stands as a symbol of the group.

Fairly common forms used to symbolize social groups are birds, fish, and animals. One may ask why it is that animals are used to stand for people. Though the animal world exists apart

This Tsimshian mortuary totem pole stands today at Git Winkul, British Columbia. Erected by a family of the Wolf *phratry*, it depicts crests from their origin myth.

from the human world, people use the animal world to talk metaphorically about the human world. The world is seen as a jungle or referred to as an animal farm. Though the world of animals and the world of people are very different, there are links between them. The world of animals is divided into species; the world of people, into social groups. Societies use the different characteristics of animal species to make systems of classification of animals, such as those discussed in chapter 3. This classification will differ from one society to the next, because each society may single out different characteristics upon which its classification is based. In a society with clans, each clan is different from the others, just as the animal species differ from one another. This is why differences among animal species are used to express differences among groups of people.

Sometimes society is conceptualized as being divided into halves, which may be symbolically represented as higher and lower, sun and moon, or right side and left side. The Yafar of New Guinea think of the two parts as male and female. Each village is divided into two sides, one side referred to as "male" and made up of several clans, and the other side referred to as "female" and also comprising several clans. In rituals, men of the male half of the village use objects conceptualized as male and associated with plants designated male, while men of the female half of the village use ritual objects that are female and connected to female plants (Juillerat 1996: 48, 49, 71). The two halves are complementary, as are male and female.

THE SYMBOLIC MEANINGS OF SPACE

Arrangements of space also make important symbolic statements about social groupings and social relationships. Among the Nuchanulth (Nootka) of the Pacific Coast of Canada, each of the large plank houses in the winter villages in which they lived in the nineteenth century represented a social group. The floor plan of the house was divided into spaces that were ranked with respect to one another (see Figure 5-1). The place of honor, the left corner of the rear of the house, was occupied by the owner, who was the highest-ranking person in the house, with the highest title, and his family. The next most important man and his family occupied the right rear corner of the house; the third most important man and his family occupied the left front corner of the house; the fourth most important man and his family were in the right front corner; the least important titled man lived with his family on the left-hand side of the house. Untitled commoners and their families lived in the remaining spaces along the sides of the house. Each location had its own hearth. The floor plan of the house was like a seating plan according to seniority. There is archeological evidence of this type of house with its status divisions that goes back at least two thousand years. However, with demographic decline and the incursion of the cash economy in the late nineteenth century, a new pattern developed in which related nuclear families lived in single family dwellings clustered behind the large houses that were now used for "sociopolitical rituals . . . [and were] transformed into potlatch houses" (Marshall 2000: 102).

In a peasant village in northeastern Thailand, space in a house is divided to symbolize not rank, but rules about marriage and sex (see Figure 5-2). The sleeping room is the most sacred part of the house. First cousins, with whom sexual relations and marriage are not permitted, may enter that

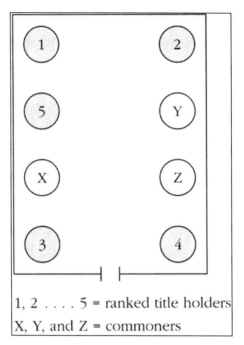

Figure 5.1   Nuchanulth house floor plan.

room but may not sleep there. More distant relatives, whom one may marry, are not allowed to enter the sleeping room and must remain in the guest room. S. J. Tambiah (1969), who has analyzed the Thai material, also relates categories of animals and their edibility to relatives whom you may and may not marry. First cousins, whom you cannot marry, are equivalent to your own buffalo, oxen, and pigs, which live under the house. You may not eat them and must give them to other people. More distant relatives, whom you can marry, are equivalent to other people's domestic animals, which you can eat. Since social space symbolizes degree of social relationship, and edibility also signifies social relationships, then the meaning of social space is also related to edibility.

Gender differences are also symbolized in the use of space. As noted earlier, husbands and wives in Papua New Guinea not only do not eat together but also live in separate houses. Women will take their husband's food to the door of the men's house but will not enter it. Space is also gendered in the Middle East, where men who are not members of the family may not enter the women's quarters.

In Mexico, the meaning and organization of domestic space is strikingly different. Houses are organized around a patio, or courtyard. Rooms for sleeping, dressing, talking when the weather is inclement, cooking, and storage open onto the patio, where all kinds of domestic activities, such as socializing, child play, bathing, and doing laundry, take place. Individuals do not have separate bedrooms. Children often sleep with parents, and same-sex siblings share a bed, emphasizing familial interdependence. Rooms in Mexican houses are locations for multiple activities that, in contrast, are rigidly separated in the United States.

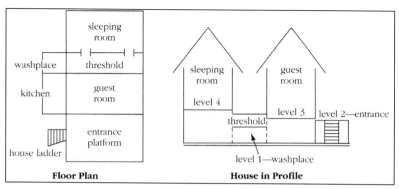

Figure 5.2 Thai house floor plan.

The households of Mexican Americans in Los Angeles represent a transition between Mexican and American usages. According to Pader, they "blur the lines between the U.S. coding system, with its emphasis on greater bodily privacy and the individual, and the Mexican system, with its emphasis on sharing and close daily interconnection" (Pader 1993: 130–31). As Mexican-American children mature, they change their ideas about family, become more individuated, and desire their own beds and bedrooms.

Gypsies, who are found in every major American city, have retained important elements of their own culture, including extended families, which form households, and their ideas about pollution and space utilization. When the Gypsies of Richmond, California, move into a house previously occupied by non-Gypsies (gaje), the house must first be ritually cleansed of the polluting effects of gaje by a thorough cleaning with disinfectants and the burning of incense. Then the inner walls are torn down and the doors removed to create communal living space, which is divided by hanging drapes. One space is devoted to palm reading, the major source of income; the other space is used as a living area for the extended family that will live there. The head of one Gypsy family moved into what had formerly been a bar and dance club in order to house the twenty-eight members of his family and the many guests the family entertained (Sutherland 1986).

In many societies like our own, individuals have their own private spaces, reflecting the premium placed upon privacy. People feel that others should not intrude into one's own space. When a teenager closes the door to her or his room, this is a sign that parents should not enter. This is in contrast to other societies, in which space is communal and has a different meaning. When space is communally shared by a group, that group may have shared responsibilities, such as collective group responsibility when a member commits a crime or shared responsibilities for payment of a bride price.

Space may also be symbolically conquered and inscribed with new meanings. In recent decades, many Muslims, members of Sufi regional cults centered in the North-West Frontier Province of Pakistan, have migrated to England, extending and expanding cult influence (Werbner 1996). At first, Muslim religious and ritual observances were conducted in mosques and in the home, where immigrants' religious observances were protected from external hostility. Expansion and conquest of new space is a significant aspect of Sufi cult organization. As Werbner notes, "The moral conquest of alien space is a test of the charismatic authenticity that legitimizes the rise of new 'living saints'" (1996: 310). Muslim men march and chant twice a year in the *julus* ceremonial procession through the Manchester, Birmingham, or London Pakistani immigrant neighborhoods, "sacralizing and 'Islamacizing' the very earth, the buildings, the streets and the neighborhoods through which they march" (Werbner 1996: 312). The "new order" with its own "living saints" is established in a foreign place, but these diasporas are still connected to home, creating a transnational network encompassing the East and the West. The march is also "an expression of the rights of minorities to celebrate their culture and religion in the public domain within a multicultural, multifaith, multiracial society" (Werbner 1996: 333).

SYMBOLS, POLITICS, AND AUTHORITY

Just as clans can be represented by things such as totems, houses, space, and personal names, so too may an entire nation be represented by an array of symbols. The combat between symbolic animals—the eagle and the bear—was used by political cartoonists to portray the conflict between the United States and the former Soviet Union. In the same way, two buildings represent the United States and Russia. News reports often indicate that the White House says this and the Kremlin says that. National flags, anthems, and food also symbolize nations. The act of desecrating the flag by burning it makes a negative statement about the country the flag represents.

Some people have assumed that "questions of symbolism are peripheral if not irrelevant to the 'real business of politics'" (Morris 2005: 1). However, as we have just noted above, desecration of a flag or even suggestions to change the design of a flag usually provoke many comments. Flags and other political symbols have a more complex series of emotional qualities and ideas associated with them than other types of symbols. They are associated with the solidarity of the groups or nations the symbols represent. This is also true of a country's name, as a symbol. Greece has prevented Macedonia from joining the European Union unless the name of the country, Macedonia, is changed. This is because Greece has a province called Macedonia and it is afraid that the country of Macedonia has designs on this territory. Morris describes the way in which the tricolor flag and "The Soldier's Song," which had inspired the Sinn Fein of Ireland in their struggle for independence from Britain, became the official symbols of the Irish Free State after it achieved its independence from the United Kingdom and its separation from Northern Ireland with its large Protestant population in 1922 (2005: 38ff).

In contrast, Northern Ireland, which remained part of the United Kingdom, though it had its own parliament, emphasized this continued connection by having the British flag, the Union Jack, as their most important symbol, which served to distance Northern Ireland from the Irish Free State. Morris notes that these highly charged political symbols played an important role in the development of Irish national identity, though at the beginning there was no unanimity about them on the part of all the political parties in what became the Irish Free State. At first, some were upset that the symbols of Sinn Fein, which had played such an important role in the fight for independence, were selected as representing the Irish nation rather than the symbols of other parties.

The symbols of Northern Ireland reiterated their continued relationship with the Crown, while the symbols of the Irish Free State represented their independence and separation from Britain.

In a number of African societies, the ruler or paramount chief represents the entire society. Thus the health of its members, as well as their fertility and the fertility of their crops, is dependent on the ruler and his health. Among the Aluund of southwestern Zaire, the paramount chief is linked metaphorically not only to the entire body politic of Aluund society but also to the kapwiip tree (De Boeck 1994). Just as the chief is the elder at the center of the community around whom the populace gathers, the kapwiip tree is the elder among trees. The chief is perceived as the trunk, and the people are the fruit surrounding the trunk. The chief rarely leaves his compound; instead, he listens (a mark of wisdom) to the people who come to him there, like the wise kapwiip tree, which remains in one place and "listens." By listening well, the chief mediates and resolves disputes. He is seen as asexual, with both powerful masculine and nurturant feminine characteristics, and is portrayed as Janus-like in carvings—one face male, and the other female. The staff he holds, made from the wood of the kapwiip tree, is carved to represent three levels—a bird (usually the fish eagle) symbolizing heaven, a female human symbolizing earth, and a snake and crocodile symbolizing the underworld. The chief is seen as mediating between these three worlds. He is "lord of the soil," responsible for all regenerative aspects of Luunda culture (De Boeck 1994: 457). Since fertility and reproduction depend on the state of the paramount chief, he must not show signs of disease, decay, or old age. The Aluund have a complex symbolic system in which metaphors are simultaneously extended in many different directions.

If authority is represented by a series of symbols, opposition to that authority is symbolically represented by an inversion of those symbols. In the 1960s in the United States, all men in authority had short hair. Young men created a symbol of opposition when they allowed their hair to grow long. If authorities have short hair, then long hair is a symbol of opposition to that authority. However, today, wearing one's hair long is acceptable. Long hair is no longer considered a symbol of opposition to society, but dyeing one's hair fuchsia, blue, or orange is. During the seventeenth century, the Cavaliers of Charles I of England wore their hair long, while those who opposed them, the Puritans led by Oliver Cromwell, wore short hair. The Puritans' hairstyle became the focal symbol of their opposition, and so they were called Roundheads (as depicted in a cartoon of the period). These examples relate to the general principle that those who oppose the established authority will select as their symbol something that is the reverse of the symbol of those in authority. Political symbols may seem trivial, but, in reality, people will die rather than deny them or give them up. People's identity or concept of self as members of a group is powerfully bound up with such symbols. To deny or reject them is to deny one's identity and worth.

Body Symbolism

The human body is often utilized as the basis for metaphors. Another common way to symbolize social groupings and social relationships is to use the human body metaphorically. Among the Teutonic tribes at the dawn of history, close and distant relatives were symbolized by close and more distant parts of the body, reckoned from the head. The father and mother were symbolized

The Cavaliers of seventeenth-century England wore their hair long, while their Puritan opposition wore their hair short. In this cartoon of the period, both men and their dogs are characterized by their respective hairstyles.

by the head; brothers and sisters were at the neck; first cousins at the shoulders; second cousins at the elbows; third cousins at the wrists; and fourth, fifth, and sixth cousins at the knuckles and finger joints. At the cutoff point of kin were seventh cousins, who were called nail relatives. Individuals beyond seven degrees of relationship were not considered kinsmen.

The internal skeletal structure of the body is also used as a metaphor for the internal structure of society. The word *bone* was used for *clan* among the Mongols, and the aristocracy was referred to as *White Bone* to distinguish them from commoners, who were referred to as *Black Bone*. A slightly different metaphor is used by the Riff of Morocco, who refer to their clan as a vein. Just as the Mongols used a skeletal metaphor, the Riff use the metaphor of blood vessels to represent the interconnection between the branching parts of their society. Americans use the metaphor of blood to represent kinship. In thinking about the biological facts of conception, we can see that the sperm from the father and the egg from the mother, which unite to form the new individual, have nothing to do with blood. Yet Americans say that the blood of their fathers and mothers flows in their veins. This is our symbolic way of talking about kinship.

Among the Ko'a on the island of Palu'e in Eastern Indonesia, "the body metaphor is applied at every socio-cosmic level" (Vischer 2003: 59). The house is considered a body through which flows the energy associated with life; the lower part of a settlement is classified as its feet and the upper part as its head. The ceremonial mound at the center, the navel of the settlement, is associated with growth. Body metaphors are also associated with the island itself, with the seaboard as the feet and the volcano and mountain as the head. Since it is seen as a living body, the blood is what rises up in the volcano, that is, the lava that eventually flows to the sea (Vischer 2003: 59). Vischer notes that "sacrificial blood is [also] hierarchically ranked according to its potency and efficacy as ritual agent" (2003: 56). The blood of humans, "big blood," generally not a part of sacrificial events, is the most potent. Water buffalo that are sacrificed also have "big blood," the only substance that can be used to directly contact the "Supreme Being." Pig's blood, which can transform a "state of conceptual heat" harmful to people into a state of coolness, is of lesser potency and is used in life crisis and agricultural rituals. Healer-sorcerers may use the blood of fowl in ritual, which is of still lesser potency. Substitutions can be made, but a vegetable can never be used as a substitute for blood, since it does not have the potency of blood.

Aho notes, "The personal body, . . . is a metaphor of the social body; orifices in particular stand for a group's weak spots (2002: 11). An example is the ancient Israelites whose polity was threatened constantly by enemies. They had a whole series of taboos relating to the orifices of members, their symbolic points of vulnerability. The dietary taboos and the need to separate from Gentiles were ways of setting the Jews apart according to God's edict. Circumcision was another means of maintaining separation. The dietary laws regarding separation of different kinds of food; preventing contamination of foods, dishes, pots, and pans; and filtering drinking water all "functioned sociologically to maintain the solidarity of the Jewish community" (Aho 2002: 37–39). Jesus moves Christianity in a different direction, suspending the dietary laws and circumcision and thus reversing the metaphor so that Christians are no longer separate from other people.

Sharp illustrates some of the ways in which "the human body is a symbolically charged landscape" in her analysis of organ transplantation (2001: 112). Organ donation and procurement, an emotionally charged area, have generated a complex set of "symbolic renderings of the body, death and mourning." Once it has been determined that brain death, the point considered to be the death of the self or the individual, has taken place, "harvesting" of the viable organs from a body still otherwise functioning can take place if the donor's kin have given their approval. To the transplant specialists, the donor has become dehumanized, and his or her organs have become "sophisticated, replaceable mechanical parts" completely separated from the identity of the donor (Sharp 2001: 115). Donated organs are not paid for at present; however, because of the shortage of such organs the suggestion has been made that a system of payment be instituted. Even now, organs are treated as if they were commodities, like other commercial medical goods that are bought and sold today (such as blood, sperm, and ova). In an effort to mask this commercialization, the donor kin are encouraged to see the transplanted organs of their loved ones as continuing to live in the bodies of unknown recipients, a life after death, so to speak. The donated organs are seen as a "gift of life," and transplant personnel use various strategies to accomplish the "veiling of procurement" (Sharp 2001: 118). The identity and life history of the donor are always kept secret, as well as the circumstances of his or her death, violent or otherwise. The message of the transplant professionals is "a greening of the body, a form of 'semantic message' that foregrounds the goodness associated with donation while simultaneously denying transplantation's more disturbing reliance on death and organ retrieval" (Sharp 2001: 120). Using logos associated with ecology, such as butterflies, trees, and foliage, on stationery, pamphlets, label pins, rings, T-shirts, posters, and bumper stickers shifts the emphasis from death to life. The use of agricultural metaphors is pervasive (e.g., organs are said to be harvested or transplanted through grafting). Some hospitals and organ procurement organizations have gone so far as to establish "donor gardens" and "donor trees," which are decorated by recipients of donated organs at ceremonies (Sharp 2001: 125). Interestingly, the kin of the donors reject such symbolism and imagery, since it dehumanizes and depersonalizes their deceased loved ones, and have begun to make donor memorial quilts similar to the AIDS memorial quilts, in which each panel commemorates a loved one who had given the "gift of life." Metaphors are used here to turn death into life.

THE SYMBOLISM OF SPORTS

As noted earlier, games in a culture are often metaphors for life. Sports in American society are children's games played by adults, but they are much more than just games. They make symbolic statements about the society, which explains their enormous popularity. In American team sports, such as football, individual achievement, which is often seen as a cultural characteristic of Americans, is subordinated to team effort. Football is an exclusively male activity in which male bonding ties individuals together in a collective effort. In this aspect, it is similar to male initiations in other societies, in which a ritual separates men from women and binds them together into a male peer group. As in such male initiation rites, in professional and college football during the training period and before games, male players are separated from women. In his analysis of American football, entitled "Into the End Zone for a Touchdown," Alan Dundes examines the folk speech involved in football and observes that "American football could be a ritual combat between groups of males attempting to assert their masculinity by penetrating the end zones of their rivals" (1978: 86). He likens football, which he sees as a form of symbolic homosexual behavior, to the initiation rites of aboriginal Australia, which also have a homosexual aspect. The male bonding of American football sets males, the participants, against females, the outsiders. This would also explain why, some years ago, the New England Patriots had strong feelings that the presence of a female reporter in their dressing room was completely inappropriate. In their eyes, she was intruding into a male ritual. The team aspect of football is also a recapitulation of the value of teamwork, pulling together for a common goal, in American society.

When a sport that originated in one culture spreads to another culture, it may take on a completely different set of symbolic meanings. With the expansion of the British Empire, cricket moved into the colonial areas that the British conquered, and today it is played enthusiastically from the Caribbean to the Pacific, especially on the Indian subcontinent. During the colonial period, it personified the quintessence of British colonialism. In fact, the expression *not cricket* means not acting like a proper Englishman and refers to stretching the rules. Nowhere is cricket played in a more spirited fashion than in the Trobriand Islands, where it was introduced by English missionaries at the beginning of the twentieth century. Over the years, the Trobrianders transformed the English version of the game, which represented colonial domination, into a cultural creation that has a multiplicity of meanings in their own Trobriand culture. In contrast to English cricket, in which all the players wear white, in Trobriand cricket the players dress in the traditional regalia for warfare, and each team may have up to forty players. The cricket game is usually part of the competition when one village challenges another to a *kayasa*, a competitive period of feasting and exchange of yams. Magic that was used in warfare, which was outlawed by the colonial authorities, is used during the cricket game, since the game of cricket is symbolically like warfare as well as like competitive exchange. When the bowler pitches the ball, he recites the magic formula that was formerly used to make a spear hit its target. In Trobriand cricket, the home team always wins; this is not supposed to happen in Western sports. The symbolism of Trobriand cricket may be seen as more like that of competitive exchange—first you "win," then I "win"—than the way sports are played in the United States, that is, to decide the "ultimate" winners. The symbolism of warfare characterizes other aspects of culture in other societies. In chapter 2, we saw such symbolism being used in the Kwakiutl marriage ritual.

UNIVERSAL SYMBOLS

It can be argued that certain symbols are found universally and carry similar meanings in all cultures. Colors are frequently associated with emotional states and sometimes with other meaningful messages as well. Some have argued that red brings about emotional arousal on the part of the viewer. In American society, red means danger and is used for stop signs in traffic control. Green is the complementary color to red and is used to symbolize the opposite of red. Since traffic lights, like all symbols, are arbitrary, the question of whether they might have originally been put forth in reversed fashion, so that red meant go and green meant stop, could be asked. Because these symbols are part of the larger category of color symbolism in our society, in which a red dress symbolizes a prostitute, the red-light district signifies a den of iniquity, and red hair means a fiery temper, it seems likely that the colors could not have been reversed. The question of whether red has the same meaning in other cultures remains to be systematically explored. In our society, black is the color of mourning; at a funeral, people wear black clothing. In contrast, white, the color of Maria Shriver's wedding gown, represents purity and virginity. A bride wears white when the relationship is established and black if the relationship is terminated by the death of her husband. In China, the color symbolism for death and mourning is exactly the opposite; there, white is the color of death and mourning, so mourners wear white clothing. It is clear that the meanings of colors vary from one culture to another.

Other symbols have been suggested as ones that have universal meaning. Hair is one of these. As noted earlier, long hair can be a symbol of rebellion when everyone else is wearing short hair. However, Edmund Leach has pointed out that, in a number of widely separate cultures, long hair, especially unkempt long hair, is a symbol of sexuality (1958). Short hair symbolizes restraint, while a shaved head often indicates celibacy, although today it has other meanings as well. Rituals that involve the cutting of hair are seen as symbolic forms of castration. The symbolism of hair is quite overt. We are not dealing here with private symbols of the type referred to earlier in this chapter, but rather with a culturally accepted and widely understood symbol. It is not a symbol whose meaning is unconscious.

SUMMARY

- Symbols and their meanings are crucial to understanding what a culture is all about.
- The term *metaphor* refers to the relationship in which one thing stands for something else, as eating is a metaphor for sexual activity.
- Metonym refers to a part of something standing for the whole, such as the crown that stands for the political authority of the Queen of England.
- Symbols are two-sided—the physical properties of the symbol as distinct from what the symbol stands for.
- Food has many different meanings in different cultures.
- Group identity may be symbolized in a number of other ways in addition to cuisine.
- Arrangements of space also make important symbolic statements about social groupings and social relationships.
- The shape of the human body has different meanings in different cultures.
- Different cultural domains, such as kinship, economics, political organization, and religion, are all imbued with symbolic meaning. To understand how these institutions work, one must understand the symbols and the cultural meanings through which they are organized.

SUGGESTED READINGS

O'Neill, Barry. *Honor, Symbols and War*. Ann Arbor: University of Michigan Press, 1999. Examines the role that symbolism plays in international relations and conflict resolution. The importance of national honor is also considered.
Watson, James I. and Melissa L. Caldwell. *The Cultural Politics of Eating: A Reader*. Malden, MA: Blackwell Publishers, 2005. Compilation of articles about the meaning of food in different cultures
Womack, Mari. *Symbols and Meaning: A Concise Introduction*. Walnut Creek, CA: Altamira Press, 2005. A general work on the various aspects of the study of symbolism.

SUGGESTED WEBSITES

www.tahititatou.com/dictionaryl.html. A handbook detailing Polynesian tattoo symbols.
www.symbols.net/food/. A website containing many different sources regarding food symbolism.
www.as.ua.edu/ant/Faculty/murphy/436/symbolic.htm. A general review of symbolic and interpretive anthropologies.

Chapter 6
Ties That Connect
Marriage, Family, and Kinship

WHAT IS "KINSHIP"? How can we identify kinship in America? In our society, we have families, and a network of relatives beyond the family. When a child grows up and gets married, he or she forms a new family. Families in America typically consist of two generations, parents and unmarried children. Some people think that this kind of kin organization is universal. However, elsewhere in the world, many societies have three or even four generational families, including grandparents, married children, and grandchildren. With such larger families the care of young children and infirm elderly grandparents is not a problem. As a consequence, they have no need for day-care centers and nursing homes that perform these functions in our society. Small, independent two-generation families are associated with the individualism characteristic of American society, though we will see later on that today American families are more diverse. An American in serious financial need usually would not go to his brother for assistance. Each brother must first look out for his own children. Besides, Americans would say, "Go to a bank. It's bad to borrow from one's relatives. That's what banks are for."

Many people in America assume that the structure of their families and their system of kinship is the one most common in the world. However, all one need do is to read the daily newspapers to find out that is not the case. In societies that newspapers refer to as "tribal societies," like those in the Northwest Territories of Pakistan and even in parts of Iraq, three-generation families are common, and brothers stand together financially and politically. In fact, sometimes, when a man dies, his brother will take his place and marry the widow. If a man is killed by a member of another clan, his brother is obliged to avenge the killing. The collective responsibilities of a kin group are shown in the following case. In 2002, a Pakistani woman was gang raped because her brother had had a sexual affair with a woman of a different caste. The sister was punished for her brother's action because families and clans are frequently held jointly responsible for the actions of one member of the group, and the honor of the group must be upheld. Ethnic groups in more complex societies often use the same extended notion of "brotherhood" or kinship to claim "we are all brothers." This collective view of brothers can be contrasted with the individualism of our own society, which pulls married brothers apart, each favoring his own immediate family.

In a "free" society like our own, one should have the right to have sexual relations with anyone one chooses. Why does the government tell us who we may or may not marry? By what right does the United States government say that we may have one, and only one, spouse? Why not permit polygamy, marriage with more than one wife? There are strict rules about sex, even in free societies like our own and they vary from one state to another. Usually sex cannot occur between parties under the age of sixteen. If you live in Massachusetts, you can marry your first cousin. In Pennsylvania or Oregon, you cannot. Though polygamy was practiced among the ancient Israelites, as described in the Bible, it is not permitted among Jews today in the United States. Mormons had to give up polygamy so that Utah could become a state.

In the societies anthropologists studied earlier, most of daily life was organized on the basis of kinship relationships. In these small-scale societies, all religious, economic, and political behavior took place within the context of a social structure based on kinship. This is why the study of kinship has been so important in anthropology. Even with increasing industrialization and globalization in so many parts of the world today kinship continues to be central. As Parkin notes, "Many societies still think in terms of lineages, affinal alliance systems, residence rules and marriage payments, while virtually all are still organized in families of some sort and use kin terms to identity and classify relatives" (1997: ix–x). Even with the increasing numbers of same-sex, gay, and lesbian families in America and Western Europe, these new types of families are vital, and kinship terminology important.

Looking at whom one can marry, that is, marriage rules, family organization, residence patterns after marriage, forms of descent and descent groups, and other aspects of kinship, one finds that there are a limited number of possibilities. Further, these rules build on one another so that where a couple lives after marriage relates to the kind of family they will have, and that is often the basis for the kinds of larger kin groups to which they belong. We must also remember that these are the rules for societies and that people's actual practices may often vary from these rules, as is always the case for all cultural rules, even rules about an explosive topic such as incest. All cultural rules are violated. For example, the records of mental institutions document that some people in our society violate the incest taboo.

In chapter 2, we saw how in weddings in two different societies, kinship played a different but still significant role in the proceedings. The Kwakiutl have groups based on kinship that they refer to as *numayms*. How does one become a member of a *numaym*? What are one's rights, privileges, and responsibilities toward other members of the *numaym*? Are all one's kin in one's own *numaym*? At the American wedding, different groupings of people based on kinship participated—the bride's side and the groom's side, immediate relatives and distant relatives. In addition, there were those who were not relatives at all but who attended as friends, neighbors, and fellow workers. What are the differences between the ways relatives are grouped in Kwakiutl society and the ways they are grouped in our own society and what do these differences mean? This chapter presents concepts that anthropologists have developed to answer these questions.

The discussion of marriage, family, and kinship that follows will deal with cultural rules found in a variety of societies. Through time, these cultural rules are frequently transformed. In the succeeding chapters on religion, politics, economics, and art, we will see that kinship still plays a crucial role in small-scale societies, despite the fact that they were shaken to their roots as they were incorporated into colonial empires, and then into new nations. Historically, before the advent of colonialism and accelerated culture change, when groups had less contact with one another, rules of kinship in these societies were much more obvious. Today, kinship and kin groups continue to be very significant in many people's lives, whether they remain in their rural villages or migrate to look for work in expanding cities like Lagos in Nigeria, or Port Moresby in Papua New Guinea. Until recently, it was widely believed that kinship relations withered in modern industrial societies. The sociologist Lewis Wirth had hypothesized that with the growth of urbanism, kinship bonds would weaken and decline in importance. Research on kinship has revealed just the opposite. New forms such as same-sex families in America and transnational families in parts of Europe, Asia, and the Americas have appeared. In the latter, relatives may not be living in the same city or country, but they still maintain contact by letter, phone, and e-mail.

MARRIAGE

Almost all known societies recognize marriage. The ritual of marriage marks a change in status for a man and a woman and the acceptance by society of the new family that is formed. However, the Nayar and the Na, which we describe later in this chapter, do not have marriage or marriage rituals. Marriage, like all other things cultural, is governed by rules that, as will be seen, are connected to one another. Just as the rules vary from one society to another, so does the ritual by which society recognizes and celebrates the marriage. In the American wedding, the bridegroom places a ring on the third finger, left hand, of the bride and repeats the ritual formula, "With this ring, I thee wed." In the Kwakiutl wedding, the bridegroom comes as a member of a feigned war party to capture the bride and "move" her from her father's house. At both Kwakiutl and American weddings, large numbers of guests are present, serving as witnesses to the marriage, signifying that marriage is more than a private affair and is recognized publicly by society. Sometimes, the ritual may be as minimal as in the Trobriand and Lesu cases, in which marriage is symbolized merely by the couple's publicly eating together.

Marriage Prohibitions

Societies also have rules that state whom one can and cannot marry. Rules about whom one cannot marry are directly related to the incest taboo, which is found in all societies and is therefore a cultural universal. The **incest taboo** forbids sexual relations between certain categories of close relatives. Almost universally, forbidden categories include mother and son, father and daughter, and brother and sister. Since sexual partners cannot be sought within the immediate family because of the incest taboo, they must be sought elsewhere. The incest taboo that forbids sexual relations also necessarily forbids marriage, since marriage almost always includes sexual access.

In many societies, there are people with whom one can have sexual intercourse but whom one cannot marry. Marriage prohibitions, therefore, are wider in scope than the prohibitions against sexual intercourse. Both the incest taboo and prohibitions against marrying certain close relatives have the effect of compelling individuals to seek sexual partners and mates outside their own group. Beyond the immediate family, there is great variation from one society to another in the rules regarding which categories of relatives one is forbidden to marry. As we noted above, even within the United States, there is variation among the states in the laws regarding which relatives one may not marry. Some states permit marriage between first cousins while others prohibit it; still others prohibit marriage between second cousins. For example, the Office of Human Services of the Commonwealth of Massachusetts decrees: "No man may marry his . . . stepmother, grandson's wife, wife's mother, wife's daughter, brother's daughter, sister's daughter, father's sister or mother's sister" in addition to other relatives (Registrar of Vital Records and Statistics, Commonwealth of Massachusetts, courtesy of Ron Palazzo). First cousins are absent from this list.

There are a few striking examples of marriage between members of the immediate family that violate the universality of the incest taboo. Among the pharaohs of ancient Egypt, such as Tutankhamen, the boy king, as well as among the royal lineages of Hawaii and the Incas in Peru, brother and sister married. In each instance, the ruler had to marry someone equal in rank, and who could be better qualified than one's own brother or sister?

Exogamy and Endogamy

Marriage within the group is called **endogamy** and marriage outside the group is called **exogamy**. The rule of exogamy, like the incest taboo, requires that members of the group seek spouses outside their own group. A rule of exogamy is frequently conceptualized as an extension of the incest taboo in that the same term is used for both. Among the Trobriand Islanders, the term *suvasova* is used for the incest taboo and is also extended to forbid sexual relations and marriage with women of one's own larger kin group, or *dala*, all of whom are called sisters. A rule of endogamy requires individuals to marry within their own group and forbids them to marry outside it. Religious groups such as the Amish, Mormons, Catholics, and Jews have rules of endogamy, though these are often violated when marriage take place outside the group. Castes in India and Nepal are also endogamous. Rules of exogamy create links between groups, while rules of endogamy preserve separateness and exclusivity, and are a means of maintaining boundaries between one group and other groups. In this sense, the brother-sister marriages referred to above reach the absolute limit of endogamy in order to preserve sanctity and power within the ruling families of those societies. More typical are those cases in which the immediate family is exogamous, while the larger group, frequently an ethnic group or religious sect, is endogamous.

Sister Exchange

Since a rule of exogamy demands that spouses come from outside one's group, relationships are created through marriage with other groups. If a man cannot marry his own sister, he gives his sister to someone in another group. According to the basic principle of exchange, something given must be returned with its equivalent. If a man accepts another man's sister, he must therefore return his own sister as the equivalent. After all, the receiver, too, may not marry his own sister. A number of societies over the world have a rule requiring that two men exchange sisters; anthropologists refer to this as sister exchange. If a man does not have a biological sister, he returns a woman for whom he uses the same kinship term that he uses for his sister. Recently, feminist anthropologists have argued that this form of marriage could just as easily be conceptualized as brother exchange. However, where men are dominant in a society, this is seen as sister exchange "from the native point of view." When Margaret Mead went to study the Mountain Arapesh in New Guinea, she asked them why they didn't marry their own sisters, expecting a response indicating revulsion at the very thought. Instead, Mead's informant stated, "What is the matter with you anyway? Don't you want a brother-in-law?" (Mead 1935: 68). This is because one hunts, gardens, and travels with one's brother-in-law among the Arapesh. Thus a marriage creates a link not only between husband and wife but also, through the wife, between two men who are brothers-in-law to each other.

Marriage Payments

In many societies marriage involves a transfer or exchange of property. Sometimes, payments are made by the groom and his family to the family of the bride, as occurs among the Kwakiutl. This payment is known as **bridewealth**. In other instances, the bride brings property with her at the marriage. This is known as **dowry**, and goods are moving in the opposite direction from bridewealth payments. In societies that practice sister exchange, there may be an option to give bridewealth if one does not have a sister to exchange. However, it is also common to find sister exchange accompanied by the payment of bridewealth, so that groups are exchanging both women and bridewealth payments. In pre-Revolutionary China, both bridewealth and dowry were paid.

Bride Service

Sometimes the groom exchanges labor for his bride, in lieu of the payment of bridewealth. When the groom works for his wife's family, this is known as **bride service**. It may be recalled that in the Old Testament, Jacob labored for seven years in order to marry Leah, and then another seven years to marry Rachel, Leah's younger sister, thus performing fourteen years of bride service for his father-in-law. Bride service was also practiced by the Yanomamo, a people living in the lowlands of Venezuela. During this time, the groom lives with the bride's parents and hunts for them. Since the Yanomamo also have sister exchange, one might say that during this period of bride service, they really are practicing brother exchange. However, since men determine whom women will marry, the Yanomamo do not conceptualize this as two women exchanging their brothers. After the period of bride service is over, the husband takes his wife back to his group. The Apu Tani, a tribal people in India, normally pay *mithun*, a large domesticated bovine as bridewealth when they marry. When a man has no *mithun* to give he performs bride service for his in-laws (Rikam 2006: 344, 354). After the service is completed he will take his wife back home, however, this bride service serves to lower his social status.

Shell rings are presented as bridewealth at an Abelam marriage.

Number of Spouses

Some societies, like our own, practice **monogamy**; that is, only one spouse at a time is permitted. However, according to the Bible, husbands could have more than one wife, as in the case of Jacob. This is known as **polygyny** and is still permitted in many societies in the world, particularly Islamic societies. Jews living in Muslim countries continued to practice polygyny up until recently. Jews coming to Israel from Muslim countries were allowed to bring several wives, but they were forbidden to marry more than one wife in Israel itself. Sometimes, as in the case of Jacob, a man marries several sisters. This practice is known as **sororal polygyny**. In the societies in which it occurs, it is usually explained by saying that sisters have a good relationship with one another, and this will help overcome the inevitable jealousy that arises between co-wives. On the other hand, many people, such as the Trobriand Islanders and the Kanuri of Nigeria, explicitly forbid sororal polygyny. The Kanuri explanation for this prohibition is that the good relationship between two sisters should not be undermined by the unavoidable friction that arises between two co-wives. This simply demonstrates that whatever rules are in effect, the people will offer an explanation for their existence that is perfectly rational in their eyes. An alternative form of marriage, known as **polyandry**, in which one woman may have several husbands, occurs but is rather rare. In almost all cases, a woman marries several brothers; this is known as **fraternal polyandry**. Today, among ethnic Tibetans in northwest Nepal, the ideal form of marriage is fraternal polyandry, in which the eldest brother is the primary husband and nominally the father of all the children, whether or not he is the biological father (Levine 1987). Sometimes, anthropologists wish to refer to plural spouses in general, either husbands or wives. In that case, they use the term **polygamy**, in contrast to the term monogamy. Because of the frequency of divorce and subsequent remarriage in the United States, it is sometimes said that Americans practice **serial monogamy**. We may not have more than one spouse at a time, but some people have numerous spouses, one after the other. Some of the Mormons in the southern part of Utah still practice polygamy, usually sororal polygamy, and the law looks the other way unless the bride-to-be is under the legal age for marriage. The discovery of oil in the Gulf States of the Middle East and the increase in wealth now permit men to marry as many wives as they wish. Up to this point, polygamy had been rare (al-Kahteeb 2007: 104).

Levirate and Sororate

The exchange of a woman for another woman or the exchange of a woman for bridewealth is an indication that marriage is a significant concern of the kin groups of the marrying couple. A further demonstration of this is found in the customs of the **levirate** and the **sororate**. Under the levirate, if a man dies, his widow then marries one of his brothers, thereby continuing the relationship between the two kin groups established by the first marriage. In the levirate, a woman marries one brother after the death of another brother, while in fraternal polyandry she is married to two brothers simultaneously. Orthodox Jews today still practice the levirate, if the brother of the deceased husband is unmarried. When a deceased wife is replaced in the marriage by an unmarried sister, this is known as the sororate. It resembles sororal polygyny, but in the sororate a man marries two sisters, the second after the death of the first. Both the levirate and sororate are practiced by the Shertukpen in India (Megejee 2006: 300). This practice illustrated what the British anthropologist Radcliffe-Brown referred to as the equivalence of siblings (1952), in which one same-sex sibling can be substituted for another.

Dissolution of Marriage

Stability of marriage varies from one society to another. Almost all societies provide a means for divorce or the dissolution of a marriage. Divorce is invariably more difficult after children have been born to the couple. Where bridewealth has been paid, it would have to be returned if the wife leaves her husband. This may be difficult to achieve if the bridewealth, paid several years before, has been spent, dispersed, or consumed. Some anthropologists have argued that the higher the bridewealth payment, the more stable the marriage and less likely a divorce, since it would require the return of bridewealth, which may be difficult in such societies. Others have said that frequency of divorce and stability of marriage are related not to the amount of bridewealth but to the degree of incorporation of a wife into her husband's family or kin group. Among the Manchus of Manchuria, who conquered China in the seventeenth century, the wife went through a fire ceremony in front of the hearth in her husband's house. This ritual served to conceptually

Nyinba polyandrous family in northwest Nepal. The eldest husband is to the left, sewing clothing; the youngest husband is to the right. The woman on the left is their common wife, holding their youngest daughter. The girl on the right is their oldest daughter; leaning against her is the family's only son.

incorporate her permanently into his kin group. In contrast, the Kwakiutl paid bridewealth to the bride's family. At a subsequent ceremony, the bride's family paid a large amount of goods to "repurchase" her, thereby reiterating her membership in the kin group of her birth. Among the Kwakiutl, the wife is never incorporated into the husband's kin group. The husband must make a new bridewealth payment if he wishes her to continue to be his wife. The bridewealth and repurchase payments of the Kwakiutl symbolize how two people may be joined in marriage and yet retain an identity in their own kin groups. The difference in these ceremonies indicates that dissolution of the marriage was more difficult among the Manchus than among the Kwakiutl.

POSTMARITAL RESIDENCE

Where the newly married couple lives after the marriage ritual is governed by cultural rules, which are referred to as **postmarital residence rule**. The nature of the postmarital residence rule determines the type of family. The postmarital residence rule in American society is that the new couple forms an independent household. This is referred to as **neolocal** residence (see Figure 6.1). When you have neolocal residence, you have nuclear families, with parents and children. In the case of a couple with two careers in two different cities, two households are often created. The rule in American society is neolocal residence, since breaching it brings sanctions. If the newly married couple lives for an extended period with the family of either the husband or the wife, it is usually because of economic hardship or the couple's student status. Gossips will make snide comments about the lack of independence of the couple, since they continue to live as though they were children. Neolocal residence characterizes other societies.

A common form of postmarital residence is when the newly married couple lives in the household of the groom's parents. This is known as **virilocal** residence (also referred to as patrilocal residence). With a rule of virilocal residence, the wife is incorporated, to a greater or lesser extent, into the household of her husband's kin, since it is she (the bride) who must leave her own family. The groom merely remains in his household as part of the virilocal extended family (Figure 6.1).

Less frequent is the case in which the newly married couple lives in the household of the bride's parents. This is called **uxorilocal** residence (also referred to as matrilocal residence) and results in a uxorilocal extended familiy. In this instance it is the husband who must be incorpo-

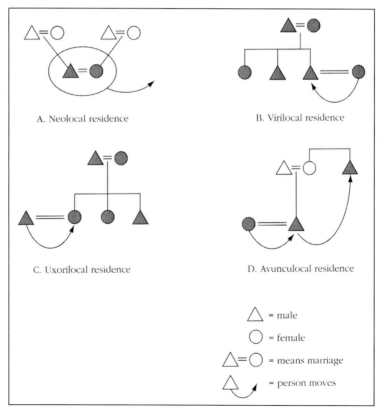

A. Neolocal residence

B. Virilocal residence

C. Uxorilocal residence

D. Avunculocal residence

△ = male

◯ = female

△=◯ = means marriage

△ = person moves

Figure 6.1   Rules of residence.

rated into his wife's family. In the past, in some Pueblo societies of Arizona and New Mexico that had a rule of uxorilocal residence, the degree of incorporation of the husband into his wife's family was so slight that the wife could divorce him simply by leaving his belongings on the doorstep. Today in the Pueblo area, neolocal residence prevails, reflecting the influence of the larger American society. When a groom performs bride service for his wife's father, as Jacob did for Laban in the Bible, he lives uxorilocally for the period of the bride service. Then, like Jacob, he usually returns with his wife to live virilocally, with his own family.

Still another rule of postmarital residence is the arrangement in which, after marriage, the wife joins her new husband, who is living with his mother's brother rather than with his own father. This is called **avunculocal** residence and results in the avunculocal extended family (Figure 6.1). This rule of residence involves two separate and distinct moves. The earlier move occurs when a man, as an adolescent, leaves his father's house to go to live with his mother's brother, from whom he will inherit later in life. The incorporation of the young man into the household of his mother's brother is associated with matrilineal descent, discussed below. After the marriage, the wife joins her husband at his maternal uncle's house. The Trobriand Islanders have an avunculocal rule of postmarital residence.

Sometimes a society will have a rule of residence stating that after marriage, the couple can live either with the bride's family or with the groom's family. They cannot establish an independent household. This is called **bilocal** residence. On Dobu, an island near the Trobriands, the married couple spends one year in the bride's village and the following year in the groom's village, alternating in this manner between the two villages every year. Among the Iban of Borneo, however, a choice must be made at some point after marriage between affiliation with one side or the other, and this choice becomes permanent.

Last, there is a postmarital residence rule in which husband and wife live with their respective kin, apart from one another. This is known as **duolocal** residence. The Ashanti of Ghana, who traditionally lived in large towns, have this form of postmarital residence. Husbands and wives live in the same town, but not in the same household. At dusk, one could see young children carrying the evening meal from their mother's house to their father's house for their father to eat.

As we have noted above, the rules stating where a couple should live after marriage result in different types of families. People who are related to one another by some form of kinship constitute a family while people who live together under one roof form a household. The members of a household may not necessarily all be related by kinship to one another. Family and household units, therefore, may not coincide. In the Ashanti example just discussed, the family unit of husband, wife, and children live in two separate households. With neolocal postmarital residence, as exists in America, the family that is formed is the **nuclear family** (see Figure 6.1). The nuclear family is an independent household that operates autonomously in economic affairs, in the rearing and education of children, and in other phases of life. After marriage, children will establish their own nuclear families.

What happens when there are plural spouses, as in societies that practice polygyny or polyandry? Among the Kanuri, where polygyny is practiced, only a small proportion of men actually have more than one wife. However, in polygynous families, each wife must have her own house and hearth. This is typical of a number of African societies. The husband must visit each wife in turn, at which time she cooks for him, and he must stay the night with her. Though he may favor one wife over another, he should treat them equally. A man's house and those of his wives form a single walled compound or household. Even though they have separate hearths and separate houses, they are all under the authority of the husband, who is the head of the household. Such a household might also include slaves belonging to the head of the household. In polyandrous societies, like Tibet, a woman and her several husbands, usually brothers, live in the same house and form a single household.

When several related nuclear families live together in the same household, they form an **extended family**. When there is a rule of virilocal residence, the household consists of an older married couple, their married sons and wives, and the unmarried children of both the older couple and their married sons. Their married daughters will have left the household to join the households of their husbands. The center of this type of extended family is a core of related men. Their in-marrying wives come from many different places and are not related to each other. Uxorilocal postmarital residence results in extended families of a very different sort. In this case, a core of related women remain together, and their husbands marry into the extended family. With avunculocal residence there is once again a core of men forming the basis of the extended family, but this core of men is linked through women. The wives in this case also marry into the family.

The most extensive extended family is one that consists of parents and married children of one sex, their spouses, and their own children. The extended family, which consists of parents and only one married son and his family, is known as a **stem family.** It occurs in parts of rural Ireland where the amount of land inherited is small and cannot be profitably subdivided. Only one son, typically the youngest one, inherits the land, while his older brothers go off to the cities, become priests, or emigrate to Boston or Hong Kong. Another type of extended family is the **joint family**, which includes brothers and their wives and children who stay together as a single family after the parents have died.

DESCENT

The kinds of family groups that we have just described are based on both kinship and common residence. Beyond the family, there are groups based upon shared kinship or descent, though members need not live in the same place. Family type and residence rules are the building blocks for such descent groups. For example, societies with virilocal residence and virilocal extended families usually have patrilineal descent groups. Membership in these groups is based upon descent from a common ancestor. These groups are sometimes called clans. Descent determines not only group membership but also rights to property and inheritance.

Patrilineal Descent and Matrilineal Descent

Societies have rules that state that the child belongs either to the mother's clan or to the father's clan. A rule that states that a child belongs to his or her father's clan is called a **patrilineal**

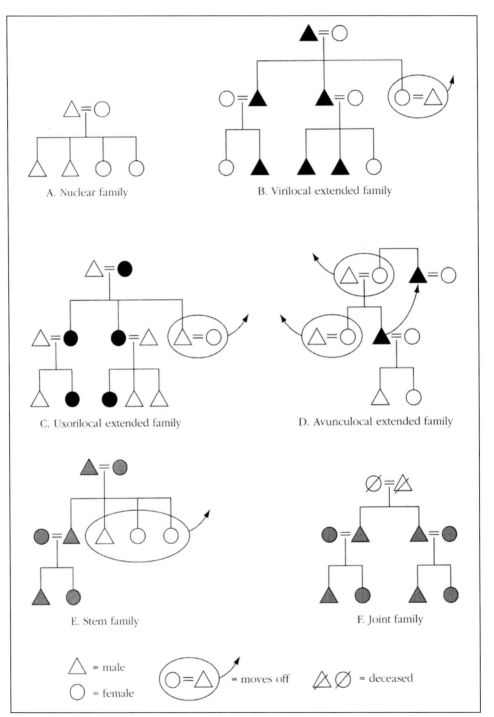

Figure 6.2   Family types.

rule of descent. This means that children belong to their father's clan, the father belongs to his father's clan, and so forth, as illustrated in the diagram (see Figure 6.2). A daughter belongs to her father's clan, but her children do not. Children share common clanship with only one of their four grandparents; however, the other three grandparents are still their relatives and kinsmen. As one goes back through the generations, ties of kin relationships form a web of kinship. A rule of descent carves out of this web of kinship a much smaller segment, which comprises the members of one's own clan. Clans continue to exist through time, beyond the lifespan of individual members, as new generations continue to be born into the clan. We have previously discussed exogamy, that is, the rule that one must marry outside one's group. In most societies that have clans, though certainly not in all, clans are exogamous, and one must marry outside one's own clan.

A **matrilineal rule of descent** states that a child belongs to the clan of his or her mother, not that of the father. The Trobriand Islanders have such a rule of descent. Among the Trobrianders, as in all matrilineal societies, the continuity of the clan is not through a man's own children but through those of his sister.

In chapter 5 we noted the way in which elements of the human body can be used metaphorically to discuss kinship. They can also be used to contrast relationships through the mother, and relationships through the father. The way in which the contrast is symbolized differs in patrilineal and matrilineal societies. In many patrilineal societies, the connection between the child and the mother is seen in terms of mother's milk and menstrual blood, which symbolize the maternal relationship. Connection to the father is seen in terms of semen or bone. The Arapesh of New Guinea believe that a child is created through the semen contributed by the father and the blood of the mother. The Arapesh are patrilineal; the child belongs to the father's clan. The child is seen as linked to the mother's clan through the blood she provided. The mother's clan continues to "own" the blood, and whenever the child's blood is shed through injury or cutting initiation scars, the child's mother's clan must be paid.

Since the Trobrianders have matrilineal descent, one would expect them to conceive of their kinship system in a different way than the Arapesh do. Among the Trobrianders, children belong to the clan of their mother, sharing common substance with their mother and other clan mates. The father is considered an affine, a relative by marriage only, in contrast to a consanguine, a blood relative. When a child was conceived in the mother's womb, the Trobrianders believed that an ancestral spirit from the mother's clan had entered her womb. Since the creation of a child is not seen as the result of the merging of substance from mother and father, they did not believe that sexual intercourse had anything to do with the conception of a child. The father, by repeated acts of intercourse, not only makes the child grow, but molds the child so that the child resembles him in appearance. The child is like a piece of clay pressed between two palms that takes on the shape of the hands that mold it. But this has nothing to do with the conception of the child in the first place, which is all the doing of the maternal ancestral spirit of the mother's clan. The child cannot be claimed by the father's clan, which had nothing to do with its creation. Though the Trobriand father is a very important relative, he is still an affine, as are all the members of his maternal clan.

Cognatic Descent

Up to now, we have discussed patrilineal or matrilineal rules of descent. Anthropologists refer to these as forms of **unilineal descent**. There are also societies that have groups based upon descent from a common ancestor, in which individuals belong to the group because either their father or their mother was a member of that group. This is called a **cognatic rule of descent**. Individuals have the choice of belonging to either their father's or their mother's group, or they may have rights in both groups, though there is usually active membership in only one since a person can live in only one place at a time. Individuals may even have rights in all four kin groups of their grandparents. Although the kin group created by a cognatic rule of descent is based upon descent from a common ancestor, the links through which individuals trace their descent are through either males or females. The kin group that the Kwakiutl refer to as a *numaym* is a cognatic descent group. A Kwakiutl boy could claim membership in both his mother's and his father's group. He usually became a member of the *numaym* of the parent of higher rank, from whom he hoped to inherit the highest titles and the most property. In addition, he inherited rights in the *numaym* of the other parent.

Double Descent

In some societies in the world, each person belongs to two descent groups, one patrilineal, in which descent is traced through the father and father's father, and the other matrilineal, in which

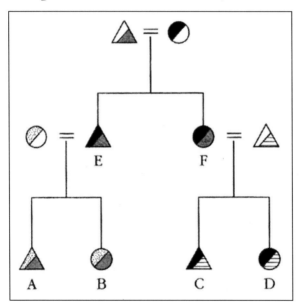

Figure 6.3   Double descent. A and B are brother and sister and belong to the same two descent groups, gray from their father and stippled from their mother. Similarly, C and D belong to the same two descent groups, striped from their father and black from their mother. E and F are also brother and sister and share the two descent groups that they get from their two parents, gray from their father and black from their mother. But their respective children, A and B, and C and D, do not have any descent groups in common.

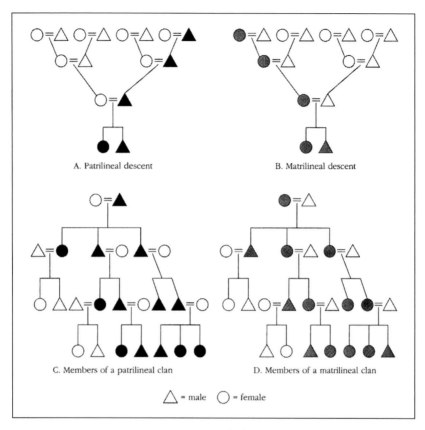

Figure 6.4   Descent and clan membership.

descent is traced through the mother and mother's mother. Anthropologists call this **double descent** (see Figure 6.3). The two groups to which an individual belongs do not conflict with one another, since each group has its own distinct functions.

DESCENT GROUPS AND THEIR STRUCTURE AND FUNCTION

The various kinds of descent groups may be based on different rules of descent and are structured differently, but they have the same kinds of functions. As we noted earlier, different kinds of descent structures are associated with particular rules of postmarital residence. Descent groups based on unilineal descent are called clans (see Figure 6.4). Because of the rule of patrilineal descent, the structure of the patrilineal clan is that of men linked through their fathers, along with their sisters who marry into other clans. It is almost always associated with virilocal postmarital residence. Sisters who marry out and wives who marry in are incorporated in varying degrees into the patrilineal clans of their husbands. In the discussion of marriage and the family in the earlier part of this chapter, we pointed out the variations in the degree of incorporation of the wife into her husband's clan. Matrilineal clans are composed of women related through their mothers and the brothers of these women. The brothers remain members of the clan into which they were born throughout their entire lives. Though they marry into other clans, in matrilineal societies, men are never incorporated into the clans of their wives. When they die, their bodies are usually brought back to be buried in their own clan land. Matrilineal clans are usually associated with avunculocal or uxorilocal postmarital residence. With a rule of cognatic descent, both men and women have membership in several cognatic descent groups, since they can trace multiple lines of descent. In this situation, husbands and wives, regardless of where they reside, are never incorporated into the descent groups of their spouses; this is the case among the Kwakiutl. The nature of descent rules and postmarital residence has consequences for the degree of incorporation of one spouse into the other spouse's kin group.

One can see the different ways in which descent groups are structured when one looks at the way in which political leadership operates (see Figure 6.5). The political functions of descent groups are carried out under the direction of leaders. In patrilineal societies like that of the Mongols, inherited leadership is usually structured in the following manner: It passes from father to son and from brother to brother. Leadership in matrilineal societies, like that of the Trobrianders, is handed down from mother's brother to sister's son or from brother to brother. In a matrilineal society, a son can never directly inherit a position of leadership from his father. In such societies, though the line of descent goes through women, the women themselves are rarely the heads of their clans. One may contrast the nature of the relationship of a man to his father in patrilineal societies and to his mother's brother in matrilineal societies. In patrilineal societies, a son will replace his father in the position of leadership and is often perceived of as a competitor and antagonist of his own father. His mother's brother, who is not in his clan, is often a source of support. In contrast, in matrilineal societies, a sister's son will succeed to the position of leadership held by

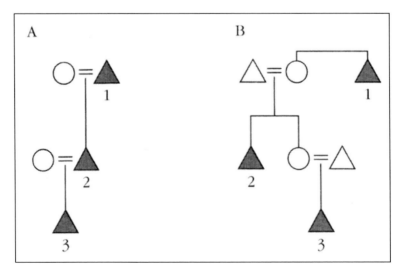

Figure 6.5   Passage of political leadership in a patrilineal society (A) and in a matrilineal society (B).

his mother's brother. The relationship between these two parallels that of the father-son relationship in a patrilineal society. In the relationship between father and son in a matrilineal society, all the elements of antagonism and potential conflict between them are removed. In societies with cognatic descent groups, like that of the Kwakiutl, a man can succeed to political leadership by virtue of descent through his mother or through his father; thus he can be the heir of either his father or of his mother's brother. While in unilineal societies, the father-son relationship is opposite to the mother's brother-sister's son relationship, this opposition does not occur in cognatic societies. The optional nature of the descent rule permits the possibility that brothers may be in different descent groups. Among the Kwakiutl, it frequently happens that two brothers are in different *numayms*, which can even fight each other. In patrilineal and in matrilineal societies, which are unilineal, this can never happen, since brothers are always in the same clan.

Clans

Matrilineal or patrilineal **clans** are still present in societies today. Some of the activities of clans concern rituals. For example, the matrilineal clan of the Trobrianders serves as host at the ceremonial distribution (*sagali*) accompanying a funeral when a member of their clan dies. Ritual objects and spells are owned by clans. Clans also have political functions and may compete with one another for power and political positions and may even fight with one another. Each clan has some kind of leadership, almost always male, to organize these political activities. The chief (the leader) of a Trobriand clan directs the accumulation of large amounts of food to be given away at a Trobriand *sagali*. Finally, what has frequently been seen as the most important function of the clan is its ownership of land. Members of a clan have the right to use its land by virtue of the fact that they are born into the clan. Clan members may work together at tasks, such as building a communal house or canoe, which benefit the clan as a whole. The common ancestor from whom all the members of a clan believe that they are descended is sometimes conceived of as an ancestral or clan spirit. This ancestral spirit may be thought of as having a nonhuman form, perhaps that of an animal. In that case, all members of the clan are thought of as having a special relationship to that animal, and they may be forbidden to eat it. Such an animal is called the **clan totem**, and, as noted in chapter 5, it is a symbol that represents the clan and could be graphically represented, as depicted in the totem pole on page 88. Patrilineal clans have similar functions.

The clan is frequently referred to by anthropologists as a **corporate descent group**, because it has many of the characteristics of a modern corporation. Like a corporation, it has an existence independent of its individual members. Old clan members die and new ones are born, while the clan continues to operate through time. The corporation owns property, and so does the clan. However, anybody can buy stock in a corporation and become an owner, but membership in a clan is restricted to certain kinds of kin, as defined by the rule of descent.

In some societies, you belong to a clan simply because your father or your mother belonged to that clan. Other people with whom you cannot trace a relationship of kinship also belong to your clan. Anthropologists say that descent is stipulated in such a clan system. Where **stipulated**

descent is found, there are no lengthy genealogies, and people usually remember back only to their grandfathers' generation. Where long genealogies are kept, written or oral, each member of a clan can trace his or her kinship back to the founding ancestor of the clan and in this way to every other member of the clan. Anthropologists call this **demonstrated descent**. In societies where clans include large numbers of people living dispersed over a wide area, each clan may in turn be divided into smaller units, referred to as subclans.

Lineages

Within clans with demonstrated descent, there are smaller units referred to as **lineages**. Sometimes all the people in the society believe themselves to be descended from a single ancestor. This founding ancestor may be historical or mythical, or a little of both. The kin groups are related to one another in an extensive genealogy. The Bedouin Arabs of Cyrenaica in eastern Libya, studied by Ernrys Peters (1960), are an example of such a society. They are nomadic pastoralists who keep herds of camels and sheep in the desert areas of their territory and cows and goats in the wooded

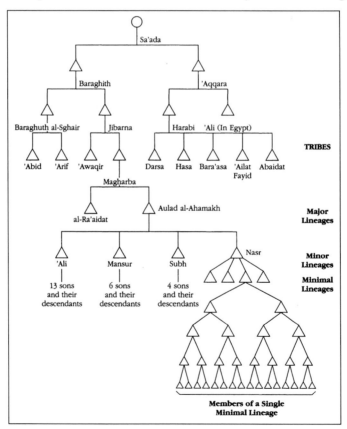

Figure 6.6   Genealogy of the Cyrenaican Bedouin.

plateau areas. All the Cyrenaican Bedouin alive today consider themselves descended from the single ancestor Sa'ada, who heads the genealogy (see Figure 6.6). Sa'ada was the mother of two sons who are said to be the founding ancestors of the two largest groups of tribes—Baraghith and 'Aqqara. The genealogy in the diagram represents the set of ideas that the Cyrenaican Bedouin use to talk about how they are related to one another and how their group is related to all other Cyrenaican groups. The genealogy is like a branching tree, extending out to its many twigs. Several twigs, or lineages, are part of a branch, and several branches, or groupings of lineages, are part of a larger limb. The larger limb represents a still larger grouping of lineages. This kind of descent system is called a **segmentary lineage system**. Groups at all the levels of segmentation are referred to as lineages. This kind of system is found in societies with patrilineal descent such as the Cyrenaican Bedouin. The constant branching out represents levels of segmentation. The branching out of the genealogy also has a close relationship to the occupation of geographical areas. The two groups of tribes, descended from each of the sons of Sa'ada, occupy the eastern and western halves of Cyrenaica. Lineages descended from brothers a few generations back graze their herds on lands adjacent to one another. Lineages that are further away genealogically occupy lands farther apart. In political action, lineages closely related to one another unite to oppose a threat from a more distantly related lineage. The Pushtuns who straddle the border between Afghanistan and northwestern Pakistan, where fighting has been taking place for years, have a segmentary lineage system, as do the Somali in Africa. We will discuss the current situation of the Pushtuns in chapter 14. In chapter 9 we examine how segmentary lineage systems operate politically.

Moieties

Another kind of grouping based on descent is one in which the entire society is divided into two halves, which are referred to as **moieties.** Moieties may be based upon a patrilineal or a matrilineal rule of descent. Sometimes in societies with moieties, a village site was divided in half, each half being occupied by the members of one moiety. As noted in chapter 5, the two parts of a moiety are often referred to in oppositional terms, such as left and right. The Abelam of the Sepik River area of New Guinea have patrilineal moieties referred to simply as "us" and "them." Among the Tlingit of the Pacific Coast of northern Canada and Alaska, the two moieties are known as Raven and Wolf, and are based on matrilineal descent. Moieties are usually composed of several clans.

Kin Groups Based on Cognatic Descent

Cognatic descent groups have the same functions as unilineal descent groups (patrilineal and matrilineal clans), though their structures are different. For example, the Kwakiutl *numaym*, a cognatic descent group, owned houses, fishing sites, berry-picking grounds, and hunting territories. The chiefs of a *numaym* acted as political leaders in potlatching and in warfare. The *numaym* acted as a unit on ceremonial occasions, such as the marriage and repurchase of the bride. Kwakiutl myths tell how the supernatural ancestors of present-day *numayms* acquired magical powers that were transmitted down the generations to their descendants.

A Na mother and child, from Yunnan Province, China. The Na are an ethnic minority society with a matrilineal descent structure in predominantly patrilineal China.

Kin Groups Based on Double Descent

The Yako of southeast Nigeria had a system of double descent. There were patrilineal clans called *yepun*, which owned land in common and possessed a single shrine and an assembly house, and whose men and their families resided together and farmed together. At the same time, each Yako individual also belonged to the matrilineal clan, or *lejima*, of his or her mother. The matrilineal clans carried out ritual and religious activities, such as funerals and periodic rites during the year aimed at maintaining fertility and harmony. While land is inherited patrilineally, movable wealth, such as valuables and household goods, is inherited through the matrilineal line. Thus, the two types of kin groups, patrilineal and matrilineal, serve different functions.

KINDREDS

The descent groups examined above are all based on a rule of descent from a single common ancestor and are said to be **ancestor-oriented**. Kindreds, on the other hand, are reckoned in an entirely different way. Earlier, we described kinship as a web. Like a spider's web, it extends out from the center (see Figure 6.7). Each person is at the center of his or her web of kinship. Anthropologists refer to the individual at the center as the ego, and the relatives who make up that web of kinship constitute ego's **kindred**. The kindred includes relatives on both ego's mother's

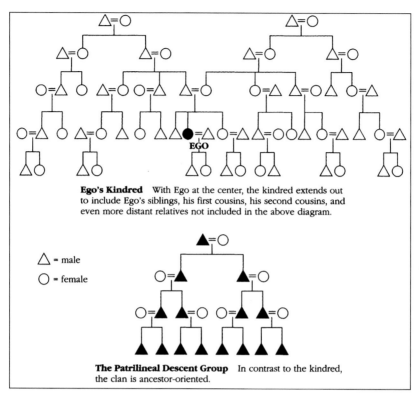

Ego's Kindred With Ego at the center, the kindred extends out to include Ego's siblings, his first cousins, his second cousins, and even more distant relatives not included in the above diagram.

△ = male

○ = female

The Patrilineal Descent Group In contrast to the kindred, the clan is ancestor-oriented.

Figure 6.7 The kindred.

and father's sides. Individuals who are descendants of ego as well as ego's ancestors and everyone descended from those ancestors are included in ego's kindred. The kindred is **ego-oriented**. The kindred as a unit does not own land or any other property; it only has coherence as a group around the ego at its center. Societies like our own, which do not have unilineal descent groups but do have kindreds, are known as **bilateral societies**. On an occasion such as the American wedding described in chapter 2, the kindreds of the bride and groom attend. If any of the first cousins of the groom, for instance, his father's brother's son, get married, a different set of relatives will be present, though there will be an overlap with his kindred. This overlap occurs since the two egos share a certain set of relatives. Kindreds do not have continuity through the generations as do corporate kin groups based on a rule of descent.

THE NA: A SOCIETY WITHOUT MARRIAGE OR FATHERS

The Na live in Yunnan Province, China, not far from the Chinese border with Myanmar. Recently, a Chinese ethnographer has described their society as one in which marriage is absent. Consequently, families have neither husbands nor fathers (Cai 2001). Earlier, we noted that marriage is almost a human universal. Do the Na believe that males are involved in procreation?

Do individuals know their biological fathers? When we look at other societies comparatively, the answers fall into place. The Na are not that different from other matrilineal societies we have looked at such as Lesu and the Trobrianders. They are only more extreme in their practices. The Na believe that sexual intercourse is necessary for procreation to occur. They say, "If the rain does not fall from the sky, the grass will not grow on the ground." But they consider that the substance of which the child is made comes solely from its mother, as the Na are strongly matrilineal. "The man is merely a waterer" (Cai 2001: 119). If the child resembles its father, they will guess who the father is (Cai 2001: 20). These beliefs are very similar to those of the Trobriand Islanders, who did not believe that a male is required for a female to become pregnant.

A Na child belongs to its mother's lineage, and kinsmen are counted solely through its mother. Each lineage has two heads: the mother, who is concerned with the internal affairs of the lineage; and the mother's brother, who is the authority figure concerned with external affairs. Several lineages constitute a matrilineal clan, the members of which are collectively responsible for payment of blood money when someone from their lineage kills an individual from another group. The father has no social role since he is not considered a relative. There is no kinship term for him or for any members of his matrilineage. The mother's brother plays the role that the father has in patrilineal societies (Cai 2001: 145).

The Na procreate through the practice of visits by "lovers" at night, in which men, unrelated to the women, visit them furtively, and leave at dawn, when the first rooster crows. Pleasure rather than procreation is the purpose of these visits. When a woman becomes pregnant, the child will belong to her lineage. The "biological" father considers her impregnation to be an act of charity on his part. The taking of lovers is very reminiscent of Lesu. In Lesu, all women take male lovers, who visit them like the Na "lovers." In matrilineal societies, offspring clearly belong to the mother, and "marriage," if it occurs, does not restrict the woman from having sexual relations with other men.

Na rules about incest are very strict. No woman may have sexual intercourse with a relative, that is, with any one matrilineally related to her (Cai 2001: 125). The strongest incest taboo concerns brother and sister. Na brothers and sisters "work, eat, and raise the children born to the sisters together" (Cai 2001: 121). Furthermore, they cannot speak about sex or make any allusions to sex (Cai 2001: 127). Today, only one sex at a time can watch TV in the village, because if sexual flirtation should occur on the TV, both sexes should not be watching it together. Brother and sister cannot sit in the same row at the movies. Since it is not always known who one's father is, it may happen that sexual relations take place between a father and his daughter (Cai 2001: 460). For the Trobrianders, father-daughter sexual relations are not absolutely forbidden.

Today, the Na, a minority group, are under strong political and legal pressure to be more like the Han Chinese, the majority population, who are patrilineal, and to practice marriage like them. However, the Na try to cling to their own cultural ways. Cai Hua, the ethnographer, who is Han Chinese, questioned them closely about such matters as "jealousy between lovers," adultery, and illegitimacy, and the Na told him that these things do not exist in their culture. These subjects are the characteristic "problems" of patrilineal societies such as the Han Chinese, since such societies are obsessed with doubts about who the father is. However, these issues are absent in matrilineal societies like the Na.

RELATIONS BETWEEN GROUPS THROUGH MARRIAGE

Sister exchange occurs when a rule of exogamy compels one group to give its women to another group in marriage, receiving the women of the other group in return (see Figure 6.8). Arapesh men state that they marry their sisters outside the group in order to obtain brothers-in-law. In general, marriages not only create links between brothers-in-law but also serve to create linkages between their respective kin groups. Groups that give women to and receive women from one another also exchange goods and services such as bridewealth, bride service, and other kinds of services at rites of passage after children are born from the marriage. These links between kin groups established by marriage are called **affinal links**. During warfare, kin groups frequently use these affinal ties and turn to their in-laws for assistance. For this reason, marriage is the basis for what is referred to as **alliance**. Although affines may be in opposition to one another and may even fight one another, the concept of alliance is nevertheless used by anthropologists to refer to these linkages between kin groups established by marriage.

In our society, marriage is based upon the decision by the bride and groom to get married. Parents and other individuals are rarely involved. As we shall see below, today families from India, now in the United States, play a more important role in the marriage choices of

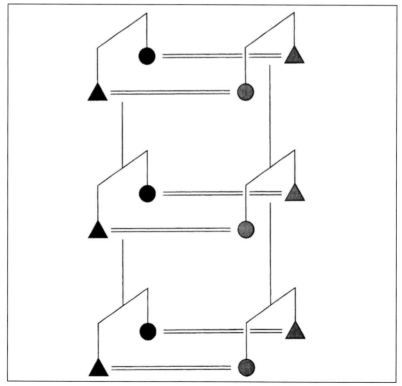

Figure 6.8 Sister exchange, or reciprocal exchange.

their American-born children. In other societies there are rules stating that one should marry someone from a certain category of relative. These rules have the effect of continuing alliance over time between groups. When groups continue to exchange sisters over generations, then women of one's own group are always marrying into the group from which wives come. This marriage pattern, sister exchange, is also referred to as a system of **reciprocal exchange** (see Figure 6.8). In such a system, the prospective husband and the prospective wife will already be related to one another. Since their parents are brother and sister, they will be first cousins. Anthropologists refer to two kinds of cousins: **parallel cousins**, who are the children of the mother's sister or father's brother, and **cross cousins**, who are the children of the mother's brother or father's sister (see Figure 6.9). In a system with reciprocal exchange, parallel cousins, who are members of one's own group, are frequently called siblings. Therefore they cannot marry. Cross cousins are never in one's own group but rather are members of the other group with which one has been intermarrying (see Figure 6.9). These cross cousins are known as **bilateral cross cousins**, since they are simultaneously the mother's brother's children and the father's sister's children. Sister exchange continued over the generations is, in effect, marrying one's bilateral cross cousin. The Yanomamo of southern Venezuela have such a marriage system of direct reciprocal exchange. A Yanomamo man must marry a woman whom he calls by the kinship term for female cross cousin (*suaboya*), and this term is at the same time the term for wife. The terms for husband and male cross cousin are also the same. Female parallel cousins, among the Yanomamo, are called by the same term as sisters. If a Yanomamo man has no biological sister to return to the man who gave him his wife, he returns a "sister" who is his parallel cousin.

There are societies in which the two kinds of cross cousins, mother's brother's children and father's sister's children, are referred to by different terms. These two types of cross cousins are not equally marriageable. Some societies have a rule that a man ought to marry the daughter of

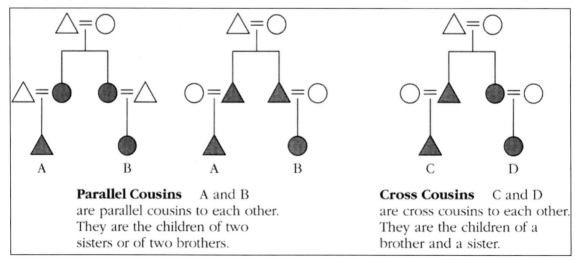

Parallel Cousins   A and B are parallel cousins to each other. They are the children of two sisters or of two brothers.

Cross Cousins   C and D are cross cousins to each other. They are the children of a brother and a sister.

Figure 6.9   Types of cousins.

his mother's brother, but he may not marry the daughter of his father's sister. Ideally, if every man married his mother's brother's daughter, in every generation, the result is as pictured in Figure 6.10. There, the groups labeled A, B, and C, linked by the marriages, are patrilineages. This marriage rule occurs much more frequently in societies with a patrilineal rule of descent, though it also occurs in societies with matrilineal descent. If a man does not have a real mother's brother's daughter to marry, he may marry a classificatory mother's brother's daughter, a woman whom a man calls by the same kinship term as his real mother's brother's daughter. She is a member of his mother's brother's patrilineage. As one can see from the figure, lineage B gives its sisters to lineage A, and lineage C gives its sisters to lineage B, in every generation. From the perspective of lineage B, lineage A is always wife-taker and lineage C is always wife-giver. This system is very different from sister exchange in that you never return a woman to the lineage that gave you a woman. Since wife-giving lineage and wife-taking lineage are always different, a minimum of three groups is required. (However, it is usually the case that more than three groups are tied together in this kind of marriage alliance.) If there are three groups, then they can marry in a circle, with lineage A giving its women to lineage C. If, for example, the royal family of Great Britain gave its daughters in marriage to the royal family of Denmark in every generation, and the royal family of Denmark gave its daughters in marriage to the royal family of Sweden in every generation, and the royal family of Sweden gave its daughters in marriage back to the royal family of Great Britain in every generation, all intermarrying in a circle, then they would have this kind of marriage system. The Kachin of Myanmar (Burma), whose political organization will be discussed in chapter 9, actually did have this kind of marriage system. It produces a structure of alliance between groups that anthropologists refer to as **generalized exchange**.

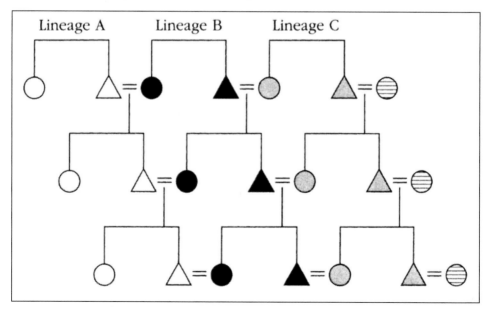

Figure 6.10   Mother's brother's daughter marriage, or generalized exchanged.

In the village of Lamalera in East Timor, this type of marriage system involving generalized exchange continues to be practiced, despite the adoption of Catholicism and substantial transformations of the village economy (Barnes 1998: 106). Though there is considerable variation in practice, 52 percent of marriages are with a man's mother's brother's daughter, and the hierarchical distinction between wife-givers and wife-takers remains significant today. Although the village of Lamalera is involved in the Indonesian national economy, clan membership is still the basis for economic cooperation in whale hunting, ownership of fishing and whaling boats, and the organization of fishing crews.

In some societies, there is the opposite preferential rule of marriage. A man cannot marry his mother's brother's daughter but should marry his father's sister's daughter. If every man married in this fashion, the result would be what is pictured in Figure 6.11. This kind of marriage rule always occurs in societies with matrilineal descent. In the figure, groups A, B, C, and D are matrilineal lineages. A man marries either his real or his classificatory father's sister's daughter. This marriage rule involves the return of a wife one generation after a wife has been given. In the first generation, D gives a woman to C, C gives to B, B gives to A, and A gives to D (if the lineages are marrying in a circle). In the next generation, the flow of women is reversed. Now D gives to A, A gives to B, B gives to C, and C gives to D. In the third generation, the flow is reversed once again. Every generation, women move in the direction opposite from the way they did in the previous generation. This resembles sister exchange in that a woman is returned to the group that originally gave a woman, but the return is made a generation later. Because the return is delayed one generation, there must be more than two groups operating in the system. A minimum of four groups is required. The Trobrianders are an example of a society with a rule for marriage with

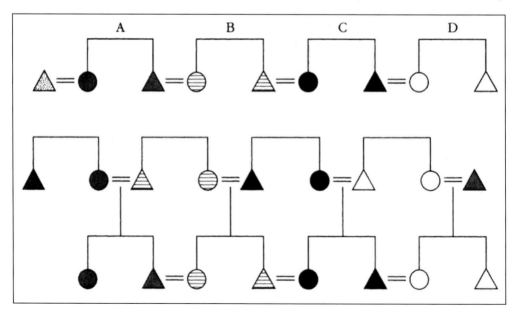

Figure 6.11   Father's sister's daughter marriage.

the father's sister's daughter, and have this form of **delayed exchange**. The Tana Wai Brama of eastern Indonesia continue today to have a pattern of delayed exchange in which the return of a woman occurs three generations later (Lewis 2003: 29).

Each of these two marriage rules produces a different structure of alliances among groups, and both are different from the kind of alliance produced by bilateral cross-cousin marriage. Marrying one's cross cousins, either mother's brother's daughter or father's sister's daughter, begins with a rule of exogamy stating that one must take a wife from outside one's group. By specifying which relatives one should marry, different patterns of alliance among groups are created. Figures 6.8, 6.10, and 6.11 represent models of these different patterns, and particular societies represent variations on these models.

Some societies, particularly in the Middle East, have a preferential marriage rule that is structurally opposite to this rule of exogamy. The rule states that a man should marry his parallel cousin, in this case, his father's brother's daughter. Since the societies of this area, like the Bedouin of Cyrenaica discussed above, are all patrilineal in descent, this marriage rule results in endogamous marriages. The Riff of Morocco, who have this marriage rule, say that they prefer to hold onto their daughters and marry them within their own group to avoid becoming entangled in alliances with other groups. This is not an explanation of what they do but rather their rationalization.

Marriage alliances may be contracted in which the procreative and sexual functions are not relevant. The Lovedu, a Bantu-speaking people of southern Africa, had a queen to whom women were given in marriage. The purpose of such marriages was to create political alliances, and sexual intercourse did not occur. In the late nineteenth century, among the Kwakiutl, where privileges were transferred as a result of marriage, one man could "marry" the foot of another, become son-in-law to the man whose foot he married, and obtain privileges through this fictive marriage at the repurchase ceremony described in chapter 2.

Kinship Terminology

Each society in the world has a set of words used to refer to relatives called **kinship terminology**. Kinship terminology is a subject that has a long history in anthropology, and the regularity of its patterning was first noticed by Lewis Henry Morgan (1877). Studying kinship terminology is vital to the anthropologist in gaining insights into how societies operate. The anthropological data that have been accumulated have revealed that there are a limited number of types of kinship terminology, and there is a general association of these types with particular kinds of social structure, as pointed out above. However, some terminologies correspond only in part to the types of social structure described above, and sometimes particular terminologies are associated with different social structural features.

There are two kinds of kinship terms, **terms of reference**, that is, the terms used to refer to other people, and **terms of address**, which are the terms one uses when talking to the person. Since languages differ, terms are not the same from one society to another. Anthropologists have found that there are a few basic types of terms of reference. Most Americans accept their own kin terminology as being the "natural" way of classifying relatives as do members of all other societies. Both your father's brother and your mother's brother are referred to as *uncle* in American usage. *Uncle* is also used to refer to your mother's sister's husband and father's sister's husband. Though the term *uncle* is used for these four relatives, two of them are blood relatives on different sides of the family, while two are relatives by marriage. Each of these four relatives is related to you in a different way, but our kinship terminology ignores these differences and groups them under one term. Anthropologists diagram kinship terminologies such as American kinship as depicted in Figure 6.12. The Yanomamo have a very different way of categorizing their relatives. They use the same term for both father's brother and mother's sister's husband, while they use a different term for mother's brother and father's sister's husband. The Yanomamo kinship terminology is pictured in Figure 6.13.

You can see that the two societies sort the terms for kin in different ways. For the parental generation, both the Yanomamo and Americans have four terms. The Americans use *father*, *mother*, *aunt*, and *uncle*; the Yanomamo use *haua*, *naya*, *yaya*, and *shoaiya*. In the Yanomamo system, father's brother and mother's brother have different terms, whereas in our society the same term, *uncle*, is used for both. Conversely, the Yanomamo class father and father's brother together, while we use different terms. In ego's own generation, we have a single term, *cousin*, for all the children of uncles and aunts. This term is unusual in that it is used for males and females. The Yanomamo are also consistent in their usage. The children of all relatives called by the same term as father and mother are referred to by the term for brother and sister. This means that parallel cousins are grouped with siblings. In contrast, the children of *shoaiya*, who are one's cross cousins, are referred to by terms different from brother and sister, *suaboya* and *heriya*. Which is more complicated? Neither. Which is more natural? Neither. These kinship terminologies are different

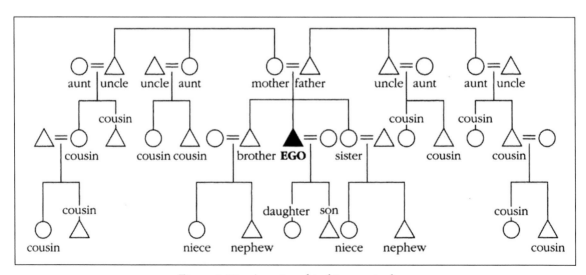

Figure 6.12   American kinship terminology.

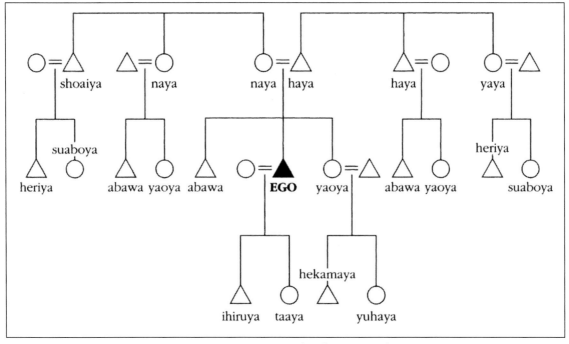

Figure 6.13   Yanomamo kinship terminology.

because each is related to a different type of social structure. The terms in a kinship terminological system group some relatives together and set apart other relatives in a way that reflects the relationship of these relatives according to the rules of residence, marriage, and descent.

The American and Yanomamo kinship terminologies conform to two of these basic types of kinship terminology. Strange as it may seem, American kinship terminology is classified as **Eskimo** since it is identical to that of the Eskimos or Inuit, as they now prefer to be called, not in the words for the terms, but in the pattern of organization. Its major characteristics are that it distinguishes between the generations and it distinguishes **lineal** relatives from **collateral** relatives (see Figure 6.14). Lineal relatives are those in the direct line of descent: grandfather, father, son, grandson, grandmother, mother, daughter, granddaughter. The rest of the relatives are referred to as collateral and can be distinguished in terms of degree of collaterality, meaning that second cousins are more remote than first cousins, and first cousins are more remote than siblings. The Eskimo type of terminology emphasizes individual nuclear families, and it is found in societies with a particular cluster of characteristics, such as neolocal rules of residence, kindreds, bilateral descent, and the absence of descent groups. Though Inuit society and our own differed in degree of complexity, subsistence pattern, and environmental setting, the pattern of organization of kinship terms and other kinship features was the same.

The kinship terminology of the Yanomamo is classified as *Iroquois*. The Iroquois type of terminology distinguishes between father's side and mother's side. However, the difference between lineal and collateral relatives is ignored; father and father's brother are classed together, as are mother and mother's sister. Generational differences are always recognized, as in Eskimo terminology. The social structure with which this terminology is usually associated is one in which one's own kin group is distinct from the kin group from which one's mother came. The group from which one's mother comes is the same group into which one's father's sister marries. In other words, the Iroquois terminology goes with sister exchange, which is the type of marriage pattern the Yanomamo have. This is why, in Yanomamo, the term for father's sister's husband is the same as that for mother's brother, and the term for mother's sister's husband is the same as that for father's brother. Female cross cousin is classed with wife and male cross cousin with brother-in-law. In every generation, "sisters" are exchanged between the two groups, and the kinship terminology reflects this. Iroquois terminology is associated with virilocal (which the Yanomamo had) or uxorilocal (which the Iroquois had) residence, but not with neolocal residence. Instead of independent nuclear families, extended families are present. This type of terminology is also generally associated with unilineal descent, but not with cognatic descent or bilateral kinship reckoning. Iroquois is by far the most common type of kinship terminology found in the world. It should be noted that societies that have Iroquois kinship terminology may not have all these social structural features, but only some of them. The Iroquois themselves had matrilineal descent and did not have sister exchange.

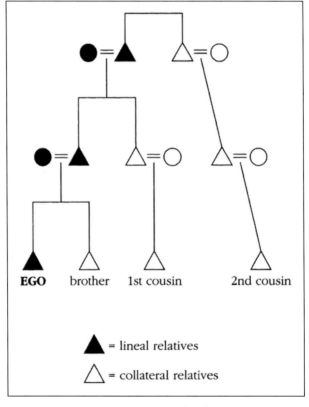

Figure 6.14   Degree of collaterality.

Besides Eskimo and Iroquois terminologies, four other major types of terminologies have been identified by anthropologists. The **Crow** type, found, for example, among the Trobriand Islanders, is almost always associated with matrilineal descent groups, avunculocal residence, and extended families. Unlike Eskimo and Iroquois terminologies, the same term may be used for members of different generations. **Omaha** kinship terminology is the mirror image of Crow. It is associated with patrilineal descent groups and, like Crow, ignores generational differences in some terms. The simplest terminology, the one having the fewest terms, is the Hawaiian type, in which only generation and male-female distinctions are made. It is usually associated with cognatic descent groups. Despite its simplicity, it has been found in association with some societies, like the Hawaiian, that have complex political economies. In the last type of kinship terminology, Sudanese, every category of relative is distinguished by a different term. It is frequently associated with patrilineal descent and economically independent nuclear families, such as those found among certain nomadic pastoral societies of the Middle East.

Some anthropologists, for example, David Schneider, have been critical of the use of the anthropological concepts for analyzing kinship presented in this chapter (1984). They see the use of this set of analytic concepts as the imposition of Western social science categories on indigenous ideas. Instead, they prefer to utilize only the native categories that the people in each society use to conceptualize kin relationships. In our view, the analysis must always begin with indigenous categories. These can and must be translated into anthropological concepts to make possible the cross-cultural comparisons that have revealed the same regularities or patterns in social structural features in societies in many parts of the worlds. The kinship variables discussed so far in this chapter, including number of spouses, degree of incorporation of spouse, type of descent rule, and structure of descent group, do not operate independently. They fit together into the particular patterns that have been revealed cross-culturally. The use of symbols and their visualization in diagrams make it easier to conceptualize these patterns.

FICTIVE KINSHIP

People also rely on social relationships made by means of ritual observances, which are known as **godparenthood**, or **compadrazgo**. Godparenthood creates a set of relationships that, though nonkin in their derivation, utilize a set of terms based on kinship. The English labels for these relationships use kinship terms such as *father, mother, daughter,* and *son,* plus the prefix—*god*—differentiating them from real kinship. This is not simply an extension of kinship, but a different kind of relationship, which uses kinship as a metaphor. This kind of relationship is found in many parts of Mediterranean Europe and in Latin America. It also occurs among the Italian and Hispanic populations in the United States. The ritual occasions upon which godparenthood is established are baptism, confirmation, and marriage, at which the godparent serves as a kind of sponsor. Real parents never carry out the role of godparents. Sometimes more distant relatives may serve as godparents, while in other cases they may not. The *compadrazgo* relationship is frequently established between individuals of different classes for social, political, and economic reasons. In peasant communities, for example, a patron who is a wealthy or powerful member of the community and probably the landlord may serve as godparent to the children of clients who are economically and politically dependent upon him. In the relationship between godparent and godchild, the godparent is expected to protect and assist the godchild, while the godchild honors the godparent, just as the patron receives support from the client when it is needed and the client receives favors from the patron. Among the Quichua-speaking Otavaleno of the Ecuadorian Andes, *compadrazgo* has not been squeezed out by the expansion of capitalism, as some anthropologists in the 1960s had predicted (Colloredo-Mansfeld 1998: 50). These indigenous people have become prosperous weavers and traders. They now select *compadres* at the marriage or confirmation of their children to extend their handicraft business by connecting with sweater-factory owners, transport operators, and shopkeepers with whom they do business (Colloredo-Mansfield 1998: 52).

In Serbia, god-parenthood, or *kumstvo*, described by anthropologist Eugene Hammel, which could only be established between nonkin, was continued from one generation to the next (1968). The word *kum* can be translated as "sponsor." Members of one group (A) stood as godparents to another group (B), and the children of those godparents in A served as godparents to the next generation of godchildren in B. Godparenthood was not reciprocal, since the group of godchildren in B did not return the favor and act as godparents to A, but instead, acted as godparents to children in still another group (C). This created a structure of alliances between groups by means of godparenthood, which is the same as the structure of alliances created by marriage with the mother's brother's daughter, which we referred to as the structure of generalized exchange.

KINSHIP IN THE CONTEMPORARY WORLD

Clans based on unilineal descent continued to exist, assuming a variety of roles, even long after the emergence of complex societies and states. When peasant societies were incorporated into nation-states, even Communist states, some larger-scale kin units continued to exist. As recently as 1987, ethnic Albanian clans in Kosovo continued to feud with one another, answering one murder with another. As is the case in clan-based societies, when ongoing feuds are involved, all clan members are held responsible for the actions of a single member. The progress of this feud was reported on Yugoslavian television. After the Turkish earthquake, which occurred in the summer of 1999, the *New York Times* reported that forty members of a clan had traveled six hundred miles from their home to try to rescue five trapped relatives. They brought their own equipment, including jackhammers, drills, electrical equipment, generators, and lights. This illustrates that members of a clan feel it absolutely necessary to come to the aid of fellow clan members in distress.

American interests are worldwide, but nowhere are they more concentrated than in an oil-rich zone extending from the Persian Gulf through Iraq, Iran, and Central Asia, the independent nations of Uzbekistan, Kazakhstan, and Turkmenia. Newspapers refer to most of this area as "tribal" and based on clanship. However, within this area, at least Iran is certainly not a "tribal" society. Sometimes the area between Afghanistan and Pakistan is called "lawless," but this is a serious misnomer. Society there is based on a different kind of law, a law rooted in kinship—based on segmentary lineages, honor, and hospitality, not one based on the state or central government.

The Gulf Cooperation Council is made up of six small states (Saudia Arabia, Kuwait, Bahrain, Oman, Qatar, United Arab Emirates), all of them monarchies. According to al-Tarrah, "kinship dominates every facet of socio-economic life. . . . Individual Gulf states have derived their social identity from their tribes, clans or factions. This has made the state a hostage of kinship, thus creating a vicious spiral of misgovernment and a sense of power entitlement in individuals. Citizens' affinities and loyalties have shifted away from the government to their tribe or clan, rendering the government weak in comparison to these social forces" (2007: 121). The implications of this statement are very significant. One must understand the system of clans and tribes in order to grasp the political organization of these small monarchies. To do business there, one must know the kinship system intimately, and how to best allocate one's capital.

In the oil-rich new nations of Turkmenistan and Kazakhstan, a similar structure of tribes and clans exists. To create a more powerful central government, Nyazimov, the former dictator of Turkmenistan, attempted "to reduce the role of clan elements in [his] country" (Blank 2007: 12; see also Collins 2006: 25). His goal was to lessen the importance of the kinship system, which was very similar to that described for the Gulf States above. The net result was a shift from the Communist system and Russian control to the worst type of dictatorship. In a later discussion of the Pushtuns along the Afghan/Pakistan border, we will see how a kinship system based on guest houses and providing hospitality to strangers supercedes the powers of the central government, preventing its control of tribal areas in Pakistan and the development of a powerful central government in Afghanistan.

Today, in China there is a tension between tradition and modernity. After the Communist Chinese conquest of the whole mainland, a series of laws were promulgated to obliterate the traditional social structure with its extended families and clans. However, "familism and its value system still affect greatly the behavior of the Chinese everywhere [today]" (Yuen 2004: 5). After 1949, the Communist government sought to eliminate what they referred to as "feudal culture." They prohibited lineage activities of all kinds as well as the practices of geomancy and divination. Villagers were still allowed to burn joss sticks and candles in front of altars in their homes. However, during the spring and fall periods of ancestor worship, they could only go surreptitiously to their ancestors' tombs to sweep them out and pay their respects. Ancestral halls were either burned or turned into meeting houses or residences for villagers, and genealogical records were destroyed (Yuen 2004: 29). Marriage laws were also passed to attempt to deal with the inequality of the sexes and to encourage freedom of choice in mate selection. Heretofore, individuals were not allowed to marry anyone with the same surname, and that practice continued. Arranged marriages were discouraged, although they still continued to take place with the help of matchmakers.

In 1978, China embarked on a policy of reform. Many villages in the Pearl River Delta shifted from agriculture, and industrialized with the construction of factories manufacturing plastic products and knitted clothing. The government allowed traditional lineage activities to be revived, including the holding of lineage meetings, and more public ancestor worship and offerings. Ancestral halls that had been destroyed were rebuilt, and genealogical records reconstructed. However, only some younger people were involved in these activities (Yuen 2004: 33). Young people sought to choose their own spouses, but some parents still used matchmakers to arrange marriages for their children. Marriage with an individual having the same surname takes place, but there must be at least five generations separating the two. Men who have become richer may now even marry a second wife (Yuen 2004: 161, 170). In conclusion, Yuen et al. note, "Traditional Chinese culture and the ideas of modern society are not completely incompatible; nor are conflicts between them inevitable" (2004: 198).

The Transnational Family

The transnational family of the twenty-first century is the consequence of more complex migration patterns than those characterizing earlier periods. Poor men and women leave their families in Asia, Africa, and Latin America in search of work, leaving husbands or wives at home to support themselves and their families with remittances. At the same time, the "transnational capitalist class," businessmen, professionals, technicians, and other highly skilled individuals primarily from Asia, seek and find employment in the United States, Australia, and Canada (Ip et al. 2006: 1–3). Ease and speed of transportation, and advances in telecommunication, have made it possible for individuals to maintain continuing links with family wherever they are located. Sometimes they may bring their families to the United States, only to leave them there when a business opportunity opens up in Hong Kong. Another example of transnational migration is the Filipino woman who comes to the United State to work as a domestic or in the health care industry and is separated from her husband and children for many years. The absence of a mother frequently results in a dysfunctional family, since men are usually the breadwinners and women the nurturers. In such cases, fathers try to pass on the care, giving responsibilities to daughters and women in the extended family, when the mother is the migrant (Parrenas 2005: 118). When men are the migrants, they are fulfilling their role as breadwinners and the family they leave behind is also affected by their absence. Their children all note that they would rather not have grown up in a transnational family. The scale of transnational adoption has also greatly increased, and is "yet another manifestation of globalization" (Howell 2006: 12).

When Pakistani men moved to Great Britain, as soon as they could afford to, they brought over their families. However, the family continued to be a "transnational family" in that there was close contact with the members of the extended family in Pakistan. The British branch of the family still owned land in Pakistan, usually tended to by a brother of the husband. When individuals died, their bodies were sent back to Pakistan for burial. Plane transportation, telephone, and Internet allowed the members of the family at home and abroad to maintain close contact. British members of the family would return to Pakistan for holidays and wedding celebrations.

The transnational family is a completely new family type. Structurally, it may be made up of kin, fictive kin, and friends, carrying out newly created roles. For example, the nature of the funeral has changed. One transnational family, scattered over five continents, went online to hold a wake; one family member delivered a eulogy online while the rest of the family watched it on their computer screens.

Kinship in America Today

As we noted in the last chapter, Americans think that a child receives half of its blood from the mother and half from the father, while more distant relatives have smaller shares of that blood, depending on the degree of distance. People think that such relationships can never be terminated because blood—the symbolic carrier of the relationship—is always present. On the other hand, relatives through marriage are different from blood relatives in every respect (Schneider 1980). These relationships are established by people making choices rather than as the result of a natural process. Such kin are termed *relatives-in-law*. Relationships that are made by people can also be terminated by people through divorce. When this happens, the in-law is no longer considered a relative. However, blood relationships can never be severed, nor can blood relatives be divorced.

The Impact of Biological Technologies on Kinship

As a result of new reproductive technologies (NRTs), Americans have begun to rethink the meaning of kinship in their own culture (see Strathern 1992). The meanings of motherhood and fatherhood have been called into question by these new reproductive technologies. Motherhood has also been called into question when test-tube fertilization of an egg takes place. An egg from the would-be mother and sperm from the would-be father are brought together and the developing embryo may be implanted in a surrogate mother. If the sperm comes from an unknown donor, who is the real father—the man who has provided the sperm or the man who has acted as the father in raising the child? When an egg in a surrogate mother is fertilized with sperm from a man who, with his wife, have contracted to be the child's parents, there may be conflict over the child between the couple and the surrogate mother. In a case described by Thompson, the egg came from the prospective mother and the sperm from the prospective father, and the surrogate was the father's sister who had had her tubes tied so that the brother's sperm could not fertilize her egg (2005: 159). In two other cases, ethnicity entered the picture when the African-American woman wanted the donor egg to come from an African American, and an Italian-American woman wanted a donor egg to come from her Italian-American friend, though the former would provide the gestational setting for the fetus (Thompson 2005: 166–67; see also Carsten 2004: 177). Children conceived by artificial insemination are now seeking the identity of their donor fathers, who are often medical students who had donated their semen merely to help infertile parents have children. If the women who donate their eggs and the men who donate semen are paid, this represents a commodification of reproduction. What formerly had been seen as a natural tie of kinship and "shared blood" between father, mother, and child is clearly much more complicated by these new technologies.

The advent of the Human Genome Project and the "current comprehensions that diseases are genetically transmitted from generation to generation . . . [has led to] the medicalization of kinship" (Finkler 2000: 3). There has been an astronomical increase in the numbers of diseases that are now attributed to genetic inheritance, and consequently there is increased emphasis on acquiring family medical histories (Finkler 2000: 15). This emphasis on genetic inheritance is in effect a focus on the faulty genes, which one may have inherited from one's ancestors. It has therefore become important to individuals to know their biological parents as well as the extended network of other biological relatives. Twenty years ago, when children were adopted, the adoption papers were sealed by the court and knowledge of their biological parentage was kept from adopted children. If Schneider's principle—that biological blood ties to parents can never be severed—is valid, then one can readily understand that such children, now adults, often feel the need to know who their biological parents are even if it invades the privacy that these biological parents sought. Today, adoption has become such an open process that the adoptive parents may establish a relationship with the biological parents even before the child is born. A *New York Times* article revealed the way in which a prospective adopting mother moved in with the biological mother weeks before the child arrived and was fully involved in all the activities leading up to the birth (October 25, 1998). The adoptive parents indicated that they intended to continue to involve the biological parents in raising the child.

A highly publicized court case, settled in 1993 after extensive litigation, highlights these issues. In Florida, two female babies were switched at birth. One of them died in early childhood, and genetic tests then revealed that she was not the biological offspring of the parents who raised her. They sued for custody of their living biological daughter, and a settlement was reached giving them visitation rights. The girl herself, who felt a strong tie to the father who had raised her, sued some time later and was permitted by the court to terminate her relationship with her biological parents, to "divorce" her parents. A biological or blood relationship, which theoretically can never be severed, was treated as if it were equivalent to an in-law relationship. This case reveals the extent to which parentage and kinship have become contested. It hinged on whether one can divorce one's biological parents. As Skolnick notes, "In some states today, unless a parent is found to be unfit or to have abandoned the child, the rights of biological parents are all but inviolate" (1998: 239).

Different Types of American Families

Until the mid-twentieth century, the usual family type for Americans was the nuclear family, which lived neolocally after marriage. Immigrant families, which included three generations, were an exception. As the age at which Americans married became later and later, single-individual households became more prevalent. A variant on this form is the household consisting of several unrelated young people, both men and women, who live together for financial reasons. The TV show *Will and Grace* portrays this form. Another household form consists of one or both grandparents and grandchildren. This occurs when the parents of the children are unable to care for them. Grandparents assume custody and responsibility instead of the state. Several websites provide information, help, and support for grandparents raising grandchildren (see Hayslip et al. 2006).

Blended Families

The high rate of divorce and the subsequent remarriage of divorced spouses have created a new type of family—the blended family or stepfamily. Thirty-five percent of children born now can expect to live with stepparents (Erera 2002: 137). The stepfather is more likely to be living with and raising young children than the biological father, though the latter may continue to be involved in child-rearing and child support. Stepmothers rarely live with their stepchildren, unless the father has custody of the children because the mother of the children has died or left the family. The stepfamily may also include nonresident children, in addition to nonresident parents. The modern stepfamily includes a variety of sibling relationships, such as full siblings, half-siblings, and stepsiblings. Half-siblings are considered blood relatives, while stepsiblings are not. Relations with in-laws and grandparents of the step family are highly varied. It may take from two to seven years for the stepfamily to "develop a sense of family with their [sic] own customs, rituals and history . . . [despite the absence of] clear behavior guides, norms or models" (Erera 2002: 143–44). Mason notes that, in contrast to the Cinderella story, adolescent stepchildren experience less conflict with residential stepmothers than do adolescent children with their own mothers in nondivorced families (1998: 98).

Gay and Lesbian Families

The increasingly public lifestyles of gays and lesbians today have also challenged American views on the definition of marriage and the family, as well as contributed to the debate on biological versus other forms of parentage. Various state legislatures and Supreme Court decisions have declared that consensual, adult sexual decisions are private, and governments should not interfere. Same-sex couples now have the right to marry legally in Massachusetts, Connecticut, and California; however, this right is being contested in the courts and legislatures. Many other states recognize a Civil Union Law, which provides a legal framework parallel to marriage (Erera 2002: 164). Some couples have chosen to go to Canada, which now permits same-sex marriage.

Gay and lesbian couples, who see themselves as equivalent to heterosexual couples, may go through a ritual they refer to as a marriage, or a commitment ceremony. At the end of a couple's "life cycle," mention of the surviving member of a homosexual couple in a newspaper obituary is another public recognition of the couple's relationship.

Originally, in the 1970s "gay liberation theorists held the heterosexual family in such contempt . . . [and roles of] lesbian and mother . . . as incompatible" (Sullivan 2004: 27). But lesbians who were previously in heterosexual marriages often tried to bring their biological children into the new family, creating a stepfamily that resembled a heterosexual family in many ways (Erera 2002: 168). Today, lesbian couples are creating families in several ways, including adoption. Though some states prohibit lesbians and gays from adopting children, independent adoption is often a route followed if possible, particularly by gay couples. Other alternatives are assisted-reproduction procedures like donor insemination. Many decide not to adopt because becoming pregnant is easier and biogenetic relatedness "would automatically trump other forms of relationship and attachment" (Sullivan 2004: 43–44). They prefer to call it alternative insemination to emphasize that it is as natural as insemination through sexual intercourse (Weston 1991: 171). Then there is the necessity of deciding which partner will become the parent. Age, work situation, and desire are the factors that couples consider. Another solution is for each lesbian parent successively to become pregnant. There are "procreative service organizations that cater specifically to lesbians, gay men, and women who desire biological children outside heterosexual marital and nonmarital relationships" (Sullivan 2004: 33). Some select known donors while other select anonymous donors. Anonymous donors may elect to release their identity when the child reaches majority. The known donor may become "a symbolic father; a flexibly defined male figure with whom the child has a relationship but to whom no parental status is imputed; or finally, an actively participating parent" (Sullivan 2004: 49–50). Some lesbians may choose to "self-inseminate," meaning finding a sperm donor themselves, perhaps among friends. Stacey notes, "Numerous lesbian couples solicit sperm from a brother or male relative of one woman to impregnate her partner, hoping to buttress their tenuous legal, symbolic, and social claims for shared parental status of the 'turkey-baster' babies" (Stacey 1998: 120–21).

At this same-sex marriage ceremony in San Francisco both parties chose to dress as brides.

If only one partner has had a child, second parent adoption is another aspect of the lesbian family. Lesbian parents frequently try to reside in states like California, New York, or New Jersey where second parent adoption is possible (Sullivan 2004: 37). Other states, such as Florida and New Hampshire, have statutes prohibiting adoptions by a second female parent, under the reasoning that a second female could not adopt a child since the child already has a "mother." The desire to have an equal relationship to the child may be accomplished by having the child use a hyphenated last name or having the child call both parents Momma A and Momma B. Couples may try to have parents and relatives on both sides as aunts, uncles, and grandparents (Hayden 2005: 125).

Many gay men also desire to have families. Gay couples choosing to become parents may use a surrogate mother, who is impregnated with the sperm of one of the gay partners, or they may adopt or foster a child (Erera 2002: 169). Adoption is a more difficult alternative. There is an Internet site that assists gay couples in finding adoption websites that are "safe," that is, accepting of gay couples as prospective parents, since many adoption agencies will not deal with gay men (Mallon 2004: 17).

Regarding sexual orientation and parenting of children in same-sex families, in 2004, the American Psychological Association concluded, "There is no scientific basis for concluding that lesbian mothers or gay fathers are unfit parents. . . . On the contrary, results of research suggest that lesbian and gay parents are as likely as heterosexual parents to provide supportive and healthy environments for their children . . . results of research suggest that the development, adjustment, and well-being of children with lesbian and gay parents do not differ markedly from that of children with heterosexual parents" (Meezan and Rauch 2005: 101; see also Cantor et al. 2006: 49, 70). More specifically, "Children of lesbian mothers have not demonstrated more gender identity or sex role confusion than children of heterosexual mothers. . . . [There is] no elevated incidence of homosexuality in offspring living with a lesbian parent" (Black 2006: 53–54). Most lesbian parents are interested in having male role models involved in the lives of their children. According to Sullivan, "When sons of lesbian mothers are exposed to real adult men with whom they have personal relationships minus the oedipal issues, they are more likely to have richer, personally meaningful sources of masculinity with which to identify" (Sullivan 2004: 91).

Earlier, the assumption was that homosexual individuals were cut off from their families of origin and formed their own "families of choice." However, studies show that "lesbian families are in regular contact with grandparents . . . but are more likely to see their biological mother's relatives than relatives of their second, non-biological mother. . . . 74% . . . with non-biological mother's mother . . . 97% with biological mother's mother" (Cantor et al. 2006: 60). Blood relatives are more likely to "come around" to acceptance of the same-sex family with the birth of a child with whom they have a biological relationship, but that is not necessarily the case (Sullivan 2004: 133, 156).

When gays and lesbians terminate their familial relationships, they sometimes end up in court arguing over the custody of the children and challenging the court system, since there are no precedents for such situations. As one might expect, biological claims of relationship are usually those that are recognized. The court has favored "the parental claims of donors who had contributed nothing more than sperm to their offspring over those of lesbians who had co-parented from the outset, even when these men [the sperm donors] had expressly agreed to abdicate paternal rights or responsibilities" (Stacey 1998: 122).

According to Hayden, "the core symbols of American kinship, [are] blood and love. . . . [but] lesbian sex provides a different model for love . . . reproducing a gender configuration that is seen to promote gender equality rather than asymmetry. . . . [but] these lesbian mothers simultaneously affirm the importance of blood as a symbol. . . . [thus] the dichotomy between straight biological families and lesbian chosen families becomes muddied. . . . [and] the so-called core symbols of kinship—the ideas that define what constitutes relatedness—are reworked and recontextualized" (Hayden 2005: 130–31). Despite these many recent changes, American kinship continues to revolve around certain basic concepts.

Kinship, Class, and Ethnicity

Carol Stack (1974) has described a kinship system among poor black people in a small midwestern city that is quite different from the one presented by Schneider (1980). Lower-class kinship was seen as an adaptation to the world of racism and poverty. On the other hand, Schneider's work on American kinship was conducted among middle-class Americans, and he assumed that it was the ideal for the entire society, including the lower class. In the situation described by Stack, various types of relatives form a wide support network within which there is reciprocation, which Stack calls "swapping" of money, child care, food, clothing, shelter, and emotional support. Those biological relatives who choose not to be involved in a support network thereby renounce their status as kin. The core of this network is a cluster of linked households, usually two or even three generations of women. Relatives such as aunts and grandmothers may carry out the role of mother for children. Males are present, but they are usually boyfriends and mothers' brothers, rarely husbands or fathers. If a young couple should marry, the newly formed nuclear family draws the individuals away from their kin and out of their support networks. Should the young husband lose his job, the couple always fall back on the resources of their respective kin networks, and the marriage is destroyed. In this situation, ties between brother and sister are stronger than those between husband and wife. In the film *Do the Right Thing*, Spike Lee captures this contradiction when he contrasts the close emotional ties between the hero and his sister, with the hero's antagonism toward his girlfriend, the mother of his child. In the kinship system described by Stack, mothers' brothers more frequently serve as role models for young male children than fathers, giving the system a matrilineal cast.

More recent research in a small African-American low-income suburb near a once-booming industrial region in the Midwest presents the same picture of interdependence of kin for financial support, and an array of essential services (Hicks Bartlett 2000: 35). Even after obtaining employment, individuals rely on their families and a network of relatives to help meet their needs for child care, funds for clothing for the new position, and money for transportation to the new job. In a study of twenty-six young low-income African-American men from the West Side of Chicago, fourteen lived with their mothers or grandmothers while nine others regarded their mother's address as their permanent address (Young 2000: 146). Only four grew up with their fathers in the home, but only intermittently. On the basis of the information provided by Stack, above, one might hypothesize that the fathers who did not live with their own children were closer to their sisters than to the mothers of their children. They serve as mothers' brothers, if their sisters have children.

In contrast, among lower middle-class families in Skylan, a housing project in a major midwestern city, there were resident fathers (Barclay-McLaughlin 2000: 60). Groveland, an African-American neighborhood in Chicago where 70 percent of the residents in single-family brick houses are homeowners, is characterized as lower middle class; however, some families had incomes below the poverty line. Though there are some intact families with resident fathers, in other families the father is absent (Pattillo-McCoy 2000: 95). The perilous economic situation of the African-American middle class in Groveland "often renders stability and mobility an extended family [concern], and sometimes even a community effort" (Barclay-McLaughlin 2000: 99).

As ethnicity became a more significant factor in American life, the U.S. Census Bureau began to pay more attention to the family organization of different ethnic groups, including Navajo, Inupiaq Eskimos of Alaska, Korean-Americans, and Latinos (Schwede et al. 2005). The Navajos, living on their reservation in the Four Corners of the Southwest, still maintain their matrilineal descent system, and have a fluid residential unit revolving around a grandmother, whose daughters and their families live in her house or adjacent to it, sharing meals, daily chores, child care, and resources, including income. It is a fluid unit in that some male and female members spend time working in the border towns because of unemployment on the reservation (Tongue 2005: 66ff).

In contrast, among the Inupiat, 78 percent of the households studied consisted of grandparents and their grandchildren, with the middle generation mostly women at school or work in another community. There are many single adult men living with a parent or grandparent who continue to participate in subsistence hunting and fishing. Local family units, an aggregate of related households, in effect a social network, continue to cooperate as a single domestic entity and in subsistence activities (Craver 2005: 109ff). Hispanics from Mexico and El Salvador living in Virginia mention the nuclear family as the ideal and the norm in their countries. After migrating to the United States, due to economic conditions, they live in complex households. These consist of extended families with a mix of spouses, children, adult siblings and their spouses and children, parents, and parents-in-law. The term *hogar*, implying emotional closeness, kinship, and shared domestic function, is used for such a unit.

SUMMARY

- This chapter presents the basic concepts of kinship that anthropologists have used to analyze the small-scale societies that were the focus of their attention when the discipline of anthropology first developed.
- The incest taboo and marriage prohibitions compel individuals to marry outside the family.
- Societies have rules regarding number of spouses and postmarital residence rules, which result in the creation of a variety of types of families.

- Societies also have rules regarding how marriage is contracted.
- Kinship rules of descent create different kinds of kin groups or clans. Though their structures may differ, the functions of such groups—land ownership and economic and ceremonial functions—remain the same.
- Different types of marriage rules result in different structures of relationship or alliance between descent groups.
- Kinship terminology in different societies reflects the pattern of descent, family type, and marriage found in those societies.
- Some societies use kinship as a metaphor to create the important relationships of godparenthood.
- Americans have their own cultural ideas about kinship, which are currently being rethought in light of reproductive technologies, surrogate parenting, artificial insemination, the emphasis on genetic inheritance of disease, step-parenthood, and adoption by gay and lesbian couples.
- Kinship continues to be important not only in our own complex industrial society but also in other societies all over the world.

SUGGESTED READINGS

Faubion, James D., ed. *The Ethics of Kinship: Ethnographic Inquiries.* Lanham, MD: Rowman & Littlefield, 2001. A series of articles concerning the relationship between ethics and kinship and the ways in which individuals are involved with families of choice rather than families of kinship.

Scott, Michael W. *The Severed Snake: Matrilineages, Making Place, and a Melanesian Christianity in Southeast Solomon Islands.* Durham, NC: Carolina Academic Press, 2007. An ethnography detailing how a matrilineal society in Papua New Guinea operates today after conversion to Christianity.

Tipton, Steven M. and John Witte, Jr., eds. *Family Transformed: Religion, Values, and Society in American Life.* Washington, DC: Georgetown University Press, 2005. A compilation of articles regarding variations of family type in America today.

SUGGESTED WEBSITES

www.umanitoba.ca/faculties/arts/anthropology/tutor/. A reference guide to general information regarding kinship and social organization.

www.mnsu.edu/emuseum/cultural/kinship/terminology.html. A discussion of kinship terminology as it relates to rules of descent.

www.stepfamiles.info/. A website to provide stepfamilies with information and resources.

---○---

Chapter 7
Gender and Age

IDEAS ABOUT MALE AND FEMALE are part of every society. These distinctions are so engrained in cultural knowledge that they are symbolic shorthand for much more complex ideas. In American society, justice is personified as female and death as male. In German culture, death is also male, but so is one's homeland—fatherland. However, for Russians, the homeland is one's motherland. Sex and age differences are universally the basis of social roles. Men may herd cattle and women milk cows in some societies, while in other societies, men and women both work as computer technicians. Senior citizens in American society may sometimes live in communities where children are not allowed to live, while in other societies, aged parents are revered members of the family and accorded the best living arrangements in the household. Ideas about age often influence ideas about male and female roles; in some societies older women are afforded power and privileges they do not have when they are presumed to be sexually active and of child-bearing age (Lamb 2000: 15–16).

Relations between the sexes in human societies throughout the life cycle are always culturally patterned. The nature of their patterning forms a powerful motif in the tapestry of culture. Many of the assumptions about gender and age categories in the social sciences draw in part from past ideas about the human body and social categories based upon it. These ideas often derive from colonial period observations of "natives" recorded as social "fact" about "others." An awareness of the sources of these ideas, counterbalanced by local people articulating their own visions, is included in most of the ethnographies about age and gender today. Many of these works combine research into historical sources in archives with fieldwork, interviews, life histories, and participant-observation.

GENDER, SEX, MALE, FEMALE

Sex is generally defined as the physical differentiation between male and female as identified by the biological and anatomical composition of genitals and related secondary sexual characteristics

141

(breast size, hair distribution, body fat, etc.). **Gender** is the culture-specific set of behavioral, ideological, and social meanings constructed around the understandings of these biological and anatomical differences. **Sexuality** refers to erotic desires and the practices associated with them (Cameron and Kulick 2003: 1). Understanding the ways in which male and female roles are culturally construed is central to anthropological theory and practice. Americans perceive differences between males and females as natural differences from which ideas about men's and women's roles derive. Differences in genitalia are understood to be signs of differences in fluids and substances that naturally divide the population into two different, mutually exclusive categories (Errington 1990). Behavior, dress, and demeanor are viewed by most Americans as determining membership in one of these two categories.

One of the primary North American constructions of identity is the binary distinction between male and female as biological, gendered, and sexually normative categories. This is now understood to be the **heteronormative** cultural vision that privileges male and female heterosexual behaviors in conceptualizing cultural and family norms. While homosexuality is no longer considered a psychological illness by psychiatrists and psychologists, the binaries of male-female, masculinity-feminity, and homosexual-heterosexual continue in the fabric of American life.

Until the mid-twentieth century, anthropologists, mostly male, focused primarily on male roles in their field research. In doing so, they were unconsciously reflecting the cultural bias of their own society, which emphasized the significance of male roles in public institutions and projected its gender ideology onto the society they were studying. The work of Margaret Mead was one exception to anthropology's male bias in the first half of the twentieth century. Due in part to feminist movements within the past thirty years, many anthropologists of both sexes began to pay attention to female as well as male roles and to the female as well as the male point of view of society, including our own. Anthropologists now focus on the cultural construction of gender and how the performance of these roles relates to other patterns in the culture (Morris 1995).

REPRODUCTION AND CULTURE

All societies recognize physiological differences in the bodies of men and women; perceptions of those differences contribute to local understandings of reproductive science. In the course of interaction between male and female some societies perceive women's sexuality and reproductive abilities as dangerous; this danger may be projected onto menstrual blood. Menstrual blood is a substance that, perhaps more than any other, is associated with femaleness; menstrual taboos are cultural expressions of the way in which some observed differences between men and women and their participation in reproduction are understood. Ideas about the effects of contact with menstrual blood tend to be part of a male vision of society that is, by virtue of the authority of male perspectives, often shared by women as well. These female substances are also empowering to women, and are associated variously with love potions, ritual calendars, and in metaphors of creation and production. Menstrual blood can be used symbolically in harmful ways in witchcraft and in a positive fashion in the manufacture of love charms (Buckley and Gottlieb 1988: 35).

In Wogeo, an island off New Guinea, the difference is based on the belief that men and women live separately in two different worlds. But realistically, men and women must come together to reproduce the society as well as to carry out the usually complementary social and economic roles upon which their society depends. Men control politics and power. Associated with these ideas about the separateness of the sexes is the belief that sexual intercourse is polluting to both sexes and that menstrual blood is harmful to men. While women menstruate naturally, in Wogeo the men incise their penises to rid themselves of the bad "menstrual" blood (Hogbin 1996 [1970]). In contrast to Wogeo, other societies play down the differences. The Wana on the island of Sulawesi, in Indonesia, conceptualize gender relationships very differently from the people of Wogeo. They minimize the differences between male and female, seeing male and female as almost identical anatomically. Husband and wife are equally involved in procreation. The Wana say that the man carries the child for the first seven days of gestation and then puts the child into a woman. It is believed that in the past men menstruated. Men's menstrual blood is said to be "white blood" and to contain the essence of humanity, which solidifies in the womb as a fetus (Atkinson 1990: 75–76).

The Mansi are a hunting and gathering society on the eastern slopes of the Ural Mountains in Siberia today. Mansi married women belong to a "'strange' clan different to that of her husband" (Fedorova 2001: 227). Women in that society are subject to a series of complex taboos that "stem from beliefs regarding the allegedly harmful essence of women related to their 'impurity'" (Fedorova 2001: 227). These taboos include moving to a special dwelling during menstruation and immediately before childbirth. After the birth, the woman stayed in the menstrual house for two or three months. The wife could not expose her face to her husband's male kin. She could not touch the "idols" in her husband's home, though after her marriage and move to the husband's house she was supposed to be protected by "his domestic gods" (Fedorova 2001: 233). During the Soviet period, education and modernization brought about a weakening of these taboos. Since the collapse of the Soviet system, many Mansi are said to be returning to "their old ways."

Reproduction and the social constructions of male and female bodies are subjects that have attracted renewed anthropological attention over the past quarter century. One focus of this literature is ethnographic analysis (often by female scholars and ethnographers) of the multiple ways women understand and use the spatial norms of menstruation and childbirth practices. The segregation of women who are menstruating or giving birth in special houses or restricted spaces has been widely noted by ethnographers for decades. The documentation of women's understandings of these forms of segregation expands our analysis of them to include women's agency in enacting their social responsibilities, and in protecting their husbands, children, and communities. The social segregation of women may create opportunities for them to spend time with their peers and young children, exchange stories and information, and cultivate alliances among their peers, unsupervised by their husbands and elders. Listening to the voices of women creates an understanding of menstrual taboos and segregation beyond a simplistic reading of menstruation as polluting. "[I]deologies of pollution should be the beginning, not the end, of ethnographic analysis. Women's own views of a patriarchal ideology can offer alternative readings of that ideology, sometimes affording women a form of personal resistance to a degrading cultural script, or allowing them to reinterpret it entirely" (Gottlieb 2002: 383–84).

Signs at the entrance to a Balinese Hindu temple request menstruating women not to enter.

GENDER AND ECONOMIC PARTICIPATION

In all societies, economic roles are based on cultural constructions of gender. In the past this was referred to as the sexual division of labor. The difference in economic roles between men and women is not an outgrowth of their biological differences. A specific task may be associated with men in one society and with women in another. As we have noted above, milking herd animals (cows, goats, sheep), for example, may be a female task in some societies and a male task in others, as is also the case with making pottery and weaving cloth. Men's economic tasks invariably have greater prestige, even though women's tasks, such as horticulture and collecting plant foods, may provide the bulk of subsistence. This is an example of **gender stratification**. Whatever the economic role of the man, it is that role which the culture values. In America and in other industrialized countries, women have become lawyers, stockbrokers, and judges, economic roles formerly reserved for men, and men have taken over some female roles, such as nurses and airline attendants, which were formerly exclusively female roles.

Earlier, we discussed the ways in which space takes on different symbolic meanings. Particular spatial areas may be associated respectively with males and females. Because women are identified with mothering, the hearth, and the home, women are associated with the domestic realm. Men,

In rural Rajasthan women (shown on the left) generally cover their heads and faces and sit separately from men and boys in community gatherings.

in contrast, are identified with the public realm. This distinction between domestic and public is one analytical tool that has been used historically in comparing male and female roles in different societies. The association of males with the public sphere and females with the domestic was widespread in the past; today this distinction is not always the case. Malagasy women conduct the haggling that takes place in the market, while in some West African societies women actually control the marketplace. A recent comparative study gives a number of examples of women traders in markets in Java, South India, Ghana, Morocco, and the Philippines (Seligman 2001).

Restrictions on women's activities outside their homes are often associated with patriarchal societies. Some women in Middle Eastern and South Asian societies follow traditions of modest dress or covering when interacting with some males of their household and unrelated men outside their home. Veiling, or covering some part of the face and body, has become the object of attack from Western feminists because it is seen as an infringement upon women's human rights. Others see this position as ethnocentric, since it ignores the particular cultural meanings of veiling. This perspective also ignores the voices of women who understand veiling as facilitating culturally appropriate ways in which they can safely and comfortably pursue their educations and careers, and actively engage in political and religious activities (Abu-Lughod 2002).

Veiling of women in the Middle East is "a language which communicates social and cultural messages, a practice which has been present in tangible form since ancient times" (El Guindi 1999: xii–xiii). However, as El Guindi notes, "there is sufficient evidence to indicate that we are dealing with multiple phenomena, layers of meaning, and diverse contexts" (1999: 4). In Egypt today, some young Egyptian women have taken up veiling as an aspect of their support of Islamic militancy. It replaces the secular dress that many of their mothers and even grandmothers wore. In Turkey, which has been secularized since the revolution of Kamal Ataturk after World War I, some young women Muslim advocates have recently begun to wear long coats and headscarves (El Guindi 1999: 129ff.). In the United States and Europe, some Muslim immigrants and citizens see dress choice as part of religious expression for both men and women. While some institutions advocate restricting particular forms of dress in public schools and other domains, other individuals and groups see choice of clothing as a form of expression widely granted to all religious and ethnic groups.

SEXUALITIES AND IDENTITIES

Contemporary sexualities are constantly being made and modified. Foucault demonstrates this in his depiction of how the modern Western idea of sexuality arose in a specific historical and social context (Whitehead and Barrett 2001; Brittan 2001: 53). Within recent years, anthropologists have explored the variation in gendered identities and sexualities. **Queer studies** theorizes and explores the construction of multiple forms of sexual identity in their cultural contexts, and stresses the lived experiences of gay, lesbian, transgendered, and bisexual identities. Originally focused primarily on male homosexuality, ethnographic studies inspired in part by queer studies perspectives now explore among other subjects gay and lesbian family and parenting, gender corrective surgery, and gender ambiguity. Queer studies in anthropology documents and theorizes local experiences and understandings of identity, as opposed to enumerating and describing multiple practices in different societies. Boellstorff states, "[T]he problem with a logic of enumeration is that . . . it presumes that concepts name preexisting entities and relations, rather than asking how the social is produced and sustained through acts of representation, including scholarly and activist representation" (2007: 19). Scholars in this area link queer theory and gender variation inquiry to postmodernism and postcolonialism (Hawley 2001; Boellstorff 2007). This research clarifies the distinction between hegemonic Euro American ideas that often originate in colonial histories, and the ways in which local communities self-identify and name relevant categories of social identities.

For example, historically documented examples of gender diversity in North American history are identified with Native American Plains societies. The term **berdache**, of French derivation, was originally used by Europeans to identify men who dressed like women and lived in socially recognized relationships with other men; this term and its association with male social behavior appears throughout twentieth century literature on gender. Scholars now recognize that there were also women in these societies who dressed like men and assumed male roles, who constituted an additional gender category (Roscoe 1998). The term *berdache* is rejected by Native

Americans and scholars alike, as it is associated with Western European categories of sexuality not relevant to Native American historical ideologies. The terms *two spirit* or *two spirited* are generally preferred although they too are inadequate to capture the wide range of gender variances they encompass (Lang 1998: xiii).

We'wha, a Zuni who was born male, was accepted as a woman in his own society as well as during a trip to Washington, D.C. in 1886 where he was received by many dignitaries, including President Grover Cleveland. He lived as a woman and was skilled at women's crafts. When he died, he was buried in a dress, with a pair of pants beneath the dress, the pants symbolizing his multiple gender statuses (Roscoe 1998: 145). Known as ***nadleehi***, these transgendered individuals are also found among the Navajo; Roscoe notes that the nadleehi tradition still continues in parts of the Navajo Reservation (1998: 65).

Roscoe cites a number of examples of women who lived as male warriors. He notes that Cheyenne female warrior chiefs "dressed like the male members of the Hohnuka, or Contrary society, who fought wearing only their breachcloths" (Roscoe 1998: 75). Some of these Cheyenne female warriors sat with the Chief Council and their opinions had weight. Similar cases occurred among the Pend d'Oreille and Flathead Indians, both from Montana, as well as the Crow and the Blackfoot. Running Eagle, a female warrior of the Blackfoot in the early nineteenth century, became a legendary subject. Her story was reprinted and given new meaning in 1984 as a positive image for young women today. The Navajo also recognized female nadleehi, giving them four culturally identified genders. Today some male nadleehi may use that label to identify themselves, being Navajo traditionalists in their belief. Younger acculturated and assimilated Navajo self-identify with the Western terms *gay* and *homosexual* and may be completely unfamiliar with the nadleehi tradition (Thomas 1997: 162, 169).

Nanda cautions against romanticizing or idealizing what appears to be non-Western cultures' "seemingly positive valuation of sex/gender diversity, the latitude they allow for the expression of gender variation or the integration of alternatively gendered individuals into society. . . . [A] positive or tolerant attitude toward gender diversity in the past does not necessarily translate into acceptance of gender diversity in the present" (2000: 4). The documentation of the lifestyles of hijras of India illustrates this conclusion (Nanda 1999; Reddy 2005). **Hijras**, "neither man nor woman," are born as males and transform their identity (sometimes with genital surgery, always as dressing and presenting themselves publically as females) into a new gender category. The representation of hijras in a growing corpus of journalism and ethnography focuses mostly on their sexual identity (Reddy 2005: 3). Reddy observes that individuals embedded in a community of hijras share religious ideologies, ideas about honor and respect, gender performance expectations, and lineage reckoning (Reddy 2005). Hijra identity also draws in large part on an idealization of asceticism; their own sexuality is therefore only one small part of a larger and complicated set of shared norms and ideas.

Hijras have been identified in South Asian history for centuries; their traditional ritual role has been to sing and dance at Hindu weddings and ceremonies following the birth of a son. These are highly auspicious occasions in Hindu society, and the presence of hijras during the completion of these rituals symbolizes their ritual power. However, they "are generally regarded with

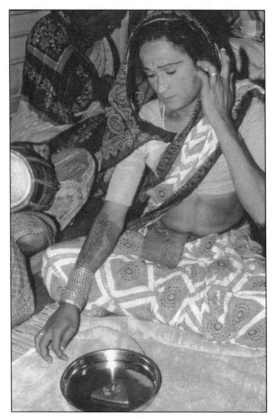

Hijras in India are born male but live as women, enacting social and religious rituals associated with their community.

ambivalence; social attitudes include a combination of mockery, fear, respect, contempt, and even compassion. . . . Hijras have the power to curse as well as to bless, and if they are not paid their due, they will insult a family publicly and curse it with a loss of virility" (Nanda 2000: 36).

The social status of hijras has declined in recent history. Their social position and ritual roles were valued and regularized during pre-colonial periods of Indian history. British rulers in nineteenth-century India abhorred their practices of surgical manipulation of genitalia, adoption of female dress and roles by men, and their association with prostitution, resulting in the criminalization of their practices (Reddy 2005: 26–28). In contemporary India, hijra participation in weddings and birth ceremonies has been dramatically curtailed by an overall decline in participation in the rituals of the past. To compensate for loss of ritual income, some hijras engage in sex work, a practice that is frowned upon by many hijras as inauthentic practice, creating status divisions and hierarchies within hijra communities (Reddy 2005: 2). Despite the ideological recognition of the "third gender" in the history of South Asian religious ideological traditions and hijra participation in public rituals, the lives of contemporary hijras are often marked by poverty, marginalization, and multiple forms of discrimination.

POLITICAL MOVEMENTS AND WOMEN'S ROLES

In our own and other industrial societies, economic, spatial, and behavioral separation of the sexes was present until the beginning of the twentieth century. Ginsburg (1989) points out that in preindustrial America, the home was basically the workplace for both men and women. With increasing industrialization during the nineteenth century, men were drawn into the factories and businesses, while women remained in the home, an essentially female domain. Women were identified with an ideology of nurturance and domesticity, despite the fact that some women worked in stores and factories for wages. Politics, the courts, businesses, banks, pubs, and so forth, were male bastions; so too were the social clubs, where real business was carried out.

At the beginning of the twentieth century, women who questioned the assignment of the male and female roles of this time formed the suffragist movement and began to agitate for the right to vote, which had been denied them heretofore. Men perceived the pioneers in this movement as very masculine women. World War II brought many women into the workforce, and since that time, ever-increasing numbers of women have become part of the American labor force. It took the feminist movement of the 1970s and affirmative action legislation to begin to raise both female and male consciousness and bring about the transformations that we see today. As women have moved into occupations such as law and medicine, formerly occupied almost exclusively by men, the society at large has come to accept women as well as men in those roles. In this way, women in American society have invaded the public realm of men, and as this has occurred, men have increasingly had more to do in the domestic realm, taking on cooking and child care.

Another example of how gender roles have changed in America concerns childbirth. In the nineteenth century, American women gave birth in the home, which, as we noted, was identified as a female sphere. At the beginning of the twentieth century, with the increasing professionalization of medicine and the growth of hospitals, the medical profession, then male-dominated, took control over the process of giving birth, and by the 1930s more births occurred in hospitals than at home. Under these conditions, birth was defined as a medical procedure, and the female reproductive process was taken over and placed in the hands of male physicians.

With the significant changes in gender roles in our society, this process is being reversed. There are more female physicians now. Interest in natural childbirth has brought about changes, and home birth is a possibility that some feminists advocate. Other aspects of the new reproductive technology, such as amniocentesis, genetic counseling, and the use of various birth control techniques, for example, intrauterine devices and birth control pills, have also been seen as giving women more choices and greater control over their lives in regard to reproductive functions. However, the introduction of these procedures does not really empower women but, rather, increases the control of technology and technologists over women and their reproductive processes (Rapp 1993; 2000).

The change in gender roles just described is in no way an inevitable progression through which all modernizing societies will pass. Anthropologists have described all sorts of changes affecting gender roles in different parts of the world in recent decades. Many women in parts of the Middle East and Asia have left their traditional domestic domains to go to work outside the home with varying consequences. For example, in Hong Kong in the 1970s, in families in which fathers were unemployed or underemployed, daughters went to work, becoming semiskilled factory workers (Salaff 1995). Their incomes played a prominent role in the household economy, though their personal gain was limited. There was some loosening of family ties, and they were freed from household duties and received small amounts of spending money. Their marriages were no longer arranged and they could choose their own spouses. However, core family values of paternal rule and filial obedience were still maintained.

The Minangkabau, who live on the island of Sumatra and are part of the Indonesian nation-state, provide us with an interesting example of the way in which the contemporary women's lives are mediated through contemporary religious and political currents. The Minangkabau have a matrilineal rule of descent and the wife's relatives play a significant role in social and economic affairs. *Adat*, the unique body of traditions related to this social system, has melded with the Qur'an since Islam was introduced in 1600. The laws of the Qur'an were developed in the context of patrilineal societies. Since the Minangkabau are matrilineal, this necessitated making compromises between adat and the Qur'an. These traditions have survived more than three hundred years of Dutch colonial rule, as well as the development of the Indonesian nation-state after the country won independence in the mid-1950s (Whalley 1998: 229).

Minangkabau began to move to the urban areas of Sumatra and to educate girls as part of the modernization and transformation of Indonesia that took place under the aegis of President Suharto. This presented many challenges to both Islam and adat. The response, in the 1980s, was an Islamic renaissance parallel to that occurring in other Islamic countries. The government itself then began to fund the building of mosques. Soon major religious events and family celebrations were emphasized, and girls began to wear Muslim dress to school. In terms of adat tradition, as early as the beginning of the twentieth century, there had been a shift from uxorilocal residence, in which the husband moved to live with the wife's relatives, to nuclear family households, though the families still lived on her lineage land and in close proximity to the wife's female relatives (Whalley 1998: 233). Despite the continuation of the matrilineal tradition, husbands began to invest more time and interest in their wives and children and less on their own matrilineage, as had been the case in the past. The growing importance of the nuclear family household has resulted in the husband's providing more subsistence for his family, as well as providing for the education of his children, allocating inheritance of personal property to them, and having more of a voice in whom his daughters marry. However, the mother's brother and matrilineage relatives, especially older women, still play a significant role in deciding schools to attend, professions to pursue, and marriages to be arranged.

With the growing importance of Islam in the 1980s, combined with the efforts at modernization, young women had to tread a narrow line to resolve the dilemma of career and family (an issue not unfamiliar to young American women). Minangkabau women are seen as being of equal moral worth with men. Islamic scholars proclaimed women to be the pillars of society given their critical roles as mothers and wives. Women's education was encouraged, in order to enable them to better raise and educate their children. The educational choices of young women today may necessitate making decisions that do not always fit with the cultural traditions of the senior generation. Young Minangkabau women have continued to wear more modest Western-style dress, though they wear traditional Muslim Minangkabau dress for ritual occasions. Islamic traditions were being aggressively taught in contrast to the Western-style education of the 1960s and 1970s. Islam was promoted as an answer to reestablishing order in a country threatened by Westernization. Recently, however, as a counter to the threats to the traditional adat, children in school are being exposed to programs emphasizing this tradition. In addition, urban middle-class Minangkabau are hosting large-scale marriage festivals that mix rock music with "all the intricate observances of high adai" (Whalley 1998: 245).

GENDER STUDIES AND FEMINIST ANTHROPOLOGY

We have considered the changing position of women in a number of societies. From these multiple examples it is clear that the religious and political policies of colonial and postcolonial states, as well as the forces of economic and social change, impact on women differently than men. Political policy and practice often specifically target women's behavior, education, and public participation in establishing social and economic norms. It is also well documented that the achievements obtained by middle- and upper-class women in many societies are not paralleled by similar attainments elsewhere. Women in lower social classes and women of color in the West feel that the feminist movements and its achievements have not always included them.

Many anthropologists, inspired by the progressive movements of the 1960s and 1970s, and the marginalization of women in the discipline prior to that period, developed intellectual agendas to focus on historicizing and analyzing constructions of female identities. **Feminist anthropology**, a women-oriented perspective, may combine inquiry with activism in that it seeks to both explore and address inequity based on gender. Feminist anthropology has evolved along with the other perspectives already discussed; influenced by postmodernist theorizing of the 1980s, feminist anthropologists challenge the essentialist reading of all social categories and representations, particularly those of "men" and "women." They are also concerned with the lived experience of women in relation to hegemonic or dominant systems of knowledge, including those that normalize cultural ideas about race, science, medicine, religion, and political participation. Feminist anthropologists cultivate methodologies to explore and theorize women's experiences in all societies, while simultaneously critiquing ideas of male and female in the theories and practices of anthropology.

MASCULINITY AND MASCULINIST STUDIES

In parallel fashion to the examination of female roles in society, it is necessary to understand the nature of **masculinity** as a series of cultural constructions "whose basis is not biological—even though the cultural construction is based on biological differences—but constructed, designed, agreed to, and upheld by a system of beliefs, attributes, and expectations" (Ramirez 1999: 28).

What constitutes masculinity changes through historic time for all societies. We also need to recognize that "masculinities" is a contested term, and there is considerable variation in what constitutes masculinity within as well as between societies (Morgan 2001: 223–24).

Guttmann, in his study of the working-class neighborhood of Santo Domingo, a *colonia* founded on the outskirts of Mexico City by "land invasion," focused on the dramatic transformation of what it means today to be male and female (2000). The following demonstrates the changes that are taking place in gender roles. It is common to hear women and men say that there used to be a lot of macho men but they are not so common today. Older men still divide the world of men into machos, meaning men of honor who responsibly provide for their families, financially and otherwise, and *mandilones*, meaning female-dominated men (Guttmann 2000: 162). The latter are seen as being bossed around by women and undependable. The term *machismo* is also associated with wife beatings, sexual episodes of infidelity, consumption of alcohol, gambling, abandonment of children, defiance of death, and bullying behavior in general (Guttmann 2000: 164).

Younger married men see themselves in a new category, "non-macho." The macho label may be rejected by the man who helps his wife and does not beat her, the latter (i.e., beating one's wife) being a characteristic of the macho man. This is clearly a divergent "cultural trajectory." The terms *machomexicano* and *la mujerabnegada*, the self-sacrificing woman, are now regarded by many working-class men as "pejorative and not worthy of emulation." Younger men rarely claim the title of macho, the model of aggressive masculinity since machos do not spend time with their children, cook, or wash dishes (Guttmann 2000: 172). However, sometimes the role of "the macho" is a playful one, which is performed on demand, and there are still depictions of macho men in dramas in places like Santo Domingo. Beyond these categories is "the broad category of men who have sex with other men . . . [including] male prostitutes who have sex for money with other men and always play the active role, and the *homosexuales*. . . . Men who have sex with other men are by some people's definition outside the bounds of masculinity altogether" (Guttmann 2000: 174). But in the final analysis, "no man in Santo Domingo neatly fits into any of the four categories, either at specific moments or throughout the course of his life" (Guttmann 2000: 174). The main point here is that for Mexicans in this *colonia* today, masculinity has shifting meanings and this has been the case historically as well.

Masculinity in American society has been examined in a variety of institutional contexts, including various industries, the military, and sports. The military is still largely male. It also "plays a primary role in shaping images of masculinity in the larger society" (Barrett 2001: 77). However, even within one of the services—the navy—for example, there are a number of different "masculinities," different strands of "hegemonic masculinity" that naval officers call upon to "secure" different forms of masculine identity (Barrett 2001: 95). For example, risk is an important value for aviators since they have more opportunities to display such behavior, while "surface warfare officers have opportunities to demonstrate physical hardships and grueling work schedules, and supply officers frequently have more opportunity to display . . . responsibility for resources" (Barrett 2001: 95). These characterizations are always seen in contrast to military men's definitions of women as emotionally unstable and less capable of enduring the physical challenges and harsh conditions of life aboard a ship.

Variations in the nature of manhood in other American settings are revealed in an examination of masculinity in various types of workplaces. Meyer, in a consideration of masculine culture on the automotive work floor during the three decades from 1930 to 1960, sees two polar forms, or ideal types, as operative during that time, which were a continuation from the nineteenth century (2001: 15). "Respectable manhood," which was related to the craft tradition, was characterized by a tempered and channeled masculinity in which mental and physical skills were used in an evenhanded fashion. In contrast, "rough manhood" related to the tradition of unskilled labor characterized by risk taking, physical strength, and disorderly behavior. Others have also associated this rough masculine culture with construction workers and steelworkers. In the northeastern part of the United States and Canada, many of these steelworkers were Iroquois who transferred the masculine warrior ethic into the daring required to walk the steel beams as skyscrapers were being constructed. As Meyer points out, under industrialization and semiskilled mass production, workers blended and merged elements of these two types, the respectable elements being fed by high wages and economic stability, while in auto plants "boylike playfulness on the shop floor . . . [and] drinking, fighting and gambling" retained aspects of the rough male identity (Meyer 2001: 19).

Majors argues that the "cool pose" of African-American men in sports is a means of countering social oppression and racism and a way of expressing their own creativity (2001: 215). Their expression of pride and respect for themselves in the "cool pose" expresses their masculinity as dominant and hegemonic, and ultimately it is about "men's domination of women." In general, according to Kimmel, our culture's definition of manhood includes a repudiation of the feminine; the necessary acquisition of power, success, wealth, and status; being strong and reliable in a crisis; never showing your emotions; exuding manliness and aggression (2001: 278). The quest to prove one's manhood is a lifelong endeavor. While male dominance is often culturally equated with male sexuality, ideologies of male and female are often transformed away from dominance toward a more egalitarian relationship between men and women.

CATEGORIES BASED ON AGE

Aging is a continuous process; however, the way in which this continuum is divided varies from society to society, as well as over time within a single society. Every society has terms for different age groups and related rituals that mark the transition from one stage to another (see chapter 10). In our own society, for example, we traditionally used terms such as *infant, child, adolescent, adult,* and *senior citizen* to identify major social categories and transitions. We now recognize more age categories, including *toddler, 'tween, teenager, baby boomer, empty nester,* and so on. In America many of our life stages reflect economic and institutional transformations over the past century. For example, the "teen-age" life stage between adolescence and adulthood is marked by physical maturity, mandatory schooling, and economic dependence, often accompanied by sexual awareness, rebellion, and parental conflict. In rural communities in America a century ago and in many contemporary agricultural societies this life stage doesn't exist in this form; adulthood begins immediately with physical maturity, often accompanied by marriage, parenting, and adult economic and social responsibilities (White 1994).

Age Grades

When age categories are formally named and recognized and crosscut the entire society, they are referred to as **age grades**; the members of one age grade constitute an **age set**. In a number of pastoralist societies (see chapter 8) in Africa, formalized age grades have importance in expressing ethnic and group identity through social organization, In early to mid-twentieth-century scholarship on these age-grade systems, they are often described exclusively from the male perspective. For example, the male age-grade system of the Nyakyusa of Tanzania was documented by Monica Wilson (1964 [1951], 1977) based on fieldwork conducted in the 1930s. Age mates, as they matured, joined to form a new village; at 10 or 11 years old, boys built huts and established a village at the edge of their fathers' village, returning to their mothers' huts for meals and to assist their fathers in agriculture. At about the age of 25, the boys, now young men, married and brought their brides to live with them virilocally in the new village. Once in a generation a great ritual was held, with administrative power and military leadership handed over by the older generation to the younger. The retiring old chief reallocated all the land and selected a headman for each new village. Therefore, all over Nyakyusaland, Wilson stated, there were three kinds of age-grade villages. They consisted of villages of grandfathers retired from leadership positions but who still performed certain ritual functions; villages of the fathers, who ruled and were responsible for defense and administration; and villages of the sons, who when necessary fought under the leadership of men of their fathers' generation.

Under the pressure of economic change, the Nyakyusa have been moving away from their traditional age villages. When men migrate from their homes for wage labor, they leave their wives with their mothers in intergenerational households. Furthermore, individuals seeking personal economic advancement create conflict with the traditional value of sharing assets between members of an age village (Wilson 1977). This situation is in contrast to that of the Samburu, a pastoral society in Kenya that retains its age-grade system. Though some Samburu have moved to towns, many of them still retain their cattle herds. Bilinda Straight, in her ethnographic research among the Samburu, concludes that they continue to rely on the male age-grade and age-set system as "indicators of men's roles (and the prestige associated with each) and referred to the centrality of livestock to their identity" (1997: 76).

Recent scholarship explores the participation of both women and men in shaping and transforming African pastoral practices and gender norms (Hodgson 2000). Dorothy Hodgson, drawing on historical sources and fieldwork among the Maasai of Kenya and Tanzania (1999, 2001), documents shifts in the practices and meanings associated with age grades, in part by exploring the sources from which these ideas emerge. Outsiders writing about the Maasai generally represent them as archetypal pastoral male warriors and as "immutable icons of traditional Africa" (Hodgson 1999: 121). These sources select and exaggerate only one "of a range of masculinities cross-cut by generation . . . shaped in relation to each other as well as to Maasai feminities" (1999: 125).

Depending upon the perspective of the author, these texts argue for either the protection of their traditional lifestyle or the necessity of its elimination in the name of modernity, economic progress, and state security. Historical and contemporary representations in part shape the Maasai's own shifting visions of masculinity and gender and ethnic identity. "Through their [own] accounts, we learn that a dominant masculinity is less a construction than a production, and thus always in tension, always relative, and always a site of mediation and negotiation" (Hodgson 1999: 144).

Drawing in part on published accounts from the 1890s to the 1930s, Hodgson describes the often-ignored responsibilities of women among Maa-speaking pastoralists in this literature. "In general, men and women had distinct roles and responsibilities in the organization of the pastoral production system premised on mutual autonomy and respect, but shared common goals in furthering the interests of their homestead" (Hodgson 1999: 125). Women were critical participants in the pastoral economy as milk managers, traders, and in caring for young and sick animals. They bartered milk and animal hides with neighboring communities. As caretakers of ritual and prayer they were responsible for the well-being of people and livestock in the community. "Women also played important roles in the rites of passage which marked the transition of men from one age grade to another" as well as in enforcing important food and sex taboos (1999: 128). Through

In Kenya, some Maasai young men demonstrate their young warrior status by performing competitively for the community, proudly wearing both traditional and modern adornments.

their songs they "regulated and commented on men's behavior . . . they used songs to mock and ridicule men who failed to live up to the standards" (1999: 129) of particular age grades, thus articulating and enforcing ideas about masculinity. "As they aged . . . their respect and authority inside and outside the homestead . . . increased. Women felt deep pride in their identity as pastoralists, and as Maasai" (Hodgson 1999: 125–26).

The Maasai age set was a group of boys and men who together moved through the ritual and spatial rituals, who were circumcised together, and were known by a shared identifying name (Hodgson 1999: 126). As younger uncircumcised boys (*ilayiok*) they herded calves and small animals, and later cattle. "They endured physical hardship, hunger, and derision as their parents and siblings worked to toughen them for the circumcision which would mark their transition to adulthood" (1999: 126). Hodgson points out that the focus of most of the published accounts of Maasai age grades is invariably the attainment of the next chronological male age-grade status of *ilmurran* ("literally 'the circumcised ones' . . . a word most often glossed as warriors" [1999: 126]). As ilmurran they enacted the ideals of communal interests and shared masculine values; they were always in the company of one or more age-set members. They protected the interests of the community, accumulated livestock, and learned to manage their herds and pastoral economy. Although not permitted to marry, they could cohabit with unmarried girls, and continued to intermittently live with and eat with their mothers. Ilmurran could not progress to the next stage of *ilpayioni*, or junior elders, until the circumcision and initiation of another ilmurran age set. As ilpayioni they could marry, reside on their own homesteads, become parents, and consolidate their political and economic power. This stage emphasized individual interests as opposed to the communal values of ilmurran, and often placed older men in conflict with their actual and classificatory sons.

According to Hodgson, in contemporary Maasai communities, "age sets are still an organizing principle of masculine subjectivity and social relations and their fundamental apparatus has remained much the same: male circumcision is still a prerequisite to becoming an adult man, each age set is still given a unique name, and men advance from age grade to more senior age grade together. But the experience, attitudes, and practices of being an age set member have changed" (1999: 142). These changes are mediated through their understanding of economic and political relationships within Maasai communities, and the institutions of colonial and postcolonial states. Change is expressed by the Maasai in part through "the contradictions produced by their encounters with modernity" (Hodgson 1999: 144), including government policies of containment, economic and agricultural development projects, education, religious conversion, and most recently, with international tourism.

For example, where previous generations of elders rejected schooling and literacy in Swahili as characteristics associated with outsiders, not ethnic Maasai, currently education for men (and increasingly for women) is being embraced for its potential in providing access to employment, political alliances, and development resources. "Whatever their current survival strategy, Maasai men of all ages now assert a very modern dream: for the village, they want a hospital, a good school, a grinding machine, more cattle medicine, a better road, and cheap public transportation to the nearby district headquarters" (Hodgson 1999: 143). This vision of modernity is however continually renegotiated by men and women within the community, and their understandings of their relationships outside the community. "Ethnohistorical analysis through the prism of masculinity demonstrates . . . that modernity is never a totalizing process, but that the contradictory structures imposed by modernist interventions can be appropriated, reshaped, and even transcended by local people in novel, if painful ways" (Hodgson 1999: 144).

RETIREMENT LIFESTYLES

We pointed out earlier how the cultural construction of gender has been changing in North America. A significant change has also taken place in the construction of the category of senior citizen. Social Security, pensions, and improvements in medical care have made postretirement lifestyles a twenty-first-century institution. By law, there is no longer a mandatory retirement age and therefore no longer a clearly defined point at which an American moves into the category of senior citizen. A person need not retire at any particular age, but individuals may begin to consider themselves senior citizens, join the American Association of Retired Persons, and retire from their employment as early as age 55. The movement toward early retirement, which characterized the 1980s and 1990s, seems to be passing; the trend now is for people to continue to do some type of work while accessing Social Security and pension benefits. This financial security allows some Americans to "age in place" while others, upon their retirement, migrate elsewhere. Those Americans who are relocating after retiring are usually younger, more affluent, and healthier than older people in general.

Many retirement communities are self-contained and focus on leisure activities (Riekse and Holstege 1996: 252). These communities, whose residents must be over 55 years of age and which do not allow children to live there, resemble a Nyakyusa village of grandfathers. As a consequence, they have no schools and therefore pay no school taxes. Retirement communities are sometimes built around religious affiliation or ethnic identity. They may also be constructed on the basis of social class. Some of them consist of mobile homes, while others contain condominiums or private homes.

Among South Asians and East Asians in the U.S., the phenomenon of **step immigration** is growing. As middle-class, professional immigrants establish themselves in new locations and professions, they reunite their parents with their families. This economic security is not always valued by the now-elderly who are uprooted from their long-term homes and communities, and introduced to a new cultural setting without familiar patterns of language, food, and socializing.

As a result of **chain migration**, when earlier migrants attract later ones from the same community, clusters of individuals having long-term relations develop. A Finnish-American retirement community of this sort exists in southeast Florida, though very few other Finns live and work in this area (Stoller 1998). The community began to develop in 1940 when Finnish Americans living in New England and the Midwest, particularly Minnesota, first came to this area to retire. Some members of the community are second-generation Finnish Americans, while others were born in Finland and came to the United States after World War II. This is not a planned retirement community, like the ones described; rather, it consists of residents scattered through a large metropolitan area and linked through informal networks and organizations. The ethnic identity manifested by the Finnish Americans in this community is the basis for informal ties and the development of solidarity and support among these older people (Stoller 1998: 289). The community contains two "Finn Halls," which sponsor cultural and social programs. Other Finnish institutions include two churches that conduct weekly services in Finnish, a Finnish language newspaper, and a Finnish-American rest home. In the community, 123 merchants and service providers identify themselves as Finnish.

Retirement communities are not exclusive to the United States. They have begun to be established in Japan. Traditionally, elderly parents lived with the family of one of their children in the extended family form known as *dokyo*. In the rural areas, 62 percent of senior citizens still live this way while in the urban areas only 33 percent do so. Fuji-No-Sato is an example of a community or "life-care" facility, located near a small fishing and farming village, which is also an upper-class summer resort area (Kinoshita and Kiefer 1992). Those desiring to live there purchase a right to live in the community rather than an apartment. They must be 60 years of age, live independently, and pay an endowment fee when they move in and then a monthly operating fee. This community, located a day trip away from Tokyo, includes primarily individuals who remain there full-time, though a quarter of the individuals use their apartments as second homes. The well-educated inhabitants are from the middle or upper-middle class. The community is self-contained, consisting of two-story buildings in a wooded environment with a shuttle bus to the village, because most of the residents do not have cars. There is a residents' association, which all must join, and a wide variety of hobby groups; Christian groups, which hold prayer meetings; and volunteer groups. Gardening is a very important activity. Since the community is an unfamiliar, unstructured, newly constituted social situation with few guidelines for behavior, people's relationships are primarily formal in nature, which characterizes Japanese behavior in such unstructured situations. Japan is relatively homogeneous ethnically compared with the United States; therefore, ethnicity cannot serve as a basis for Japanese retirement communities. In this community social class can function in this way.

Expectations about care-giving of the elderly often reflect gender and social norms within society. In some agricultural societies, in the absence of pensions and state support for the elderly, people are financially dependent on their children who are, in a sense, their "Social Security." In rural communities of northern India that are organized around agricultural production, with patrilineal descent and virilocal postmarital residence, married sons are expected to care for their elderly parents in the household they inherit from their father. This contrasts with contemporary America, where care of elderly parents often becomes the responsibility of adult daughters; in families with an unmarried adult daughter there is a strong expectation that she will become the primary caregiver of elderly parents. As India becomes increasingly industrialized and urbanized with traditional extended households, virilocal residential patterns are also being modified. Neolocal postmarital residence is increasing as a younger generation leaves family farms to find occupations in towns and cities. "Old age homes" and institutionalized non-kin settings for the care of the elderly, commonplace in North America and Europe, are now emerging as a normalized but not highly valued option to "aging in place."

CONCLUSION: THE BODY
AND CONTEMPORARY ANTHROPOLOGY

An explosion of scholarly interest on the part of social scientists and historians about the human body over the past decade has taken place in print; it is a rare book or journal article in anthropology that does not from some perspective theorize or provide a local perspective on an aspect or function of the human body as social, historical, or cultural construction. This interest in contextualizing gender, age, sexuality, reproduction, life stages, physiology, the unborn, reproductive technologies, organs, even the very boundaries of life and death, as cultural issues, is new in some ways, and familiar to anthropologists in others.

New vocabularies and methodologies drawing from postmodernist perspectives encourage looking at ideas about various aspects of the body as historically contingent, normalized through political rather than scientific discourses. Understanding science as containing cultural norms and ideas calls into question a single body of knowledge about the natural world. The rejection of meta-narratives, or universalizing explanation, for sociopolitical phenomena is now a basic part of the anthropological canon. And yet there is something familiar about this "new" way of thinking about science and the human body. Its dependence upon understanding the historical and cultural logic embedded in all systems of knowledge, through the documentation of local voices and ideas, would be familiar to and consistent with the comparative foundations of cultural anthropology.

SUMMARY

- Age and sex are the most common bases for distinction between social roles in every society.
- Categories based on age and sex do not simply build upon biological differences, but are defined by culture.
- Anthropologists distinguish between sex, which is physical differentiation between male and female, and gender, the culture-specific ideas constructed around the understanding of these differences.
- With the growth of the feminist movement within the past thirty years, many anthropologists of both sexes began to pay attention to female as well as male roles and to the female as well as the male point of view of society.
- The cultural expressions of gender vary from society to society. For example, the Wogeo believe that men and women are very different and live separate and complementary lives though they come together to reproduce.
- In many societies menstrual blood is believed to be polluting to males. Particular spatial areas may be associated respectively with males and females.
- Many societies recognize "third" and "fourth" genders, and accommodate into their societies men or women who choose to live as the opposite gender.
- The feminist movement of the 1970s and affirmative action legislation raised both female and male consciousness and brought about the transformations that we see today in the occupational and legal expectations of people around gender and sexual identity.

- The shift in gender roles described for industrialized societies is in no way an inevitable progression through which all modernizing societies will pass.
- Masculinity, like femininity, is a series of cultural constructions that are not based simply on biological differences. It is constructed, designed, and upheld by a system of beliefs and attitudes.
- The macho man as a symbol of masculinity is beginning to be rejected by a younger generation of Hispanic men.
- Every society has terms for different age groups, but the number of terms varies. In our own society, we use such terms as *infant, toddler, child, adolescent, adult*, and *senior citizen*.
- When the age categories are formally named and recognized and crosscut the entire society, they are referred to as age grades. The Maasai, pastoralists in Kenya and Tanzania, have age grades for men and complementary participation in the life cycle for women.
- Retirement communities, populated entirely by aging individuals and couples, are becoming more commonplace in many societies around the world.
- The anthropological study of gender and aging is part of a growing contemporary interest in theorizing and documenting the wide variety of social practices focusing on the human body.

SUGGESTED READINGS

Nanda, Serena. *Gender Diversity: Crosscultural Variations.* Prospect Heights, IL: Waveland Press, 2000. How sex/gender diversities are understood in seven different cultures.

Lamb, Sarah. *White Saris and Sweet Mangoes: Aging, Gender, and Body in North India.* Berkeley: University of California Press, 2000. Based on fieldwork in West Bengal, India, a detailed ethnography focusing on how women in rural communities view themselves, their families, and their aging bodies.

Robertson, Jennifer, ed. *Same-Sex Cultures and Sexualities: An Anthropological Reader.* Malden, MA: Blackwell Publishing, 2004. The multiple chapters and case studies in this edited volume explore same-sex sexualities from the perspectives of theory, language, transsexuality, and globalization.

SUGGESTED WEBSITES

www.who.int/topics/gender/en/. The website of the World Health Organization includes multiple entries on international health issues from a gendered perspective.

www.aarp.org/. The website of the American Association of Retired Persons (AARP) outlines the political and economic issues that engage people over 50 in anticipation of retirement.

www.civilrights.org/issues/glbt/. News and updates on political issues and movements on gay, lesbian, bisexual, and transgendered (GLBT) issues in the United States.

Chapter 8

The Economic Organization of Societies

Production, Distribution, and Consumption

THE ECONOMIC ORGANIZATION of a society is the way in which that society, in a regularized fashion, goes about providing the material goods and services it needs to reproduce itself. Economic organization is a cultural construction that operates according to sets of cultural rules. Rules relating to economic organization are similar to rules that govern the other aspects of culture. Individuals may interpret the rules to their own advantage. In economic terms, this is known as **maximizing**. Human and animal labor, man-made technology, and natural resources are brought together for the provisioning of society. In small-scale societies economic behavior operated to a large extent within the context of the kinship structure. In such situations, rules governing who owns the resources, how work is organized, who uses or eats the product, and so forth, were governed by kinship rules. As societies expanded in scale, economic behavior was separated from the realm of kinship, and economic institutions became more and more delimited as separate systems. Today, the world can be said to be a single economic system as a consequence of globalization. We will show how the societies we will be discussing in this chapter have become part of the world system, in one way or another. Though in this chapter we deal with economic organization separately from political organization, the subject of the next chapter, the two topics are intertwined. Economic decisions always have political implications, and political decisions likewise have economic implications, as reflected in the term **political economy**. For purposes of analysis, we will consider economic organization in terms of production, distribution or exchange, and consumption.

PRODUCTION

Production is the process whereby a society uses the tools and energy sources at its disposal and the labor of its people and domesticated animals to create the goods necessary for supplying society as an ongoing entity. **Technology** is that part of culture which enables people to exploit their environment. Technology encompasses the manufacture and use of tools according to a set of cultural rules. Tools relate to and impact on other aspects of culture. Artifacts have important symbolic meanings. Elaborate yam houses and canoes in the Trobriand Islands are significant symbols of chiefly power. Not only the finished object, but the process of manufacture also has religious and symbolic meaning.

Today, the anthropology of technology includes the study of tool manufacturing and use not only in small-scale and in prehistoric societies but also in modern industrial societies, despite the differences in the types of tools. Hence, production design and development has recently become a subject of anthropological research (see Suchman 2001: 163–78; Aronson, Bell, and Vermeer 2001: 179, 193).

Hunting and Gathering

For the greatest time of their existence on earth, some 5 million years, human beings subsisted by means of a combination of hunting wild animals; gathering roots, seeds, and plants; and fishing and collecting sea life along the shores. This mode of exploitation of the natural environment is referred to by anthropologists as foraging or hunting and gathering. It represented "a mode of existence characterized by the absence of direct human control over the reproduction of exploited species and little or no control of . . . the behavior . . . of food resources" (Panter-Brick et al. 2001: 2). Hunting-and-gathering as a subsistence base represented an amalgam of traits including individual autonomy, regardless of gender and age, extreme egalitarianism, and a relatively loose attachment to the group as a consequence of mobility. This enables the hunters and gatherers to readily adapt and alter ways under changing circumstances (Kent 1996: 13–14).

By the early twentieth century, when anthropologists began to do fieldwork, they discovered that societies dependent primarily on hunting and gathering were found only in a range of marginal environments. The Inuit (or Eskimo) of the Arctic region, the Pygmies of the Ituri Forest in Zaire in Central Africa, the San (or Bushmen) of the Kalahari Desert in southern Africa, and the Washo of the Great Basin on the California-Nevada border are examples of societies that formerly depended exclusively on hunting and gathering for their subsistence. These hunting and gathering societies occupied very different kinds of environments with very different flora and fauna. Nevertheless, several generalizations can be made about their mode of subsistence. All these societies had sparse populations with very low population densities. The plants and animals they depended on were scarce or abundant according to the seasons. Migratory animal species were absent for much of the year and then present for a short time in superabundance. Similarly, nuts, fruits, tubers, and seeds ripened during a particular time of the year, at which point they needed to be harvested. They often processed resources at special-purpose field camps and brought these processed resources back to their base camps to be stored (Rowley-Conwy 2001: 41). In order to deal with variations in availability, hunters and gatherers typically had to exploit all the resources present in their environments. Variation in the diet of hunters and gatherers follows latitude, which clearly relates to climate. The degree of dependence on vegetable food declines as one moves farther from the equator. The percentage of meat rises until one gets to the far north where meat constitutes almost 100 percent of the diet (Kuhn and Steiner 2001: 103–104; see also Jenike 2001). There is more diversity nearer the equator where birds, small mammals, and reptiles complemented the vegetable diet.

Hunter-gatherer societies followed a migratory cycle because it was necessary to be in particular areas to harvest what had become available in those areas at that time. While there were regular sites to which they returned every year, they did not have year-round, permanent village settlements. Larger agglomerations of individuals came together when greater amounts of food were available in one locale. This was usually the case when some single food resource was abundant (migratory caribou, spawning salmon, ripening pine nuts, and the like). Religious festivals were frequently held at such times. At other times of the year, small dispersed groups of one or more nuclear families migrated as a unit.

The technology of hunting-and-gathering people utilized natural materials taken directly from the environment, such as stone, bone, wood, and sinew. Manufacturing techniques were relatively simple. Hunters and gatherers had an intimate knowledge of the environment, including animal behavior and the growing patterns of plants. For example, the Inuit hunted seal in many different ways, depending upon climatic conditions, seasons, and seal species. Every part of the animals captured was used for food or the manufacture of a whole variety of goods. In hunting-and-gathering societies, there were no specialists whose only occupation was to make tools. Everyone made his or her own tools. Children were taught how to manufacture tools as part of their education.

Task differentiation was primarily between males and females, with men hunting and fishing while women gathered plants, collected shellfish, and took care of domestic tasks, such as clothing manufacture, food preparation, and child care. Children began to learn tasks at a young age, and at puberty assumed adult economic roles. Successful hunters and fishermen, who excelled at their tasks, were accorded respect and prestige, and their advice was often sought. Hunting-and-gathering societies tended not to have social class divisions. Nor did they usually rank individuals as higher or lower in social status.

The environment itself changes as a result of human exploitation. Ecological balance is altered as people harvest those species they utilize. In some societies, an effort was made to limit exploitation of the environment by imposing some controls on the hunting of certain species or animals of young ages. In other cases, the environment became permanently degraded. For example, centuries ago in New Guinea, fire was used as an aid in hunting, and as a consequence the primary forests were destroyed and replaced by grassland, totally altering the ecosystem and the fauna of the area. Today, in the United States, we are suffering the consequences of having overfished halibut and cod on the Grand Banks off Nova Scotia and on the New England seacoast.

Hunting-and-gathering populations were never isolates, trading with other hunters and gatherers. They began to have long-term exchange relationships with agriculturalists and pastoralists of the same or different ethnic groups once these other modes of production developed (Headland and Reid 1989; Bird-David 1992; Shott 1992). Before the present political upheavals, the Twa of Rwanda were hunters who were part of a hierarchical, caste-like structure. They exchanged the products of the hunt with Hutu agriculturalists and Tutsi pastoralists. Archeological evidence supports the antiquity of this kind of interaction. The Dobe San sites on the edge of the Kalahari Desert show remains of ceramics, iron, and cattle from the eighth to the eleventh century (Layton 2001: 297).

Although most hunting-and-gathering societies were egalitarian, the Kwakiutl and other Northwest Coast societies of British Columbia were an exception because of the presence of ranked differences. Their environmental resources were so rich, particularly in sea life, that they were able to support a much denser population than is usual in hunting-and-gathering societies. They had permanent winter villages with wooden plank houses, though they migrated from these villages at other times of the year to exploit particular resources. They had full-time craft specialization. Their political system was more complex and they had inherited titles and chiefly positions. There are several reasons for this series of differences between Northwest Coast societies, and hunting-and-gathering societies in other parts of the world. The rich environment of the Northwest Coast provided both mammals and birds; many species of edible plants; numerous varieties of fish, shellfish, and sea mammals; and lastly, but importantly, the several species of salmon that annually spawned in the rivers. The preservation and storage of this wide range of products enabled them to produce surpluses; maintain large, permanent village communities; and support a more complex culture. The development of large, oceangoing plank canoes, for example, among the Nuchanulth (Nootka), who lived on the west coast of Vancouver Island, enabled social interchanges and exchange of goods to take place over wide areas. They were also extremely useful in raiding and warfare, the hunting of sea mammals, and fishing for various kinds of ocean fish. How they utilized the surplus produced for social purposes such as holding potlatches will be discussed below.

How Contemporary Hunters and Gatherers Have Adapted to the Modern World

Hunting and gathering as an economic endeavor and a way of life still continues today. The environment is still an important source of subsistence for people in Alaska, northern Canada, and Siberia. But even in these areas, it is always combined with other kinds of economic activities, in mixed economies (Hitchcock and Biesele 2000: 6). Foraging provides subsistence as well as market-oriented items to be sold for cash, which is used to purchase manufactured items. This modified mode of subsistence is always integrated, to a greater or lesser degree, into national and international economies. People who still pursue a hunting-and-gathering mode of subsistence as a part-time endeavor use such modern tools as rifles, steel traps, and snowmobiles. Today, foragers depend on human labor, are closely attached to the land, have common property resource management systems, and have a worldview that combines nature with spiritual phenomena (Hitchcock and Biesele 2000: 7). Since mineral and petroleum deposits have been found in some areas where foragers traditionally lived, they have had to cope with the problem of whether and to what degree they will accept commercial development of these resources, while promoting conservation and the survival of their ecosystem. Though the Kwakiutl and Nuchanulth still fish, their catch of halibut or salmon goes to the cannery or fish market. Then it can be sold locally, or it is sent to other parts of the world since they are now an integral part of the Canadian economy and beyond that, the world economy. Most of the food they eat is purchased at the store with money they have earned. Among the Tlingit, subsistence fishing, done in a different location than commercial fishing, and seal hunting are still pursued and remain an important sector of the economy (Dombrowski 2001: 85,105; Thornton 2008).

In the early 1970s, the government of Zaire tried to sedentarize the Mbuti, who are hunters and gatherers, by settling them in villages along major roads, and turning them into agriculturalists, giving them seed and machetes with which to cultivate their own fields. This plan soon failed and the Mbuti moved back into the Ituri forest to continue their nomadic hunting-and-gathering life (Ichikawa 2000: 263–64). They continue to have a *kpara* (patron-client relationship) with neighboring agricultural villagers, bartering meat for commodities that are today manufactured around the world. The Mbuti also have begun a commercial meat trade whereby they sell meat to town dwellers. The meat not only provides animal protein but is valued by the town people because it is seen as a source of "wild power" not obtained from fish or domestic animals (Ichikawa 2000: 269). In addition, the Mbuti also exchange day labor for food, beer, iron implements, women's cloth, and so on. According to Ichikawa, "Although the Mbuti have contacts with the market economy, their own economy remains 'uncaptured' by the nationwide monetary economy" (2000: 275).

The Misstassini Cree of eastern Canada still spend part of the winter season in multifamily communal dwellings in the forest, trapping animals with modern steel traps. The skins of the marten, lynx, mink, and weasel they trap end up in the fur markets of New York. When protesters demonstrated against the wearing of fur coats because it represented what they saw as the needless killing of fur-bearing animals, this directly affected the livelihood of Cree families.

This controversy is similar to the Inuit problem with animal rights groups who are against the "large-scale industrial" harvesting of seals, particularly harp seal and hooded seal pups in the North Atlantic. These groups argue that the Inuit should use traditional technology and should restrict use of the products of the hunt to subsistence only. The Inuit argue that their tradition centers on maintaining a way of life in the same environment as in the past. To be Inuit today means to maintain traditions, such as sharing the products of the hunt within kinship networks. Traditional religious beliefs and practices can be maintained within an economic system that includes modern hunting equipment as well as other products of modern technology. They sell part of their harvest to purchase store-bought items (Hovelsrud-Broda 1997). In an even further extension of globalization into the Inuit hunting-and-gathering economy, Inuit sell the right to hunt walruses to white trophy hunters at $6,000 a piece. Inuit guides lead the trophy hunter up to the walrus, who dispatches it with one well-placed shot, carefully avoiding the tusks and the head, which the white hunter takes. The Inuit crew butchers the carcass in the traditional manner, intestines and all, to be stored and eaten throughout the winter by the entire Inuit community (*New York Times Magazine*, August 25, 2002).

The Australian Aborigines, who were hunters and gatherers, held communal title over access to and use of biological resources, that is, the plant and animal species used for food and medicines. This "traditional knowledge" of Australian plants has been used in the commercialization of those plants often without recognition of their contribution. This information on the Australian Aboriginal use of plants for particular purposes was sometimes published by anthropologists and others. The Aborigines have "demanded the right to control access over that knowledge and the resources" (Biber-Klemm et al. 2006: 105,108). For example, the Duboisia plant is currently being cultivated in northern New South Wales and southern Queensland in order to produce a sedative for use with motion sickness without any recompense to the indigenous people. There is even question about whether they agreed to its commercialization (Biber-Klemm 2006: 56). "Smokebush" grows in Western Australia and its healing properties were known to Aborigines over a long period of time. The western Australia government gave the U.S. National Cancer Institute a license to collect these plants, which were later found to be useful against the HIV virus, and this discovery was patented by the latter. Subsequently, AMrad-Victoria, an Australian company, was given a worldwide license to develop the patent, and later to develop the anti-AIDS drug. The Australian Aborigines were not acknowledged financially or otherwise "for their role in having first discovered the healing properties of smokebush" (Biber-Klemm et al. 2006: 97). To prevent this injustice from occurring in the future, the Australians later developed a model contract to be used in negotiations on access to traditional knowledge in which benefits are shared. It is their attempt to integrate indigenous customs into their modern legal system.

In addition to plant life, land rights are another issue for the Aborigines. The contemporary Aboriginal owners of the land comprising the Kakadu National Forest are the direct descendants of people who have lived in the area for 50,000 years. Some of them live in the park while others live nearby. The park land is owned by twelve clans. "Historically, tourism has been seen as an intrusion and the traditional owners have mostly been passive beneficiaries . . . via shared ownership of tourism properties and as beneficiaries of land rent payments and a share of park fees provided for in park lease agreements" (Wellings 2007: 94). Today, they are much more interested in engaging in "ecotourism" to generate more income, for employment opportunities for young people so they can remain on the land. Culturally based tourism is seen as maintaining interest in and valuing of their cultural heritage, as well as passing it on to their children. The Board of Management, established in 1989, and which plays an important role in the management of the park, contains a majority of indigenous members who jointly manage the park with the Australian government. Its goal is to protect the park as well as promote it as a tourist attraction with natural features, as well as cultural attractions, while the indigenous population continue to be able to use their land for hunting, fishing, and ceremonies, and to continue to hold private their sacred stories, sites, and rituals (Wellings 2007, 95–100). In Australia, the traditional practice of controlled burning has been incorporated into the management of Kakadu and Uluru National Parks, and the park rangers have reached a degree of cross-cultural understanding that enables them to accept the fact that "traditional owners had retained the necessary skills . . . [and] applied them systematically" (Layton 2001: 311).

Agriculture

The domestication of plants and their use for subsistence, beginning some 8,000 to 10,000 years ago, represented a significant transformation of human society. This change depended upon the development of a new corpus of information by means of which human beings acquired much greater control of the environment and, in turn, transformed it in a much more significant way than had been done by hunters and gatherers. Social groups were tied to territories differently than they had been with hunting and gathering. With a shift to agriculture, social groups utilized a smaller area, and population was more dense and concentrated in hamlets and villages. In the same manner as hunting-and-gathering societies, agriculturalists operate on the basis of a seasonal cycle, especially where there is a marked climatic difference between winter and summer or rainy and dry seasons. The agricultural year is usually divided into planting time, growing time, and harvest. Even when they are under the threat of starvation, agricultural people must restrain themselves from eating their seed or they will have no crop during the following year. The factors to be considered in an examination of different economic systems based on agriculture include how people utilize their labor, how they work the land, how they use water resources, which crops they grow, and whether they grow crops for their own subsistence or for sale in the market.

Horticulture

Throughout South America and Melanesia, **horticulture** is the mode of production. It is based upon crops that are grown in gardens through vegetative propagation, using a part of the plant itself, rather than through the planting of seeds. Systems of production based on horticulture vary in terms of the number of crops grown in a garden, the length of the fallow period, and whether the water necessary for plant growth is controlled. A continuum of New Guinea societies reflects greater and greater complexity of horticultural techniques for cultivating gardens and achieving higher crop yields and more permanent gardens. The simplest form of horticulture, known as **swidden**, or **shifting cultivation**, involves making gardens by burning down the forest and planting the garden in the ashes, which acts as a fertilizer. No other means of fertilizing is used. Because the soil is rapidly exhausted, a new garden in a new location must be planted every few years. Gardens contain many kinds of plants on a single plot. A digging stick was often the only tool used. This type of horticulture is supplemented by hunting and the collection of wild plants. In lowland New Guinea, the sago palm, a wild plant whose pith is used for food, is an important supplement to what is produced in the gardens. For example, as much as 90 percent of the diet of the Tor in western New Guinea may come from wild sago. Each Tor tribe has its own territory, with boundaries known by all. Their sparse population makes them like hunting-and-gathering societies, though they live in villages surrounded by their yam gardens.

The Abelam of New Guinea illustrate an intermediate type of horticulture. Many varieties of short yams, taro, sweet potatoes, and a range of other plants are grown in gardens that are used several times and then allowed to remain fallow and uncultivated. Each lineage owns garden land, which is distributed by the headman to families. The Abelam also grow a special species of long yam, which may be eight to ten feet long and is used in ceremonial exchange, described later in this chapter. Its cultivation involves special techniques such as mounding the soil to create a plant bed and erecting trellises for vines. Soil around the growing point may be carefully loosened to allow the tuber to grow. Abelam villages are much larger and more permanent than those of the Tor.

The most complex forms of horticulture in New Guinea are found in the mountains of the central highlands. There, people like the Enga use a variety of labor-intensive techniques. The gardens may be used for a generation or more. Clans own land used for hunting and fishing, while arable land within clan territory is owned by individual families. Each garden consists of a regular series of mounds formed from soil and mulch, separated by ditches, and used only for sweet potato cultivation. These single-crop gardens are separated from mixed gardens in which most other crops are grown. The yields from the mounded gardens of the Enga are considerably greater than the yields from the two types of horticulture described earlier. The Enga number over 150,000, so there is considerable pressure for land, and Enga clans may fight one another over land. The complex exchange system of the Enga, which will be described below, is linked to their great productivity. The horticultural systems just described depend upon rainfall for water. However, root crop cultivation can also involve water control. The Dani of the Grand Valley in western New Guinea have used dams, ditches, and drainage systems to turn a natural swamp into a productive cultivation area.

Just as hunting-and-gathering peoples have intimate knowledge of the plant and animal species that they exploit, horticulturalists display an extensive knowledge of soils, food plants, and cultivation techniques. This practical know-how is frequently combined with magical practices performed during the process of production. In general, in societies with horticulture, the land cultivated is usually owned by clans. Individual families, members of the clan owning the land, plant and harvest from their own plots. There is increased competition for good land, and warfare was frequently waged by one clan to drive another from its land.

Grain Agriculture

In the more temperate areas of several continents of the world, agriculturalists use swidden agriculture to grow maize in the New World, millet and sorghum in Africa, and rice in Asia. In preparing fields for growing grain, the same technique of cutting down trees and burning off brush is used as in swidden horticulture. There is also a long fallow period after several plantings. The only source of water is rainfall. Agricultural societies in much of Europe and Asia growing grain depended on a technology that involved crop rotation, the use of the plow drawn by draft animals, and animal manure as fertilizer. Wheat, rye, and barley were the predominant crops in the Old World. The use of draft animals required raising crops such as hay to feed those animals.

Millennia ago, grain agriculture, which was dependent on the use of elaborate irrigation systems, was developed. It was more extensive than the type of water control practiced by the Dani. An enormous input of labor was required to create the necessary artificial environment of lakes, ponds, dikes, and terraces that made up the irrigation systems. The advent of such systems in Mesopotamia and China was associated with the development of urban civilizations and states. Increased productivity per acre of land, the basis for increasing cultural complexity, depended on several factors. Establishing elaborate irrigation systems initially required great outputs of labor; maintaining them also requires a certain amount of labor. The crops on which people subsisted also vary in terms of their storage potential, which affects how crop surplus will be utilized for social purposes. The nature of the technology is also an important factor. Steel axes and machetes are more efficient than stone axes. Animal labor is more efficient than human labor, except in places of high population density, such as China. Machines and the mechanization of agriculture, as has occurred in the United States and elsewhere, represent a quantum jump in efficiency and therefore in productivity.

Agriculture in Today's World

Each technological advance produced its own set of problems. Mechanized agriculture, for example, has resulted in overproduction and the need to store vast agricultural surpluses; the use of chemical pesticides has led to widespread pollution of soil and water. In the United States, fewer farmers grow more and more food, and the family farm has become a corporation and may even be listed on the stock exchange.

Throughout the world, people in rural areas have been affected by the penetration of globalization and new international division of labor. There is an international flow of goods and of technological information and new political forms that serve as challenges to local ways of life. The effects of globalization may include changes in local political structures and in gender relations, sometimes resulting in more economic power for women, as well as changes in economic formations. But local people have responded in a variety of ways and such connections do not always mean a loss of local power. In the New Guinea highlands today, subsistence horticultural practices are supplemented by the extensive cash-crop production of coffee, while in the lowlands and the Bismarck Archipelago, coconuts are grown for oil to manufacture soap.

Among the Asante, an ethnic group with matrilineal descent dominating the forest area of Ghana in West Africa, both men and women actively farm. Men grow coca, a cash crop that is exported. Both men and women participate in commercial food production for Ghanaian cities and to provide food, including tomatoes, cassava, eggplant, plantains, and yams, for those farmers who specialize in cocoa and other cash-crop production (Clark 1994: 253–70). There are also centers where food crops, locally produced, are marketed. Women dominate the farming and trade of food crops and control the marketplaces. The flexible market system with its many marketplaces also provides a market for secondary crops and craft products that are "fall-back" options for the periods when crop production suffers in bad years. Women farmers, suffering from gender disparities in resource allocation, restricted from the planting of cocoa, and discouraged from expanding their farms, have diversified into food processing and trading (Clark 2000: 259–60). Female farmers and traders gain income from trading and are able to demonstrate their personal autonomy in the agricultural and commercial sectors.

Throughout Java, the colonial system emphasized the production of products for export even within the sector of peasant subsistence agriculture. In the postcolonial period, this involved engagement with the "development" plans of whatever political regime was in power. The To Pamona of Central Sulawesi had been forced by the Dutch colonial government to move from their hilltop hamlets, where they practiced swidden cultivation of rice, to narrow valleys to develop irrigated or wet rice agriculture. Though they were engaged in a market economy, they still maintained their earlier multifamily households, feasting pattern, and gift exchange (Schrauwers 1999: 105). This limited capital accumulation and resulted in a "Janus-faced" economy, which is seen by the Indonesian state as hindering development.

Even after decades, some indigenous people in Brazil are still struggling to guarantee their land rights and territories. Multinational companies are now interested in indigenous knowledge of plants that might have commercial value, especially for the development of prescription drugs. The case of the Wapichana Indians is an example of this type of exploitation (Avila 2001 as quoted in Ramos 2006). Clovis Ambrosio, their leader, is quoted as saying, "[W]e use a plant named *cunami* for fishing. We also produce medicines extracted from a tree known as *tibiru* or greenheart . . . a chemist named Conrad Gorinsk[y], the son of a Wapichana woman and a German man researched the *cunami* and the *tibiru*, while promising to help our communities with medicine. He never did. . . . Mr. Conrad Gorinsk[y] has patented the cunaniol and the *rupununi* in the United States, Europe and Great Britain" (Ramos 2005: 254). In Brazil, this kind of exploitation of the plant knowledge of indigenous people is now being referred to as "biopiracy" (Ramos 2005: 255). In contrast, the Kayapo of Brazil have made an agreement to market Brazil nut oil, a native product. According to Nugent, "participation in the commodification of previously noncommercial products provides the Kayapo with income" (2006: 277).

Animal Domestication

In most areas, the domestication of animals followed soon after the domestication of plants. In the Old World, a wide variety of animal species were domesticated, most of which furnished meat and milk. Some animals, such as the horse, donkey, bullock, and buffalo, were also used for transportation. The hair of others, such as sheep and goats, was woven into cloth. In the New World the only significant animal domesticates were the carnelids, such as the llama and alpaca. The animals were selectively bred to enhance those characteristics that make them more controllable and more useful to humans, and to eliminate characteristics such as intractability. Humans have shaped the biological characteristics of these animals through the process of domestication. At the same time, pastoral societies adapted to the needs of their animals, particularly in the migration cycle. This way of life was more widely practiced in the past than in the present. However, as we shall see below, when governments try to end nomadic pastoralism they face opposition.

Societies that are completely dependent upon their domesticated animals are known as **nomadic pastoral societies**. Only rarely do they cultivate. This specialized mode of subsistence developed from an earlier economy that included both domesticated plants and animals. Nomadic pastoral societies, with one or two exceptions, were found in the Old World, particularly in arid zones. Sheep, goats, camels, horses, cattle, yaks, water buffalo, or reindeer constituted the basic herd animals for these societies. All these animals are social, not solitary, in their habits. In most cases one or two types of animals formed the basis for herds. Nomadic pastoralists depended on their herd animals for a range of products. Daily yields of milk and milk products such as cheese were central to their diet. From earliest times, live animals, wool, and milk products were exchanged by the pastoralists with sedentary people for essentials, such as tea, sugar, and flour. Since wealth was measured in numbers of animals in the herd, pastoralists were loath to kill animals for their meat alone; therefore, this was done only on special occasions.

The animal species upon which particular nomadic pastoral societies depend was related to the nature of the environment that was exploited. Some species, such as camels, are best adapted to arid desert areas, and others, such as horses, to well-watered grassy plains. Some can withstand extremes of temperature, while others cannot. Some, such as goats, do best in steeper mountain environments, while others, such as water buffalo, can live only in flat, swampy lowlands. The way of life of nomadic pastoralists involved seasonal movement or migration in a regular pattern from one place to another. The community and its herds might move from summer to winter pasturage or from wet to dry locations. In their seasonal movements, pastoral nomads resemble hunters and gatherers, particularly those who hunt large herds of migratory animals, such as the caribou. However, there is a crucial difference in that hunters followed the migratory herd wherever the herd went in its natural migration, whereas the herds that belong to the nomadic pastoralists follow the people who herd them.

The most widespread form of nomadic pastoralism involves the herding of sheep and goats. Excellent examples are the Basseri, Bakhtiari, and Qashqai pastoral nomads in Iran. Their migration cycle takes them from winter pasturage in the southern lowlands, roughly at sea level, to summer pasturage in the Zagros Mountains, at an altitude of 10,000 feet. The sheep herded by the Basseri are so adapted to the migratory cycle that they can survive neither the cold winters of the mountains nor the torrid summers of the lowlands. In addition to sheep and goats, the Bakhtiari have a species of cow in their herds that is small and agile and can make the arduous migration. Though most nomadic pastoral societies have this as their dominant mode of production, combinations are frequently found. For example, the Bakhtiari practice some agriculture and hunting and gathering in addition to nomadic pastoralism.

Nomadic pastoralism in Mongolia depended on a mix of horses, sheep, goats, camels, and sometimes cattle. Before the revolution, pasture land was held in common by kin, though its use was sometimes controlled by lords or monastic leaders. Later, pasture land was controlled by the collectives and the state planning bureaus, which also owned herds, machinery, and the like. Herders have always dwelt in yurts or gers, using dried dung for fuel. All the different animals herded are milked, with the milk being used to make an alcoholic drink, *kumis*, and a great variety of cheeses. Flour, tea, tobacco, and other products came from the outside as a consequence of trade in pastoral products. During the period of the collectives, control of animals, herd movements, and pasture use as well as marketing was done by the collective, and people received wages and then pensions.

The desert zone of the Arabian plateau was inhabited by an Arabic-speaking group, the Rwala Bedouin. In the past, they were mainly herders of camels, but they also had some sheep, goats, and horses. The camels were herded by men and boys, often at some distance from the nomadic camp. The products of the camel included milk and hair, but even more important, the animal was a mode of transportation. The Rwala bred camels for sale to sedentary oasis dwellers and to transporters who needed the animals for long-distance caravan trade. The seasonal cycle of the Rwala involved moving into the desert in the spring, when available water has allowed grass cover to grow. As the year progressed, the climate became drier, and the Rwala moved closer to the desert oasis sources of water. Since goats and sheep as well as camels were herded, the Rwala needed to be mindful of the water requirements of these different animal species.

Not all people who had animals were nomadic pastoralists. Some domesticated animals foraged in the bush for their food but returned to places of permanent human settlement at night. The mithan, a type of domesticated ox found in Southeast Asia among the Nagas and Chin of Myanmar, was allowed to roam freely, depending completely upon forage for food. Only its meat was used, and then only on ceremonial occasions. In contrast, in Europe, the dairy cow, a relative of the mithan, was kept in a stall and fed with fodder, or on ranges in enclosed pastures, and was milked daily. The dairy cow and the ox were part of the mixed farming complex in Europe and North America. In the American west, cattle were allowed to range freely, being rounded up once or twice a year, calves were branded, and adult animals moved to market to be sold and used for meat.

The Marsh Arabs of Iraq inhabited the swampy area at the confluence of the Tigris and Euphrates rivers. They relied completely on their herds of water buffalo. Since they depended solely on the buffalo, they had to trade the dairy products produced from the milk of their buffalo for grain and other foodstuffs from sedentary peoples, who are culturally the same except for mode of subsistence.

Can Nomadic Pastoralism Be Maintained Today?

Most nomadic pastoral societies have undergone great changes under political pressure from their national governments. As a result of wars, revolutions, and famines, their way of life has been transformed. Sheep and goat herders in Iran and Syria no longer migrate with their herds. Instead, they move their animals and their belongings from one pasture site to another by truck, rather than using traditional draft animals such as camels or donkeys. They need not even set up camp near a water source, since tank trucks bring water to wherever they set up camp, which may even be next to a highway. The Rwala no longer raise camels, since trucks have replaced the camel as the principal means of transportation in the desert.

The homeland of the Marsh Arabs became a major battleground of the Iran-Iraq war in the 1980s and was a center of military activity during the Gulf War. The nomadic groups of Iran were forcibly sedentarized by Reza Shah in the 1920s in order to exercise political control over them, resulting in the loss of their herds and livelihood. Migration was resumed after the abdication of Reza Shah in 1941. Sedentarization was attempted again by Mohammad Shah, Reza's son, in the 1960s, with the same disastrous results. There is no information on how the nomadic tribes of Iran have fared since the Khomeini revolution. Since nomadic pastoral peoples usually occupy marginal lands that are not suitable for agriculture, when they are forced to sedentarize, usually for political reasons, we often find them returning to nomadic pastoralism when political pressure is relaxed.

In 1921, the Mongolian Revolutionary Party seized control of the state with the support of Soviet troops. Monastery herds, which were huge, were distributed to families. Collectivization of the pastoral sector did not occur until the 1950s (Humphrey and Sneath 1999). Collectivization involved the detailed establishment of joint work teams, the organization of herd movement, the introduction of new breeds of sheep, and the production of hay in some areas for use as fodder (Humphrey and Sneath 1999: 110). After the Soviet state fell, Mongolia held elections in 1992 and the communists lost control of the government. Privatization of the herds had begun in 1990 with the adoption of the Mongolian privatization law. The number of herders has increased since that time, though the quality of livestock has fallen as a result of climatic disasters such as drought over the past few years, resulting in a return to a subsistence economy. District heads try to control the "adminstration of pastoralism" but with little success. There are companies that have flocks, in part, cared for by individuals who receive wages and advances for products produced. However, many individuals had their own herd, and belonged to no organization. Because of the extensive availability of pasture and the low rate of stock per pasture, Mongolians have been able to avoid degradation of the environment, which remains relatively unpolluted. They still keep large herds of horses that are not marketed but kept for prestige purposes. Herders today are better able to plan their migrations because of their knowledge of how different grass species grow and the behavior of animals. There is now much more economic and class diversity in Mongolia, but the multimillionaire who has made his money from entreprenurial activity may still live next to a very poor household (Humphrey and Sneath 1999: 110, 114, 132–33).

The Nentsy remain a nomadic pastoral people, dependent on reindeer herding in western Siberia, in an area of tundra where the Ob River empties into the Arctic and agriculture is not possible. After the revolution, they were collectivized but only to a degree, since the Soviet officials allowed the Nentsy to keep private herds. After the collapse of the Soviet economic system, their economy reverted to privatization and regional economic marketing. Many other reindeer pastoralists in Siberia have undergone economically difficult times after the Soviet collapse, but the Nentsy have thrived. They sell not only the meat of the reindeer, but also the antlers while they are in "velvet." Newly grown antlers are cut in summer, when bony substance is not yet present. Velvet reindeer antlers are rich in amino acids, and are used to make medications that "strengthen the human immune system and . . . for Asian clients, increasing strength, improving the blood, and building masculine virility" (Stammler 2005: 306). China and Korea are the primary markets.

When reindeer are slaughtered for the market by the Nentsy, knives are used and there is no ritual associated with it. According to Stammler, the ethnographer, "When slaughtered for sale, it becomes a commodity, becomes alienable and is treated as an object in the market sphere of exchange" (2005: 176). The sale of reindeer meat is a source of income, permitting them to buy commodities they need—flour, tea, fuel, and guns and ammunition for hunting, and so forth. Reindeer slaughtered for subsistence are lined up facing east and strangled, so that not a single drop of blood falls to earth. If the reindeer has been sacrificed, a short speech is addressed to the spirit. First the owner of the deer drinks the warm blood, then the men of the camp share a meal of raw meat and warm blood, finally the women and children share in the meal (Stammler 2005: 173–78). Though the Nentsy are active participants in an impersonal market economy, they still retain their own emphasis on communal reciprocity and exchange. Wealthy families with large herds of reindeer continue to provide leadership for the Nentsy as a whole. Each Nenets family is still strongly dependent on other families for help, labor, and food.

The Organization of Work

As Durrenberger and Marti note, "[L]abor is embedded in all relationships from kinship and house-hold organization to non-kin social networks, to market based employee/employer relationships to political relationships" (2006: 1). How are work organized and labor recruited in a particular social order? The organization of work in a society relates to the nature of postmarital residence and the formation of kinship groups in that society. Cooperative endeavors in which people work commu-nally serve to reinforce the social solidarity of the group. When the most important subsistence tasks are performed by men, the residence pattern after marriage tends to be virilocal, whereas when the tasks are performed by women working together, the postmarital residence pattern tends to be uxorilocal. Chiefs were frequently instrumental in organizing certain kinds of production. For example, Trobriand chiefs organized the activities of their clan members in building a canoe, and Kwakiutl chiefs organized the members of their *numaym* when they built a new house.

The productive tasks performed by men and women are culturally determined in all societ-ies, as noted earlier. In hunting-and-gathering societies, there was a sexual division between the female domain of gathering and collecting and the male domain of hunting. Often the gathering activities of women provided the bulk of the food on which the group subsisted. The products of the hunt brought back by the men, however, represented the most desirable food. Hunting was a more prestigious activity than gathering, reflecting the relative valuation of male and female roles in the society. The productive tasks assigned to men in one society may be assigned to women in another. In some New Guinea societies, such as the Tor, women cut down the sago palm to get its pith, while in other societies, such as the Abelam, men do this. In our own society today there are many tasks that men formerly performed that are now performed by women.

Within both male and female domains, some work tasks are done individually and others in cooperative groups. The hunting of herd animals, such as caribou by the Nunamiut Eskimo was carried out communally. However, for animal species that tend to move individually, hunting was done on an individual basis. Gathering and collecting by women also tended to be done on an individual basis. Myanmar (Burmese) women, who work together at the different tasks involved in the manufacture of silk, sing as they work. It would seem that working communally is more pleasurable than when each person goes off to work by himself or herself. In our own society today many people now work as freelancers or consultants out of offices set up in their homes, having left their offices where they were part of a large, multinational company. The invention of computers, e-mail, and Fed Ex has made this possible.

Where the mode of subsistence is crop cultivation, men tend to be concerned with the prepa-ration of the garden plot or field, and also with water-control systems. Both men and women may be involved in planting, weeding, and harvesting. In New Guinea societies a clear distinction is made between certain crops, such as bananas and sugarcane, which are referred to as male crops, and other crops, such as sweet potatoes, grown by women, referred to as women's crops. When plows and mechanized agricultural implements are introduced, the whole range of agricultural tasks usually becomes the province of men, and women, if they are involved in agricultural tasks at all, are limited to growing vegetables in gardens. In nomadic pastoral societies, the task of herding and moving the camp is in the male realm, while women milk the animals and manufacture milk products.

The Organization of Work in Contemporary Societies

The organization of work in contemporary societies has become the subject of anthropological investigation. In many societies over the world today, more and more women are leaving their homes for full- or part-time work. Earlier, we noted that Asante women dominated the marketplace. Javanese market culture, for example, also seems to be gendered in that women play a substantial role in the more localized small-scale trading that occurs, while men are more frequently the "wholesalers" (Alexander 1998).

How does globalization of work operate in what one might call a transnational work force? One example is call centers that have been established in India in the past few years. As a consequence of the installation of high-capacity phone lines, customers in North America can call "customer service" or "technical support" for Dell Computers, Hewlett Packard, American Express, and many other large companies, and the call will be directed to an Indian operator in a call center in New Delhi, Bangalore, Mumbai, or Chenai for assistance. Between 2000 and 2003 the number of call centers increased from sixty to eight hundred with some five hundred companies outsourcing work to them. Operators in these centers also do telemarketing calls trying to sell banking and financial plans, computer hardware, and other products. Mirchandani's investigation of these call centers reveals transnational corporate practices and the way in which Indian workers deal with them. Companies ensure that the calls are seamlessly connected so the customer does not know where the operator is located. The transnational company subcontractor provides the workers with language training to "neutralize" their accents and speech patterns. The workers see this as an attempt to Americanize their speech patterns so American customers can understand them (Mirchandani 2004: 360). Each worker is assigned an American-sounding name. There is a predefined script the worker must follow. Workers must mask their geographic location by avoiding questions about it, and must sometimes sign nondisclosure agreements (Mirchandani 2004: 365). As Mirchandani notes, "Revealing that service work has been subcontracted to India may give rise to customer dissatisfaction for a wide variety of reasons, ranging from racism and ignorance towards Indians, concern about local jobs and assumptions about exploitative transnational corporate practices" (2004: 366). The operators say they are taught to be humble to the customer, to treat them as gods. However, in reality, they see Americans as uneducated, not knowing anything about computers but with high disposable incomes. The parochialism of some Americans comes out when customers say they want to speak to an American. Because of the 12- to 16-hour time difference between India and America, Indian workers must work night shifts. This transforms their usual lives. Though call center work is promoted as highly skilled, and highly desirable since workers are paid twice what they would receive locally, they know that they are receiving half of what an American worker doing the same work would receive. The workers Mirchandani interviewed revealed themselves not to be "cyper-coolies," or a passive workforce, but rather individuals who voiced objection to the dehumanizing nature of the scripting and the routine, but who do not want the subcontracting to end because by Indian standards they are receiving high wages.

DISTRIBUTION

Earlier in the last century—before globalization, development, and all the things that contact with Western societies and subsequently colonialism wrought, societies in many parts of the world had very distinctive ways of organizing their social life, as well as their exchanges, ritual and otherwise. Exchange ceremonies played a central role in the ritual life of many communities, and there were regularities in the patterning of ceremonial distributions of food and other material goods. Comparative research has revealed that there was a limited range of structures or forms of distribution to be found in very different places. Below, we will describe these structures of exchange and provide examples of how they operated in different societies. Such patterns and structures have been transformed over the past century in many societies. However, as we have pointed out in several examples earlier in this chapter, though the To Pamona of Indonesia and the Nentsy of Siberia have been drawn into the global market, at the same time they retain traditional exchanges and ritual obligations of gift-giving to their affines today. In Papua New Guinea, the Tanga use *bisnis* and *kastom* to mark this distinction.

In discussing systems of distribution or exchange one is concerned with who gives what to whom, when, where, and how. In every society, the system of distribution is determined by the operation of cultural rules and the way in which individuals in the system interpret them. Even where distribution of goods is carried out in markets, such as in our own society, supply and demand are culturally constructed. Sometimes the structure of the distribution of material goods is identical to the structure of relationships between groups established by marriage. Certain general principles apply universally to systems of exchange. Exchange may be broken down into three components: giving, receiving, and returning. When an object is offered, the process of exchange begins. It may be accepted or declined. If the object is accepted, then its equivalent must at some point be returned. The acceptance creates a relationship through time, until the return is made. The refusal to accept creates a relationship of a negative sort, diametrically opposite to the relationship created by acceptance. Giving, receiving, and returning may constitute a process over time. From the initial offer until the return, two individuals or two groups are linked to each other in a relationship. The acceptance of something offered constitutes the assumption of an obligation to return—recipients place themselves in debt to the givers. If such indebtedness continues for a long period of time or if goods go repeatedly in the same direction and are not returned, the recipients become inferior in their own eyes, as well as others, and the givers superior. Mauss (1954) long ago recognized that giving, receiving, and returning create links; exchange may be the basis for seeking assistance, recruiting allies, and creating alliances. But there is also an aggressive component, since the process usually involves competition. Recipients who are in an inferior position and cannot return may even perceive the initial offer as an aggressive act designed to shame them in the eyes of others. Some analysts see "deception as an integral part of exchange"

(Gerschlager 2001: 8). In fact the word for exchange in German, *tauschen*, is similar to the word for deceiving, *tauschen*. One might add that deception is often present, in particular, in market exchange. An old expression, going back to Roman times, says *caveat emptor*—let the buyer beware! Though exchange may be perceived primarily as an economic phenomenon, in fact, it is frequently linked to the political structure and differences in rank, hence the utility of viewing these conjointly as political economy. All the exchange systems we will discuss below have been penetrated to a greater or lesser degree by market exchange and globalization,

Distribution in Egalitarian Societies

Several types of exchange systems characterized egalitarian societies in which rank differences were absent, and they can be arranged in a continuum of increasing complexity. The simplest type of exchange system involves two sides, of equal status, in continuing exchange with each other. The two sides could be two parts of a village, two clans, or two moieties. This type is referred to as reciprocal exchange (see Figure 8.1). It is identical to the exchange of women in marriage referred to as direct reciprocal exchange (see page 122).

The Abelam of New Guinea, whose mode of production has already been described, have reciprocal exchange (Kaberry 1940, Rubel and Rosman 1978). Their exchange system involves only the exchange of goods between moieties, since they do not have direct sister exchange or bilateral cross-cousin marriage. The moieties are not named, but are referred to as *us* and *them*. The Abelam live in patrilineal clan-hamlets that are paired with one another. Men in one clan-hamlet have *tshambura*, or exchange partners in another clan-hamlet. Earlier, we talked about the Abelam gardens in which men alone grow long yams of a different species solely for purposes of exchange. Women grow yams used for subsistence. The exchange yams are selected and bred for their great length. The head of the clan uses his special magical knowledge to make the yams grow very long. He himself must abstain from sexual intercourse for the whole growing period of the yams, since sexual contact with

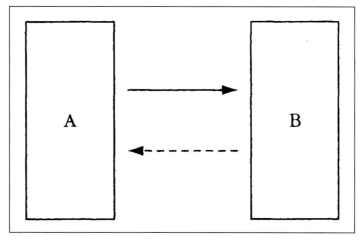

Figure 8.1   Reciprocal exchange.

women will prevent the yams from growing long. The strength, prowess, and magical power of the group are measured by the length of their yams.

The long yams are carefully harvested and individually decorated with flowers, feathers, and masks (see photo). They are then displayed at the ceremony, from which all women are barred, where they will be distributed to the exchange partners of the group. All the important men from surrounding hamlets are present as witnesses to the exchange, and to partake of the feast that accompanies it. The giver of the yam keeps a record of the length and circumference of that yam since the return must be the equivalent of what has been given. The return is not immediate, but is delayed until the group that has received is ready to give. Exchange partners also exchange pigs and important services in connection with the initiation of their respective sons (Rubel and Rosman 1978). Reciprocal exchange systems such as that of the Abelam exhibit the following characteristics: They involve two sides that are equal in status. Though they may compete to outdo one another in their continuing exchanges, the rule of equivalence in exchange keeps that sort of competition in check. Each side needs the other to perform important services for one another such as boys' initiation.

When changes occur in the rules of exchange, and one host group gives to several groups simultaneously, a more complex system develops, and the pattern becomes significantly different from that of reciprocal exchange (see Figure 8.2). The Maring of the New Guinea highlands have

Decorated long yams are displayed before exchange by the Abelam.

such a system of economic distribution or exchange (Rappaport 1984). These groups are equal in status. The distributive system is part of a religious ceremony referred to as the **kaiko**, which extends over many months. A group of closely related patrilineal clans serve as hosts of the kaiko. The guests at the kaiko come in groups from the surrounding territories. The host group has intermarried with these neighboring groups and is allied with them in times of war. Guests come brandishing their weapons and singing war songs, and hosts and guests dance in an aggressive display. This again demonstrates that there is a symbolic relationship between warfare and exchange. The aggressiveness is present despite the fact that guests and hosts intermarry, are allied to one another, and distribute food and valuable goods to one another. Cooked pork from many pigs is distributed at the final kaiko event. Production is directed toward amassing pigs for the kaiko distribution. Each of the guest groups, who come from a wide area, will in the future hold its own kaiko, at which it will fulfill its obligations to make a return. All the groups are relatively equal in status. The host group is invited in turn to the kaiko that each guest group will hold in the future. Despite the fact that the Maring are involved in plantation wage labor and grow some coffee for sale, they continue to hold the kaiko up to the present (LiPuma 2000: 197ff., 202).

A complex system of exchange develops when groups are linked in a chain so that goods move from group to group serving to tie together an entire region. This is an example of **generalized exchange** and is identical to the structure created by marriage with the father's sister's daughter. The **Te** distribution system of the Enga, whose production we described earlier, is of this type (Meggitt 1974). Enga patrilineal clans, occupying contiguous areas, fight with their neighbors but also exchange women and goods with them. People who are affines may also become exchange partners, or Te partners, to one another. An Enga man will have two groups of Te partners, one set in clans to the east of his clan and a second in clans to the west of his clan. He transmits goods he has received from his eastern partners at their Te ceremonies to his western partners at the *Te* ceremony that his clan hosts, and vice versa (see Figure 8.3). This is a system of delayed exchange in which goods move from one group to the next until they reach the end of the chain, and the exchange reverses direction. People who were givers of valuables such as stone axes, shells, plumes, and small pigs in the first stage become receivers of live pigs in the second stage. Live pigs move down the chain as

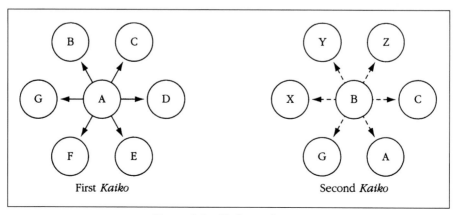

Figure 8.2   Kaiko exchange.

they are distributed at successive Te distributions held in turn by each clan. At the end of the chain, there is a second reversal, when the last receiver of live pigs becomes the first distributor of cooked pork. The distribution of cooked pork completes one cycle of the Te (see photograph on page 181). It will begin again when initiatory gifts go in the direction opposite to the pork.

Giving and receiving in the Te exemplify the ambivalence seen in exchange in general. Members of neighboring clans, though potential enemies, are dependent on one another to pass on the objects of the Te. If warfare breaks out in the middle of a Te cycle, the Te is disrupted. It is in the interest of Te partners in other clans to make peace between the combatants so that goods can continue to move along the Te chains. The Enga value their pigs greatly; yet their distribution system sends out the pigs that they raise along a line of exchange partners until the pigs eventually come back as roast pork (Rubel and Rosman 1978). The value they place on their pigs is what the pigs in size and number will bring in renown when they are distributed to one's exchange partners. Today, the Enga no longer hold the Te ceremony. The reasons for this are not clear.

Systems of Exchange in Societies with Flexible Rank

The kinds of exchange systems in the societies we have discussed so far stressed the equivalence in status of groups that constitute givers and receivers. There are, however, societies in which rank differences, which are an integral part of the political structure, play a significant role in the exchanges. Here we will be dealing with societies in which the rank of individuals and groups is constantly subject to modification.

Kwakiutl

The Kwakiutl wedding potlatch, described in chapter 2, was a kind of distribution in which rank and rank differences were central to the exchanges. Theoretically, every person in Kwakiutl society holds an inherited rank position, associated with a name owned by his or her *numaym*, or cognatic

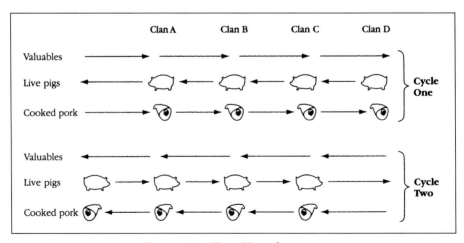

Figure 8.3   Enga Te exchange.

Sides of cooked pork are displayed on an enormous platform, 90 feet long, before they are distributed at an Enga Te ceremony held in the summer of 1974.

descent group. However, rank can be raised through potlatching or lowered by the absence of potlatching. A number of rite-of-passage events were occasions for potlatches. One hundred years ago, accumulation for a potlatch meant gathering and storing smoked salmon, olachen grease (oil from the candlefish), berries, and other food, and accumulating blankets and valuables such as jewelry, masks, and even canoes, referred to as *trifles*, as described in chapter 2. Potlatches may be hosted by one *numaym* or by a group of *numaym*, or tribes. At each potlatch, the person whose rite of passage is being celebrated receives a new name or title. A succession of potlatches was held for a great chief's son as he grew older. At each one he got increasingly more important titles. At the most important potlatch he assumed the name associated with the position of chief.

The guests who come to a potlatch serve as witnesses to the event, for example, the succession to chiefly power, and receive goods for this service. The guests, affines of the hosts, are seated according to their rank and receive goods in that order. The guest *numayms* must at some future time reciprocate by making a return potlatch. Kwakiutl potlatches were sometimes described as if the motivation for them was competition and the desire to shame one's rivals. But all exchange involves some form of competition, and maybe deceit. Since guests at a Kwakiutl potlatch are also affines, the Kwakiutl potlatch is no more competitive than some other examples of affinal exchanges such as the Maring *kaiko* and the Enga *Te*. One must hold a potlatch in order to raise one's rank, but one needs equally high-ranking competitors to challenge. Once again, as in all exchange systems, the givers and receivers are dependent upon and need one another, while they are competing with one another.

By the end of the nineteenth century, the Kwakiutl were involved in the Canadian cash economy. Hudson Bay blankets, power boats, sewing machines, tea cups and saucers, and other goods from the Euro-Canadian economy purchased with wages began to be distributed at potlatches. Like other societies being drawn into the world system, the Kwakiutl were using wages and manufactured products in their traditional ceremonial distributions. As early as 1895, the Canadian government made its first attempt to outlaw the potlatch. Such large-scale distributions and the destruction of property went against the Protestant ethic and the modern Canadian capitalist economy, which missionaries and government officials thought the native population should emulate. However, potlatches continued to be held in secret. The prohibition against

Tlingit men at a potlatch at Klukwan, Alaska, October 14, 1898.

holding a potlatch ended in 1951, and large-scale potlatches have been held since then by many Kwakiutl groups.

The potlatch as a form of ceremonial exchange was found in other Native American societies on the Pacific Coast of Canada and Alaska, but took a somewhat different form, depending on the nature of the kinship system of the society. The Tlingit have a social structure based on matrilineal descent, matrimoieties, matrilineal clans, avunculocal residence, and a preference for marriage with the father's sister's daughter. This means that each Tlingit clan intermarries with two other matrilineal clans, both of them in the opposite moiety (see chapter 6, Figure 6.11). The Tlingit had basically only one occasion for a potlatch. When a chief died, his heir, his sister's son, sponsored a mortuary potlatch and assumed the title, name, and political position of his mother's brother. The two other matrilineal clans who intermarried with the host clan were guests at the potlatch, since one clan had built a new house for the heir, and the other clan had buried the dead chief and carved the mortuary totem pole in his honor. (See the totem pole pictured in chapter 5 on page 88.) According to Thornton, more and more Tlingit are carrying out mortuary potlatches today, in the twenty-first century. These remain the central ceremonial occasions which tie them to their "ancestral places" (2008: 188). The structure of the potlatches and the occasions on which they take place relate to the differences between a matrilineal society such as the Tlingit and a cognatic society such as the Kwakiul.

*Trobriand Islanders: How Different Exchange
Systems Coexist in the Same Society*

In the Trobriand Islands three different types of exchange systems were present: **sagali**, **urigubu**, and **kula**. The Trobriand Islanders are horticulturalists and very different from the Tlingit who are hunter-gatherers. But the Trobriand *sagali* or large-scale ceremonial distribution of yams and other foodstuffs is structurally identical to the potlatch of the Tlingit, though they take place on two occasions, not one. Like the Tlingit, the Trobrianders have matrilineal clans, avunculocal residence, and father's sister's daughter marriage (see chapter 6, Figure 6.11). Trobriand funerary rites include the mortuary *sagali*, a distribution to the clan of the wife of the dead chief in exchange for all the funerary services provided by clan members. Contenders for the chiefly position compete to be the organizer of the funerary *sagali*. The Trobrianders also hold a *sagali* when the chief's sister becomes pregnant. It is her son who will succeed to the position of chief in this matrilineal society. The guests at a pregnancy *sagali* are the father's lineage of the chief and his sister, who have performed various services for the chief's sister during her pregnancy and are receiving the ceremonial distribution of food, yams, areca nuts, and bananas in exchange. Thus among the Trobrianders, the two clans that intermarry with the host clan are guests at two separate *sagali*, a funeral *sagali*, and a pregnancy *sagali*, whereas in the Tlingit potlatch these two groups of guests are present at the same time but are seated on opposite sides of the house (see chapter 6, Figure 6.11).

The second type of exchange is a distribution of yams called **urigubu**, which occurs after every harvest. Marriage initiated this annual payment of yams, the *urigubu*, by a man to his sister's husband (see Figure 8-4). The *urigubu* yams are displayed in a yam house that is built by a man's

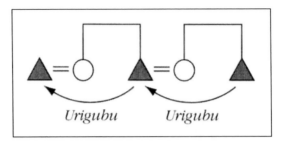

Figure 8.4   *Urigubu* payments.

brother-in-law, who will be giving him the yams. The Trobrianders have a mixed garden and a taro garden for their own subsistence, while the main yam garden produces the *urigubu* that goes to the sister's husband. At harvest time, the accumulating piles of yams are displayed and then ceremonially carried to the house of the sister's husband in another village and presented to him to be stored in his yam house. Meanwhile, the giver of yams will in return be receiving yams from his wife's brother. Great care and productive effort are given to these particular yams, which will eventually be given away. Yams for *urigubu* represent the prestige of the giver as a gardener and as a kinsman fulfilling an obligation. But these yams are consumed by households other than that of the producer. To market economists, the most rational, economically efficient system would be for everyone to grow and then eat his own yams. The *urigubu* distribution system of the Trobrianders makes sense only in terms of their social system. The *urigubu* is paid to the husbands and fathers of the matrilineal lineage for carrying out the important social role, not the biological role, of father. Malinowski referred to *urigubu* as economic tribute for chiefs since they took many wives, up to twenty or more, given to them by village headmen in their districts. With so many brothers-in-law, the chief accumulates many yams after each harvest, which he then redistributes as rewards to his followers on the various occasions for feasts (Malinowski 1935). In addition, at harvest time, there are competitive yam feasts, called *kayasa*, between villages. The game of cricket played by the Trobrianders, discussed in chapter 5, is part of the competitive *kayasa* being held between villages.

Kula, another type of Trobriand exchange, links the Trobriand Islands with a circle of other islands that are different culturally and linguistically. Trobrianders considered these islands dangerous places because warfare and cannibalism were endemic in precolonial times (see Figure 8.5). The goods exchanged in the *kula* are two kinds of shell valuables—red shell necklaces, which move clockwise around the circle of islands, and white armshells, which move counterclockwise. According to the rules of the *kula*, those who are to receive in the exchange always sailed their small native crafts to the givers' island. Nowadays they use motorboats. To receive armshells, the Trobrianders would sail east in a clockwise direction to the island of Kitava. To receive red shell necklaces, they would sail south in a counterclockwise direction to the island of Dobu. Thus, *kula* partners are always exchanging red shell necklaces for armshells, and vice versa, but never armshells for armshells or necklaces for necklaces. *Kula* exchange is identical in structure to generalized exchange, that is, the structure of matrilateral cross-cousin marriage described in chapter 6.

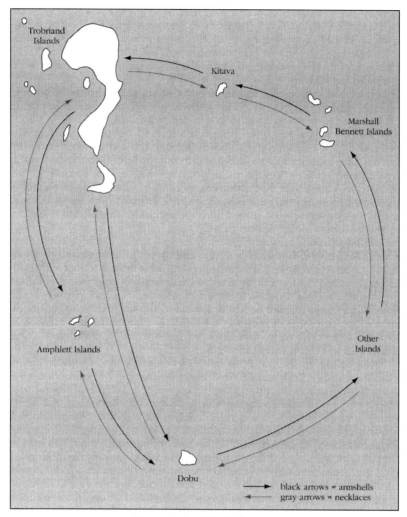

Figure 8.5   The Kula ring.

The exchange of shell valuables in the *kula* created alliances between individuals living in potentially hostile areas. While the *kula* exchange, with its elaborate ceremony, is being carried out, direct barter of food, pottery, and other manufactured utilitarian objects is also taking place between the *kula* visitors and their hosts. This barter, which does not take place with *kula* partners but with others on the island, involves the exchange of items that are scarce or absent in one place but not another. For example, when the Trobrianders go for *kula* objects to the Amphlett Islands, they bring food, plentiful on their island, to exchange for the pottery made there. *Kula* exchange, which involves ceremonial behavior, is delayed, while barter is immediate. *Kula* does not involve bargaining while barter involves trying to get the best deal for oneself, as occurs in market exchanges. The Massim area, before extensive contact with Europeans, was an area of chronic

Armshell valuables brought from the island of Kitava are to be given to *Kula* exchange partners on Trobriand Island. Photographed by Bronislaw Malinowski during his 1914–1918 fieldwork.

warfare; the pre-contact *kula* exchange system alternated with warfare, and the *kula* system described by Malinowski operated as it did because of European pacification (Keesing, 1990: 152). This relationship between *kula* exchange and warfare appears to parallel that between warfare and the Enga *Te* exchange described earlier.

These exchange systems, though modified, continue to operate among the Trobrianders today, who are now citizens of Papua New Guinea (Schiefenhovel and Bell-Krannhals, 1996). A recent description of *kayasa* on Kaileuna indicates that it is now a contest among men of a village to see who can grow the most yams. The *kayasa* organizer uses this as a means of increasing his prestige. Chiefdomship is still a matter of ascribed status, but success in competitive events such as the *kayasa* is also an important element in becoming a chief (Schiefenhovel and Bell-Krannhals, 1996: 249). Visitors come to the final stages of the ceremony as witnesses. *Urigubu* is also a matter of competition, since men gain prestige from giving large amounts of *urigubu*. Though today they travel in fiberglass boats and are Christians, "in many respects the Trobrianders of today seem to have stepped from the pages of their famous ethnography" (Schiefenhovel and Bell-Krannhals, 1996: 236).

Although the Trobrianders, Tlingit, and Kwakiutl have different modes of production, all three have flexible rank systems. All three societies produce economic surpluses. Distribution of goods at potlatches and at *sagali* serves to enhance one's rank and prestige. Goods are given to chiefs by their followers in their kin groups as a kind of **tribute**, which is redistributed on ceremonial occasions. When the chief serves as a host at such a ceremonial redistribution, he validates his claim to high rank. The acceptance of the redistributed goods by the guests means they recognize this claim. Rank in these societies is flexible, in that the more one distributes, the higher one's rank becomes.

Systems of Exchange with Fixed Rank

When rank differences are permanent the nature of exchange is significantly altered. In such systems, aristocrats are separate from commoners, lords from vassals, patrons from clients, and high castes from low castes, as occurs in India. The groups in such systems differ not only in rank and prestige but also in the economic resources that they control. Societies with fixed rank systems have groups that are economically specialized and have a permanent division of labor. The systems of economic distribution always symbolically emphasize the inferiority of vassal, client, commoner, and low-caste individual, and the superiority of aristocrat, lord, patron, and high-caste individual. When superiors give to inferiors, the act is seen as generosity or largess. When inferiors give to superiors, it is considered tribute. No matter how much tribute the inferiors give, it does not raise their status; it merely further enhances the prestige of their superiors. At the same time, the greater generosity and continual distributions of the superiors enhance their status, not that of the inferiors. These cultural formulations are not contrary to the principle of exchange in which the person who receives more than he returns becomes lower in status. Rather, it is a demonstration of the way in which the social structure and political organization determine the meanings of the exchanges. If high-status individuals are defined as superior, their superiority is demonstrated both when they give and when they receive, regardless of the amounts. Objects given by inferiors as tribute and objects that are the largesse of aristocrats are usually different types of objects. They derive their cultural meanings solely from the status of the giver, whether the goods move up to a higher-ranked individual or down to a lower-ranked individual.

In India, castes were endogamous, highly specialized occupational groups. In any particular place, all the castes form a system in which members of the various castes perform their services for one another under the supervision and control of the landholders. The castes are hierarchically ordered, from the Brahmans, who are priests, at the top, to the untouchables, who are tanners, washers, and sweepers who carry away human excrement. Though Indian castes are relatively fixed in rank, individual castes or sub-castes may disagree on their placement within the system. Today they quite frequently attempt to change their position with respect to other groups. As we noted earlier in chapter 5, caste members may start to eat food formerly forbidden to them. Though the caste system has been outlawed in India, it is still operating in many places.

Where rank differences in the social system are fixed, we find economically specialized occupational groups that are tied together in an interdependent system of economic exchanges. Economic subsistence in these societies is completely dependent upon exchange. Distributions in egalitarian societies serve to create and maintain ongoing social relations between groups that are equal in status. In societies with flexible rank, distributions allow different groups to improve their rank. Distributions in societies with fixed rank maintain the status of some groups over others. The different types of exchange systems we have discussed are all related to particular types of political organization. Again, this is why many anthropologists prefer to talk about political economy, reflecting the interrelationship between the two.

Barter

Barter is a type of distribution that conforms in part to principles of exchange. It involves direct, immediate exchange, always of different objects. As a consequence, barter does not create ongoing relationships. It usually involves goods and commodities that each party does not have in its own environment. Occurring within a context governed by cultural rules, it includes haggling and bargaining (Humphrey and Hugh-Jones 1992). These characteristics make barter much more like monetary exchange.

Since barter usually does not create or lead to continuing social relationships, it is often seen as the most simple and direct type of exchange. However, in recent years barter takes place in the collapsed ruins of former communist economies in Eastern Europe. It is particularly important in Russia and the other republics that have replaced the Soviet Union. Barter is currently employed in what formerly were planned socialist economies that used money and credit. In Russia, barter increased from 5 percent of GDP in 1994 to 60 percent in 1998 (Marin and Schnitzer 2002: 2). According to Marin and Schnitzer, "Barter trade has become a dominant phenomenon in the domestic economies of the former Soviet Union" (2002: 103).

Why has this transformation from money to barter occurred? The most common reason given for using barter, rather than cash, is that the buyer simply doesn't have cash. Money is in short supply. Though this is the common excuse offered, it may not be true. Other reasons are that people have no trust in the value of money, and that payments in goods are faster than payments in cash (Marin and Schnitzer 2002: 123). Banks today are mistrusted and avoided. "It is feared that they may crash or arbitrarily freeze personal accounts" (Humphrey 2002: 77). Finally, many contemporary economic transactions are illegal, and barter helps in evading taxes, circumvents customs procedures when importing goods, and allows for the use of fake documents and fake contracts and for payment of "presents" for the service of solving problems (Seabright 2000: 310).

How does this system of widespread use of barter work? The return in barter transactions may not be immediate. If manufactured goods are involved, the "seller" of some products may still have to wait until they are available to receive his or her return. The result is that this type of barter is a form of delayed exchange (Humphrey 2002: 78). One side is in debt until the goods become available. Unlike the simple form of barter in which exchange is immediate—like the yams exchanged for pots, which occurs alongside *kula* exchange—Russian barter depends on trust, since the return isn't made until sometime in the future. It is more like the potlatch, *Te*, or *kula*, all of which also depend on some degree of trust. This requires working and exchanging within a community (called a "suzerainty" by Humphrey) and having a powerful and successful boss who can protect you from the authorities (Humphrey 2002: 18). This is particularly important when most of this economic activity is marginally criminal.

For the tribal people of Siberia, like the Evenki (formerly called Tungus), present-day barter has some of the characteristics of their exchange system of sharing, and gift-giving to one's affines. Under the Soviet system, the Evenki, who are reindeer herders and hunters and gatherers in the Siberian taiga forest, were collectivized. Before that, under the Czar, taxes were collected from the Evenki, who were reduced to a form of serfdom (Ssorin-Chaikov 2000: 358). Under their traditional system, the hunter cannot eat game that he has killed but gives it to affines. This is similar to the way in which the Arapesh and Abelam must exchange their yams and pigs (see chapter 5). Today, the furs are given to intermediaries in a form of gift-exchange. The Evenki hunter gives them to a nonrelative or trader. (The same term for affine is also used for trader.) The hunter receives a countergift of flour and other food supplies, which the community shares. What one side (the trader) perceives as barter, the other side perceives as gift exchange with one's "affine" (Ssorin-Chaikov, 2000: 359). It is not uncommon for two sides in a relationship to perceive that relationship differently. National Public Radio has recently reported that systems of barter have developed in the United States to deal with the difficult economic situation.

The Market System

The term *market* has two meanings. The first refers to the location, or site, where food commodities and craft items are bought and sold. The second meaning characterizes an entire economic system based upon the determination of prices by the market, that is, in terms of supply and demand. This is the exchange system with which Americans are familiar. Its characteristics are different in many respects from those of the exchange systems we have discussed so far. Perhaps the most distinctive feature of market exchange is that the buyer need have no other social relationship with the seller. While one may deal with the same grocer, butcher, supermarket, or stockbroker over many years, one may shift overnight and carry out the same transactions with another store or stockbroker. The relationship between buyer and seller has its basis solely in the fact that the seller has something that the buyer wants or needs and is willing to pay for. The basic premise of a market system is to make a profit, which means to buy cheap and sell for more than you have paid. Transactions in a market system are governed by bargaining, or haggling over price, in which the buyer tries to buy something as cheaply as possible. It is not determined by social relationships. This is in contrast to a Kwakiutl potlatch, which is based on continuing social relationships, in which the more that is given to others, the greater the prestige of the giver.

A market system depends on the presence of money. Societies that did not have market systems did not have money in the usual sense of that term. Money serves a number of purposes. With a market system, money can be used as a standard of value, because any commodity, service, or labor can be expressed in terms of its monetary worth. Money can be used as a store of value, because it can be hoarded and used later to obtain commodities or services. But most important, money can serve as a medium of exchange, whereby one commodity can be converted into money and then that money can be used to exchange for any other kind of goods or services. The money used in our society is considered all-purpose money, because it can be exchanged for anything in the society. The valuables discussed in connection with ceremonial distribution, such as the armshells and necklaces in the **kula**, are objects that have value but can be used only for particular ceremonies, such as the *kula*. The restricted use to which such valuables are put is in sharp contrast to the many purposes that money serves.

Markets served to articulate peasant communities with the economy of the city, when cities first arose some 5,000 years ago. There are different kinds of market structures. One kind of market structure links a number of different communities to a central market town. In addition to its subsistence activities, each of these communities may specialize in a different craft activity, such as weaving, manufacture of pottery, or manufacture of tiles. People from each of these communities come into the market, often once a week, to sell their wares and to buy the goods, frequently of Western manufacture, which they require but do not make for themselves. In some places markets are held in different villages and towns on successive days of the week. In places like the Golden Triangle area of Myanmar (Burma), the Five Day market moves between five different villages during the week. The sellers are primarily women from different tribal villages, who come to the market in their tribal dress to sell garden crops and food (see photograph). Western products such as sneakers, shoes, shirts, jackets, and baby clothing are also sold. The same items are sold in all the villages that make up the Five Day market. The buyers on a particular market day are from the villages surrounding that market. These kinds of marketing structures define a region.

The Market Economy and Globalization

The market economy, as Collins notes, "is a dynamic economic system that is accumulative and expansive. Once established, its tentacles spread and envelop peripheral societies both in industrial nations and in those at the margins" (2000: 1). This spread of the market system is referred to today as **globalization.** It means not only the penetration of entrepreneurship, technology, technological knowledge, and modes of production, but most recently the development of multinational corporations and the movement of capital and goods to as well as from most places in the world without concern for national boundaries or different currencies. The establishment of global institutions such as the World Trade Organization, the World Bank, and the International Monetary Fund, which provide money as well as expertise, has had an impact in many parts of the world. Not only do the tentacles of capitalism and market exchange spread from the Western world to other societies, but they also spread from economic institutions to other institutions such as religion, politics, and the art world. International treaties such as the North American Free Trade Agreement also have an important effect on the movement of goods and people. Though it has the potential to integrate the economies of Canada, Mexico, and the United States, at the present time there is a backlash from workers in danger of losing their employment as a consequence of it (Cook 2004: 267ff.).

In a market economy under capitalism, all economic behavior is evaluated in market terms, with individuals making decisions in order to cut the best deal for themselves. Anthropologists have been interested in the factors that determine how decisions are made and whether these decisions are based exclusively on expectations of economic gain or loss. Such studies often assume that individuals make rational choices and that their purpose is always to maximize their

Meo women dominate in the Five-Day market in the Golden Triangle region of Myanmar (formerly Burma).

own position. In a market economy, labor also operates according to the laws of supply and demand. Workers go to places where employment is available. If a factory closes, its workers are expected to move freely to other places where work is to be found. In Europe, this sometimes means moving to another country. Sometimes, a U.S. industry like TV set manufacturing loses out to foreign competition, or the company becomes multinational, outsourcing the manufacture of these TV sets to a country where labor costs are low. In this case, the workers in that industry are expected to retrain themselves for other work. Most of the world today operates as a single market. However, what is good for workers manufacturing sewing machines in the modernized economies of Taipei or Hong Kong creates hardships for workers who have lost their jobs as a result of the closing of a plant manufacturing sewing machines in Elizabeth, New Jersey.

Whereas in nonmarket economic systems, the economy is embedded in a larger cultural matrix, the growth of a market economy in an industrialized capitalist society marks the development of an economic institution that at first was viewed as separate from other institutions and its cultural matrix. Social scientists assumed that market economies operated rationally and were not influenced by cultural factors. However, now they recognize that the economy is "embedded" and "Japanese capitalism may be quite different from Chinese, and both in turn from American"

(Hefner 1998: 11). Japanese and Americans both manufacture cars within capitalist market systems. Since there are differences in these two cultures, the social organization of factories and the relationships between managers and workers are different. Business as it is conducted by overseas Chinese in Southeast Asia, for example, is based on particularistic relationships in which family as well as reciprocal relationships known as *guanxi* are significant in the conduct of business. The traditional family firm as a basis for conducting business has given the Chinese in Southeast Asia the edge over the less commercially oriented Thai, Javanese, Malay, Burmese, or Vietnamese (Mackie 1998: 129). The overseas Chinese have been economically successful in Thailand for hundreds of years despite many political and economic changes (Hamilton 2006: 266). The small- and medium-sized Chinese family businesses in Taiwan underlie Taiwan's dynamic form of capitalism (Hamilton 1998). Family-owned Asian firms, which have been in existence a long time, have good will, enabling them easier access to the capital of institutional investors (Yeung 2007: 99–100). With the development of the global system, these differences in the cultural settings of capitalism and market economies in different countries sometimes cause miscommunication and misunderstanding. Ong details how foreign enterprises wishing to do business in Shanghai must "indigenize" their operation by replacing foreign expatriate managers with local staff who come with technical training, but must be inculcated with "company and Western business culture" (2006: 169). Some people even believe that if a few bribes or kick-backs are necessary to conduct business, then bribery is not immoral, especially if the bribes are given to individuals outside the United States. Similarly, for South Korea, "[c]ulture has been an important driver for ICT [information and communication technologies] . . . which has become a convenient means to enrich this social norm [of word of mouth communication among the many groups to which they belong] by forming numerous communities" (Lee 2007: 123).

Even a fishing community in Malaysia can be affected by the expanding global economy. The ethnic Malay fishermen have large families that they must support from the sale of fish harvested under recently instituted fishing licenses for fish and gear. This restricts the amount of fish caught "to balance sustainability with the fishermen's needs." However, the establishment of factories in the area has brought about inflation in the price of basic food items. The desire for piped water, electricity, telephones, and other items formerly considered luxuries has placed a strain on Malay family income because of the need for more cash. The inflation in bridewealth, the "new consumerism" (meaning the inclusion of nontraditional Western items as part of such exchanges), and the greater elaborateness of marriage feasts have also increased the need for money. As the need for increased income rises, fishing is no longer seen by Malay man as a desirable occupation. A study of fishermen in a community such as New Bedford, Massachusetts, would reveal many of the same economic factors, such as declining fish yields, declining income, and increased costs for family maintenance and college education for children. But people feel that they should remain in the community where they grew up and should not move to where jobs are, despite a worsening economic situation.

The world system of money and markets has penetrated even the most remote societies. In places such as Papua New Guinea, and other places in the Pacific, it coexists with reciprocal and generalized exchange. Sometimes, as on the island of Tanga in Papua New Guinea, Westernization, or modernization, and its attendant goods become a separate category, *bisnis*, in opposition to *kastom*, that is, those traditional practices continued from the past (Foster 1992). The market principle, which is based upon the law of supply and demand, assumes that nothing exists within our society that cannot be purchased with money. However, in our society other kinds of exchanges continue to coexist alongside the market system. We have cultural rules about reciprocal gift exchange between relatives and friends who are considered equals. People who give gifts expect to be reciprocated, at some future time, with gifts that are roughly equivalent. Our rules do not require the recipient to return like for like, as the Abelam do. People often bring gifts when invited for dinner. It is appropriate to bring wine or flowers but not considered appropriate to bring a pound of ground sirloin or to give the hostess a $20 bill.

Capitalism and the market economy also involve other kinds of "gifts." Gift exchange as we have just described it is different from the case of the congressmen who receive gifts from constituents or lobbyists and who are exchanging these "gifts" for influence since the purpose of such gifts is different. The givers of these gifts will have influence in the setting of rules and the passage of legislation favorable to their businesses. Under capitalism, the giving of large monetary gifts can thereby serve to undermine government law-making. Gift giving may also be involved in competition. In the dress industry, gifts may be given by dress manufacturers to the buyers of dresses of a department store chain in order to have the chain buy dresses from that company and not another. The line between giving gifts to lobbyists, which is legal, and gifts to "facilitators" who help in the avoidance of true tax assessment of property, which is not, is a fine one. What one person may call a gift, another will call a bribe.

CONSUMPTION

In its most general sense, consumption means the way in which people use goods that they have obtained. As with other aspects of culture, consumption is determined by cultural rules. There is a relationship between the consumption of goods and the nature of the social system as well as the system of cultural meanings within which it is embedded. In the small-scale societies anthropologists formerly studied, food and other material goods were consumed in relation to subsistence as well as in the context of ritual. In many instances these goods were grown or manufactured and used within the local community. But we also saw how yams as *urigubu* were ceremonially moved from one Trobriand community to another. In this example, goods manufactured in one place were ceremonially distributed and then taken to be utilized elsewhere. Hence, the aim of production was distribution or exchange. In complex societies, as we shall see below, people's demands for a product stimulate production.

With the development of complex modern industrial society came the notion of the consumer. Consumers used goods referred to as commodities, which are manufactured by someone else. **Commodities** were sometimes further subdivided into goods required for subsistence and luxury items whose acquisition was usually related to high rank or elite status. The anthropological focus shifted to the way such commodity consumption was mediated by global capitalism, which had produced the commodities in various places all over the world, and how such objects become incorporated into the local scene. Consumption may communicate social differentiation. The material goods one possesses or wears mark one's identity (Miles et al. 2002: 3). These material goods define a consumer's lifestyle.

Sometimes religious beliefs dictate the nature of product consumption. A visit to Lancaster, Pennsylvania, or Shipshewana, Indiana, the location of Amish communities, will immediately demonstrate the way in which their religious beliefs have dictated the use of horse and buggy rather than car and pickup truck, and the wearing of very modest clothing, blue or black in color, rather than the latest fashion. They still farm and depend on the products of their fields and herds and carefully control the commodities that enter their world as well as what is excluded based on their religious beliefs. Their sphere of social relations has resisted "commodification." One can find examples of this process in many other parts of the world.

The Changing Nature of Consumption

Today, consumption and consumerism in the Third and Fourth Worlds are sometimes directly related to consumption in the industrialized world. We know that clothing plays a significant role as a consumer item in the West. Styles for both women and men change if not seasonally then yearly. What is in fashion one year is discarded the next. Though clothing is a commodity, its purchase represents an expression of the self. What happens to this clothing when it is discarded? In the United States, some of it ends up in Salvation Army stores to be reused by members of the underclass, who usually cannot afford what is in fashion. Other items may end up in "resale stores" to be purchased by frugal members of the middle class. However, much of it is sold in 100-pound lots by dealers. As part of an international trade, these same items are sent overseas to Africa and parts of Asia, not only from the United States but from Canada and Europe. Clothing, shoes, hats, belts, and the like, for men, women, and children, as well as linens and towels, may end up as far away as the bazaar in Chakhcharan in the middle of Afghanistan or in markets in Zambia, in Africa. They are recommodified and reconceptualized in their new context. In Zambia, this clothing, discarded by Westerners, is referred to as *salaula* and perceived as a very desirable commodity. *Salaula* means "rummaging," which describes the process whereby buyers select the garments they want to purchase from the opened bales of secondhand clothing that come to Zambia as a consequence of the large international secondhand clothing trade. In Zambia as elsewhere, this clothing also represents self-identity, as well as well-being (Hansen 2002: 225). There have been complaints that this secondhand clothing industry has had a negative affect on the domestic clothing industry and thus on textile production in Zambia. In part, this trade in secondhand clothing marks the impoverishment of Third World peoples from the Western point of view, since they are wearing "our" discarded clothing. At the same time, it represents new styles in the form of the introduction of Western fashion from the Zambian point of view.

The sale of religious objects in Cairo, Egypt, represents a reversal of what occurs among the Amish. In these sales "sacred" objects have been turned into commodities (Starrett 1995). Religious objects are mass-produced in factories, sometimes even in other countries, such as Japan, for sale to devout Muslims. Such objects include a wide variety of items, such as copies of the Qur'an in velvet boxes, which are commonly displayed in the back windows of automobiles or taxis. These objects are displayed in order to obtain God's blessing and protection, to ward off the evil eye, and to signal the owner's Muslim identity. There are differences of opinion about such objects, and their religious meanings are contested. Educated Muslims feel that employing such manufactured commodities in this way reduces religion itself to the level of mass consumption. This use of sacred objects, which is very widespread, has produced a backlash among more scholarly Egyptian Muslims, who claim such a use of sacred objects is really resorting to magical charms and is counter to Islamic values.

Sometimes commodification of a particular product for sale in an international market can result in significant changes in a people's way of life. The lives of the Otavalo, indigenous Quecha-speaking people with their distinctive dress and customs, have been significantly transformed as a consequence of their success in the weaving trade (Meisch 1998). The Otavalo had been weavers even before the Spaniards arrived, but the introduction of the Spanish loom in the twentieth century resulted in an upsurge in their production of woven woolen tweeds. Indian products became popular tourist items when the extension of the Pan-American highway made Otavalo accessible. Many Otavalos moved to towns and cities in other parts of Latin America, Spain, and the United States and set up weaving workshops and stores, which maintained ties with the home community. All Otavalos are textile producers, though many still plant crops for their own consumption. Tourism led to expansion of the marketplace and other businesses such as restaurants and folk music clubs, from which the indigenous people profited. Textiles are sold to tourists, to other Ecuadorians throughout the country, and even to foreign exporters (Meisch 1998: 20). The prosperity of the Otavalos, now half the population of the town, has significantly altered their position in society and brought about a transformation in ethnic and power relations in the valley. They now buy refrigerators, cars, trucks, and stereos, and send their children to universities to become doctors and lawyers (Meisch 1998: 24–25). Another consequence of this now transnational textile industry has been the increase in the elaborateness of *compadrazgo* feasts, including the introduction of new dishes, and an increase in the number of *compadres* honored (Colloredo-Mansfield 1998: 57).

Food is another important object of consumption, the examination of which reveals much about cultural structure and cultural representations. For most of human existence, basic foods came from no more than a dozen miles away. This is in contrast to today's far-flung international trade in food, in which tomatoes can move from Mexico to Canada and rice from India to the United States. The use of canning, freezing, and other preservation methods has made it possible for the volume of food moving from continent to continent to greatly increase (Mintz 2006). Interestingly, there has been a countermovement in many areas of the United States to return to locally produced foods, to be cooked as "Slow Food" in contradistinction to the Fast Foods obtained at McDonald's and Taco Bell.

Yap, part of the Federated States of Micronesia, exemplifies the kind of accommodation that is made between the declining indigenous food system and the growth in the amount of imported foods such as rice, canned meats and fish, and frozen chickens and turkey tails. As Egan et al. note, "Food is perhaps the quintessential means through which Yapese express important cultural values" (2006: 31). Most households still produce local food. Women grow taro in irrigated patches, yams, bananas, and so on. The labor of a woman in her husband's taro patch has important ceremonial significance in solidifying her claim and that of her children to positions within the estate owned by her husband's group. Men fish and obtain other sources of protein. There is a clear conceptual and cultural separation between the foods produced by women's as opposed to men's labor. Besides ceremonial transfers of food, family food producers regularly, sometimes daily, "help" kin, neighbors, and friends with contributions of vegetable food, sea turtle, or fish to express sociality and fulfill cultural obligations. The fisherman must decide on the allocation of his catch in terms of to whom to give, what to give, and how much to market if necessary. Much of the time these food producers are also wage earners holding down regular full-time positions. A Yapese meal should consist of products produced in the gardens by women and the protein that the men have obtained. Imported foods have even come to be re-contextualized as male protein, with rice and bread as female foods, and are presented as ceremonial gifts at special events. But as Egan et al. note, "Carry-out pizza freshly made from imported ingredients at local stores are served at children's birthday parties. Family outings . . . [break to] eat macaroni salads and barbequed hot dogs" (2006: 44–45). Despite what appears as a dual economy, it is local food production and re-contextualized imported foodstuffs that still continue to encode important social meanings and values.

Earlier studies of modernization and modernity assumed that when industrializing people adopted the use of money and began to purchase jeans, transistor radios, canned food, and other items of Western manufacture, the result would be either incorporation and global homogenization of material culture or some form of mass resistance to Western culture. These goods often came to stand for becoming modern, and people could, by the use or nonuse of such objects, signify Americanization and Westernization or a conscious rejection of such identification. Frequently, material goods have been accepted re-contextualized. Sometimes, objects used in the past have come to stand for a nostalgia for that past and a continuity of identity. The Japanese tea ceremony performs that function for modern Japanese today. The passion many Americans have for collecting toy trains, metal lunch boxes from the 1950s, and antique baseball cards derives from that same sense of nostalgia for the past, loss of youth, and remembrance of a more tranquil period in the nation's history. There is a market for such items; they have become commodities.

SUMMARY

- The economic organization of a society is how that society goes about providing the material goods and services it needs to reproduce itself. Economic organization is a cultural construction and operates according to sets of cultural rules.
- For most of their time on Earth, humans subsisted by hunting wild animals and gathering plants, an economic system long superceded by other systems. This way of life still continues today for a small group of people but always combined with other kinds of economic activities.

- More complex modes of production than horticulture, or vegetative propagation, such as grain agriculture produce storable surpluses that are used to support full-time specialists and social hierarchies.
- Societies that are completely dependent on domesticated animals are known as nomadic pastoral societies. A series of economic factors have significantly transformed this way of life.
- In society there is a division of labor based on gender and age.
- In societies with flexible rank, distributions are the means by which the ranking of groups is raised or lowered.
- The term *market* has two meanings. The first refers to location, or site, where food commodities and craft items are bought and sold. The second characterizes an entire economic system based on the determination of market prices, that is, in terms of supply and demand.
- Whereas in nonmarket economic systems, the economy is embedded in a larger cultural matrix, the growth of a market economy in an industrialized capitalist society marks the development of an economic institution that is separate from other institutions.
- In its most general sense, consumption means the way in which people use goods they have obtained. As with other aspects of culture, consumption is determined by cultural rules.

SUGGESTED READINGS

Gudeman, Stephen J. *The Anthropology of Economy: Community, Market, and Culture.* Malden, MA: Blackwell, 2001. An approach that emphasizes the community as the core of the economy.

Hann, C. M., ed. *Property Relations: Renewing the Anthropological Tradition.* New York: Cambridge University Press, 1998. A series of essays considering the cultural, social, and symbolic aspects of property, as well as its material component in a number of different societies.

Wilk, Richard, ed. *Fast Food/Slow Food: The Cultural Economy of the Global Food System.* Lanham, MD: AltaMira Press, 2006. A survey of the social aspects of the food industry, food habits, and changes in food usages that have taken place in many parts of the world.

SUGGESTED WEBSITES

wwww.openair.org. A website that surveys various types of markets in different parts of the world.
www.auburn.edu/~johnspm/gloss/barter. A glossary of terms relating to political economy.

Chapter 9
Power, Politics, and Conflict

WHAT IS POLITICS? Does politics always involve the use of power? What does it mean "to get an offer you can't refuse"? In American society, that metaphor represents the exercise of power in many different contexts. It may be a way of forcing someone to do something he or she doesn't want to do, or getting a competitor to remove himself or herself from competition. How do power and politics operate in different societies? A Trobriand man aspiring to chiefly office might seize the opportunity of his mother's brother's death to organize the latter's funeral *sagali* to give him an advantage in inheriting the chieftainship. Thus, a Trobriand funeral *sagali* is a political as well as a social, religious, and kinship event. So too are the funerals of a Mafia boss and a dictator in a totalitarian state. In these examples, though the successor comes from a small circle of eligible individuals, there is no fixed rule regarding succession.

Questions about politics and power may be illuminated by comparing the processes of political organization in two contrasting small-scale societies, the Trobrianders and the Yanomamo. Durkheim long ago pointed out that one or two detailed examples were useful explanatory devices. Trobriand political organization involved the division of the main island of Kiriwina into a number of districts, each of which contained several villages. Members of its four matrilineal clans were dispersed throughout the districts, though sub-clans were localized. Within a particular district, one sub-clan would rank higher than all the others, and its **chief** would be the paramount chief of the district. The other villages in the district had headmen who were subordinate to the chief and gave their sisters to him as wives, therefore furnishing him with yams, *urigubu* as tribute. His real or classificatory sisters' sons competed with one another to succeed to the position. Before the man who succeeded to the position could make the funerary *sagali* for his predecessor, he had to demonstrate that he had many followers who would support him as the new chief and assist him at the *sagali*. The chief controlled resources as well as labor and was the titular owner of all the land in the district, although the garden magician and actual users of the land also had some rights to it. The chief decided when the time was propitious to declare a *kayasa*, a period of feasting and competitive games such as cricket, between his own village and another to be held at harvest time. As a result of the chief's decision, all the people of the village were bound to work their hardest so the *kayasa* would be a success.

Malinowski (1929) mentions that the chief had "special henchmen" to punish people who did not obey him. They might even inflict capital punishment. Frequently, people obeyed the chief because they were afraid that he might command that evil magic be used against them. Several political symbols were associated with Trobriand chieftainship. Special signs of deference were shown to the chief. No man's head might be higher than that of the chief, so either the chief sat on a high platform or people bent when they walked past him. The chief's large, elaborately decorated yam house, displaying the *urigubu* yams given him as tribute, was another symbol of his political authority. Only the members of the chief's sub-clan could wear a certain kind of ornament, red spondylus shell disks, on their foreheads. The food taboos that had to be observed by people of rank were also symbols of political authority.

Yanomamo political organization provides a clear contrast (Chagnon 1997). Every Yanomamo man is his own boss; no other Yanomamo can give him orders. Each Yanomamo village is a completely independent unit. One village will entertain and feast another village in order to win its support as an ally. Villages that are enemies of one another will raid each other to capture women. Every Yanomamo village has a **headman**, a man who has demonstrated leadership qualities. These include fearlessness in war, as well as wisdom and judgment in planning the course of action for the village—in making alliances with other villages, in planning attacks on other villages, and in moving the village to another area when gardens are depleted. The position of headman is not hereditary. The headman of the village must obtain the agreement of all the men of the village when a decision about any course of action must be made. The headman does not direct individuals to do things; first he does them himself, setting an example for the others to follow. Headmen are constantly challenged by others who aspire to the position. A man is headman only as long as the villagers have confidence in his judgment. Another individual with supporters can begin to oppose the headman in his decisions. As this opposition grows, the headman, if the people lose confidence in him, may be supplanted by his rival, or the headman may inspire his villagers to use force to drive out the opposing leader and his followers to form their own village.

Since there is no fixed rule of succession, the younger brother or son of a headman is no more likely to succeed as headman than any other adult man in the village. No one performs labor for the headman; he works his own garden. The headman has no special magical knowledge. Since there are no rank differences among the Yanomamo—all adult males are equal—there are no outward signs of rank, no special deference, and no special food customs to differentiate the headman from other villagers, or those with power from those without it. The equal status of all adult Yanomamo males is consonant with the egalitarian relationship they have in exchange (see chapter 8).

Concepts in Political Anthropology

These examples provide us with a framework within which to examine the concepts that are employed to analyze political systems found in different societies, including our own. **Power** is the key concept used in defining political organization. Power is the ability to command others to do certain things and to get compliance from them. One can immediately see the contrast between the Yanomamo and Trobrianders. The Yanomamo headman does not have the power to compel villagers to act in a particular way, whereas the Trobriand chief demonstrates his power in a whole range of activities. Power must be distinguished from **authority**. When power becomes institutionalized, we say it has been transformed into authority. This means that there is a recognized position, or office, the occupant of which can issue commands that must be obeyed. It is apparent that the Trobriand chief has authority as well as power, which derives from his chiefly office, and his commands are always obeyed. Does the Yanomamo headman have any authority? He holds a recognized position or **office**, but since the headman has no power to compel people to obey him, he has no authority. Nevertheless, he is a leader, since others will follow him if he is able to influence them. **Influence** is the ability to persuade others to follow one's lead. They will continue to follow him and he will have influence over them as long as they have confidence in his leadership ability. Some form of leadership is found in all human groups. When leadership is not vested in a formal institutionalized position and is based solely on influence, as is the case of the Yanomamo headman, loss of confidence means loss of followers and loss of leadership position. Influence represents informal power, in contrast to the power vested in formal political positions.

A distinction is also made between **government** and **politics**. Government refers to the decisions made by those in office on behalf of the entire group in carrying out common goals. This may involve going to war to maintain the defense of the group, a decision a president must make. It also involves dealing with the day-to-day matters of law and order. Thus, the Trobriand chief carries out important governmental functions. For example, when he decides to hold a competitive *kayasa* with another village, as we have described in Chapter 8, he organizes the production of those under him. The chief initiates the overseas *kula* exchange, and is the owner of the canoe used. *Kula* deals with overseas relations between Trobrianders and other peoples, in effect, foreign affairs. In contrast, among the Yanomamo, the consensus of the whole group is what is important, even though they have a headman as their leader.

Politics is concerned with an entirely different aspect of political organization. Whereas government involves the carrying out of shared goals, politics involves competing for power. Politics concentrates on the manipulation of people and resources, the maneuvers intended to enhance power, the rise of factions that compete for power, and the development of political parties with differing points of view. Politics emphasizes opposing points of view and conflict, divergent rather than common goals. Of course, in our own society as well as others, those vying for power in the political arena usually claim that they are operating for the common good and not just for their own personal aggrandizement. They may actually believe this to be true.

Politics also operates among both the Trobriand Islanders and the Yanomamo. When a Trobriand chief dies, the choice of a new chief is open to political maneuvering and competition among the individuals in the group of people eligible to succeed. These candidates must demonstrate their political abilities to followers who are their fellow sub-clansmen. At this point, potential claimants to the chiefly office make promises and point to their demonstrated skills in organizational leadership and their wealth. The man who is recognized as the new chief now has the authority to govern and assumes the appropriate Trobriand symbols of political authority. Politics is constantly present among the Yanomamo, since Yanomamo headmen regularly face the potential opposition of those who also aspire to leadership in their village. Even the decision to hold a feast may be the basis for political maneuvering. A rival for the position of headman may himself try to organize a feast. He tries to convince others in the village that this is a wise deci-sion politically. If he succeeds in enlisting the support of the majority of the villagers, then he has in effect become the new headman. If he can mobilize only partial support, he will come to lead his own faction in the village, and he may try again in the future. He may also fail to get any support, in which case he retires to the sidelines and sulks. Anthropologists refer to a position that depends on personal qualifications and individual ability as an **achieved status**, in contrast to an **ascribed status**, which one inherits.

Forms of Political Organization

Some form of authority and leadership has always existed in all human societies. The forms of political organization we describe will provide us with a picture of how successively more complex political structures developed. This process of greater and greater political complexity involved increasingly more sharply defined positions of leadership. The forms of political organization that we will describe characterize societies that are all now parts of nation-states.

Informal Leadership

In the simplest form of political organization, leadership was manifested intermittently. This type of organization may be called **informal leadership**. The Iglulingmiut, an Inuit (Eskimo) group of eastern Canada, formerly had this form of political organization. The name given to the group means "the people" (*miut*) of Iglulik, who were all those living in that area. There were no fixed political offices, and a number of men, but never women, exerted leadership in certain situations. These temporary leaders, whom Kurtz calls episodic leaders, did not have the power to compel people to obey them (2001: 460). Generally, people who were respected made decisions, adju-dicated disputes, and represented the community in discussions with outsiders (Hitchcock and Biesele 2000: 19). There were winter villages along the coast, consisting of kin-related families, though not the same ones every year, which exploited ocean resources. The men of influence and leadership in the winter village were the "boat owners," the senior males of the kin units that owned the boats used to hunt seals. The hunting of caribou in the summer, done jointly by several families, was conducted under the leadership of a man with hunting expertise. At the end of the hunt, the families scattered, and the leader was no longer a leader. Leadership operated only through influence, and different men exercised their influence in those areas in which they had special knowledge or ability. This kind of political organization was found only among peoples whose subsistence was based exclusively upon hunting and gathering.

Band Organization

Some hunting-and-gathering societies had a more complex form of political organization known as **band organization**. Bands had a more fixed membership that came together annually to carry out joint ritual and economic activities. The Ojibwa—hunters and gatherers in the forests of the eastern Canadian sub-arctic—had this type of political organization. During most of the year, small groups of related families moved from one hunting area to another. In the summertime, the whole band frequently came together on the shores of a lake and remained as a unit for the summer. The men with influence were leaders of the group. Though fluid in its membership, the band had more cohesiveness than societies with only informal leadership. The band acts as a unit under recognized leadership, though that leadership is based on influence, not on authority.

Big Man Structure

A still more complex political organization is the **Big Man structure**. There is usually a term for this position, and frequently, it literally means "big man." The Big Man structure represents a greater delineation of the leadership position, in comparison with that of band organization. As leadership becomes more clearly defined, so does the group of followers (see also Kurtz 2001: 47–48). In Melanesia, the Big Man takes the initiative in exchanges with other groups. In contrast, ordinary men fulfill their obligations in exchanges with affines and kin and contribute to what is accumulated by the Big Man of their group, as described in Abelam and Enga exchange ceremonies in chapter 8. The Big Men organize their group's production and are the nodes in the exchange system. The Big Man derives his power from his direction of the ceremonial distribution of the goods accumulated by his group and the decisions he makes in the redistribution of goods within his own group. The Abelam Big Man wears the emblem of his office around his neck (see photo).

The Big Man also directs a range of other activities. As noted in the previous chapter, the Abelam Big Man organizes the labor involved in the production of long yams for exchange, but he also acts as the ritual expert, since he alone knows the magical spells that make the yams grow so long. On behalf of his entire group, he maintains sexual abstinence for the whole growing period. Artistic ability as a carver or painter of designs is also a desirable characteristic in an Abelam Big Man, but the most important characteristic is his ability to produce the long yams on which the prestige of the entire group depends. Throughout New Guinea, the oratorical skills of the Big Man are essential, since he must deliver speeches at ceremonial distributions as the representative of his group. The Big Man should also show prowess in warfare, though his involvement is usually in the organizational area. Since women cannot be near any phase of the growing or exchange of long yams among the Abelam, they cannot be Big Men.

An Abelam political leader wearing emblems and ornaments signifying that he is a Big Man.

The position of Big Man is an achieved status, dependent on personal qualifications and individual ability. As he ages, a Big Man may no longer be able to carry out all the activities necessary to maintain his influence in his group. In that case, his leadership position may be challenged by other aspiring Big Men. Competition between challengers involves political skills and maneuvering. Although in a patrilineal society the Big Man's son may have an initial advantage, he will not be able to become a Big Man himself if he lacks the necessary abilities. A man who has leadership qualities, although he may be from another family in the clan, may surpass the Big Man's son in gaining followers and, in time, be recognized as the new Big Man.

Though women have influence and play an important role in exchange in many societies of Melanesia, they rarely occupy the Big Man position. The women of the island of Vanatinai in the Coral Sea, one of the islands in the *kula* ring, are an exception. The term that literally means "giver" is a gender-neutral term referring to Big Men and Big Women (Lepowsky 1990). These Big Women are central nodes in the exchange of goods and valuables. They lead *kula* expeditions, organize mortuary feasts, and orate at ceremonies, just like Big Men do.

The Big Man political structure is associated with reciprocal exchange systems in egalitarian societies, as we have described in chapter 8. In societies like that of the Abelam, they organize the ceremonial distribution of yams.

Chieftainship

The introduction of fixed positions of rank and some method of succession leads to a fourth type of political organization—chieftainship. In this form of political organization, individuals as well as the kin groups of the descent system are ranked with respect to one another. The Trobriand example, with which we began this chapter, exemplifies this type of organization. As shown earlier, the chief does not merely exert influence over others but has real authority, which means that he has the power to enforce his decisions. Power and authority are vested in the chiefly office, and whoever occupies that position exercises authority and has power. In the Big Man structure, any man can become a Big Man if he has the ability and works hard. In chiefdoms, which are ranked societies, the chiefly position is restricted to certain high-ranking individuals. Among the Kwakiutl, who also have a ranked system and chiefs, the oldest child, regardless of sex, inherits the chiefly position through **primogeniture** and the highest-ranking name in the *numaym*, or kin group. Though a Kwakiutl female may inherit the chiefly name, a male kinsman usually carries out the duties of the office. Succession may go through females, and a man may inherit the highest position from his mother. In chieftainships, there is a hierarchy of other political positions that are ranked with respect to one another. The Trobriand chief heads a district with villages whose headmen give their sisters to the chief as wives, and who therefore pay *urigubu* to the chief. Malinowski (1929) called this *tribute*. These village headmen are the chief's affines, brothers-in-law, though they are not of the chiefly sub-clan, but are from other sub-clans lower in rank than the chief's.

The political economy of chieftainships is a more complex redistributive system than that associated with the Big Man structure. In a chieftainship, because there are more levels of political organization, villagers give to their village headmen, who in turn give to the chief. This is exactly what happens at a Trobriand *kayasa*, when two villages compete with one another. Yams are presented to the chief by the heads of the two villages. The chief later redistributes what he has received in feasts to reward the villages in his district for various services. Chieftainship is also associated with potlatch exchange systems like those of the Kwakiutl and Tlingit. While some chiefdomships are associated with flexible rank such as the Kwakiutl and Trobriands, others are associated with systems of fixed rank. Chiefdomships have been identified archeologically in various parts of the world such as Chaco Canyon in North America and the early Bronze Age chiefdoms in Denmark (Earle 2002: 16, 50). The political entity referred to as a tribe in the anthropological literature is a postcontact colonial formation.

Transformation from Big Man to Chieftainship and Back Again

As described by Leach (1954) in the 1940s, the Kachin, a hill people of Kachin Province, northern Myanmar (Burma), had a patrilineal lineage structure. Their unique example shows how the Big Man structure could develop into chieftainship and chieftainship could collapse into the Big Man structure. In its Big Man form, which the Kachin called *gumlao*, a number of Kachin villages, all equal in rank, were tied together by a patrilineal genealogy. Each village had a headman, who could be the eldest male from any lineage in the village, and there was also a council of elders (from each lineage) for every village. At village ceremonies and festivals, the heads of lineages sacrificed separately to a variety of spirits. The Kachin marriage rule favoring marriage with the mother's brother's daughter separates lineages who take women (wife-takers) from those who give women (wife-givers) (chapter 6, Figure 6.10). Among those Kachin with the gumlao structure, there were no differences in rank between wife-givers and wife-takers. If one lineage in a village grew wealthier or stronger than the others, it might try to raise its status by offering to pay a higher bride-wealth and by seeking wives from high-ranking lineages in other villages. If successful, it could transform itself into a chiefly lineage that dominated the other lineages in its own village, sponsoring village feasts, which would further raise its prestige. Succession to the position of village headman would become ascribed rather than achieved. The rule of succession was **ultimogeniture**, which meant that the new chief was the youngest son. His line became the aristocratic lineage of a village. If he succeeded in gaining control of other villages, the Kachin would say that the political form was of the *gumsa* type, with the chief ruling over a number of villages, or a domain.

In the *gumsa* form, the chief held both a political and ritual position, and only he made sacrifices on behalf of the domain to his ancestral lineage spirit, which was now taken to represent the ancestral spirit of all the lineages in the domain. Since the chief was entitled to receive a hind leg of all animals killed either in hunting or for sacrifice from everyone in his domain except his own lineage, he was referred to as the "thigh-eating chief." The chief had the right to erect a special kind of house post, as well as have the people in his domain build his house and work on his agricultural land. Whereas under the *gumlao* system, all lineages were equal in rank and married in a circle, in the *gumsa* form, there was a ranked series of lineages, and a lineage that gave women to another lineage was superior to it. The men of the chiefly lineage had to get their wives from the aristocratic lineages of other domains. Not only could the unranked *gumlao* (Big Man structure) turn into the *gumsa* (chieftainship), but the reverse process could also occur. When the *gumsa* structure placed great economic strains upon the people, there was a revolt and the egalitarian *gumlao* system was reestablished. It appears that the Kachin marriage pattern has the potential for the development of rank differences from a form in which all lineage groupings that exchange women are equal.

The transformations Leach described for the Kachin, from *gumlao* to *gumsa* and back, are, according to him, all due to internal forces. However, Ho, who studied Kachin across the border in China, reports that external forces such as money, markets, and trade in opium, were equally important in bringing about changes in political structure among the Kachin in China and Burma (2007: 211–56). Ho argues that when markets were introduced to the Kachin area in the nineteenth century, Kachin concepts of property and ownership changed from a sense of communal ownership in which clans were ranked (*gumsa*) to one of personal property and individual ownership. With the florescence of opium production, individual mobility replaced clan mobility, and a greater tendency toward *gumlao* (egalitarian) political structure followed (Ho 2007: 212, 253–55). Thus, contrary to Leach's theory, according to Ho, the transformation between *gumsa* and *gumlau* was due to external forces. The state had little control over this area, and opium production could continue unabated.

The State

The last type of political organization that we will discuss is that of the **state.** Archaeologists have been interested in the conditions that produced the earliest states in Egypt, Mesopotamia, the Indus Valley, China, Mexico, and Peru. Cultural anthropologists focused upon still-functioning indigenous states that existed as a consequence of the colonial policy of indirect rule. Many of the well-studied examples are to be found in Africa and Southeast Asia. The state differs from the other types of political organization in a number of significant ways, the most important of which is a difference in scale. Though some states may be quite small, the state has the potential for encompassing millions of people within its orbit. It is organized on a territorial basis, made up of villages and districts, rather than on the basis of kinship and clanship. In the state we find social stratification, rulers, aristocrats, commoners, and various low-status groups. These strata may be endogamous, and are never tied together by kinship. All those under the control of the state are its citizens or its subjects. Frequently today, states contain not only small-scale societies like the Yanomamo but also multiethnic populations who speak different languages and are culturally different from one another.

The state is governed by a ruler whose legitimate right to govern and command others is acknowledged by those in the state. Many of the early states were theocracies; that is, the ruler was head of both the religious hierarchy and the state at the same time. In many indigenous states, the ruler was not only the political symbol but also the religious symbol of the whole society. This was particularly true in East African states. In the symbolism of the Aluund of southwestern Zaire (discussed in chapter 5), the paramount chief is the lord of the soil and must not show disease, decay, or old age, since the productivity of crops depends on the state of his health. The administrative functions of the state are carried out by a bureaucracy that grows in size and complexity as the state expands. Customary law becomes formalized into a legal code. The adjudication of disputes by the leader grows into a court system, which enforces its decisions through the police. The tribute given to the chief is transformed into taxes paid to the state, which support the growing bureaucracy. The state expands by conquering neighboring peoples, who become culturally distinct subject peoples, and whose territories are incorporated within the state.

The way in which an indigenous state functioned in the twentieth century can be seen from a description of the empire of Bornu, the Kanuri state on the borders of Lake Chad in northern Nigeria. This state was studied in 1956 when it was still under British colonial rule, by Abraham Rosman, one of the authors of this book. When the British entered the area at the turn of the century, they resurrected the partially collapsed indigenous state and governed through the Shehu of Bornu, the head of state. This highly stratified society included the royal family, aristocratic families, commoners, including village farmers, and slaves. Only the Shehu could grant aristocrats titles, which sometimes came with land, including entire villages. The slaves were war captives and their descendants, who became the personal property of the Shehu. They could become titled aristocrats, though still slaves.

Prior to the arrival of the British, there was an empire of Bornu, located at the southern end of a strategic caravan route that led from the Mediterranean Sea across the Sahara to the populous states of West Africa. Caravans brought manufactured goods from Libya and returned there with slaves, ivory, and other raw materials. Muskets, introduced through the caravan trade, were monopolized by the state. The army of Bornu, completely controlled by the Shehu, had generals who were slaves of the Shehu. The army defended the borders of Bornu from incursions by other states, particularly Bornu's enemies, the Hausa states to the west. As a result of conquest, non-Kanuri people, such as the Babur and some Bagirmi, permanently became part of the empire of Bornu. In the fourteenth century, Islam spread to Bornu, following the same path as the caravan routes. Islam was adopted by the entire population when the ruler of Bornu converted. Judges trained in the Qur'an and in Islamic law were appointed by the Shehu to hear criminal cases. The Shehu and his appointed district heads heard and arbitrated civil cases involving personal and family disputes. The Kanuri believed that persons in authority at every administrative level up to the Shehu must be available every day to hear the disputes and complaints of their people.

The administrative structure of the state was centered in the capital city. There were also districts, with their capitals, where district heads, titled aristocrats, resided. Titles, positions, and their associated districts tended to be inherited along family lines, but these appointments were ultimately at the discretion of the Shehu, who could also depose the titleholders. Though the village headship tended to be inherited along family lines, the officeholder had to demonstrate

Mounted retainers of a Kanuri district head in northern Nigeria demonstrate their allegiance to their leader. This photo was taken in 1956 when Nigeria was a British colony.

loyalty to the district head, who could appoint or depose him. Members of the district head's retinue, freemen or slaves, collected taxes from villages and nomadic pastoral peoples, like the Fulani. Politics operated with regard to succession to the position of Shehu. Only the son of a Shehu could himself become Shehu. But the Shehu had many wives, including slave wives, so there were always many contenders. After the death of a Shehu, the eligible contenders vied for support among the members of the council of aristocrats, who made the final decision. When a new Shehu came to power, the district heads had to shift their loyalty to him or else lose their positions. On the other hand, the new Shehu would appoint as many of his own supporters to district head positions as he wished. In the same way, a reshuffling of power at the district level led to the appointment of new village heads.

Under British colonial rule, referred to as **indirect rule**, Kanuri officials of the indigenous state structure, including the Shehu, carried out the actual administration of districts, applied native law, and collected the taxes under the supervision of British officials. They were directed by a lieutenant governor who resided in the provincial capital. Real authority was in the hands of the colonial masters. Under British pacification, the Kanuri army had been disbanded. After Nigeria gained independence in 1960, Bornu became a province within the new state, which had a democratic government for a brief time. Then it was ruled by military governments. Several years ago, democratic elections were held. A civilian government is currently in control, though the head of state is a general.

WAR AND PEACE

Going to war is one of the most important decisions made by those in positions of authority. Warfare, feuds, and revenge seeking between social groups are resorted to when there are no lawful, mutually acceptable means of resolving conflicts peacefully. Feuding is defined as hostile action between members of the same group, and warfare as hostile action between different groups. Feuds, conducted according to rules, involve collective, not personal, responsibility. When feuds occur, revenge can be taken against any member of the group. In a segmentary lineage system, such as that found among the Enga, discussed earlier, it is hard to tell the difference between feuding and warfare, because sub-clans within the same clan may fight each other on one occasion but come together as a single clan when fighting another clan. It is then hard to say which is feud and which is war.

The question of how to define warfare has been raised again recently. The "omnibus" definition held by "hawks" sees war as "nearly ubiquitous, or very nearly so." This ties in with a view held by some sociobiologists that humans are basically, even "genetically" aggressive (Sponsel 2000: 838; see also Otterbein 1999). The contrary view, held by the "doves," is that humans are basically peaceful beings with an occasional homicide here and there.

Clearly, if one defines warfare and human aggression more narrowly, then it would not be considered a human universal. For example, "'Bushman,' 'Pygmies,' and 'Semai' [are seen as] . . . 'ethnographic classics' of peaceful societies" . . . [while] warlike societies [are the] Yanomami,

Maring, and Dani" (Sponsel 2000: 838–39). Dani warfare, which we would consider more ritual than war, involves the killing of one or two individuals, after which both sides retreat. This is a very different kind of "aggression" than the idea of "total annihilation." We must remember that warfare is "embedded" in culture. Head-hunting, cannibalism, torture, and mutilation are clearly aggressive acts that could be considered warfare. Anthropological accounts of warfare are all postcontact and often reflect the efflorescence of warfare that was a response to conquest. The Yanomamo and the people of New Ireland are excellent examples of this phenomenon.

According to Otterbein, warfare began when humans began to hunt and early hunters attacked competing groups of hunters. Foragers who were primarily gatherers domesticated plants and became peaceful, sedentary agriculturalists. Once city-states emerged, warfare based on battles and sieges developed (Otterbein 2004: 10–11, 61). Kelly has done a comparative study of the origins of warfare in human societies (2000). He argues that we first see clear evidence of warfare in the Upper Paleolithic, about 12,000 years ago, in contrast to Otterbein, who sees warfare beginning in the Lower Paleolithic. Evidence for warfare in the archeological record is found "in the form of skeletal evidence of violent death, the relocation of habitations to defensive sites, changes in weapons technology and the like" (Kelly 2000: 148). A number of comparative studies reveal that hunters and gatherers tend to be relatively peaceful. Like the Hadza, they resolve disputes by the disputants going their separate ways and getting out of one another's way. Kelly states that warfare involves collective responsibility. When a wrongdoer is punished and a murderer is killed, the perpetrator is held responsible for his or her actions. In cases of collective responsibility, all members of the murderer's lineage, clan, or tribe are held equally responsible. Earlier, we have called this type of collective responsibility feuding when it takes place within a group, and warfare when it is between groups. Kelly argues that warfare evolves side by side with increasing complexity of political organization (2000). As societies become more complex, warfare becomes more frequent and is carried out for a variety of reasons.

Contrary to the belief that warfare is a no-holds-barred action aimed at exterminating one's foe, it operates according to cultural rules, like all other forms of cultural behavior. Peacemaking, the opposite of warfare, is also governed by cultural rules, as we shall see below. Anthropologists have attempted to comprehend warfare as it operated in small-scale societies in order to try to understand it in today's complex societies. Unfortunately, by the time anthropologists went to do field research, those small-scale societies that they studied had been conquered and pacified and were under colonial rule or were parts of nation-states. It is only from field descriptions of societies in Amazonia and New Guinea, where warfare continued despite contact with Europeans and colonial rule, that we have some understanding of indigenous ideas about warfare, its causes, and how it was conducted. There is also ethno-historical data on how warfare was conducted by Native Americans during the early period of European colonization.

One of the fullest accounts of warfare practiced by a small-scale society is that of the Yanomamo in Amazonia (Chagnon 1997). However, this account is now contested. There are several levels of hostility among the Yanomamo, though hostilities could terminate at any level. The chest-pounding duel, which can arise from accusations of cowardice, stinginess with food, or gossip, is halfway between a sporting contest and a fight. It can take place between two individuals of the same village or, at a feast, between the men of two different villages. The next, more intensive level is the side-slapping contest, whose provocations are the same. The third level is the club fight, usually provoked by arguments over women. It can also take place within or between villages. Two men attack one another with long wooden clubs. These contests end when one opponent withdraws. The most intensive kind of hostility is the raid, conducted by one village against another, which one could define as warfare. Villages that have a history of being enemies raid one another to take revenge for past killings. Women are frequently captured in the course of a raid and become another reason to continue to raid. Preemptive first strikes may take place even after a feast because the Yanomamo say that you can never trust another Yanomamo.

Periods of warfare alternate with periods of peace for the Yanomamo and "peacemaking often requires the threat or actual use of force" (Chagnon 1997: 7). The Yanomamo ceremonial dialogue, or *wayamou*, is a ritual that takes place as a way of making peace when relations between villages that normally have close ties are deteriorating or when people from more distant, potentially hostile villages come to visit. Stylized body movements, rapid speech, and particular rhetorical features, such as metaphors, metonyms, repetition, and incomplete sentences, are utilized. Goods are often requested, which will be returned when the present hosts of the feast are invited to a feast at some future time.

Anthropologists have been very concerned with offering explanations for warfare. Most find unsatisfactory the frequently offered explanation that warfare is due to instinctive human aggressiveness. Warfare is prevalent at certain times and not others, and under certain conditions and not others. The task of the anthropologist is to explain why warfare occurs when and where it does. Proposing a universal human aggressive instinct cannot explain this variability. Earlier, Chagnon argued that the Yanomamo went to war in order to maintain their political autonomy (1983). More recently, he has adopted a sociobiological approach. He notes that successful warriors, men who have killed many individuals, have more wives and over three times as many children as do other men. Therefore, the cause of warfare is ultimately biological or reproductive success (Chagnon 1997: 205). In a recent reanalysis of all the historical and ethnographic data on the different Yanomamo groups in both Venezuela and in Brazil, Ferguson argues that "the actual practice of war among the Yanomami is explainable largely as a result of antagonisms related to scarce, coveted and unequally distributed Western manufactured goods" (1995: 8). He claims that before Western contact, warfare was limited or absent among the Yanomamo (Ferguson 1995: 75). When Western goods were introduced, access was unequal, leading to conflict between different Yanomamo groups and increased warfare. Peters, the ethnographer of the Xilixana Yanomami of Brazil, sees an abundance of steel goods in their area and considers the reasons for warfare to rest, rather, with avenging sorcery and revenge in general (Ferguson 1995; Peters 1998: 216–17). Koch (1974) offers another kind of explanation for warfare as it occurred in small-scale societies based on his research among the Jale in New Guinea. He claims that warfare breaks out when no third party exists to settle disputes. In his view, war is just another means of dispute settlement. Anthropological explanations for warfare must be distinguished from those of the combatants. The Yanomamo themselves say that they go to war to avenge a previous killing and as a result of conflicts over women (Lizot 1994).

Many of the points made about warfare in small-scale societies are also applicable to complex societies. The motives of those who carry out the war, both the soldiers and the planners, are different from the causes of war as seen by analysts. For example, the United States declared war on Japan after Pearl Harbor was bombed. We, as natives, explain the war as a result of Japan's aggressive act. A disinterested analyst might explain the war as a result of the fact that Japan, an increasingly more powerful and industrializing state, needed to expand its sphere of influence to obtain more raw materials, such as oil from Indonesia (then the Dutch East Indies). They thereby impinged on the United States' sphere of influence in the Pacific.

Like the wars fought by the Yanomamo, our wars are also conducted according to rules. After World War I, the use of poison gas in warfare was outlawed by an international agreement, the Geneva Convention. The Korean War was conducted as a limited war—limited in that nuclear weapons were not used. When certain unspoken agreements about the geographical extent of the war were violated and the United States moved its troops north of the Yalu River, the People's Republic of China entered the war and the level of conflict escalated. Materialist or ecological explanations of warfare seem to be as applicable to modern complex societies as they are to small-scale societies. The desire to obtain more land or other important strategic resources, such as oil and mineral wealth, has often caused warfare in modern times. Sometimes modern states carry out preemptive strikes, that is, attacks on the enemy when they believe that the enemy is about to launch an attack. The United States carried out a preemptive strike against Iraq. During this war, the United States chose to ignore and violate the Geneva Convention in its treatment of prisoners. Yanomamo villages also carry out preemptive strikes even when they are not under attack in order to prevent other villages from attacking them first, to maintain their political autonomy.

A distinction should be made between societies that have been characterized as peaceful, such as the San (Bushmen), the Semai, and Mbuti (Pygmies), and the act of making peace after hostilities as we have described for the Yanomamo. In a recent study, Fry notes that many societies have an anti-war, anti-violent ethos including those as diverse as the Mehinaku and Wauja of the Amazon, the Sami of Norway, and the Lepcha of the Himalayas (2006: 18, 19, 58). Fry claims that "the view that humans are fundamentally warlike stems much more from the *cultural beliefs* of the writers than from . . . data" (2005: 20). He concludes that though humans engage in warfare, they have a strong capacity for peace (Fry 2006: 246).

THE ANTHROPOLOGY OF VIOLENCE

The focus on what has come to be known as the "anthropology of violence" began with the shift in anthropology, under the influence of postmodernism, to a consideration of cultural life from the subjective point of view. As Scheper-Hughes and Bourgois note, "Violence itself defies easy categorization . . . [but one can speak] of a continuum of violence. . . . The social and cultural dimensions of violence are what give violence its power and meaning" (2004: 1, 2). The anthropology of violence also includes a concern with the "culture of terror," "torture," and how these are used to establish "hegemony," or the domination of one group over another (Taussig 2002: 172–73). The focus has been upon the way in which narratives "are in themselves evidence of the process whereby a culture of terror was created and sustained" (Taussig 2002: 179).

Scheper-Hughes and Bourgois see conquest and colonialism as historically central to the contemporary patterns of violence and genocide across the world (2004: 5). But one can certainly argue the Holocaust and the "killing fields" of Cambodia are separate issues, not related to colonialism. As Hinton notes, "[the] Khmer Rouge ideology glorified violence against the 'enemy' . . . adapting traditional cultural knowledge to its lethal purposes" (2004: 167). Competition between groups over political power and resources and the suspension of traditional values and relationships as in Rwanda and Darfur may result in genocide. State terror and political kidnapping, as occurred in Latin America in Chile and Argentina, may also be subsumed under the category of violence (Scheper-Hughes and Bourgois 2004: 17–18).

There are those who link conflict to violence, seeing violence as "an assertion of power or a physical hurt deemed legitimate by the performer and some witnesses" (Schroeder and Schmidt 2001: 3). This is a broader conceptualization, which includes what we have considered under warfare, above. But this newer perspective on the larger category of violence also focuses on the subjective aspect and on the role played by memory, as for example, in the connection between wars and prior conflicts (Schroeder and Schmidt 2001: 3, 9). President Bush makes connections between our need to make a preemptive strike on Iraq, and the Desert Storm war in 1991, September 11, and even to the December 7 attack on Pearl Harbor and the need for us to protect our country against preemptive strikes. Narratives keep alive the memory of former wars and conflicts. Since, by and large, anthropologists do not observe violent events directly, the anthropologist deals with the participants' narratives after the event (Schroeder and Schmidt 2001: 11).

Collective large-scale violence is also seen as connected to "massive trauma" and the reshaping of cultural identity (Suarez-Orozco and Robben 2000: 1). The reactions of Americans, particularly Manhattanites, to 9/11 brought about a rethinking of themselves and their cultural identity. These were encoded into cultural narratives such as stories, books, television programs, and documentaries. It was an example of how violence "penetrates people's psychic constitution" (Gampel 2000: 59).

LAW AND SOCIAL CONTROL

At various points in this chapter, we have touched upon the subject of **law**. Anthropologists have been interested in the way disputes have been settled in the small-scale societies they have studied. In the absence of any written legal codes or formal courts before which lawyers argued cases, anthropologists in the field would listen to and record the manner in which disputes were aired and conflicts resolved. By doing this, they tried to get at the rules, what constitutes proper behavior in light of those rules, what is the acceptable range of deviation from the rules, what is unacceptable behavior, and how it is dealt with and punished. The legal principles or bases upon which disputes are resolved were frequently not explicitly verbalized by the people. They emerge only through the analysis of specific cases, from which anthropologists have abstracted the legal principles that are the basis for decision making.

Anthropologists have come to realize that "classic" studies of indigenous legal systems, written in the decades between the 1930s and the 1960s, were studies of legal systems that had already been transformed as a consequence of European contact and encapsulation within colonial empires. As Fuller notes about one of the South African societies whose legal system had been intensively studied, "Tswana 'law and custom,' in other words, became more law-like as the indigenous normative order was reconstituted within the new colonial environment, in which Christianity and trade were at least as crucial as the colonial legal system itself" (1994: 10). This transformed system was the one studied by anthropologists.

Societies without written legal codes had a variety of ways to settle conflicts or disputes. Sometimes the two parties thrashed it out themselves; the solution might be a fair one, or the stronger party would force the weaker to capitulate. Sometimes each side mobilized support from people with whom they had economic relationships (as among the Ndendeuli of southern Tanzania). Song contests might be held in which an audience decided the winner (as among both the Inuit and the Tiv of Nigeria), or the disputants might simply disperse (which is what the Hadza of Tanzania did). Interestingly, today, since the Inuit have moved into permanent settlements, personal communications broadcast over the radio, received by a large audience, have some of the same characteristics of the song duel (Briggs 2000: 120).

Some societies have an authority who, as a third party, acts to resolve disputes and either decides the case on its merits or plays the role of a **mediator**. Such authorities may be political leaders or judges who have the power or influence to force the disputants to accept their decisions or recommendations. The legal principle applied in a particular case becomes the legal principle for future cases. This idea of universal application is what makes it a principle of law, rather than simply the political decision of someone in authority. When a legal decision is made after a violation of the law, some sort of sanction must be applied, possibly the use of force. A punishment just as severe may result if the community avoids someone or shames a person by public flogging. Other methods of social control in addition to the law include gossip and accusations of witchcraft. Informal negotiations, without recourse to state institutions, also occur in the Western World. Ruffini describes the way in which shepherds in Sardinia employ negotiations between the parties, mediation, or arbitration using "kinship, ritual kinship, patron-client relations, neighborhood, and friendship bonds [to settle the dispute]" (2005: 133).

In complex societies, a distinction is made between civil, or private, law and criminal, or public, law. **Civil law** deals with private disputes between individuals, in which society acts as an arbitrator. For example, if a car stops short on a highway and your car plows into it, the owner of the car will take you to civil court and sue you for damages to his or her car. **Criminal law** deals with crimes, such as theft, assault, and murder, which are considered offenses against society as a whole. The wronged party against whom a crime has been committed is not allowed to punish the offender himself; the accused perpetrator is tried in criminal court. Private disputes in small-scale societies rend the fabric of the social structure, and they are dealt with as actions against society as a whole. No distinction is made between civil and criminal law.

Moore notes that today, anthropologists have widened their scope of investigation. She observes, "[T]oday that [anthropology's] comparative perspective has informed new approaches to the familiar. Anthropologists now consider the socio-legal aspects of the modern state in two very different milieus: the unofficial but organized subfields which exist within nation-states, and the transnational or global fields that criss-cross and transcend states, some of them official and some unofficial" (Moore 2005: 1). For example, Merry studied the way three nongovernmental but institutional entities in Hilo, Hawaii, responded to violence against women (2005: 249ff.). Snyder, focusing on the manufacture of Barbie dolls, shows how international is the manufacture of such dolls, the many "players" involved, and the various institutional structures in the different nation-states that are involved and the way in which international trade regulations and a form of "global legal pluralism" have developed to regulate this global market (2005: 218ff).

Law is also associated with morality and value systems. When viewed as a series of statements of what constitutes proper behavior, the law differentiates right from wrong, good from bad. In our own legal system, some of our laws represent, in effect, the continuation of ancient religious commandments, such as "Thou shall not steal." For most individuals, laws of this sort have been internalized. That is, most people do not break such laws, not because they are afraid of being punished but because if they did break such laws, they would feel guilty. The enforcer of the law is the person's own conscience.

Law in the Postcolonial Period

Postcolonial nation-states, like the Sudan and Papua New Guinea, have been very interested in anthropological studies of customary law. They have sought to take into account the various forms of customary law found within their borders in creating legal codes for their nations, rather than simply adopting Western-oriented legal systems. The concept of **legal pluralism**, which refers to the relationship between indigenous forms of law and the foreign (European or American) law that developed in colonial and postcolonial societies, may also be used to describe the situation that develops when people migrate from postcolonial states to European countries. This has occurred in France when Muslim people from Algeria and other parts of North Africa migrated there with their Islamic culture and Islamic legal ideas (Botiveau 1992–1993). There are two possibilities—either the Islamic migrants submit completely to the hegemony of the French legal system (as Muslims migrating to the United States submit to the United States legal system), or the French legal system takes into account the Islamic legal system. During the colonial period, Islamic law had already been codified in accordance with the French legal system in both Egypt and Algeria, so migrants were familiar with more modern procedures. For example, the modern legal systems in Arab states such as Syria, Jordan, and Morocco require that civil marriages or the civil registration of a marriage takes place before the Muslim religious ceremony.

At present, with regard to matrimonial matters, foreign Muslims in France to some extent may choose the law that they wish to be applied. French mayors cannot celebrate polygamous marriages, but a Muslim man can choose to have a polygamous consular marriage, though this marriage has no legal status in France. When polygamous marriages have taken place prior to emigration, the French courts have recognized the husband's obligation to support each wife. Nor could the second wife of a polygamous North African migrant be denied entry into France. However, if a North African man first marries a French woman and then a North African woman, the latter's right to inherit is barred by the French courts. Islamic revivalism has developed today in France, and Islamic law is accepted by the French if there is no contradiction "with public order." When Muslims become French citizens, the definition of equality of rights is at stake and "Islamic positive law" is becoming a part of French legal culture (Botiveau 1992–1993: 96).

In recent years, Native Americans have more and more frequently been engaged in legal battles with federal and state governments as well as with non-Native Americans. They assert their hunting and fishing rights, or their rights over land promised them in treaties, or the freedom to pursue their own religious practices, or their rights to tribal cultural objects now in the hands of various museums. These cases represent an affirmation of Native American **sovereignty** clashing with the sovereignty of the United States. This confrontation can be seen, for example, in cases involving the use of Native American sacred sites. In the past, tribal people have been discouraged from using the courts to protect their freedom of religious expression because legal doctrines often equate such customary religious expression with fringe nonindigenous religions, which mainstream Americans regard with great skepticism (Carrillo 1998: 277). In 1978, Congress passed the American Indian Religious Freedom Act, which was supposed to protect Native American religious expression. Though this act was supported in principle, only sometimes did the courts uphold Native American claims. In other cases, such as *Lyng v. Northwest Indian Cemetery Protective Association*, in which a road construction project was to invade sacred sites that were significant in the belief systems of native people of northwestern California, the Native American litigants lost their case (Carrillo 1998: 7).

However, in another case, Earl Platt was unsuccessful when he tried to prevent the Zuni from crossing his land when they made their regular quadrennial summer solstice pilgrimage from their reservation to the mountain area they called Kohlu/wala:wa in northeastern Arizona (*U.S. on Behalf of the Zuni Tribe v. Platt*, 7300 F.Supp. 318 1990, in Carrillo 1998). In this case, the United States government acted on behalf of the Zuni when in 1985, Platt, one of the largest landowners in Arizona, challenged the right of the Zuni to cross his land and sought to interfere with their pilgrimage. Evidence was presented indicating that the pilgrimage had been taking place at the time of the Spanish conquest, and until recently had been largely uncontested. The area is believed by the Zuni to be their place of origin and the home of their dead. The trek, which takes four days and is 110 miles long, has been consistently the same. The Zuni had lost control over the ancestral land, which the pilgrimage traversed, after 1876. To the Zuni, the pilgrimage was the fulfillment of a religious obligation (Meshorer 1998: 318).One of the problems encountered during the trial, which has characterized other court cases regarding Native American religious practice, was the need to present evidence to support the case while at the same time trying to avoid revealing ritual place-names and esoteric information that normally remains secret. Since Zuni witnesses were reluctant to testify, archaeological, ethno-historical, and contemporary information from non-Indian local inhabitants was provided to demonstrate that the Zuni pilgrimage continued to be held. In its decision, the court deemed that the defendant, Platt, was aware that the pilgrimage had been taking place and went across his property, that such usage was "actual, open and notorious, continuous and uninterrupted," that "such use was known to the surrounding community," and that the Zuni believed that their crossing was a matter of right (*Zuni Tribe v. Platt*, in Carrillo, 1998: 318). The court then ordered that the Zuni be granted an easement over Earl Platt's land for 25 feet in either direction of the route of their pilgrimage for a two-day period every four years during the summer solstice, without rights to use Platt's water or light fires on this pathway, and with the necessity to notify Platt at least 14 days before the pilgrimage

As has happened in many parts of the world, the modern Western forms of social control that were introduced did not completely replace the older indigenous forms, but existed side by side with them. In Ghana, a police force was established soon after conquest by the British (Abotchie 1997). The British colonial government curtailed the authority and jurisdiction of the indigenous political leadership. Jurisdiction over all criminal and civil cases was vested in a Supreme Court, with colonial district commissioners dealing with lesser offenses. Postindependence governments modernized the police force and expanded the court system when the level of crime rose.

According to Abotchie, "traditional modes of crime control such as trial by ordeal . . . has persisted side by side with modern methods of crime control" (1997: 7). Many people, though nominally Christian (Abotchie calls them "Christians of little faith"), still believe in the traditional deities and express fear of them. As a consequence, traditional forces serve as a greater deterrent to criminal activity than do modern police methods and the fear of imprisonment (Abotchie 1997: 116–19). The Ghanaian police are seen as corruptible. They are easily bought, and one may escape from them. Prison is not viewed as a reforming experience, and police activity is seen as retarding justice. Supernatural forces, however, are inescapable, and their penalties are more severe. Though lineage leaders and chiefs have lost their politico-legal authority, their "religious functions, and [the] sanctions of the lineage head and the chief, however, remain effective . . . ; besides, both rulers still hold themselves accountable to the supernatural forces" (Abotchie 1997: 128). Ceremonies such as female puberty rites and marriage rituals serve to reinforce the traditional system of values and norms. It is evident that earlier forms of social control have continued despite the introduction of modern political and legal forms and police practices. This represents the same kind of "two-sided" system we saw operating in the realm of economics.

After 1952, the Mae Enga of highland Papua New Guinea made use of the Courts for Native Affairs and the Native Lands Commission to resolve land and other types of disputes. The Village Courts established in 1973 dealt with more local matters. Often the district officer acted as the arbiter in attempting to apply village "custom" to settle disputes, and the police enforced the decision. Peace and Good Order Committees were established in order to deal with the resurgence of fighting after independence. Police action and coercive punishment were favored to deal with guilty parties. Young notes, interestingly, that "the relationship between Engans and the modern but weak Papua New Guinea State is quite different from their relationship with the Colonial Administration which was perceived as 'strong'" (2004: 166–67). During the Colonial period, Australians did not allow guns and confiscated spears after battles. Young notes that the Enga regard the present state, run by Papua New Guineans, as if it was another clan, and would be likely to seek "payback revenge" if a fellow clansman were executed (2004: 166).

NATION BUILDING IN THE POSTCOLONIAL PERIOD

After the colonial period, states in Africa, Asia, and Latin America that were created and fashioned at independence were organized on a Western model. The Western European idea of state development had global influence, but not everywhere. For example, in the Islamic Republic of Pakistan, "Islam constitutes the moral-symbolic language of Muslim politics" (Verkaaik 2001: 347). But there are varieties in Islamic interpretation, which range from the strict fundamentalism of the Wahabi regime in Saudi Arabia to the more modernist interpretation that inspired the founders of Pakistan. In the twentieth century, the equation of the state, the economy, the society, and the nation was predominant. However, in today's postcolonial world there is a challenge to the state, and state power as a locus of territorial sovereignty and cultural legitimacy, by ethnic separatism, the globalization of trade and capital movement, and the migration of immigrants and refugees (Hansen and Stepputat 2001: 1–2). Demands upon the new states by ethnic groups for autonomy, and often independence, on the one hand, are countered by the need for the state to be a part of supranational organizations such as the UN, the World Bank, and NATO.

Colonialism and the emergence of new nation-states in Africa and Asia have brought about great political changes. The newly emerged states of Africa and Asia were successors to colonies that were arbitrarily carved out by the colonial powers, without regard to the boundaries of indigenous political entities. These nation-states tried to develop a national culture to unify the new nation. Traditional forms of leadership and politics were transformed as they were integrated into the state systems of these new nations. Today's postcolonial nation-states contain culturally diverse tribal populations. Lewis has recently made the point that precolonial states in Africa, such as the kingdom of Ethiopia and the Zulu, Bemba, and Ganda states, were also multiethnic in their composition (1999: 58ff.). This was also true of other conquest states, like the empire of Bornu, described earlier in this chapter, which included non-Kanuri peoples such as the Fulani and the Bagirmi. After independence was gained, in many countries, tribalism was seen as a problem to be overcome in forging a new national identity. However, tribalism does not die; rather, it is transformed and then maintained as ethnic difference. Though the ideology of ethnicity is new, the members of an ethnic group have returned to a conceptualization of themselves as all related by bonds of kinship. When the state developed, the kinship links tying a community together disappeared, only to return as an ideology when ethnicity has become important. Ethnic differences become the basis of political competition in the new nation-states. The drive to establish a national culture may be (or is often seen as) an attempt by the dominant and most powerful group or the numerically superior ethnic group to establish its culture as the national culture. This was the case with the Javanese, who dominate Indonesia.

All the indigenous societies we have described that were part of colonial empires are now encompassed within the boundaries of modern-day states. The Trobrianders, Abelam, Maring, and Enga are all part of the nation-state of Papua New Guinea, where today both Big Men and chiefs run for the office of representative in the New Guinea parliament or for the position of Councilor in the local District Council (on the Maring, see LiPuma 2000: 83). In the Trobriands, in particular, despite involvement in national politics, Trobriand chiefs are still strong and "hold the reins in their hands, much to the dismay of the national administration and missions" (Schiefenhovel and Bell-Krannhals 1996: 236). But Schiefenhovel and Bell-Krannhals also note that "the Trobrianders thus have an interesting mix of ascribed chieftainship, and men who achieve their rank and influence by merit. The latter position, as a rule, cannot be transferred to the first position" (1996: 249). Those who run for office often act like Big Men in their political activities. Today, Trobriand chiefs are sometimes members of the Papua New Guinea Parliament, continuing this chiefly control over external affairs.

Today the Yanomamo are to be found in both Venezuela and Brazil. They have been in indirect contact, via trading networks, with the outside world for a very long time (Ferguson 1995). When missionaries arrived in numbers in the 1950s, they established themselves in an area "by giving away vast amounts of goods" (Rabbens 2004: 93). In the mid- to late 1980s, some 40,000 miners, armed with guns and airplanes, attracted by the discovery of gold, invaded Yanomami territory. Cassiterite (the basis for tin) was also sought. At least 15 percent of the Yanomami populations died of new diseases to which they had no resistance, or as a result of conflicts with the miners (Rabbens 2004: 12). The invasion of miners and others has resulted in the introduction of venereal diseases and the birth of mixed-race children who will no longer have rights as Yanomamo (*New York Times*, October 1, 2002). Only a few villages remain in remote areas, away from "civilization," and many have moved to mission stations, where the power is in the hands of the missionaries. In Brazil, the army, with assistance in the form of $1.5 billion, has begun to construct new military bases, and expand old ones in territories that had been set aside for the Yanomamo and other "tribes," and have also begun to recruit Yanomamo young men for the army. The so-called "tribal leaders" have protested and with the help of Indian advocates have instituted legal action to stop this intrusion.

The Kayapo and other Brazilian Indian groups headed by a young leadership have become strong advocates for the protection of the territory of indigenous groups against the so-called "march of progress" by mining, hydroelectric, and forestry interests who, along with the Brazilian military, sought to exploit the resources in indigenous territories. International groups such as Amnesty International and the U.S. Congressional Human Rights Caucus have helped them in this endeavor (Rabbens 2004: 23). Davi Kopenawa Yanomami is probably the only Yanomami leader to gain international attention. He is a shaman who had worked as an interpreter for FUNAI, the Brazilian National Indian Foundation. He spoke eloquently in 1992 before the General Assembly of the United Nations at the opening ceremony for the International Year of Indigenous Peoples. He is also a bridge person to village Yanomami, trying to bring together village leaders to discuss the cessation of feuding and internal warfare in order to move beyond the confines of the villages to unite as a single people and concentrate on common endeavors such as the improvement of medical care and education for the next generations (Rabbens 2004: 120ff.).

Today, the Kachin live under the military government of Myanmar, and the *duwa*, the traditional leader or chief, no longer has political power. Conflicts between the central government and ethnic groups, like the Kachin, have been mostly peacefully resolved. As Lawtaw notes, "Since the beginning of the 1990s, religious organizations and a few NGOs have started community development programs . . . at the grassroots level" (2007: 237). There were three separate armed Kachin groups up until 2005, which today work to protect the rights of the Kachin people, two of the groups becoming militias in the areas of Kachin State in which they operated. The separate traditional Manau festivals, which were organized by different villages, have today been consolidated into a single celebration, the "Traditional Manau Dance Festival," which takes place at the same time as Kachin State Day. Its aim is to unite the separate Kachin linguistic groups and the other non-Kachin ethnic groups, as well as the different segments of the Kachin population, to rebuild the unity that the Kachin people had in 1948 (Lawtaw 2007: 243). It is attended even by Kachin who live in India and China. A Kachin National Consultative Assembly was formed to create good will, bring together the various Kachin armed groups, prevent violence, and promote "the establishment of a genuine democratic nation" (Lawtaw 2007: 244–45). In addition, according to Lawtaw, the patrilineal Kachin still maintain the following sets of kin relationships: the *htingaw* (patrilineal kin group of brothers—*kahpu-kanau*), *mayu* (lineages from which brides come), and *dama* (lineages into which female members of kin group marry) (2007: 245), which we have described in chapter 6. She notes, "The social network among the *kahpu-kanau, mayu* and *dame* is still very strong and nowadays one can say that the Kachin social network functions as a kind of 'insurance' or 'social security' system in Kachin society" (Lawtaw 2007: 245).

Empowerment

At the beginning of this chapter, we talked about power as the ability to command others and authority as the institutionalization of power. **Empowerment** has been used variously to refer to actions by the people to get what they want, populist action, revolt from below to subvert those in authority, and the devolution of power to place it in the hands of the have-nots, the subalterns. Using the ideas of Foucault (1972) about the way in which power is vested in **discourse**, one can say that with empowerment, the have-nots gain a voice. When successive African states gained their independence, empowerment of the African populace was a primary policy.

In Zimbabwe, for example, when independence was gained in 1980, there was a presidential directive on Africanization of the Zimbabwean civil service, and the empowerment of the African population. Though the public sector and various types of funds are now managed by indigenous Zimbabweans, most Zimbabweans continue to participate in the economy as unskilled, seasonal, and unpaid domestic and agricultural laborers. The policy of indigenization and empowerment of the black population has been primarily articulated by the male, black, self-employed business lobby. The rest of the black population, however, was convinced that black politicians and leading bureaucrats were interested only in empowering and enriching themselves (Gaidzanwa 1999: 118–19). Those Zimbabwean groups lobbying for empowerment, such as the Indigenous Business Development Council, a black business lobby; the Affirmative Action Group, which included the War Veterans' Association; and the Indigenous Businesswomen's Organization, were still involved, by and large, in patronage politics. Even the businesswomen's group, which was organized to combat the problems women encountered in venturing into business in a male-dominated world, and which explicitly supported the economic empowerment of black women, supported Robert Mugabe in the 1996 election and they have continued to rely on the patronage of his ruling party. There have been no plans for the democratization of landholding, from which women are barred, though they are the sources of labor and management. The emphasis has been on acquiring land from white farmers. More recently, the political situation has changed and President Mugabe has assumed dictatorial power and ordered the confiscation of land belonging to white farmers. The War Veterans' Association is the group taking over the land. It is clear that the term *empowerment* serves as an effective political slogan; in Zimbabwe the policy of indigenization and empowerment, in practical terms, has meant the empowerment of a limited, predominantly male, political circle, consisting of the supporters of Mugabe.

India has also initiated programs that emphasized empowerment and development. A group in Uttar Pradesh, the *Mahila Samakhya*, sought to "empower low-cast poor rural women, through collective consciousness-raising and mobilization to challenge caste, class, and gender oppression, engender social change, and develop themselves and their community" (Sharma and Gupta 2006: 14). Since Indian officials emphasized "procedure," application filing, and the ability to write, the staff and clients of this program were forced to learn these skills. But being able to write and read meant "empowerment" to the nonliterate clients. Demands for village development such as digging a well or constructing a road had to be in writing to the local level bureaucrats, and literacy enabled the members of the group to follow the "paper trail" of their request (Sharma and Gupta 2006: 14, 16).

POLITICS IN THE CONTEMPORARY NATION-STATE

Many political anthropologists are interested in the modern nation-state. It is necessary at this point to distinguish between state and nation, or nation-state. States may be culturally homogeneous but, more likely, include members of several different cultural or ethnic groups. The **nation, or nation-state**, developed in Europe with the rise of nationalism, which assumed that a people who had a culture and a language should constitute a separate nation, or nation-state. The concept of nation-state links an ethnic ideology with a state organization. **Ethnonationalism** refers to the desire on the part of a minority ethnic group in a multiethnic state to have its own nation-state. Ethnonationalism has led to the breakup of a number of European states such as Czechoslovakia and Yugoslavia.

The term **neo-nationalism** has begun to be used by European anthropologists to describe the reemergence of nationalism at the end of the Cold war "under different global and transnational conditions" (Banks and Gingrich 2006: 2). This form of nationalism is a reaction to the enormous increase in transnational migration. The 2001 election in Denmark clearly illustrated the strength of the neo-nationalist position, the voting strength of the right-wing parties, and their antagonism toward the 17,000 refugees from Bosnia-Herzegovina, and the immigrants from Turkey, Pakistan, and Somalia.

In the former Soviet Union there had been efforts to develop a "communist" culture, but this became, by and large, an attempt to Russify the distinctly different Central Asian and Caucasian peoples who were part of the Soviet State. This policy was met with opposition but little overt conflict because of Soviet suppression. Under the policy of *glasnost*, which opened up Soviet society, ethnicity and nationalism reasserted themselves, and many republics, such as the Baltic states, Moldavia, the Ukraine, Tadjikistan, Kazakstan, Kyrgyzstan, and Uzbekistan, became politically independent. For the non-Russian republics, this meant moving out from under the domination of Russian culture. These independent states now have the problems of defining themselves as nations, and states such as Georgia are dealing with their own internal ethnic minorities. The collapse of the Soviet Union was soon followed by the requests from the now independent countries such as Latvia and Lithuania to join NATO for the advantages thereby bestowed

An interesting political phenomenon occurred when Kazakhstan was created. Under the Soviets, the Kazakhs, an ethnic minority, were forced to transform their economic and political institutions to conform to communist ideology. With the collapse of communism, Kazakhstan reverted to a different political structure that included a Parliament and a president. However, in the 1990s under President Nazarbaev, it soon became a totalitarian state. In addition, during this time, the earlier form of political organization based on clans and on kinship that the Soviet authorities had attempted to suppress was also resurgent. Up until the early twentieth century, the Kazakhs were nomadic pastoralists with a segmentary lineage structure as described in chapter 6. Though a considerable Russian minority remained after "independence," Kazakh ethnicity and the Kazakh language were emphasized in the new state. According to Schatz, "clan and umbrella clan genealogies experienced a revival as traits that distinguished ethnic Kazakhs from the non-titular [Russian] citizens of independent Kazakhstan. . . . In short, genealogical knowledge was understood to be axiomatic (even if it required reviving in the 1990s) [to establish Kazakh identity]" (2004: 117). Clans rose in importance and streets and schools were named after clan-based heroes (Schatz 2004: 118). Opposition between clans, a characteristic of segmentary lineage structures, became a major feature in the postindependence inter-clan and local level politics of Kazakhstan. Patronage networks were also based on clan identity. Old clan politics and the new parliament-president political organization combine with the riches of oil. This makes Kazakhstan an important actor in the world's current energy crisis.

Although this is the postcolonial period, nation-states in Europe that have been in existence for hundreds of years may still exhibit tribalism, meaning identity with a particular group likened to a tribe, and exhibit ethnic differences in ways similar to postcolonial nations in Africa and Asia. The southern area of Belgium, Walloonia, where French is spoken, has been in conflict with the northern area, where Flemish, a Dutch dialect, is spoken. If this is the result of postcolonialism, then the colonialism that it involves is that of the ancient Romans, whose colony extended up to the Flemish-speaking border, but not beyond it (see chapter 4). The conflict concerns not only language but also control over economic resources. Each of these areas of Belgium now has its own legislature and regional executives, and the central government includes a fixed proportion of ministers from each group.

Factionalism

One of the recurring themes in the study of local-level politics has been **factionalism**. Many of the earlier anthropological studies of peasant communities in the Old and New Worlds explored the operation of political factionalism as it related to the way national politics was played out on the local level. Leaders of factions vying for power may build their followings in a number of different ways, depending upon the structure of the community. The faction consisting of the leader and his followers resembles the Big Man and his followers. Like the Big Man, the leader of a faction is in opposition to other faction leaders. The faction leader vies with other leaders to attract followers, as does the Big Man. There is an exchange relationship between the faction leader and his followers, as there is between the Big Man and his followers, and both types of leaders need to continue supporting and rewarding followers in order to hold onto his followers. When the leader in either case loses power or dies, the faction or group of followers dissolves. In this aspect, factions contrast with political parties, which continue to exist though individual leaders may come and go. However, within political parties in the United States, factions may be found on a level of local communities, where party leaders and their supporters compete for control of the party apparatus at that level. More than one hundred years ago, the ward boss (Boss Tweed in New York) operated like a Big Man distributing largess to his followers. In nation-states, factionalism may be based on differences in ethnic background. In such situations factionalism is transformed into ethnic conflict.

Warlords

Today, the term **warlord** is frequently used with reference to leaders in Afghanistan, Somalia, and Myanmar (Burma). A warlord and his followers are structurally similar to a faction and its leaders. A warlord is like a militarized Big Man. One warlord may be a military commander with an extensive regional following and the ability to use his personal prestige to secure benefits for his followers, like General Dostum (see photo) and the late General Massoud, in Afghanistan. Another "strongman" has a more limited militarized ethnic or clan formation mobilized locally, such as is found in Somalia (Rich 1999b; for Somalia, see below). Warlordism has become a growing phenomenon in contemporary international politics as can be seen from reading the daily newspaper. The *New York Times* has reported that the State Department of the United States was disappointed with Hamid Karzai, president of Afghanistan. They hoped that he would "crack down on corruption" and arrest the warlords who controlled the drug trade (*New York Times*, June 7, 2008). Instead of arresting General Dostum after the latter was said to have attacked a rival warlord with a beer bottle, President Karzai was reported to have said that "he did not want to pick a fight with General Dostum for fear of alienating his backers." General Dostum, a leader of Uzbeks in Afghanistan, operates outside President Karzai's sphere of influence and range of control. Karzai, who is Pushtun, needs to keep General Dostum and his Uzbeck followers as supporters of his Afghan government. He does this by offering inducements, not by threats of punishment (*New York Times*, June 7, 2008).

Some warlords and their groups are the consequence of the post-cold war disappearance of "superpower hegemony," subsequent to which, multiplicities of ethnic and other loyalties emerged to become the basis for these new groupings of warlords and followers. It is like a "barbarians at the gates" phenomenon that occurs at the end of imperial eras (Rich 1999a: xi–xii). Warlordism is confined, primarily, to what one might consider to be peripheral, more undeveloped areas. These are the areas in which anthropologists have frequently done their research. Warlords are

Uzbek Warlord Rashid Dostum of Afghanistan, greeted by residents of the northern town of Shibergan.

often involved in the illicit trade of opium and other narcotics, as well as in the arms trade, all of which have become completely globalized. The emergence of mercenary armies, a new kind of "warrior class," is also associated with warlordism, which serves to undermine "the authority of conventional governments" (O'Brien 1999).

In Somalia, the population of nomadic pastoralists was culturally and linguistically homogeneous, subsumed under a single overarching segmentary lineage system. Under colonialism, titular clan leaders were officially recognized by the colonial government. The postcolonial democracy elections pitted sixty-five parties, which represented important lineages and sub-lineages, against one another. After the assassination of the president of the country in 1969, clans and clan families became the basis for militias, with modern weaponry introduced by the United States and the Soviet Union. These militias were run by warlords. The warlords and their groups in opposition to one another, in effect, represented different parts of the segmentary lineage system (Rosman and Rubel 1999).

Patron-Client Relationships

The **patron-client relationship** discussed in connection with *compadrazgo* in chapter 6 also has important political dimensions. In the past, patrons, frequently landowners, played roles as intermediaries between the peasants of a village and the provincial or national government. Problems with tax collectors and the court system brought clients to their patrons, who were always of a higher class, for assistance. Because of their wide social contacts with their social equals in the towns and cities, patrons could help clients whose social contacts were limited to their own villages. Though there were no links of actual kinship between patrons and clients, the *compadrazgo* ties between the families of patron and clients were perpetuated over generations. Patrons as landlords and clients as tenants were distinguished by their differential access to land and by their class differences as gentry and peasants. These social and economic differences were the basis for a difference in political power. Patron-client relationships are usually superseded when opposition between socioeconomic classes serves to separate and oppose them.

Today, a form of patron-client relationship continues to be important in the political economy of Bangladesh. At first a homeland for Bengali Muslims and a province of the Islamic republic of Pakistan, Bangladesh became an independent nation in 1971after a bloody civil war. An earlier class structure of commoners and nobility has been replaced by a system based on land ownership, wealth, education, and power, in which a hierarchical network of interpersonal patron-client relationships dominates (Kochanek 1993: 44). In the countryside, this system is reinforced by economic forces, such as scarcity of credit, land, tenancy contracts, and employment opportunities, along with political factors, such as the need for protection. The concept of *daya*, meaning "grace" or "blessing," constitutes the intellectual underpinning of the reciprocal patron-client relationship. Individuals feel that they have the moral right to demand food and subsistence from those "well placed." The well-placed individuals, who acquire their prosperity from a higher moral authority, are expected to give generously to their clients. The patrons who distribute are expected to be authoritarian and to be feared and obeyed (Kochanek 1993: 45).

This pattern of patron-client relationship has extended beyond the rural area and has come to dominate not only the whole of the Bangladesh political process but the business community as well. Though Bangladesh has formal legal, constitutional, and administrative governmental structures, these have come to be monopolized by a "traditional pattern of patron-client relationships based on *tadbir*, a process of personal lobbying" (Kochanek 1993: 251). Policymaking and implementation always require personal connections. For example, the entire governmental structure of General Erhsad from 1982, when he came to power as a result of a military coup, to 1990 was based on the patron-client pattern. He traveled through the countryside "like a ward boss distributing benefits in exchange for support" (Kochanek 1993: 265). The business community, which is in its early stages of development and modernization, is characterized by the same pattern, with primary emphasis on personal relationships. Businessmen often obtain exemptions from rules and other kinds of business benefits by manipulating the regulatory system and the administration of policy, using their personal connections. Patron-client relationships, from the countryside to the capital, are a way of life in Bangladesh.

POLITICS IN AMERICAN SOCIETY

The concepts we have discussed in this chapter can be applied to our own society as well. The operation of leadership in terms of power and exchange, the politics of empowerment, bureaucracy and administration, the emergence of leaders through political maneuvering, factionalism, police corruption, and patron-client relationships are as relevant to political situations in our own society as they have been in the situations described thus far in this chapter. If Ghanaian citizens are afraid that the police can be bought off, many segments of American society feel the same way. Just as Bangladeshi businessmen manipulate the regulatory system of the government, so do businessmen in our country. In the past, the ward boss in big American cities was like a New Guinea Big Man in redistributing patronage in the form of material benefits among the "ward heelers." Factions representing different political positions and coalitions operate at every level of our political system. They may coalesce around individuals or around an issue, such as abortion, equal rights for women, or affirmative action for minorities. Ethnic politics are as active today in American cities as they are in any nation-state in Asia or Africa. Elections pit Poles against African Americans in Chicago, Hispanics against Anglos in Texas and California, and Cubans against African Americans in Miami.

The Mafia

The Mafia organization was originally brought over by Sicilian immigrants at the turn of twentieth century. It easily adapted itself to the politics of corruption, which was operative at the time in New York and the cities to which it spread. A number of structural similarities can be found in criminal organizations like the American Mafia in other parts of the world such as the Sicilian Mafia, the Russian Mafia, and the Colombian drug cartels. These organizations begin with marginal criminal activities, such as prostitution and gambling, and soon move into trafficking in drugs. They operate when weak, corrupt governments are present, which was the situation when the Soviet system collapsed. They offer "protection" against predators, and use their political influence to serve as "fixers." Internally, they use kinship, godfather/godchild relations, and patron/client relations to maintain loyalty. However, Schneider and Schneider point out that each of these criminal organizations operates in a different cultural context, affecting the type of relationship it has with external forces and authorities. The alliance that the Sicilian Mafia had with the Masons and with Italy's right-wing military secret service was quite different from the Colombian drug cartels' relationship to its governmental bureaucracy (2004: 314–16).

The American Mafia is based on the patron-client relationships characteristic of the Sicilian rural scene from which the men in the American Mafia emigrated. A study of the Mafia in Sicily and in Detroit explicitly likens the don to a Big Man (Louwe 1986). The Big Man in the Mafia family provides a source of income for his "family," and protection against the risks of making money illegally; in return, family members pay him respect, grant him complete obedience and loyalty, and give him a share of their profits from criminal enterprises. His status is achieved through the demonstration of his ability. The don maintains his influence by manipulating his connections with the police, politicians, and judges. The greatest threat to the family is the member who is turned into an informer by the police. There is no clear rule of succession, though a son may succeed his father as don and continue as patron to his father's clients. However, more in keeping with the Big Man structure, the clients whose patron has died may move to become followers of another don. The film *The Godfather* and the TV program *The Sopranos*, which we will discuss in chapter 11, present a very sympathetic portrait of a Mafia family, focusing on succession, and on the personal as well as professional problems of the don.

Within the past decade, the media have been referring to the Russian Mafia in the United States. Not much is known about the organization of crime among the Russians, many of them Jewish, who began to emigrate to the United States in large numbers in the late 1970s. They settled in that part of Brooklyn known as Brighton Beach, now often referred to as "Odessa by the Sea" (McCauley 2001: 72; Friedman 2000: 13). In a recent study, *Russian Mafia in America*, there was disagreement about whether Soviet emigré criminal groups operated like La Cosa Nostra, or were less organizationally complex and hierarchical. However, particular leaders have been identified as "capo di tutti capi" (Finckenauer and Waring 1998: 164). Many Brighton Beach residents, in discussing crime in their area, used the term *Russian Mafia* and saw the Italian Mafia and Soviet emigré crime groups as being very similar in their mode of organization. Salter argues that because they engage in "risky business" there is a great need for trust, and therefore Mafias rely on kin and ethnic ties, characterized as kin ties, in the conduct of their business (2002: 5).

POLITICAL ECONOMY

At the beginning of this chapter, we noted that political organization and economics are intimately interwoven and that this interrelationship is referred to as political economy. What are the ways in which the forces of production shape the culture and political organization? As shown throughout this chapter, the various types of political organization are associated with different forms of distribution and often different forms of production. For example, chieftainship is interwoven with a redistributive system, as described in chapter 8, in which surplus goods funnel into the central political position, that of the chief, and are distributed on ceremonial occasions to other chiefs, who in turn redistribute to their followers. The chief maintains political authority by controlling and disbursing economic goods, while the economic system is dependent on the establishment of fixed positions of authority. Markets are always associated with state structures. The state as a political system, as we have pointed out, operates on a territorial basis beyond the level of kinship and clanship. The less personal relationships of a market are in accord with this type of system.

Ortner's landmark discussion of political economy as a framework of analysis points out its advantages (1984). She notes that an approach in terms of political economy is very open to symbolic analysis. Throughout this chapter, we have indicated how symbols are used to express rank and authority—as, for example, among the Trobrianders. Among the Kachin, who oscillate between two forms of political structure, the Big Man of the *gumlao* type and the chieftainship of the *gumsa*, symbols are used in different ways to express these opposing structures. In the context of the modern nation-state, symbols become a powerful means of constructing ethnic identity, and they are employed to express ethnic conflicts as well as class struggles.

As opposed to an emphasis on particular societies as isolates, political economy promotes a regional perspective. As we pointed out, systems of ceremonial exchange such as the *kula* demonstrate how societies with differing political systems were joined in a regional system of ceremonial exchange and barter. A focus upon political economy also reveals the way in which capitalist forces of production in Latin America have shaped the way of life of oppressed people. An emphasis on political economy can show how societies have been drawn into a world system.

SUMMARY

- Power, the key concept in defining political organization, is the ability to command others to do certain things and to get compliance from them. When power becomes institutionalized, it has been transformed into authority, with a recognized position, whose occupant must be obeyed.
- Anthropologists refer to a position that depends on personal qualifications and individual ability as an achieved status, in contrast to an ascribed status, which one inherits.
- In the simplest form of political organization, leadership was manifested intermittently while band organization had a more fixed membership that came together annually to carry out joint ritual and economic activities. The position of Big Man was dependent on personal qualifications and individual ability. The political economy of chieftainships is a more complex redistributive system with more levels of political organization.
- The state differs from the other types of political organization in scale. It is organized on a territorial basis, rather than on the basis of kinship and clanship. In the state we find social stratification—rulers, aristocrats, commoners, and various low-status groups.
- Feuds, conducted according to rules, involve collective, not personal, responsibility, so revenge can be taken against any member of the group. Warfare is hostile action between different groups. The task of the anthropologist is to explain why warfare occurs when and where it does.
- The legal principles or bases upon which disputes are resolved emerge only through the analysis of specific cases. Law is a cultural system of meanings that the anthropologist must interpret.
- The faction consisting of the leader and his followers resembles the Big Man and his followers.
- After independence was gained in many new nation-states, tribalism was seen as a problem to be overcome in forging a new national identity. However, tribalism does not die but is transformed and maintained as ethnic differences, which then become the basis for political competition.
- The concepts—the operation of leadership in terms of power and exchange, the politics of empowerment, bureaucracy and administration, political maneuvering, factionalism, police corruption, and patron-client relationships—are all relevant to political situations in our own society.

SUGGESTED READINGS

Lazhnev, Sasha. *Crafting Peace; Strategies to Deal with Warlords in Collapsing States.* Lanham, MD: Lexington Books, 2005. Case studies of warlords in Sierra Leone and Tajikistan and a general discussion of warlordism and ethnicity.

Schroeder, Ingo W., and Bettina E. Schmidt, eds. *Anthropology of Violence and Conflict.* New York: Routledge, 2001. A series of articles concerning the role that violence and conflict play in contemporary world politics.

Vincent, Joan, ed. *The Anthropology of Politics: A Reader in Ethnography, Theory, and Critique.* Malden, MA: Blackwell Publishers, 2002. An excellent survey of both historic and contemporary ideas that deal with political anthropology.

SUGGESTED WEBSITES

www.anthro.uiuc.edu/faculty/cfennell/syllabus/anth560/anthlawbib.htm. Details a variety of sources on anthropology and law.

www.onewal.com/. The American Mafia Website presents a variety of historic and contemporary information on the Mafia. http://warlordsofafghanistan.com/. Presents information on the history of various warlords in Afghanistan and their present situation.

Chapter 10
Religion and the Supernatural

MANY PEOPLE IN THE WORLD believe in an order of existence beyond the observable universe, that is, in what we call the supernatural. For example, the Trobriand Islanders believe that when a person dies, his or her spirit splits in two. One part goes to live on the island of Tuma in the village of the dead, to remain there until it is reincarnated in the spirit of a newborn child. The other part of the spirit haunts the favorite places of the deceased, and its presence is frightening to the villagers still alive. They are even more afraid of sorcerers, especially flying witches, who are thought to have caused the death in the first place. Beliefs in sorcery, spirits, and witchcraft are not limited to societies like that of the Trobriand Islanders. One can ride along a country road in England and see a billboard announcing an impending meeting of a local witches' coven to be held the following week. Meetings of American witches' covens are also announced in the newspaper. Popular television programs feature teenage witches and individuals with the power to communicate with the dead.

The fundamental right to religious belief protects believers in witchcraft, like the followers of many other faiths in America today. However, periodically religious followers run afoul of the law in the practice of their religion. In the course of their religious rituals, serpent handlers in some states of the Appalachian region hold up venomous snakes or ingest poisons. They base these practices on the belief that if they are free of sin, worshipers will not be harmed. Practitioners cite New Testament Scriptures stating that "[believers] shall speak with new tongues; they shall take up serpents; and if they drink any deadly thing, it shall not hurt them" (Mark 16: 17–18). Members of these religious communities, like many other Christian groups described as "fundamentalist," take the Bible literally. Some people bitten during the ritual survive; others subsequently die. Worshipers believe that those who die in this way are being punished for their sins. The snake, in this instance, is seen as acting as an agent of God. Whether a person is pure or sinful determines if the snakebite or poison will be fatal. The outcome is understood by the participants to be the result of the intervention of supernatural forces. From the perspective of law, the practice presents a danger to participants and observers, requiring state intervention (Burton, 1993). Enforcement of these statutes is sporadic, and most cases go unprosecuted unless highly publicized in the media.

The Trobriand belief in the power of sorcerers and the serpent handlers' belief that the purity of their character will protect them from snakebites and poisons go beyond what one can observe. Such explanations rely on phenomena that fall into the domain of the supernatural. From the Western point of view, empirical explanations of the observable world are considered scientific. Explanations that do not depend on empirical evidence, but instead rely on strongly held beliefs in nonempirical or supernatural forces are categorized as religious. However, people in other societies, like the Trobrianders, consider their spiritual culture heroes and the ghosts of their ancestors absolutely real, no less real than the physical world around them.

In American society, scientific explanations that involve the forces of nature are generally perceived to be distinct from religious beliefs and ideas about the supernatural. The intersection of religion as a belief in the supernatural and the other parts of culture is encountered in our discussions of family, economics, and political organization, as well as in our discussions of religion. Nonreligious or secular institutions in America routinely invoke the symbolism of religion; the phrase "In God We Trust" appears in courtrooms and on every dollar bill.

Religious phenomena involve the use of symbols that evoke powerful emotional responses. One has merely to consider the difference between water and holy water and the emotional response evoked in Catholic ritual by the latter to realize this. Symbols that evoke strong feelings are to be found throughout cultures, in domains considered religious and those considered to be secular or nonreligious. Political symbols, such as the flag and the national anthem, produce strong shared emotions; religious symbols and ideas amplify the emotions of political rituals.

Religious ideas inspire individuals to enact or perform in culturally sanctioned ways, blurring the division between how the mind understands ideology and the body enacts these ideas. Religious ideologies also invariably shape ideas about the body and bodily experience. The recent focus in anthropology on the cultural construction of the human body as enacting internalized values, referred to as **embodiment**, is an important contemporary approach to understanding the lived experience of religion and ritual.

Religious ideology invariably normalizes gender roles, and is invoked to maintain the status quo of social divisions or mobilize people around collective acts of violence. It can also provide the basis for resistance to societal norms, and mobilize movements of social justice and change. Religious ideology not only motivates individual and group behavior but is invariably encoded in various degrees into national identity and state policy. Considering these multiple ways religion functions in human societies, it is not surprising that there is considerable debate among scholars about defining it.

RELIGION STUDIED / RELIGION DEFINED?

The history of the anthropological study of religion is intertwined with European economic expansion and colonialism. The late nineteenth- and early twentieth-century "armchair scholars" derived their various theories from the comparative information that forms the collective body

A domestic shrine in Rajasthan, India, contains images of important household deities; they are presented with offerings of food and money and dressed according to the season.

of knowledge about the global diversity of religious and ritual practices. This information was gathered by or collected with the approval of colonial officials who recognized the benefit of understanding local belief systems to new rulers. Later ethnographic information on religious systems relied on the extensive direct observations and field experiences of anthropologists. Some scholars argue that these observations and the resulting written accounts of non-Western religions identify local experience as religious phenomena because of the inevitable imposition of European and American categories of ideology and practice. This critique cautions contemporary scholars to clearly define, to the best of their ability, the underlying assumptions and approaches that guide their observations and conclusions.

Religion is traditionally defined by anthropologists as the cultural means by which humans deal with the supernatural, but many humans also believe that the reverse is true—that the supernatural deals with humans. In this interaction, the supernatural is usually seen as powerful and human beings as weak. In another approach, Saler (1993) defines religion in terms of a pool of elements that tend to cluster together. They include a belief in God, gods, or "spiritual beings" with whom humans can have spiritual contact; a moral code believed to emanate from extrahuman sources; belief in a human ability to go beyond human suffering; and rituals that involve humans with the extrahuman (Saler 1993: 219). The "spiritual beings" and the extrahuman of Saler's definition can be equated with what we call "the supernatural." Klass (1995) argues that defining religion in terms of the supernatural reflects a Eurocentric assumption about the separation of the "natural" and "supernatural" realms of existence. He therefore defines religion as "that instituted process of interaction among the members of that society—and between them and the universe at large as they conceive it to be constituted—which provides them with meaning, coherence, direction, unity, easement, and whatever degree of control over events they perceive as possible" (1995: 38).

A system of religious belief is found in every culture, and is therefore generally acknowledged to be a cultural universal; beliefs and practices, however, vary between and among communities and practitioners. This universality has prompted scholars to question what it is about life and the world in which that life is lived that compels humans to propose that the world is governed by forces beyond their empirical observations. Many theorists over the years have attempted to answer this question. Max Weber (1930) argued that since life is made up of pain and suffering, human beings developed religion to explain why they were put on Earth to suffer. St. Paul constantly asked God why he was afflicted with a "thorn in the flesh," without ever receiving an answer. Sigmund Freud (1928) proposed that religious institutions represented society's way of dealing with childish needs of dependency on the part of individuals. What would otherwise be a neurotic trait thereby finds expression in the form of all-powerful gods and deities who control an individual's destiny. Melford Spiro (1966) suggests three kinds of needs that religion fulfills. The first is called the cognitive need, that is, the need to understand; this is the need for explanations and meanings. The second is the substantive need to bring about specific goals, such as rain, good crops, and health, by carrying out religious acts. The third is the psychological need to reduce fear and anxiety in situations in which these are provoked. Emile Durkheim (1915) and others who have followed Durkheim's approach saw religion as the means by which society inculcates values and sentiments necessary for the promotion of social solidarity and the society's ultimate survival.

Recent explanations have involved what is referred to as the **cognitive science of religion**. This approach examines religious phenomena as a result of how the human brain has evolved over time to process and categorize information. Boyer (2001) claims that religious symbolism and representations are constrained cognitively by the universal properties of the mind-brain: "Religious concepts are probably influenced by the way the brain's inference systems produce explanations without our being aware of it" (2001: 18). He characterizes religious expressions as "counter-intuitive ontologies" (2001: 65). For example, holy water is chemically no different from tap water; however, believers see it as different, and this is counterintuitive. Rituals represent behaviors that are separate from everyday life, and religious representations "violate" what people consider to be natural phenomena. He suggests that the universality of religious experience is best understood by questioning "what makes human minds so selective in what supernatural claims they find plausible" (2001: 31). Other scholars of religion and cognition are investigating neurophysiological and neurobiological manifestations of religious phenomena such as trance and meditation; some cite the role played by the temporal lobe of the brain in these expressions of religious ideas, emotions, and practices.

From these different considerations of why religion exists and what explanations have been offered for the universality of religious phenomena, we can suggest some tentative answers to the questions we have posed. Human beings are part of a social world as well as a natural world. They are dependent on the actions of other humans, as well as on the forces of nature. Some of these actions and forces can be controlled through their own behavior. However, they are helpless in the face of other actions and forces. Humans attempt to understand and at least influence or control through a belief in the supernatural what is otherwise uncontrollable and unexplainable. By doing this, they alleviate their anxieties about their helplessness in the situation, although Boyer points out that many religious ideologies engender anxiety and "create not so much reassurance as a thick pall of gloom" (2001: 20). The organization of the supernatural world that is constructed by human beings reflects the society in which they live. The sentiments and emotions generated by the supernatural are an important force in the enhancement of social solidarity.

RELIGION, SCIENCE, AND INTELLIGENT DESIGN

Many aspects of the natural world that were formerly explained by religious ideology are now explained by means of science. In the seventeenth century, the Catholic Church insisted that the earth was at the center of the solar system, and persecuted Galileo for his scientific research, which demonstrated that Copernicus's earlier conclusion was correct: that the sun, not the earth, was at the center of our solar system. Despite conclusive evidence supporting this scientific view of the solar system, it took the Catholic Church hundreds of years to officially accept the scientific explanation.

To many people the distinction between religious and scientific systems of knowledge and explanation is not readily apparent. Recent responses to the teaching of the theory of evolution in public schools are an example of the contemporary debates over conflicts between religious and scientific explanation. Based on the Old Testament book of Genesis, Judeo-Christian belief states that God created the universe, the earth, humans, and all species of life on earth. The seventeenth-century clergyman Bishop Ussher determined for Christians that creation occurred in the year 4004 BC. Until the late nineteenth century, this was the accepted belief about creation in the Western world. In the mid-nineteenth century, Darwin proposed his theory of the evolution of species based upon empirical evidence from comparative anatomy, geology, botany, and paleontology. This scientific theory proposed an alternative explanation for the development of all the species in the world and the appearance of human life. For a time, both religious and scientific explanations of creation competed with one another.

Today, many people accept the academic, scientific theory of evolution. However, approximately half the American people surveyed in a 2001 Gallup Poll expressed a belief in a creationist approach to human origins, broadly generalized as the belief that each of the species on earth was created and placed here by God as spelled out in the Book of Genesis. In reality there are multiple versions of creationist belief systems, among them Flat Earthers, Geocentrists, Young Earth Creationism, and Progressive Creationism, all of which hypothesize models of species and geological diversity based on varying interpretations of Biblical and scientific sources (Scott 1999). Creationists in the United States have challenged the exclusive teaching of Darwinian scientific evolution in public schools, and have argued, in courts, school boards, and state legislatures, that both creationism and evolutionary science should be taught to public school students as alternative theories for the origins of life on Earth. In the early 1980s the state legislatures of Louisiana and Arkansas passed laws stating that when evolutionary science was taught in the public schools, creationism also had to be taught as an alternative theory. The Louisiana legislation was challenged in the Supreme Court and in 1987, in *Edwards, Governor of Louisiana, et al. v. Aguillard et al.* the Supreme Court ruled against this legislation, holding that teaching creationism in public schools was unconstitutional because it attempted to advance a particular religious perspective.

As a result of this Supreme Court decision, proponents recast creationism into **Intelligent Design** (ID) theories, which in various versions accept some of the scientifically proposed theories for the age of the earth and its biological complexity, but require the presence of deistic agency for the creation of the earth and its life forms (Ross 2005). In the late 1980s in Dover, Pennsylvania, the School Board instituted a requirement that ninth-grade science students be informed of the equivalence of ID and evolutionary science theories in their classes. Several parents sued, and in *Kitzmiller, et al. v. Dover Area School District, et al.* the U.S. Federal District court ruled that teaching Intelligent Design violated the First Amendment, on the grounds that intelligent design is not science and "cannot uncouple itself from its creationist, and thus religious, antecedents." For those who accept Darwin's theory of evolution, religion has not ceased to be important. However, these judicial rulings have established that both creationism and intelligent design theories are religious paradigms that cannot be used to explain how humans came to be on Earth in public school classrooms.

Observations of the world are the basis for scientific knowledge for people in all societies. The Trobrianders used their empirical knowledge and were capable of accurately predicting the displacement of objects in the water and about wind currents, when they constructed outrigger canoes. However, they had no scientific explanation based on empirical evidence for why the wind blows or why storms come up; in these unpredictable realms they resorted to supernatural explanations. They tried to control the wind through the use of wind magic (Malinowski 1974). In American society, some people also resort to nonscientific explanations. Scientific knowledge cannot at present determine why some children contract leukemia while others do not. If such a disease strikes a child in a family, the family may search for nonscientific cures such as faith healing or the "laying on of hands."

Science, magic, and religion are all ways of understanding and influencing the natural world. Magic and religion differ from science in that what is unexplained by science in the natural world is explained in magic and religion by recourse to the concept of the supernatural. Magic and science are similar in that the aims of both are specific, and both are based upon the belief that if one performs a set of specific actions, one will achieve the desired result. Magic and science differ in that they are based on different theories of knowledge—magic (which is part of religion) is based on the belief that if spells or rituals are performed correctly, the supernatural will act in such a way that the desired end within the natural world will result. **Magic** is based on the idea that there is a link between the supernatural and the natural world such that the natural world can be compelled to act in the desired way if the spell is performed as it should be. **Science**, on the other hand, is based on empirically determined logical connections between aspects of the natural world that will regularly result in predictable outcomes. Hypotheses concerning these logical connections are subject to change if new empirical data suggest better hypotheses. Science is based on empirical knowledge obtained through the five senses, whereas the defining feature of religion is the supernatural, a belief in a reality that "transcends the reality amenable to the five senses" (Lett 1997: 104). The competition between religious explanations and scientific explanations that we described above continues to be present today.

Magic differs from other aspects of religion in that people attempt to manipulate the supernatural through direct intervention. If the right magical formula is used, success is inevitable because magic is seen as being able to bend the supernatural to the will of the practitioner. Other religious practices, on the other hand, are not as specific in their aims. Religious rites emphasize the degree of human beings' powerlessness and do not compel direct results in the way that magic does. Religious rites involve people making appeals to the gods, which may or may not be granted. Magic is therefore manipulative and religion is supplicative. Magical knowledge manipulates on behalf of individuals, whereas religion is the belief system and ritual practice of a community.

CONCEPTIONS OF THE SUPERNATURAL

Ideas about ghosts and spirits are part of a larger category of beliefs about the spiritual or noncorporeal counterparts of human beings. Tylor (1871), the nineteenth-century evolutionist, termed this **animism**. He theorized that animism was the seed from which all forms of religion grew. He hypothesized that what he referred to as "primitive people" saw all living things, including the forces of nature, as composed of a corporeal, or bodily, form and a spiritual aspect. This was an extension of the idea that each person has a body and a separable other self or soul. This other self was seen in the person's shadow, or in the reflection in a pool, and it traveled far and wide in the person's dreams. Ideas about animism were the cornerstone for Tylor's development of an evolutionary history of religion, in which animism evolved into a pantheon of deities (polytheism) and finally into monotheism. Most contemporary scholars, who find in all religious systems of the past and present the coexistence of supernatural entities and deities, question this evolutionary framework.

People who believe in any religion see the supernatural world as inhabited by a variety of superhuman creatures, agents, and forces whose actions will bring about good fortune or misfortune, rain or drought, famine or fertility, health or disease, and so forth. The natural world serves as a model, though not an exact one, for people's conceptualizations of the supernatural. It would be too simplistic to say that the supernatural world is simply a mirror image of people's life on Earth. Nevertheless, there is a relationship between the social structure of a society and the way in which its supernatural world is organized. Similarly, the power relationships in the supernatural world are related to the kind of political organization found in society.

The kinds of **spirits**, the general term for those that populate the supernatural realm, may be grouped into types using English terms to describe them. This is seen by some scholars as the imposition of Western or English language concepts on non-Western indigenous categories. These terms therefore represent an English translation and not an exact equivalent. Spirits of the dead may be categorized chronologically in relation to the living, as ghosts of the recent dead, ancestor spirits of remote generations, and the ancestral spirits of the ancient past, who were group founders in mythological times. In societies with totemic clans, such as the Kwakiutl (see chapter 5), founding ancestors may be represented as animals. This belief in nonhumans as ancestors directly links the identity of human groups with particular animals, and is usually accompanied by prohibitions against killing and eating the totemic animal by group members.

Some believe that all animal and plant species have both physical and spiritual components. The natural world is then seen as having its spiritual counterpart. Inanimate forces such as rain, thunder, lightning, wind, and tide may also be seen as spirits themselves, or as motivated by spiritual beings, or controlled by deities or gods. If the spirit is directly perceived as having human characteristics as well as supernatural power, then it is referred to as a **god** or **deity**; the population of gods and deities recognized by a society is a **pantheon**. The relationships between the gods of a pantheon are frequently conceived of in human terms. The gods show jealousy, have sexual intercourse, quarrel, and live much like human beings. Human characteristics of this sort are also attributed to ghosts and ancestral spirits in many societies.

The origins and activities of supernatural beings are depicted in myths (see chapter 11). Any particular combination of different kinds of spiritual entities may be found in a given society. The supernatural world conforms to its own logic. Often people identify with an ideological system such as Judaism, Christianity, and Hinduism, and still maintain beliefs in ghosts, witches, and spirits of nature as parallel systems. This will become apparent as we examine the supernatural worlds of different societies.

The Kachin, an ethnic group now referred to as Jingpaw in Myanmar (Burma) (see chapters 6 and 9), were studied by Edmund Leach who conducted fieldwork in northern Burma between

1939 and 1945. His fieldwork and publications began during British control of Burma and continued despite the battles between British and Japanese forces in the region during World War II (Anderson 2007). His now classic study *Political Systems in Highland Burma* (1954) describes the Kachin prior to World War II. Kachin State, the northernmost region of Burma, was created as an autonomous region of Burma in 1948. Kachin State borders on China and India; these borders have historically been porous. Interaction between related ethnic groups across these borders was not explored by Leach, but is considered by contemporary scholars of Southeast Asia to be significant to the region's history and sociopolitical development (Robinne and Sadan 2007). Long-term anthropological field study in this region has been impossible for several decades because of the political instability of the area. Myanmar is a predominantly Buddhist country, although a significant minority of ethnic Kachin have converted to Christianity.

Kachin social organization described by Leach consists of a patrilineal segmentary lineage structure with mother's brother's daughter's marriage, so there is a division between wife-givers and wife-takers. The Kachin supernatural world is made up of spirits called *nats*, who are hierarchically ordered like the hierarchical gumsa world of Kachin political organization. Shadip, the chief of the nats and the reincarnation of the creator of everything, is responsible for good fortune and fertility. Beneath him are his children, the sky spirits. Since the Kachin have a rule of succession of ultimogeniture, the senior-most sky spirit is Madai, the youngest of the sky spirits. Nats, like people, belong to lineages. Madai's daughter is said to have married a human being who was the first ancestor of all Kachin chiefs. The Madai nat gave a woman to the first Kachin chief and is therefore wife-giver to the most senior Kachin line of chiefs. This links the world of the supernatural to human beings through marriage alliance. The sky spirits are superior to humans because they are wife-givers to humans. Below the sky spirits are the ancestor nats, the spirits of the ancestors of the various Kachin lineages. The sky nats are approached by making offerings to one's ancestor nat, who acts as an intermediary. Only the senior chief can make offerings to Madai directly, because his ancestor was wife-taker to Madai.

Another category of nats is seen as inferior to humans because they are the offspring of a human girl and an animal. These inferior spirits are said to cause all kinds of misfortunes to humans, such as death in childbirth and fatal accidents. Witches, who are human beings, also have a relationship to the supernatural. Witchcraft is inherited in a particular lineage, and the people in the lineage themselves are unaware that they possess this attribute. They unknowingly cause misfortune and illness to people who are their affines, those to whom they give wives.

It is apparent that the Kachin picture of the supernatural world described by Leach is an extension of and directly correlated with their social organization. The relationships among the spirits and between the spirits and human beings are the same as the relationships between individuals and social groups on the human level. Like human beings, the spirits are also organized into lineages, with wife-takers always lower in rank than wife-givers. The Kachin example supports Durkheim's idea that the supernatural world mirrors the organization of human society and that human propitiation of the supernatural world through prayers and sacrifices has the function of reinforcing human society and reinforcing social solidarity. Human worship of the supernatural is, in effect, the worship of a projection of society. The relationship between the social structure and the organization of the world of the supernatural is often not such a simple one-to-one relationship. For example, the Kaguru of East Africa believe that witches, unlike humans, walk upside down on their hands. In this case, the supernatural world is an inversion of the real world.

RITUAL—APPROACHING THE SUPERNATURAL

Generally speaking, human beings approach their conception of the supernatural by carrying out ritual acts, usually involving a combination of speech and patterned behavior that alters the emotional state of the participants. Recording and analyzing rituals and theorizing about their meaning and underlying belief-systems has engaged anthropologists since the inception of the discipline. Some scholars analyze ritual primarily as the enacting of belief systems about the composition of the world—putting religious beliefs into practice. Others focus on the social solidarity of ritual practices as particular groups of people enact shared experience. **Ritual** is also understood as a performance that symbolically communicates values and ideas to both participants and observers; these values include communicating appropriate gender roles and behaviors and the appropriate behaviors of subordinates to those superior to them. A single intellectually satisfying definition of ritual is elusive because of the multiple aspects of personal and group experience, meaning, symbolism, expression, and functions enfolded in its performance. The following ethnographic examples identify some of the types of rituals described by scholars, and illustrate various approaches to their analysis.

Hortatory rituals consist of exhortations to the supernatural to perform some act (Firth 1951). In the event of a shipwreck, the captain of a Trobriand canoe would exhort the supernatural powers to send the marvelous fish to guide the drowning victims to a friendly shore. The Trobrianders have a native term for this category of exhortation. The term means "by the mouth only." Prayer, involving words only, differs from hortatory ritual in its method of approach and intent. Prayer emphasizes people's inferior position to all kinds of gods since they beseech the gods to act on their behalf.

Sometimes, the gods can be approached only by going into a self-induced or drug-induced **trance**, an altered state of consciousness associated with the performance of ritual. The Yanomamo blow the hallucinogenic substance *ebene* up their noses to induce a trance and enable contact with the spirit world. In the trancelike state produced by the drug, individuals may hallucinate that they are flying to the spirit world. Sometimes trances may be induced without the use of any drugs. Many North American Indian societies had the **vision quest**, in which a man, through starvation, deprivation, and sometimes even bodily mutilation, attempted to induce a trance in which a supernatural being would visit him and thenceforth become his guardian spirit and protector. Among the Crow of Montana, an adolescent boy would go out into the wilderness and fast and thirst for days in order to induce a vision. He might even mutilate himself by cutting off a joint of a finger on his left hand if the vision was not forthcoming. The vision usually came on the fourth night, since for the Crow the number four had magical significance. Supernatural visitors came most frequently in the form of animals, sometimes powerful ones such as buffalo and eagles, at other times animals such as dogs or rabbits. The Crow believed that the supernatural spirit adopted the individual who saw him, and thereafter the spirit acted as a protector, teaching its protégé a sacred song, instructing him in special medicines, and imposing special dietary restrictions. The man wore tokens of his vision and accumulated a medicine bundle consisting of sacred objects connected to the first and subsequent visions of his spirit protector. Part of the man's power could be used to protect others whom he adopted for this purpose, as his spirit protector had adopted him.

Trance states are also interpreted by anthropologists as performative vehicles that unconsciously give "actors license for actions and expressions not available to them in their 'ordinary' state" (Bourguignon 2004: 557). Bourguignon, in an analysis of multiple trance state religions, focuses on the prevalence of women performing these rituals. While men are generally the exorcists in such religions, women often evidence possession and enact the presence of the spirits (Bourguignon 2004: 557). Bourguignon theorizes that "[a]cting out the identity of spirits in ritual possession trance offers women an acceptable, and consciously deniable, way to express unconscious, forbidden thoughts and feelings, particularly in situations of social subordination" (2004: 558). In a possession trance state, women in social systems who have otherwise been socialized to subordination have temporary access to power by acting out the personalities and roles of the spirits. They are held blameless for their actions in these states as "they are neither responsible for nor aware of what is going on and do not remember it after the fact" (Bourguignon 2004: 572).

Another way of approaching the supernatural is by making sacrifices. The Kachin attempt to intercede with the nats, or spirits, when they cause sickness or misfortune by making sacrificial offerings. There is a relationship between the size and value of the sacrificial offering and the importance of the spirit to which it is offered. The inferior nats are offered rats, dogs, pigs, and chickens, but never cattle. Household ancestral spirits are offered only chickens. The village headman's ancestral nats are given offerings of pigs. Sky nats are given offerings of pigs and buffalo. Shadip, the creator, is given a sacrifice of a whole pig, which is not eaten but is buried. Sacrifices are made on ritual occasions to ensure the supernatural protection of crops and their fertility. Eating the meat from sacrificial animals is eating sacred food, which brings humans into contact with the gods. Today, these ceremonies have become a single large ceremony held in a stadium, in which a single mithan, a wild ox, is sacrificed. As a consequence of the advent of Christianity, and the movement for political autonomy among the Kachin, the performance of this ritual expresses cultural and political identity through a religious ceremony.

The widespread sacrifices and offerings of live animals, food, vegetables, incense, and even money are a way of approaching the supernatural by bearing gifts. Since the relationship between humans and the supernatural emphasizes the subordination of the humans, people can only hope for supernatural support in fighting wars; in warding off misfortune, sickness, and death; and in providing fertility in exchange for their gift.

Rites of Passage

Rites of passage are communal ritual ceremonies that publicly mark the changes in status an individual or group experiences through the progression of the life cycle as it is culturally constituted. The beginning and end of life are always marked by some kind of ritual. In addition, one or more points between life and death at which one's status changes, such as a girl's first menstruation or marriage, may be marked with a public ceremony. Cultures may emphasize a biological event, such as the onset of menstruation, in their rites of passage or other milestones such as the first catch of a fish or a child's first haircut. An example of the cultural determination of such rites is demonstrated in the variation in the age at which a male child is circumcised and the presence or absence of this practice in societies over the world.

Van Gennep (1960), in his analysis of rites of passage, pointed out that all such rites involve three stages. The first stage marks the separation of the individual from the category or status previously occupied. Next is a period of transition in which the individual is in a kind of limbo. During this period, the individual is frequently secluded from the rest of the society. Victor Turner (1967: 93–111) has characterized this period as a particularly sacred one, a **liminal period** in which the individual is literally "in between," no longer in one status and not yet in another. Liminality may be quickly resolved by reincorporation, such as the assumption of adulthood after a bride's wedding, or extended, as in the permanent "outsider" status of religious practitioners who live their lives outside mainstream society. The last stage is one of reincorporation, in which the individual is ceremonially reintegrated into society, but this time in the new status. Frequently, this three-stage process is represented by means of the metaphor of death and rebirth. The individual in the former category "dies" and is "reborn" into the new category. In the third stage of the ceremony, the person is often given a new name and puts on a different type of clothing, marking the birth of a new person.

Rites of passage generally reflect gender divisions within society; the Arapesh of New Guinea celebrate several different kinds of rites of passage that separate male and female initiates and symbolically convey the social norms and expectations for each group. Though the Arapesh have a patrilineal rule of descent, they believe their blood comes from the mother while the father contributes the semen. When one's blood is spilled, the mother's group must be recompensed by the payment of shell valuables. This principle underlies all rites-of-passage ceremonies, as well as other aspects of Arapesh culture. After the birth of a child, the child's father "pays for the blood" by giving shell rings to the child's mother's brother. Through this act the child now belongs to the father's group, though the mother's lineage is still said to "own" the child's blood.

At puberty, several boys are initiated at the same time to make them into men. The rites involve isolation from females, with whom the boy has spent most of his time, the observance of a series of taboos, and the incision of the boy's penis. He is also introduced to the secret male Tamberan Cult, where he learns that the Tamberan spirit is the sounds of the drums and the flute secretly played by the men. This information is kept from women and children. During initiation, the boy is beaten by his mother's brother and his penis is incised by a man designated the Cassowary, who removes the "female" blood from the initiate. The initiate then drinks blood that has been contributed by all the old men of the group and is thereby reborn as a man. At the end, he is reincorporated into society as a man at a feast made by his father to honor the boy's mother's brother, who must be paid for the shedding of the boy's blood. Finally, the boy, now a man, goes on a trip and meets all his father's trading partners, signifying his new status.

Male and female initiatory rites are found in societies with matrilineal as well as patrilineal descent rules; however, there is a difference at boys' initiation between patrilineal and matrilineal societies. Lesu, in New Ireland, is a matrilineal society. Before the colonial period and missionary activity, boys were initiated and circumcised. But even in this matrilineal society, boys were forcibly removed from their protesting mothers and turned into men. This initiatory rite, as well as girls' initiation, was performed in conjunction with mortuary rites. Young girls were secluded, fed special foods, and tattooed during this period of seclusion. Both boys and girls emerged as initiated into their respective roles as men and women during the final stages of the mortuary ceremony.

Rites of Passage in American Culture

Different kinds of rites of passage characterize American culture, with its multiethnic complexity and religious diversity. These include the Jewish circumcision rite, Christian baptism, bar mitzvah, confirmation, different types of wedding ceremonies, the retirement party, and various types of funerals. The same stages of separation, transition, and reincorporation can be seen in these rites of passage as in those of other cultures. Just as the Arapesh payment of shell rings marks the entry of the child into his or her father's patrilineal group, circumcision and baptism perform the same function. At birth the child moves from being a neonate into a liminal state, not yet part of society. At the christening, the priest or minister dabs the child's forehead with water and names the child, thereby marking its entry into Christian society. On the occasion of the Jewish circumcision, the cutting of the foreskin by the mohel marks the male child as a Jewish male. The recently introduced naming ceremony for Jewish girls soon after birth performs the same function.

Many of the rites of passage described above involve some form of violence to the body of the initiates; tattooing, scarification, male and female circumcision, starvation, and multiple other forms of physical mutilation are found in rites of passage around the world. For decades anthropologists have documented the physical ordeals associated with initiation; contemporary theorists are now focusing on this near-universal aspect of religious ritual. Whitehouse (2000) focuses on the violence of ritual as the basis of identifying two types or modes of religiosity: doctrinal and imagistic. Using a cognitive framework, he suggests that the intensity of the memory of the violence of initiation rituals serves psychological and sociological functions. The memory of the initiation, because of the pain and intensity of emotions surrounding it, is imprinted on the brain as long-term memory. He contrasts the information transmitted through this memory of episodes of intense physical experience ("imagistic") with the kind of religious information transmitted through scripture, sermons, or other forms of religious instruction ("doctrinal"). "The doctrinal mode, which relies on semantic memory, is more sober, organized, and verbal; the 'imagistic' mode, which relies on episodic memory, is more emotional and personal, and ideas are conveyed nonverbally to a much greater degree" (Laidlaw 2004: 4). The binary division of all religious practice into imagistic and doctrinal is challenged by some scholars (Whitehouse 2000 and Laidlaw 2004). However, this approach has the advantage of including pain and violence inflicted on the human body during initiation rituals into a theory of religious beliefs and practices.

Rites of Intensification

Another major category of ritual—**rites of intensification**—is celebrated communally either at various points in the yearly cycle, such as spring, fall, or the winter and summer solstices, or at times when the society is exposed to some kind of threat, during periods of conflict or natural disaster. Societies may hold rites of intensification to mark planting, in hope of a good crop, or to mark the harvest, in thanks for what has been given. The Kachin ceremonial sacrifices known as *manau*, carried out by the chief on behalf of the whole community, were rites of intensification that served to reiterate the social structure and reinforce the solidarity of the group.

When an event of importance to the whole community on Wogeo takes place, such as appointing the official heir to the chief, a rite of intensification, known as a **warabwa**, is held. The *nibek* spirit monsters are summoned. The community as a whole sponsors the warabwa and is host to many other villages. The climax of the ceremony is a great distribution of food and pork. One of the occurrences at a Wogeo warabwa takes place the day before. At this time, there is a free-for-all, at which the rules regarding the respect relationship between certain categories of relatives are suspended, and they may insult and humiliate each other.

The suspension of rules in this case serves, in a negative fashion, to emphasize the rules of the group. The rites allow the expression or release of tension in a ritual context that could not be permitted in the everyday course of events. A similar reversal of everyday behavior occurs in North and South American cultures at Mardi Gras, just before Ash Wednesday, which marks the beginning of the forty-day period of penance leading to Easter. Mardi Gras rites, marked by great exuberance and extravagant behavior, contrast with the restraint and somberness of Lent that follows. The celebration of Holi in Hindu cultures is another example of public exuberant behavior that reverses, for one day, the usual behaviors of social order. In northern India, this religious festival is celebrated each spring in part by people throwing colored powders and colored water on each other; usually submissive wives playfully confront their husbands and other relatives to whom they generally show respect and douse them with colored water and powders. In rural communities in Rajasthan, lower-caste men reverse the usual norms of inter-caste behavioral norms by flinging powders, waters, and animal dung at upper-caste men, actions that would not be tolerated on any other day of the year.

Thanksgiving, the giving of thanks, is a rite of intensification celebrated by Americans of European descent. It invokes the Pilgrims' celebration in the Plymouth Colony in Massachusetts, in 1621, when they gave thanks to God for their survival, contributed to in great part by the cooperation of Native Americans, during their first year in the New World. Presidents Washington, Jefferson, Adams, and Madison all issued proclamations declaring national days of "thanksgiving" for various military and political events. Thanksgiving as a national holiday celebrated on the last Thursday in November was established by presidential decree in 1863. To Lincoln and nineteenth-century Americans, Thanksgiving recognized potential threats to national unity, including the Civil War and the influx of immigrant populations (Siskind 1992). Today, most Americans participate in a Thanksgiving meal and, by their participation, give thanks in a way that is mostly secular; the religious aspect, if present, may involve saying grace at the start of the meal. This

American rite of intensification demands that particular foods be eaten to symbolize Thanksgiving. Turkey, not lamb chops or meatballs, symbolizes this celebration, although it is unlikely that turkey was actually part of the Pilgrims' celebration. Though Native Americans are recalled to have contributed to the survival of the Pilgrims and were included in the first Thanksgiving celebration, today most do not celebrate the day as a rite of intensification; for them it is remembered as the beginning of the conquest of America by Europeans.

Ritual does not simply mirror society and culture, but helps shape its defining features. Ritual can also challenge the existing order. Today, rituals are seen as dynamic and flowing, ever responsive to the changing aspects of modern and postmodern life. Experimentation and the development of new rituals, such as the Wicca rituals we will discuss below, or commitment ceremonies marking same-sex marriages, have become important foci of anthropological research. Anthropologists study the performative aspects of ritual and are interested in how participants constitute ideas about themselves through their actions. However, there is a tension or dialectic between the traditional rules of ritual and innovation or experimentation in actual performances; not all people will agree with the value or ideology being articulated by new approaches to ritual and ideology. The anthropologist's goal in documenting and studying contemporary rituals is understanding the meaning of the ritual and its subjective aspects as encompassed in the participant's point of view.

RELIGIOUS SPECIALISTS

The supernatural is often approached indirectly, through intermediaries, who have access to it because they possess some special gift. Many have been through extensive training, or have inherited esoteric knowledge or ability. Religious specialization is found in small-scale societies as well as in complex, hierarchically organized societies. Religious specialists often have a primary function, such as curing illness or predicting the future. The English labels for these specialists—diviner, oracle, magician, shaman—usually refer to that function, though the translation of the indigenous terms for these specialists may not be exact. Religious specialists may operate on a full- or part-time basis; this distinction is generally linked to the sociopolitical system of the society being described.

In small-scale societies, the **shaman** was usually the only religious specialist. These part-time specialists used their powers primarily to diagnose illness, cure illness, and sometimes cause illness as well. They also had other functions, such as divining the future. Early travelers referred to these individuals as "witch doctors" to highlight their curing functions. This was a particularly unfortunate translation. The term *shaman* comes from the Tungus of Siberia. Shamans were found throughout Asia and among a great many indigenous societies of North and South America. Kehoe (2000) traces the generalized use of the term *shaman* from a specific Siberian set of practices to a global category of religious practitioner as a consequence of the work of the religion scholar Mircea Eliade, who in various publications in the mid-twentieth century generalized and popularized the use of the term. Kehoe argues that Eliade's vision of shamanism as a widespread practice associated with nonliterate societies reifies Eurocentric dichotomies between "simple" and "complex" societies, and ignores diversity of practice and belief systems in Siberia and elsewhere.

An early twentieth-century Tlingit Shaman wearing ritual paraphernalia, shakes his oyster-catcher rattle while dealing with a witch.

The practices and functions of the Kwakiutl shaman typify some shamanic activities ethnographically identified elsewhere. Kwakiutl shamans were classified on the basis of the level of their expertise or power. The least powerful were those who were able only to diagnose and locate the disease, that is, determine the place in the body where the object causing the disease was lodged. But the most powerful could not only cure diseases but could also cause illness in others. Both Kwakiutl men and women could become shamans. One became a shaman as a result of an initiation by a supernatural spirit that came to the person while he or she was sick. The most common spirits were wolf, killer whale, and toad. The spirit taught the novice songs and dances and gave the shaman a new name, which was always used by the shaman when acting in that capacity.

The Kwakiutl healer wore certain paraphernalia—a neck ring of shredded red cedar bark to which was attached a pouch bearing small objects, which represented the diseases the shaman could cause—and used a special rattle and a ring of hemlock branches for purifying patients. In keeping with the ranked social structure of the Kwakiutl, great chiefs "owned their shamans," who protected them by throwing disease into their enemies. The Kwakiutl are now Christians and there is no information as to whether there are any practicing shamans and whether they are still curing people today. In other parts of the world, shamanism is practiced today alongside other religions.

In a nonranked society such as the Inuit, shamanistic activity was not limited to curing or causing disease. The Inuit shaman intervened with the supernatural in attempting to control the forces of the environment. When game was unavailable, shamans were asked to call on their spirits to divine where animals were located. Shamans were also said to control thunder and stop snowstorms and the cracking of the ice. The Inuit believed that sickness was caused by the sufferer's loss of his or her soul or by evil ghosts and spirits who were usually angered by the breach of some taboo. An Inuit boy became a shaman by joining the household of an elderly shaman as a novice, where he observed special taboos, had visions, and was taught special shamanistic techniques. The novice also had to refrain from sexual relations.

Shamanism in contemporary Siberia is found among the Buddhists of the Buryat Republic, and in Tuva, an autonomous, Turkic-speaking republic in the geographical center of Asia, both of which are part of the Russian federation. Tuvan shamans are healers dealing with various diseases and with the loss of the soul. They treat the sick by holding séances, which begin at nightfall and last until dawn, during which time the shaman contacts the spirits and "voyages" to the three worlds: the subterranean, the celestial, and the middle world of humans (Kenin-Lopsan 1997: 110). The shaman employs spirit-helpers, animals ranging in size and power from bears to moths, and these spirit-helpers are artistically portrayed on wands, which the shaman employs in the ceremony. In addition, the Tuvan shaman wears a decorated coat and boots, and uses a drum and a rattle.

The Tuvan shaman may also be called in to divine the location of game for a hunter. A childless couple may seek help from the shaman to "summon the soul" of an unborn infant to their home, a felt yurt (Kenin-Lopsan 1997: 127). Kenin-Lopsan, a Tuvan ethnographer who collected many poetic chants, or songs, performed by Tuvan shamans, pointed out that these songs were a major form of Tuvan artistic expression and served to keep the Tuvan language alive. Tuvan shamans in their shamanic performance employed the "throat singing" for which Tuva is famous. In this special kind of singing, they imitated the languages of their animal spirit-helpers (Kenin-Lopsan 1997: 132–33). Tuvan shamans may be female or male. Kenin-Lopsan's maternal grandmother was a famous shaman imprisoned several times by Stalin. She died in prison in the mid-1940s. The renewal of Tuvan shamanism in the post-Soviet era is demonstrated by the fact that in 1992 a Society of Tuva Shamans was formed and was subsequently recognized by the Tuvan Ministry of Justice (Kenin-Lopsan 1997: 132). Tuvan shamanism continues to be an integral part of Tuvan culture, and today, in particular, is part of their ethnic identity; Russian, European, and American tourists travel to Siberia seeking encounters with "shaman gurus" (Kehoe 2000: 19).

These examples show responses to two universal dilemmas: One of them is the loss of self, and the other is that something, perhaps a spirit or cancer cells, is invading in a person's body. These concerns are found in all societies. The shamanic solution, to travel to the spirit world for the answer, is but one of many solutions. Through a variety of means, shamans go into an altered state of consciousness, or a trance, during which they have direct contact with the spirit world. They use spirit-helpers and can call spirits to be present during their séances (Townsend 1997: 431–32).

Instead of being replaced by scientific theories of curing, shamanism has actually undergone a present-day revival (Winkelman 2000, McClennon 2002). Shamanism, for both of these writers, has to involve "soul flight" and "ecstatic communication with the spirit world." Winkelman argues that shamanism "manipulates self-identity and social identity" (2000: xiii) by emphasizing "integrative brain functions." In his view, the soul journey, which the shaman helps the patient to undergo, and the search for a guardian spirit constitute forms of self-objectification. They are a form of role-playing that serves to expand human socio-cognitive dynamics (Winkelman 2000: xiv). Shamanism provides a mechanism for stepping outside one's self, to take a journey to another land, to return in a reborn form, and thereby to acquire a new self awareness.

Diviners are part-time religious specialists who use the supernatural to enable people to make decisions concerning how they should act in order to have success. The Chinese, in general, have always placed great emphasis upon omens. Archaeological information has revealed that the Chinese many millennia ago interpreted the cracks in tortoise shells to foretell the future. They

A contemporary Tuvan shaman wearing special garb prepares for a ceremonial performance.

also used **geomancy**—the interpretations of the future from cracks in dried mud—and fortune telling. Diviners use other methods to gain their information; chickens or other animals are killed and their entrails inspected and interpreted to determine what action to take in the future. In our own society, many people seek help to divine what their future holds for them. Gypsy fortune-tellers in storefronts in many cities, large and small, as well as at rural county fairs are paid to read palms, tea leaves, and Tarot cards, and to look into crystal balls to foretell the future. The services of astrologers, who foretell the future from the positions of the stars, are sought out by Americans of all religions and classes; former White House Chief of Staff Donald Regan claimed that First Lady Nancy Reagan, wife of the president, regularly sought out the services of an astrologer in scheduling public appearances to protect her husband's safety. As part of his functions, in addition to curing, the Inuit shaman would also tell hunters where they would find animals. They took the shoulder blade, or scapula, of an animal such as a reindeer, a moose, an elk, an otter, or a seal and placed it on a fire until cracks appeared, forming a pattern. This practice is called **scapulimancy** and is similar to the Chinese use of tortoise shells. The pattern of cracks was then interpreted to locate the place where animals were to be found.

Sorcerers and witches, as religious specialists, concentrate upon doing evil things, causing illness and death rather than curing. Sorcerers and witches are the English terms into which indigenous terms are translated, and they may be inexact. Since there is a logical connection between curing illness and causing it, in many societies the same specialist sometimes performs both functions. Anthropologists define **sorcery** as a set of skills that are learned, whereas people are born with a propensity toward **witchcraft**. Witchcraft and sorcery involve the use of supernatural means to cause bad things to happen to one's enemies, or to the enemies of individuals who engage the services of a sorcerer. These enemies may be persons outside one's own group or persons within one's own group with whom one is in opposition. Kwakiutl shamans could use sorcery against enemy groups. Among the Trobrianders, as noted in chapter 9, the people of a district feared that their chief would use sorcery against them if they went against his commands. Sorcery here, as in other societies, was being used as a means of sociopolitical control.

In many societies, when a person in the prime of life becomes sick or dies, it is necessary to ascertain what caused the illness or death. This means going beyond the immediate cause of a death, such as the tree that fell or the lightning that struck, to the more important underlying reason this particular person died. There is often a belief in such societies that the illness was caused by witchcraft or sorcery. British social anthropologists working in Africa, especially E. E. Evans-Pritchard and Max Gluckman, adopted an approach in which they saw such sorcery and witchcraft accusations as the product of tensions and conflict within the community. When a person in the prime of life dies, investigators try to divine through supernatural means the person who caused the death. Like the detective in a murder mystery in our own society, the diviner asks who has the most to gain to determine the most likely suspect.

Claims of witchcraft are usually made in such a way that they reveal the cleavages in a society. According to Douglas (1991), who analyzed the witch trials of sixteenth-century England and the accusations of witchcraft among Yao villagers from Malawi in the 1950s, the witch is someone on the opposite side of a power conflict. He or she is accused of antisocial behavior or libeled by his or her accuser. The person accused of antisocial behavior may be charged with eating food that is repellent to the accuser, even human bodies; aberrant sexual behavior, such as sex with the devil; or the murder of children for occult ritual purposes.

Women are particularly vulnerable to charges of witchcraft in societies that practice virilocal postmarital residence patterns. Bhil women in Rajasthan who marry into their husbands' villages are strangers to the community (Weisgrau 1997). If they are widowed and childless, they lose their fragile ties to their communities of residence. Accusations of witchcraft (*dakani*) against them may be used by their husband's kin to undercut potential claims to inheriting an interest in her husband's property. Contemporary Indian civil law supports widow inheritance, but in practice few Bhil women invoke these claims through the courts. "Her status as an outsider—and a witch—may be brought to bear particularly if it is in the interests of her husband's patrilineage to drive her out of the community, or at least the realm of respectability, in cases of dispute over property and inheritance" (Weisgrau 1997: 130).

Magic, witchcraft, and sorcery all involve the manipulation of the supernatural. **Magicians** direct supernatural forces toward a positive goal—to help individuals or the whole community. In parts of Melanesia one frequently finds societies in which there are several part-time religious specialists who carry out magical rites to bring rain, promote fertility in the gardens, and ensure successful fishing. The garden magician among the Trobrianders is one of the most important people in the village. He recites his magical spells and performs his rituals at every stage of the process of growing yams, and what he does is seen as being as essential to the growth and maturation of crops as weeding and hoeing. He officiates at a large-scale ceremony involving all the men of the village that takes place before any gardening begins. He carries out specific rites at the planting and weeding and in assisting the plants to sprout, bud, grow, climb, and produce the yams. Since the garden magician must perform his rites before each stage of production, through his spells he acts, in effect, to coordinate and regulate the stages of work throughout the entire village (Malinowski 1935). Each village has its own special system of garden magic, which is passed on by matrilineal inheritance, so a sister's son succeeds his mother's brother as garden magician.

Magical practices have always coexisted with universal religions such as Christianity, Islam, and Judaism in many Old World societies. The institution of the evil eye operates in the same way as witchcraft. If misfortune occurs, it is assumed to have happened because of the use of the evil eye by some enemy. People believe that it is dangerous to praise a child as beautiful, strong, or healthy, since this will create jealousy on the part of others and cause them to invoke the evil eye. Various kinds of magic, including protective devices and verbal ritual formulas, are used to ward off the evil eye. Among the Basseri, a nomadic pastoral society of Iran, a mirror is placed on the back of the horse on which the bride is taken to her groom, since a joyous occasion such as a wedding is likely to promote envy on the part of some onlookers. The mirror is used to reflect the evil eye back to its sender. Communities of believers from Cairo to New York City recite magical spells to ward off the evil eye, wear charms and religious medals to bring good fortune, and nail religious symbols to walls and doorways to serve as magical charms to protect households. These are all forms of magic practiced today. The religious objects whose commoditization and sale in

Cairo discussed in chapter 8 all represent magical ideas set within the context of Islam (Starrett 1995). The refracting vinyl stickers of raised hands and unopened copies of the Qur'an displayed in automobiles are intended to ward off the evil eye. Islamic religious leaders consider these practices as running counter to the basic teachings of Islam, for the Qur'an is to be read, not to be used as a charm for protection.

With the emergence of class divisions in earlier and later states, religion became more elaborated and more differentiated as a separate institution. In contrast to the shaman and the magician, who operate as individual practitioners and part-time specialists, **priests** are full-time religious practitioners who carry out codified and elaborated rituals, and their activities are associated with a shrine or temple. The body of ritual knowledge, which is the priest's method of contacting the supernatural, must be learned over a lengthy period of time. Archaeological data on Mesopotamia reveal that in societies that were the forerunners of full-fledged states, there was a single figure that was both the political and religious head of the community, and there was a priestly class. Subsequently, as the state evolved, there was a separation of political and religious positions. In chapter 9, we noted that formal legal codes evolved out of religious codes in early states. The class of religious specialists was but one of a number of stratified classes in an increasingly more hierarchically organized society.

Priestly classes were intimately associated with development and control of the calendar in the early civilizations of the Maya and the Aztecs, and in Egypt and Mesopotamia. It is not known whether priests invented the calendar, but it was used for determining when communal religious rites should take place. In these early civilizations the priesthood seems also to have been associated with scientific observations of the heavens. In ancient Egypt, the flooding of the Nile was absolutely regular; its onset could be dated 365 days from the last onset. The development of a solar calendar, in place of the more widespread lunar calendar, enabled the flooding to be predicted. The development of this solar calendar depended on a certain amount of astronomical knowledge. The ability to predict natural phenomena, such as the yearly flooding, was connected, in the eyes of the people, to priestly proximity to the supernatural. This in turn gave the leader of the theocracy—the priest-king—great power over the ordinary agriculturalists.

RELIGIOUS SYNCRETISM: OLD RELIGIONS IN NEW GUISES

All religions believe that their rituals have been practiced since time immemorial; in reality religious institutions all respond to changing conditions and are influenced by other belief systems. The term *syncretism* refers to the integration of cultural traits into existing cultural practices. As we've documented, people practicing Judeo-Christian religions wear amulets to ward off the evil eye, seek advice from fortune-tellers, and go to faith healers to be cured by the laying on of hands. Various earlier pre-Christian beliefs, including belief in local spirits, were incorporated into Christianity as it spread through Europe. This also occurred as Islam moved through the Middle East and parts of Africa. When missionaries carried Christianity throughout the world, the same process was also operative. This missionary activity, which continues today, did not result in the eradication of earlier traditional beliefs and activities.

In America, this process has produced new forms of Christianity and Islam, for example, Mormonism (Church of Jesus Christ of Latter-Day Saints), Christian Science (Church of Christ, Scientist), and the Nation of Islam. Sometimes entirely new religions, such as Scientology, emerge. Although the forms of religious expression may change, the functions they fulfill for their followers remain constant.

The imposition of colonialism and the events of the postcolonial period invariably transform local visions of the supernatural. Among the Kaliai of West New Britain there has been a syncretism of traditional Kaliai forms of sorcery with European culture (Lattas 1993). Men who have traveled widely while working for Europeans and serving in the constabulary have the reputation of being sorcerers. Their great power derives from their connection to Europeans and from the sorcery knowledge they have had the opportunity to acquire while working in other areas. In fact, the nation-state, conceptualized as a white institution, is itself seen as imbued with the powers of sorcery.

Shamanism has taken on a modern appearance in Westernizing societies in Asia. Before Korea began its rapid industrialization, shamanic rituals were held in response to life-threatening illnesses and to promote the health, harmony, and prosperity of the small farming families. These families were primarily rural in outlook, though they were tied to urban commercial markets (Kendall 1996: 522). In the 1970s, Korea embarked on a course toward modernity. In the clash between modernity and superstition, between rationality and magic, shamanism was considered to be superstition. Government policy stressed that shamanism "deluded the people" and fostered "irrational" beliefs (Kendall 2001: 29). In popular practice, however, shamanic rituals aimed at "reconciliations between the living members of the household and their gods and ancestors who appear . . . in the person of costumed shamans." As time went by, these rituals were increasingly accepted as part of "national culture" because they are considered ancient Korean traditions. Today these same shamanic rituals, or *kut*, have spread from the rural farmers to a new class of small-businesspeople and entrepreneurs living in the cities, who are holding kut ceremonies to ensure success in their business enterprises as well as to cure their illnesses. For those engaged in high-risk enterprises, business is precarious and success or failure seems arbitrary and beyond their control. Thus, "doing well by the spirits" is important. Since financial distress and worry can often lead to illness, it is understandable that the kut ceremony has dual functions (Kendall 1996: 516–18).

In the United States, we have also had a period of religious transformation and innovation, which began in the 1970s following the demise of the counterculture movements of the "flower children" of the 1960s. At first, the development of these alternative religious movements, sometimes referred to as **New Age Movements** or New Religious Movements, was paralleled by an erosion of the "major" religions—Judaism, Catholicism, and Protestantism. However, in the most recent past, the growth of Christian Fundamentalism and the resurgence of Orthodox Judaism have marked a turnaround for these dominant faiths. Nontraditional religious movements have a long history in the United States. Some of these groups, for example, the Shakers, are only minimally present today, while others, the Mormons (Church of Jesus Christ of Latter-Day Saints), for example, continue stronger than ever. In recent years, the immigration of many non-Westerners,

Buddhists, Muslims, Hindus, and others into our now multicultural, pluralistic society have introduced still other religious belief systems into the mix. Many of the New Religious Movements are cultural transplants representing groups of Asian origin, such as the Hare Krishna movement (International Society for Krishna Consciousness). These New Religious Movements are seen as "different responses to the failure of mainline religious traditions to provide a meaningful moral context for everyday life" (Bromley 1998: 330).

For the same reasons that New Religious Movements have become popular, shamanism has also grown in importance in America and Europe. Westerners disillusioned with their own religious institutions have turned to "neoshamanism." As Atkinson notes, "It [shamanism] presents in the 1980s and 1990s what Buddhism and Hinduism provided in the preceding decades, namely a spiritual alternative for Westerners estranged from Western religious traditions" (1992: 322). Neoshamanism claims to be nonhierarchical in comparison with traditional Western religions, emphasizes self-help, and links participants to nature. Consequently, it is appealing to seekers of alternative religious experiences.

Witchcraft has existed in America, in one form or another, from the seventeenth century on (Melton 1982). There have been periodic infusions from Europe, as its popularity waxed and waned. Though witches today see themselves as the reborn victims of witch-hunts in past centuries, in fact, there have been no accusations of witchcraft paralleling those in sixteenth-century England and seventeenth-century Salem (Orion 1995: 52). The flowering of what has come to be known as the neopagan religion, or Wicca, began in the 1960s. In 1954, shortly after the repeal of anti-witchcraft laws in Britain, Gerald Gardner published an account of witchcraft that stimulated its revival. While in Gardner's version of Wicca, covens, the minimal religious unit, were characterized by levels of initiation, a hierarchical organization, and a more codified set of traditions and rituals, Wicca in America is democratized, individualized, highly creative, and inventive. Its major focus has been to disown, by lifestyle, word, and philosophy, the religious and political ideas that dominate the rest of American society. Christian conservatives and fundamentalists understandably see this opposition to American society and to Christianity as a direct threat. Interestingly, those who identify themselves as members of Wicca come primarily from Protestant and Catholic backgrounds (Orion 1995: 63). Wicca is therefore a pointed rejection of Christianity: it is both pre-Christian and the object of Christian persecution.

Wicca rituals usually involve the sacred circle, formed of individuals whose constant circular movement generates a cone of energy directed to specific tasks to better the earth. This is also seen as a form of therapeutic "healing magic," releasing and dissipating "maladaptive emotional states" for the individual as well as for the earth by creative energy. Wicca celebrations mark the solstices, equinoxes, and key occasions of the agricultural year, as well as biweekly sabbaths. They also have come to include rite-of-passage ceremonies, such as Wiccaning—the blessing and presenting of infants to the pagan spirits; girls' and boys' puberty rites or initiation; handfasting, the tying together of the hands of the couple at a ceremony to signify trial or permanent marriage, heterosexual or homosexual; and ritual preparation for death. The Wicca pantheon has the Mother Goddess, giver of life and incarnate love; the Sun; and the Moon at the core. In addition, magical beliefs from ancient Egypt, Greece, Babylonia, and the Jewish Kabbalah, as well as Celtic, Druid,

Norse, and Welsh pagan beliefs, have been eclectically included (Melton 1982). Women enjoy a special status, and the person of the high priestess is venerated.

Wicca in America has all the organizational characteristics of a religion. In fact, a federal appeals court in 1986 ruled that Wicca was a religion protected by the Constitution. As a consequence, believers in Wicca are today trying to change the public view of their belief system. Its practitioners feel that Wicca should be protected by the same laws that protect the practice of other religions. Fundamentalist Christians, however, still associate witches and Wicca with Satanism and campaign against its public practices,

An emphasis on feminist spirituality, which developed as an offshoot of radical feminism in the 1970s, influenced Wicca and the American neopagan movement and gave rise to the "American Goddess movement." It is an eclectic movement with "beliefs and practices that are becoming increasingly idiosyncratic . . . dynamic, [with an] increasingly diverse form of popular religiosity that has emerged among women" (Gottschall 2000: 60). In southern California, for example, Goddess believers gather to celebrate summer and winter solstices, and pagan holidays such as Hallomas and Lammas as large public rituals with belly dancers, drummers, poets, and vocalists (Gottschall 2000: 61–62). Several men came to one ritual studied by Gottschall, but by and large most Goddess events, like the first International Goddess Festival, are for "women only."

A contemporary Wiccan coven in Salem, Massachusetts, site of the seventeenth-century witch trials.

Goddess worshipers see their practice of Wicca religion as challenging the patriarchal religious framework that characterizes the major world religions.

Cyberspace and Religion: "Give Me That Online Religion"

One can go on the Internet, into cyberspace today, click on the Digital Avatar site, and the cyber version of a Kali temple welcomes you with the image of the god Shiva and a menu of worship experiences from the mystical utterance of Vedic praise, which affirms the totality of creation, to meditation while watching a mystical, rapid alteration of Shiva images. In 2001, there were more than 1 million online religious websites in operation, and the number is increasing daily (Brasher 2001: 6). All the major religions in the world, as well as newer religious groups, recognize the vast audience they reach in cyberspace, far beyond the churches, synagogues, ashrams, mosques, and temples to which religions were formerly confined, and they are intent on exploring the global arena. All mainstream religions have become active in cyberspace. Their websites include "an introduction to their beliefs, a directory of congregation locations, a calendar explaining upcoming religious events, and a prayer room" (Brasher 2001: 70).

In addition to the official Vatican site, there are other Roman Catholic sites—for example, the Christ in the Desert site of the Benedictine Monastic Order. This site includes such options as "Today's Martyrology," the monastery gift shop, online monastic chants, how to request prayers, the week's homily, and how to learn more about the order's retreat house. The majority of all religious sites online are Protestant, such as those belonging to the Church of Christ, which attempts to use its three hundred sites in cyberspace to bring converts to the physical church. Most Protestant denominations have their own websites. The Christian Fundamentalists part of evangelical Christianity in America, which has a long tradition of preaching their beliefs, first in churches, then on the radio, and now on television, have a large variety of websites.

Muslims use the website to announce prayer times in a host of cities. However, there is limited access to the Internet in some Muslim countries, though there are some Islamic chat rooms and sites devoted to Sufism (Zaleski 1997: 55, 68). American Buddhism, Tibetan Buddhism, and Zen Buddhism are well represented, as are sites for Hindu temples and gurus such as Sri Sathya Sai Baba. Even the Amish, in Pennsylvania, who do not use cars but ride in horse-drawn carriages, have a website, as do neopagans who are "revising customary neopagan rituals for a virtual environment . . . and designing new ones for cyberspace" (Brasher 2001: 87, 88). There is even a cyberheaven where one can memorialize one's deceased relative with a picture and brief tribute to that relative. The producers of the site see it as analogous to heaven; hence angels against a background of clouds are presented as the introduction to the site. This site is part of a category of sites not connected to any religious group; it allows an individual to create a site as a virtual sacred place and preach his or her own religious ideas and include music and created rituals (Brasher 2001: 69). Cyberspace has also become the location for apocalyptic websites, as well as those devoted to religious satire. The Internet, in theory, provides equal opportunity for both mainstream and alternative voices to represent their perspectives; Brasher suggests that online religious activity "could become the dominant form of religion and religious experience in the next century" (2001: 19).

The intersection of religion and the Internet is undeniable, but the nature of that intersection is debated; scholars are only recently exploring the implications of cyberspace and the human-technology interface for religious belief systems. "Boosters of the Internet in its earliest days saw the 'information superhighway' as it was dubbed, as having a utopian potential to revolutionize social relationships. . . . It soon became evident that in many ways, the Internet mirrored existing social relationships (Henderson 2007: 62).

While the Internet presents the possibility of endless streams of information about both traditional and nontraditional religious practices, access to this information is mediated by familiar forms of market capitalism; "A user's access to websites reflects his or her computer's operating system and software. . . . Not all search engines gain access to all sites. An individual user's preferred search engine, or browser—and different versions of this—determines search outcomes" (Henderson 2007: 68). Search engines will invariably return hundreds or thousands of possible sites for searches based on the number of times the search term appears; most users will look only at the first ten or so (Henderson 2007: 69). The "digital divide"—the lack of access to computers and Internet technology—globally remains a reality, as "[f]ar more people around the world lack access to the Internet than have it" (Cowan 2005a: 262).

Cowan (2005b) identifies major differences between online interactive ritual and the virtual experience. Online, these rituals are text-based rather than experiential; instructions and responses are read and typed. The ritual environment must be imagined rather than experienced; the use of a candle for example as a word typed into a computer as opposed to experienced through sight and smell on an altar will result in very different responses. "To speak of virtuality and popular Internet usage both overstates the case for activity that occurs in computer-mediated environments such as the World Wide Web and blurs important technological distinctions between activity that does take place in 'virtual reality' versus that which simply comes and goes online" (Cowan 2005b: 52). The practice of religion, Cowan argues, is not likely to be replaced by online experience. "While we may interact with each other through the computer, we do not live 'life on the screen.' Indeed, throughout our online experience, the offline world constantly impinges; it continually reminds us of its presence and its power" (Cowan 2005b: 262).

POLITICS, RELIGIONS, AND STATES

In today's world, religion plays an extremely important role in politics. In a sense, we have come full circle. When states and civilization began in the Middle East, they were theocracies, and politics and religion were intertwined. This connection between politics and religion has been widespread throughout history and in different societies. For example, today, political parties in Europe often have religious labels, such as the Christian Democratic party in Germany. Conflict in Sri Lanka is mobilized around the two major religions in the country: Buddhism and Hinduism. Former American President George W. Bush regularly and publicly discussed his religious identity as a "born-again Christian" and the effect of his religious ideas on national and international policy formation.

The label **fundamentalism** is widely and often ambiguously applied to an ever-widening range of political and religious ideologies. This term, used first in discussions of Protestant Christian ideologies, historically "connotes an attachment to a set of irreducible beliefs or a theology that forestalls further question" (Nagata 2001: 481). It is now attached to a wide range of religious and political movements in both scholarly and journalistic sources; its very ambiguity often invokes emotional responses in the reader. Nagata (2001) identifies some characteristics of its use in multiple sources; it is invariably used to describe an "other" and is rarely a term of self-identification in religious or political discourse. "Since 1979 (the year of the Iranian revolution), academic, political, and public attention has turned toward Islam, where most examples of fundamentalism are of sociopolitical movements, usually representing challenges to the elites and regimes in their home states" Nagata 2001: 486). Through general usage, "fundamentalism" invokes a religious perspective; however, it is also used to describe a wide range of political ideologies including ultranationalisms, extreme ethnic chauvinisms, as well as often-violent movements for linguistic and cultural purity (Nagata 2001: 493).

Islam has become a very significant dimension in Middle Eastern and Central Asian politics with worldwide effect. Throughout their history, Islamic peoples have responded to the call of religious leaders such as the Mahdi, "the rightly guided one," who, in the Sudan in the late nineteenth century, called for a renunciation of corruption and a return to the true moral values of Islam. Present-day political leaders are following earlier examples. Reza Shah Pahlevi, the Shah of Iran, had embarked on a program of Westernization and modernization after World War II. Women were no longer required to wear veils and were encouraged to attend schools and colleges. Western clothing, Western music, and Western ideas were emphasized. In the late 1970s, the Ayatollah Khomeini, with his political strategy involving a strict interpretation of Shi'ite Islam, succeeded in overthrowing the Shah. This Shi'ite-based policy of Iran has been influential in many parts of the Muslim world, reverberating in Nigeria, Pakistan, and Iraq where Shi'ite and Sunni Muslims have been battling for political control.

In widely separated Muslim countries such as Algeria, Egypt, and Turkey, political movements attempting to take over the governments of these countries claim to govern strictly according to the Qur'an. Afghanistan, a monarchy attempting to modernize, was invaded by the Soviet Union in 1978, resulting in a civil war. The Taliban movement was originally formed by students from rural areas, studying in Islamic religious schools (*madrassas*) in the Kandahar region of Afghanistan. Young men eager to end the factionalism and fighting swelled their number. The Taliban movement, with direct support from the American government, drove out the Soviets and took control of most of the country. Al Qaeda, an international militant terrorist alliance, with support of the Taliban government, claimed responsibility for the destruction of the World Trade center in New York City on September 11, 2001. In the autumn of 2001 the Taliban was driven out of power as the result of military invasion by the United States. While they ruled, the Taliban instituted decrees banning women from attending school or working, permitting them to leave their houses only when completely veiled. Men had to give up Western clothing and had to wear full beards. Children were forced to abandon music, dancing, kite flying, and playing marbles. The United States, in the search for Al Qaeda's leader Osama bin Laden, took control of the country and installed Hamid Karzai to lead Afghanistan into its transition to a democratic government..

Islamic-based political movements expanded from Afghanistan to Turkmenistan, Uzbekistan, Tajikistan, and Kyrgyzstan, now independent republics, formerly part of the Soviet Union. Armed Islamic fighters seek to undermine the post-Soviet governments of these republics. Living standards for a majority of the populations in these republics have plummeted since the collapse of the Soviet Union; disaffected and unemployed young men are particularly attracted to the rhetoric of social and political transformation espoused by radical Islamicists.

Christian fundamentalists in America today are calling for a return to Christian values and a strict interpretation of Biblical text. Christians mobilize their followers to help bring this about at the ballot box by electing individuals who support their aims. Many Christian fundamentalists were formerly mainline Protestants who joined evangelical denominations practicing an unambiguous, stricter morality. Members of such religious groups may teach their children at home instead of sending them to school, thereby controlling the content of their education. They seek to keep the interactions of the members of their families within their own religious community. They listen to their own kind of music on Christian radio stations, read books written for Christians and purchased in Christian bookstores, and watch Christian television. As members of the new Christian Right political movement, they have tried to shape elections from local school boards to presidential politics by being active in the Christian Coalition. There are also Orthodox Jews who adhere to a very strict interpretation of Jewish tenets to guide their lives. Fundamentalism, wherever it is found, is characterized by a certainty of its principles, focus on difference rather than shared interests with others, a rejection of relativism, and "a retreat from ecumenism and dialogue" (Nagata 2001: 494).

WHY RELIGION?

Much of religious behavior has an instrumental goal; that is, the individual has some particular goal in mind when the religious ritual is performed. Those who carry out the rites and perform the spells desire to produce results, such as stopping a storm, bringing rain, or ensuring fertility for their crops. The Inuit shaman contacts his spirits to find out where the hunter should go to find his prey. The Trobriand garden magician recites the particular spells that will make the yams grow. The Kachin sacrificed to the nats to ensure that their crops would successfully grow to maturity. In many cultures, women perform religious rites to help them become pregnant. For example, in Poland, Catholic women go to the tombs of Catholic saints and Jewish rabbis to recite prayers to enable them to become pregnant. Orthodox Jewish women in Israel go to the tomb of Rachael, in Hebron, with the same goal. The motives and goals in all these cases are to bring about quite specific results—to make natural forces and natural processes respond to human need.

Sometimes religious action has particular effects that the individual may not be aware of. These are different from the conscious goals and purposes of the participants themselves.

American baseball players use magic rituals and formulas in areas of the game most fraught with uncertainty—hitting and pitching (Gmelch 1971). Reducing anxiety for the pitcher or the hitter and giving the individual a sense of confidence, even if it is false confidence, improves performance. Anxiety is reduced for the Korean businessman after he goes through the performance of a shamanic ritual. He feels more confident as a consequence. One could argue that anxiety itself has important functions in dangerous situations. Under such circumstances adrenaline should be flowing and all one's senses should be alerted to potential danger. When a person is faced with uncertainty in possibly dangerous situations, alertness to the real dangers and confidence in one's ability to cope with the situation are the most desirable mix and can be brought about by performing some magical or religious ritual.

Predictions of social scientists in the mid-twentieth century that economic development and modernization would result in global secularization have not come to pass. Religious ideology and identity dominate national and international policy. They shape the outcome of elections and motivate invasion and military action. In pluralistic states such as India, religious identity continues to be the basis of discrimination and violence against religious minorities. In the beginning of the twenty-first century it's impossible to think about contemporary state and geopolitics without thinking about the religious identities of those in and out of power.

SUMMARY

- Religion is generally defined as the cultural means by which humans deal with the supernatural; some religious systems integrate the supernatural realm into their overall system of beliefs about the world in general.
- Religion fulfills certain universal functions, such as the allaying of anxiety; explanatory functions, which answer such questions as why humans came to be on Earth and the meaning of life; and expiatory function, in which individuals are assisted with guilt and misfortune.
- Humans attempt to understand and at least influence or control through a belief in the supernatural what is otherwise uncontrollable and unexplainable, and by doing this, they alleviate anxieties about their helplessness in the situation.
- Today, we would say that many aspects of the natural world, which were formerly explained by religion, are now explained by science.
- In terms of its explanatory function, religion is to be distinguished from science in that the latter is based on observations and the former on belief.
- Magic and religion differ from science in that what is unexplained by science in the natural world is explained in magic and religion by recourse to the concept of the supernatural.
- Societies have a variety of ways of conceiving of the supernatural. These conceptualizations are directly related to the ways in which their societies are organized, and are reinforced through national ideologies and practices.
- The population of gods and deities recognized by a society is a pantheon. The relationships between the gods of a pantheon are frequently conceived of in human terms.

- In some societies, such as the American Indians who lived on the Plains, individuals go out alone to seek a vision of an animal spirit, who then becomes their protector and guardian spirit throughout life.
- Often people believe in a monotheistic religion such as Judaism, Christianity, and Islam, and still maintain beliefs in ghosts, witches, and spirits of nature as parallel systems.
- Generally speaking, human beings approach the supernatural by carrying out ritual acts, usually involving a combination of speech and patterned behavior that alters the emotional state of the participants.
- Rites of passage are found in all societies; they recognize and mark the transition of life stages, as well as enforce gender norms associated with each life stage.

SUGGESTED READINGS

Bacigalupo, Ana Mariella. *Shamans of the Foye Tree: Gender, Power, and Healing among Chilean Mapuche.* Austin: University of Texas Press, 2007. An ethnographic study that describes shamans' gender identities through performance in social, political, and ritual contexts.

Bowie, Fiona. *The Anthropology of Religion: An Introduction.* 2nd edition. Malden, MA: Blackwell Publishing, 2006. An overview of major classic and contemporary theories and approaches in the anthropology of religion.

Klass, Morton. *Mind Over Mind: The Anthropology and Psychology of Spirit Possession.* Lanham, MD: Rowman & Littlefield Publishers Inc., 2003. An accessible discussion integrating anthropological and psychological approaches to the study of spirit possession.

SUGGESTED WEBSITES

www.adherents.com/. National and international statistics, news and descriptions concerning the world's religions and emerging forms of religious practice.

www.history.com/minisites/thanksgiving/. Video content and discussions, historical myths and realities about Thanksgiving celebrations in America.

www2.hsp.org/exhibits/Balch%20exhibits/rites/rites.html. Rites of passage in America, described for multiple ethnic and religious groups, based on a traveling exhibition created by the Balch Institute for Ethnic Studies.

Chapter 11
Myths, Legends, and Folktales
Past, Present, and Future

PEOPLE ATTEMPT TO EXPLAIN the unknowable by constructing a supernatural world; they also talk about that world. They tell folktales about supernatural creatures. They relate legends about the distant past of unrecorded history in which knights slew dragons. They tell myths about the origins of the world and of people and their social groups. They tell the myths of how God gave them the very land on which they dwell. They tell stories about the exploits of supernatural animals that talk; about big bad wolves that swallow grandmothers; about the brother of the wolf, the coyote, who acts as a trickster. They tell stories about fairies, elves, and the Little People. These different types of stories all deal with universal themes, such as birth, growing up, male-female relations, and death. In America, today, the media for such stories, for the most part about universal themes, include television, films, and other modern forms of mass communication.

Myths, legends, and folktales represent a continuum. They are Western categories, but they provide a useful framework for organizing this material. Myths deal with the remote past, often with the time of the origin of things both natural and cultural—how the world and its people were created, how fire was discovered and cooking began, and how crops were domesticated. Myths were associated with the sacred, especially in ancient and small-scale societies (Von Hendy 2002: 77). As the time period becomes less remote, myths fade into **legends**, which are sometimes thought to have a basis in historical fact. **Folktales** deal with an indeterminate time, which, in European folktales, is indicated by the standard opening, "Once upon a time." To the tellers as well as the audience of these stories, they constitute accounts of real people and real events. Needless to say, the boundaries of these categories are very fluid, and the distinctions are often those made by the analysts. For example, in a recent volume, *African Myths of Origin*, Belcher notes "[I]n this collection of stories the historical element regains its importance . . . [and the stories could be called] 'traditions of origin' leaving out the word 'myth' . . . [though they] . . . describe cultural origins for the people involved . . . [and] have been handed down from one generation to another, although always with changes and adaptations to keep them relevant to their contemporary audiences" (2005: xiv).

MYTHS

The people of Wogeo have a myth that tells how the flutes that represent the *nibek* spirits came to be. As is typical, this myth takes place in the distant past when the culture heroes who created everything in the world lived. Two female heroes dreamed of making flutes. They cut two sticks of bamboo and bored a hole in each, forming flutes that immediately began to play. They were overjoyed with the self-playing flutes. When they went to work in the gardens, they stoppered the holes to prevent the flutes from playing. An adolescent boy then stole the flutes from the two women, and tried to blow them, causing the women to return. On seeing that the boy had stolen the flutes, the women told him that the flutes would never again play by themselves. Since a male had stolen them, no female could ever look at the flutes. The women told him that it would be hard to learn to blow the flutes, but, in order to become men, boys had to make the effort. The two women then left the island of Wogeo in disgust. They eventually settled on Kadovar and Blupblup Islands, and the mainland of New Guinea. These places are the only locations where bamboo for flutes can currently be found.

Various theoretical approaches have been proposed to explain the existence of myths. One views myths as literal history. Such an approach would interpret the Wogeo myth as signifying that there was an earlier period of matriarchy, when women controlled those aspects of society that men now control. Nineteenth-century evolutionists such as Lewis Henry Morgan and Johann Jakob Bachofen would see this myth as an indication of an earlier stage of matrilineal social organization and matriarchy, which they saw all societies going through as they developed. In such a unilineal, universal framework, patrilineal social organization and patriarchy would then follow. This method of interpreting myths as literal history, as well as the unilineal theory of the evolution of societies, was discredited by anthropologists long ago.

Malinowski, who was anti-evolutionist, saw the necessity of analyzing a myth in relation to its social and cultural context. To Malinowski, myths were charters for how and what people should believe, act, and feel. Just as our Declaration of Independence states that all men are created equal, a body of myths lays out ideals that guide the behavior of members of a culture. Malinowski's approach to myth as charter requires that the Wogeo myth be examined in terms of Wogeo cultural facts. There is a men's cult focused upon the men's house where the sacred flutes are kept. Women are kept away from the men's house and are never allowed to see the sacred flutes. At adolescence, boys go through a rite of passage, which involves initiation into this cult. Their tongues must be scarified so they can be rid of the effects of their mother's milk. After this, they can they learn to play the flutes. Boys must be taught to incise their penises with sharpened clamshells while standing in the ocean. The blood must flow into the ocean and not on the body, since it is dangerous and can pollute the boy. Men do this periodically to rid themselves of the pollution resulting from sexual intercourse with women. Both men and women are seen as pol-

Wogeo flutes, which can be seen only by men, are played by initiated men and represent the voices of the *nibek* spirits.

luted by sexual intercourse. Women get rid of this pollution naturally, through menstruation. The people of Wogeo say, "Men play flutes, women bear infants." Malinowski would see the Wogeo myth as providing the justification and rationale for men's performing certain ritual and ceremonial roles from which women are excluded.

Clyde Kluckhohn stressed the interdependence of myth and ritual, with both fulfilling the same societal needs (see also Von Hendy, 2002: 178ft). In many instances, according to Kluckhohn, myths provide statements about the origins of rituals, as well as details of how they are to be performed. Both the telling of the myth and the performance of the ritual arouse the same emotional feelings. Kluckhohn also saw myth and ritual as serving the psychological function of alleviating various forms of anxiety. There is a direct connection between the myth and the ritual in Wogeo. The flutes are the voices of the *nibek* spirits, in ritual. The initiation of boys when they learn how to play the flutes is directly connected to the mythic statement about a boy's growing up only when he learns to play the flute. More recent approaches to the interpretation of myths include the Freudian psychoanalytic approach adopted by Alan Dundes. A Freudian interpretation of the Wogeo myth would see the flutes as masculine objects, clearly phallic symbols. The myth signifies penis envy on the part of the women, and anxiety about castration on the part of the men. Individuals express unconscious fears and anxieties in symbolic form through dreams. Myths are seen as reflecting the collective anxieties of a society, and giving cultural expression to these anxieties. Freud considered certain repressed anxieties and frustrations to be universal, that is, connected to pan-species characteristics related to growth and development.

Lévi-Strauss has pursued a large-scale, detailed analysis of myths from North and South American Indian societies (Lévi-Strauss: 1963, 1971). To Lévi-Strauss, myths provide explanations for contradictions present in a culture that cannot be resolved. The Wogeo myth emphasizes the separation of women from men, after men obtained possession of the flutes. In Lévi-Strauss's terms, the myth attempts to resolve the contradiction between the ideal of keeping males and females apart and the need for them to come together to reproduce society through sexual intercourse. Like all other myths, this myth, too, fails to provide a permanent solution to this contradiction.

Most anthropologists analyzing myths today would agree that myths must always be understood in connection with other cultural facts. In Wogeo, the aphorism "Men play flutes, women bear infants" is important. Male and female are seen as separate but complementary. Women bear children as part of a natural biological process. Flutes are cultural objects manufactured by men. Hence, women are associated with natural things, and men with cultural things. Playing the flutes connects men to the *nibek* spirits, whose voices are the flutes. At this time they must practice sexual abstinence. While women get rid of the bad blood of sexual intercourse naturally, through menstruation, men must do this by means of culturally learned behavior—the incising of their penises. Ideally, life for each sex should be separate. However, in order for women to bear children, as they should, the sexes must come together. This is the only way that society can reproduce itself. By means of the various ceremonies of boys' initiation, they are symbolically separated from women, being re-born from the *nibek* spirits as men. Women dreamed, and then made the flutes, which played by themselves during a time when men and women were not separate. After the boy stole the flutes, the flutes would no longer play by themselves and men had to learn to play them. Men separated themselves from women. The same pattern of the aphorism "Men play flutes, women bear infants" is repeated in the initiation ceremonies and in the myth. Men, representing culture, are separated from women, representing nature. Boys, associated with their mothers from birth, have not yet learned the secrets of their culture. These are learned at initiation, and they thereby acquire culture. But the myth also says that, at one time, women were superior to men, bearing children, and having the flutes as well. The present domination of men rests upon their having stolen what was once women's. Because they could bear children, and cleanse themselves naturally through menstruation, by nature, they were superior in the past because for them, the flutes played by themselves. Men have to do everything the hard way by means of cultural practices that must be learned. But, when men took control of culture, they were able to dominate women. Ultimately, the myth is about the origins of culture and the tension inherent in male-female relations.

There are echoes of the same theme in ancient Greek mythology. Both the Amazons, super-human women who controlled their society, and the Fates, women who, through their weaving, determined the destiny of all humanity, are taken to be evidence in the myths for a matriarchal stage of society. Robert Graves has linked these myths to an earlier matriarchal stage in the development of European society (1955). Interest in what Greek myths tell us about matriarchy still continues today. A recent reanalysis of Greek myths concludes, "If there ever was a time when men ruled the world, or even served as the central focus of a civilized society, Greek myth does not record it" (Lefkowitz 2007: 186). Lefkowitz notes that in Greek myths women are seen as advising male rulers, and even taking over some of their responsibilities. However, it is barbarians such as the Amazons who ruled themselves and fought wars, and the Lycians who used mother's rather than father's name and whose citizenship was based on mother's status, which the Greek myths as well as Herodotus see as societies in which women dominated (Lefkowitz 2007: 3). These Greek myths tell us about contradictions in ancient Greek society. As we can see, the universal theme of male-female relations is handled in similar ways in very different societies.

An interesting support for the continuity of the structure of myths comes from Scheub's analysis of what he calls Zulu "archetypical rites of passage and mythic paths." He focuses on two Zulu "storytelling" women who lived one hundred years apart, the earlier material having been recorded by a Christian missionary and the later information recorded by Scheub himself. He notes "the evolving of stories from one generation to the next. At the core of their stories are identical structural underpinnings [though]; the façade of those stories varies to the point that the narratives seem wholly unlike" (2006: 4, 50–51). This similarity occurs despite the fact that the stories of both tellers reflect their times, and different responses to apartheid, British in the first and Afrikaner for the second.

In recent years, analysts have begun to utilize a variety of newer techniques in the study of the myths of ancient societies in which direct narrative data were not present. For example, in the study of Etruscan mythology, it was necessary to utilize artistic representations, evidence from archeological sites, as well as indirect evidence from Greek and Roman texts (de Grummond 2007: xii). The Etruscan language is part of the Tyrsenian language family, which is an isolate, like Basque. Knowledge about it is incomplete, though individual words are known because of the alternation of Greek and Etruscan in some inscriptions. These myths consisted of a body of sacred stories that explained how the universe was created and organized in a specific way with particular divine creatures such as the mother goddess, and also how to approach the gods by means of specific rituals (de Grummond 2007: xiii). Not unexpectedly, many of these sacred stories or myths were linked to the Etruscans' "highly developed religious practice, and the relationship between myth and ritual, a common concern in world mythology . . . " (de Grummond 2007: xiv).

Sahlins demonstrated the role that myth played in structuring the interaction between the Hawaiians and Captain Cook and his death at their hands, when the former assumed that Cook was the god Lono (1985). Keegan has recently shown the way in which Taino myths structured Taino interactions with Christopher Columbus. In both instances myths are also seen as "structuring social reproduction" (Keegan 2007: 3). Lutz et al. focus on "contact stories" of peoples in Australia, New Zealand, and the United States, looking at explorer and indigenous accounts and the way in which indigenous peoples have recorded, verified, and used contact stories within their own oral and written histories (2007).

LEGENDS

Myths treat the ancient past and the origins of things, while legends deal with the less remote past, just beyond "the fringe of history." Legends are about heroes who overcome obstacles, slay dragons, and defeat conquering armies to establish the independence of their homelands. Such legends are retold to justify the claim of a people to their land and their integrity as a people. The traditions of Polynesian societies, as they have been retold over the generations, illustrate the way myths fade into legends. For example, the Polynesian Maori, who first settled New Zealand, have a myth of how Maui fished up the islands of New Zealand from the ocean depth. Later, he was the culture hero who obtained fire. Kupe, another culture hero, rediscovered the islands while chasing a supernatural octopus, and reported back to the Maori living in their earlier homeland. The first settlers set sail, using Kupe's directions, reaching the islands now called New Zealand. Maori genealogies, which go back as far as forty generations, are repeated down through the generations, linking the present population to the first settlers and Kupe. Maori legends are concerned with the several migrations to New Zealand, and how each tribe and kin group came to occupy its land. Today, legends, recorded in the nineteenth century by English missionaries and scholars, are being used by the Maori as they assert their ethnic identity and demand restitution for lost land. The Hawaiians, like the Maori, are great genealogists, with a tradition of migrations by canoe from Tahiti to the islands of Hawaii. The genealogy of the Hawaiian royal family, the *Kumulipo*, is a prayer chant that traces descent directly back to the gods. The gods appear to be like men in their appearance and actions, and it is hard to separate them from chiefs who lived and were later deified. Thus the world of myth imperceptibly becomes the world of legend and finally, the known world of history. Interestingly, Hawaiian legendary traditions are today being used "to reinforce a tourist-oriented image of Hawaii . . . an ongoing 'process of cultural construction' . . . situated in the preoccupations and negotiations of the present, . . . where every teller engages with the past and interprets it so as to affect listeners or readers" (Bacchilega 2007: 30).

Legend Becomes History: King Arthur and the Knights of the Round Table

King Arthur and his Knights of the Round Table had been considered legend for many centuries, with people in each century recreating the story in their own fashion. In fact, some, who place him in the category of culture hero, argue that "the story of his life and death has been the principal myth of the island of Britain" (Castleden 2000: 1; see also Higham 2002: 1). He was surrounded by such mystery that it was believed he never lived. However, recently there has been a reexamination of various historical documents, such as the *Historia Britionum*, written in 830 by the monk Nennius. It is based on sources, going back to the sixth century, the one in which Arthur lived, which now attest to his actual existence. Archeological materials support this. Whether he was actually a king is disputed, though one source, dated around 1100, describes him as "Chief of the Kings of Britain" (Higham 2002). This would make him a Celtic king, a commander and a chief, during this time. Unfortunately, Arthur was mortally wounded by the Saxon armies, who eventually conquered the southwest part of Britain, earlier a Celtic domain. According to Higham, "Arthur sounds like the very best post-Roman British aristocracy" (2002: 113). This supports the continued influence of Roman culture in Britain despite their earlier defeat. The story of King Arthur is an important example of how historical reality was distorted and overlaid by medieval romances, and later literary treatments until Arthur's very existence was doubted. He had been transformed into a legendary, even mythic figure who became identified with the nation.

FOLKTALES

Folktales are set within a timeless framework. They are concerned with imparting moral values, and usually take the form of demonstrating what happens to individuals who violate the moral code of the society. Often animals freely interact with humans as heroes or villains; at other times tales may be about animals who talk, act, and think like human beings. One of the most common folktale motifs is that of the trickster. Among many North American Indian societies, the trickster takes the form of a coyote, though among the Kwakiutl, the trickster is a raven. There are many sides to the character of coyote. Sometimes he is depicted as being very cunning—he feigns death in order to catch game; he cheats at races and wins. At other times he is singularly stupid. In some tales he is a glutton, and in others he is involved in amorous and ribald adventures. The trickster figure seems to be a universal folklore figure that represents the incongruous combination of monster, loutish liar, braggart, creator and destroyer, and duper, as well as the one who is always duped himself (Goldman 1998). According to Peck, "European immigrants brought to North America tales in which a human trickster outwits other people, and such stories have never waned in popularity" (1998: 203). In European tales, the trickster is almost always a human male, while in Native American tales he is usually personified as an animal, though he may sometimes assume a human shape (Erdoes and Ortiz, 1998: xiii). Goldman identifies two main strands of "trickster scholarship" among those who have studied the trickster motif. In the first, the trickster enables breaches of the accepted order to occur within the realm of the imagination, allowing adults and children to be amused by behavior categorized as antisocial while at the same time being socialized. The second deals with the marginal, liminal status of the trickster who is a mediating being, resolving dilemmas of human existence. It is a way of talking about ourselves in a satiric, ironic, and comedic fashion (Goldman, 1998: 90).

With the expansion of cultural studies, the concept of the **trickster**, which originated as coyote or raven in Native American tales, has been applied in analyzing the literary works of Mark Twain, Herman Melville, and Jack London, as well as to the analysis of many aspects of popular culture such as Bugs Bunny and Roadrunner (Reesman 2001). In the writings of Mark Twain, especially in *Huckleberry Finn*, the trickster is the deadpan storyteller, Mark Twain himself. Melville, however, uses John-the-slave, a well-known trickster in African-American folklore, as a character in his classic novella *Benito Cereno*. John-the-slave can be either a trusted slave or a black slave driver who deceives and manipulates his master. While appearing to be the trusted slave, John-the-slave really is the master. In *Benito Cereno*, an American ship comes upon a seemingly deserted slave ship. In fact, the ship is under the complete control of the slaves after a slave

An early portrayal of King Arthur and the Knights of the Round Table.

revolt. Baba, leader of the revolt, and his son Mure appear to be the groveling retainers of the Spanish captain; however, like John-the-slave, they really are totally in control.

Folktales are characteristic of particular groups, distinguishing them culturally from other groups. "The folktale is thus a vehicle for transmitting to members of the group their collective traditions, perceptions, and values" (Alexander-Frizer 2008: x). Although those of Judeo-Spanish background have been dispersed from their homeland, Spain, since 1492, an oral tradition embodied in the Judeo-Spanish folktale has been passed down in Judeo-Spanish (Ladino) or Hebrew over many generations. In each country where the exiles settled, "there developed . . . a unique Judeo-Spanish culture in relation to the geographical and cultural surroundings" (Alexander-Frizer 2008: ix). These factors shaped the folktales. For example, the "moral tale" dealing with values and matters of conscience was dominant in the stories told by Judeo-Spaniards from Salonika. Legends about general Jewish figures such as Elijah the Prophet and the Ten Lost Tribes are also included (Alexander-Frizer 2008: 96, 97). Folktales can also be much more recent. Bar-Itzhak has analyzed the three main fields of Jewish folklore in Israel: stories about the initial rural settlement of the kibbutzim in Palestine, folklore brought to the newly established State of Israel by waves of immigrants such as the Polish and Yemenite Jews (and that was transformed

"The Spirit of Haida Gwaii" by the Haida artist Bill Reid, includes multiple figures in Haida mythology, including Grizzly Bear (far left), the Bear Mother, Grizzly's human wife (center with oar), the human Shaman (center in conical hat), and the trickster Raven (holding oar far right). This sculpture stands outside the Canadian Embassy in Washington, D.C., in a sense representing Canada as a whole.

by the new problems the immigrants faced in Israel), and the ethnic folklore emerging, which is a return to traditional ethnic patterns but now influenced by the Israel milieu (2008: x–xi).

FAIRY TALES

Just as Coyote tales taught morality to children, fairy tales, according to Bruno Bettelheim, teach children what it means to grow up. While myths are about extraordinary, superhuman heroes or gods, the characters in fairy tales are ordinary mortals. "Whatever strange events the fairy tale hero experiences, they do not make him superhuman, as is true for the mythical hero. This real humanity suggests to the child that, whatever the content of the fairy tale, it is but fanciful elaborations and exaggerations of the tasks he has to meet, and of his hopes and fears" (Bettelheim 1977: 40). Fairy tales were transmitted orally, told around the fire after the work of the day. Consequently, they changed as the centuries went by, as all oral literature does, until they began to be recorded, first by Charles Perrault in the late seventeenth century, and then by the brothers Grimm during the nineteenth century. Recent research has revealed that the fairy tales recorded by the brothers Grimm, such as that of Little Red Riding Hood, have earlier medieval versions as recorded in Medieval Latin literature (Ziolkowski 2007: 4–5). Fairy tales perform an important function in that they are "among our most powerful socializing narratives. They contain enduring rules for understanding who we are, and how we should behave" (Orenstein 2002: 10). One might say that they convey universal and timeless truths.

A fairy tale such as "Red Riding Hood," up until the nineteenth century, was "a bawdy morality tale, quite different from the story we know today" (Orenstein 2002: 3). There have been changes in the meanings of the characters, and although the wolf has always signified evil, in the earlier adult version Red Riding Hood was the unchaste woman. Most fairy tales are stories that are familiar throughout Europe and North America. However, fairies and their stories in Ireland seem to be particular to Irish culture. Irish fairies are an intimate part of Irish culture even today. For example, Purkiss notes that "on Internet newsgroups, a troll is a person who haunts Usenet in an attempt to stir up controversy by posting inflammatory statements" (2000: 306).

PERFORMANCE

Originally, myths, legends, and folktales were transmitted orally, and each telling was a performance. They were retold from generation to generation, to the awe and amusement of successive audiences. Each time a story was retold, it came out slightly differently. Variations were introduced, different episodes were included, and, eventually, different versions of the same story developed. Stories usually diffused from one society to another over a wide area, and in each of these societies a somewhat different version of the story could be found. Anthropologists collect as many versions of a single story told in a particular society as they can. By comparing these different versions, they are better able to ascertain the meaning of the story. In similar fashion, the same and related stories in different societies over a wide area are collected and compared by anthropologists. Lévi-Strauss analyzed different versions of the same myth and related myths in different South American Indian societies (Lévi-Strauss 1971). His analysis revealed the presence of the same themes and contradictions in mythologies throughout this large area.

When we shift to an examination of the performance aspects of myths, legends, and tales—which are, in effect, oral narratives—the factor of creativity enters the picture. Huntsman points out that the different presentations of the same story move from a veneration of "tradition" to a celebration of "creativity" (1995: 124). Tokelau tales, or *kakai*, which are fictitious tales told as entertainment, must contain the episodes, chants, songs, and key phrases that the audience expects. But the tellers of these tales have a wide latitude to elaborate and embellish a story as long as they include what their listeners expect (Huntsman 1995: 125). In contrast, Tokelau *tala*, which are myths, legends, historical narratives, or accounts of the pre-Christian past, have as their primary purpose to inform, though they may also be entertaining. Specific geographic place-names "'ground' the narrative as an account of events that happened at known, named places" (Huntsman 1995: 154). These place-names must be narrated accurately. Huntsman also makes the point, made by many others, that storytellers and raconteurs "tailor" their narrative performances to their audiences (1995: 154). Tellers of stories and tales also vary in their storytelling abilities.

Consideration of the performance aspects of oral narratives places them within a temporal framework, which brings up the question of the continuities and changes of such accounts. The ghost narratives of the Cook Islands, or *tupapaku*, recount stories about spirits in animal form, which are deeply rooted in Polynesian history. Recently, they have come to include stories about cows, pigs, dogs, goats, horses, and cats—introduced domesticates—as spirit vehicles. As Clerk notes, *tupapaku* accounts "have never been separated from the life of the community as a whole. They have adapted consistently to new circumstances, incorporating new experience, yet maintaining a continuity with traditions of great antiquity" (1995: 173; see also Alexander-Frizer 2008: part 3). Continuity and change also characterize all other aspects of culture. As we noted for the potlatch in previous chapters, although people now give away power boats and tea sets instead of elk skins, the organization of the potlatch remains the same. The contents of myths, tales, and potlatches change much more rapidly than does their structure.

When myths, folktales, and legends are written down, an oral narrative becomes written literature. The stories may form the basis for the literary tradition of the society. The legends of King Arthur and the Knights of the Round Table ceased to be stories told by bards, or professional storytellers, and became English literature, as we noted above. The fact that the story is now written down does not mean that it will not continue to change. It may be rewritten by poor writers or by good writers and may change with each retelling. The characters, motifs, and central themes of these stories may often be used by poets, novelists, and dramatists in their own works. For example, in Mary McCarthy's novel *The Group* (1963), the knights have been transformed into female students at Vassar in the 1950s. The American musical *Camelot* also retells the legend of King Arthur and the Knights of the Round Table. *Camelot* later became the referent for the Kennedy presidency.

LEGENDS AND FOLKTALES IN AMERICAN CULTURE

One may pose the question, does our culture have myths, legends, or folktales? Myths deal with the remote past and with superhumans who created the world, the people in it, and all their material objects and cultural institutions. American culture does not include these kinds of myths. However, stories about how American culture was forged and about its origins are our American myths. Legendary figures abound. Some were historical people, such as Billy the Kid, Davy Crockett, Daniel Boone, Kit Carson, Annie Oakley, and Buffalo Bill. Stories about their lives became legends, but other legends about them had no basis in fact. Other heroes, who are the subjects of folktales, such as Pecos Bill, John Henry, and Paul Bunyan, probably never lived. The setting for all these legends was the expanding American frontier. The stories demonstrated how these people conquered natural obstacles and made the frontier livable. They were scouts who led the wagon trains across the dangerous and endless Plains. They were river men who opened up the rivers to settlement and commerce. They were railroad builders who laid the steel track across an expanding nation. They were the sheriffs and marshals who made the frontier safe. In American legends, the theme is a characteristically American one—the conquest of the frontier and the settlement of the land. As occurs in legends in general, American heroes, by their bravery, their ingenuity, and their labor, assert the claim of a people to their land. This, of course, totally ignored and overrode the claim of the Native American population who were on the land first.

Sometimes the heroes of the legends, such as Paul Bunyan, assumed superhuman proportions. He was a legendary lumberjack and logger. As the lumber industry moved across America from Maine to Michigan and Minnesota, and then later to Washington and Oregon, the Bunyan stories moved with it, and Paul Bunyan, at first a regional hero, became a national hero. Bunyan, his ax, and his blue ox Babe are of enormous and superhuman size. Bunyan's feats are distinctive because of both his cleverness and his great strength, and many of the stories are humorous (Peck 1998: 131ff.). In some of the stories he creates natural landmarks, like Puget Sound. Many stories demonstrate his ability to conquer nature. In one story he makes a river run backward in order to break up a log jam. Paul Bunyan stories are also told in the oilfields of Texas and Oklahoma. Here, Bunyan is an oilman who is even given credit for inventing the tools and methods of drilling for oil. The Bunyan stories began in the tales told in the lumber camps of northeastern Michigan and reached a maximum popularity and audience when they became the subject of newspaper columns and advertising copy in the second decade of the twentieth century. Newspaper advertisements turned Paul Bunyan from a folkloric hero into a popular superhero of that time. It is interesting to note that today the work of press agents and publicists is to turn their clients, ordinary human beings, into mythic figures, like Elvis Presley.

While the legends of Paul Bunyan and other tall tales are indigenously American, many folktales and fairy tales told in America are largely derivative, having come with people from other countries. Joel Chandler Harris was a journalist and also a writer of short stores and the Uncle Remus tales. It was "his studies into folklore, and his writing of the tales told to him by American Blacks . . . that made him one of the nation's leading folklorists" (Brasch 2000: xxii). Though a white man, his Uncle Remus stories are said to be a relatively accurate translation of African-American English, which we discussed in chapter 3. As a young man, Harris worked for a publisher who owned a plantation and slaves. While sitting in the cabins of the slaves on the plantation, he learned about their culture and heard the language and the stories, which he later transformed into the Uncle Remus stories. Brer Rabbit, a central character in the stories, is clearly a trickster figure, with his trickery, deceit, and deviousness. He and the other animals in the stories represent transformations of the animals with which the slaves, who came from West Africa, were familiar. Portraits of the rabbit as a trickster also appear in the tales of the Creek, Natchez, and other southeastern Native American groups. Scholarly analysis has shown that the tales were borrowed by the Native Americans from the slaves. Harris considered himself merely a "compiler" of the stories. It is interesting to note that in a recent collection, *From My People: 400 Years of African American Folklore*, edited by Daryl Cumber Dance, Harris is nowhere mentioned. The volume includes folktales—a number about Brer Rabbit and Brer Fox, folk music, soul food, and proverbs, among other categories.

American Films as Legends and Myths

Legends and tales are rarely told by storytellers in present-day America. Parents may read stories to small children, and perhaps these stories may be read in required literature courses. The major themes of such stories, however, continue to be repeated, but now in the media of mass communications. It is in films and television that these same themes from legends and tales reappear. One has only to think of the Western film to understand this point, since Westerns have become inextricably linked to American identity. The hero of the classic Western, like the heroes of American legends, is a rugged individualist who tames the frontier. But Americans have an ambivalent attitude about taming the frontier. They look back with fondness to the time when the frontier represented escape from the constraints of society—a time when individuals took the law into their own hands. The cattlemen who used the open range for cattle grazing represent the beginning of law and order. But they fought the farmers who wanted to fence in the range and who represented a further step in the process of control over nature.

In the classic film *The Man Who Shot Liberty Valence*, director John Ford captures the ambivalence between the wilderness of the frontier, represented by the outlaw Liberty Valence; civilization, represented by Senator Ransom Stoddard; and Donovan, the real hero, who straddles both worlds. The tension in the film is between Liberty, the outlaw, and Ransom, the civilized man. The story of the killing of Valence, the villain, is told in a series of flashbacks from a civilized present time to an earlier frontier time. But a sense of loss and nostalgia for that earlier period pervades the film. Despite the changes in emphasis of the 1960s and 1970s, "the Western's overall thrust sanctified territorial expansion, justified dispossession of the Indians, fueled nostalgia for a largely mythicized past, exalted self-reliance and posited violence as the main solution to personal and societal problems" (Coyne 1997: 3). However, the usual representation of American identity in the Western was white and male. To some extent this picture was transformed in the late 1970s, when the TV miniseries *Centennial*, based on a novel by James Michener, presented the history of a Colorado town, emphasizing the multicultural composition of the frontier and condemning the mass slaughter of the Indians by a racist army officer (Coyne 1997: 184). More recently, *Dances with Wolves*, which many might not call a Western, clearly presents a different picture of Native Americans than do classic Westerns such as *Stagecoach*. President Bush has used the themes of the Western in his discussion of international affairs. Osama bin Laden is wanted "Dead or Alive." We have assumed a "go it alone stance" in our relations with other countries, a "cowboy" stance. We are in a struggle of good and evil and you are "either with us or against us." This is the rhetoric of the classic Western.

The legend of Billy the Kid has been told and retold in films, plays, novels, and ballets. How did Billy the Kid, who was a real person, turn into a legend, and what are the characteristics that differentiate the legendary Billy from the real Billy? Billy the Kid was shot and killed by Pat Garrett (himself a legendary figure), the sheriff of Lincoln County, New Mexico, in July 1881. He had been arrested for murder and sentenced to hang seven months earlier, but he shot and killed his two guards and escaped from prison. Garrett and his posse tracked him down to Fort Sumner, an abandoned army fort, where they killed him. Shortly thereafter, Garrett, with the help of a former newspaperman, wrote the book *The Authentic Life of Billy the Kid,* and the myth was launched. Since so many false stories were being told about Billy at that time, Garrett wanted to set the record straight. According to Garrett, Billy committed his first murder at the age of 12 to defend his mother's honor. Billy carried out later murders in Lincoln County after the execution of his friend John Tunstall, becoming an avenging angel until Sheriff Garrett, with a heavy heart, ended his life. Much of the information in Garrett's account was either mistaken (including Billy's real name) or invented.

Years later, a researcher collecting folklore as part of an oral-history project in New Mexico interviewed a Hispanic member of Sheriff Pat Garrett's posse. The Billy that he recalled was very generous, spoke fluent Spanish, and wore moccasins. "Everybody liked Billy the Kid." He claimed that Garrett's account was all wrong and that Billy was much too smart to be caught in the room where Garrett said he shot him. Though for two weeks the posse surrounded the house where the shooting took place, they never caught sight of Billy or recovered his body.

Each teller of the Billy the Kid story expands a different aspect of the "myth." What do we know about the real person who was Billy the Kid? He was born Henry McCarty, probably in New York City. While he was still young, his mother took him and his brother out West, ending up in Silver City, New Mexico. Before he came to Lincoln County, New Mexico, Henry McCarty, at the age of 18, seems to have killed a man in a gunfight in Arizona in 1877. After that, he assumed the name William Bonney. The Lincoln County "war" into which Henry McCarty was drawn was, in reality, a battle between two factions of the county for political control. One faction consisted of a group of Irish Catholics. The other faction consisted of Protestants led by John Tunstall, the Englishman who was killed. The Lincoln County war has been interpreted as a continuation of the ethnic-religious conflict that was taking place in Northern Ireland (O'Toole 1999). McCarty, born a Catholic, was not in the Irish-Catholic faction in this war. Since Henry's mother remarried when he was 13 to a Scotch-Irish Protestant man, it appears that Henry and his mother converted. Therefore, Henry, now Billy, became a member of the gunfighters for the Protestant faction, which ended in his capture and trial for murder and his killing by Pat Garrett after he escaped from jail.

What are the elements in the myth of Billy the Kid that resonate and touch the emotions of so many Americans? From the very beginning, we see the figure of Billy as the avenging angel and the fighter for justice. Though an outlaw, he is no wanton killer. Garrett sees the first murder that Billy committed as justified, because he was defending his mother's honor. Billy was driven to commit this crime. He is an outsider, yet he understands and obeys a code of honor. He honors friendship and loyalty. He is generous to the poor, and consequently, they help him escape from the authorities, who are evil. Like the wind, Billy cannot be captured. He lives on somewhere. The characteristics attributed to Billy were those of legendary outlaws and heroes such as Jessie James and, much earlier, Robin Hood. Finally, Billy the Kid is only 21 when he is killed. His youth itself is an important part of the myth. These features may not, in fact, describe Henry McCarty, but they are all characteristics of the myth of Billy the Kid. They explain why his story has been and will continue to be retold in films, with Robert Taylor, Paul Newman, Val Kilmer, Kris Kristofferson, or some unknown young actor playing the role of Billy.

The only known photograph of Billy the Kid, whose life became an American legend.

In addition to seeing Western films as contemporary versions of American legends, some analysts have examined American films as myths whose meanings encode somewhat different symbolic patterns characterizing American society. Nathanson, for example, has analyzed the classic film *The Wizard of Oz*, which continues to be re-shown today, in terms of the way its specific mythic properties relate to the important problems of human existence (1991). As Nathanson notes, "The Wizard of Oz may be called a 'secular myth' because, though not overtly religious, it functions in a modern ostensibly secular society, to some extent, the way myths function in traditional and religious societies" (1991: 312). The use of fantastic imagery, the inclusion of supernatural forces and beings, and the fact that it relates to basic human questions, such as where we have come from, where we are going, where we belong, and who we are in relation to others, situate it in the realm of myth. *The Wizard of Oz* is about coming of age and building new relationships and also about going home. Though the Wizard himself initially appears to be a fraud, he is the source of important folk wisdom: The qualities Dorothy and her companions are searching for—a heart for the Tin Man, courage for the Cowardly Lion, a brain for the Scarecrow, and the capacity to be grown-up for Dorothy—are to be found within oneself. The heroine, Dorothy, comes of age in the Emerald City where she is transformed from a child into an adult, after which she is transported back to Kansas. The film was made during the Depression, a very unsettled time, and films from this period often depict explicitly going home and implicitly growing up. Various American symbolic landscapes can be identified in the film, including Munchkin City—a small midwestern city; the Emerald City—the eastern metropolis; the Haunted Forest—the wilderness, threatening and hostile untamed nature; the Yellow Brick Road—a path that pierces the wilderness and represents the unification of America, as well as the freedom and hope of the open highway; and, finally, the Frontier Farm—home, order, and civilization. The Wizard also communicates the notion of the progressive urban setting as set against the traditional rural countryside of the populist worldview, the ultimate resolution of the two being technological agriculture in a bucolic paradise (Nathanson 1991: 173). Kansas is the beginning, the paradise; Oz is the world in which Dorothy searches for order in chaos (the Haunted Forest). At the end of the film, she repeats the mantra, "There's no place like home," and she's back in her bedroom in Kansas (Mackey-Kallis 2001: 137). This represents one of the most important themes of the film, the need to return home, having grown up. The fear of losing one's home was a particularly poignant theme in the 1930s when the film was made.

The film gives mythic expression to what are seen as the deepest feelings of the American people, a nostalgia for the past combined with a hope for the future. The myth of Dorothy in Oz has been more recently recycled in the film *Tootsie*. Michael Dorsey, an out-of-work actor, a failure whom nobody will hire, becomes Dorothy Michaels. In the course of life as Dorothy, he learns about himself. He observes, at the end, "I was a better man as a woman than I ever was as a man." Like Dorothy in *The Wizard of Oz*, Michael Dorsey grows up by finding the truth inside himself. *The Wizard of Oz* is one of the fifty most popular movies ever televised (Mackey-Kallis 2001: 129).

The *Star Wars* films have been said to represent "one of the great myths of our time," combining the theme of a heroic journey with that of the eternal battle between good and evil (Henderson 1997: 3). As noted above, Westerns as a film genre popular from the end of World War I to the early 1970s were no longer very significant in either films or television after that point. *Star Wars* is the "quintessential hero quest" (Mackey-Kallis 2001: 202, 214ff.). However, in the *Star Wars* series, George Lucas, the filmmaker, recycled some Western themes that resonate with more general American conceptualizations. At the beginning of the first film, *Star Wars: Episode IV; A New Hope*, Luke Skywalker is living with his foster parents on the remote desert planet Tatooine, the frontier of civilization, which is also occupied by the Sand People, the equivalent of the Native Americans, as the uncivilized Other. Luke starts on his heroic journey of revenge after his foster parents are killed and his home destroyed. This parallels the destruction by Native Americans of frontier settlements established on Indian territory by American pioneers, who saw the area as a wilderness to be occupied and tamed, and the survivors who sought revenge. Some of the characters in the film recapitulate prototypical figures from Westerns, for example, Han Solo (the loner), the quick-on-the-draw gunfighter, and Greedo, the bounty hunter. This first film in the series is climaxed by a classic Western-style shoot-out with the Death Star, with the Evil Empire as the O.K. Corral (Henderson 1997: 129). In *Return of the Jedi*, Luke, representing the force for good, returns to his home planet, now overrun by a powerful criminal and his gang, and turns out the villains. This theme in *Return of the Jedi* is a recapitulation of the themes of the classic American Western films *Dodge City* and *My Darling Clementine*.

Since the beginning of the twentieth century, Americans have been captivated by technology and its great potential; this is a significant theme in the *Star Wars* series. To Americans, science not only has the potential to solve the world's problems but also can eventually provide knowledge about all aspects of nature. Science fiction, in the form of literature, comic books, and film, was the setting in which this category of themes was explored. In the *Star Wars* films, intergalactic travel is an everyday occurrence, and the level of technological development is accelerated to a degree far beyond what today's humans experience or can even imagine. American faith in the future of technology began to be undermined, to some extent beginning in the 1970s, following the publication of Rachel Carson's *Silent Spring* (1962) and Charles Reich's *The Greening of America* (1970), among others, which depicted how technology run wild was despoiling our environment and threatening the future of the earth. Today, we are very concerned about climate change and global warming. Both sides of the dilemma of how humans maintain their humanity in relating to technology are depicted in *Star Wars*. In the Empire, technology is supreme and the aim is to turn human beings into machinelike servants to technology, suppressing their humanity. The Empire becomes a dystopia, the opposite of a utopia, a place where totalitarian power and violence reign supreme (Henderson 1997: 152–53). Luke Skywalker must use his interior strength and fortitude to fight the system, not to oppose machines as the Luddites of the last century did, but to put humans and their feelings and emotions in control of the machines, instead of having the machines control humans. Another theme is the fear of the Evil Empire, which could be interpreted as a fear of aliens or Others. In this battle between good and evil, Luke takes on heroic characteristics. In the Republican primary contest of 2000, John McCain referred to himself as Luke Skywalker because, like Skywalker, he fought against the system. The *Star Wars* series also echoes the King Arthur stories, in that Luke grows up in "relative obscurity" and finds Obi-Wan Kanobi, his Merlin (Mackey-Kallis 2001: 206ff., 226).

The Sopranos: An American Myth

The Sopranos, the spectacularly popular television series, has also been analyzed in terms of its mythic qualities. Why have the Mafia characters of *The Sopranos* and *The Godfather* films risen to become mythic figures like Jesse James and Billy the Kid, who also were lawbreakers? What do they tell us about American culture? *The Sopranos* operates at three levels: a representation of the real world, the underworld of the Mafia, and the world of fantasy that is told to therapists. The title immediately reveals two things. Sopranos are women who have high voices, and to use Soprano as the family's last name means that Tony is likened to a woman. The implication is that his manhood is threatened, perhaps by castration. Tony himself says, "This whole war could have been averted. Cunnilingus and psychiatry brought us to this" (Barreca 2002: 7). The title of the series also tells us that we are dealing with soap opera, with the emphasis on opera.

Tony Soprano, pondering over the collapse of Western civilization, is Everyman (Barreca 2002: 3). He is also the Hamlet of New Jersey. Tony and Hamlet are both "profoundly introspective and prone to self-doubt, intimidated by formidable mothers, worried about public roles, concerned about treacherous uncles, and irresolute about matters of the heart. . . . The worlds inhabited by Tony and Hamlet appear to them as stale, flat, and unprofitable (or, as Tony puts it, 'I'm losing my mind here')" (Barreca 2002: 3). Tony is like the rest of us and deals with real-life problems. He is a husband, a father, a brother, and a son. In these roles, he interacts with forceful and determined women. Livia, his mother, pretending to be the suffering woman, knows and effectively uses her emotional power over Tony. His wife, Carmela, equally forceful, confronts Tony about all the problems at home, like financial security and Tony's lack of a pension. Tony worries about his daughter Meadow getting into a good college. When she gets into Columbia, she scornfully throws it up to him that he doesn't even know the canon of dead, white males, which she is forced to read at Columbia! But Meadow admits that Tony is no different from other fathers, or other husbands or other sons (Barreca 2002: 38).

The myth of the Mafia, told in *The Godfather* and reiterated in *The Sopranos*, is that the underworld and the real world operate according to the same basic values. In both worlds, factions compete and war with one another. When Mafiosi "waste" an opposing member, they go out of their way to point out that it's nothing personal. When asked by Dr. Melfi if he will go to hell for his actions, Tony replies, "Soldiers don't go to hell. It's business, we're soldiers, we follow codes, orders" (Barreca 2002: 31). Tony's creed is "You gotta do what you gotta do." There are bad guys, like Ralph everywhere—in the movie business, in accounting, in academia, and so on, as there are good guys. Tony is different from Ralph because Tony is a good guy. There is a Mafia code: you act forcefully when you have to, meaning you murder someone or have someone murdered. The other side of the code is strong loyalty to superiors and inferiors. Tony strictly observes this Mafia code. In this respect, Tony is no different from the average "good soldier" in the everyday world.

The level of therapy, or psychiatry, constitutes still a third level. What people tell their therapist reflects something other than reality. It reflects their distortions, their desires, and sometimes their fantasies. The interaction between Dr. Melfi, the therapist, and Tony Soprano represents one of the most popular themes in *The Sopranos*. Real-life patients even discuss her with their therapists. The idea of a Mafia killer bearing his breast to his female therapist is a brilliant device, because it reveals Tony's rationalizations about his actions. We quoted Tony as saying, "I'm losing my mind here," meaning he recognizes that he needs help, since he is ambivalent and indecisive. If anyone in his organization were to find out about this, it would be disastrous for Tony. He must always appear to be totally in control (like Vito Coreleone). This action of going to a therapist could never happen to real Mafiosi because it would undermine their power. Like all therapists, Dr. Melfi has a serious problem of counter transference. One literary critic, in her analysis of the series, is very taken with the character of Dr. Melfi. She says, "Dr. Melfi is (or might be) me—me watching with concern, distaste . . . and eventually a kind of fascination" (Barreca 2002: 25).

Americans are fascinated by gangsters, especially Mafia gangsters. Programs and films such as *The Sopranos* and *The Godfather* show the way in which the Mafia represent a dialectic between beloved American values—family, home, loyalty, and roots—and the murder and rapaciousness of the underworld. Interestingly, rapaciousness itself has been and continues to be an aspect of American capitalism, making some corporate executives resemble Mafia kingpins. It is the leadership ability of these dons as depicted in film that Rudolph Guiliani admires when he holds Don Coreleone up as a model leader (Guiliani 2002: 36, 312). Inculcating obedience in followers is one of the principles of leadership, and Tony Soprano is a good soldier who follows orders. For him this is the justification for his violent acts. Yet, in doing so, he often suffers pain and experiences panic. That is what makes *The Sopranos* so appealing.

Urban Legends

What are **urban legends** and how do they reflect modern life? An urban or contemporary legend can be defined as "a story in a contemporary setting (not necessarily a city), reported as a true individual experience, with traditional variants that indicate its legendary character . . . [and the stories] typically have three good reasons for their popularity: a suspenseful or humorous story line, an element of actual belief, and a warning or moral that is either stated or implied" (Brunvand 2000: 6). There is a very broad range of such legends and clearly some drop out as others begin to be told.

Earlier, we recounted some of the political repercussions of the events of 9/11. 9/11 also produced a flood of urban legends, referred to as "twin tower" legends (Harding 2005: 109–117). We are all aware that the attack on the Twin Towers really happened. Why should we, therefore, consider these stories not to be true? Harding notes, "Urban Legend and conspiracy theory blend neatly together" (2005: 110). One such legend is that the 9/11 attack was carried out by Israel, but blamed on Arab terrorists, and that Jewish employees were warned in advance, and therefore none were killed. Though Osama bin Laden has claimed responsibility for the attacks, and many Jews in fact were killed, the legend persists. Another legend involves the mysterious stranger, often of Middle Eastern origin, who, in response to a good deed like the return of his lost wallet, warns his benefactors not to go to a specific place, like New York City on a certain date. The point of such a legend is to say that if you help someone else and become involved, he, in turn, will help you to avoid a chance attack. Still another legend reports that Bin Laden has been sighted in Utah, or some other place. This is part of another set of legends, that in some unseen part of our house, our town, our nation, a dangerous and mysterious stranger is lurking. After 9/11, a legend appeared claiming that Bin Laden, or the Bin Laden family, owned Citibank. According to Harding, "Bush family ties to the Bin Laden family, however, are said to exist" (2005: 114). This, coupled with the evacuation of over one hundred members of the Bin Laden family within 24 hours of 9/11, gave fuel to this particular urban legend. Nine months after the Twin Tower attacks, hospitals saw a sharp increase in births, according to still another urban legend, suggesting that faced with annihilation, humans sought desperately to reproduce themselves. The urban legends arising after the events of 9/11 reveal the fears and concerns running through American culture. Among them are governments that lie to us in order to win our support, faceless corporations and banks who are willing to collaborate with our enemies, and the "Fear of the 'evil foreigner' bent on the destruction of our way of life" (Harding 2005: 117).

Organ theft narratives also constitute urban legends, that is, "a body of beliefs which can be summarized thus: organized criminal groups engaged in the organ trade are using large-scale kidnapping and murder, preferably of children, in order to supply human organs to a vast network of professional but criminal medical personnel, who practice clandestine transplants, bring huge profits to themselves and to those in the trade" (Campion-Vincent 2005: 3). It includes stories about the pseudo-adoption or purchase of the babies of poor women destined to be cut up and used in organ transplants, children kidnapped for their eyes, or tourists kidnapped for their kidneys (Campion-Vincent 2005: 4, 13, 25). Despite the fact that organ transplants are a life-giving and legitimate medical procedure, hostile attitudes toward medicine and the actual fact of a modern trade in organs have made the accusations in these stories "more plausible" (Campion-Vincent 2005: 38).

The mass media often play a key role in the dissemination of urban legends, which lends a further aura of truth to the story. Koven points out that "[t]elevision programs not only draw upon urban legend material for their stories but also, by retelling these legends, redistribute these stories to new generations" (2008: 69). Brunvand observes that "the stories do tell one kind of truth. They are a unique, unselfconscious reflection of major concerns of individuals in the societies in which the [urban] legends circulate" (1998: 146). In this sense, urban legends in our culture are no different from the myths we discussed earlier, which also deal with such major concerns.

SUMMARY

- Myths deal with the remote past, often with the time of the origin of things both natural and cultural, and are associated with the sacred.
- Several interpretations of myths include Malinowski's, which emphasizes that myth was a charter for how people should believe, act, and feel; Kluckhohn, who stressed the interdependence of myth and ritual; and Lévi-Strauss, who viewed myth as providing explanations for cultural contradictions that cannot be resolved.
- Myths fade into legends, which are sometimes thought to have a basis in historical fact.
- The story of King Arthur exemplifies the way in which historical reality was distorted to the point where his very existence was doubted, and he had been transformed into a legendary figure.
- Folktales, which deal with an indeterminate time, often feature a trickster, who appears in Native American stories as a coyote or raven. He represents a combination of monster, loutish liar, braggart, creator, and destroyer.
- When transmitted orally, each telling of a myth, legend, or folktale was a performance. When they are written down, they become literature.
- American films and television employ themes from legends and tales; Westerns, for example, are contemporary versions of American legends.
- Americans are fascinated by portrayals of the Mafia in film and television because they represent a dialectic between beloved American values such as family, loyalty, and roots and the murder and rapaciousness of the underworld.
- An urban or contemporary legend is a story in a contemporary setting, reported as a true individual experience, which has an element of actual belief and a warning or moral.

Suggested Readings

Dance, Daryl Cumber. *From My People: Four Hundred Years of African American Folklore.* New York: Norton, 2002. A collection of many African-American folktales that have survived and been adapted through the centuries.

Loy, R. Philip. *Westerns in a Changing America, 1955–2000.* Jefferson, NC: McFarland, 2004. A number of basic themes are explored in a wide variety of Westerns.

Von Hendy, Andrew. *The Modern Construction of Myth.* Bloomington, IN: Indiana University Press, 2002. A consideration of the anthropological theories about the invention and evolution of myth.

Suggested Websites

www.pitt.edu/~dash/folktexts.html. An encyclopedic compendium about folklore and mythology.

www.snopes.com/info/top25uls.asp. The details of twenty-five urban legends currently circulating.

www.britannia.com/historyh12/html. The sites associated with King Arthur are discussed along with the historical evidence for his existence.

Chapter 12

The Artistic Dimension

EVERY CULTURE UNIVERSALLY produces what we of the Western world label art. Objects that are formed to meet utilitarian needs are also frequently embellished and decorated and are referred to in the West as the decorative arts. Other objects have no utilitarian purpose, but are created solely for aesthetic reasons. Language communicates information, thought, and emotion, but art is also a mode of communication. Anthropologists such as Anthony Forge and Nancy Munn see art as a system of visual communication. Forge (1973) also includes dance and gesture, along with painting, sculpture, and architecture, as part of this system of visual communication. Munn has analyzed the art of the Walbiri of Australia in terms of the fundamental graphic elements of which it is composed (1973). Each element has a range of meanings, and the elements are ordered in regular ways according to rules of combination, similar to rules of grammar in language. The artistic products of the Walbiri, such as sand drawings or decorated objects used in ceremonials, contain representations of totemic myths, known as dreamings. These are stories about the mythical totemic ancestors of the Walbiri and their travels. Poetry and song are heightened, more expressive, and embellished ways of communicating the same things as everyday language.

On the Northwest Coast, masks, totem poles, sculpted house posts, painted house fronts, decorated ceremonial bowls, and other utilitarian objects include designs that represent particular clans. (A totem pole is illustrated on page 88.) These designs depict the mythological ancestors of the clan, such as the wolf, the grizzly bear, the sea bear, the raven, the eagle, and the killer whale. The message conveyed is that the art object represents the kin group. The kin group and its representation are conceptually one. Art objects are used at rituals, as for example the masks worn by chiefs at the Kwakiutl wedding potlatch (described in chapter 2). During such rituals, myths recounting the adventures of the mythological ancestor will be told, or the dance or song associated with that myth will be performed. Forge points out that in Arnhem Land, in Australia, art, myth, and ritual are also completely interlocked and interdependent (1973). There are three different ways of expressing the same thing—in words, in actions, and in visual form. The interconnection between art, myth, and ritual on the Northwest Coast illustrates the same point.

Art also communicates emotion. The emotion may be awe, as is the case when statues represent powerful supernatural spirits. It may be terror, as invoked by Poro masks from West Africa. It may be mirth and pleasure, as when masked dancers carry out their antics or when satirical art caricatures pomposity. Is it possible to talk about a universal aesthetic impulse? Are masterpieces of art produced in one culture recognized as such by people in all cultures? Or does the aesthetic appreciation of art objects extend only to the members of the society within which they were made? Each society has particular standards by which it judges its art. However, there are masterpieces that are appreciated aesthetically by people of very different cultures. In some instances, the emotional impact of the object appeals to some universal sense and does not require particular cultural knowledge in order to be appreciated. In an experiment carried out by Irvin Child, a psychologist, and Leon Sirota, an anthropologist, photographs of BaKwele masks from Central Africa were shown to BaKwele elders, including carvers, all of whom were knowledgeable about masks (1965). These men ranked the masks in terms of their aesthetic value, from the best mask to the worst. The same photographs of the masks were then shown to a group of art history students at Yale University, and they too ranked the masks according to their opinions of the aesthetic value of each mask. There was significant agreement between the two groups of judges. Though the American students knew nothing about the masks or about BaKwele culture, they tended to agree with the BaKwele experts about which masks were aesthetically superior and which masks were mediocre. This research seems to indicate that there is some universal aesthetic sense in what we call the arts, manifested in all cultures.

Beyond this universal aesthetic impulse, cultures differ from one another with regard to the form of their artistic expression. The Tikopia stress poetry but have little in the way of visual arts. The Chimbu of Highland Papua New Guinea decorate their bodies, while the Kwakiutl used to decorate their houses. This kind of concentration on one or another of the "arts" is also found in many societies in the Western world if one examines them over a long span of time. In German culture, the highest achievement among all the arts is to be found in music; English culture excels in literature; painting finds its highest expression in Holland and in Italy. Still others seem to stress each of the arts equally. The reasons a culture emphasizes one art and not another are unclear.

The interpretation of the meaning of a work of art in a culture can be made only in terms of that culture's symbolic system. Witherspoon, in his work on the Navajo, shows the nature of the relationship among the categories of the beautiful, the good, and the evil, and the ways these are reflected in Navajo rug design and sand painting. However, as we noted in our discussion of the BaKwele experiment, people from other cultures can appreciate a work of art in terms of its aesthetic qualities, without understanding its meaning in the culture that produced it. Each culture has its own distinctive style that expresses its symbols in the same way that a tapestry does.

Up until recently, only in the Western world was art produced for art's sake, to be hung in museums, galleries, and homes or to be performed in concerts before large audiences. This was also the case in complex societies such as China and Japan, which had Chinese opera and Kabuki performances. In the kinds of small-scale societies that anthropologists first studied, art was embedded in the culture. Ritual performances employed art, and the meanings that the art communicated related to the meaning of the ritual and the mythology associated with it. But today Australian aboriginal artists and artists from the Northwest Coast produce art in Western genres (silkscreen prints or acrylic paints) embodying traditional styles, which is exhibited in sophisticated urban art galleries.

In our own culture, much of what is labeled art is created solely to give aesthetic pleasure, to be admired. This point has so influenced the definition of art in our society that we make a distinction between that which is useful, or utilitarian, and that which is art and has no practical use. Utilitarian objects are often recognized as art at a later time, when they are valued for their aesthetic beauty and referred to as decorative arts. Furniture and other objects made by the Shakers and quilts made by the Amish are examples of this type. Today, the term *decorative arts* has come to include objects in current use that are admired for their aesthetic qualities. In small-scale societies there was no such thing as pure art; therefore, in those societies this distinction has no relevance.

STYLE

Art can be examined in terms of **style**, beyond its communicative function. The function of art is the role it plays in society, its use in rituals, the information conveyed, and the aesthetic pleasure that it communicates through its content. Structure is the component parts and the way they are put together. That is its style. For example, the art of the Northwest Coast is characterized by a particular style, as is apparent from the illustrations in this chapter. What are the characteristics of that style that make it distinctively different? The art of the Northwest Coast area is primarily three-dimensional carving in wood. This undoubtedly relates to the fact that the societies of the Northwest Coast are located in the northern coastal rain forest, where massive trees such as cedar and spruce provided excellent raw material for the carver. The colors used in Northwest Coast art were predominantly yellow, black, red, and green-blue, with the unpainted natural wood as a background color. The pigments used were made from natural materials—fungus, berries, ochre, moss, charcoal. The distinctive green-blue used was produced by allowing native copper to corrode in urine.

Because of the emphasis on sculpture, round, oblong, oval, circular, and curvilinear forms predominate, even on flat surfaces. The interlocking of animal and sometimes human forms, such as that found on totem poles, is typical. Franz Boas noted that the depiction of animals in Northwest Coast art is characterized by the emphasis of certain features—eyes, mouths, ears, fins, feathers, and tails (1955). Each animal species, from killer whale to dragonfly, can be identified by the representation of the features unique to that species. Thus, the curved beak is the distinctive feature of the eagle, and the snout, the distinctive feature of the wolf. The same techniques for carving wood were adapted for use in other media, such as stone, bone, and metal. Besides carving in the round, Northwest Coast artists also worked on two-dimensional surfaces. The change from three dimensions to two dimensions required a transformation of design. The tech-

Painting from a Tsimshian house front representing a bear.

nique adopted on the Northwest Coast for two-dimensional designs is called split representation. The painting on a Tsimshian house front on the illustration depicts this technique. The bear has been sliced in half and the two sides placed next to each other to make up the house front. This represents a bear—the two sides in profile—but together they form a bear looking frontward. Two other features of Northwest Coast art style are also important. Design elements cover an entire surface, leaving no blank spaces, and eyelike shapes are used as fillers and in place of joints. The portrayal of eyes in masks indicates the great importance of eyes in Northwest Coast society. All these features, taken together, form the distinctive style of the art of the Northwest Coast.

There is a hierarchical aspect to the concept of style. One can speak of the style of the individual artist, that is, the features that are characteristic of the work of a particular artist. Sometimes the art style of a village, city, or region can be identified. It is more frequent to refer to the art style of a single society, such as Kwakiutl. Certain general features delineate the art style of a larger area as we have shown above for the Northwest Coast. Contemporary Northwest Coast artists, such as the remarkable Haida carver Bill Reid, use the traditional content and the distinctive style of Northwest Coast art but add their own individual quality to it. The style of each artist is therefore different, as is the case for European and American contemporary artists. The sculpture in bronze, patinated to look like argillite, by Bill Reid, entitled "The Spirit of Haida Gwaii" (see photograph on page 267), exemplifies the combination of traditional themes from Haida mythology, united with the genius of a creative artist.

The hierarchical concept of style applies to the art of complex societies. One can speak of the style of Renaissance art, of the Italian Renaissance in particular, of the schools of Venice or of Florence, and of the particular style of Raphael, which differs from that of Tintoretto. The concept of style is applicable at each level. It is also applicable to music and literature, where it has the same hierarchical structure.

THE ARTIST

In the past, scholars questioned whether one could speak of the style of the individual artist in small-scale societies, as comparable to the style of Raphael in terms of its uniqueness. Art in such societies was embedded in social, ritual, and ceremonial contexts, and it therefore had to be produced within a set of constraints, since it had to convey certain messages. The artist who carves a Kwakiutl potlatch mask must operate under such a set of constraints, but beyond that he can show some degree of inspiration and individualism. After all, he does not merely copy a previously existing mask. He carves a representation of a known spirit in terms of his conceptualization of that spirit. He gets his inspiration in dreams. Accounts from other societies indicate that there, too, inspirations are said to come from dreams. As we will show in our discussion of *malanggan* carvers on New Ireland, the carver dreams the image he will carve. Dreams are the sources of individual creativity since each person's dreams differ. William Davenport reports that wood-carvers in the Solomon Islands receive their inspiration from the supernatural, which comes to them in dreams (1968). Creativity or genius in some people and not in others is a difficult phenomenon to explain, and people the world over resort to external factors, such as divine inspiration from the supernatural or the Muses, to account for it. In addition to inspiration, the artist must also have the technical skills to translate a vision or a dream into a work of art. Thus craftsmanship is also a part of creativity. Carvers and artists differ in their degree of creativity and craftsmanship. People in all societies distinguish between good and bad art. They do this by applying a set of aesthetic standards.

Seeing the art of small-scale society as the product of an anonymous artist working within a communal tradition and the art of our society as the product of the creativity of the individual artist is an erroneous construct of Western society (Price 1989).Within the cultural context and in the community in which the art is produced, the creativity of the individual artist in small-scale societies is recognized and rewarded, and the names of superior artists are known far and wide. Such art is made anonymous when it is extracted from its original cultural context by Westerners and transformed into objects in their museums representing "primitive" art or "the other."

The fame of Yoruba artists and carvers was known well beyond the towns in which they lived (see Walker, cited in Abiodun et al. 1994: 91). However, when King Tezifon of the Yoruba kingdom of Alada sent a carved divination board to King Felipe IV of Spain in 1659, the carver's name was not included. Like almost all examples of art from small-scale societies that wound up in European museums, the artist who carved it became "Anonymous." The carved divination board now resides in a German museum. In response to this gift, Felipe IV sent twelve Capuchin missionaries, bringing with them a translation of Christian doctrine into the language of Alada. We can therefore assume that the Alada divination tray was, in a sense, equal in Christian eyes to the text on Christian doctrine brought by the missionaries. As Yai, a Yoruba scholar, explains

A contemporary *malanggan* carver from New Ireland holding his adze beside an unfinished carving.

it today, "The king of Alada, in an attempt to establish an equal cultural and political exchange must have thought of sending to European kings a divination tray that he perceived as a perfect equivalent of the text European missionaries carried with them along the West African coast. . . . It was a carved text par excellence. Tezifon was therefore engaging the contemporary European elite in a cultural dialogue, an exchange of texts or discourses" (1994: 111). The tray was used by an oracle or diviner and was meant to hold the blood of sacrifices. As Bassani points out, the carving on the tray portrays the Yoruba cosmos that the diviner employs in his ritual performances (cited in Abiodun et al. 1994: 81–82). The Yoruba artist's task is to translate this cosmos or text into another form—into artistic, visual expression.

Like the New Ireland carver, who translates a myth into a *malanggan*, the Yoruba carver translates one medium into another; he translates words into visual art. Though the identity of the carver of this divination tray can probably never be recovered, anthropologists today attempt to find out who the artists were who carved many of the masterpieces to be found in museums. They are very often successful, as in the case of Olowe, a carver who died in 1938, considered by many the most important Yoruba artist of the twentieth century. Although he was famous in Nigeria, ethnographers of the time paid no attention to the identity of this outstanding carver (Walker 1998: 91). Though individual artists make masks among the Poro, the link between the carvers and the masks that they manufacture is denied. Like his work—the mask, which is a combination of the natural and the supernatural—the artist who creates this thing is himself somewhat outside society. Artists in a great many societies, including our own, are frequently considered marginal people who are not bound by the norms of usual behavior.

THE VISUAL ARTS

The visual arts include such modes of representation as painting, sculpture, body decoration, and house decoration. Masks are a special kind of sculpture, found in a number of societies around the world, but certainly not universally. We have chosen to examine masks as an exemplification of art in culture because they have certain intrinsic features, yet their meaning and use differ from one culture to the next. The two stone masks pictured have been acclaimed as works of art. What makes them works of art? What do we know about their place in the culture that made them? These two masks were collected from the Tsimshian of British Columbia in the late nineteenth century. They were found in two different locales by two different individuals and ended up in two different museums, one in Ottawa and the other in Paris. An anthropologist, Wilson Duff, thought they matched. In 1975 he brought them together for an exhibit at Victoria, British Columbia, and found that the sighted mask fit snugly into the back of the unsighted one, the two forming a single entity. The inner mask had holes drilled in it for the wooden harness with which it was attached to a human head. We know, therefore, that they were used as masks, but this is the only direct information that we have on their use. The two masks form a set, and their meaning must be interpreted in that light. The alternation of sighted and unsighted has a particular meaning for us, but what did the masks mean in Tsimshian culture?

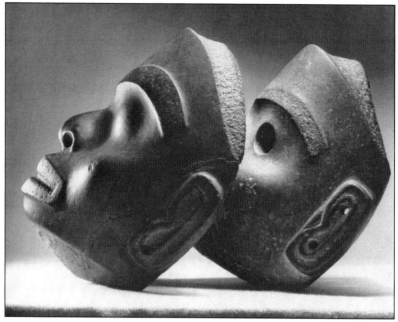

Tsimshian stone masks, one with eyes open and another with eyes closed, fit together as a set.

We do know a good deal about the meaning of masks and how and when they were used in ritual and ceremonial life among the Kwakiutl, southern neighbors of the Tsimshian. Using these data, in addition to what we know about Tsimshian culture, we gain some insights into their uses among the Tsimshian. In the Kwakiutl wedding potlatch, described in chapter 2, chiefs wear masks and costumes that depict the supernatural ancestors who are the mythological founders of their *numayms*. Each chief makes a speech in which he relates how his privileges, including the right to wear a particular mask, have descended to him from mythological times. A mask described in chapter 2 is called the Devourer of Tribes and represents a sea bear, a mythological monster combining characteristics of the bear and the killer whale. The father of the bride is able to call forth this supernatural creature because his *numaym* is descended from it, and only that *numaym* has the right to make a mask representation of it and personify it in a ritual. The Kwakiutl masks, which now hang inertly on museum walls, were used in dramatic ritual performances to enact the myths of the spirits they represented.

The Tsimshian, carvers of the twin stone masks, used masks in a way similar to that among the Kwakiutl. Tsimshian masks represent supernatural spirits. They were used at potlatches and at supernatural dance society rituals. Contact with supernatural spirits operated along lineage lines, and at initiation, power from the supernatural spirits, associated with a boy's own lineage, was "thrown" into him. Somewhat later he was initiated into a secret society. He then had the right to sing the song of his spirit and wear its mask at ceremonies. When a chief wore his mask, the supernatural spirit was in him. Its presence was also indicated by the sound of a whistle, which represented the voice of the spirit. Among the Tsimshian, carvers of masks, artists, song composers, and dramatists were all men who had received supernatural power. Returning to the stone masks, we can imagine these masks, now in museum cases, being used in a Tsimshian ceremony. It is dead of winter in a village on the Skeena River, and the *halaiit*, the sacred dance of the Tsimshian, is being held. Whistles announce the approaching spirit, and before the entranced audience the chief appears with the face of the sightless stone mask. As he slowly dances, the stone mask miraculously opens its eyes. The great power of the spirit residing in the chief has caused this miracle. The two stone masks represent a single face, which opens and closes its eyes. What does this mean? Wilson Duff suggests that the sighted/sightless states represent looking outward and looking inward or self-recognition, sight and memory, seeing and imagining, looking ahead and seeing the past (1975).

Among the Igbo of southeastern Nigeria, masking is an important part of public performances as well as secret society rituals. As Ukaegbu notes, "Igbo masking is a social performance derived from a common cultural base and although any number of its many displays share essential characteristics, they still exhibit an astonishing degree of interpretational variation" (2006: 1). In addition, the structure of particular performances of Igbo masking changes over time. Before the establishment of British colonial rule, Igbo religion impacted every aspect of life. At that time, the major focus of the institution of masking was to provide a religious setting in which the Igbo interacted with and reinforced their relationship with the various forces of the universe (Ukaegbu 2006: 30). The shift to Christianity was a blow to masking. At that point, "[t]he masking tradition was either appropriated for the service of colonialism or banned . . . [and] experienced maskers left the tradition in droves" (Ukaegbu 2006: 5). At first, the masking tradition retreated into the realm of secrecy. But just before Nigerian independence was declared, Christians returned to the masking tradition, reinvigorating it, which resulted in the development of new forms of masking emphasizing the artistic aspect and not the religious significance. However, masks are often used at initiations into full membership in the community, as well in adult initiation into cults.

The Agaba mask-type found in varying forms and importance throughout the Igbo area is not only a mask design but also an associated performance form. The Agaba masks, worn only by men, represent otherworldly figures that are superior to men. Though each mask is unique, a common structure emphasizes grotesqueness to accentuate their terrifying appearance. Variation exists within a flexible framework of core features that is able to accommodate new ideas and interpretations in design and production. As Ukaegbu notes, "Agaba is the most flexible of the mask types, designs and performances . . . [in that it acquires] new functional purposes and designs wherever it goes" (2006: 7). Men actively participate in all the aspects of masking, and women are only marginally involved, except for some women who have special relationships with particular masks.

Masks are also used by the Poro Society, which is found among a group of tribes in Liberia and adjacent Sierra Leone. When a person dons a mask, the spirit is said to be present in him. Among the Mano, as among the Tsimshian, whistles and horns symbolize the voice of the spirit. There are basically two kinds of Poro Society masks—portrait masks, the repositories of the spirits of important deceased leaders and the ancestor spirits, and grotesque masks portraying half-animal, half-human creatures associated with the spirits of nature, other spiritual beings, and various gods. The masks were smeared with the blood of sacrificed animals such as chickens or sheep. The Poro Society was a secret male cult with several initiatory grades. Individuals accused of crimes were brought before the masks for a judgment. The Mano would say that the mask punished or even executed someone since the wearer carried out the mask's decision. People conformed to societal rules because they feared the power of the spirits, which were contained in the masks of the Poro Society.

Among the Kwakiutl, summer and winter were clearly separated as the secular and sacred periods, and the art objects employed in the different rituals in summer and winter contrasted in style (Rosman and Rubel 1990). Summer was the time for potlatching, such as the wedding potlatch discussed in chapter 2, and on these occasions claims to rank were demonstrated. Chiefs wore masks illustrating their mythological ancestors. Between the secular world of summer and the sacred world of winter, there was a ritual period of transition when the spirits came into the village and the Winter Ceremonial was held. The Kwakiutl Winter Ceremonial dances, which lasted several months, parallel the *halaiit*, the sacred dance of the Tsimshian discussed earlier. Young people who were seized and devoured by the spirits were initiated into secret societies and then subsequently emerged during a ceremony. The spirits were portrayed by individuals wearing masks that represented particular spirits. The initiated members of the secret society were considered shamans, since they crossed the border from the natural world into that of the supernatural and became dangerous cannibal spirits. The art style used in these Winter Ceremonial masks was an exaggerated and distorted one, in contrast to that used in the masks of secular summer rituals. It was a style appropriate to the supernatural world of the shaman. The illustrations show how the strongly curved beak of the eagle in the secular potlatch mask becomes the greatly distorted beak of the Crooked Beak of Heaven. The pronounced snout of the wolf in the secular potlatch mask becomes the exaggerated mask worn in the Winter Ceremonial.

Masks have characteristics that differentiate them from other forms of art. A mask is worn by a person and is always a face. When people don masks they become a different person, what is represented by the mask. It can represent the face of a human being, an ancestor; the face of an animal; or the face of an imaginary creature, such as a monster or a supernatural being, in which human and animal features are combined in the face portrayed on the mask. In Bali, Indonesia, the face itself is considered a mask. While the Balinese do wear masks in ritual performances, donning a mask and leaving the face bare are symbolically equivalent. The masks in Kwakiutl, Tsimshian, Mano, and Igbo societies represent statements about the nature of the individual. Each society has a particular view of the individual—what his or her relation is to others in the society, where he or she came from, how he or she came to be, and what his or her place is in the natural world. Masks are embedded in culture and play a significant role in the performance of religious rituals. The masks along with the dances and songs performed by the wearer usually symbolize central ideas in the culture and convey important information relevant to kinship, social relationships, myths, and political activities, as in the Kwakiutl Winter Ceremonial. In contrast, once the masks are removed from the society they assume a completely different character as inert art objects displayed in museums.

Top two images are the masks of the wolf and eagle worn during secular potlatches. The eagle (middle image) is a transformation mask that opens up to reveal another mask representing the face of a man. These masks contrast in style with the wolf and Crooked Beak (eagle) of the sacred Winter Ceremonial (bottom).

New Ireland Malanggans, Yesterday and Today

Malanggan mortuary sculptures from northern New Ireland, now part of Papua New Guinea, are striking examples of visual art. The carvings were used in the religious ritual held to commemorate the deaths of several individuals of a single clan and simultaneously to initiate the boys of that clan. European explorers of the early nineteenth century were sufficiently captivated by the sculptures to bring back examples to Europe and America. When Christian missionaries came to New Ireland in the late nineteenth century, they tried to suppress the *malanggan* ceremony and the carvings associated with it, since these represented earlier pagan beliefs. However, the *malanggan* ceremony did not die and continues to be celebrated today. The Catholic Church no longer sees a conflict between the *malanggan* rite and Catholicism and has even incorporated *malanggan* sculpture into church architecture. The designs for *malanggans* are still owned and sold by one clan to another. When a *malanggan* sculpture is ordered for an upcoming ritual, the owner of the design tells the carver the myth embodying the design and what the carving should look like. The carver then translates the words into a visual image. Sometimes the process of translation for the carver involves dreaming the image, which he will then carve. The carver of a *malanggan* works within a set of constraints such that the design can immediately be recognized as a member of a particular named category of images. Further, the owner of the design must be able to recognize it as his particular design. Since the carver does not use a sculpture from a previous *malanggan* ceremony as a model, a degree of artistic creativity is always involved. Carvers are evaluated in terms of how well they express the design, and several have island-wide reputations.

Before contact, after the *malanggans* were used in a ceremony, they were burned or left to rot. After European colonization, *malanggans*, since they were no longer valued after the ceremony, were given or sold to Europeans, and many wound up in museums all over the world. Today, in New Ireland, after they are used in ceremonies, *malanggans* may sometimes be sold to tourists and collectors. Modern carvers use steel chisels and commercial paints. When shown pictures of *malanggan* carvings 100 years old and now in the Australian Museum, they admired the workmanship of the earlier carvers, particularly since the earlier carvers had only stone tools to use. However, the present-day carvers felt their own carvings were superior. The three-dimensional *malanggan* art of New Ireland has also provided the inspiration for the New Ireland printmaker David Lasisi.

Ethnic Identity and Toraja Art

The architecturally based carvings of the Toraja have graced museum walls over the world for a hundred years. Heretofore, art had been treated as a minor and passive aspect of Toraja ethnic identity marking, but it can be "an active ingredient in identity politics . . . as well as a critique of established ethnic, colonial, or political hierarchies" (Adams 1998: 328–29; see also Adams 2006). The Sa'dan Toraja of highland Sulawesi, a province of Indonesia, have been marginalized in the multiethnic Indonesian state not only by their small numbers and geographic isolation, but also because they are Christians in a predominantly Muslim country. The Toraja area has recently become a mecca for international tourists who travel seven hours by bus to see the interesting architecture and elaborate carving of the houses and the slaughter of bulls that accompanies what seems to be a never-ending series of funeral rituals. The carving on the Toraja house, or *tongkonan*, is the visual embodiment of the ancestry and elite rank of the family that occupies it. Nowadays, non-noble Toraja tourist guides often introduce newer explanations of motifs, such as the cross motif used long before Toraja conversion, which is said to represent "evidence of their ancestors' intuitive proximity to Christianity" (Adams 1998: 333). A few carvings represent the postindependence period of upheaval. One carved panel shows troops of the Darul Islam movement of lowland Sulawesi, who sought to establish a separate Muslim state, shooting a Toraja man. In the 1960s, the Indonesian government and the Protestant Toraja church encouraged the abandonment of this type of house, with its elaborate carvings, because it represented a visible sign of Toraja "backwardness," and the Toraja were encouraged to move into houses built of cinder block (Adams 1998: 337).

However, in the 1970s and 1980s, both the government, which began to celebrate regional diversity as a cornerstone of Indonesian national identity, and the church reversed their positions. Churches began to be embellished with Toraja motifs, and new churches were built that resembled *tongkonan*s in their architecture, like the New Ireland churches that were embellished with *malanggan* sculpture. Tourism had become more and more important, and the house architecture that had formerly represented elite power now came to represent Toraja ethnic identity. *Tongkonan* images began to be seen decorating pubs and intersections in Rantepo, the Toraja capital, on T-shirts, on model houses, and on silver jewelry. More recently, Toraja carvers have begun to produce finely carved wall plaques, or carved paintings, which the carvers themselves see not as ornaments or handicrafts but as art (Adams 1998: 341). Miniatures of Toraja houses are affixed to automobile windshields to symbolize ethnic identity (Adams 2006: 191ff). This new medium of expression is frequently used to portray the symbols of political dissent. Toraja carvings and motifs have also begun to appear in Ujung Pandang, the south Sulawesi port city occupied by Bugis and Makassarese people, rival ethnic groups. As a consequence, there have been changes in ethnic conceptualizations and relationships. Whereas the Toraja were formerly seen as the victims of Bugis-Makassarese raiders, the relationship is being renegotiated. The Toraja see this use of their traditional motifs and house architecture as a minor ethnic triumph, while the Bugis and Makassarese have misgivings about this and feel vague ethnic malaise. Even the Indonesian government has co-opted the image of the *tongkonan*, featuring it on the 5,000 rupia banknote.

Decorating the Body

A rather special kind of visual art involves the decoration of the human body. People all over the world "use the skin as a surface for artistic expression and embellish themselves with decorations which carry a wide variety of meanings" (Reichel-Dolmatoff 1998: 12). The messages conveyed by body decoration range from statements about social, economic, or political status and class, the different phases of a life, to those referring to the sacred and profane. Body decorations must always be examined within a cultural context that may change over time in order to decode their meanings. For example, Maori tattooing, performed with a chisel-like implement by a revered and highly paid expert over a period of years, was a very significant aspect of Maori culture up to the nineteenth century. Today, Maoris use the same tattoo designs for ceremonial purposes, but they are applied with pigment.

Tattooing or modification of the skin is a form of body modification. As such, it is part of a larger category, and related to other practices such as knocking out the incisors (which occurs among some east African societies), cutting off a finger joint (practiced by some Plains societies), or circumcision. The simplest form of skin modification is scarification, a very widespread custom that occurs typically at initiation. A child, female or male, is "born again" through rites of initiation, which confer tribal status. Scarification, therefore, involves a transformation from nature and one's unblemished skin, to culture, with its tribal markings. The elaboration of scarification becomes tattooing, a form of art. The *moka* facial tattooing of the Maori and the total body tattooing of the Marquesans unquestionably use the body as a "canvas" for their art. At the same

Facial tattooing, or the art of *moko*, was characteristic of the Maori of New Zealand. Wi Te Manewea was a famous nineteenth-century warrior and chief of the Ngati-Raukawa.

time, the person being tattooed goes through the painful ordeal typical of initiation (Atkinson 2003: 52).

Body decoration, or body modification as it is sometimes called, is also practiced in modern American society. Tattooing and piercing are popular ways of embellishing the body. Hewitt sees a parallel between the transformation of the body and religious conversion since such self-alterations are, in effect, acts of self-transformation, ways of creating a new identity, or expressing one's individuality or affiliation with a particular alternative sub-cultural group (1997: 3, 4). Body tattooing with a hot needle, originally associated with the exoticism of the circus in America, became popular with lower-class and blue-collar workers at the beginning of the twentieth century (Hewitt, 1997: 71). In the 1950s, there was a tattoo renaissance as a new, safer technology was introduced (Hewitt 1997: 71, 73). Clients with more income and better education often design their own tattoos, making the tattoo into an aspect of self-expression and self-identification. Atkinson refers to subcultures in Canada that utilize tattooing as part of their "style" (2003: 99). Various types of body piercing have also recently become popular, especially among Generation X females. Piercing has moved from a countercultural sign of identity to become a trend and a fashion, represented in mainstream magazines. Americans have transformed a marginal practice into a trendy one (Hewitt, 1997: 84). Over time, nonconformity has become conformity. Rush describes the way in which piercing and implants of lips, breast, buttock, thighs, and penis in a number a different cultures are designed to "attract interest and correct those 'flaws' inherited from mommy and daddy" (2005: 94–98).

Among the peoples of the central highlands of New Guinea, body decoration was a most important type of art, since these people did little carving, painting, or mask making. The decorations people wear and the painting of the body at ritual performances and exchange ceremonies, such as the *kaiko* of the Maring (discussed in chapter 8), convey messages about the social and religious values of the people and also demonstrate the relationship of the people to their clan ancestral spirits. Certain ideals and emotions are evoked for audience and participants by the wearing of the decorations. The Melpa of the New Guinea Highlands had an elaborated system of body painting before they became Christians. Now they use body painting only in association with cultural performances for tourists (Strathern and Strathern 1971; Stewart and Strathern 2007). Similarly, darkness and brightness relate to the opposition between men and women.

Collecting "Artificial Curiosities"

The removal of artifacts from exotic places began with the Age of Exploration. Captain Cook brought back many specimens that people in Europe saw as representative of the way of life of the people he encountered. He also brought back a living specimen, Omai, the Tahitian, along with "artificial curiosities" and "natural curiosities" such as fossils, rocks, and shells. These found homes in the collectors' cabinets of royalty and the aristocracy. Such collections were the nuclei around which, in the nineteenth century, museums such as the British Museum were formed. In the heyday of colonialism, large quantities of such objects were taken by traders, missionaries, and government officials from small-scale societies that had become parts of colonial empires. These objects were sent to museums in all the capitals of Europe, as well as to America. They now hang on museum walls, removed from the cultural context in which they were created and used, and their creators were reduced to anonymity. Artifacts now in the museums of the capitals of colonial empires represent the success of colonialism, the conquest of pagan gods, and the transformation of the indigenous people into producers of cash crops.

At the turn of the twentieth century, European artists such as Vlaminck, Matisse, and Picasso began to appreciate and to collect what Westerners began to call "primitive" art. These creators of modern art were seeking new ways to depict the world about them, in particular, the human form. Much of the art they collected came from the French colonies in Africa. In these carvings and sculptures, the Western artists saw what was for them a completely new way of conceiving of and depicting the human figure, and they used these conceptualizations in their own sculpture and paintings. Just as Western artists borrowed artistic ideas from the peoples of colonized areas, so did the artists of colonized areas borrow from Western societies. Numerous examples from all over the world showing how the art of subject peoples reflected their views of their colonial masters were provided in Julius Lips's book *The Savage Hits Back* (1937). This art makes pointed political comments and is both humorous and satirical in nature.

The Art World Today

Traditional styles of what were small-scale societies like those of New Ireland and the Northwest Coast continue today, vibrant and alive, translated into new media. In these new forms, the art has become part of a commercial art market, exhibited in elegant galleries and sold to buyers from all over the world. The translation of a sculptural style into modern graphics has occurred not only in New Ireland, but on the Northwest Coast as well. For example, the Kwakiutl artist Tony Hunt is a printmaker as well as a sculptor. Australian artists exhibit their unique paintings in art galleries from Sydney to Santa Fe. Bill Reid, the contemporary Haida artist whose sculpture is pictured on page 297 also created jewelry in silver and gold.

When tourism develops in an area, simplified versions of traditional art and objects embodying traditional motifs in new media frequently begin to be manufactured as tourist art. In the mid-nineteenth century, the Haida of British Columbia began to carve miniature totem poles, platters, and boxes out of argillite, a soft, black, easily carved form of coal, using traditional designs for sale to tourists. This is a medium that the Haida had not used before European contact. Some argillite carvings portrayed Europeans, such as ship captains and their wives. What has been called airport art can be found from Nairobi to Port Moresby. When style and content are dictated by what tourists buy, and Navajos make crosses and Stars of David out of silver and turquoise to be sold in Albuquerque, traditional art styles no longer completely retain the characteristics of an earlier period. Silver jewelry in the American Southwest is itself an introduced art form. Sometimes, the designs of tourist art become so popular that miniature ivory totem poles, symbols of the Northwest Coast, are made in Japan and sold in Vancouver, and Navajo silver and turquoise jewelry, mass-produced in Hong Kong, is sold in Santa Fe. This tourist art is clearly distinct from creative translations of traditional forms by artists such as Reid, Hunt, and Lasisi.

In the 1970s, cultural anthropologists began to investigate modern urban society, and it turned its gaze upon new kinds of communities. The New York art world is the core of one such community, composed of commercial, communicative, and social networks that spread from there all over the world (Sullivan 1995).This art world includes the artists, dealers, art critics and theorists, collectors, curators of corporate collections, curators and directors of museums, and auction house personnel who decide what will be the important images to be illustrated in international art magazines and shown at museum shows, and who formulate what will become art in the modern world. The community is defined not only in terms of a shared identity, common interests, and a network of social relations, but also in terms of politics and economics.

Sullivan focuses on this community and the changes that have transformed it over the past thirty years (1995). At the beginning of the 1960s, a communications explosion took place that changed the way people encountered art by expanding the number and the types of settings—studios, new museums, and public collections—within which such an encounter could take place. There was also a concomitant growth in the number of art publications devoted to reviewing and critiquing contemporary art. Artists perceived themselves as increasingly alienated from their art and losing control over it. They felt that they were not benefiting sufficiently from their art and demanded legal agreements from purchasers to ensure some remuneration to them in resales, which were becoming increasingly frequent. Art was being treated as a commodity, especially by artists, to be purchased and resold, most often at auction. The 1970s found many artists, whose works were increasing in value, becoming economically successful and entering the leisure class, with affinities with middle- and upper-class collectors and dealers. This was in contrast to the peripheral position artists had earlier held in American society and in other societies as well, as we have noted above.

Curators' decisions on what to exhibit and critics' decisions about the quality of the art determined the aesthetic value of the artwork. Their decisions crucially determined which artists were favored and were selling their art and which were not. Art dealers and gallery owners were in a parallel position, deciding whose work to include in a show and whose work to advise collectors to purchase. At the apex of this structure were the world-famous artists, collectors and dealers, and museum directors. In the 1970s this world began to change as contemporary art moved into the auction galleries and price was determined publicly rather than by means of the backroom negotiations that dealers and clients had formerly engaged in. Collectors began to shop at auctions, paying astronomical prices for works by world-famous artists. New money was entering the scene, and financiers of many nationalities, interested in art as an investment, were bidding up prices. In the meantime, the prices of art from earlier times were also rising. Van Gogh's painting Irises sold for $53 million in 1987, and his portrait of Dr. Gachet sold in 1990 for $82.5 million, the highest price ever paid for a painting up until that time. Even museums moved into the auction market to reconstitute their collections, deaccessioning works "not of museum quality" in favor of what their directors thought represented important trends, to broaden their collections. Museum directors learned "the art of the deal" in sales as well as exchanges. This process also occurred in the area of ethnographic art. Sotheby's auctioned off a Maori house post, whose sale price was over a million dollars, and Navajo blankets, which sold for hundreds of thousands of dollars.

By focusing on the art "community," which represents the type of unit anthropologists have always studied, one can see the ways in which the roles and positions of people in the art world have changed. Art, like the religious artifacts in Cairo discussed in chapters 8 and 10 on economics and religion, has become a commodity, purchased by the wealthy as an investment and to show their good taste. All forms of art have now become commodities, which is characteristic of capitalism and free markets. Both the art market and the meanings of the art have been transformed in the process.

The Native American Graves Protection and Repatriation Act (NAGPRA), passed in 1990, acts to transform Native American art objects that have become commodities back into objects that have religious and cultural significance. All museums are required to survey their collections and publish an inventory of human remains, funerary and sacred objects, and "cultural patrimony," identifying geographic origin, cultural origin, and the facts regarding the accession of the objects (Dubin 2001: 23, Fine-Dare 2002: 119). After the inventories were published, tribes could then make claims to objects. The cultural artifacts repatriated were seen by the tribes as essential to the continuance of their traditions. Even prior to the passage of the act, the Zuni had started to try to repatriate the wooden anthropomorphic carvings of their war gods, stimulated by the great increase in Native American political activity, "the Red Power movement" that had begun in the late 60s. These war gods were a significant aspect of Zuni religion, and by 1993 "sixty-five War Gods had been located and repatriated to the Zuni" (Fine-Dare 2002: 06). The Pecos Pueblo started the repatriation process of artifacts from the Harvard Peabody Museum in 1991, but the more than 130 crates of material were not returned until 1999 (Fine-Dare 2002: 2).The NAGPRA act also "bans trade" in funerary and sacred objects.

Even before the passage of NAGPRA, as early as the 1930s and 1940s tribes such as the Osage and North Carolina Cherokee had set up their own museums, though it was not until the 1960s and 1970s that the tribal museum movement really "took off" (Watt 2007: 70). These museums, owned and operated by tribes, were seen as a means not only of perpetuating tribal history and culture, but also as a "a benchmark or milestone of a tribe's collective self-worth . . . 'a declaration that we are important' and culturally worth maintaining" (Watt 2007: 73). The two audiences for these museums are first, and most importantly, the tribal community and then the general public. The messages conveyed by exhibits need to present a balance between what is directed to these separately constituted "publics." Further, Issac describes how for the A:shiwi A:wan Museum set up by the Zuni, the Zuni approach to knowledge and its transfer, and the conflict between the elder and younger generations regarding knowledge production and transfer, are both relevant to how the museum decides to exhibit material (2007). Today there are more than 120 tribal museums in the United States. Tribal museums have also been established by First Nations in Canada such as U'mista, which has the potlatch material confiscated by the Canadian government in the 1920s and subsequently returned many years later (McLoughlin 1999).

THE CULTURAL SETTING OF MUSIC AND DANCE

Like painting and sculpture, music and dance are considered arts because they evoke emotion and can be evaluated in terms of aesthetic qualities. In contrast to painting and sculpture, music and dance are like spoken language in three important aspects. All three unfold through time. Every sentence, every musical composition, every dance has a beginning, a middle, and an end. This is not true of a painting or a carving, which has no beginning or ending and for which the dimension of time is irrelevant. Once made, it continues to exist. Musical compositions and dances are ephemeral. They find expression in performances, but once the performance is over, they no longer exist. The musical instrument upon which the composition was performed is still there, and an idea of how the piece should be performed persists; however, the performance of the piece dies away unless it has been recorded on tape or film, a modern phenomenon. Like the tale or legend told by a bard, the musical piece exists as a concept in people's minds, and each performance is a slightly different manifestation of that idea. In this conceptualization of a piece of music, it is like the mental template a potter uses to make and decorate a certain kind of pot. Only in Western societies were musical compositions written down, using some form of musical notation. Until recently, dances were performed and only memory guided the next performance. Now there are systems of dance notation that are analogous to written language. Ethnomusicologists and anthropologists, when they studied music and dance in small-scale societies, were studying a tradition, transmitted orally and by performance. In these societies, music and dance, like oral literature and folktales, were taught and passed on without benefit of written notational systems.

The anthropological emphasis has always been on the relationship between music and dance and other aspects of culture. In our discussion of the visual arts in small-scale societies, we saw that art was not produced simply to be admired but was integrated with other aspects of culture. The same is true of music and dance. In fact, when anthropologists first began to study dance, they were more interested in the cultural context of the dance than in the dance itself. There is a great range of ritual and ceremonial settings in which music and dance play important roles. Birth, initiation, weddings, and funerals are typically occasions for music and dance. The Kwakiutl and American weddings described in chapter 2 both included music and dancing. These two examples illustrate the contrasting ways in which music and dance function in the two societies. The dances and songs performed at the Kwakiutl wedding were owned by the *numayms* of the chiefs who performed them, as were the crests on the masks worn by the performers, in contrast to the dance music played at the American wedding by a hired band. In Kwakiutl culture, in addition to the message of ownership, the songs and dances of the groom's side convey the power, based on supernatural contacts, that is necessary to move the bride. We must also consider who has the right to perform a piece of music or dance and who owns it. There is a great range of variation regarding the degree of specialization involved in the performance of music and dance, even within societies. Sometimes, as is the case among the Kwakiutl, songs and dances are privately owned and may be performed only by their owners. There are dances that may be performed only at a particular stage in life, such as dances for a male initiation.

The Kwakiutl wedding involves music, dance, and what in the Western world would be called theater, all of which come together in a performance. This is now referred to as the anthropology of performing arts (Royce 2004: 1). The discussion of the performing arts would involve not only an examination of the forms and the rules that characterize the particular "genres," but also how those are acquired, the degree of mastery necessary, the nature of the interpretation in the particular performance, virtuosity, that is, the level of mastery of the performer, and how and whether audiences understand and appreciate what they are seeing. Earlier, Boas and others had merely recorded music or photographed dance without seeking to understand how these forms related to the other aspects of the culture in which they were performed, nor did they compare any aspects of the performance and its parts cross-culturally. Earlier we discussed body decorations and their meanings as signifiers of knowledge about cultural values and institutions, and they are clearly part of any performance. Royce analyzes the place that a particular Tewa ritual and dance plays in their ritual cycle, as well as who dances, who makes the choices about the dates of the dance, the songs that must be composed, the musicians and singers who will perform, the choreography and "grammar" of the Tewa dances, as well as many other aspects (2004: chapter 6). She even deals with the distinctions between dances now being performed for the non-Indian world, and the annual cycle of ritual performances for the pueblo alone.

Music

While the function of music and dance is similar to that of the visual arts, each is characterized by a different kind of structure. The elements of music are sounds, and their characteristics are pitch and duration. Sounds produced consecutively constitute melody, while sounds produced simultaneously form harmony. Melody, harmony, and rhythm, which is a steady succession of beats marked by regular accents, represent the basic concepts for analyzing the structure of music, which varies from one culture to another. For example, most of the music of our society is based upon a system of eight tones, an octave—usually taught as do, re, mi, fa, sol, la, ti, do. However, from time to time, other structures have also been used, such as Schoenberg's use of a twelve-tone scale. Many other societies in the world base their music on a scale in which there are only five tones. This is called a pentatonic scale and, in fact, it is more common in the world than our octave, or eight-tone scale. Rhythm is also subject to cultural variation. In our own society, each musical composition is usually characterized by a single, regular rhythmic impulse. A waltz has one kind of rhythm, and a march another kind of rhythm. Recent music in Western culture may shift rhythms throughout the piece. This is in contrast with other societies, such as those in Zaire in Africa, where a single musical composition can have two different rhythms carried on simultaneously. These and other marked variations make the music of other cultures sometimes sound strange to our ears. In addition, the instruments created to produce musical sounds are enormously varied.

Music is a form of communication. The music at an American wedding conveys a message. When the organ plays as the bride, dressed in white, marches down the aisle, the audience silently repeats the words, "Here comes the bride, all dressed in white." The message conveyed is the ideal of the purity and virginity of the bride. This message is carried by the whiteness of the bride's gown, by the words of the song, and even by the melody of the music. Music also plays a role in funerals. In this instance, music can convey the emotions of grief and sadness better perhaps than any other medium. Because music is a powerful vehicle for expressing emotions as well as ideas, it can be a central mechanism for symbolizing culture and cultural differences.

The style of playing panpipes (a group of pipes bound together, each one emitting a different note) among the Aymara, the indigenous people of highland Peru, was distinctive of their culture. From the 1920s on, it has had an interesting diffusion, which reveals the nature of asymmetrical power relations in Peru (Turino, 1991). This musical style among the Aymara, who were the clients of mestizo patrons living in the town of Conima, was characterized by ad hoc musical ensembles organized in an egalitarian fashion playing music in several different traditions at various kinds of fiestas. This was in keeping with the emphasis on equality and on group solidarity in Aymara communities. Any man could play in an Aymara panpipe ensemble. The mestizo rural elites held the Aymara in disdain until the 1920s, when a movement, *indigenismo*, made people begin to take an interest in the local indigenous culture. Aspects of Aymara culture, such as the panpipe tradition, began to be selected as symbols to stand for Peruvian national identity. In this process, however, the panpipe tradition of the Aymara was transformed into one with fixed membership, regular rehearsals, the maintenance of performance quality, and change in the nature of the harmony. This transformation took place in the town of Conima, and the changed musical form was later brought to Lima and other cities when the newly organized group traveled there to perform. During the 1970s, by which time Lima was swollen with rural migrants from the highlands, the panpipe tradition from Conima began to be performed by migrants who had heretofore been ashamed to perform their music in the city because of social prejudice against Aymara Indian culture. Radicalized middle-class students in the city also began to perform the panpipe music and subsequently brought it back to the rural towns from which these students had come. Young Aymara people in the villages, increasingly influenced by national culture, now ignore the majority of indigenous musical instruments and community traditions in favor of the urban panpipe movement. This example illustrates the way in which an indigenous musical tradition is altered in form when it moves to an urban environment and it comes to symbolize Peruvian national culture. It is then brought back to the countryside where it displaces earlier musical forms.

In many societies, men and women have two rather differentiated spheres of expressive activity. Concurrently with the increased interest in gender roles, researchers have begun to more systematically explore women's musical practices (Koskoff 1987). Since a woman's identity is believed to be embedded in her sexuality, women's role in music frequently expresses this. Musical performance is seen as enhancing sexuality, and female court musicians in the past in India, Indonesia, and Tunisia were associated with sexuality and profane pleasures. In many societies, the genre (or type) of music performed, the style of the performance, and the location of the performance are different for males and for females.

Ethnomusicologists and anthropologists investigate music in complex societies, from Iran, Japan, and Bali to the urban environment of Lima and Vienna. After a diaspora of millennia in many different countries, the Bukharan Jews ended up in Vienna beginning in the 1960s where they became what they called the Sephardic community. The older generation still speaks "Bukhori," a dialect of Tajik, while the younger generation speaks Hebrew, though both groups have learned German (Lechleitner 2007: 93ff). There are three synagogues, schools, and two organizations. Several musical forms are represented at celebrations such as Passover, Rosh Hashana, and musical school events. These include Bukharian traditional music as well as songs about Bukhara in Tajik, using a drum accompaniment that is appreciated by the older generation, modern versions of these traditional songs, popular well-known Jewish songs, and comedy sketches involving music. The Bukharians like to maintain the music and song of their forefathers to the extent that they can despite the various influences that have impacted them through the centuries. They also appreciate the more modern versions of these traditions (Lechleitner 2007: 97–98). They see these musical activities as a way of keeping the Bukharian community together within the culturally diverse environment of Vienna.

Musicians

As societies become more complex, musicians as well as dancers often become full-time specialists. For example, Kanuri musicians, referred to as praise singers, are a full-time, highly trained, and specialized group who occupy a particular position in the social structure (see photo). The performers include a vocalist, drummers, and a player of an oboe-like reed instrument. The musicians are male, but the vocalist may be female. They frequently are attached to a patron, an aristocrat, who supports them in exchange for singing his praises on ceremonial occasions. They can also travel and perform as a group, living on the money they receive from their audiences. They are generally considered to be of low status by the Kanuri populace, since the way they earn their living is considered to be begging. Nevertheless, virtuoso performers are greatly admired by everyone. Though the performers are aware of what other people think of them, they consider themselves artists. They value their own talents and thrive on the admiration of the audience. Artists' talents are admired, yet the creativity that makes them different from other people also makes them suspect. The Kanuri musician wears an earring in one ear, unlike ordinary Kanuri males.

The praise singers of Mali, called *jeli* but also referred to by the term *griots*, were, like Kanuri, praise singers, a separate, endogamous group in the social structure. However, their position has undergone a transformation (Schulz 1998). In the past, praise singers were attached to freeborn

An ensemble of Kanuri praise singers and musicians in Geidam, Nigeria.

upper-class families in a patron-client relationship. In exchange for citing the illustrious genealogies and extolling the virtues of their patrons, praise singers were provided with food and housing for life. With increasing modernization and urbanization, praise singers began to appear who were not *jeli*, and who would sing anyone's praises for money. When radio and television came to Mali, praise singers became media stars. But they were considered "inauthentic" because they performed for financial payments. They would sing the praises of the ancestors of people they didn't even know, newly rich people who gloried in these praises. Praise singing, like other forms of art, had become a commodity, to be bought and sold. Nevertheless, praise singers on TV were thought to be carrying on an important tradition of the culture. These new "media stars" on TV and in urban theaters would sing about the evil and corrupting effects of money, though people would rush to the stage to shower them with money.

Sometimes performers are of a different ethnic group from the majority of the society. The Gypsies, speaking Romani, their own language, have spread from India throughout Europe, a persecuted minority without a homeland. In Afghanistan and Pakistan, Gypsies are traveling performers and musicians, and are considered a low-status group, completely outside the existing social structure. Gypsy music has had an enormous impact on Western culture generally, as well as on each country into which they moved. The Gypsies of Romania and Hungary are professional musicians who play a particular style of violin music, which is closely associated with these countries. In Spain, the distinctive Flamenco style of music and dance is Gypsy music and dance. Gypsy musicians and performers are described by Dostoyevsky in his novels because they were an important part of Russian culture. The Belgian Gypsy guitarist Django Reinhard was the greatest jazz guitarist of all time. Chico Iliev, a Bulgarian Gypsy musician, in describing his relationship to music says, "I find it [Gypsy music] difficult to describe but there is no Gypsy existence without music. We have such a heavy life and if we didn't have the music we would kill ourselves. The music is our medicine. Our Opium" (quoted in Cartwright 2005: 12).

Dance

Dance has been defined as those cultural practices that "formalize human movement into structured systems in much the same way that poetry formalizes language" (Kaeppler 1985: 92). There may or may not be an indigenous conceptualization that translates into the category of dance. Kaeppler has proposed that the anthropological consideration of dance focus upon the movement dimensions of particular cultural activities and the messages such movements are conveying, to develop a cultural conceptualization of dance for a particular society (1985). A formal description of the structure of dance would include the steps, spatial patterns, relationships to music, and postural positioning. Beyond the description, the focus of anthropological analysis of dance is on its cultural setting and its meaning. Dances, like all other forms of art, encode particular cultural messages. They may be visual manifestations of social relations, or they may be part of a visual aesthetic system. Westerners frequently isolated the formal movement aspects of rituals and ceremonials as dance, neglecting the role such movements played in the total social phenomena within which they were performed. In doing this, they were utilizing a Western categorization, since in our society, dance, for the most part, has become entertainment, disassociated from ritual and ceremonial.

The culture of the Swahili, a Muslim people living in East Africa, represents a syncretism of Islamic cultural codes and indigenous Swahili culture. The Swahili have a category, *ngoma*, that means "drum," "dance," or "music," illustrating the inextricable connection between music and dance. *Waungwana*, or high status, was marked by the possession of tall white-washed stone houses with enclosed courtyards, within which women were secluded, in keeping with the custom of *purdah*. The courtyards were the settings for rituals and ceremonials, and poetry and dance competitions (Franken 1992). Two *ngoma* performed were exclusive to the Swahili high-status class. The *ngoma la hazua* was a men's line dance performed in spotless white prayer robes and richly embroidered prayer caps at weddings and circumcisions, with music and a singer who recounted the heroic deeds and distinguished ancestors of the family. Today this dance is held outdoors at weddings during the week celebrating the birth of the Prophet. The *lelemama* was performed by married women as a rite of passage. It was also a line dance in which the dancers wore special costumes and finger cymbals.

The *ngoma* of the lower-class people, who are the recent arrivals to town, economically poor, lacking important ancestors, and not very religiously observant, is different from that of the upper class. The men's dance, the *uta*, or the "coconut-cutters' dance," is held outdoors, during the birthday week of the Prophet on a sandlot between houses (Franken 1992: 206). The dancers, wearing men's work clothing and leg rattles, dance in a circle, leaning on canes and stamping their feet in unison to the rhythm of *uta*. The second lower-class dance, the *mwaribe*, is performed outdoors during the week of the Prophet's birthday by young men who wear Western street clothes, to a drum accompaniment. It is clear that the movements in these dances communicate contrasts about status. But they also demonstrate the inextricable connection between music and dance.

Dance can also enable individuals to assume "exotic new identities" through social dancing or through professional immersion in dance careers (Shay 2008: 1). The United States and Canada seem to be the only locations where such a phenomenon took place during the 1960s and 1970s when multiculturalism and the search for ethnic roots and identities became important. Shay notes, "During this post 1950s period, literally millions of mainstream Americans . . . [became interested in] . . . various exotic dance genres: . . . Balkan dances of various ethnicities, Latin American dance traditions such as the samba, tango, . . . a wide variety of Asian genres . . . like Chinese opera, Balinese, Cambodian, Javanese classical traditions, and Middle Eastern dance genres of various types but particularly belly dancing which alone attracted over a million women by the 1980s" (Shay 2008: 12). Obviously, there is variation in degree of difficulty in learning the dance forms and the length of time and training required to achieve a competent performance. During this time, individuals spent a great deal of money on classes, workshops, costumes, films and videos of the dances, and even visits to the country of origin of the dance form they were particularly interested in. What happens to these dance forms as they are transmitted from one culture to another? Several studies talk about such transformations. For example, "the tango was commodified and colonized in an uneven movement from the developing world to the First

World" (Savigliano in Shay 2008: 41) and the "oriental dance, in which the myriad orientalist images that abound in the United States are (mis)appropriated and perpetuated in performances, is even more widespread" (Shay 2008: 31). The appropriation of dance forms can go in the other direction. As Shay notes, "Belly dancers in Egypt between the 1930s and the 1970s frequently appropriated movements, costumes and other elements for the dances from Hollywood films" (2008: 31).

SUMMARY

- Art is a mode of communication, communicating ideas as well as emotions and involving an aesthetic impulse—what constitutes beauty.
- There seems to be a universal aesthetic impulse, though cultures may express aesthetics in many different ways using different art forms.
- One culture may emphasize visual arts such as carving while another places greater emphasis on music and dance.
- Art can be analyzed structurally in terms of what is known as style. Style characterizes the art of all societies and can also be used to characterize the art of an individual or a particular historical period.
- The various arts operate within a set of traditional constraints. Yet every carver, painter, musician, and dancer adds his or her individual conceptualization, his or her own interpretation to the final product. It is in this aspect of art that creativity is to be found, and this creativity forms the basis for the audience's judgment of the aesthetic worth of the art produced.
- Masks, which are to be found in a variety of societies, illustrate the meanings that can be attached to what is a single form of art, and they also make statements about a culture's view of the self.
- Various forms of art may be used to express ethnic identity, as illustrated by Toraja carving.
- In the eighteenth century, the collecting of the artifacts of the small-scale societies that anthropologists were to later study was referred to as the collection of "artificial curiosities."
- Global tourism has resulted in the production of tourist art, the manufacture of objects by local artists to meet the demands of consumers, that is, tourists, who want a remembrance of the places they visited.
- The art world has become a community of buyers and sellers as a consequence of the commodification of art and the development of a worldwide auction market.

SUGGESTED READINGS

Krutak, Lars. *The Tattooing Arts of Tribal Women.* London: Bennett & Bloom, 2007. A discussion of tattooing of women in a number of societies, detailingthe history of the tattooing and how it relates to culture and social life.

Morphy, Howard and Morgan Perkins. *The Anthropology of Art: A Reader*. Malden, MA: Blackwell Publishing, 2006. A collection of articles, past and present, on a variety of topics relating to the anthropology of art.

Stone, Ruth M. *Theory in Ethnomusicology*. Upper Saddle River, NJ: Pearson Prentice Hall, 2008. A survey of a variety of ethnomusicology topics.

SUGGESTED WEBSITES

http://42explore.com/mask.htm. A general survey of masks and their uses in different parts of the world.

www.native-languages.org/northwest.htm. A compilation of general information about Northwest Coast art.

www.art-pacific.com/artifacts/nuguinea/malagan.htm A guide to the different forms of art to be found on New Ireland, Papua New Guinea.

Chapter 13
Living/Working in the Globalized World
Colonialism, Globalization, and Development

IN THE FIRST PART OF THE PAST century, anthropologists looked at cultures as if they were static, unchanging entities. Malinowski, who carried out several years of fieldwork among the Trobriand Islanders between the years 1912 and 1917, recorded his observations without paying attention to the changes taking place before his very eyes. In reality, cultures are constantly undergoing change, but in today's world change occurs at a very rapid rate.

The forces for change in the world today are numerous and powerful. Colonialism, which was one of the strongest forces for change, is all but gone, and in its place is a series of new nation-states based on the geography of colonial empires rather than on sameness of culture. Postcolonial nation-states are building national cultures in their attempt to supplant and suppress the various indigenous cultures within their borders, in the same way that, in the past, the nation-states of Europe attempted to forge national cultures with varying degrees of success. Despite political independence, economic interdependency of one-time colonies on former colonial powers, in many places, constitutes **neocolonialism**. Over several centuries, changes have greatly altered earlier economic institutions. These changes include the introduction of cash crops, production and consumption of modern manufactured goods, foreign exploitation of local resources, and the need for labor. The enormous expansion of cities in these new nations presented economic and cultural inducements that attracted many migrants from rural areas. When they returned to their villages, they brought urban culture with them, introducing changes into village culture. Even those remaining in remote villages are now familiar with urban ideas and technologies.

In many industrializing nations the strategies and institutions of economic development are part of everyday life. Developing states adopt agricultural, industrial, educational, health, tourism, and resource exploitation strategies to raise incomes and enhance the quality of lives of their citizens. These projects, financed historically by Western-dominated multilateral (multi-state) lenders and donors, are now increasingly being supported through domestic financial markets.

306

New forms of credit and lending practices, such as the **microfinance** approach developed by Bangladesh's Grameen Bank, provide small business loans to poor individuals and groups of people who otherwise would not have access to credit. **Nongovernmental organizations (NGOs)**, structurally independent of state-based institutions of development, are familiar worldwide as local links to national and international funds and information networks. Cell phones, computers, and globally circulated media bring images, ideas, and expertise from urban centers to the countryside. Anthropologists participate in these activities in various ways. Some document the experiences of, and resistance to, economic transformation, mass communication, and labor migration; others apply their anthropological knowledge to formation and evaluation of development strategies and policies.

GLOBALIZATION AND ANTHROPOLOGY

Colonialism and its aftermaths can be examined at several different levels. **Postcolonial studies** focus on the effects of colonialism on former European colonies; often interdisciplinary, these studies combine the use of historical and literary texts with ethnography. The unit that anthropologists usually study in the field is the micro analytic level. However, they do not study it alone, but in relation to like units and to the more inclusive political levels. The next more inclusive level of analysis is that of the nation-state, where the focus of the anthropologist has been on the construction of a national culture and the creation of national identity. Since nation-states operate as independent, politically autonomous units, political decisions and economic planning take place at this level. Consequently, the unit of analysis of economic development is also the nation-state. At a still higher, more inclusive level of analysis is the **world system**. This concept, developed by Immanuel Wallerstein (1974, 2004), refers to the historic emergence of the economic interrelationship of most of the world in a single economic system, in which the concept of the division of labor, usually seen as operative in a single society, is projected onto the global capitalist economy.

Wallerstein sees the system developing after the breakdown of feudalism and the rise of capitalism and entrepreneurship and the succeeding Industrial Revolution. During and after the Age of Exploration, Europeans vastly expanded their search for sources of raw materials and mineral resources, as well as for markets for their manufactured goods. These European countries formed the core of a world system, and the colonies and protectorates that they dominated formed the periphery. The world system operates according to capitalist market principles, with profits constantly reverting to the investors of capital, who are located, for the most part, in the core. Anthropologists have been particularly concerned with the effects of the penetration of the world system on indigenous peoples all over the world and their active responses to this penetration. Eric Wolf (1982), in *Europe and the People without History*, explored this topic, focusing, for example, on how the Kwakiutl and other native people of North America responded to the fur trade network set up by the Hudson's Bay Company in the eighteenth century. World systems theory focused primarily on the existence of structures, such as core and periphery, with anthropological research directed toward the examination of the dynamics of the relationship between the smaller, local parts of the system in the periphery and the larger parts of the core.

Within recent years, the term *globalization* has come to signify the multiple rapid transformations in the lives of people in most parts of the world due to "speeding up of the flows of capital, people, goods, images, and ideas across the world, thus pointing to a general increase in the pace of global interactions and processes" (Inda and Rosaldo 2008: 11). There are multiple consequences to this intensification of interaction and connections, including cross-border interaction and the impact of developments in one part of the world rapidly being felt in distant areas. "All told, globalization can be seen as referring to those spatial-temporal processes, operating on a global scale, that rapidly cut across national boundaries, drawing more and more of the world into webs of interconnection, integrating and stretching cultures and communities across space, and time, and compressing our spatial and temporal horizons" (Inda and Rosaldo 2008: 11–12).

Globalization has been brought about in part by the development of a worldwide network of finance and capital. This has occurred on a greater scale than ever before, and at an increasingly rapid rate as a result of enormous advances in telecommunications and computer technology. As transnational or multinational corporations expand and "globalize," they move beyond the scope of regulation by nation-states, and the latter lose the power to regulate and control them. Within various parts of the industrializing world, globalization has resulted in great economic successes, for example, in South Korea, Malaysia, and India, while other parts of the world, such as some Central American and African countries, have fallen behind, no longer being seen as profitable targets of global investment.

New technologies have not only facilitated globalization, they have also streamlined resistance against it. Internet and e-mail networks allow those who have access to these technologies to receive and send information reflecting multiple perspectives. This mobilization of concerned individuals and groups facilitated by electronic technologies is seen at the World Trade Organization meetings in various cities around the world. The WTO attempts to integrate states into a global economy. At WTO meetings local citizens regularly demonstrate their resistance to this goal from various perspectives. Some demonstrators are concerned about ecological devastation and global environmental threats. Labor unionists are dissatisfied with changes in tariffs and labor rights, which threaten workers' jobs and deregulate wages and working conditions. At the Seattle WTO meeting in 1999 some demonstrators expressed a general unhappiness that Americans may no longer have complete control of their economy. The latter speaks to the issue that nation-states in a globalized economy no longer have the ability to make fundamental decisions regarding exchange rates, tariffs, taxation, and wages.

Though globalization seems to be similar to colonialism and the neocolonialism of the latter part of the twentieth century, in reality it represents a quantum leap in the reach, penetration, and power of global capitalism (Appadurai 1996; Loker 1999: 13–14). Among the anthropologist's roles in the study of globalization are to examine the various colonial contexts where one might say that globalization had its beginnings, and to focus on the lived experience of people in different communities: to "put human faces on what would otherwise would be anonymous, impersonal statistics" (Orlove 1999: 196).

Factory production, labor, and patterns of consumption are among the variables scholars analyze to document historic changes and local variations associated with globalization. Political economy theorists and historians make the distinction between periods in American economic history designated as Fordism and Post-Fordism, referencing the characteristics of Henry Ford's methods of automobile production in the early and mid-twentieth century. **Fordism** refers to the assembly-line production system, characterized by mass production of identical or similar products by generally unskilled laborers along a moving assembly line. These industrial innovations greatly reduced the production costs and increased profitability of Ford's automobiles. This mass production system also lowered the cost of automobiles to consumers, including a new generation of factory workers who could afford to buy the products they were producing. Despite initial resistance by manufacturers, labor unions made great inroads into organizing factory workers and providing wage and other benefits in exchange for increased levels of production. Fordist production contributed to America's post-World War II growth and was the primary economic approach to industrialization through the 1970s. Post-Fordism emerged with the shift in the American and other Western economies from manufacturing to service industries, the simultaneous growth of new information technologies. Company headquarters are no longer associated with centralized manufacturing facilities, and are instead linked by communication technologies to decentralized globally situated sites of labor, service support (such as the "call centers" in India), and product assembly. Reductions in trade barriers and tariffs, and the creation of regional and global trading networks facilitate trade, capital transfers, and production.

Many of the products now consumed in Western markets are produced in **Free Trade Zones (FTZ)** of developing countries, which offer financial incentives and labor regulation concessions to multinational corporations to attract foreign export production facilities. Also known as Export Processing Zones (EPZ), Free Trade Zones are usually located in underdeveloped areas of the host country, requiring migration of labor to staff the factories producing garments, electronics, sneakers, and other consumer goods for export. Governments of developing countries create these zones to provide their citizens with employment in the hope of stimulating economic growth and poverty alleviation. However, the concessions made to foreign companies include the suspension of wage, labor, and environmental protection regulations they are subject to in their home countries. As a result, laborers are rarely protected with basic rights to minimum wage, secure employment, and healthy working conditions. They can rarely afford to buy the products they labor to produce.

Ethnographic studies of export production facilities around the world (e.g., Ong 1987, Rothstein 2007, Hewamanne 2008) document the gender and labor inequalities that characterize globalized Post-Fordist capitalism. Women, often young and unmarried, are targeted as preferred factory workers and "dominate the lowest levels both of pay and authority, whereas men occupy most positions of supervisory and managerial rank" (Mills 2003: 43). The feminization of the globalized labor pool has parallels in the nineteenth-century Industrial Revolution in Europe, but the contemporary gendered and flexible labor recruitment that characterize late capitalism "encompasses every corner of the globe" (Mills 2003: 42). Most of the ethnographic studies of global labor document women's labor conditions and the social consequences they face by join-

Vietnamese workers assembling shoes in a Nike factory on the outskirts of Ho Chi Minh City. Nike, an American company, is a major employer of women in Vietnam.

ing the local flexible workforce. By engaging in nontraditional employment and travel away from their homes, they may subsequently be deemed "unmarriageable" or "dishonorable" and may be subjected to multiple forms of violence. Men are also targeted for labor recruitment based on presumed gendered and ethnic norms. Male labor migrants, particularly those crossing borders in pursuit of employment, endure harsh working conditions and discrimination as ethnic and religious minorities (Mills 2003: 52). These dangerous and unprotected work environments are increasingly providing the impetus for laborers to unionize, and to form alliances with other domestic and international workers to protect their rights and safety (Mills 2003: 51).

THE HISTORIC BACKGROUND TO GLOBALIZATION: THE MANY FACES OF COLONIAL RULE

It is important to understand colonial history as the precursor to the flow of labor, capital, and consumer goods today in the globalizing world. Colonialism over the course of history has taken many forms, with different effects on the peoples colonized. There were various reasons for the establishment of colonies. Sometimes it was the search for raw materials and markets. At other times, colonies were established because of the need to protect the boundaries of an empire from marauding peoples or other empires. Sometimes, only colonial administrators and people involved in the extraction of resources lived in the colony. In other instances, many people came to the colony as settlers. At the beginning of the colonization of North America, the only contacts that Native American societies had were with explorers and governmental representatives of the British and French colonial empires. Over time, a large and more powerful immigrant population engulfed these societies; new social and political systems emerged marked by grossly unequal power and coercion.

The initial motivation for the establishment of colonies was economic gain, which frequently took the form of exploiting raw materials as well as providing markets for the goods of the mother country. The Industrial Revolution in Western Europe led to shortages of resources locally and the need to find them abroad. Often, a single large trading company, such as the British East India Company, the Hudson's Bay Company, or the Dutch East India Company, held a monopoly on trade; these trading companies eventually attained political control as well.

There were important differences in the ways colonial powers, established after the Industrial Revolution, governed. The British developed the policy of **indirect rule**, which was then applied throughout the British Empire. A relatively small number of English administrators controlled large colonial territories by integrating local political leaders and bureaucrats into the British-controlled administrative system. In contrast, the French ruled directly, establishing military garrisons and large administrative staffs throughout their empire. The French had a policy of accepting an educated individual from their colonies, who was then referred to as an *évolue*, as a citizen of France. In contrast the British integrated educated Indian, Pakistani, and African locals into the colonial administration but maintained social and political divisions. Though the indigenous population was usually much larger than the foreign population, power and wealth were all in the hands of the representatives of the colonial power. The nature of these contacts was in every respect an unequal one.

Anthropologists writing about colonialism document the complexity of the dimensions of colonial life and the reach of colonial powers into the social and political lives of the colonized (Pels 1997, Stoler 2006). These interventions continue to resonate in postcolonial social, political, and religious constructions of identity (see chapter 14). The colonizers felt that it was constantly necessary to define the social boundaries between themselves and the colonized, whose "otherness" was perpetually being redefined. European colonizers had a variety of intentions toward the indigenous populations. Methodist missionaries hoped to turn the tribes of southern Africa into yeoman farmers modeled on the yeomanry of eighteenth-century England (Comaroff and Comaroff 1986). Other colonizers attempted to transform the existing social organization to provide laborers who would work in the mines. The boundary between the European colonizers and the local population was sometimes eroded by sexual relations between European men and local women, which produced an intermediate population with an ambiguous identity in the European racial system of classification (Stoler 2002).

The nature of initial contact varied from colony to colony. Colonial control was sometimes set up in the form of patrol posts in the native territory. The Australian government used this method to achieve control over the tribal peoples of highland New Guinea, who were frequently hostile to the colonizers. First contact was often peaceful. Military resistance usually occurred later, as in the case of the Maori, when people realized that they were losing their independence, autonomy, cultural distinctiveness, and ability to determine their own destiny. The fighting between British and Maori ended with the Treaty of Waitangi in 1840. The Maori were treated as a sovereign state with which treaties were made. Under the terms of the treaty, the British Crown received all rights and powers of sovereignty over Maori territory, though the Maori chiefs thought they were giving up only partial rights. In 1996, an official report found that an entire province in New Zealand had been illegally taken from the Taranaki Maori tribes by the Treaty of Waitangi. The report recommended that the Maori be given back the land surrounding Mount Taranaki, or equivalent financial compensation.

The complexities of the colonial period are relevant to anthropological research of postcolonial settings in the present day. Each example of Western colonial expansion may appear to be different from any other case. Nevertheless, the establishment of the colony and the course of events that followed can be described in terms of a number of variables. These include land policy, resource exploitation, type of labor recruitment, and intensity and type of missionary activity.

Different colonial empires had somewhat different policies with respect to the rights of native peoples over their land. Furthermore, these native peoples themselves had a variety of different conceptualizations about land rights. In the Australian case, the colonial government understood the native pattern of land utilization and the claims of various Australian bands to ancestral homelands, but it chose to ignore them and claim the entire continent as unoccupied wasteland, recognizing neither the land rights nor the sovereignty of the natives.

In America, both the British colonial government and the American government, in the Ordinance of 1787, recognized Native Americans' rights to land and these relationships were maintained with Native American tribes through the nineteenth century. As the immigrant population of the United States grew and with it the demand for land, the Indian land base began to be reduced by successive treaties that the Indians were forced to conclude with the United States government. The fight over land continues today, but the positions are reversed. Tribes like the Passamaquoddy of Maine have gone to court to lay claim to their traditional land, on the basis of their contention that the United States government broke treaties made with the tribes in centuries past.

Exploitation of resources other than land was critical in defining the nature of the colonial experience and is profitably examined at the level of the world system. The Western demand for rubber illustrates the way the economic fates of people on three different continents were linked. The natural stands of rubber trees in the Amazon and Congo river basins were exploited during the wild rubber boom of 1895 to 1910. In both places, tribal peoples, who had been subsistence agriculturalists, provided the source of labor for the tapping of latex from the rubber trees in the tropical forest. British entrepreneurs took wild rubber plant seedlings from the Congo and Amazon basins and transported them to the British colony of Malaya, where they established rubber plantations to provide a steady source of this raw material. Rubber from these plantations captured the world market, bringing to an end the boom in wild rubber from the Congo and Amazon basins. Subsequently, the Firestone Rubber Company of America developed rubber plantations in Liberia, and this rubber also gained a share of the world market. Since rubber was the dominant cash crop, Firestone controlled the entire economy of Liberia at that time. The shift to synthetic rubber, developed during World War II, signaled the great reduction in importance of plantation-grown rubber.

Exploitation of resources in colonial areas and their successor nation-states required labor. This need for labor was met in a variety of ways, which had profound effects on the indigenous peoples, dislocating their economies and their traditional forms of family and social organization in varying degrees. In the earliest period of the colonization of the New World, the demand by the colonizers for a large-scale labor force to exploit resources was satisfied by the enslavement of native tribal peoples such as the Tupi-speaking coastal peoples of Brazil. The Portuguese enslaved them and their population was decimated as a result of disease and the conditions of slavery. From the sixteenth century to the beginning of the nineteenth century, some 8 to 10 million Africans were brought to the New World as slaves to furnish labor for the plantations there. As Africans from different cultures speaking different languages were forced to adapt to the new conditions of slavery and to the cultures and languages of their plantation masters, new cultures were forged.

Plantation labor was also obtained by means of indenture. This was the case for indentured laborers from India who went to Trinidad, British Guiana, Fiji, and South Africa. Local **corvee labor** was the method of the colonial government used in the Congo to force people to work as rubber tappers. In the Pacific, **blackbirding**, as the kidnapping of Melanesians was referred to, was used to fulfill the labor requirement of the sugar plantations on Fiji and in Australia. These forms of labor recruitment eventually gave way to contract labor, which was used to exploit the mineral resources of southern Africa. Men migrate from the tribal areas to the mines for a period of nine to eighteen months. In the past, the South African government controlled the flow of workers through Pass Laws, preventing those without a contract from leaving tribal areas for the towns and cities. This migration left the tribal areas bereft of men, children without fathers, and wives without husbands. The earlier organization of the family was undercut and weakened, and women alone raised the children. During the time they worked in the mines, the men became increasingly familiar with urban life and new associations such as unions developed. Leadership based on skill and on education superseded tribal leadership in most situations.

When a colonial administration was set up, concerted efforts were made to abolish those practices that violated the colonizers' moral code; headhunting, cannibalism, and non-Western family forms and marriage patterns were especially targeted for abolition. Anglican and Methodist missionaries in northwestern Canada among the Haida considered the potlatch a heathen custom, since it was a significant native religious rite that they felt impeded the spread of Christianity among these people. The missionaries particularly objected to the accumulation and redistribution practices of the potlatch, which they considered irrational economic behavior. In other settings missionaries recorded and transcribed languages that existed only in oral forms; the creation of vernacular bibles was in many cases the first attempt to record and preserve rapidly disappearing indigenous languages.

NEW IRELAND: AN EXAMPLE OF INCREASING INCORPORATION INTO THE GLOBAL SYSTEM

It is useful to examine the ways in which the variables we have just discussed operate in a particular case, New Ireland, now part of the nation-state of Papua New Guinea. New Ireland is located in the Bismarck Archipelago, close to the equator and east of the much larger island of New Guinea. The first Western explorer known to have made contact with New Irelanders, in 1619,

European missionaries brought various forms and practices of Christianity to the people of New Guinea in the early 1900s.

was the Dutchman Schouten. He was searching for trading opportunities in the Pacific outside the geographic area over which the Dutch East India Company had established a monopoly. Schouten tried to exchange beads with the New Irelanders for needed supplies, but the exchange could not be transacted because, as one would expect, neither side understood the other. When the New Irelanders attacked Schouten's men with their slings and clubs, he responded with cannon fire, killing ten or twelve of them. This initial contact with the West was certainly a violent one, not easily forgotten by the New Irelanders. Over the next two centuries some seven European expeditions sought to replenish their supplies on New Ireland. They offered trade goods, such as beads and cloth, which did not seem to interest the New Irelanders, and consequently they were given little in the way of supplies in return.

During the first decades of the nineteenth century, ships began to put in more and more frequently at New Ireland locations. By this time, the New Irelanders knew that the European ships anchoring in their harbors wanted to reprovision with coconuts, tubers, and pigs, and the Europeans had become aware of the New Irelanders' desire for iron. Iron hoops, used to hold casks of whale oil together, were cut into three- or four-inch segments, and given in exchange for supplies. They were greatly prized by the New Irelanders since they were used to make adzes and axes, which made gardening much easier. The process of carving *malanggan* mortuary sculptures also became much easier. In the early nineteenth century, English and American whalers put in to the bays of New Ireland for fresh water and supplies, giving in exchange hoop iron, along with buttons, bottles, strips of cloth, and, later, tobacco. A number of seamen became castaways on New Ireland at this time. In 1825, Thomas Manners, an English whaler, asked to be put ashore, where he subsequently lived with the villagers, took wives, and fathered children. As a result of Manners's presence, the Big Man of his village seemed to have had more political power. For men such as Manners, the islands of the Pacific were a romantic escape from the alienation of industrializing European society.

During this period, the island was, for the first time, enmeshed in the world system when traders came seeking tortoise shell to be sent to Europe for the manufacture of combs and other decorative items, which became the rage of fashionable Europe. *Beche-de-mer* (sea cucumbers) were also collected and then dried and sold to the Chinese as a food delicacy. By this point, a mutually agreed-upon barter system had been established, and some New Irelanders were able to communicate in Pidgin English. The New Irelanders thus became part of the global system of trade.

The first European trading post was set up on New Ireland in 1880 by the German trader Eduard Hernsheim to purchase coconuts. From his base on Matupi Island in New Britain, Hernsheim set up a network of trading stations, including a number on New Ireland. His agents at these stations—Englishmen, Scandinavians, and, later, mostly Chinese—bought unhusked coconuts (later, only the nuts) from the New Ireland villagers in exchange for tobacco, beads, and ironware from Europe. The price the villagers received for coconuts varied, depending on the price of copra (dried coconut meat) on the world market, the price of beads in Europe, and the number of competing traders in the area. These were factors from the world economic system over which villagers on the local level had no control. In the indigenous system of exchange, shell valuables and pigs did not fluctuate in value. Hernsheim transported copra on his own ship to be sold in Hamburg, where he was raised and where he sent his profits. The success of his business enterprise depended on the world price of copra.

Relying on villagers to bring in their coconuts did not produce a steady supply of copra. As Hernsheim notes in his memoirs, "It was impossible to make long-term agreements with these savages; there were no chiefs and no large villages" (1983). Because the New Irelanders had Big Men, rather than chiefs, there was no one in a position of central political authority with whom traders and later political administrators could make binding agreements and sign treaties. There was no single indigenous political structure that unified the whole island. The alternative to the unpredictable supply of copra provided through trading stations was the establishment of a plantation system, which began on New Ireland at the beginning of the twentieth century. Land for plantations had to be purchased by Europeans from New Irelanders. Since land on New Ireland was owned by matrilineal clans, only clan representatives could negotiate such sales.

Labor recruiters began in the 1880s to call at locations in New Ireland to recruit workers for plantations in Fiji and, later, Australia, often resorting to blackbirding. Captain Wawn, one of the first labor recruiters, or blackbirders, in the area, recruited for the sugar plantations in Queensland, Australia. Despite the fact that some of the men changed their minds and jumped overboard, the remainder were forcibly taken to Queensland to work as laborers. When they returned home three years later, the recruits brought back boxes filled with Western goods, which they used to maximize their positions in the political arenas of their own villages, becoming leaders and Big Men. Many came back to New Ireland speaking Pidgin English, and this enabled them to deal more successfully with the European traders on the island. The sugar produced in Queensland and the copra from Fiji and Samoa where the New Irelanders worked were destined for sale on the world market.

Missionary activity began in New Ireland in 1875 when the Methodist Reverend George Brown, an Englishman, stationed two Fijian religious teachers there, where no colonial administration existed. Fijian teachers were important to the Methodist missionary enterprise because they could more effectively spread the message of Christianity than Europeans. The Methodist missionaries voiced their strong opposition to local habits and tried to eliminate the New Irelanders' customs such as wearing no clothing, ritual dancing—which the missionaries considered lewd—and cannibalism. The progress of missionizing was impeded by the absence of authoritative leadership and the many languages spoken on the island. When a chief converts, as in Fiji, an entire chiefdom converts with him; Big Men do not have the same kind of authority over their followers. Catholic missionaries visited New Ireland in 1882. The Catholic approach to missionizing differed from that of the Reverend Brown. It involved setting up mission stations run by Europeans to which the local people would come for religious instruction and schooling. The legacy of the Reverend George Brown is the many Methodist congregations all over the island led by indigenous religious leaders. The Catholic mission stations of the island are now run by expatriate American priests of the Order of the Sacred Heart, while the diocese of New Ireland is headed by a German bishop.

Although traders of several nationalities were operating in the Bismarck Archipelago after 1880, German companies dominated the area economically. Australia, then a British colony, was concerned about German influence on the island of New Guinea and proceeded to annex the southern half of that island. Within a year an agreement was signed in which Germany took control over northern New Guinea and the Bismarcks and the English were to control the remainder of New Guinea. The German flag was raised over New Ireland in November 1884. While it had already been tied to the rest of the world economically for several decades, New Ireland now politically became part of the German colonial empire.

It was not until 1900 that a government station was established at Kavieng, the present provincial capital, with Franz Boluminski as district commissioner. For the first time in its history, the whole island constituted a single political entity, a district within the colony of German New Guinea, instead of many autonomous villages. Former employees of the large German trading companies began to apply for land to establish plantations in such numbers that shortly thereafter the colonial government had to enact regulations to prevent the New Irelanders from losing all their land. The monument Boluminski left in New Ireland was the coastal road, stretching for over 100 miles from Kavieng, built by means of corvee labor extracted from the villages along its path.

During the German administration, great efforts were made by the colonial government to end the state of perpetual feuding between local communities and to end raiding and looting of European trade stations by the New Irelanders. Beyond the retaliatory raids against offending communities by the local native police organized and led by the Germans, pacification took the form of moving villages to the coast, where they could be more easily supervised. This movement of inland villagers to the coast tore whole communities away from their ancestral clan lands, bringing them into the coastal villages as intruders. This left the interior of New Ireland relatively deserted. Headmen, called *luluais*, not always the traditional leaders, were appointed for each village by the German administration. Sometimes the men who had worked in plantations overseas, learned Pidgin English, and had subsequently become Big Men were appointed *luluais*.

Most of the earlier European traders, like Hernsheim, went to Australia or returned to Europe after they had made their fortunes. In contrast, Chinese traders, who came somewhat later, stayed on in New Ireland, intermarried with the local people, and eventually took control of the trade stores. The Chinese traders did not feel the same way as Europeans did about maintaining sharp social boundaries between colonizers and colonized.

The Germans were stripped of their colonies, including New Ireland, after their defeat in World War I, and Australia took over the administration of New Ireland under a mandate from the League of Nations. The Australians expropriated German-owned plantations and sold them at low rates to Australian ex-servicemen, who employed local New Irelanders from nearby villages. In other respects, life for the New Irelanders did not change much when colonial control passed from the Germans to the Australians. When the price of copra rose on the world market in the 1920s, Australian plantation owners became quite successful, but when it fell during the Depression, they lost money. Villagers had to sell coconuts from their own trees to raise cash to purchase trade goods and to pay the newly imposed head tax. Patrol officers encouraged the villagers to cut and dry the meat of the coconut kernels themselves so that they could sell it as processed copra and receive a higher price for it than for the kernels.

The Australians established patrol posts at various locations over the island and continued to use the *luluai* system put in place by the Germans. Patrol officers periodically visited almost every village to collect the head tax; adjudicate disputes, particularly over land; examine health conditions; see that labor recruitment rules were adhered to; and conduct censuses. In this way, the colonial bureaucracy increasingly penetrated many aspects of the daily life of the New Irelanders. By this time, Pidgin English had developed as the *lingua franca* for New Ireland, as well as many other areas of the southwest Pacific. The Europeans used it to communicate with the local people. New Irelanders from different parts of the island, who spoke different languages, used it to converse across linguistic boundaries.

The Japanese occupied New Ireland during World War II and the primary hardship of the indigenous population arose from Japanese confiscation of pigs and foodstuffs. The Australians returned after World War II to administer Papua New Guinea as a United Nations Trusteeship Territory, with independence as the eventual aim. The Australian owners reopened their plantations, and the economy continued much as it had before the war, though new crops, such as cocoa, began to be grown alongside the coconut palms. In the 1950s, as a first step toward independence, the Australians introduced a system of elected local government councils, which took over some of the functions that had been carried out by patrol officers. A House of Assembly was established in Port Moresby, with representation from districts all over Papua New Guinea. In 1975 the independent nation of Papua New Guinea was established. New Ireland was set up as a province, with its own elected provincial assembly and a provincial government headed by a prime minister.

Since independence, Australian expatriates have been withdrawing from the economic system of New Ireland, though they still own some of the plantations. Some of the plantation laborers are New Irelanders, while others have been brought in from the Sepik River area of New Guinea. The world price for copra has been very low in recent years, and many of the plantations are run at a minimal level since the owners do not wish to take a loss. As plantations are abandoned, they revert to the local villages, which still basically have a subsistence economy of gardening, raising pigs, and fishing. In addition, the local villagers have moved into cash cropping, producing copra and cocoa to sell to government marketing boards, which then sell these products on the world market. Sometimes villagers have organized themselves into cooperatives to buy and operate a truck or a boat. In recent years, Malaysian and Japanese companies have exploited the timber resources in the interior part of the island; fixed royalties are paid to national and provincial governments and to local people. Rainforest conservation in Papua New Guinea is increasingly becoming the subject of national and international action; in 2008 the government announced plans to phase out raw log exports by 2010.

The significant unit for most New Irelanders continues to be their village. Villages had been politically independent before New Ireland became a colony. Today, though there are still Big Men and matrilineal clans, every village is part of an electoral district and the majority of New Irelanders participate in provincial and national elections. In contrast to people elsewhere who have become exclusively wage laborers or who depend exclusively on cash crops, New Ireland villagers have resisted being completely absorbed into a market economy. Many prefer to sell products only when they need cash. However, they are increasingly forced to view themselves in regional terms, as New Irelanders, and in national terms, as Papuan New Guineans. Changes at the world level affect them economically and politically, and they see themselves as necessarily part of the world system. This now includes participating in international systems of tourism, art and artifact production and consumption, commercial fishing, wage labor in the nearby Lahir gold mine, and palm oil production.

DEVELOPMENT AND ANTHROPOLOGY

The flow of money, expertise, and ideas from the West to underdeveloped countries around the world began after World War II and continues to this day. While originally viewed by some as evidence of Western humanitarianism, this transfer of capital and technology is now recognized to be deeply embedded in geopolitical interests and conflicts. Ideas about development as socio-economic and sociopolitical transformations are viewed today as examples of discourses (Escobar 1991, 1995) with particular sites of production, political uses, goals, and histories. With the rise of the global development industry and the international bureaucracies that finance and administer it, anthropologists play an increasingly large role in shaping and executing development policy and strategy worldwide. Applied or practicing anthropologists, working outside academic settings, often hired as consultants to facilitate development programs, are self-reflexive about the ethical dilemmas they routinely confront and develop strategies for attempting to resolve these dilemmas The uses of anthropological field methods and data in nonacademic settings, including those of state policy, development strategy, humanitarian efforts, military operations, and law enforcement, continually challenge both academic and practicing anthropologists to develop standards, methodologies, and ethics to incorporate the rights and interests of local communities (Morris and Bastin 2004, Whiteford and Trotter 2008).

Development History and Strategies

After World War II, revolutionary movements led to the establishment of many new states in Africa and Asia. Though the colonial yoke had been thrown off, many newly independent states were crippled economically by policies of resource exploitation and extraction and industrial suppression. These states faced wide gaps in wealth and education levels between classes, and growing hunger and poverty among most of its citizens. In comparison to the "developed" world of America and its European allies, these states were collectively referred to in development discourse as "undeveloped." The economic underdevelopment of many non-Western countries was recognized as a political threat to Western interests; President Harry Truman in his 1949 inaugural speech offered American scientific advances and technology for the improvement of underdeveloped areas of the world as part of his agenda for combating the spread of Soviet communism.

The term *Third World* came into use in the early 1950s in American and Western European political discourse to designate impoverished, under-industrialized states of Africa, Asia, and Central and South America. The term *First World* referred to the industrialized Western democratic capitalist states; the *Second World* was the communist bloc and its member states under the domination of the Soviet Union. The terms *Northern* and *Southern* states came into use later for First and Third World states, referencing their general distribution above and below the equator as well as the demise of the Soviet Bloc. Later the term *Fourth World Peoples* collectively designated tribal or indigenous people in Third World countries.

Some American economists and social theorists of the 1950s and 1960s stated that underdevelopment was the result of the retention of so-called traditional social and political institutions in independent states that prevented "rational" or Western-style economic transformation. The most influential of these **modernization** theorists, Walt W. Rostow, was the author of the highly influential book *The Stages of Economic Growth: A Non-Communist Manifesto* (1960), as well as a political advisor on the war in Vietnam to Presidents John Kennedy and Lyndon Johnson. Rostow's version of modernization theory hypothesized an evolutionary meta-narrative for economic development. He stated that all countries pass through the same stages of development, and that the ultimate stage of modernization, associated with urbanization and intensive consumer consumption, required the replacement of traditional values and institutions with Western-style technology, economic markets, and political systems. Those states that were not developed into Western-style modern industrialization were believed to be stalled at one of the earlier critical stages of transformation and required external inputs to "jump start" their economies into the single proposed trajectory of development. This unilinear model of development was criticized for a number of its assumptions, particularly its Western bias in articulating one single possibility for development dependent upon the emulation of Western- style capitalism. It was also criticized for its nonhistorical perspective; the cause of underdevelopment was explained exclusively by reference to traditionalism within the underdeveloped nation-state, with no reference to the historical relationships between states before and after colonial encounters.

Andre Gunder Frank and other scholars associated with **dependency theory** saw underdevelopment in a different way. They stressed the alliance of interests between elites in underdeveloped countries with those of Western capitalists in the developed countries. Third World countries are dependent upon the Western capitalist markets for their raw materials and labor; the extraction of these resources benefited a small class of people who controlled the export of resources. Frank and other dependency theorists saw these elites as unwilling to forgo the economic benefits of continuing the dependency of their nation's export economies on Western markets. These export industries generated little significant economic growth or employment opportunity for the majority of the local population, and generally did not create a profitable industrial base in most Third World countries. Dependency theorists suggested that autonomous national development, free from ties to the world economy, would create significant economic growth and a sustainable development strategy in the national interest, rather than serving the interests only of elites of developing countries.

With the downfall of the Soviet communist system, **neoliberalism** emerged as the dominant economic and political philosophy driving most state development initiatives. Neoliberalism harkens back to many ideas about free market capitalism articulated by Adam Smith in his 1776 publication *The Wealth of Nations*, in which he argued for laissez-faire economics and few governmental interventions in markets and production systems. Neoliberalism in contemporary political discourse actually has much in common with American conservative political strategy that seeks to greatly limit government controls and interventions in economics, trade, and even the delivery of social services. One example of this perspective in the United States is the growing trend towards decentralization and privatization of primary and secondary schools. With its emphasis on privatization, free enterprise, and unfettered competition in the marketplace, neoliberalism is seen by some as facilitating the distribution of globalization's benefits. Proponents encourage unregulated national and regional networks of trade and production between states. Within developing states this perspective encourages the participation of individual entrepreneurs in the local and national economy through credit schemes, microfinance, and other business incentives.

Development is also seen as replacing "local and rational technologies" with capitalist forms, ignoring local knowledge. Today local knowledge is seen as crucial, and one must pay attention to it in suggesting any forms of change. Local knowledge means "the culture, values, and social institutions of the place," which are and always have been, in effect, the principal foci for anthropologists. This has also been referred to as "indigenous knowledge" (Sillitoe 2002: 8). There has been a shift in emphasis from "top-down" intervention to a "grassroots" participatory perspective (Sillitoe 2002: 2). People at the local level want to share in technological advances with the West but on their own terms. An example of this strategy is the interaction of First Nations (Canadian Indians) with the Canadian government regarding the resources on First Nations lands. Each Nation has worked out its own agreement. "Various mixtures of this indigenous knowledge with Euro-American approaches have produced some spectacular successes, greatly improving some communities in 25 years" (Croal and Darou 2002: 83).

Over several decades, nongovernmental organizations (NGOs) have arisen in many countries, facilitating delivery of development, education, and health programs to local communities. Through "participatory development," NGOs try to involve community members in program planning and execution, addressing local priorities and problems (Sillitoe 2002: 8). NGO budgets derive from either the state or the international donor organizations, obscuring the distinction between "governmental" and nongovernmental organizations (Weisgrau 1997: 102–16). NGO representatives are often members of the elite from the city, of a different social class from the villagers. NGOs introduce plans and proposals initiated from outside the community, reflecting international or state development priorities (Mosse 2005). Anthropologists are sometimes called in to evaluate program outcomes on behalf of donor organizations that fund NGO projects.

Development initiatives often involve the introduction and marketing of tourism. From Highland New Guinea to Bali, tourist dollars have become an important source of income. Mt. Hagen "Sing-Sings" are a "must" stop on tours of Highland Papua New Guinea. The Chimbu in the Highlands has created special dances, utilizing local myths and costumes from a variety of rituals, to perform before tourists who come on special tours. These encounters, once considered too frivolous for scholarly consideration, are now taken seriously by anthropologists who study tourism (Chambers 2000, Henderson and Weisgrau 2007).

Tourism and its related infrastructures dominate the economies of many southern countries; tourism ebb and flow has serious consequences on labor markets and employment levels. Tour-

Village women of Rajasthan, India, meet with the representatives of a nongovernmental organization to discuss voting and employment issues.

ism-oriented transportation infrastructures often privilege foreigners and side-step the needs of citizens and local communities. Many of the advertising images of tourism brochures and websites market the so-called "exoticism" of people and destinations with images that perpetuate gender, racial, and ethnic stereotypes as well as historical inaccuracies. Some of the conflicts that arise around tourism strategy are the degree to which local destinations control their own representations in national and global discourse, and the distribution of economic benefits deriving from tourism enterprises.

Anthropology and Change: Academic and Applied Perspectives

As has been discussed, contemporary anthropologists play multiple roles in the lived experiences of development and globalization. One is the investigation of different cultures for the knowledge about how other people live their lives, for the production of intercultural understanding, and for the general theoretical information gained concerning similarities and differences between cultures and societies. Another is through historical anthropology, which uses archives and other historical data to understand the experiences of different groups in the past. An additional perspective is that of **applied anthropology**, which is concerned with the application of anthropological knowledge and methodologies to the solution of practical problems, initiating direct action, or contributing to the formation of a broad range of policies.

Even before the emergence of anthropology as a discipline, missionaries and government officials were involved in gathering anthropological information to implement their policies of conquest and conversion. During the colonial period, ethnographic studies were always included in the training of government administrators destined to work in colonies all over the world, who instituted many changes in all aspects of life of the people they controlled, as we have documented earlier. They often saw these changes as bringing "progress" to peoples, doing away with "savage" practices such as nakedness and cannibalism, helping to make them "modern"—that is, civilized and Westernized. The Bureau of American Ethnology, founded in the 1850s, "an early manifestation of anthropology in the United States . . . was created as a policy research arm of the federal government" (Willigen 2002: 23). The people most directly affected did not desire most of the changes that were instituted, but their opinions were rarely sought. This legacy of anthropological involvement in United States policy administration has created distrust between some Native American communities and anthropologists.

Anthropologists gathered ethnographic information in the form of policy-focused basic research for the American government during the 1930s on the subject of rural life (Goldschmidt 1947). During World War II anthropologists put together ethnographic handbooks used to prepare administrators for areas being recaptured from the Japanese, to provide intelligence on the Japanese and other adversaries, and to give the government advice on how to improve national morale (Willingen 2002: 25–29). Many of those involved, such as Margaret Mead, Gregory Bateson, and Ruth Benedict, straddled the academic and applied fields during that time. Ethical questions began to be raised during the Vietnam War when some anthropologists were involved in providing ethnographic information that suggested the most efficient ways of carrying out local resettlement strategies. These debates continue over the role of American cultural anthropologists employed by the Department of Defense and working with the American military in Iraq and Afghanistan.

Many in the discipline now understand that there is no such thing as "value-free research." Earlier, during the colonial period, some anthropologists had tried to "increase the fairness and humaneness of various domestic and international colonial systems" (Willingen 2002: 31). However, it became quite clear that that was impossible. Value-explicit research meant that anthropologists thenceforth had to clearly define their goals and values for the communities within which they wished to work. These and other ethical issues are often discussed and debated within the discipline; the American Anthropological Association established and continues to reformulate codes of ethical conduct for ethnographic research projects.

The demand for more involvement of anthropologists in policy research resulted in the development of applied anthropology professionals. Practicing anthropologists work with community leaders, nonprofit institutions, corporations, and governments to create, implement, and evaluate programs and policies, in domestic settings as well as abroad. The applied anthropologist is often hired to do a rapid assessment of a particular situation and come to some conclusions regarding a policy that might be implemented. In that type of situation, the degree of collaboration with the local community varies. Trained to make cross-cultural comparisons and explore cultural diversity, anthropologists are increasingly recruited by corporations to develop international business strategies and personnel training programs. Academic anthropologists, usually affiliated with a college or university social science department, engage with many of the same subjects as practicing anthropologists, through ethnographic research and writing. They explore the history of ideas about development, local understandings of these concepts, and the often competing visions expressed by state institutions, international development agencies, and local community members.

Paige West (2006) documents the interactions between scientists and NGO workers representing an international biodiversity conservation project with communities of Gimi-language speakers in Papua New Guinea. West's ethnography is "multi-sited and multi-temporal" in that it connects diverse sites of the production of knowledge about biodiversity in Papua New Guinea over long periods of time. She explores the connections between consumer markets in New York

Coffee is grown and prepared for export in the Papua New Guinea Highlands. It is marketed globally using images and claims that appeal to consumers in Western markets.

City and rural, "out of the way" communities near the eastern highlands of Papua New Guinea where she has conducted seven years of fieldwork. She traces the history of ideas about nature, wildlife, and biodiversity management produced in northern environmental protection organizations and academic institutions. In this "imagining" of Papua New Guinea, its animal and plant life is exotic, threatened, and in need of protection.

To this end, the Crater Mountain Wildlife Management Area (CMWMA) was established in the early 1980s. Funded by the U.S.-based Wildlife Conservation Society, the CMWMA encompassed Gimi-speaking and other communities within its boundaries. The CMWMA was envisioned by the nongovernmental organizations that created and administered it as a site of economic development and conservation. This goal would engage local communities in production and marketing of local products and the development of tourism while employing strategies of environmental sustainability. "It was imagined that these markets would allow for the flow of cash income to people who live in highly biologically diverse places. In turn, these people would work to conserve the biological diversity on which the markets were based" (West 2006: xii). The NGO workers and conservation planners imagined this undertaking as a social contract between themselves and local community members that would create income and employment opportunities through sustainable environmental practices that would also attract scientists and researchers to the area.

Throughout the ethnography, West explores the multiple misunderstandings and contradictory visions of development and the environment among the principal actors and participants. To some Gimi, their participation in this project meant access to their vision of the modern, including "medicine, education, technology, and knowledge and wealth, the things they see as development" (West 2006: xiii). Their engagement with their natural environment is meaningful and active; its resources are integral to their physical and cultural lives. The conservationists imagine the "environment" as "existing apart from the Gimi and indeed as being threatened by Gimi practices and social life" (West 2006: 218). Both sides imagined an appropriate development strategy from their historical, cultural, and practical perspectives; neither side understood the other's perspective. Nor did they understand the role of the American ethnographer in the midst of this contested environment. West's goal in this complicated story that continues to unfold is to "disentangle the connections" and "contradictions" of conservation, development, and commodity production. Her study explores among other issues how "the past imaginaries of New Guinea and its nature and culture as untouched, exotic and spectacular drove people who wished to protect it, sell it, explore it, and study it, and that these same imaginaries drive environmental conservation in Papua New Guinea today" (2006: 4).

People on the Move

Migration, or the movement of populations, has characterized the evolving human species from the beginning. The most recent information from physical anthropologists tells us that our ancestors moved out from Africa in wave after wave to populate Asia, Europe, and finally the New

World and the Pacific Islands. Humans have always been on the move, as we have seen in the last chapter. We have already mentioned that one of the many characteristics of both colonialism and globalization is labor migration; people move to where labor is required with varying degrees of autonomy and compulsion. We shall now consider in more detail the different kinds of migration, as well as some of the resulting situations and cultural outcomes.

Internal Migration

Internal migration refers to population movements within a nation-state. Such migrations have been taking place in our own country since its settlement almost 500 years ago. The expansion of our country from the original thirteen colonies represents a form of internal migration. The nineteenth-century movement of population ever westward to the Pacific Ocean continued this pattern. At the beginning of the twentieth century, large numbers of African Americans, dissatisfied with life in the segregated rural South, began their movement to the northern urban cities where they hoped to find work and freedom from the segregated culture of the South. This movement continued for many years. During the twentieth century, migration from rural areas to cities represented another significant movement of population. Whereas in the nineteenth century most of the population of the United States lived in the rural areas of the country, increasingly, in the twentieth century, the urban and suburban populations have come to dominate. The mechanization of farming and farm consolidation forced many farming families to seek their fortunes in the cities of the nation.

Labor migration, the movement of people to where jobs are available, is also a form of internal migration. After World War II, many people sought their fortunes in "sunny California," where they saw new employment opportunities. People have also moved from the urban Northeast to seek employment elsewhere, since the industries of that area were moving to other parts of the country or even overseas. Senior citizens, referred to as "snowbirds," whose retirement communities we discussed in a previous chapter, move from northern states, with their cold winters, to Florida, California, and the Southwest, where the climate is more to their liking. One might even consider professors as exemplifying internal migration, since, during the course of their careers, they may teach at different colleges and universities in different parts of the country.

Transmigration

Transmigration refers to populations who migrate far from their homelands to many different parts of the world. These people may be completely assimilated into the culture of their new country. Through **assimilation** they adopt the language and culture of their new country. Many people who were persecuted in their homelands or who were dissatisfied with their lives in the countries of their birth came to America and desired to be completely assimilated.

Historians such as Sobel (2002) have examined the process of migration from Europe and Africa to America during the eighteenth century by looking at autobiographical statements the migrants wrote. While many of them looked forward to the advantages offered by living in the

New World, especially religious and political freedom, migration meant giving up a culture and a social structure that they were comfortable with, and it sometimes meant learning a new language as well. The autobiographical narratives reveal that the migrants underwent significant changes in their personal identity as they adapted to life in colonial America and became Americans. Often they underwent important religious changes such as conversion to new Christian denominations such as the Moravian Church, or they became Baptists or Quakers. The migrants first encountered these religious denominations in America. The new sense of self felt by the migrant was also frequently accompanied by a newly discovered sense of "otherness" (This is what I am. It is completely different from those deceitful others). For example, Venture Smith was brought to America as a slave at the age of six. From that point on, he saw whites as the enemy, who valued lying and deception, and blacks as valuing truth and integrity (Sobel 2002: 189). "Freedom," said Venture Smith, "is a privilege which nothing else can equal" (Sobel 2002: 189).

The phenomenon of "being born again" occurs often in the narratives (Sobel 2002: 199). The process of migration to a new land, to a new culture, involves remaking one's self and creating a new identity for one's self. It is as though one were "born again" in the New World. After the American Revolution, a collective identity was consciously being constructed. The importance of the concept of the "not-me" in American culture and the construction of American identity are reflected in the continued racism directed at African Americans and Native groups (Sobel 2002: 202).

Diasporas

Some migrants maintain their original ethnic identity for centuries and today are known as **diaspora populations**. In recent years, the overseas migration of groups such as the Chinese and Indians (described below) have come to be known as diasporas. This term is now applied to populations who have moved to other parts of the world and retained some connection to their homelands. The word *diaspora* was originally a Greek term that meant "dispersion." It came to be applied to the uprooting of the Jewish people after the destruction of the Second Temple in AD 70, their exile from the Holy Land and subsequent dispersion throughout the Old World and, later, the New World.

The term *diaspora* is now applied to diverse migrant groups that settled in countries away from their homelands for a variety of reasons. Some analysts have argued that "the term should be reserved for groups forced to disperse, and whose members conscientiously strive to keep past memories, maintain their heritage and are involved in a survival struggle" (Tatla 1999: 3). Such diaspora groups have faced ethnocide-forced cultural integration—or even genocide in the effort to eliminate or exterminate them. Cohen (1997) has suggested a number of specific features that all diasporas have in common. First, they all represent dispersal from a homeland. Members of the diaspora always maintain a collective memory about their homeland, including its location, history, and achievements, idealizing their ancestral home. They have a collective commitment to its maintenance, restoration, safety, and prosperity, and to its re-creation if it no longer exists as a separate political entity. Frequently, a movement to return to the homeland among members of the diaspora becomes important to the group. Diasporas also sustain strong ethnic group consciousness over a long period of time, based on a sense of distinctiveness compared to their neighbors, a common history, and the belief in a common fate. They may have a troubled relationship with the host soci-ety, which does not accept them, and in such situations there is always the possibility that another calamity, a wave of persecution or perhaps another dispersal, will befall the group. In contrast, in some situations, in which the host country constitutes a plural society, members of a diaspora may continue to have a distinctive creative life. Diaspora populations also have a strong sense of empathy and solidarity with co-ethnic members residing in other countries (Cohen 1997: 26).

The reasons for the dispersal of a diaspora population may vary. Armenians, Africans, and Jews represent "victim diasporas." That is, their movement was a consequence of forced removal, as was the case for the Africans who were brought to the New World, or persecution and threats of death, which forced the Armenians to flee from Turkey and the Jews to flee from the pogroms in Poland and the Ukraine. The Armenian diaspora population of London represents individu-als from a number of different countries, such as Cyprus, Lebanon, and Iran. They speak either the eastern Armenian dialect and trace their ancestry to Iran or Armenia, or western Armenian that was spoken in eastern Turkey before the genocide of the Armenians of Turkey in 1915. This distinction was often the basis for divisions in the London Armenian diaspora. The mostly first-generation immigrants belong to "a shifting set of voluntary organizations which sponsored a small cultural centre, two churches . . . a Sunday school and wide variety of less regular activities from lectures to movies to musical recitals to teas or fund-raising dances" (Amit 2002: 268). Since this Armenian population interacts with non-Armenians, especially those born in Britain, their ethnicity was only a "part-time" ethnicity. Since the Armenians were not residentially organized, their Armenian identity and its reproduction in the next generation required effort and self-con-scious recognition of their ethnic background. Families maintained extensive personal networks and contact with relatives in Lebanon and the United States in the manner of the transnational families we will describe below (Amit 2002: 272).

Sometimes, like South Asians or Turks, men had to leave families and their homelands, in which employment was scarce, and go in search of work abroad. The Chinese and Lebanese rep-resent the movement of people to other countries in search of trade opportunities (Cohen 1997). "Overseas Indians" are to be found in Fiji, East Africa, and in Trinidad. "Overseas Chinese" have lived for generations in many countries in Southeast Asia, Indonesia, Papua New Guinea, Cuba, and elsewhere. These populations also constitute diasporas. They are well established in these countries and are frequently very successful economically. Their ethnic identity still remains Chinese or Indian. Anthropologists, who have been concerned with the adaptations that the Chinese and Indians have made in different cultural settings and the means by which they have maintained their ethnic identities, have studied these "overseas" populations extensively. South Asian populations have been subject to discrimination in, and eventual expulsion from, Uganda under the rule of Idi Amin, transforming them into a secondary diaspora population. In Fiji South Asians have been threatened with expulsion and are targeted for political and economic discrimi-nation by native Fijian politicians.

The overseas Chinese were originally viewed as "**sojourners**," that is, individuals who migrated because of economic opportunities, sending a portion of their wages home, with the intention of returning. They were identified in terms of the provinces or areas from which they came, such as Canton, Hong Kong, or Shantung, perhaps because the dynasty was Manchu, not Chinese. After the formation of the Chinese Republic, their identity was shifted to a Chinese national identity. In the latter part of the twentieth century, after the Communist Revolution, the Chinese shed their sojourner status, but even though they emigrated with the intention of setting up permanent residences, they were still identified as overseas Chinese. The ethnic Chinese played an important role in economic development in East and Southeast Asia. Many of these overseas Chinese continue to identify with Chinese culture and language. There are also Chinese who have been identified as transnationals, in that they are interested in economic gain and opportunity wherever it can be found. Chinese transnational families exist in which siblings may be citizens of the different countries where their families have invested and established businesses. Kinship, culture, and commerce keep these families together. Many Chinese families have assimilated, since they have lived in the countries to which their ancestors moved for several generations. However, even these individuals are identified as Chinese, though they may not be culturally or linguistically Chinese. This is where what is identified as the "race" factor comes into play. Identity is "forced" on an individual as a consequence of appearance. Chinese who are remote from their culture may visit China, their ancestral home. Such encounters, "diasporic encounters," have begun to occur with some frequency, as we noted earlier. These encounters are increasingly the subject of films and other popular culture forms.

More recently, the process of globalization has had an effect on diasporas. Air transportation has made international migration much easier. People migrate more frequently and, rather than permanently settle in another country, remain in continuous contact with their homelands, to which they often return upon retirement. Cities have become more international, more cosmopolitan in their acceptance of cultural differences. Overseas nationals play an increasingly important role in the economies of their countries of origin by investing capital earned abroad in stock and bond markets. Notions of plural societies and multiculturalism in many places have coexisted with or replaced the idea of a national culture. Complete assimilation and the idea of the "melting pot" no longer operate in our country or in others.

Transnationalism

Transnationalism refers to family members who migrate from their homes to another country, such as the United States, and continue to maintain close contact with those left behind, thus forming new kinds of families (Kearney 1995). Other relatives may follow them, in a pattern of **chain migration**. These family members now in the United States maintain a kind of dual existence. They live and work in our country, sometimes even in different cities, but remain members of their families back home, sending money, owning property, and even voting. They may become United States citizens and still maintain these close connections. In chapter 6 we referred to this type of transnational family, which regularly uses e-mail, telephone, and airlines as ways of maintaining close contact.

Terms such as *internal migration, transmigration, diasporas,* and *transnationalism* represent relatively new concepts in the anthropological vocabulary. However, anthropologists for decades have been studying ways of life of immigrants abroad. These new terminologies are of assistance analytically, enabling anthropologists and others to have a better understanding of what is happening. For example, they permit us to describe more accurately a new type of family, the transnational family. By using the concept of diaspora populations, we can more readily recognize the necessity of looking at African Americans, Afro-Cubans, and Afro-Brazilians in terms of what they have in common historically. These commonalities, however, do not obscure the social and political particulars of individual diaspora populations. These are also not essential characteristics of groups of people; the diaspora population of one generation may be a national or ethnic group in the next generation.

SUMMARY

- Cultures are constantly undergoing change at a very rapid rate in today's world.
- Colonialism, which was one of the strongest forces for change, is all but gone, and in its place is a series of new nationalities, based on the geography of colonial empires rather than on sameness of culture.
- The new postcolonial nation-states are industrializing, and forming national cultures in their attempt to integrate various indigenous cultures within their nation-state.
- Globalization has been brought about by the development of a worldwide network of finance and capital. It represents historical continuities with colonialism and the neocolonialism of the latter part of the twentieth century.
- The initial motivation for the establishment of colonies was economic gain, which took the form of exploiting raw materials as well as providing labor and markets for the goods of the mother country.
- The British developed the policy of indirect rule using the indigenous political structure, which was then applied throughout the British Empire. In contrast, the French ruled directly, establishing military garrisons and large administrative staffs throughout their empire.
- The establishment of a colony and the course of events that followed can be described in terms of land exploitation, type of labor recruitment, and intensity and type of missionary activity.
- Different colonial empires had somewhat different policies with respect to the rights of native peoples over access to land. Furthermore, these native peoples themselves had a variety of different strategies about land rights.
- Exploitation of resources in colonial areas and their successor nation-states required labor, which was met in a variety of ways. Labor recruitment dislocated economies and the traditional forms of family and social organization of colonized populations.
- Applied anthropology is concerned with the production and application of anthropological knowledge to the solution of practical problems.
- Some anthropologists work with the U.S. government and military in conflict areas; many in the discipline recognize that there is no such thing as "value-free research."

- A major characteristic of globalization today is the movement of people across borders for economic, political, and social reasons. Internal migration, transmigration, transnational families, and diaspora populations are some of the categories used to describe contemporary population movements.

SUGGESTED READINGS

Nash, June C. *Practicing Ethnography in a Globalizing World: An Anthropological Odyssey.* Lanham, MD: Altamira Press, 2007. How ethnography illuminates a wide array of global problems, written for students by an esteemed anthropologist and ethnographer.

Hewamanne, Sandya. *Stitching Identities in a Free Trade Zone: Gender and Politics in Sri Lanka.* Philadelphia: University of Pennsylvania Press, 2008. The impact on their lives of working in a Free Trade Zone, through the words and experiences of young women in Sri Lanka.

Crate, Susan A. *Cows, Kin, and Globalization: An Ethnography of Sustainability.* Lanham, MD: AltaMira Press, 2006. An ethnography of the Sakha indigenous people of northeastern Siberia, Russia, with a focus on how exploitation of natural resources of the area link the Sakha to the global economy.

SUGGESTED WEBSITES

www.globalization101.org. A comprehensive website designed for students of globalization with links to literature on history, politics, economics, and activism.

www.cwis.org/index.php. The website for the Center for World Indigenous Studies contains multiple links to news and scholarship about indigenous peoples around the world.

www.sscnet.ucla.edu/southasia/Diaspora/diaspora.html. A website exploring the history and current issues in the South Asian Diaspora.

Chapter 14

States and Identities

Ethnicity, Race, and Nationalism

IN TODAY'S WORLD, STATES ARE universally recognized as the sole legitimate political entity; borders are generally recognized and maintained by international consensus, treaties, and organizations. State sovereignty in the twenty-first century is sometimes seen as being challenged by the forces of globalization. In the previous chapter we discussed the impacts of the flow of people, ideas, jobs, and capital across borders. In the United States outsourcing of customer service and data processing is now a familiar aspect of American corporate strategy. Increasingly, state bureaucracies, facing the same financial pressures as private corporations, are outsourcing administrative jobs to reduce administrative costs. Both corporate and governmental outsourcing are generating a backlash by various groups that seek to protect jobs in the United States; legislation has been introduced in some state senates banning the outsourcing of government contracts and reserving government jobs for American citizens. This is just one example of the ongoing conflicts raised by globalization from the perspectives of citizenship and state sovereignty. "[T]he rhetoric of legislation against the flight of jobs abroad seamlessly weaves together national belonging, citizenship, culture, race, state work, and state control. It articulates a fear of the loss of sovereignty to globalization, which in turn presumes a certain understanding of the state and of the state's role in governing a territory and the resources and population within that territory" (Sharma and Gupta 2006: 5).

As we discussed in chapter 9, states are organized on a territorial basis, and encompass diverse groups of people. The term *state* suggests a particular political structure and sovereign territory; *nation* suggests shared cultural identity that may derive from common ideas about origins, history, family, and religion, as well as language use. The term ***nation-state*** is used when nation and state are coterminous. In reality, this is more likely to be a multicultural state with a national identity existing alongside multiple ethnic identities. **Nationalism** is a political movement to claim or reformulate shared ideas about identity among citizens within a state's borders. Nations are composed of one politically autonomous ethnic group, while *state* is the term used to refer to any politically autonomous entity, whether it is composed of one or many different ethnic groups.

One goal of newly independent states is to create a national culture incorporating diverse population groups within its borders. The creation and maintenance of a national identity selectively employs myths, symbols, and history to forge shared sentiments; competing visions of the past and identities in the present are often the basis of conflict between groups of people in pluralistic states. As suggested above, the forces of globalization are increasingly being integrated into the cultural framing of national identities. Despite the predictions of some social scientists that globalism and transnational migration would reduce the potency of national identity, anthropologists regularly document how cultural ideas about states, nationalism, and citizenship are strengthened and contested in globalized settings.

The terms *ethnic identity*, *ethnic group*, *nationalism*, *multiculturalism*, and *race* are among the conceptual tools used by anthropologists and other social scientists. They are also part of the language of television news programs and newspaper headlines and are therefore themes for our times. Ethnic groups share common cultural norms, values, identities, patterns of behavior, and language. Their members recognize themselves as a separate group and are so recognized by others. They may or may not be politicized. Ethnic identity, or ethnicity, is seen by some analysts as based on primordial sentiments, that is, sentiments that are conceptualized as going back to ancient times and that tie group members to one another emotionally, despite persistent attempts to assimilate them. To others, ethnic identity is a resource or an instrument to be employed in pursuit of economic or political goals; it is therefore understood as situational, invoked in some contexts but not in others. Ethnic differences may also parallel class differences; in some societies, the underclass is a separate ethnic or racial group. Under those conditions, ethnic conflict may be characterized as class conflict.

Religion is one of the important factors serving to distinguish one ethnic group from another. In a number of examples discussed below, we will see that in addition to ethnic differences, meaning cultural differences, there are also religious differences. When religious differences are present, the ethnic conflict is heightened and intensified. Each side finds support in the moral authority of its own religion for continuing the conflict and for using violent action against those whom it characterizes as heretics. The former Yugoslavia illustrates this very well. The dominant Serbs are an Orthodox population, who view themselves historically as Christian martyrs who suffered under the Muslim Ottoman Empire. Bosnians and Albanians, in Kosovo, are Muslims. Croatians, on the other hand, are Roman Catholics. Despite similarities in language and culture among these ethnic groups, their religious differences have exacerbated the ethnic conflict and are sometimes used to justify violence against members of the other ethnic group.

Race and racial classifications often are a basis for making distinctions between ethnic groups. Many people tend to think of race as a scientific concept based on biological systems of classification. Scientists have challenged the genetic basis for claiming that there are separate identifiable races by which all human variation can be classified. However, the cultural idea persists that racial classifications are discrete, fixed categories to which people can be assigned based on physical appearance and presumed ancestry. In reality the concept of race differs from one society to another; racial systems are socially constructed over time within specific social and political contexts (Smedley 2007).

The cultural construction of race is illustrated by the "one drop of blood" concept in the American system of racial classifications. This social interpretation of principles of genealogy includes the rule of **hypodescent**, which classifies anyone with any identifiable African-American ancestry as black, not white.

In comparison, in Brazil, color of complexion forms an element in the conceptualization of status and group; the lighter the complexion, the higher the class status of the individual. Hundreds of different races are recognized in Brazil based on phenotype, or appearance; as an individual's appearance changes, so does the assignment of his or her racial category (Harris 1970). In Brazil race is a continuum and an achieved status; in the United States it is clearly a fixed, bipolar category and an ascribed status.

Racism, discrimination on the basis of race, is expressed at both individual and institutional levels. Forces of racism work to separate the two categories of white and African American in the United States. As anthropologist John Gwaltney's African-American informants in *Drylongso* expressed it, oppressed by the white majority, they were one of two "nations" in the United States (Gwaltney 1993). Social scientists have echoed this point, from Gunnar Myrdal, who called America's treatment of African Americans *An American Dilemma*, to Andrew Hacker's view of *Two Nations: Black and White, Separate, Hostile, Unequal.*

In some parts of the United States racial identities are complicated by patterns of property ownership, occupation, political alliances, and religion that cross strictly bipolar racial categories (Adams and Gorton 2006). Genetic identity projects, including the proliferation of commercial enterprises that trace individual ancestry, reify the traditional cultural categories of race through a new methodology of individual genomic identity (Palmie 2007). "The new molecular biology and its attendant practices of biotechnological intervention are giving race a new lease on life" (Abu El-Haj 2007: 284) as social categories with political implications.

NATION BUILDING

The idea of nation building began in Europe, the nation being defined as a sovereign political state with a single national culture (Gellner 1983, Hobsbawn 1992). France, Italy, and England began to develop their nation-states before other European countries. The development of national cultures involved conscious culture building on the part of the hegemonic group in political control of the state—the goal being the elimination of regional ethnic cultures in favor of a national culture. Anthropological research has revealed the way this process of conscious, national culture building, in Africa, for example, takes place in various media such as radio, TV, and newspapers.

Archaeology, the interpretation of the past through material remains, is utilized in the service of creating national identity, as is the case in Pakistan and Israel. States choose to emphasize one aspect of their archeological past rather than another, in keeping with the messages about the past, which the archaeological results are meant to support. Each state tells its own myth about its past. Domestic and foreign tourism, and the information communicated by tour guides at historical sites, is a significant aspect of contemporary nationalism projects. In Israel, archaeology has always served the function of conveying the rights of Israelis to its national borders. Israel chooses to emphasize archaeological research related to religious rather than secular sites. It concentrates on the periods of the First and Second Temples, that is, the Iron Age through early Roman times, ignoring earlier sites such as the Mount Carmel caves where Neanderthal skeletal material was found. Archaeological sites, like that of Masada, are used as widely promoted tourism destinations as well as the locations for national ceremonies to imbue Israeli national values. Emphasis on this particular archaeological information builds a cultural past for Israel that is invoked in contemporary political discourse (Abu El-Haj 2001). In Pakistan, during the colonial period, Buddhist sites such as Taxila were important locations for archaeological investigation. When the Islamic state of Pakistan was established, there was no longer any scientific interest in these sites by the Pakistani state, which emphasized only its Muslim historical roots. As Kohl points out, "Control of the past provides a source of legitimization for control of the present" (1998: 236).

The imposed national culture was usually that of the hegemonic or dominant group. In Great Britain, that meant that the language and culture of the English, the politically dominant group, were to supersede the Celtic cultures and languages of Wales, Scotland, and Ireland. Regional differences between the people of Cornwall and Yorkshire should disappear in favor of standard English language and culture. The same process occurred in France and somewhat later in Germany and in Eastern Europe. Despite attempts to impose a national culture emanating from the capital, London or Paris, regional cultural and dialect differences persisted and national identity never really fully penetrated the countryside, especially the more remote areas. More recently, in Great Britain, the Scottish people have moved beyond the assertion of their ethnic identity. The establishment of the Scottish Parliament is an expression of their movement to ethnonationalism. Wales now has its own national assembly, and the Welsh language is taught to youngsters in public schools and can be heard in radio broadcasts.

Sometimes the process of nation building involves the breakup of older empires. For example, in the nineteenth century the intellectual elites in the Czech area of the Austro-Hungarian Empire sought the freedom to have their own nation-state. Through the process of ethnogenesis, they set out to rediscover and re-create a national cultural repertoire, consciously selecting cultural items, often from rural folk culture, that they identified as Czech. Some people went to the trouble of inventing a Czech ancestry using bogus early records, such as medieval manuscripts supposedly discovered in Bohemia in 1817 and 1818 (Lass 1988).

The process of nation building accelerated in Europe after World War I with the creation of several nations out of both the old Ottoman Turkish and Austro-Hungarian Empires. However, the new nations that resulted, such as Czechoslovakia, Poland, Romania, and Yugoslavia, ended up being multiethnic states, like the new states in Africa. These states included one dominant ethnic group and several minority groups. For example, Poland included Germans, Ruthenians, Kashubians, and Jews as minority groups. In Czechoslovakia, the Czechs were the dominant group. Recently, they and the Slovaks decided that they wanted to be separate nation-states. Czechoslovakia was peacefully divided into the Czech and Slovak nations. However, even within the Czech Republic there are Moravian and Silesian people who demand a measure of autonomy and self-government (Bugajski 1994: 306–310). Gypsies, present in considerable numbers in the former Czechoslovakia, are not welcome in either the Czech Republic or Slovakia.

Both the process of nation building and its obverse—in which nation-states, once created, then collapse—are to be found not only in Europe but also in Africa and Asia (Fox 1990). These nation-states include indigenous groups, whom anthropologists have been studying since the beginning of the discipline; now the focus is on the adjustment of these societies to the penetration of the newly developed national culture.

CULTURAL IDENTITY REASSERTED
AND TRANSFORMED IN MODERN STATES

In the previous chapter we saw the way the German colonial government established a single political entity, New Ireland, where previously there had been independent, autonomous villages speaking different languages. The term **tribe** was originally used by anthropologists to refer to cultural groupings, each of which spoke its own language. Anthropologists now understand that the concept of the tribe was, in effect, created by colonial governments to enable them to deal more efficiently with groups with a common culture and language and unfamiliar forms of leadership, whose most complex political groupings were villages or bands (Fried 1975). In common usage, *tribal* is often ambiguous and even pejorative, indicating insular affiliations and traditions. In contemporary states the claims of indigenous peoples to land and other resources are acknowledged to varying degrees. The tensions between tribal identity (now conceptualized by anthropologists as ethnic identity) and national identity are continually confronted by indigenous groups in different political settings.

Most tribal people recognize that the introduction of changes from the industrialized world, which is also constantly undergoing change, has had and will continue to have a profound effect on their cultures. Frequently, people are ready and willing to accept those changes that they perceive as immediately useful, such as access to medical care and education. Sometimes change is forced upon them, and sometimes they forcibly resist change. One form of resistance is to run away, as the Kreen-akore of the tropical forest of Brazil ran from attempts to contact and pacify them. But you can only run so far and for so long, and eventually, even the Kreen-akore stopped running. Other tribal groups retain their identity and uniqueness by conscious efforts to preserve the traditional and customary and to reject the new. As a Menomini man defiantly said to the former Commissioner of Indian Affairs, "You can make the Menomini reservation into Menomini County but you can't make a white man out of me."

It has been recently pointed out that predictions made in the first half of the twentieth century about what would happen to small-scale tribal societies have turned out to be incorrect (Sahlins 1999). An earlier generation of anthropologists, typified by Boas and Malinowski, assumed that such societies could not withstand the onslaught of industrialization and Westernization; they would either become like "us" or would disappear entirely. Throughout the northern areas of the globe, peoples who formerly practiced hunting and gathering have accepted new technologies to carry out subsistence practices. They use rifles, snowmobiles, and modern traps. They have transformed their technology while retaining other aspects of their culture. The distribution of results of the hunt is carried out as it was done in the past. As we noted at several junctures, structure, like the pattern of distribution after the hunt, changes more slowly than its content—the use of snowmobiles to hunt for the animals. For example, the relationship to animals of the Yup'ik-speaking people of Alaska has continued in the same manner as in the past. As one Yup'ik informant puts it, "When we bring animals into our houses, we treat them as guests" (Sahlins 1999: xvi). Despite their long and intensive interaction with the global market economy, northern hunters such as the Yup'ik "have not fundamentally altered their customary organization of production, modes of ownership and resource control, division of labor, or patterns of distribution and consumption; nor have their extended kinship and community bonds been dissolved or the economic and social obligations thereof fallen off; neither have social (cum 'spiritual') relations to nature disappeared; and they have not lost their cultural identities, not even when they live in white folks' towns" (Sahlins 1999: xvii). The last point is a particularly important one. It is precisely when they live in "white folks' towns" and cities that there is a need to assert their cultural identity as different. The manner in which cultural identity is asserted differs according to the social context, for example, multicultural America versus ethnonationalistic European nations. As Sahlins states it, "I am simply making the point that the Eskimo are still there—and still Eskimo" (1999: vii). So are the Kwakiutl; so are the Trobrianders.

When a national identity is being built, political pressure is applied to suppress cultural differences, as noted in chapter 9. Frequently, this pressure has the opposite effect from what was intended. In response to such pressure, cultural identity is often reasserted. Malaysia has been dominated by Muslim Malay speakers since it gained its independence, after World War II. The non-Muslim Iban, who live in Sarawak, the part of Malaysia on the island of Borneo, have recently begun to reassert their cultural identity. In the past, the Iban had been headhunters and pirates in the South China Sea. Today, when Iban boys leave home to go to school, search for work, or join the military or the police, that is seen as symbolically equivalent to the traditional journey into the unknown that an Iban boy made as part of his initiation into manhood. The Iban rite of passage from boyhood to manhood is being maintained, but in a new form. Iban politicians talk about preserving their traditional lifestyle while at the same time fighting for a larger share of civil service and other employment in the Malaysian government for their people.

People develop various ways to assert their continued cultural identity. The ways they separate themselves from the dominant society are known as **boundary maintenance mechanisms**. For example, the Rio Grande Pueblos of New Mexico—Tewa and Keres—who were in contact with the Spanish missionaries and explorers in the seventeenth century, have divided their religious life into two separate domains: the indigenous one with its *katchinas* (religious figurines), priests, and *kivas* (underground religious chambers), which are operated in secret, closed off from the outside world, including the village structure of the Catholic Church. By preserving their language and much of their ritual structure, the Rio Grande Pueblos have been able to maintain their culture and their identity for more than three hundred years, despite their nominal conversion to Catholicism and their integration into the U.S. economy. In contrast, the Navajo living in the same general area have been more receptive to changes, from their acceptance of livestock raising, silver working, and rug weaving from the Spaniards, to their embrace of new ideas brought back by Navajo veterans who served in World War II.

REVITALIZATION MOVEMENTS

Often, after changes have taken place in significant aspects of their culture, people recognize that they are in the process of being stripped of their own culture but have not been assimilated into the hegemonic culture. The uncertainty of their position makes them ready to follow a religious innovator, who has a more concrete vision of a better future. Out of these conditions, religious cults are born, which have been termed **nativistic movements** or **revitalization movements**. These religious movements synthesize many traditional cultural elements with elements introduced from the dominant society.

An example of such a movement is the Handsome Lake religion of the Seneca, one of the six tribes that constituted the League of the Iroquois. By the end of the American Revolution, the Seneca had suffered partial devastation of their villages, decimation of their population, and the general dislocation of many aspects of their culture. In the 1780s, Handsome Lake, who was a *sachem*, or tribal leader, of the Seneca, had a series of visions, during which he had contact with the various Iroquois deities and foresaw what the life of the Seneca should be like in the future. What he envisioned was an amalgam of older Iroquois traditions and new ideas derived from the Quakers and other missionaries. The social organization of the Seneca had been based on matrilineal descent and uxorilocal postmarital residence. In contrast, Handsome Lake stressed the importance of the nuclear family and deemphasized matrilineage. The Quakers had come as missionaries to the Seneca, and many of their economic values, such as thrift, were adopted by Handsome Lake. At the same time, much traditional Seneca ceremonialism was also maintained. Handsome Lake had many adherents during his lifetime, although there were other political leaders who opposed and competed with him. After his death, his doctrines were written down and formed the Code of Handsome Lake. Though it was revolutionary when it first appeared, over the centuries the Handsome Lake religion, as it came to be called, became a conservative force as new changes were accepted by the Seneca. Today the supporters of the Handsome Lake religion are among the more conservative members of the Seneca tribe living on their reservation in upstate New York. What began as a vision of Seneca accommodation to the culture of the white population was transformed over time into a bulwark resisting change.

Cargo Cults

A particular type of revitalization movement in Melanesia is the **cargo cult**. Cargo cults made their appearance early in the twentieth century. However, they proliferated after World War II, which was a period of more intensive contact with outsiders, particularly with the American soldiers who drove out the Japanese and used the islands of Melanesia as a staging base. The

Melanesians were astonished by the technological might of the Western world, as represented by the American armed forces. Like all revitalization movements, these cargo cults revolved about a charismatic leader or prophet who had a vision of deceased ancestors rising from the dead. They would arrive in a big ship or plane, bringing an inexhaustible cargo of steel axes, razor blades, tobacco, tinned beef, rice, and rifles. More recently, the expected cargoes include transistor radios, wrist watches, and motorcycles. People built piers into the sea, erected huge warehouses, and even prepared landing strips when planes were expected. They neglected their gardening and often killed off their pigs, since the expectation was that no one would have to work anymore after the cargo arrived. Sometimes elements of Christianity were included in the visions of the prophet, so that Jesus Christ was expected to arrive along with the cargo.

Like all other revitalization movements, cargo cults are a synthesis of the old and the new. In a situation of culture contact in which tribal peoples find themselves helpless and overwhelmed by the power of the dominant society, a prophet appears who preaches turning to the ancestors to seek their help in acquiring the very things that make the dominant society so powerful. The cargo is seen as the secret of the white people's power. Like all forms of religion that attempt to explain the inexplicable, cargo cults attempt to offer a supernatural explanation of what it is that makes white people so powerful. Converts to the cargo cult have faith that the secret of white people's power, the cargo, will come to them as a result of supernatural forces. Cargo cults are religious movements, though many of them are short-lived. At the same time, however, they make statements about power relations; for when the cargo comes, the present situation will be reversed and the powerless will become powerful. Cargo cults exemplify how the force and emotive power of religious belief can add great strength to a political movement. In the past, such religious cults in East and West Africa were dreaded by colonial powers. Nativistic movements, revitalization movements, and cargo cults represent responses to colonialism that combine cultural continuity as well as cultural change. The particular forms they take not only represent responses to colonialism but also reveal a great deal about the cultures in which they are found.

Rebuilding Cultural Identity

Sometimes, a group loses everything except its sense of its own cultural identity. The Mashantucket Pequot Tribal Nation of Connecticut is such a group. The Pequot were nearly obliterated as a people in the Pequot War of 1637and stripped of most of their land. However, they were able to demonstrate to the Department of the Interior that their tribal existence never ceased, enabling them to receive recognition as a tribe from the American government on October 18, 1983. The introduction of high-stakes gambling in 1992 has made the tribe wealthy and influential and has enabled members to fund events that are part of a conscious attempt to "re-create" their culture. They have approached the task of cultural building or rebuilding on two different fronts. First, they have sponsored Mashantucket Pequot historical conferences, which bring together scholars to discuss topics such as the history of the Indians of New England and the current state of knowledge about native peoples of New England and their adjustment to the encounter with Euro-Americans. To this end they have established their own museum, which focuses on Native

American culture in general and on Pequot culture in particular. Second, they sponsor a powwow, or Schemitzun, translated as "Feast of Green Corn and Dance," which brings together American Indian performers from many tribes all over the country. The performers are attracted in part by the richest purse offered on the competitive powwow circuit. After almost three hundred years, the traditions of the Pequot are almost forgotten, along with their language and ceremonial songs and dances. The Pequots are endeavoring to re-create their own culture by borrowing and adapting what they can from other tribes. The process the Pequot are now going through, as they attempt to construct a tribal or cultural identity, is identical to that involved in the fashioning of ethnic identity that is now going on in multicultural America.

Blood, Culture, and Race

The Cherokee of Oklahoma illustrate the way identity can be "socially and politically constructed and how that process is embedded in ideas of blood, color and race" (Sturm 2002: 2). The federal government requires that American Indians must have one Native grandparent in order for them

Dance contestants in the Mashantucket Pequot Tribe Feast of Green Corn and Dance held in 2006 at the Pequot's Foxwoods Resort Casino. Representatives from five hundred tribal nations from the United States and Canada participated in this annual exhibition and dance competition.

to obtain social services such as health care, housing, and food commodities. They need to present a certificate in which the Bureau of Indian Affairs and their tribe have authenticated the fact that they are Indians. Despite this "racial" restriction, the Cherokee nation has a multiracial population of more than 175,000 members of which as many as 87,000 have less than 1/16 Cherokee ancestry. Cherokee tribal law merely requires that an individual be a lineal descendant of a tribal member (Sturm 2002: 2). Informants use the metaphor of blood as the most important thing about Cherokee identity. One may ask how the concept of blood is understood to be significant in this situation, since the range in the population is from full-blood to a miniscule amount (Sturm 2002: 201).

Before the arrival of Europeans, the Cherokee had a class of slaves who were captives taken during intertribal warfare. If they were adopted, then they became full members of the tribe; otherwise, they were individuals in bondage. After the arrival of the Europeans, a large-scale Indian slave trade developed, whereby individuals captured from other communities were exchanged for European goods. By the middle of the eighteenth century with the African slave trade at its height, the Cherokee shifted to a trade in runaway African slaves. In fact, the Cherokee themselves had African slaves up until 1863. Euro-American conceptualizations about race were adopted despite the fact that sexual relations and intermarriage between Africans and Cherokee had begun to take place. The council of the Cherokee nation passed an act forbidding such intermarriages as well as intermarriage with whites.

Today, tribal membership is claimed by multiracial individuals, some of whom are "black" and the descendants of "freedmen" and former slaves, and others who are "white." Though they may be able to document the necessary descent by blood, they may still be rejected by some Cherokee and other Native Americans. The question of who is to be counted as Cherokee is an important one. To Native Americans like the Cherokee, the metaphor of blood is the "measure of racial, cultural, social and national belonging . . . [and] Federal Indian Policy and Cherokee national policy both have fetishized and objectified Native-American blood" (Sturm 2002: 203). Cherokee have conflated ideas about blood, race, color, and culture, with blood becoming a "particularly potent substance for Cherokee identity" (Sturm 2002: 203).

ETHNOGENESIS

Contact and colonialism can produce a process by which a people assert a new ethnic identity and take on a new name. This is known as **ethnogenesis**. William Sturtevant first used the term to refer to the process through which the Seminole historically differentiated and separated themselves from the Creek, the larger group of which they were a part. Nancy Hickerson (1996) has noted that the historic record reveals the disappearance, often quite abruptly, of certain peoples (such as the Mayan Empire) and the sudden appearance of others (such as the Scythians), likening this process to the three-stage sequence that Van Gennep (1960) proposed for rites of passage, discussed in chapter 10. The first phase is separation, the severing of a group's previous loyalties; the second is a liminal phase during which surviving ties wither away and new ones are initiated; the third is the birth of a new identity, which is affirmed through the adoption of new rituals and a new mythology to validate them. This last phase "may obscure all traces of the earlier history (or histories) of the population and even promote a belief in a miraculous origin or special creation" (Hickerson 1996: 70). Manipulation of the historical past is one of the distinctive characteristics of the process of ethnogenesis. As Hill observes, "Ethnogenesis is not merely a label for the historical emergence of culturally distinct peoples but a concept encompassing people's simultaneously cultural and political struggles to create enduring identities in general contexts of radical change and discontinuity" (1996: 1).

In the ebb and flow of populations after the arrival of the Europeans in the New World, ethnogenesis occurred many times as groups were physically dislocated from the areas they had traditionally exploited. During the sixteenth and seventeenth centuries, Tanoan-speaking people known as the Jumano, who were bison hunters and traders, were exploiting an area east of the Rio Grande in the southern Plains. As a consequence of unsuccessful warfare with the Apache over trade routes and access to trade centers, they appear to have dispersed, many moving north. The use of the name *Jumano* then declined, but subgroups with their own names continued. The term *Kiowa* later appeared as the label for these groups, now in their new homeland in the Platte-Arkansas River area. Today, the people of the modern Kiowa nation have an origin myth that begins with their ancestors' emergence from the underworld in a cold land far north—thought to be in the Yellowstone River Valley. The ancestors subsequently moved south and east to their historic territory (Hickerson 1996: 83). Here we see a sequence in which the Jumano disappear and "die" and a new people, the Kiowa nation, are born.

ETHNONATIONALISM

The process of ethnogenesis not only is applicable to the tribal or ethnic groups in the New World but also parallels the development of **ethnonationalism** in Europe. When European ethnonationalists are able to take control of the state, they co-opt the state's use of force, which they now turn to their own nationalistic purposes. Ethnogenesis in Europe has a long history. The French Revolution may be seen as the expression of emerging French national self-identity (Pickett 1996). Under the banner of "Liberty, Equality, and Fraternity," Napoleon brutally brought France's "civilizing principles" to the rest of Europe. Though pretending to spread universal principles, he was actually expanding the scope of French nationalism and hegemony. As often happened throughout history, one group's ethnogenic awakening produced a reaction among that group's neighbors. German ethnogenesis and the movement toward German unification in the latter half of the nineteenth century was a reaction to what was happening in France. This led Germany to develop a sense of its own special destiny.

As Pickett points out, "Ethnogenesis is hostile to knowledge" (1996: 16). Ethnogenesis ignores science in favor of its newly created myths; it denies history in order to distort it and control it. French hegemony under Napoleon—that is, nationalism under the guise of universal principles—proved ephemeral. In the same way, Soviet Russian hegemony—Russian nationalism under the guise of universal socialist principles—has also disappeared, as will be discussed below.

Multiculturalism

A multicultural state is composed of several ethnic groups, none of which is officially recognized as dominant. Instead, all are ideologically considered equal. In the nineteenth century, when the United States welcomed large numbers of immigrants seeking refuge from persecution, they became Americans, part of what was referred to as the "melting pot." American, as a national identity, was being constructed, and an American culture was developing. However, since the 1960s we have come to think of ourselves differently. Most of us now view ourselves as a multicultural society. This means a recognition of diversity, highlighting "neglected aspects of our social history, particularly the histories of women and minorities" (Trotman 2002: ix). Other nations, for example, Great Britain, are reflecting on whether they have become multicultural states. In contrast, the French state has officially rejected multiculturalism. However, as noted in chapter 9, the French legal system has accepted Islamic law in cases involving family law. Muslims from North Africa who have settled in France are challenging the official suppression of ethnically based identity. Multiculturalism is distinctly different from the characteristically European situation in which one ethnic group is the national core. In that case, the values of the dominant group constitute the national culture, politically and religiously, and that group dominates smaller minorities, creating two classes of citizenship.

As noted above, in Great Britain today, political power and linguistic recognition have now been given to the Scottish and Welsh people. However, those people who migrated to Great Britain from other parts of the commonwealth have been dealt with in a different way. Earlier waves of people coming to England as conquerors, like the French, left marks of their culture and language. Other migrants, in later centuries, have been assimilated into mainstream English culture and life, so that by the middle of the twentieth century there was a widespread belief that British culture was homogeneous, though, in reality, it was dominated by English culture.

After World War II, large numbers of migrants from the Caribbean and, more particularly, India and Pakistan came to Great Britain to better themselves economically, accepting work that the English no longer wished to do. Though it was originally thought that they would return to their homelands, instead, they sent for their families and settled permanently. Language and religious differences set apart the South Asians, especially, from the rest of the population. Islam provides its adherents with a communal way of life with separate religious institutions—mosques, separate schools, the right to wear their type of clothing and eat *halal* meat—all of which challenge assimilation. Though the British authorities have made concessions in the direction of multiculturalism, British Muslim activists have been challenging Islamophobia, which has not diminished with time (Ellis and Khan 1999: 45). In fact, since 9/11 Islamophobia in Britain has increased. State support for separate Muslim schools has been an especially thorny issue. Multiculturalism, as currently practiced in Britain, still does not allow for full participation in the society if one chooses a public Muslim identity rather than an accommodation that confines one's Muslim identity to the domestic and local community environments.

Although the political discourse of multiculturalism is publically voiced, Britain has remained essentially a homogeneous, Western, Christian society rather than a pluralist society accepting of people who are significantly different in religion or race. Economic advancement is not the same for the "ethnic population" as it is for British whites, since a racial barrier exists, and nonwhites with PhDs find it hard to find work suitable to their education level. The British white population and British ethnic minorities still lead mostly separate lives and the hyphenated Britons do not feel that they are a part of Britain. The education system is sometimes the only arena that is multiethnic. Links with those "back home" are still maintained by sending remittances and by frequent visits.

ETHNICITY AND NATIONALISM AFTER COMMUNISM

After the Russian Revolution in 1917, the Union of Soviet Socialist Republics was created out of the Russian Empire. This empire had been based on the conquest of many non-Russian peoples, just as the Ottoman Empire had included many non-Turkish people and the Austro-Hungarian Empire had incorporated peoples who were neither Austrians nor Hungarians. This example reveals the dialectic between hegemonic state culture and different ethnic groups who desire to have their own nation-states. The Marxist Soviet government tried to construct a Soviet culture as the national culture of the Union of Soviet Socialist Republics. This Soviet culture included the idea that workers of the world should unite as a class and rise above national sentiments. The government's attitude toward the different "nationalities" vacillated between the celebration of ethnic differences and the suppression of ethnic national identity, which was seen as challenging Soviet identity. When the Soviet Union crumbled at the end of the 1980s, its fifteen constituent republics became independent sovereign states. Ethnic minorities, who formerly had had their own autonomous republics or autonomous *oblasts* (districts) contained within the newly established independent states, demanded self-determination in the form of cultural and political autonomy or independence. Such ethnic minorities exemplify ethnonationalism as they strive to establish independent sovereign states.

These identities, which had been suppressed during the Communist era, propel politics in all the areas of the former Soviet Union today. The newly independent republics must cope with the legacy of seventy years of Soviet rule. This means that they must deal with larger or smaller numbers of individuals who are culturally Russian or members of other ethnic groups who migrated there or were moved there by the Soviet government. They must also contend with territorial borders that were drawn by the Soviet state. Within the Russian state itself, ethnonationalism has emerged and is being dealt with.

The Chechen region of Russia presents an unusual sort of problem involving ethnonationalism and ethnic violence, which has long historical roots. The Chechens, a Muslim people who speak a Caucasian language totally unrelated to Russian, were conquered by the czarist empire in the nineteenth century. They resisted Russian domination and control. During World War II the Chechens sided with Nazi Germany and fought against their enemy Russia. In response to their traitorous actions, Joseph Stalin deported many of them to Siberia and few lived to return home. The eve of the post-Soviet Russia found the Chechens, an ethnic minority fighting for self-determination, facing the majority Russians who considered them gangsters and traitors. The Russian government is determined not to grant them their independence—in contrast to the autonomy granted to Tajiks, Uzbeks, Kirgyz, Turkomen, and others. The Chechens have turned to fighting for their freedom and independence. Terror is one of the weapons they use. After the occurrences of 9/11, the American government grouped Chechen revolutionaries with other Islamic terrorists like Al Queda, to the delight of the Russian government. The U.S. government has also supported Georgia in its fight against rebellious Muslim groups, which spread from Chechnya into Georgia. At the same time, as we shall see below, the Georgians are fighting another Muslim people within the state of Georgia, the Abkhasians.

The new nation-state of Georgia, in the Caucasus Mountains south of Russia, contains several non-Georgian ethnic groups with sizable populations, such as the South Ossetians and the Abkhazians. In addition, Georgia has ethnic Russians, Armenians, and Azerbaijanis. Meskhetians originally lived in Georgia but were expelled by Stalin after World War II and sent to live in Uzbekistan. Under Soviet rule, the Abkhazians and Ossetians had some degree of political and cultural autonomy, though the Georgians were politically dominant in the Republic. The Abkhazians are linguistically and culturally distinct from the Georgians, though they are physically similar to West Georgians (Benet 1974). Their mythic history stresses their distinctiveness. However, they have historically been oriented toward the Mediterranean since Abkhazia is on the Black Sea. Christianity entered Abkhazia in the sixth century, and Islam much later, in the fifteenth and sixteenth centuries. While most Abkhazians are nominally Muslim, a small minority have remained Christian. Abkhazians retain their cultural distinctiveness through their style of dress, dance, folklore, legends, kinship system, and other cultural items. Their exceedingly difficult language, which Russians, Georgians, and Armenians rarely learn, also serves to set them apart. Within the Abkhazian Autonomous Republic, the Abkhazians form only a quarter of the population; the other three-quarters are Russians, Georgians, Greeks, Turks, and Armenians.

The forces of ethnonationalism propelled the Georgian Republic to independence. However, the attempts of the Abkhazians and South Ossetians, with their own ethnonationalistic feelings, to gain their independence or autonomy were seen as threats to the Georgian state and Georgian political hegemony. Though political leadership at the local level was in the hands of Abkhazians and South Ossetians, they were overrepresented in low-class manual and rural occupations (Jones 1992). The Georgians considered these ethnic groups not entitled to their own sovereignty. In fact, all those who were not ethnic Georgians were seen as having no rights, as foreigners in Georgia. South Ossetians and others, such as Russians, were viewed as invaders who should return to where they came from. Government policy favored Georgian expansion into non-Georgian areas. The aim of the educational system was to indoctrinate all students in Georgian language and culture, regardless of their ethnic background. The Abkhazians and Ossetians declared their independence, resulting in fighting on all sides. The Abkhazian fight for independence has become a subject for the international media, as shown by the accompanying photograph. The South Ossetians of Georgia would like to unite with the North Ossetians, who live in Russia, which is now a separate country. The Abkhazians have succeeded in gaining control over their territory. In fact, some 200,000 Georgians who fled Abkhazia claim that they have been subjected

A soldier of the Abkhaz army during an operation in the Kodori gorge on October 17, 2001, which separates the breakaway Georgian republic of Abkhazia from Georgia; Abkhazians have been fighting the Georgians since the breakup of the Soviet Union.

to a policy of ethnic cleansing. Russia continues to maintain several military bases in Georgia. The Georgian case exemplifies a situation in which a politically dominant group's attempts to homogenize a population of different ethnic groups result in demands by those groups not merely for cultural autonomy but for complete political independence.

Like Georgia, the newly independent nation of Uzbekistan in Central Asia is ethnically diverse. The Uzbeks themselves, two-thirds of the population, are Muslims who speak a Turkic language. They are in the process of making decisions about which part of their historic past constitutes their true Uzbek heritage. This would then be used as a rallying point for building Uzbek national culture and developing an Uzbek national identity. Is the focus of Uzbek nation-building to be the heritage represented by Turkic Runic script and the Chaghatai Turkic language (Menges 1967) or the Islamic tradition with its Arabic script, which the Arabs brought into the area when they overran the Turks in the seventh and eighth centuries? The question of whether to shift from Cyrillic, introduced by the Russians, to Arabic or Turkic Runic script represents the dilemma of whether Uzbek heritage is to be Islamic or pre-Islamic. The building of national identity is always a creative as well as a political process. This often involves choosing to emphasize one aspect rather than another from a very complicated multiethnic history. The choice of one script over another, as in this case, becomes an important political decision.

Most recently, the state institutions of Uzbekistan have been under attack by an Islamic fundamentalist insurgency, known as the Islamic Movement of Uzbekistan, which desires to purge the current government of corruption. The resurgence of Islam in Central Asia as a whole has led some people in this area to talk about an Islamic state—a revival of an earlier idea of a grand Turkestan, or, in more modern terms, a United States of Asia, which would join Uzbekistan with Kyrgyzstan, Kazakhstan, Tadzhikistan, and Turkmenia, all nations with Islamic backgrounds (Hall 1992). The Uzbek Islamic fundamentalist movement has sent fighters from its bases in northern Tajikistan into Kyrgyzstan to use villages in an Uzbek enclave in that country as bases from which to attack Uzbekistan. Russia and Uzbekistan sent support to the Kyrgyzstan government to repel this attack. There are Uzbeks also living in Afghanistan where they are a minority population. We will discuss their relationship with the American-supported Afghan government below.

ETHNIC DIFFERENCES, ETHNIC VIOLENCE, AND THE NEW NATION OF AFGHANISTAN

Afghanistan provides us with an excellent example of why it is so important to understand the culture, the social structure, and the political system of other regions of the world today, particularly regions with which the United States is directly involved. After 9/11, American forces went into Afghanistan to seek out and destroy Al Qaeda and the Taliban, who were governing Afghanistan and providing protection for the Al Qaeda forces. After the Taliban were no longer in control of Afghanistan, our troops moved in and we became involved in nation-building in a country with a shallow tradition of "nationhood" and with a mix of many ethnic groups. The Afghanistan situation was very different, for example, from the ethnonationalism of the former Yugoslavia, which was found in part of Kosovo, Bosnia, Serbia, and Croatia, where people speaking a common language (Serbo-Croatian) were each demanding their own nation-states.

In this discussion of Afghanistan we will focus on the Pushtuns, the largest ethnic group in the country. They number perhaps 10 to 12 million people and straddle the border between Afghanistan and Pakistan. Perhaps 7 million Pushtuns are in Afghanistan (Magnus and Naby 2002: 93). The remainder are in Pakistan. As a result of colonialism, the Pushtuns are found on both sides of the Afghanistan/Pakistan border. As czarist Russia extended its empire southward, it came into contact with British India. During the nineteenth and early twentieth centuries, Britain and Russia waged the "Great Game," which was a war over the land of the Pushtuns (also known as "Pathans" in the writings of Rudyard Kipling and others). The Durand line marks the present boundary between Pakistan and Afghanistan. After colonial England fought and lost three Afghan wars trying to conquer Kabul, Afghanistan's capital, the buffer nation of Afghanistan was created with Russia's approval, which separated Russia from India, with an eastern "tail," the Wakhan Corridor, which served to further separate China from India and Russia.

As a consequence, the nation of Afghanistan includes a large number of ethnic groups. To the north are Tajiks, Uzbeks, Turkomen, and Mountain Khirgiz, each of which at the present time also has its independent nation-state outside Afghanistan as a result of the breakup of the Soviet Union. Other ethnic groups are the Hazaras, Baluch, Aimaqs, and Nuristanis who were non-Muslims in the nineteenth century but were conquered and converted at the end of that century. The Pushtuns, the largest ethnic group, had ruled Afghanistan through a monarchy until 1978. Though the Pushtuns dominated the political system and exercised hegemony over Tajiks, Uzbeks, and all the others, they did not try to make them into Pushtuns. The pattern had been set more than two hundred years ago by the great Afghan ruler Ahmed Shah Durrani (1747–1773), who conquered and ruled over an empire that extended from Persia to Delhi in northern India. Over his own people, the Afghans, he ruled as an "elected tribal chief," but over conquered peoples he exacted tribute (Magnus and Naby 2002: 30).

The border between Afghanistan and Pakistan is sometimes referred to as a lawless area, but it is not lawless at all. It is simply beyond the control of the state governments of Afghanistan and Pakistan. The law that governs this tribal area is the customary law of the Pushtuns. Various Pushtun tribes are found on both sides of the border. Many are nomadic pastoral peoples. Earlier we noted that pastoralists move with their herds to rich summer pastures high in the mountains, and back down to lowland areas when autumn comes. Pushtun nomads move their herds into the Sulayman Mountains of Afghanistan in summer, and back down to the Indus Valley in Pakistan in winter. When they moved with their herds, Pushtun men were always armed—Enfield rifles in the past, Kalashnikovs more recently. This has always been one of the world's most porous borders. When American military forces tried to pin down Al Qaeda forces along this border in Operation Anaconda, they found that the Al Qaeda (and probably Osama bin Laden as well) simply crossed into Pakistan. The new Afghan government, with little tax revenue to depend on, is trying to collect customs taxes more diligently along this border. However, Pushtuns living there have depended on smuggling from time immemorial. In fact, their definition of "freedom" is not to be under the yoke of a central government, which collects taxes from them.

In an earlier chapter we discussed the use of the term *warlord* as used in newspaper accounts. Control of the drug trade has created a number of warlords in this area. These warlords operate much like Big Men or Mafia dons do. Their access to resources (arms, smuggling, the drug trade) enables them to act as centers of redistribution of resources to their followers, who are predominantly from the same tribe. Barth, who studied Pushtuns of the Yusufzai tribe in Swat, Pakistan, observes that every Yusufzai "chief" had his men's house. Allegiance to a particular chief is expressed by visiting his men's house and eating the food he provides. Barth observes that "only through his hospitality, through the device of gift-giving, does he create the wider obligations and dependence which he can then draw upon in the form of personal political support—in the final resort, military support" (1959: 12). Chiefs in Afghanistan are acting as warlords. These leaders are now also being referred to as "field commanders." They head armed militias, bound to their leader by Pushtun concepts of loyalty. During conflict, however, the leader may ally himself with one faction or another.

The customary code of the Pushtuns is known as Pushtunwali. "Equality of all adult members of the group is, at least in theory, one of the key principles of Pushtun life" (Vogelsang 2002: 24). Another principle is hospitality. Hospitality is obligatory to outsiders, and Pushtun leaders show their generosity by feeding strangers, along with their followers, in their guest houses. In return, one has obligations of loyalty. However, the Pushtun concept of loyalty is to a personal leader, not to a principle or to an ideology (Caroe 1958: 256). An extension of hospitality is the obligation to offer sanctuary. Someone fleeing the law may request sanctuary. To refuse the request would stain one's honor (Caroe 1958: 351). Finally, revenge against someone who has killed a member of one's clan is an obligation (Barth 1959: 83–86). This type of customary law, which bases carrying out criminal punishment on the kinship system rather than on central government, is an anachronism in many ways. Yet it prevails among Pushtuns in the tribal areas of Pakistan and in large parts of Afghanistan. This is not simply the absence of law. This very different customary legal system is in effect in the Pushtun tribal area.

The social structure of the Pushtuns is one that we have encountered before. It is the segmentary lineage system described for the Cyrenaican Bedouin (on page 116), and for the Somali. All Pushtun believe that they are descended from a common ancestor, named Qays (Caroe 1958: 11). Pushtuns are subdivided into a number of tribes, perhaps thirty or forty, stretching from Quetta and Kandahar northeast into Swat, in Pakistan. The tribes, in turn, are divided into clans and subclans. The Pushtuns are patrilineal, and practice patrilocal postmarital residence, as do all their neighbors in Afghanistan, the central Asia peoples to their north, and the Persian-speaking peoples to their west. The central feature of segmentary lineage systems is to foster a balance of power. If one lineage, clan, or tribe grows more powerful, another opposing lineage, clan, or tribe will rise up to challenge the first. When there is an external threat from a common enemy, like the British in colonial times or the Soviets in the 1970s and 1980s, Pushtuns will unite to meet the threat.

The early history is dominated by Ahmed Shah Durrani, of the Abdali tribe. He took the name Durrani, meaning "pearl of pearls," for the group of tribes centering in Kandahar. They constitute the Durrani major section of the segmentary lineage system. Opposing him and his successors were the leaders of the Ghalji (or Ghilzai) tribes, another major section, centered in Ghazni, many of whom were nomadic pastoralists. In the wars during the eighteenth and nineteenth centuries over control of parts of northern India, the Durrani and Ghalji vied with one another, though the Durrani managed to maintain control during this whole period until Mohamad Zahir Shah, a Durrani of the Populzai tribe, abdicated in 1973. Da'ud Khan, his cousin and of Durrani descent as well, led a military coup and established a republic. In 1978, Nur Mohammad Taraki, of the opposing Ghalji faction, came to power and established a communist state. He carried out a purge of all Durrani elements in the government, and Da'ud and his family were killed. The opposing segments of the segmentary structure had regained control from the Durranis.

The present government of Hamid Karzai, a Durrani from the Populzai tribe, established after the overthrow of the Taliban regime and supported by the "nation-builders" from America, rests on a very precarious balance. Pushtuns in general are not accustomed to a strong central government, and the balance of power inherent in their segmentary lineage structure favors a decentralized structure. Military commanders (sometimes called warlords) are traditionally found dispersed in various clans and tribes. In addition to balancing the forces within the Pushtun political system, it is also necessary to balance political leaders of the various different ethnic groups in the country—especially Tajiks and Uzbeks, with their own array of field commanders and warlords. This is the culture and the underlying social structure that American-led state-building policy in the area must cope with.

ETHNIC PROCESSES IN SRI LANKA

The ethnic conflict that has continued in Sri Lanka for decades exemplifies the way ethnic identity is heightened and transformed under colonial conditions: the role played by differences in religion and language, the operative economic factors, and the ways majority-minority relations can worsen to the point of civil war in postcolonial states (see Tambiah 1986, 1988; Daniel 1996). The conflict is between two ethnic groups: the Sinhalese, who speak an Indo-European language, and the Tamils, who speak a Dravidian language. Both languages have borrowed significantly from one another over the centuries. Since 74 percent of the population is Sinhalese, that language became the official language when Sri Lanka gained its independence from Britain. However, public education continued to be provided in parallel Tamil and Sinhalese tracks. The majority of the Sinhalese are Buddhist, with some Christians, mostly Roman Catholics; the Tamil are primarily Hindu, also with a Roman Catholic minority. There is, in addition, a small Muslim population descended from Arab, Persian, and Malay seafarers and people from the Malabar Coast of India. There are many cultural similarities between the Sinhala and Tamil groups, despite these differences in language and religion and different mythic charters.

The Tamils consider the northern part of the island of Sri Lanka their traditional homeland, though much of the Tamil population is scattered among the Sinhalese in the rest of the island. The two were separate ethnic communities until the advent of British colonial rule in 1796. The British developed a colonial economy on the island, then known as Ceylon, that was based on tea plantations. A small English-speaking elite, educated in English-style schools run by missionaries, included both Tamils and Sinhalese. However, for some time the Sinhalese have resented what they see as a Tamil monopoly of the white-collar and professional positions that were the rewards of such an education.

Sri Lanka became independent in 1948. During the postwar period, Sri Lanka went through the uneven economic development that characterized many developing countries. It tried to organize a welfare state to improve the educational and health systems for its people, but its economy did not improve. The plantation economy declined, attempts to develop exports failed, living standards fell, and rising expectations went unfulfilled as young people left school educated but with no employment prospects. The underclass began to suffer, but protests were organized in terms of ethnic differences rather than along class lines. This is an example of what we noted earlier in this chapter, the way class differences may be expressed as ethnic differences. Animosity was directed by the Sinhalese majority, who saw themselves as the original population, against the Tamils, whom they characterized as outsiders.

From the beginning of the colonial period, a revival of Buddhism was spearheaded by Buddhist monks who borrowed the evangelical techniques of the Christian missionaries who had come to Ceylon under the colonial umbrella. Their role became a more secular one involving social service and eventually politics (Seneviratne 2001: 15). While the urban, English-speaking elite had political power, a group of Sinhalese-speaking rural leaders, schoolteachers, indigenous medical practitioners, traders, and merchants began to see themselves as the conservators of Sinhalese language, culture, and religion. They joined forces with the monks in the 1950s in a Sinhala revival, which emphasized not only the Sinhalese language and Buddhism, but also a view of the Sinhalese as an Aryan race who were claimed to be different from the allegedly dark-skinned, Dravidian-speaking Tamils. This use of "Aryan" raised the "bogey of racist claims" (Tambiah 1986:5). It represented the imposition of a conceptualization from India, where "fair-skinned Aryans" were the invaders from the north who conquered the "dark-skinned" people of the south. The Sinhalese looked to a mythic history that saw their destiny as conquerors and rulers over the whole island for the glory of Buddhism and the expulsion of the Tamil invaders in the north.

The strength of this mythic history is seen as the reason the Sinhalese majority still persist in exploiting the Tamil minority, despite the fact that the alleged Tamil overrepresentation in education and employment was corrected. In recent years the consequence has been Tamil reprisals and violence, and the Sinhalese have responded in kind. The Tamil now demand self-determination, recognition as a nationality, and a guarantee that they will be able to continue to live in their traditional homeland. The government of India became involved when Prime Minister Rajiv Gandhi, who had originally sided with the Tamil separatists, tried in 1985 to broker a peace settlement between the Sri Lankan government and the Tamil rebels. When he sent Indian troops into Sri Lanka in 1987 as peacemakers, they clashed with Tamil guerrillas and the relationship soured. In 1991 Gandhi was assassinated, reputedly by a Tamil rebel group. For some time the Tamil have been using "suicide bombers" and as a consequence have been labeled terrorists by the United States and Britain.

The prospects for a lasting peace are still in question. The Tamils seek an independent country as their objective, with the cities held by the Tamils constituting the territory of the Tamil state, Eelam. The Tamil rebel movement "maintains itself through an international network with offices in London and Paris and through the financial contributions of expatriate Tamils all around the world" (Eller 1999: 139–40). This is one example of the role of members of a diaspora supporting an ethnonationalist movement.

Anthropological comparison of the Tamil-Sinhalese conflict in Sri Lanka with similar conflicts in other parts of the world reveals the same militant, rampant ethnonationalism related to religious differences. In Sri Lanka, a resurgent Sinhalese Buddhism felt itself threatened by Tamil Hinduism from the north. Once again, class intersected with ethnicity, as resentment was expressed against Tamils, who were seen as educated and successful in greater numbers than they should have been. Although there were indeed real differences between Sinhalese and Tamils in Sri Lanka, their ethnic identities were invented and constructed, based on both mythic histories and differing

Saffron-robed Buddhist Sinhalese monks staged a protest in Colombo, Sri Lanka's capital, in 1996 to condemn Tamil attacks on innocent civilians. The political conflict in Sri Lanka continues to mobilize religious and linguistic symbols associated with Buddhist Sinhalese and Hindu Tamils.

views of recent history, as well as in oppositional terms—"we are the opposite of them." Each side defined itself in terms of its opponent. Troops from other nations or international organizations sent in as peacekeepers do not always succeed in keeping combatants apart; in this case, Indian military forces ended up fighting the Tamil insurgents. Military combatants and civilians on both sides suffer in such fierce ethnic conflicts through repeating cycles of violence and retribution.

IMMIGRATION AND MULTICULTURALISM IN THE UNITED STATES

As we noted in chapter 1, modern human beings have always migrated from one place to another; in the process they inevitably confront the cultures and institutions of other groups of people. With the advent of modern states, people crossing borders must negotiate the legal and cultural systems of the receiving state; they are classified and regulated according to the norms and practices of those institutions. Diverse groups within the borders of the United States confront the contradictions of American cultural and political institutions that promote the rhetoric of diversity while simultaneously privileging some groups over others. Restrictions on immigration and citizenship are continuous themes in American history. These debates in different periods of

American history illustrate how ideas about race, ethnicity, and multiculturalism are constructed in political discourse and enforced through state law and policy.

According to archaeologists and geneticists, the first settlers of North America started coming across the Bering Strait perhaps as early as 25,000 or 30,000 years ago; migration into North and South America is estimated to have begun sometime after approximately 16,500 years ago (Goebel et al. 2008). In their construction of their cultural past, as we have seen with the Kiowa, American Indians view their mythic ancestors as having emerged from places in their native areas. Hence, they have always been in America, which is what their mythology tells them, tying them to the landmarks of their territories from time immemorial. They see the "story," told by scientists of the peopling of the New World by populations originating in Asia and crossing the Bering Strait as an attempt to turn them into immigrants in America. This migration narrative undercuts their hard-won battles with the American state for cultural and territorial autonomy based on claims of indigeneity.

These conflicting narratives of identity and history moved from anthropological journals into mainstream journalism with the discovery of a skeleton in southeastern Washington State in 1996. "Kennewick Man" was accidentally discovered on federal land administered by the Army Corps of Engineers. Scientists who first examined the remains estimated the skeleton to be approximately 9,000 years old, and originally classified its cranial features as "Caucasoid." A facial reconstruction of Kennewick Man attracted widespread media attention, due in large part to its similarity to the actor Patrick Stewart. Historian Vine DeLoria Jr. pointed out striking similarities between Kennewick Man's facial reconstruction and a portrait of Chief Black Hawk painted in 1833 (Thomas 2000: xxv); however, these images did not attract equal media attention.

An alliance of five Northwest tribes claimed their rights to the remains. Citing the **Native American Graves Protection and Repatriation Act (NAGPRA)**, they invoked their right to bury the remains promptly, consistent with their religious norms for proper handling of a dead ancestor. A group of scientists sought access to the skeleton to study it for the important information this unique find could reveal about early human populations in the New World. The battle over control of the remains moved into the American court system. In 2004 a federal appeals court ruled that the tribes failed to establish the cultural identity of Kennewick Man as American Indian. The remains were moved to the Burke Museum at the University of Washington where they remain under the control of the Corps of Engineers. The case of Kennewick Man raises important questions about the political uses of science in discourses about race, identity, and history. "[T]he pivotal issue at Kennewick is not about religion or science. It is about politics. The dispute is about control and power, not philosophy. Who gets to control ancient American history—governmental agencies, the academic community, or modern Indian people?" (Thomas 2000: xxvii).

The Europeans who came to North America in the 1600s as colonists called themselves English, Irish, Scottish, Dutch, Swedish, German, French, Spanish, and Russian. Slaves who were brought from Africa were imported by the colonists to work the plantations that had been established. An American culture began to develop from an English-Continental base, and earlier national identities merged to become an American identity. In the 1840s, American culture was portrayed by Alexis de Toqueville as emphasizing entrepreneurship, the "self-made man," personal advancement, individualism, restlessness, and the upholding of a biblical tradition. The

British had a social structure based on an inherited aristocracy, a monarchy, an official religion headed by the monarch, king or queen, and a class structure. This was clearly different from the American culture, religious organization, and social structure.

As immigration swelled in the late nineteenth and early twentieth centuries, the idea was that all who came to the United States would be assimilated into the emerging American culture. The picture the United States had of itself was that of a "melting pot," a receiver of people from many different cultures and societies who would learn the language of the country—English—and its culture, and assimilate into the developing American culture and society. Immigrants had chosen to come here because they saw it as a land of opportunity, and they were welcomed by the new society with open arms. America was industrializing. There was a great need for labor, and jobs were plentiful.

The influx of immigrant labor created a backlash, expressed in part through racial and ethnic discrimination. In the late nineteenth and early twentieth centuries the immigration and citizenship rights of Chinese and other Asians were restricted by federal law. One feature of this restrictive policy barred Chinese women from the United States, creating a generation of male-only Chinese immigrants. Immigration from Mexico was subject to increasing scrutiny by border patrols. The Immigration Act of 1924 banned further immigration from most Asian countries. This act restricted the number of immigration visas issued and allocated them on the basis of quotas by nationality. One section of the law, the Johnson-Reed Act, limited total European immigration to 150,000 per year, and limited the number of immigrants by nationality to 2 percent of the total already living in the United States. This had the effect of greatly increasing immigration from Great Britain and other northern European countries, and curtailing immigration of Italians from southern Europe and Jews from eastern Europe.

Italians and Jews of European descent had an ambiguous racial identity in the United States in the early twentieth century. Although they were acknowledged as white they were "both white *and* racially distinct from other whites" (Foner 2005: 14, emphasis in original). Under the prevailing racial system, when it came to southern and eastern Europeans "characteristics other than color—believed to be innate and unchangeable—were involved in defining them as separate races" (Foner 2005: 14). Racialized discourses of the time referenced presumed facial characteristics of Jews and the complexion of Italians as markers of racial distinction from, and inferiority to, unambiguously white populations of the "Nordic" type from Western Europe. "It seems clear that the Johnson-Reed Act was an effort to preserve the racial status quo on the part of those who acted out of a particular sense of white racial consciousness and who saw their privileged position threatened by the changing complexion of America" (Rees 2007: 56).

Many of the immigrants who came from Eastern Europe in the middle of the nineteenth century used ethnic terms, rather than terms referring to a nation-state, to identify themselves, demonstrating the weakness of national identity in some places in Europe like the Austro-Hungarian Empire at this time. These ethnic identities continued to be maintained in the domestic realm and within the community, despite the ideology of the melting pot. Silesians and Kashubians, in the communities they established in Pennsylvania, for example, retained much of their language and culture, as well as their religious affiliation.

Scotch-Irish immigrants were descendants of a Protestant group from Scotland, moved by the conquering English into Ulster County in Northern Ireland. They subsequently emigrated to America in the eighteenth and nineteenth centuries. They came from economically poor areas and moved into equally marginal frontier areas in the United States. The Scotch-Irish retained their ethnic identity in the border areas of Appalachia, providing us with the images of the feuding Hatfields and McCoys. They also gave us such self-made entrepreneurs as Andrew Mellon, patriots such as Patrick Henry, and five presidents of the United States—Polk, Buchanan, Jackson, Arthur, and Wilson.

American immigration policy underwent transformation again in the 1950s and 1960s. New policies encouraged reunification of immigrants with close family members from abroad, and the immigration of people with professional skills to meet service-oriented and technological labor market demands. The majority of the "**new immigrants**" to the United States came from Carribbean, Latin America, and Asian countries, in contrast to the "old immigrants" who were mostly from European countries (Foner 1987: 2). Among the new immigrants were people from East Asian and South Asian countries, seeking economic and professional opportunities. Dominican and Haitian immigrants were largely motivated by political instability and economic pressures. Vietnamese immigrants left their country due to the impact of war. In the 1980s, large numbers of people from former Soviet republics emigrated to the United States.

As with previous waves of immigration, the influx of new immigrants prompted new formulations of identity categories and new debates over the use of racial and ethnic categories. To cite one example, "Asian" was an option of racial self-identification in the U.S. census for the first time in 2000 when it was disaggregated from the 1990 category "Asian and Pacific Islander." Proponents of this move argue that it will facilitate more precise data-gathering on socioeconomic status, health conditions, and other demographic factors. Those who question its usefulness cite the enormous variation in countries of origin, languages, religions, and ethnicities encompassed in this collective terminology that includes people from South Asia, continental China, other East Asian countries, and the Philippines. The single "Asian" racial category obscures a wide variety of ethnicity and is implicated in the generation of stereotypes. The label of "model minority" mythologizes the economic and educational success of "Asian" immigrants. While at first glance complimentary, the model minority myth, like any other stereotype, is dangerous and misleading on several levels. "[T]he myth is a gross simplification that is not accurate enough to be seriously used for understanding 10 million people. Second, it conceals within it an invidious statement about African Americans along the lines of the inflammatory taunt: 'They made it, why can't you?' Third, the myth is abused both to deny that Asian Americans experience racial discrimination and to turn Asian Americans into a racial threat" (Wu 2002: 49).

Culture Unassimilated, Reiterated, and Renewed in America

As we noted above, in retrospect, the idea of the melting pot was a myth for all Americans. The ideal, when the Founding Fathers wrote the Declaration of Independence, the Constitution, and the Bill of Rights, was to have no single dominant ethnic group. In contrast, in other countries, such as Great Britain, France, and Germany, one religion was the state religion and the culture of one group was dominant. However, what was written on paper was not the case in reality. Immigrants who came here learned English, and Christmas was a legal holiday, but not Hanukkah or the Prophet's birthday. Though people conformed to majority norms in the public spheres of work, school, government, and so on, ethnic cultural practices were often retained in the private spheres of life. While assimilation was being emphasized, the persistence of ethnic practices in any form was officially ignored and even denied, being revealed only in scholarly articles. Over the past forty years the United States has recast its image and replaced the melting-pot symbol with that of a multiethnic, multicultural, pluralistic society. Americans are now enjoined to become more aware of and to respect the differing cultural backgrounds of ethnic groups other than their own. All the groups, taken together, are seen to constitute American culture today. The implications of this shift in our image of ourselves from assimilation to multiculturalism continue to reverberate in school curricula, in urban politics, on television, and in films. Now that multiculturalism and multiethnic images occupy center stage, we are also paying more attention to cultural continuities with the past and to ethnic practices that continue from yesterday, in a reworked form.

African Americans and Their Heritage

The defiant reiteration, strengthening, and redefinition of ethnic identity by various ethnic groups in recent years was in response to the civil rights movement in the 1960s, which gave birth to the idea of black power—the empowerment of African Americans—and the conscious construction of African-American culture. In the mid-1960s, African Americans proclaimed that "black is beautiful" and strengthened their identity by reiterating their African traditions and constructing their heritage anew.

With today's emphasis on different ethnic traditions, scholars of African-American culture are investigating continuities with African cultures in contemporary communities. For example, rural African Americans in southern states such as Georgia, Alabama, and South Carolina had a tradition of cooking, washing, and sharing gossip in swept yards surrounding their houses. This custom is now found only among members of the older generation. Swept yards were the center of family activity during the slave period and after. This use of space has been linked by Westmacott to West African village practices (1992). Cultural continuities with both West African and Central African cultures have been traced in a number of other areas. African-American speech, discussed in chapter 3, shows African retentions in verb tense usage (Asante 1990) and the use of many lexical items from African languages (Herskovits 1941, Turner 1949). Some of these African words, like the terms *gumbo* and *goober*, have been borrowed by white speakers of English. Africanisms also survived in the various musical traditions including the gospel tradition, jazz, and the blues (Maultsby 1990).

The strengthening of African-American identity involved cultural creativity. Alex Haley's television miniseries *Roots*, first aired in the 1970s, graphically depicted the epic history of his family as he reconstructed it, beginning with his West African ancestor who was enslaved and transported to America. All America watched *Roots*, but it had an especially powerful impact on African Americans and their sense of ethnic identity. *Roots* served to directly connect African-

African-American family members light candles together in celebration of Kwanzaa.

American culture to West African culture. Learning Swahili, wearing Kente cloth, using African greetings, and learning to cook African foods were tied to a cognizance of a Pan-African heritage of historic accomplishments.

This connection to West African culture also stimulated travel and tourism to domestic and African destinations associated with the Mid-Atlantic slave trade and its aftermaths. Anthropologists and other social scientists analyze these tourism sites to document the struggles over the representation of events and their participants in heritage-related travel sites. Leisure destinations that claim educational authority, such as Colonial Williamsburg, present a vision of history as authoritative fact. Behind the scenes, political struggles take place over control of the narratives of American history and the contributions of people of African descent presented in reconstructions, displays of material remains, and tour guide scripts (Gable et al. 1999).

Similar debates over the representations of history occur at Elmina Castle in Ghana. The castle and its grounds are a historically significant travel destination for African Americans and other groups in the black diaspora worldwide, as they were important sites of imprisonment and subsequent disembarkation for African slaves during the height of the Mid-Atlantic slave trade from 1700 to 1850 (Bruner 1996). Tourists from the black diaspora, particularly African Americans, want to see this tragic, barbaric association of this site with the slave trade enshrined and commemorated exclusively. Ghanaians have a more complicated set of historical narratives and references associated with this site. "For Ghanaians, Elmina Castle represents a part of Ghanaian history, from the Portuguese who built Elmina in 1482 primarily to facilitate trade on the Gold Coast, to the Dutch who captured the castle in 1637, to the British who gained control of Elmina in 1872, through to Ghanaian independence in 1957" (Bruner 1996: 292).

In her ethnography about narratives of slavery period history in Ghana, Bayo Holsey observes: "I found that the high visibility of the slave trade within the tourism industry stands in sharp relief to its practical invisibility in other arenas of Ghanaian society, where it is rarely mentioned. When I asked local residents whether or not they had ever learned about the slave trade from any sources outside of the tourism industry, from members of their families or other people in their communities, they told me that they had not. . . . Many told me that the castles are just for tourists and expressed little interest in them" (Holsey 2008: 2). These competing visions of this significant period in history form the basis of conflict over the use and control of space, and the narratives presented to foreign tourists and Ghanaians, in the castle and on its grounds.

The celebration of holidays of Kwanzaa and Juneteenth are examples of recognizing cultural practices that draw on African-American history and practices. Juneteenth, also known as Freedom Day or Emancipation Day, commemorates the day of official enforcement of the abolition of slavery in Texas, June 19. Juneteenth has been an official state holiday in Texas since 1980; currently over half of the states recognize its observance officially. Kwanzaa was developed in 1966 by a professor of black studies at California State University at Long Beach and is widely celebrated today all over the country with the sending of Kwanzaa cards and gift-giving. The seven-day cultural festival, held from December 26 to New Year's Day, is observed by African Americans of all religious faiths.

Kwanzaa is particularly associated with the purchase of goods associated with African identity, though these objects are purchased at other times of the year as well. A market has been created, and Africans from West Africa have begun to bring goods from Africa for sale to African Americans. These African entrepreneurs sell in street markets in New York and other cities with sizable African-American populations. American businessmen have also found a niche in this holiday market; greeting cards and gifts that represent the African tradition and African-American history are exchanged (Stoller 2002: 82). This marketing of Afrocentrism represents an attempt to replicate the signs and symbols of Africa through consumer goods that tie African Americans to their heritage.

As we have discussed previously, the one-drop rule held that "offspring of interracial unions were defined racially as African American, regardless of the racial identity of their other parent" (Daniel 2002: x). The grandchildren, great-grandchildren, and so on, down the generations were also thus categorized. Recently, those of multiracial background have begun to feel that all the backgrounds of their ancestry are important and should be recognized—European, American Indian, and so forth. The 2000 census included categories of self-identification that allow for respondents designating multiple racial and ethnic categories. These new multiracial identity categories are seen by some as undermining the goal of unifying African Americans into a strong political force. However, as Daniel notes, "The new multiracial identity, rather than imploding

African American identity, can potentially forge more inclusive constructions of blackness and whiteness" (2002: 175). Those who argue for integrative pluralism encourage recognition of cultural and racial diversities as well as commonalities.

Diversity in America—Challenges and Debates

We used to view ethnicity as a perpetuation of cultural traditions from the past. We now understand that the utilization of symbols of ethnic identity has always involved creativity and inventiveness (Sollars 1989, Stern and Cicala 1991). The question of authenticity of customs is frequently raised when they have been invented recently, but customs invented a century ago are accepted as authentic; the age of a custom or the number of years an event has been celebrated has nothing to do with its authenticity.

Many ethnic groups, following African Americans, began reasserting and reiterating their own ethnic identity and group solidarity and building their own cultural traditions in an increasingly public manner. New York City, a receiving destination for immigrants for two centuries, provides a spatial landscape on which to observe the expression of ethnic identity by both "old" and "new" immigrant groups (Foner 1987). Parades along Fifth Avenue in New York, occurring on many weekends, reflect the kaleidoscope of groups publicly displaying and reiterating their ethnic identity with floats, bands, costumes, and dignitaries.

While ethnic parades of the Irish and the Pakistanis in Great Britain symbolize each ethnic group's claim to certain spaces, ethnic parades in New York make a different symbolic statement. Most of the ethnic groups use the same space—Fifth Avenue in New York City. They are proclaiming and celebrating their ethnic identity as hyphenated Americans. Among the ethnic parades on Fifth Avenue during the year are the Irish, Greek, South Asian, Puerto Rican, Scottish, Polish, German, and Turkish Day parades. The largest ethnic parade of all is that of the West Indians, who march in Brooklyn on one of the days of the West Indian Labor Day celebration.

Whether it is Slovenians who settled in Cleveland several generations ago, or Somalis who have recently settled in Lewiston, Maine, or those of Nordic descent who are recapturing the culture of their ancestors, we are becoming more and more aware of the diversity of cultural background of new and old Americans. New minorities, such as Hispanic Muslims in California, constantly proclaim their existence. We are made aware of ethnic celebrations such as the Persian New Year—Nowruz—which is the ancient beginning of the spring equinox, or the distinctive thanksgiving ritual dedicated to the Prophet Elijah, which is celebrated at weddings by the Jews from India, the Bene Israel.

America is a nation based on religious freedom, and from the beginning, it attracted religious believers persecuted in their European homelands. Despite this, there is a strong streak of religious intolerance in the country, sometimes coupled with racism. The majority's intolerance of African-American Muslims, or Native American churches that practice the peyote "cult," or Caribbean "sects" like Santeria, seeking to carry out animal sacrifice, exemplifies this streak. The rituals of these religious groups offend the Christian majority, which legally tries to eliminate these practices. Since 9/11 Muslim Americans of all ethnicities and countries of origin have

Ethnicities and identities are celebrated throughout the year by parades and festivals in New York City. This float celebrates Indian independence in the annual Indian-Pakistan Independence Day Parade in 2007.

experienced discrimination, legal persecution, and racial profiling, sometimes in the name of enforcing national security.

How do third- and fourth-generation individuals with mixed ethnic heritages deal with ethnic identity today? Such Americans are now making choices regarding which of several ancestries they want to stress and which they will omit through selective memory (Waters 1990). People may choose to express their ethnicity situationally, in domestic and ritual settings, or through participation in periodic public events such as parades or annual identity festivals. The United States is now a multicultural, multiethnic, and pluralist society. The ongoing debates regarding how to implement multicultural curricula in colleges, high schools, and elementary schools reflect our groping for new ways to symbolize and express the multiple aspects of our cultural traditions. We continue to negotiate the ways in which national economic and security interests can be protected while respecting the rights of all ethnic and religious minorities. The significance of these debates is that they have almost eclipsed the consideration of what remains of a shared American culture and value system, which includes religious tolerance and the principles embodied in the Bill of Rights and the Constitution.

SUMMARY

- In today's pluralistic, multicultural world, the terms *ethnic* and *ethnic identity*, a way of identifying oneself, are frequently used as alternatives to culture and cultural identity.
- Ethnic groups share common cultural norms, values, identities, patterns of behavior, and language.
- Racial classification systems are culturally constructed, based on culture-specific ideas about identity, although many people tend to think of race as a scientific concept of human variation based on biological characteristics.
- The building of national identity is always a creative political process that draws on various forms of identities and the use of historical and archaeological interpretation by the state.
- Indigenous peoples around the world have adopted multiple religious and political strategies to resist or accommodate their integration into state systems.
- Following the collapse of the Soviet empire, newly independent sovereign states adopted a variety of political strategies to forge new national identities within borders and territories created by the former Soviet rulers.
- In Afghanistan the stability of the central government is challenged by ethnic- and kin-based affiliations of its leaders and their followers.
- The ethnic conflict that has continued in Sri Lanka for decades exemplifies the way in which ethnic identity is heightened and transformed under certain conditions. These include the role played by differences in religion and postcolonial economic factors.
- While the idea of the melting pot was dominant in the United States, and assimilation was being emphasized, the persistence of ethnic practices in any form was officially ignored and even denied. However, over the past thirty years the United States has recast its image and replaced the melting-pot symbol with that of a multiethnic, multicultural, and pluralistic society.
- The reiteration, strengthening, and redefinition of ethnic identity by various ethnic groups in recent years was in response to the civil rights movement in 1968, which gave birth to the idea of black power—the empowerment of African Americans—and the conscious construction of African-American culture.
- Other ethnic groups also began reasserting and reiterating their own ethnic identity and group solidarity and building their own hyphenated cultures in an increasingly public manner.
- Individuals with mixed ethnic heritages deal with ethnic identity today in America by making choices regarding which of several ancestries they want to stress under different circumstances and situations.

SUGGESTED READINGS

Sharma, Aradhana and Akhil Gupta, eds. *The Anthropology of the State: A Reader*. Malden, MA: Blackwell Publishing, 2006. Classic theoretical works and contemporary scholarship on states, development, violence, citizenship, and popular culture.

Kempadoo, Kamala. *Sexing the Caribbean: Race, Gender and Sexual Labor*. New York: Routledge, 2004. An analysis of how the history of colonialism and racial ideologies intersect with tourism and contemporary forms of sex work in the Caribbean.

Smedley, Audrey. *Race in North America: Origin and Evolution of a Worldview*. 3rd ed. Boulder, CO: Westview, 2007. A comprehensive history of the origins and manifestations of racial categories and constructions in North America, traced through intellectual, philosophical, scientific, and migration histories.

SUGGESTED WEBSITES

www.foxwoods.com/pequots/. The official website of the Mashantucket Pequot with descriptions of their history, museum, and details on the annual Schemitzun ceremony.

www.slaveryinamerica.org. An encyclopedia, database, and personal narratives of the transatlantic slave trade and its lived experience in the Americas.

www.lankalibrary.com/. Continually updated reports and news stories on Sri Lanka.

www.pbs.org/wgbh/pages/frontline/shows/jefferson/mixed/. A website developed by PBS for a documentary on the relationship between Thomas Jefferson and Sally Hemmings, including essays on race, mixed race categories, and the "One Drop of Blood Rule" in contemporary America.

Epilogue

THE GOAL OF ANTHROPOLOGY is to demonstrate that there are many cultures in the world and that our culture is but one of them. The mission of the anthropologist is to explore cultural differences to see the ways in which cultures are similar and the ways they differ. Today, many anthropologists study complex cultures in North America, Europe, and Asia and use historical and linguistic methods. They may also study groups in their own culture that are usually different from themselves in ethnic background and class membership.

Throughout this book, we discuss globalization as processes that are having a significant impact on our world. Anthropology, with its associated methodologies, is particularly well suited to explore the ways these global processes affect local communities. The anthropological perspective reveals the ways people "on the ground" are reacting to the larger forces beyond their communities that directly affect their lives. It can show the ways peoples' lives have been changed in response to the building of new factories locally, which are owned by multinational companies; or as a result of the availability of new technologies originating beyond the borders of their countries; or how family members maintain their ties while living in multiple countries around the world. The local level where people live their lives, and the way it articulates with the regional, national, and international, is the central focus of the contemporary anthropological approach.

Respect for cultural diversity is one of the central messages of anthropology and of this book. It leads one to conclude that our cultural practices are but one possible way of doing things, and that our way is not the "right way" or "only way." Cultural diversity and cultural differences are linked to the central concept in anthropology, that of culture. The culture concept is a holistic idea, which forces one to consider the many aspects of culture (religion, gender, kinship, art, politics, etc.) as they relate to one other.

The metaphor of the tapestry of culture, which we have used as the framework for this book, relates to the interrelationship, or interweaving, of these various aspects of culture or cultural institutions. Like the colors and designs of an enormous tapestry, every thread—meaning people's activities and individual behaviors as they live out their lives, observed by the anthropologist in the field—contributes to the pattern. However, not even the most elaborate medieval tapestry can approach the splendor and complexity of any single culture. But this is only a metaphor. It is an abstraction about how people lead their lives according to cultural rules; about good and evil; about rules and transgressions. Members of a community are themselves often in vigorous disagreement about the underlying values of their own culture. Today, the metaphor of the tapestry must be seen in the light of the disjunctions that have occurred as a consequence of colonialism, postcolonialism, and globalization.

In today's ever-changing world, decisions are constantly being made concerning the future direction of particular societies and ethnic groups. These decisions should be made by the people of these groups, and they should be informed decisions. This is where anthropology, in the form of applied anthropology or the practice of anthropology, comes in. Basic anthropological knowledge can be provided by anthropologists from other places coming in to work with the members of the society, or it can be provided by trained anthropologists from that culture who have an understanding of culture change. In this manner, anthropology works in the service of humanity, by contributing to cultural understanding worldwide.

References

Abiodun, Rowland, Henry Drewal, and John Pemberton. *The Yoruba Artist: New Theoretical Perspectives on African Arts.* Washington, D.C.: Smithsonian Institution Press, 1994.

Abotchie, Chris. *Social Control in Traditional Southern Eweland of Ghana: Relevance for Modern Crime Prevention.* Accra: Ghana Universities Press, 1997.

Abu El-Haj, Nadia. *Facts on the Ground: Archaeological Practice and Territorial Self-Fashioning in Israeli Society.* Chicago: University of Chicago Press, 2001.

———. "The Genetic Reinscription of Race." *Annual Review of Anthropology* 36 (2007): 283–300.

Abu-Lughod, Lila. "Do Muslim Women Really Need Saving? Anthropological Reflections on Cultural Relativism and Its Others." *American Anthropologist* 104, no. 3 (2002): 783–90.

Adams, Jane and D. Gorton. "Confederate Lane: Class, Race and Ethnicity in the Mississippi Delta." *American Anthropologist* 33, no. 2 (2006): 288–309.

Adams, Kathleen M. "More than an Ethnic Marker: Toraja Art as Identity Negotiator." *American Ethnologist* 25, no. 3 (1998): 327–51.

———. *Art as Politics: Re-Crafting Identities, Tourism, and Power in Tana Toraja, Indonesia.* Honolulu: University of Hawaii Press, 2006.

Ahearn, Laura. "Language and Agency." In *Annual Review of Anthropology* 30 (2001): 109–137.

Aho, James. *The Orifice as a Sacrificial Site: Culture, Organization and the Body.* New York: Aldine De Gruyter, 2002.

Alexander, Jennifer. "Women Traders in Javanese Marketplaces." In *Market Cultures: Society and Morality in the New Asian Capitalisms*, edited by Robert W. Hefner. Boulder, CO: Westview Press, 1998.

Alexander-Frizer, Tamar. *The Heart Is a Mirror: The Sephardic Folktale.* Detroit: Wayne State University Press, 2008.

Alim, H. Samy. *You Know My Steez: An Ethnographic Study of Styleshifting in a Black American Speech Community.* Duke University Press: American Dialect Society, 2004.

Al-Issa, Ihsan. "Culture and Mental Illness in Algeria." In *Al-Junun: Mental Illness in the Islamic World*, edited by Ihsan Al-Issa. Madison, CT: International Universities Press, 2000, pp. 101–20.

al-Khateeb, Salwa. "The Oil Boom and Its Impact on Women and Families in Saudi Arabia." In *The Gulf Family: Kinship Policies and Modernity*," edited by Alanoud Alsharekh. London: The Middle East Institute, SOAS, 2007.

al-Tarrah, Ali. "Family in the Kinship State." In *The Gulf Family: Kinship Policies and Modernity*, edited by Alanoud Alsharekh. London: The Middle East Institute, SOAS, 2007.

Amit, Vered. "Armenian and Other Diasporas: To Reconcile the Irreconcilable." In *British Subjects: An Anthropology of Britain*, edited by Nigel Rapport. Oxford: Berg Publishers, 2002.

Anderson, Robert. "The Biographical Origins of Political Systems of Highland Burma." In *Social Dynamics in the Highlands of Southeast Asia: Reconsidering Political Systems of Highland Burma by E. R. Leach*, edited by F. Robinne and M. Sadan. Leiden: Brill, 2007.

Appadurai, Arjun. *Modernity at Large: Cultural Dimensions of Globalization*. Minneapolis: University of Minnesota Press, 1996.

Aronson, Meredith, David Bell, and Dan Vermeer. "Coordination of Technological Practice and Representation at the Boundaries." In *Anthropological Perspectives on Technology*, edited by Michael Bryan Schiffer. Albuquerque: University of New Mexico Press, 2001.

Asante, Molefi Kete. "African Elements in African-American English." In *Africanisms in American Culture*, edited by E. Holloway. Bloomington: Indiana University Press, 1990.

Atkinson, Jane Monnig. "How Gender Makes a Difference in Wana Society." In *Power and Difference: Gender in Island Southeast Asia*, edited by Jane Fishburne Collier and Sylvia Junko Yanagisako. Stanford, CA: Stanford University Press, 1990.

_____. "Shamanisms Today" *Annual Review of Anthropology* 21 (1992): 307–330.

Atkinson, Michael. *Tattooed: The Sociogenesis of a Body Art*. Toronto: University of Toronto Press, 2003.

Atkinson, Quentin D. and Russell D. Gray. "How Old Is the Indo-European Family? Illumination or More Moths to the Flame?" In *Phylogenetic Methods and the Prehistory of Languages*, edited by Peter Foster and Colin Renfrew. Cambridge: Short Run Press, 2006.

Axel, Brian Keith. "Introduction: Historical Anthropology and Its Vicissitudes." In *From the Margins: Historical Anthropology and Its Futures*, edited by Brian Keith Axel. Durham, NC: Duke University Press, 2002.

Azhar, M. Z., and S. L. Varma. "Mental Illness and Its Treatment in Malaysia." In *Al-Junun: Mental Illness in the Islamic World*, edited by Ihsan Al-Issa. Madison, CT: International Universities Press (2000), pp. 163–86.

Bacchilega, Cristina. *Legendary Hawaii and the Politics of Place: Tradition, Translation, and Tourism*. Philadelphia: University of Pennsylvania Press, 2007.

Baker, Philip and Peter Muhlhausler. "Creole Linguistics from Its Beginnings, through Schuchardt to the Present Day." In *Creolization: History, Ethnography, Theory*, edited by Charles Stewart. Walnut Creek, CA: Left Coast Press, 2007.

Baldwin, Dare and Meredith Meyer. "How Inherently Social Is Language." In *Blackwell Handbook of Language Development*, edited by Erika Hoff and Marilyn Shatz. Oxford: Blackwell Publishing, 2007.

Baldwin, John R., Sandra L. Faulkner, and Michael L. Hecht. "A Moving Target: The Illusive Definition of Culture." In *Redefining Culture: Perspectives across the Disciplines*. New Jersey: Lawrence Erlbaum Associates, 2006.

Banks, Marcus and Andre Gingrich. "Introduction: New-Nationalism in Europe and Beyond." In *Neo-Nationalism in Europe and Beyond: Perspectives from Social Anthropology*, edited by Andre Gingrich and Marcus Banks. New York: Berghahn Books, 2006.

Barclay-Mclaughlin, Gina. "Communal Isolation: Narrowing the Pathways to Goal Attainment and Work." In *Coping with Poverty; The Social Context of Neighborhood, Work, and Family in the African American Community*, edited by Sheldon Danziger and Ann Chih Lin. Ann Arbor: University of Michigan Press, 2000.

Bar-Itzhak, Haya. *Israeli Folk Narratives: Settlement, Immigration, Ethnicity.* Detroit: Wayne State University Press, 2008.

Barnes, Robert H. "Alliance, Exchange, and the Organization of Boat Corporations in Lamalera (E. Indonesia). In *Kinship, Networks, and Exchange*, edited by Thomas Schweizer and Douglas R. White New York: Cambridge University Press, 1998.

Barreca, Regina. "Introduction." In *A Sitdown with the Sopranos: Watching Italian-American Culture on TV's Most Talked about Series*, edited by Regina Barreca. New York: Palgrave-Macmillan, 2002.

Barrett, Frank J. "The Organizational Construction of Hegemonic Masculinity: The Case of the US Navy."In *The Masculinities Reader*, edited by Stephen M. Whitehead and Frank J. Barrett. Cambridge: Polity Press, 2001.

Barth, Fredrik. *Political Leadership among Swat Pathans.* London: Athlone Press, 1959.

Behar, Ruth. *An Island Called Home: Returning to Jewish Cuba.* New Jersey: Rutgers University Press, 2007.

Belcher, Stephen. *African Myths of Origin.* New York: Penguin Books, 2005.

Benet, Sula. *Abkhasians: The Long-Living People of the Caucasus.* New York: Holt, Rinehart and Winston, 1974.

Berger, Peter L. "The Cultural Dynamics of Globalization." In *Many Globalizations: Cultural Diversity in the Contemporary World,* edited by Peter L. Berger and Samuel P. Huntington. New York: Oxford University Press, 2002.

Berger, Peter L. and Samuel P. Huntington. *Many Globalizations: Cultural Diversity in the Contemporary World.* New York: Oxford University Press, 2002.

Berlin, Brent and Paul Kay. *Basic Color Terms: Their Universality and Evolution.* Berkeley: University of California Press, 1969.

Bettelheim, Bruno. *The Uses of Enchantment: The Meaning and Importance of Fairy Tales,* 1977. Reprint. New York: Vintage Press, 1989.

Bhatt, Rakesh M. "World Englishes." *Annual Review of Anthropology* 30 (2001): 526–50.

Biber-Klemm, Susette, Thomas Cottier, Phillippe Cultel, and Danuta Szymura Berglas. "Rights to Plant Genetic Resources and Traditional Knowledge: Basic Issues and Perspectives." In *Rights to Plant Genetic Resources and Traditional Knowledge*, edited by Susette Biber-Klemm and Thomas Cottier. Wallingford, England: CABI Publishing, 2006.

Bickerton, Derek. *Language and Human Behavior.* Seattle: University of Washington Press, 1995.

Bird-David, Nurit. "Beyond 'the Hunting and Gathering Mode of Subsistence': Culture-Sensitive Observations on the Nayaka and Other Modern Hunters and Gatherers." *Man* 27 (1992): 19–44.

Black, James C. "Same Sex Parents and Their Children's Development." In *Same Sex Marriage: The Legal and Psychological Evolution in America*, edited by Donald J. Cantor, Elizabeth Cantor, James C. Black, and Campbell D. Barrett. Middletown, CT: Wesleyan University Press, 2006, pp. 81–100.

Blank, Stephan J. *Turkmenistan and Central Asia after Nizyazov.* Carlisle, PA: Strategic Studies Institute, 2007.

Blok, Anton. *Honour and Violence.* Malden, MA: Blackwell Publishers, 2001.

Blommaert, Jan. "Language Policy and National Identity." In *An Introduction to Language Policy: Theory and Method*, edited by Thomas Ricento. Oxford: Blackwell Publishing, 2006, pp. 238–54.

Boas, Franz. Introduction to *Handbook of American Indian Languages*. 1911. Reprint. Lincoln: University of Nebraska Press, 1966.

_____. *Primitive Art*. New York: Dover, 1955.

_____. *Kwakiutl Ethnography*, edited by Helen Codere. Chicago: University of Chicago Press, 1966.

Boellstorff, Tom. "Queer Studies in the House of Anthropology." *Annual Review of Anthropology* 36 (2007): 17–35.

Bolin, Inge. *Growing Up in a Culture of Respect: Child Rearing in Highland Peru*. Austin: University of Texas Press, 2006.

Botiveau, Bernard. "Islamic Family Law in the French Legal Context." *Cambridge Anthropology* 16 (1992/1993): 85–96.

Bourdieu, Pierre. *Outline of a Theory of Practice*. Cambridge: Cambridge University Press, 1977.

Bourguignon, Erika. "Suffering and Healing, Subordination and Power: Women and Possession Trance." *Ethos* 32, no. 4 (2004): 557–74.

Boyer, Pascal. *Religion Explained: The Evolutionary Origins of Religious Thought*. New York: Basic Books, 2001.

Brasch, Walter M. *Brer Rabbit, Uncle Remus and the 'Cornfield' Journalist: The Tale of Joel Chandler Harris*. Macon, GA: Mercer University Press, 2000.

Brasher, Brenda. *Give Me That Online Religion*. San Francisco: Jossey-Bass, 200l.

Brass, Paul R. *The Politics of India Since Independence*, 2nd ed. Cambridge: Cambridge University Press, 1994.

Briggs, Jean "Conflict Management in a Modern Inuit Community." In *Hunters and Gatherers in the Modern World: Conflict, Resistance, and Self-Determination*, edited by Peter P. Schweiter, Megan Biesele, and Robert K. Hitchcock. New York: Berghahn Books, 2000.

Brittan, Arthur. "Masculinities and Masculinism" In *The Masculinities Reader*, edited by Stephen M. Whitehead and Frank J. Barrett. Cambridge, UK: Polity Press (2001), pp. 51–55.

Bromley, David G. "New Religious Movements." In *Encyclopedia of Religion and Society*, edited by William Swatos. Walnut Creek, CA: AltaMira/Sage Publications, 1998.

Brown, Donald E. *Human Universals*. Philadelphia: Temple University Press, 1991.

Brown, Julie V. "Afterword." In *Madness and the Mad in Russian Culture*, edited by Angela Brintlinger and Ilya Vinitski. Toronto: University of Toronto Press, 2007.

Brown, Michael E. and Sumit Ganguly. *Fighting Words: Language Policy and Ethnic Relations in Asia*. Cambridge, MA: MIT Press, 2003.

Brown, Penelope. "Everyone Has to Lie in Tzeltal." In *Talking to Adults: The Contribution of Multiparty Discourse to Language Acquisition*. Mahwah, NJ: Lawrence Erlbaum Associates, 2002.

Brown, Roger. "The Language of Social Relationship." In *Social Interaction, Social Contest, and Language*, edited by Dan Slobin, Jule Gerhardt, Amy Kyratzis, and Jiansheng Guo. Mahwah, NJ: Lawrence Erlbaum, 1996.

Bruner, Edward M. "Tourism in Ghana: The Representation of Slavery and the Return of the Black Diaspora." *American Anthropologist* 98, no. 2 (1996): 290–304.

Brunvand, Jan Harold. "Urban Legends." In *What's So Funny: Humor in American Culture*, edited by Nancy A. Walker. Wilmington, DE: Scholarly Resources Books, 1998.

_____. *The Truth Never Stands in the Way of A Good Story*. Urbana: University of Illinois Press, 2000.

Buckley, Carina, and James Steele. "Evolutionary Ecology of Spoken Language: Co-Evolutionary Hypotheses are Testable." *World Archaeology* 34, no. 1 (2002): 26–46.

Buckley, Thomas, and Alma Gottlieb. *Blood Magic: The Anthropology of Menstruation*. Berkeley: University of California Press, 1988.

Bugajski, Janusz. *Ethnic Politics in Eastern Europe*. Armonk, NY: M. E. Sharpe, 1994.

Bunn, Henry and Craig W. Standford. "Conclusions: Research Trajectories on Hominid Meat-Eating." In *Meat-Eating and Human Evolution*, edited by Craig B. Stanford and Henry T. Bunn. New York: Oxford University Press, 2001.

Burton, Thomas. *Serpent-Handling Believers*. Knoxville: University of Tennessee Press, 1993.

Buss, David M. *The Handbook of Evolutionary Psychology*. NJ: John Wiley and Sons, 2005.

Bybee, Joan. "Language Change and Universals." In *Linguistic Universals*, edited by Ricardo Mairal and Juana Gil. New York: Cambridge University Press, 2006.

Cai Hua. *A Society without Fathers or Husbands: The Na of China*. New York: Zone Books, 2001.

Cameron, Deborah and Don Kulick. *Language and Sexuality*. Cambridge: Cambridge University Press, 2003.

Campion-Vincent, Veronique. *Organ Theft Legends*. Jackson: University of Mississippi Press, 2005.

Cantor, Donald J. et al. *Same-Sex Marriage: The Legal and Psychological Evolution in America*. Middletown, CT: Weslyan University Press, 2006.

Caroe, Olaf. *The Pathans: 550 B.C.–A.D. 1957*. New York: St. Martins Press, 1958.

Carrillo, Jo. *Readings in American Indian Law: Recalling the Rhythm of Survival*. Philadelphia: Temple University Press, 1998.

Carsten, Janet. *After Kinship*. Cambridge, UK: Cambridge University Press, 2004.

Cartwright, Garth. *Princes amongst Men: Journeys with Gypsy Musicians*. London: Serpent's Tail, 2005.

Casique, Irene. *Power, Autonomy and Division of Labor in Mexican Dual-Earner Families*. New York: University Press of America, 2001.

Castleden, Rodney. *King Arthur: The Truth behind the Legend*. New York: Routledge Press, 2000.

Cattell, Ray. *Children's Language: Consensus and Controversy*. New York: Continuum Publishing, 2007.

Cavalli-Sforza, Luigi Luca. *Genes, Peoples, and Languages*. New York: North Point Press, 2000.

Chagnon, Napoleon. *Yanomamo: The Fierce People*. New York: Holt, Rinehart and Winston, 1983.

_____. *Yanomamo*, 4th ed. New York: Harcourt Brace Jovanovich, 1997.

Chambers, Robert. *Native Tours: The Anthropology of Travel and Tourism*. Prospect Heights, IL: Waveland Press, 2000.

Child, Irvin and Leon Sirota. "BaKwele and American Aesthetic Evaluations Compared." *Ethnology* 4, no. 4 (1965): 349–60.

Chomsky, Noam. *On Language*. New York: The New Free Press, 1998.

_____. "On the Nature, Use, and Acquisition of Language." *In Handbook of Child Language Acquisition*, edited by William C. Ritchie and K. Bhatia. New York: Academic Press, 1999.

_____. *New Horizons in the Study of Language and Mind*. New York: Cambridge University Press, 2000

Clark, Gracia. *Onions are My Husband: Survival and Accumulation by West African Market Women*. Chicago: University of Chicago Press, 1994.

Clerk, Christian. "'That Isn't Really a Pig': Spirit Traditions in the Southern Cook Islands." In *South Pacific Oral Traditions*, edited by Ruth Finnegan and Margaret Orbell. Bloomington: Indiana University Press, 1995, pp. 161–76.

Clifford, James. "Introduction." In *Writing Culture: The Poetics and Politics of Ethnography*, edited by James Clifford and George Marcus. Berkeley: University of California Press, 1986.

Coates, Jennifer. *Men Talk: Stories in the Making of Masculinities*. Oxford: Blackwell Publishing, 2003.

_____. *Women, Men and Language: A Sociolinguistic Account of Gender Differences in Language*, 3rd ed. New York: Longman, 2004.

Cohen, Robin. *Global Diasporas: An Introduction*. Seattle: University of Washington Press, 1997.

Collins, Kathleen. *Clan Politics and Regime Transition in Central Asia*. New York: Cambridge University Press, 2006.

Collins, Thomas W. "Introduction." In *Communities and Capital: Local Struggles Against Corporate Power and Privatization*, edited by Thomas W. Collins and Charles Wingard. Athens: University of Georgia Press, 2000, pp. 1–4.

Colloredo-Mansfield, Rudi. "The Handicraft Archipelago: Consumption Migration, and the Social Organization of a Transnational Andean Ethnic Group." *Research in Economic Anthropology* 19 (1998): 31–68.

Coman, Mihai. "Cultural Anthropology and Mass Media: A Processual Approach" In *Media Anthropology*, edited by Eric W. Rothenbuhler and Mihai Coman. Thousand Oaks, CA: Sage, 2005.

Comaroff, Jean and John L. Comaroff. "Christianity and Colonialism in South Africa." *American Ethnologist* 13, no. 1 (1986): 1–22.

Cook, Scott. *Understanding Commodity Cultures: Explorations in Economic Anthropology with Case Studies from Mexico*. New York: Rowman & Littlefield, 2004.

Cook, V. J. and Mark Newson. *Chomsky's Universal Grammar: An Introduction*. Oxford: Blackwell Publishing, 2007.

Cosmides, Leda and John Tooby. "Neurocognitive Adaptations Designed for Social Exchange." In *The Handbook of Evolutionary Psychology*, edited by David M. Buss. New Jersey: John Wiley & Sons, 2005.

Cowan, Douglas E. "Online U-Topia: Cyberspace and the Mythology of Placelessness." *Journal for the Scientific Study of Religion* 44, no. 3 (2005a): 257–63.

_____. *Cyberhenge: Modern Pagans on the Internet*. New York: Routledge, 2005b.

Coyne, Michael. *The Crowded Prairie: American National Identity in the Hollywood Western*. New York: I.B. Tauris, 1997.

Craver, Amy. "Household Adaptive Strategies among the Inupiat." In *Complex Ethnic Households in America*, edited by Laurel Schwede, Rae Lesser Blumberg, and Anna Y. Chan. New York: Rowman & Littefield, 2005.

Croal, Peter and Wes Darou. "Canadian First Nations' Experiences with International Development." In *Participating in Development: Approaches to Indigenous Knowledge*, edited by Paula Sillitoe, Allan Bicker, and Johan Pottier. London: Routledge, 2002.

Crosette, Barbara. "Central Asian University Aims to Train Region's Next Leaders." *The New York Times*, August 26, 2002.

Daniel, E. Valentine. *Charred Lullabies: Chapters in an Anthropology of Violence*. Princeton, NJ: Princeton University Press, 1996.

Daniel, G. Reginald. *More than Black? Multiracial Identity and the New Racial Order*. Philadelphia: Temple University Press, 2002.

Dasgupta, Jyotirindra. "Language Policy and National Development in India." In *Fighting Words: Language Policy and Ethnic Relations in Asia*, edited by Michael Brown and Sumit Ganguly. Cambridge, MA: MIT Press, 2003.

Davenport, William. "Sculpture of the Eastern Solomons." *Expedition* 10 (1968): 4–25.

De Boeck, Filip. "Of Trees and Kings: Politics and Metaphor among the Aluund of Southwestern Zaire." *American Ethnologist* 21, no. 3 (1994): 451–73.

De Bose, Charles E. "Codeswitching: Black English and Standard English in the African-American Repertoire." In *Readings in African American Language: Aspects, Features and Perspectives*, vol. 2, edited by Nathaniel Normant, Jr. New York: Peter Lang, 2005.

De Grummond, Nancy Thompson. *Etruscan Myth, Sacred History, and Legend.* Philadelphia: University of Pennsylvania Museum of Archeology and Anthropology, 2007.

Diesendruck, Gil. "Mechanisms of Word Learning." In *Blackwell Handbook of Language Development.* Oxford: Blackwell Publishing, 2007.

Dillard, Joseph L. "Perspectives on Black English." In *Readings in African American Language: Aspects, Features and Perspectives*, vol. 2, edited by Nathaniel Norment, Jr. New York: Peter Lang, 2005.

Dirks, Nicolas B., Geoff Eley, and Sherry B. Ortner. "Introduction." In *Culture/Power/History: A Reader in Contemporary Social Theory*, edited by Nicholas B. Dirks, Geoff Eley, and Sherry B. Ortner. Princeton, NJ: Princeton University Press, 1994.

Dissanayake, Wimal. "Globalization and the Experience of Culture: The Resilience of Nationhood." In *Globalization, Cultural Identities, and Media Representations*, edited by Natascha Gentz and Stefan Kramer. Albany: State University of New York Press, 2006.

Dombrowski, Kirk. *Against Culture: Development, Politics, and Religion in Indian Alaska.* Lincoln: University of Nebraska Press, 2001.

Donald, Leland. *Aboriginal Slavery on the Northwest Coast of North America.* Berkeley: University of California Press, 1997.

Donham, Donald L. "Thinking Temporally or Modernizing Anthropology." *American Anthropologist* 103, no. 1 (2001): 134–49.

Douglas, Mary. "Witchcraft and Leprosy: Two Strategies of Exclusion." *Man* 26, no. 4 (1991): 723–26.

_____. "Deciphering a Meal." In *Implicit Meanings: Selected Essays in Anthropology*, 2nd ed. New York: Routledge, 1999.

Draguns, Juris. "Psychological Disorders of Clinical Severity." In *Handbook of Cross-Cultural Psychology*, vol. 6, Psychopathology. Boston: Allyn and Bacon, 1980.

Droschel, Yvonne. "Queering Language: A Love That Dare Not Speak Its Name Comes Out of the Closet." In *Language, Sexualities and Desires: Cross-cultural Perspectives*, edited by Helen Sauntson and Sakis Kyratzis. New York: Palgrave Macmillan, 2007.

Dubin, Margaret. *Native America Collected: The Culture of an Art World.* Albuquerque: University of New Mexico Press, 2001.

Duff, Wilson. *Images: Stone: B. C.: Thirty Centuries of Northwest Coast Indian Sculpture.* Seattle: University of Washington Press, 1975.

Dundes, Alan. "Into the End-zone for a Touchdown: A Psychoanalytic Consideration of American Football." *Western Folklore* 37 (1978): 75–88.

Durkheim, Emile. *The Elementary Forms of Religious Life.* 1915. Reprint. Translated by Joseph W. Swain. New York: Free Press, 1965.

Durrenberger, E. Paul and Judith E. Marti. "Introduction." In *Labor in Cross-cultural Perspective*, edited by E. Paul Durrenberger and Judith E. Marti. New York: AltaMira Press, 2006.

Earle, Timothy. *Bronze Age Economics: The Beginnings of Political Economies.* Boulder, CO: Westview, 2002.

Egan, James A., Michael L. Burton, and Karen L. Nero. "Building Lives with Food: Production, Circulation and Consumption of Food in Yap." In *Fast Food/Slow Food: The Cultural Economy of the Global Food System*, edited by Richard Wilk. New York: AltaMira Press, 2006.

El Guindi, Fadwa. *Veil: Modesty, Privacy and Resistance*. Oxford: Berg Publishers, 1999.

Eller, Jack David. *From Culture to Ethnicities to Conflict: An Anthropological Perspective on International Ethnic Conflict*. Ann Arbor: University of Michigan Press, 1999.

Ellis, Patricia and Zafar Khan. "Hopes and Expectations: Kashmiri Settlement in the United Kingdom." In *Dominant Culture as a Foreign Culture: Dominant Groups in the Eyes of Minorities*, edited by Janusz Mucha. New York: Columbia University Press, 1999.

Engels, Frederick. *The Origin of the Family, Private Property, and the State*. 1884. Reprint. New York: International Publishers, 1972.

Erdoes, Richard, and Alfonso Ortiz. *American Indian Trickster Tales*. New York: Viking, 1998.

Erera, Pauline Irit. *Family Diversity: Continuity and Change in the Contemporary Family*. Thousand Oaks, CA: Sage Publications, 2002.

Erikson, Erik H. *Childhood and Society*, 2nd edition. New York: W. W. Norton, 1963.

_____. *Gandhi's Truth: On the Origins of Militant Nonviolence*. New York: W. W. Norton, 1969.

Errington, Shelly. "Recasting Sex, Gender and Power: A Theoretical and Regional Overview." In *Power and Difference: Gender in Island Southeast Asia*, edited by Jane Monnig Atkinson and Shelly Errington. Stanford, CA.: Stanford University Press, 1990.

Escobar, Arturo. "Anthropology and the Development Encounter: The Making and Marketing of Development Anthropology." *American Ethnologist* 18, no. 4 (1991): 658–82.

_____. *Encountering Development: The Making and Unmaking of the Third World*. Princeton: Princeton University Press, 1995.

Ewing, Katherine. "Consciousness of the State and the Experience of the Self: The Runaway Daughter of a Turkish Guest Worker." In *Power and the Self*, edited by Jeannette Marie Mageo. New York: Cambridge University Press, 2000.

Fedorova, Elena G. "Mansi Female Culture: Rules of Behavior." In *Identity and Gender in Hunting and Gathering Societies*, edited by Ian Keen and Takako Yamada. Osaka: National Museum of Ethnology, 2001.

Ferguson, R. Brian. *Yanomami Warfare: A Political History*. Santa Fe, NM: School of American Research Press, 1995.

Finckenauer, James O. and Elin J. Waring. *Russian Mafia in America: Immigration, Culture and Crime*. Boston: Northeastern University Press, 1998.

Fine-Dare, Kathleen S. *Grave Injustice: the American Indian Repatriation Movement and NAGPRA*. Lincoln: University of Nebraska Press, 2002.

Finkler, Kaja. *Experiencing the New Genetics: Family and Kinship on the Medical Frontier*. Philadelphia: University of Pennsylvania Press, 2000.

Firth, Raymond. *Elements of Social Organization*. London: Watts, 1951.

Foner, Nancy. *New Immigrants in New York*. New York: Columbia University Press, 1987.

_____. *In a New Land: A Comparative View of Immigration*. New York: New York University Press, 2005.

Forge, Anthony. *Primitive Art and Society*. London: Oxford University Press, 1973.

Foster, Robert. "Commoditization and the Emergence of 'Kastom' as a Cultural Category: A New Ireland Case in Comparative Perspective." *Oceania* 62, no. 4 (1992): 284–93.

Foucault, Michael. *Archaeology of Knowledge*. New York: Pantheon, 1972.

Fox, Richard G. *Nationalist Ideologies and the Production of National Cultures*. American Ethnological Society Monograph Series, no. 2, 1990.

Frake, Charles. "Fine Description." In *Fine Description: Ethnographic and Linguistic Essays by Harold Conklin*, edited by Joel Kiupers and Ray McDermott. Monograph # 546, Yale Southeast Asia Studies, 2007.

Franken, Marjorie A. "The Dance and Status in Swahili Society." *Journal for the Anthropological Study of Human Movement* 7 no. 2 (1992): 77–93.

Frazier, E. Franklin. *The Negro Church in America.* New York: Schocken Books, 1963.

Freud, Sigmund. *The Future of an Illusion.* London: Hogarth Press, 1928.

Fried, Morton. *The Notion of Tribe.* Menlo Park, CA: Cummings Publishing, 1975.

Friedman, Robert L. *Red Mafiya: How the Russian Mob Has Invaded America.* Boston: Little, Brown, 2000.

Fromm, Erich. "Individual and Social Origins of Neurosis." *American Sociological Review* 9 (1944): 38–44.

Fry, Douglas. *The Human Potential for Peace: An Anthropological Challenge to Assumptions about War and Violence.* New York: Oxford University Press, 2006.

Fuller, Chris. "Legal Anthropology, Legal Pluralism and Legal Thought." *Anthropology Today* 10, no. 3 (1994): 9–12.

Fung, Heidi. "Affect and Early Moral Socialization: Some Insights and Contributions from Indigenous Psychological Studies in Taiwan." In *Indigenous and Cultural Psychology: Understanding People in Context*, edited by Uichol Kim, Kuo-Shu Yang, and Kwang-Kuo Hwang. New York: Springer, 2006.

Gable, Eric et al. "On the Uses of Relativism: Fact, Conjecture and Black and White Histories at Colonial Williamsburg." *American Anthropologist* 19, no. 4 (1992): 791–805.

Gaidzanwa, Rudo. "Indigenisation as Empowerment? Gender and Race in the Empowerment Discourse in Zimbabwe." In *The Anthropology of Power: Empowerment and Disempowerment in Changing Structures*, edited by Angela Cheater. New York: Routledge, 1999.

Gampel, Yolanda. "Reflections on the Prevalence of the Uncanny in Social Violence." In *Cultures Under Siege: Collective Violence and Trauma*, edited by Antonius C. G. M. Robben and Marcelo M. Suárez-Orozco. Cambridge: Cambridge University Press, 2000.

Gathercole, Virgina, C. Mueller, and Erika Hoff. "Input and the Acquisition of Language: Three Questions." In *Blackwell Handbook of Language Development.* Oxford: Blackwell Publishing, 2007.

Geertz, Clifford. "Deep Play: Notes on the Balinese Cockfight." *Daedalus* 101 (1972): 1–37.

_____. "From the Native's Point of View: On the Understanding of Anthropological Understanding." *Bulletin of the American Academy of Arts and Sciences* 28, no. 1 (1974).

Gellner, Ernest. *Nations and Nationalism.* Ithaca, NY: Cornell University Press, 1983.

Gerken, Lou Ann. "Acquiring Linguistic Structure." In *Blackwell Handbook of Language Development*, edited by Erika Hoff and Marilyn Shatz. Oxford: Blackwell Publishing, 2007.

Gerschlager, Caroline. "Introduction." In *Expanding the Economic Concept of Exchange: Deception, Self-Deception and Illusions*, edited by Caroline Gerschlager. Boston: Kluwer Academic Publishers, 2001.

Gilligan, C., N. Lyons, and T. Hammer. *Making Connections: The Relational Worlds of Adolescent Girls at Emma Willard School.* Cambridge, MA: Harvard University Press, 1990.

Ginsburg, Faye D. *Contested Lives: The Abortion Debate in an American Community.* Berkeley: University of California Press, 1989.

Gmelch, George. "Baseball Magic." *Trans-Action* 8, no. 8 (1971): 39–47.

Goebel, Ted et al. "The Late Pleistocene Dispersal of Modern Humans in the Americas." *Science* 319, no. 5869 (2008): 1497–502.

Goldman, L. R. "A Trickster for All Seasons: The Huli iba Tiri." In *Fluid Ontologies: Myth, Ritual and Philosophy in the Highlands of Papua New Guinea*, edited by L. R. Goldman and C. Ballard. Westport, CT: Bergin and Garvey, 1998.

Goldschmidt, Walter. *As You Sow: Three Studies in the Social Consequences of Agribusiness*. Glencoe, IL: Free Press, 1947.

Good, Byron J. "Culture and Psychopathology: Directions for Psychiatric Anthropology." In *New Directions in Psychological Anthropology*, edited by T. Schwartz, G. White, and C. Lutz. Cambridge, UK: Cambridge University Press, 1992.

Goodenough, Ward. *Description and Comparison in Cultural Anthropology*. Chicago: Aldine Publishing Company, 1970.

Goren-Inbar, Naama. "Stone Age Combustion: Fire Use Proposed at Ancient Israeli Site." *Science*, April 30, 2005.

Gottlieb, Alma. "Afterword." In "Special Issue: Blood Mysteries: Beyond Menstruation as Pollution." *Ethnology* 41, no. 4 (2002): 381–90.

Gottschall, Marilyn. "The Mutable Goddess: Particularity and Eclectism within the Goddess Public. In *Daughters of the Goddess: Studies of Healing, Identity and Empowerment*, edited by Wendy Griffin. Walnut Creek, CA: AltaMira Press, 2000.

Graves, Robert. *The Greek Myths*. New York: George Braziller, 1955.

Greenberg, Joseph. *Language Universals*. The Hague: Mouton, 1966.

Gregg, Gary S. *The Middle East: A Cultural Psychology*. Oxford: Oxford University Press, 2005.

Gregor, Thomas. *Anxious Pleasures: The Sexual Lives of an Amazonian People*. Chicago: University of Chicago Press, 1985.

Guiliani, Rudolph. *Leadership*. New York: Hyperion, 2002.

Gusterson, Hugh. *Nuclear Rites: Weapons Laboratory at the End of the Cold War*. Berkeley: University of California Press, 1996.

Guttman, Mathew C. "A (Short) Cultural History of Mexican Machos." In *Gender Matters: Rereading Michelle C. Rosaldo*, edited by Alejandro Lugo and Bill Mauer. Ann Arbor: University of Michigan Press, 2000.

Gwaltney, John Langston. *Drylongso: A Self-Portrait of Black America*. New York: New Press, 1993.

Hall, Gary and Clare Birchall. *New Cultural Studies: Adventures in Theory*. Athens: University of Georgia Press, 2006.

Hall, Michael. "From Marx to Muhammad." *Cultural Survival* 16, no. 1 (1992): 41–44.

Hamilton, Gary G. "Culture and Organization in Taiwan's Market Economy." In *Market Cultures: Society and Morality in the New Asian Capitalisms*, edited by Robert W. Hefner. Boulder, CO: Westview Press, 1998.

_____. *Commerce and Capitalism in Chinese Societies*. New York: Routledge, 2006.

Hammel, Eugene. *Alternative Social Structures and Ritual Relations in the Balkans*. Englewood Cliffs, NJ: Prentice-Hall, 1968.

Hansen, Karen Tranberg. "Commodity Chains and the International Secondhand Clothing Trade: Salaula and the Work of Consumption in Zambia." In *Theory in Economic Anthropology*, edited by Jean Ensminger. Walnut Creek: AltaMira Press, 2002.

Hansen, Thomas and Finn Stepputat. *States of Imagination: Ethnographic Explorations of the Postcolonial State*. Durham, NC: Duke University Press, 2001.

Harding, Nick. *Urban Legends*. Harbenden, UK: Pocket Essentials, 2005.

Harris, Marvin. "Referential Ambiguity in the Calculus of Brazilian Racial Identity. *Southwestern Journal of Anthropology* 26, no. 1 (1970): 1–14.

Harrison, K. David. *When Languages Die: The Extinction of the World's Languages and the Erosion of Human Knowledge*. New York: Oxford University Press, 2007.

Harrison, Simon. "The Past Altered by the Present: A Melanesian Village after Twenty Years." *Anthropology Today* 17, no. 5 (2001): 3–9.

Hawley, C. John. *Postcolonial, Queer: Theoretical Intersections*. Albany: State University of New York Press, 2001.

Hayden, Corinne. "Gender, Genetics and Generation: Reformulating in Lesbian Kinship." In *Same-Sex Cultures and Sexualities: An Anthropological Reader*, edited by Jennifer Robertson. Malden, MA: Blackwell Publishing, 2005.

Hayslip, Bert and Julie Hicks Patrick. *Custodial Grandparenting: Individual, Cultural and Ethnic Diversity*. New York: Springer Publishing Company, 2006.

Headland, Thomas N. and Lawrence A. Reid. "Hunter-Gatherers and Their Neighbors from Prehistory to the Present." *Current Anthropology* 30 (1989): 43–66.

Hefner, Robert W. "Introduction: Society and Morality in the New Asian Capitalisms." In *Market Cultures, Society and Morality in the New Asian Capitalisms*, edited by Robert W. Hefner. Boulder, CO: Westview Press, 1998.

Henderson, Carol E. "Virtual Marketing: Making Heritage, Marketing Cyberorientalism? In *Raj Rhapsodies: Tourism, Heritage and the Seduction of History*, edited by Carol Henderson and Maxine Weisgrau. Aldershot, UK: Ashgate Publishing Company, 2007.

Henderson, Carol E. and Maxine Weisgrau. *Raj Rhapsodies: Tourism, Heritage and the Seduction of History*. Aldershot, UK: Ashgate Publishing Company, 2007.

Henderson, Mary. *Star Wars: The Magic of Myth*. New York: Bantam Books, 1997.

Hernsheim, Eduard. *South Sea Merchant*. Port Moresby: Institute of Papua New Guinea Studies, 1983.

Herskovits, Melville J. *The Myth of the Negro Past*. 1941. Reprint. Boston: Beacon Press, 1951.

Hewamanne, Sandya. *Stitching Identities in a Free Trade Zone*. Philadelphia: University of Pennsylvania Press, 2008.

Hewitt, Kim. *Mutilating the Body: Identity in Blood and Ink*. Bowling Green, OH: Bowling Green State University Popular Press, 1997.

Hickerson, Nancy P. "Ethnogenesis in the South Plains: Jumano to Kiowa." In *History, Power, and Identity: Ethnogenesis in the Americas 1492–1992*, edited by Jonathan D. Hill. Iowa City: University of Iowa Press, 1996.

Hicks-Bartlett, Sharon. "Between a Rock and a Hard Place: The Labyrinth of Working and Parenting in a Poor Community." In *Coping with Poverty: The Social Contexts of Neighborhood, Work, and Family in the African-American Community*, edited by Sheldon Danziger and Ann Chili Lin. Ann Arbor: University of Michigan Press, 2000.

Higham, N. J. *King Arthur: Myth Making and History*. London, Routledge, 2002.

Hill, Jonathan D. "Introduction: Ethnogenesis in the Americas, 1492-1992." In *History, Power, and Identity: Ethnogenesis in the Americas,1492-1992*, edited by Jonathan D. Hill. Iowa City: University of Iowa Press, 1996.

Hinton, Alexander Laban. "Why Did You Kill? The Cambodian Genocide and the Dark Side of Face and Honor." In *War and Peace: An Anthology*, edited by Nancy Scheper-Hughes and Philippe Bourgeois. Malden, MA: Blackwell, 2004.

Hitchcock, Robert K. and Megan Biesele. "Introduction." In *Hunters and Gatherers in the Modern World: Conflict, Resistance and Self-Determination*, edited by Peter P. Schweitzer, Megan Biesele, and Robert K. Hitchcock. New York: Berghahn Books, 2000.

Ho, Ts'ui-p'ing. "Rethinking Kachin Wealth Ownership." In *Social Dynamics in the Highlands of Southeast*

Asia: Reconsidering Political Systems of Highland Burma by E. R. Leach, edited by François Robinne and Mandy Sadan. Boston: Brill, 2007.

Hobsbawn, E. J. *Nations and Nationalism since 1780: Programme, Myth, Reality*, 2nd ed. Cambridge, England: Cambridge University Press, 1992.

Hodgson, Dorothy L. "'Once Intrepid Warriors': Modernity and the Production of Maasai Masculinities." *Ethnology* 38, no. 2 (1999): 121–50.

_____. *Once Intrepid Warriors: Gender, Ethnicity and the Cultural Politics of Maasai Development*. Bloomington: Indiana University Press, 2001.

_____, ed. *Rethinking Pastoralism in Africa: Gender, Culture & Myth of the Patriarchal Pastoralist*. Oxford: James Curry, 2000.

Hogbin, Ian. *The Island of Menstruating Men: Religion in Wogeo, New Guinea*. 1970. Reprint. Prospect Heights, IL: Waveland Press, 1996.

Holmes, Janet. *Gendered Talk at Work: Constructing Gender Identity through Workplace Discourse*. Oxford: Blackwell Publishing, 2006.

Holodynski, Manfred and Wolfgang Friedlmeier. *Development of Emotions and Emotion Regulation*. New York: Springer, 2006.

Holsey, Bayo. *Routes of Remembrance: Refashioning the Slave Trade in Ghana*. Chicago: University of Chicago Press, 2008.

Hovelsrud-Broda, Greta K. "Arctic Seal-Hunting Households and the Anti-sealing Controversy." *Research in Economic Anthropology* 18 (1997): 17–34.

Howell, Signe. *Kinning of Foreigners: Transnational Adoption in a Global Perspective*. New York: Berghahn Books, 2006.

Hume, Lynne and Jane Mulcock. "Introduction: Awkward Spaces, Productive Places." In *Anthropologists in the Field: Cases in Participant Observation*, edited by Lynne Hume and Jane Mulcock. New York: Columbia University Press, 2004.

Humphrey, Caroline. *The Unmaking of Soviet Life: Everyday Economies after Socialism*. Ithaca, NY: Cornell University Press, 2002.

Humphrey, Caroline and Stephen Hugh-Jones. *Barter, Exchange and Value: An Anthropological Approach*. Cambridge, England: Cambridge University Press, 1992.

Humphrey, Caroline and David Sneath. *The End of Nomadism? Society, State and the Environment in Inner Asia*. Durham, NC: Duke University Press, 1999.

Huntsman. Judith. "Fact, Fiction and Imagination: A Tokelau Narrative." In *South Pacific Oral Traditions*, by Ruth Finnegan and Margaret Orbell. Bloomington: Indiana University Press, 1995, pp. 124–60.

Ichikawa, Mitsuo. "'Interests in the Present' in the Nationwide Monetary Economy: The Case of the Mbuti Hunters in Zaire." In *Hunters and Gatherers in the Modern World: Conflict, Resistance, and Self-Determination*, edited by Peter P. Schweitzer, Megan Biesele, and Robert K. Hitchcock. New York: Berghahn Books, 2000.

Inda, Jonathan X. and Renato Rosaldo. "Tracking Global Flows." In *The Anthropology of Globalization: A Reader*, 2nd ed., edited by Jonathan Inda and Renata Rosaldo. Malden, MA: Blackwell Publishers, 2008.

Ingold, T. "Culture, Perception and Cognition." In *Psychological Research: Innovative Methods and Strategies*, edited by J. Haworth. London: Routledge, 1996.

Ip, David, Ray Hibbins, and Wing Hong Chui. "Transnational Chinese Migration." In *Experiences of Transnational Chinese Migrants in the Asia-Pacific*, edited by David Ip, Raymond Hibbins, and Wing Hong Chui. New York: Nova Science, 2006.

Issac, Gwyneira. *Mediating Knowledges: Origins of a Zuni Tribal Museum*. Tucson: University of Arizona Press, 2007.

Jenike, Mark R "Nutritional Ecology: Diet, Physical Activity and Body Size." In *Hunters and Gatherers: An Interdisciplinary Perspective*, edited by Catherine Panter-Brick, Robert H. Layton, and Peter Rowley Conway. Cambridge, UK: Cambridge University Press, 2001.

Jobling, Mark A., Matthew Hurles, and Chris Tyler-Smith. *Human Evolutionary Genetics: Origins, Peoples and Diseases*. Abington: Garland Science, 2004.

Jones, Stephen F. "Indigenes and Settlers." *Cultural Survival* 16, no. 1 (1992): 30–32.

Juillerat, Bernard. *Children of the Blood: Society, Reproduction and Cosmology in New Guinea*. New York: Berg, 1996.

Kaberry, Phyllis. "The Abelam Tribe, Sepik District, New Guinea." *Oceania* 21 (1940): 233–58, 345–67.

Kaeppler, Adrienne. "Structure Movements in Tonga." In *Society and the Dance*, edited by P. Spencer. Cambridge, England: Cambridge University Press, 1985.

Karmiloff, Kyra and Annette Karmiloff-Smith. *Pathways to Language: From Fetus to Adolescent*. Cambridge, MA: Harvard University Press, 2001.

Kautzsch, Alexander. *The Historical Evolution of Earlier African American English: An Empirical Comparison of Early Sources*. New York: Mouton de Gruyter, 2002.

Kearney, M. "The Local and the Global: The Anthroology of Globalization and Transnationalism." *Annual Review of Anthropology* 24 (1995): 547–65.

Keegan, William. *Taino Indian Myth and Practice: The Arrival of the Stranger King*. Gainsville: University of Florida Press, 2007.

Keenan, Elinor. "Norm-Makers, Norm-Breakers: Uses of Speech by Men and Women in a Malagasy Community." In *Explorations in the Ethnography of Speaking*, edited by Richard Bauman and Joel Sherzer. Cambridge, England: Cambridge University Press, 1974.

Keesing, Roger M. "New Lessons from Old: Changing Perspectives on the Kula." *Finnish Anthropological Society Transactions* 27 (1990): 139–63.

Kehoe, Alice Beck. *Shamans and Religion: An Anthropological Exploration in Critical Thinking*. Prospect Heights, IL: Waveland Press, 2000.

Kelly, Raymond C. *Warless Societies and the Origin of War*. Ann Arbor: University of Michigan Press, 2000.

Kendall, Laurel. "Korean Shamans and the Spirits of Capitalism." *American Anthropologist* 98, no. 3 (1996): 512–27.

_____. "The Cultural Politics of 'Superstition' in the Korean Shaman World: Modernity Constructs Its Other." In *Healing Powers and Modernity—Traditional Medicine and Science in Asian Societies*, edited by Linda H. Connor and Geoffrey Samuel. Westport, CT: Greenwood, 2001.

Kenin-Lopsan, M. B. *Shamanic Songs and Myths of Tuva*. Los Angeles: International Society for Trans-Oceanic Research, 1997.

Kent, Susan. "Cultural Diversity among African Foragers: Causes and Implications." In *Cultural Diversity among Twentieth Century Forgers*, edited by Susan Kent. Cambridge: Cambridge University Press, 1996.

Kimmel, Michael S. "Masculinity as Homophobia: Fear, Shame, and Silence in the Construction of Gender Identity." In *The Masculinities Reader*, edited by Stephen M. Whitehead and Frank J. Barrett. Cambridge: Polity Press, 2001.

Kinoshita, Yasuhito and Christie W. Kiefer. *Refuge of the Honored: Social Organization in a Japanese Retirement Community*. Berkeley: University of California Press, 1992.

Kitayama, Shinobu, Sean Duffy, and Yukiko Uchida. "Self as Cultural Mode of Being." In *Handbook of Cultural Psychology*, edited by Shinobu Kityama and Dov Cohen. New York: The Guilford Press, 2007.

Klass, Morton. *Ordered Universes: Approaches to the Anthropology of Religion*. Boulder, CO: Westview Press, 1995.

Klass, Morton and Maxine K. Weisgrau. *Across the Boundaries of Belief: Contemporary Issues in the Anthropology of Religion*. Boulder, CO: Westview Press, 1999.

Kleinman, Arthur, and Byron Good. *Culture and Depression: Studies in the Anthropology and Cross-Cultural Psychiatry of Affect and Disorder*. Berkeley: University of California Press, 1985.

Kluckhohn, Clyde. "Myths and Rituals: A General Theory." *Harvard Theological Review* 35 (1942): 45–79.

_____. "Universal Categories of Culture." In *Anthropology Today: An Encyclopedic Inventory*, edited by A. L. Kroeber. Chicago: University of Chicago Press, 1953.

Koch, Klaus-Friedrich. 1974. *War and Peace in Jalémó: The Management of Conflict in Highland New Guinea*. Cambridge, MA: Harvard University Press, 1974.

Kochanek, Stanley A. *Patron-Client Politics and Business in Bangladesh*. Newbury Park, CA: Sage Publications, 1993.

Kohl, Philip. "Nationalism and Archeology: On the Construction of Nations and the Reconstructions of the Remote Past." *Annual Review of Anthropology* 27 (1998): 223–46.

Koskoff, Ellen. *Women and Music in Cross-Cultural Perspective*. New York: Greenwood Press, 1987.

Koven, Mikel J. *Film, Folklore, and Urban Legends*. Lanham, MD: The Scarecrow Press, 2008.

Kuhn, Steven L. and Mary C. Stiner. "The Antiquity of Hunter-Gatherers." In *Hunter-Gatherers: An Interdisciplinary Perspective*, edited by Catherine Panter-Brick, Robert H. Layton, and Peter Rowley-Conwy. Cambridge: Cambridge University Press, 2001.

Kurtz, Donald. *Political Anthropology: Power and Paradigms*. Boulder, CO: Westview Press, 2001.

Labov, William. *Sociolinguistic Patterns*. Philadelphia: University of Pennsylvania Press, 1972.

_____. "Co-existent Systems in African-American Vernacular English." In *African-American English: Structure, History and Use*, edited by Salikoko S. Mufwene, John R. Rickford, Guy Bailey, and John Baugh. New York: Routledge, 1998.

Laidlaw, James. "Introduction." In *Ritual and Memory: Toward a Comparative Anthropology of Religion*, edited by Harvey Whitehouse and James Laidlaw. Walnut Creek, CA: AltaMira Press, 2004.

Lakoff, George and Mark Johnson. *Metaphors We Live By*. Chicago: University of Chicago Press, 2003.

Lamb, Sarah. *White Saris and Sweet Mangoes: Aging, Gender, and Body in North India*. Berkeley: University of California Press, 2000.

Lang, Sabine. *Men as Women, Women as Men: Changing Gender in Native American Cultures*. Austin: University of Texas Press, 1998.

Lass, Andrew. "Romantic Documents and Political Monuments: The Meaning-Fulfillment of History in 19th-century Czech Nationalism." *American Ethnologist* 15, no. 3 (1988): 456–71.

Lattas, Andrew. "Sorcery and Colonialism: Illness, Dreams and Death as Political Languages in West New Britain." *Man* 28 no. 1 (1993): 51–78.

Lawtaw, Ja Nan. "Peace Initiatives among Ethnic Nationalities." In *Myanmar: State, Society and Ethnicity*, edited by N. Ganesan and Kyaw Yin Hlaing. Singapore: Institute of Southeast Asian Studies, 2007.

Layton, Robert H. "Hunter-Gatherers, Their Neighbours and the Nation-State." In *Hunter-Gatherers: An Interdisciplinary Perspective*, edited by Catherine Panter-Brick, Robert H. Layton, and Peter Rowley-Conwy. Cambridge: Cambridge University Press, 2001.

Leach, Edmund. *Political Systems of Highland Burma: A Study of Kachin Social Structure*, 1954. Reprint. Boston: Beacon Press, 1965.

_____. "Magical Hair." *Journal of the Royal Anthropological Institute of Great Britain and Ireland* 88 (1958): 147–64.

Lechleitner, Gerda. "The Community of Bukarian Jews in Vienna." In *Cultural Diversity in the Urban Area: Explorations in Ethnomusicology*, edited by Ursala Hametek and Adelaida Reyes. Vienna: Institut fur Volksmusikforschung und Ethnomusikologie, 2007.

Lechner, Frank J. and John Boli. *World Culture: Origins and Consequences*. Oxford: Blackwell Publishing, 2005.

Lee, Sang M. "Information Technology and Economic Development Strategy." In *Globalization and Change in Asia*, edited by Dennis A. Rondinelli and John M. Heffron. Boulder, CO: Lynn Rienner Publisher. 2007.

Lefkowitz, Mary R. *Women in Greek Myth*, 2nd ed. Baltimore: Johns Hopkins University Press, 2007.

Lepowsky, Maria. "Big Men, Big Women and Cultural Autonomy." *Ethnology* 29, no. 1 (1990): 35–50.

Lett, James W. *Science, Reason and Anthropology: The Principles of Rational Inquiry*. Lanham, MD: Rowman & Littlefield, 1997.

Lévi-Strauss, Claude. *Tristes Tropique*. New York: Atheneum. 1961.

_____. "The Structural Theory of Myth." In *Structural Anthropology*. New York: Basic Books, 1963.

_____. *L'Homme Nu: Mythologique* 4. Paris: Plon, 1971.

_____. *La Voie des Masques*. Paris: Plon, 1979.

_____. *The Raw and the Cooked*. Chicago: University of Chicago Press, 1990.

Levine, Nancy E. "Fathers and Sons: Kinship Value and Validation in Tibetan Polyandry." *Man* 22, no. 2 (1987): 267–86.

Levine, Robert A. and Karin Norman. "The Infant's Acquisition of Culture: Early Attachment Reexamined in Anthropological Perspective." In *The Psychology of Cultural Experience*, edited by Carmella C. Moore and Holly F. Mathews. Cambridge, England: Cambridge University Press, 2001.

Lewin, Ellen. "Weddings without Marriage: Making Sense of Lesbian and Gay Commitment Rituals." In *Queer Families, Queer Politics: Challenging Culture and the State*, edited by Mary Bernstein and Renate Reimann, New York: Columbia University Press, 2001.

Lewis, E. Douglas. "Ritual, Metaphor, and the Problem of Direct Exchange in a Tana Wai Brama Child Transfer." In *Framing Indonesian Realities: Essays in Symbolic Anthropology in Honour of Reimar Schefold*, edited by Peter J. M. Nas, Gerard Persoon, and Rivke Jaffee. Leiden, The Netherlands: KITLV Press, 2003.

Lewis, I. M. *Arguments with Ethnography: Comparative Approaches to History, Politics and Religion*. New Brunswick, NJ: Athalon Press, 1999.

Lieberman, Daniel E., and Robert C. McCarthy. "The Ontogeny of Cranial Base Angulation in Humans and Chimpanzees and its Implications for Reconstructing Pharyngeal Dimensions." *Journal of Human Evolution* 36, no. 5 (1999): 487–517.

Lieberman, Philip. *Eve Spoke: Human Language and Human Evolution*. New York: W. W. Norton & Company, 1998.

Lips, Julius. *The Savage Hits Back*. 1937. Reprint. New Hyde Park, NY: University Books, 1966.

LiPuma, Edward. *Encompassing Others: The Magic of Modernity in Melanesia*. Ann Arbor: University of Michigan Press, 2000.

Litosseliti, Lia. *Gender and Language: Theory and Practice*. London: Hodder Arnold, 2006.

Lizot, Jacques. "Words in the Night: the Ceremonial Dialogue—One Expression of Peaceful Relationships among the Yanonami." In *The Anthropology of Peace and Non-Violence*, edited by Leslie E. Sponsel and Thomas Gregor. Boulder, CO: Lynne Rienner Publishers, 1994.

Loizos, Peter. "Disenchanting Developers." *Anthropology Today* 7, no. 5 (1991): 1–2.

Loker, William M. "Grit in the Prosperity Machine: Globalization and the Rural Poor in Latin America." In *Globalization and the Rural Poor in Latin America*, edited by William M. Loker. Boulder, CO: Lynne Rienner Publishers, 1999.

Louwe, Heleen, "Police-Reformers: 'Big Men' Failing Their Followers." In *Private Politics: A Multi-Disciplinary Approach to "Big Man" Systems*, edited by Martin A. Van Bakel, Renee R. Hogesteijm, and Pieter von de Velde, vol. 1. Leiden, The Netherlands: Brill (1986), pp. 174–81.

Lowe, Kathy. "Gendermaps." In *Gender in Early Childhood*, edited by Nicola Yelland. New York: Routledge, 1998.

Lukanuski, Mary. "A Place at the Counter: The Onus of Oneness." In *Eating Culture*, edited by Ron and Brian Seitz. Albany: State University of New York Press, 1998.

Lutz, John Sutton. *Myth and Memory: Stories of Indigenous-European Contact*. Vancouver: UBC Press, 2007.

Lynch, John. *Pacific Languages: An Introduction*. Honolulu: University of Hawaii Press, 1998.

Mackey-Kallis, Susan. *The Hero and the Perennial Journey Home in American Film*. Philadelphia: University of Pennsylvania Press, 2001.

Mackie, Jamie. "Business Success among Southeast Asian Chinese." In *Market Cultures: Society and Morality in the New Asian Capitalisms*, edited by Robert W. Hefner. Boulder, CO: Westview Press, 1998.

MacNeilage, Peter F. and Barbara L. Davis. "The Evolution of Language." In *The Handbook of Evolutionary Psychology*, edited by David M. Buss. Hoboken, NJ: John Wiley & Sons, 2005.

Magnus, Ralph and Eden Naby. *Afghanistan: Mullah, Marx and Mujahid*. Boulder, CO: Westview Press, 2002.

Majors, Richard. "Cool Pose: Black Mascuinity and Sports." In *The Masculinities Reader*, edited by Stephen M. Whitehead and Frank J. Barrett. Cambridge: Polity Press, 2001.

Malinowski, Bronislaw. *Argonauts of the Western Pacific*. 1922. Reprint. New York: E. P. Dutton and Co., 1961.

_____. *The Sexual Life of Savages in Northwestern Melanesia*, New York: Harcourt, Brace and World, 1929.

_____. *Coral Gardens and Their Magic*. New York: American Book Co., 1935.

_____. *Magic, Science and Religion and Other Essays*. London: Souvenir Press, 1974.

Mallon, Gerald P. *Gay Men Choosing Parenthood*. New York: Columbia University Press, 2004.

Manganaro, Marc. *Modernist Anthropology: From Fieldwork to Text*. Princeton, NJ: Princeton University Press, 1990.

Marcus, George E. "Ethnography in/of the World System: The Emergence of Multi-Sited Ethnography." *Annual Review of Anthropology* 24 (1995): 95–117.

Marin, Dalia and Monika Schnitzer. *Contracts in Trade and Transition: The Resurgence of Barter*. Cambridge, MA: The MIT Press, 2002.

Marshall, Yvonne. "Transformations of Nuu-chah-nulth Houses." In *Beyond Kinship: Social and Material Reproduction in House Societies*, edited by Rosemary A. Joyce and Susan D. Gillespie. Philadelphia: University of Pennsylvania Press, 2000.

Mascolo, Michael and Jin Li. "Editors' Notes." In *Culture and Developing Selves: Beyond Dichotomization*. San Francisco: Jossey-Bass, 2004.

Mason, Mary Ann. "The Modern Step Family: Problems and Possibilities." In *All Our Families: New Policies for a New Century*, edited by Mary Ann Mason, Arlene Skolnick, and Stephen D. Sugarman. New York: Oxford University Press, 1998.

Maultsby, Portia K. "Africanisms in African-American Music." In *Africanisms in American Culture*, edited by Joseph E. Holloway. Bloomington: Indiana University Press, 1990.

Mauss, Marcel. *The Gift*. 1925. Reprint. Translated by Ian Cunnison. London: Cohen and West, 1954.

McCarthy, Mary. *The Group*. New York: Harcourt, Brace and World, 1963.

McCauley, Martin. *Bandits, Gangsters and the Mafias: Russia, the Baltic States and the CIS Since 1992*. New York: Longman, 2001.

McClenon, James. *Wondrous Healing: Shamanism, Human Evolution and the Origin of Religion*. DeKalb, IL: Northern Illinois University Press, 2002.

McGee, R. Jon and Richard L. Warms. "Postmodernism and Its Critics." In *Anthropological Theory: An Introductory History*, edited by R. Jon McGee and Richard L. Warms. New York: McGraw Hill, 2008.

McGrew, W. C. "The intelligent Use of Tools: Twenty Propositions." In *Tools, Language, and Cognition in Human Evolution*, edited by K. R. Gibson and T. Ingold. Cambridge: Cambridge University Press, 1993.

McKnight, David. *People, Countries, and the Rainbow Serpent: Systems of Classification among the Lardil of Mornington Island*. New York: Oxford University Press, 1999.

McLoughlin, Moira. *Museums and the Representation of Native Canadians: Negotiating the Borders of Culture*. New York: Garland Publishing, 1999.

McWhorter, John H. *Defining Creole*. New York: Oxford University Press, 2005.

Mead, Margaret. *Sex and Temperament in Three Primitive Societies*, 1935. Reprint. New York: Mentor Books, 1950.

Megejee, Rinchin. "Marriage Rules, Practices and Emotions in Shertukpen Marriage Ceremony." In *Marriage and Culture: Reflections from Tribal Societies of Arunachal Pradesh*, vol. 2, edited by Tamo Mibang and M. C. Behera. New Delhi: Mittal Publications, 2006.

Meggitt, Mervyn. "System and Sub-System: The Te Exchange Cycle among the Mae Enga." *Human Ecology* 1, no. 2 (1974): 111–23.

Meezan, William and Jonathan Rauch. "Gay Marriage, Same-Sex Parenting, and America's Children." *The Future of Children* 15, no. 2 (2005): 97–115.

Meisch, Lynn A. "The Reconquest of Otavalo, Ecuador: Indigenous Economic Gains and New Power Relations." *Research in Economic Anthropology* 19 (1998): 11–30.

Melton, J. Gordon. *Magic, Witchcraft and Paganism in America: A Bibliography*. New York: Garland Publishing, 1982.

Menges, Karl H. "People, Languages, and Migrations." In *Central Asia: A Century of Russian Rule*, edited by Edward Allworth. New York: Columbia University Press, 1967.

Merry, Sally Engle. "Rights, Religion and Community: Approaches to Violence against Women in the Context of Globalization." In *Law and Anthropology: A Reader*, edited by Sally Falk Moore. Malden, MA: Blackwell, 2005.

Mertz, Elizabeth. "Legal Language: Pragmatics, Poetics, and Social Power." *Annual Review of Anthropology* 22 (1994): 435–45.

Meshorer, Hank. "The Sacred Trail to Zuni Heaven: A Study in the Law of Prescriptive Easements." In *Readings in American Indian Law: Recalling the Rhythm of Survival*, edited by Jo Carrillo. Philadelphia: Temple University Press, 1998.

Meyer, Stephen. "Work, Play and Power: Masculine Culture on the Automotive Shop Floor, 1930–1960." In *Boys and Their Toys: Masculinity, Technology and Class in America*, edited by Roger Horowitz. New York: Routledge, 2001.

Miles, Steven, Kevin Meethan, and Alison Anderson. "Introduction: the Meaning of Consumption, the Meaning of Change?" In *The Changing Consumer: Markets and Meanings*, edited by Steven Miles, Alison Anderson, and Kevin Meethan. New York: Routledge, 2002.

Miller, Martin A. "The Concept of Revolutionary Insanity in Russian History." In *Madness and the Mad in Russian Culture*, edited by Angela Brintlinger and Ilya Vinitsky. Toronto: University of Toronto Press, 2007.

Mills, Mary Beth. "Gender and Inequality in the Global Labor Force." *Annual Review of Anthropology* 32 (2003): 41–62.

Mintz, Sidney. "Food at Moderate Speeds." In *Fast Food/Slow Food: The Cultural Economy of The Global Food System*, edited by Richard Wilk. New York: AltaMira Press, 2006.

Mirchandani, Kiran. "Practices of Global Capital: Gaps, Cracks and Ironies in Transnational Call Centres in India." *Global Networks* 4, no. 4 (2004): 355–73.

Moore, Sally Falk. "General Introduction." In *Law and Anthropology: A Reader*, edited by Sally Falk Moore. Malden, MA: Blackwell, 2005.

Morgan, David. "Family Gender and Masculinities." In *The Masculinities Reader*, edited by Stephen M. Whitehead and Frank J. Barrett. Cambridge: Polity Press, 2001.

Morgan, Lewis Henry. Ancient Society. 1877. Reprint. New York: World Publishing, 1963.

Morgan, Marcyliena. "Theories and Politics in African-American English." *Annual Review of Anthropology* 23: 325–45, 1994.

Morris, Barry and Rohan Bastin. *Expert Knowledge: First World Peoples, Consultancy and Anthropology.* New York: Berghahn Books, 2004.

Morris, Ewan. *Our Own Devices: National Symbols and Political Conflict in Twentieth-Century Ireland.* Dublin: Irish Academic Press, 2005.

Morris, Rosalind C. "All Made Up: Performance Theory and the New Anthropology of Sex and Gender." *Annual Review of Anthropology* 24 (1995): 567–92.

Mosse, David. *Cultivating Development: An Ethnography of Aid Policy and Practice.* London: Pluto Press, 2005.

Mufwene, Salikoko S., John R. Rickford, Guy Bailey, and John Baugh. *African-America English: Structure, History and Use.* New York: Routledge, 1998.

Muhlhausler, Peter. *Linguistic Ecology: Language Change and Linguistic Imperialism in the Pacific Region.* New York: Routledge, 1996.

Munn, Nancy. "The Spatial Presentation of Cosmic Order in Walbiri Iconography." In *Primitive Art and Society*, edited by Anthony Forge. London: Oxford University Press, 1973.

Nanda, Serena. *The Hijras of India: Neither Man Nor Woman*, 2nd ed. Belmont, CA: Wadsworth, 1999.

_____. *Gender Diversity: Crosscultural Variations.* Prospects Heights, IL: Waveland Press, 2000.

Nagata, Judith. "Beyond Theology: Toward an Anthropology of 'Fundamentalism.'" *American Anthropologist* 103, no. 2 (2001): 481–98.

Nathanson, Paul. *Over the Rainbow: The Wizard of Oz as a Secular Myth of America.* Albany: State University of New York Press, 1991.

New York Times. "As Ills Persist Afghan Leader is Losing Luster," June 7, 2008.

New York Times. "An Intrusion of Soldiers Threatens Amazon Tribe," October 10, 2002.

_____. "Secrecy and Stigma No Longer Clouding Adoptions," October 25, 1998.

New York Times Magazine Section. "A Big Game," August 25, 2002.

Nugent, Stephen. "Euphemism in the Forest: Ahistoricism and the Valorization of Indigenous Knowledge." In *Human Impacts on Amazonia: The Role of Traditional Ecological Knowledge in Conservation and Development*, edited by Darrell Addison Posey and Michael J. Balick. New York: Columbia University Press, 2006.

O'Brien, Kevin A. "Privatizing Security, Privatizing War? The New Warrior Class and Regional Security." In *Warlords in International Relations*. London: MacMillan Press, 1999.

Ong, Aihwa. *Spirits of Resistance and Capitalist Discipline: Factory Women in Malaysia*. Albany: State University Press of New York, 1987.

_____. *Flexible Citizenship: The Cultural Logic of Transnationality*. Durham, NC: Duke University Press, 1999.

_____. "Corporate Players, New Cosmopolitans, and *Guanxi* in Shanghai." In *Frontiers of Capital: Ethnographic Reflections on the New Economy*, edited by Melissa S. Fisher and Greg Downey. Durham, NC: Duke University Press, 2006.

O'Reilly, Karen. *Ethnographic Methods*. New York: Routledge, 2005.

Orenstein, Catherine. *Little Red Riding Hood Uncloaked: Sex, Morality and the Evolution of a Fairy Tale*. New York: Basic Books, 2002.

Orion, Loretta. *Never Again the Burning Times: Paganism Revived*. Prospect Heights, IL: Waveland Press, 1995.

Orlove, Benjamin. "Working in the Field: Perspectives on Globalization in Latin America." In *Globalization and the Rural Poor in Latin America*, edited by William M. Loker. Boulder, CO: Lynne Rienner Publishers, 1999.

Ortner, Sherry B. "Theory in Anthropology since the Sixties." *Comparative Studies in Society and History* 26, no. (1984): 126–66.

O'Toole, Fintan. "The Many Stories of Billy the Kid." *The New Yorker* 74, no. 10 (1998): 86–98.

Otterbein, Keith F. "The Doves Have Been Heard From, Where Are the Hawks." *American Anthropologist* 102, no. 4 (1999): 841–44.

_____. *How War Began*. College Station: Texas A&M University Press, 2004.

Pader, Ellen J. "Spatiality and Social Change: Domestic Space Use in Mexico and the United States." *American Ethnologist* 20, no. 1 (1993): 114–37.

Palmié, Stephan. "Genomics, Divination, 'Racecraft.'" *American Ethnologist* 34, no. 2 (2007): 205–222.

Panter-Brick, Catherine, Robert H. Layton, and Peter Rowley-Conwy, eds. *Hunter-Gatherers: An Interdisciplinary Perspective*. Cambridge: Cambridge University Press, 2001.

Parkin, Robert. Kinship: *An Introduction to Basic Concepts*. Malden, MA: Blackwell Publishers, 1997.

Parrenas, Rhacel Salazar. *Children of Global Migration: Transnational Families and Gendered Woes*. Stanford: Stanford University Press, 2005.

Patillo-McCoy, Mary. "Negotiating Adolescence in a Black Middle-Class Neighborhood." In *Coping with Poverty: The Social Context of Neighborhood, Work, and Family in the African-American Community*, edited by Sheldon Danziger and Ann Chili Lin. Ann Arbor: University of Michigan Press, 2000.

Peck, Catherine. *A Treasury of North American Folk-Tales*. New York: W.W. Norton, 1998.

Pels, Peter. "The Anthropology of Colonialism: Culture, History, and the Emergence of Western Governmentality." *Annual Review of Anthropology* 26 (1997): 163–83.

Pennycook, Alastair. *Critical Applied Linguistics: A Critical Introduction*. Mahwah, NJ: L. Ehrlbaum, 2001.

_____. "Global Englishes, Rip Slyme, and Performativity." *Journal of Sociolinguistics* 7, no. 4: (2003): 513–33.

Peters, Emrys. "The Proliferation of Segments in the Lineage of the Bedouin of Cyrenaica." *Journal of the Royal Anthropological Institute of Great Britain and Ireland* 90 (1960): 29–53.

Peters, John F. *Life among the Yanomami: The Story of Change among the Xilixana on the Mucajai River in Brazil.* Peterborough, Ontario: Broadview Press, 1998.

Pickett, Terry H. *Inventing Nations: Justifications of Authority in the Modern World.* Westport, CT: Greenwood Press, 1996.

Pinker, Steven. *The Language Instinct.* New York: Harper Perennial, 1994.

_____. "The Semantic Bootstrapping Hypothesis." In *First Language Acquisition: The Essential Readings,* edited by Barbara Lust and Claire Foley. Oxford: Blackwell Publishing, 2004a.

_____. "Implications for the Semantic Bootstrapping Hypothesis." In *First Language Acquisition: The Essential Readings,* edited by Barbara Lust and Claire Foley. Oxford: Blackwell Publishing 2004b.

_____. *The Stuff of Thought.* New York: Viking, 2007.

_____. "The Moral Instinct." *New York Times Magazine,* January 13, 2008. pp. 32–37, 52, 55–58.

Pinker, Steven and P. Bloom. "Natural Language and Natural Selection." *Behavioral and Brain Sciences* 13, no. 4 (1990): 707–784.

Polka, Linda, Susan Rvachew, and Karen Mattock. "Experiential Influences on Speech Perception and Speech Product in Infancy." In *Blackwell Handbook of Language Development,* edited by Erika Hoff and Marilyn Shatz. Malden, MA: Blackwell Publishing, 2007.

Powdermaker, Hortense. *Life in Lesu.* 1933. Reprint. New York: W. W. Norton, 1971.

Poynton, Cate. *Language and Gender; Making the Difference.* London: Oxford University Press, 1989.

Price, Sally. *Primitive Art in Civilized Places.* Chicago: University of Chicago Press, 1989.

Purkiss, Diane. *Troublesome Things: A History of Fairies and Fairy Stories.* London: Penguin Press, 2000.

Rabbens, Linda. *Brazil's Indians and the Onslaught of Civilization: The Yanomami and the Kayapo.* Seattle: University of Washington Press, 2004.

Radcliffe-Brown, A. R. *Structure and Function in Primitive Society,* Glencoe, IL: Free Press, 1952.

Ramirez, Rafael I. *What It Means to Be a Man: Reflections on Puerto Rican Masculinity.* New Brunswick, NJ: Rutgers University Press, 1999.

Ramos, Alcida Rita. "The Commodification of the Indian." In *Human Impacts on Amazonia: The Role of Traditional Ecological Knowledge in Conservation and Development,* edited by Darrell Addison Posey and Michael Balick. New York: Columbia University Press, 2006.

Rapp, Rayna. "Reproduction and Gender Hierarchy: Amniocentesis in America." In *Sex and Gender Hierarchies,* edited by Barbara D. Miller. Cambridge, England: Cambridge Press, 1993.

_____. *Testing Women, Testing the Fetus: The Social Impact of Amniocentesis in America.* New York: Routledge. 2000.

Rappaport, Roy A. *Pigs for the Ancestors: Ritual in the Ecology of a New Guinea People,* 2nd ed. New Haven, CT: Yale University Press, 1984.

Reddy, Gayatri. *With Respect to Sex: Negotiating Hijra Identity in South India.* Chicago: University of Chicago Press, 2005.

Rees, Richard W. *Shades of Difference: A History of Ethnicity in America.* New York: Rowman & Littlefield, 2007.

Reesman, Jeanne Campbell. *Trickster Lives: Culture and Myth in American Fiction.* Athens: The University of Georgia Press, 2001.

Reichel-Dolmatoff, Elizabeth. "Foreword." In *Body Decoration: A World Survey of Body Art*, edited by Karl Groning. New York: Vendome Press, 1998.

Ricento, Thomas. "Theoretical Perspectives in Language Policy: An Overview." In *An Introduction to Language Policy: Theory and Method*. Oxford: Blackwell Publishing, 2006.

Rich, Paul B. "Introduction." In *Warlords in International Relations*, edited by Paul B. Rich. London: Macmillan Press, Ltd., 1999a.

_____."The Emergence and Significance of Warlordism in International Politics." In *Warlords in International Relations*, edited by Paul B. Rich. London: Macmillan Press, Ltd., 1999b.

Rickford, John R. "The Anglicist/Creolist Quest for the Roots of AAVE: Historical Overviews and New Evidence from the Copula." In *Studies in Contact Linguistics: Essays in Honor of Glenn G. Gilbert*, edited by Linda L. Thornburg and Janet M. Fuller. New York: Peter Lang, 2006.

Rickford, John R. "The Creole Origins of African-American Vernacular English: Evidence from Copula Absence." In *African-American English: Structure, History and Use*, edited by Salikoko S. Mufwene, John R. Rickford, Guy Bailey, and John Baugh. New York: Routledge, 1998.

Riekse, Robert J. and Henry Holstege. *Growing Older in America*. New York: McGraw-Hill, 1996.

Rikam, N. T. "Exchanges in Nyishi Marriage: Bride Price or Balanced Reciprocity of Marriage Gifts." In *Marriage and Culture: Reflections from Tribal Societies of Arunachal Pradesh*, vol. 2. New Delhi: Mittal Publications, 2006.

Robben, Antonius C. G. M. and Marcelo M. Suárez-Orozco. *Cultures Under Siege: Collective Violence and Trauma*. New York: Cambridge University Press, 2000.

Robinne, François and Mandy Sadan. *Social Dynamics in the Highlands of Southeast Asia: Reconsidering Political Systems of Highland Burma by E. R. Leach*. Leiden, The Netherlands: Brill, 2007.

Rogoff, Barbara. *The Cultural Nature of Human Development*. Oxford: Oxford University Press, 2003.

Roscoe, Will. *Changing Ones: Third and Fourth Genders in Native North America*. New York: St. Martin's Press, 1998.

Rosman, Abraham and Paula G. Rubel. "Structural Patterning in Kwakiutl Art and Ritual," *Man* 25 (1990): 620–40.

_____. "Colonialism and the Efflorescence of Warfare." In *War and Society*, edited by Stephen P. Reyna and R. E. Downs. London: Gordon and Breach Publishers, 1999.

Ross, Marcus R. "Who Believes What? Clearing Up Confusion Over Intelligent Design and Young-Earth Creationism." *Journal of Geoscience Education* 49, no. 1 (2005): 30–35.

Rostow, Walt Whitman. *The Stages of Economic Growth: A Non-Communist Manifesto*. Cambridge: Cambridge University Press, 1960.

Rothstein, Frances. *Globalization in Rural Mexico: Three Decades of Change*. Austin: University of Texas Press, 2007.

Rowley-Conwy, Peter. "Time, change and the archaeology of hunter-gatherers: how original is the "Original Affluent Society'?" *In Hunger-Gatherers: An Interdisciplinary Perspective*, edited by Catherine Panter-Brick, Robert Layton, and Peter Rowley-Conwy. Cambridge, UK: Cambridge University Press, 2001.

Royce, Anya Peterson. *Anthropology of the Performing Arts: Artistry, Virtuosity, and Interpretation in a Cross-Cultural Perspective*. New York: AltaMira Press, 2004.

Rubel, Paula G. *The Kalmyk Mongols: A Study in Continuity and Change*. Indiana University Publications, Uralic and Altaic Series, vol. 64. Bloomington: Indiana University Press, 1967.

Rubel, Paula G. and Abraham Rosman. *Your Own Pigs You May Not Eat*. Chicago: University of Chicago Press, 1978.

Ruffini, Julio L. "Disputing Over Livestock in Sardinia." In *Law and Anthropology: A Reader*, edited by Sally Falk Moore. Malden, MA: Blackwell, 2005.

Rush, John A. *Spiritual Tattoo: A Cultural History of Tattooing, Piercing, Scarification, Branding and Implants.* Berkeley: Frog Ltd., 2005.

Saffran, Jennie R. and Erik D. Thiessen. "Domain-General Learning Capacities." In *Blackwell Handbook of Language Development,* edited by Erika Hoff and Marilyn Shatz. Oxford: Blackwell Publishing, 2007.

Sahlins, Marshall. *Islands of History*. Chicago: University of Chicago Press, 1985.

_____. "What Is Anthropological Enlightenment? Some Lessons of the Twentieth Century." *Annual Review of Anthropology* 28 (1999): i–xxiii.

Salaff, Janet W. *Working Daughters of Hong Kong: Filial Piety or Power in the Family.* New York: Columbia University Press, 1995.

Saler, Benson. *Conceptualizing Religion: Eminent Anthropologists, Transcendent Natives, and Unbounded Categories.* Leiden, Holland: E. J. Brill, 1993.

Salter, Frank K. "From Mafia to Freedom Fighters: Questions Raised by Ethology and Sociobiology." In *Risky Transactions: Trust, Kinship and Ethnicity*, edited by Frank K. Salter. New York: Berghahn Books, 2002.

Saussure, Ferdinand de. *Course in General Linguistics*. 1915. Reprint. New York: McGraw-Hill, 1966.

Sax, William S. *Dancing the Self: Personhood and Performance in the Pandav Lila of Garwal.* New York: Oxford University Press, 2000.

Schatz, Edward. *Modern Clan Politics: The Power of "Blood" in Kazakhstan and Beyond.* Seattle: University of Washington Press, 2004.

Scheper-Hughes, Nancy and Philippe Bourgois. "Introduction: Making Sense of Violence." In *Violence in War and Peace: An Anthology*, edited by Nancy Scheper-Hughes and Philippe Bourgois. Malden, MA: Blackwell, 2004.

Scheub, Harold. *Storytelling Songs of Zulu Women: Recording Archetypal Rites of Passage and Mythic Paths.* Lewiston, NY: Edwin Mellen Press, 2006.

Schiefenhovel, Wulf and Ingrid Bell-Krannhals. "Of Harvests and Hierarchies: Securing Staple Food and Social Position in the Trobriand Islands." In *Food and the Status Quest: An Interdisciplinary Perspective*, edited by Polly Wiessner and Wulf Schiefenhovel. Providence, RI: Berghahn Books, 1996.

Schieffelin, Bambi. "The Acquisition of Kaluli." In *The Cross-Linguistic Study of Language Acquisition*, vol. 1, edited by D. I. Slobin. Hillsdale, NJ: Lawrence Earlbaum, 1985.

_____. "Teasing and Shaming in Kaluli Children's Interactions." In *Language Socialization across Cultures*, edited by Bambi Schieffelin and Elinor Ochs. Cambridge, England: Cambridge University Press, 1986.

Schieffelin, Bambi B. and Elinor Ochs. "The Microgenesis of Competence: Methodology in Language Socialization." In *Social Interaction, Social Context, and Language*, edited by Dan L. Slobin, Julie Gerhardt, Amy Kyratzis, and Jiansheng Guo. Mahwah, NJ: Lawrence Erlbaum, 1996.

Schneider, David M. *American Kinship*, 2nd ed. Chicago: University of Chicago Press, 1980.

_____. *A Critique of the Study of Kinship.* Ann Arbor: University of Michigan Press, 1984.

Schneider, Jane and Peter T. Schneider. "Mafias." In *A Companion to the Anthropology of Politics.* Malden, MA: Blackwell Publishing, 2004.

Schrauwers, Albert. "'It's Not Economical': The Market Roots of a Moral Economy in Highland Sulawesi." In *Transforming the Indonesian Uplands: Marginality, Power and Production*, edited by Tania Murray Li. New York: Harwood Academic Publishers, 1999.

Schröeder, Ingo W. and Bettina E. Schmidt. "Introduction: Violent Imaginaries and Violent Practices." In *Anthropology of Violence and Conflict*, edited by Bettina E. Schmidt and Ingo W. Schröder. New York: Routledge, 2001.

Schulz, Dorothea E. "Morals of Praise: Broadcast Media and the Commoditization of Jeli Praise Performances in Mali." *Research in Economic Anthropology* 19 (1998): 117–32.

Schwede, Laurel, Rae Lesser Blumberg, and Anna Y. Chan. *Complex Ethnic Households in America*. New York: Rowman & Littlefield, 2005.

Scott, Eugenie C. "The Creation/Evolution Continuum." *National Center for Science Education Reports* 19, no. 4 (1999): 16–25.

Seabright, Paul. *The Vanishing Rouble: Barter Networks and Non-Monetary Transactions in Post Soviet Societies*. Cambridge: Cambridge University Press, 2000.

Sebba, Mark. *Contact Pidgins and Creoles*. New York: St. Martin's Press, 1997.

Seligmann, Linda J. *Women Traders in Cross-Cultural Perspective: Mediating Identities, Marketing Wares*. Stanford, CA: Stanford University Press, 2001.

Seneviratne, H. L. "Buddhist Monks and Ethnic Politics." *Anthropology Today* 17 (2001): 15–21.

Shady, M. E., L. A. Gerken, and P. W. Jusczyk. "Some Evidence of Sensitivity to Prosody and Word Order in Ten-month-olds. In *Proceedings of the 19th Boston University Conference on Language Development: Vol. 2* edited by D. MacLaughlin and S. McEwan. Somerville, MA: Cascadilla Press, 1995.

Sharma, Aradhana and Akhil Gupta. "Introduction: Rethinking Theories of the State in an Age of Globalization." In *The Anthropology of the State: A Reader*, edited by Aradhana Sharma and Akhil Gupta. Malden, MA: Blackwell Publishing, 2006.

Sharp, Leslie A. "Commodified Kin: Death, Mourning, and Competing Claims on the Bodies of Organ Donors in the United States." *American Anthropologist* 103, no. 1 (2001): 112–33.

Shay, Anthony. *Dancing across Borders: The American Fascination with Exotic Dance Forms*. London: McFarland & Company, 2008.

Sherman, Suzanne. *Lesbian and Gay Marriage: Private Commitments, Public Ceremonies*. Philadelphia: Temple University Press, 1992.

Shott, Michael J. "On Recent Trends in the Anthropology of Foragers: Kalahari Revisionism and Its Archaeological Implications." *Man* 27 (1992): 843–71.

Shweder, Richard A. "Rethinking the Object of Anthropology and Ending Up Where Kroeber and Kluckhohn Began." *American Anthropologist* 103, no. 2 (2001): 437–40.

Sillitoe, Paul. "Participant Observation to Participatory Development: Making Anthropology Work." In *Participating Development: Approaches to Indigenous Knowledge*, edited by Paul Sillitoe, Alan Bicker, and John Pottier. London: Routledge, 2002.

Siskind, Janet. "The Invention of Thanksgiving." *Critique of Anthropology* 12, no. 2 (1992): 167–91.

Skolnick, Arlene. "Solomon's Children: Psychological Parenthood, Attachment Theory, and the Best Interests Standard." In *All Our Families: New Policies for a New Century*, edited by Mary Ann Mason, Arlene Skolnick, and Stephen D. Sugarman. New York: Oxford University Press, 1998.

Smedley, Audrey. *Race in North America: Origin and Evolution of a Worldview*, 3rd ed. Boulder, CO: Westview Press, 2007.

Smitherman, Geneva. "Word from the Hood: The Lexicon of African-American Vernacular English." In *African-American English: Structure, History and Use*, edited by Salikoko S. Mufwene, John R. Rickford, Guy Bailey, and John Baugh. New York: Routledge, 1998.

Sobel, Mechal. "Migration and Collective Identities among the Enslaved and Free Populations of North

America." In *Coerced and Free Migration: Global Perspectives*, edited by David Eltis. Stanford, CA: Stanford University Press, 2002.

Sollars, Werner. *The Invention of Ethnicity*. New York: Oxford University Press, 1989.

Snyder, Francis. "Governing Economic Globalization: Global Legal Pluralism and European Union Law." In *Law and Anthropology: A Reader*, edited by Sally Falk Moore. Malden, MA: Blackwell, 2005.

Spiro, Melford. "Religion: Problems of Definition and Explanation." In *Anthropological Approaches to the Study of Religion*, edited by Michael Banton. London: Tavistock Publications, 1966.

Sponsel, Leslie. "Response to Otterbein." *American Anthropologist* 102, no. 4 (2000): 837–41.

Ssorin-Chaikov, Nickolai. "Bear Skins and Macaroni: The Social Life of Things at the Margins of a Siberian State Collective." In *The Vanishing Rouble: Barter Networks and Non-Monetary Transactions in Post Soviet Societies*, edited by Paul Seabright. Cambridge: Cambridge University Press, 2000.

Stacey, Judith. "Gay and Lesbian Families: Queer Like Us." In *All Our Families: New Policies for a New Century*, edited by Mary Ann Mason, Arlene Skolnick, and Stephen D. Sugarman. New York: Oxford University Press, 1998.

Stack, Carol B. *All Our Kin: Strategies for Survival in a Black Community*. New York: Harper & Row, 1974.

Stammler, Florian. *Reindeer Nomads Meet the Market: Culture, Property, and Globalisation at the End of the Land*. Munster: LIT Verlag, 2005.

Starrett, Gregory. "The Political Economy of Religious Commodities in Cairo." *American Anthropologist* 97, no. 1 (1995): 51–68.

Stern, Stephen and John Allan Cicala, eds. *Creative Ethnicity: Symbols and Strategies of Contemporary Ethnic Life*. Utah: Utah State University Press, 1991.

Stevens, Williams. "Black and Standard English Held Diverging More." *The New York Times*, March 14, 1985, p. A14.

Steward, Julian. *Theory of Culture Change*. Urbana: University of Illinois Press, 1955.

Stewart, Pamela and Andrew Strathern. "Self-decoration in Hagen and Duna (Papua New Guinea): Display and Disjuncture." In *Embodying Modernity and Post-Modernity: Ritual, Praxis and Social Change in Melanesia*, edited by Sandra Bamford. Durham, NC: Carolina Academic Press, 2007.

Stoler, Ann Laura. *Carnal Knowledge and Imperial Power: Race and the Intimate in Colonial Rule*. Berkeley: University of California Press, 2002.

———. *Haunted by Empire: Geographies of Intimacy in North American History*. Durham, NC: Duke University Press, 2006.

Stoller, Eleanor P. "Informal Exchanges with Non-Kin among Retired Sunbelt Migrants: A Case Study of a Finnish American Retirement Community." *Journal of Gerontology: Social Sciences* 53 B (1998): S287–S298.

Straight, Bilinda. "Gender, Work, and Change among Samburu Pastoralists of Northern Kenya." *Research in Economic Anthropology* 18 (1997): 65–91.

Strauss, Sarah. *Positioning Yoga: Balancing Acts Across Cultures*. New York: Berg, 2005

Stoller, Paul. *Money Has No Smell: The Africanization of New York City*. Chicago: University of Chicago Press, 2002.

Strathern, Andrew and Marilyn Strathern. *Self-Decoration in Mount Hagen*. London: Gerald Duckworth, 1971.

Strathern, Marilyn. *Reproducing the Future: On Anthropology, Kinship and the New Reproductive Technologies*. New York: Routledge, 1992.

Sturm, Circe. *Blood Politics: Race, Culture, and Identity in the Cherokee Nation of Oklahoma*. Berkeley: University of California Press, 2002.

Suarez-Orozco, Marcelo M., and Antonius C. G. M. Robben. "Interdisciplinary Perspectives on Violence and Trauma." In *Cultures under Siege: Collective Violence and Trauma*, edited by Antonius C. G.M. Robben and Marcelo M. Suarez-Orozco. Cambridge, UK: Cambridge University Press, 2000.

Suchman, Lucy A. "Building Bridges: Practice-Based Ethnographies of Contemporary Technology." In *Anthropological Perspectives on Technology*, edited by Michael Brian Schiffer. Albuquerque: New Mexico Press, 2001.

Sullivan, Maureen. *The Family of Woman: Lesbian Mothers, Their Children, and the Undoing of Gender.* Berkeley: University of California Press, 2004.

Sullivan, Nancy. "Inside Trading: Postmodernism and the Social Drama of Sunflowers in the 1980s Art World." In *The Traffic in Culture: Refiguring Art and Anthropology*, edited by George E. Marcus and Fred R. Myers. Berkeley: University of California Press, 1995.

Sutherland, Anne. *Gypsies—The Hidden Americans*. Prospect Heights, IL: Waveland Press, 1986.

Tambiah, S. J. "Animals Are Good to Think and Good to Prohibit." *Ethnology* 8, no. 4 (1969): 423–59.

_____. *Sri Lanka: Ethnic Fratricide and the Dismantling of Democracy*. Chicago: University of Chicago Press, 1986.

_____. "Ethnic Fratricide in Sri Lanka: An Update." In *Ethnicities and Nations: Processes of Interethnic Relations in Latin America, Southeast Asia, and the Pacific*, edited by Remo Guidieri, Francesco Pellizzi, and Stanley J. Tambiah. Austin: University of Texas Press, 1988.

Tatla, Darshan Singh. *The Sikh Diaspora: The Search for Statehood*. UCL Press, 1999.

Tattersall, Ian. *Becoming Human: Evolution and Human Uniqueness*. New York: Harcourt Brace, 1998.

Taussig, Michael. "Culture of Terror-Space of Death." In *The Anthropology of Politics: A Reader in Ethnography, Theory, and Critique*, edited by Joan Vincent. Oxford: Blackwell Publishers, 2002.

Thomas, David Hurst. *Skull Wars: Kennewick Man, Archaeology, and The Battle for Native American Identity*. New York: Basic Books, 2000.

Thomas, Wesley. *Two-Spirit People: Native American Gender Identity, Sexuality, and Spirituality.* Urbana: University of Illinois Press, 1997.

Thompson, Charis. *Making Parents: The Ontological Choreography of Reproductive Technologies*. Cambridge, MA: The MIT Press, 2005.

Thornton, Thomas F. *Being and Place among the Tlingit*. Seattle: University of Washington Press, 2008.

Tomasello, Michael and Elizabeth Bates. "Introduction." In *Language Development: The Essential Readings*, edited by Michael Tomasello and Elizabeth Bates. Malden: Blackwell, 2001.

Tongue, Nancy E. "I Live Here and I Stay There: Navajo Perceptions of Households on the Reservation." In *Complex Households in America*, edited by Laurel Schwede, Rae Lesser Blumberg, and Anna Y. Chan. New York: Rowman & Littlefield, 2005.

Townsend, Joan B. "Shamanism." In *Anthropology of Religion: A Handbook*, edited by Stephen D. Glazier. Westport, CT: Greenwood Press, 1997.

Trotman, C. James. "Introduction. Multiculturalism: Roots and Realities." In *Multiculturalism: Roots and Realities*, edited by C. James Trotman. Bloomington: Indiana University Press, 2002.

Turino, Thomas. "The History of a Peruvian Panpipe Style and the Politics of Interpretation." In *Ethnomusicology and Modern Music History*, edited by S. Blum, P. Bohlman, and D. Neuman. Urbana: University of Illinois Press, 1991.

Turner, Jonathan H. *On the Origins of Human Emotions: Sociological Inquiry into the Evolution of Human Affect*. Stanford, CA: Stanford University Press, 2000.

Turner, Lorenzo. *Africanisms in the Gullah Dialect*. 1949. Reprint. New York: Arno Press, 1968.

Turner, Victor. *The Forest of Symbol: Aspects of Ndembu Ritual.* Ithaca, NY: Cornell University Press, 1967.

Tylor, Edward B. *Primitive Culture: Researches into the Development of Mythology, Philosophy, Religion, Language, Art and Custom,* 2 vols. London: John Murray, 1871.

Ukaegbu, Victor. *The Use of Masks in Igbo Theater in Nigeria: The Aesthetic Flexibility of Performance Traditions.* Lewiston, NY: The Edwin Mellon Press, 2006.

Van Gennep, Arnold. *The Rites of Passage.* 1909. Reprint. Translated by Monika B. Vizedom and Gabrielle Caffee. Chicago: University of Chicago Press, 1960.

Vaughn-Cooke, Fay. "Are Black and White Vernaculars Diverging?" In *Readings in African American Language: Aspects, Features and Perspectives,* edited by Nathaniel Norment, Jr. New York: Peter Land, 2003.

Verkaaik, Oskar. "The Captive State: Corruption, Intelligence Agencies and Ethnicity in Pakistan." In *States of Imagination: Ethnographic Explorations of the Postcolonial State,* edited by Thomas Blom Hansen and Finn Stepputat. Durham, NC: Duke University Press, 2001.

Vischer, Michael P. "Substitution, Expiation and the Idiom of Blood in Ko'a Sacrificing: Comparative Issues in Austronesian Ethnography." In *Framing Indonesian Realities: Essays in Symbolic Anthropology in Honor of Remar Schefeld,* edited by Peter J. M. Nass, Gerard Persoon, and Rivke Jaffe. Leiden, The Netherlands: KITLV Press, 2003.

Vogelsang, Willem. *The Afghans.* Malden: Blackwell Press, 2002.

Von Bremen, Volker. Dynamics of Adaptation to Market Economy among the Ayoreode of Northwest Paraguay." In *Hunters and Gatherers in the Modern World: Conflict, Resistance, and Self-Determination,* edited by Peter P. Schweitzer, Megan Biesele, and Robert K. Hitchcock. New York: Berghahn Books, 2000.

Von Hendy, Andrew. *The Modern Construction of Myth.* Bloomington: Indiana University Press, 2002.

Walker, Roslyn Adele. *Ọlọ́wẹ̀ of Isẹ̀: A Yoruba Sculptor to Kings.* Washington, DC: National Museum of African Art, Smithsonian Institution, 1998.

Wallerstein, Immanuel M. *The Modern World System: Capitalist Agriculture and the Origins of the European World Economy in the Sixteenth Century.* New York: Academic Press, 1974.

_____. *World-Systems Analysis: An Introduction.* Durham, NC: Duke University Press, 2004.

Waters, Mary C. *Ethnic Options: Choosing Identities in America.* Berkeley: University of California Press, 1990.

Watt, Lisa J. "Today's American Indian Tribes and Their Museums." In *American Indian Nations: Yesterday, Today, and Tomorrow.* New York: AltaMira Press, 2007.

Weber, Max. *The Protestant Ethic and the Spirit of Capitalism.* London: Allen and Unwin, 1930.

Weisgrau, Maxine K. *Interpreting Development: Local Histories, Local Strategies.* Lanham, MD: University Press of America, 1997.

Wellings, Peter. "Joint Management: Aboriginal Involvement in Tourism in the Kakadu World Heritage Area." In *Tourism and Protected Areas: Benefits beyond Boundaries,* edited by Robyn Bushell and Paul Eagles. Oxfordshire: CAB International, 2007.

Werbner, Pnina. "Stamping the Earth with the Name of Allah: Zikr and the Sacralizing of Space among British Muslims." *Cultural Anthropology* 11, no. 3 (1996): 309–333.

West, Paige. *Conservation Is Our Government Now: The Politics of Ecology in Papua New Guinea.* Durham, NC: Duke University Press, 2006.

Westmacott, Richard. *African-American Gardens and Yards in the Rural South.* Nashville: University of Tennessee Press, 1992.

Weston, Kath. *Families We Chose: Lesbians, Gays, Kinship.* Columbia University Press, 1991.

Whalley, Lucy A. "Urban Minangkabau Muslim Women: Modern Choices, Traditional Choices in Indonesia." In *Women in Muslim Societies: Diversity within Unity,* edited by Herbert I. Bodman and Nayereh Tohidi. Boulder, CO: Lynne Rienner Publishers, 1998.

White, Leslie. "Energy and the Evolution of Culture." *American Anthropologist* 45, no. 3 (1943): 335–56.

_____. *The Science of Culture.* New York: Farrar, Straus and Giroux, 1949.

_____. *The Evolution of Culture.* New York: McGraw-Hill, 1959.

White, Merry. *The Material Child: Coming of Age in Japan and America.* Berkeley: University of California Press, 1994.

Whiteford, Linda M. and Robert T. Trotter II. *Ethics for Anthropological Research and Practice.* Long Grove, IL: Waveland Press, 2008.

Whitehead, Stephen M. and Frank J. Barrett, eds. *The Masculinities Reader.* Cambridge: Polity Press, 2001.

_____. "The Sociology of Masculinity." In *The Masculinities Reader,* edited by Stephen M. Whitehead and Frank J. Barrett. Cambridge: Polity Press, 2001.

Whitehouse, Harvey. *Arguments and Icons: Divergent Modes of Religiosity.* Oxford: Oxford University Press, 2000.

Wierzbiecka, Anna. *Emotions across Languages and Cultures: Diversity and Universals.* Cambridge: Cambridge University Press, 1999.

Willigen, John Van. *Applied Anthropology: An Introduction,* 3rd ed. Westport, CT: Bergin and Garvey, 2002.

Wilson, Monica. *Good Company.* 1951. Reprint. Boston: Beacon Press, 1964.

_____. *For Men and Elders: Change in the Relations of Generations and of Men and Women among the Nyakyusa-Ngonde People 1875–1971.* New York: Africana Publishing, International African Institute, 1977.

Winkelman, Michael. *Shamanism: The Neural Ecology of Consciousness and Healing.* Westport, CT: Bergin and Garvey, 2000.

Winzeler, Robert L. *Latah in Southeast Asia: The History and Ethnography of a Culture-Bound Syndrome.* Cambridge, UK: Cambridge University Press, 1995.

Wirth, Louis. "Urbanism as a Way of Life." The American Journal of Sociology. 44 (1938): 1–44.

Wolf, Eric R. *Europe and the People without History.* Berkeley: University of California Press, 1982.

Woodbury, Anthony C. "A Defense of the Proposition, 'When a Language Dies, A Culture Dies.' " *Texas Linguistic Forum* 33 (1993): 1–15.

Workman, Lance and Will Reader. *Evolutionary Psychology: An Introduction.* New York: Cambridge University Press, 2004.

Wrangham, Richard W., James H. Jones, Greg Laden, David Pilbeam, and NancyLou Conklin-Brittain. "The Raw and the Stolen: Cooking and the Ecology of Human Origins." *Current Anthropology* 40, no. 5 (1999): 567–94.

Wu, Frank H. *Yellow: Race in America beyond Black and White.* New York: Basic Books, 2002.

Yai, Olabiyi Babalola. "In Praise of Metonymy: The Concepts of 'Tradition' and 'Creativity' in the Transmission of Yoruba Artistry Over Time and Space." In *The Yoruba Artist: New Theoretical Perspectives on African Arts,* edited by Rowland Abiodun, Henry J. Drewal, and John Pemberton. Washington, D.C.: Smithsonian Institution Press, 1994.

Yeung, Henry Wai-chung. "Globalizing Asian Business: Dynamics of Change and Adjustment." In *Globalization and Change in Asia,* edited by Dennis A. Rondinelli and John M. Heffron. Boulder, CO: Lynne Rienner Publishers, 2007.

Young, Alfred Jr. "On the Outside Looking In: Low-Income Black Men's Conceptions of Work Opportunity and the Good Job." In *Coping with Poverty: The Social Context of Neighborhood, Work, and Family in the African-American Community*, edited by Sheldon Danziger and Ann Chili Lin. Ann Arbor: University of Michigan Press, 2000.

Young, Douglas W. *"Our Land Is Green and Black": Conflict Resolution in Enga*. Goroka, Papua New Guinea: Melanesian Institute, 2004.

Yuen, Sun, Pui-Iam Law, and Yuk-ying Ho. *Marriage, Gender, and Sex in a Contemporary Chinese Village*. Armonk, NY: M.E. Sharpe, 2004.

Zaleski, Jeff. *The Soul of Cyberspace: How New Technology Is Changing Our Spiritual Lives*. San Francisco: Harper Edge, 1997.

Zicker, John P. "Kinship and Exchange among the Dolgan and Nganasan of Northern Siberia." *Research in Economic Anthropology* 19 (1998): 191–238.

Ziolkowski, Jan M. *Fairytales From Before Fairy Tales: The Medieval Latin Past of Wonderful Lies*. Ann Arbor: University of Michigan Press, 2007.

Glossary

acculturation the process of culture change resulting from the contact between two cultures.

achieved status position in a social structure dependent upon personal qualifications and individual ability.

adaptation the process in which a population or society alters its culture to better succeed in its total environment.

affinal link connections between kin groups established by marriage.

African-American Vernacular (AAVE) speech patterns and norms adopted in some settings to demonstrate community affiliation.

age grade categories of individuals of the same age that are recognized by being given a name and that crosscut an entire society.

age set a group of individuals of the same age that moves as a unit through successive age grades.

agency refers to the fact that individuals are active responders to their culture.

alliance a linkage between kin groups established through marriage for the mutual benefit of the two groups.

allomorph a variant form of a morpheme.

allophone a variant form of a phoneme.

ancestor-oriented group a social unit that traces kin relationships back to a common ancestor.

animism a belief in the spiritual or noncorporeal counterparts of human beings.

applied anthropology the application of anthropological knowledge and methodologies to the solution of practical problems, direct action and/or development policy.

archaeology examines history of cultures through their material remains.

ascribed status an inherited position in the social structure.

assimilation adoption of the language and norms of a new culture.

authority an institutionalized position of power.

avunculocal residence a form of postmarital residence in which the bride goes to live with her husband after he has moved to live with his mother's brother.

band organization a type of social group with a fixed membership that comes together annually for a period to carry out joint ritual and economic activities.

barter an immediate exchange of unlike objects, which may involve bargaining.

berdache Native American term for a man who assumes a woman's role and dresses as a woman.

Big Man structure an achieved position of leadership in which the group is defined as the Big Man and his followers.

bilateral cross cousin cross cousins through both the mother's and father's side.

bilateral societies societies with kindreds but without unilineal descent groups.

bilocal residence a form of postmarital residence in which husband and wife alternate between living with the husband's relatives for a period of time and then with the wife's relatives.

blackbirding the term for the kidnapping of Melanesian laborers to work on colonial plantations in Fiji and Australia.

blended family, or stepfamily, a family created by the divorce and remarriage of spouses and the combining of parents, step parents, step siblings, and half siblings.

boundary maintenance the ways in which a social group maintains its individual identity by separating itself from the dominant society.

bride service a custom whereby the groom works for the bride's family before marriage.

bridewealth payments made by the groom's family to the family of the bride.

cargo cult a particular type of revitalization movement that first appeared in the early twentieth century in Melanesia and represents a synthesis of old and new religious beliefs.

chain migration, when earlier migrants attract later ones to the same community, resulting in residential clusters of individuals having long-term social and economic relationships.

chief the leader of a society with faxed positions of leadership (see chieftainship)

chieftainship a type of political organization in which fixed positions of leadership are present along with a method for succession to those positions.

civil law the part of a legal system that regulates family and property issues.

clan a social group based on common descent but not necessarily common residence.

clan totem an animal from which members of a clan believe themselves descended and with whom they have a special relationship that may prohibit the eating of that animal.

code-switching the use of one or more languages or speech styles in conversation.

cognate a relative traced through either the mother's or the father's line.

cognate (linguistic definition) words in two different languages that resemble one another and demonstrate that the two languages are related to each other.

cognatic rule of descent a rule of descent in which group membership may be traced through either the father or the mother.

cognitive science of religion examines religious phenomena as a result of how the human brain has evolved over time to process and categorize information.

collateral relative a relative not in the direct line of descent.

commodity any product produced for sale to a consumer other than the producer.

community a naturally bonded social unit.

compadrazgo ritual godparenthood found in Mediterranean Europe and Latin America.

comparative approach comparing societies to uncover similarities and reveal differences.

complex societies heterogeneous, culturally diverse societies with regional, class, occupational, religious, and ethnic differences.

components the criteria used to characterize and differentiate any kind of category.

consumption the processes by which products are used by humans.

corporate descent group a social group based upon common descent that owns property collectively.

corvee labor a system of forced labor associated with colonial plantations.

creationist belief systems theories of species and geological diversity based on varying interpretations of Biblical sources.

creole a pidgin language acquired by children as their native language.

criminal law the part of a legal system that determines and punishes criminality.

cross cousins children of one's mother's brother or one's father's sister.

cultural evolution the anthropological theory that refers to the development of culture into ever more complex forms.

cultural relativism the emphasis on the unique aspects of each culture, without judgments or categories based on one's own culture.

cultural rules internalized rules of behavior covering all aspects of life.

cultural universals cultural features that are to be found in all societies.

culture the way of life of a people, including their behavior, the things they make, and their ideas.

culture shock effect upon the observer of encountering a cultural practice different than one's own.

deity a spirit perceived as having human characteristics as well as supernatural power.

delayed exchange the return of goods or of women a generation after their giving; associated with preference for marriage with father's sister's daughter.

demonstrated descent a system of descent in which kinship can be traced by means of written or oral genealogies back to a founding ancestor.

dependency theory views underdevelopment as the consequence in former colonies of their economic suppression, coupled with continued economic dependence on colonial-based networks of trade and political alliances.

dialects variations within a single language between one speech community and another.

diaspora a population spread from its original homeland to other countries, which continues to maintain affiliation with its homeland.

diffusion the process by means of which a culture trait that originates in one society spreads to another.

direct reciprocal exchange a continuing exchange of like for like between two parties.

discourse an institutionalized way of thinking or speaking about a subject that comes to be the normalized and accepted worldview through political processes.

distinctive features see components.

distribution the manner in which products circulate through a society.

diviners part-time religious specialists who use the supernatural to enable people to succeed in specific undertakings.

double descent the presence of matrilineal and patrilineal descent rules in a single society.

dowry goods that are given by the bride's family to the groom's family at marriage.

duolocal residence a postmarital rule of residence in which husband and wife live with their respective kinsmen, apart from one another.

ebene hallucinogenic substance used by the Yanomamo.

ego-oriented group a kinship unit defined in terms of a particular ego.

embodiment the perspective that considers the cultural construction of the human body as enacting internalized values that contribute to the lived experience of religion and ritual.

empowerment the ability of groups or individual to achieve their political rights and goals.

enculturation the process by which culture is learned and acquired by particular individuals.

endogamy a rule requiring group members to marry within their own group.

ethnic groups distinctive groups within a state who preserve cultural items from their past.

ethnocentrism the idea that what is present in one's own culture represents the natural and best way to do things.

ethnogenesis the creation of a new ethnic group.

ethnohistory work on the history of societies with no record that draws on archaeology, oral histories, or archives.

ethnonationalism the desire of ethnic groups within a state to have their own nation-states.

ethnosemantics the anthropological investigation of native systems of classifications.

evolutionary psychology the application of Darwinian principles of natural selection.

exogamy a rule requiring group members to marry outside their own social group.

extended family several related nuclear families living together in a single household.

factionalism local groups building support under a powerful individual or idea vying for influence locally and within state systems.

fairy tales stories set in recognizable historical timeframes imparting morals or lessons particularly to children.

feminist anthropology explores cultural practices and inequities based on gender.

fictive kinship social relationships in which unrelated individuals use kin terms to establish and recognize their relationships. Oftentimes, the relationship is established by ritual observances.

folktales stories about fanciful creatures set in indeterminate times that impart morals or lessons.

Fordism the economic, production, and consumer-oriented innovations associated with Henry Ford's assembly line mass production of automobiles.

Fourth World Peoples oppressed tribal peoples living in Third World nations.

fraternal polyandry a form of marriage in which a woman is simultaneously married to several brothers.

Free Trade Zones (FTZs) (also known as Export Processing Zones) areas in developing countries set aside for foreign-owned export production facilities.

function the way a particular unit or structure operates and what it does.

fundamentalism a range of political and religious ideologies generally connoting a set of beliefs accepted as irreducible that forestall further inquiry or debate.

gender the culture-specific set of behavioral, ideological, and social meanings of constructed biological and anatomical differences.

gender stratification the comparative ranking of economic and political activities associated with men and women in any society.

generalized exchange a form of marriage in which women move from wife-givers to wife-takers but never in the opposite direction.

geomancy the interpretation of the future from physical objects.

globalization the worldwide connection between societies based upon the existence of global market connections and the spread of cultural items everywhere.

godparenthood see *compadrazgo*.

government the process by which those in office make and implement decisions on behalf of an entire group in order to carry out commonly held goals.

grammar the complete description of a language, including phonology, morphology, and syntax.

guardian spirit among North American native peoples, an animal spirit that becomes the protector of an individual as a result of his quest for a vision.

gumlao the egalitarian form of the Kachin political organization.

gumsa the chieftainship form of the Kachin political organization, in which wife-givers are higher in rank than wife-takers.

headman a leader of a group with no power or authority and with no fixed rule of succession.

hekura supernatural creatures that are part of the Yanomamo religious belief system.

heteronormativity cultural perspective that privileges male and female heterosexual indentity in conceptualizing social and family norms.

Hijras in India communities of individuals born as males who transform their identity into a new gender category.

historical particularism theoretical approach emphasizing each culture's uniqueness.

hortatory rituals exhortations to the supernatural to perform some act.

horticulture a form of cultivation in which crops are grown in gardens without the use of a plow.

hypodescent a cultural rule that classifies individuals as members of a lower-status group by virtue of their marriage of parents' identity groups.

idiolect the distinctive linguistic features or cultural features characteristic of an individual.

incest taboo prohibition of sexual relations between certain categories of close relatives.

indirect rule the system of rule associated with the British Empire by which a small number of English administrators controlled large colonial territories by integrating local political leaders and bureaucrats into the administrative system.

influence the ability to persuade others to follow one's lead when one lacks the authority to command them.

informal leadership a type of political organization in which there is no single political leader but rather leadership is manifested intermittently.

informants (or consultants) individuals within a fieldwork setting who provide cultural information to an anthropologist.

innovation the process of bringing about cultural change through the recombination of existing ideas into creative new forms.

Intelligent Design theories of speciation and geological history that accept some scientifically proposed evolutionary models but require the presence of deistic agency for the creation of the earth and its diverse life forms.

intracultural variation variability within a culture.

internal migration population movements within a nation-state.

joint family a type of extended family in which married brothers and their families remain together after the death of their parents.

kaiko a lengthy Maring religious ceremony.

kayasa a competitive period of feasting, including a competitive giving of yams to the chief, and games like cricket among the Trobrianders.

key informats individuals with whom the anthropologist forms a personal, ongoing relationship and who serve as mentors and important sources of information.

kindred a kin group oriented in terms of a particular individual.

kinship terminology a set of terms used to refer to relatives.

kula an exchange system involving one kind of shell valuables moving in a clockwise direction and another kind moving in a counterclockwise direction that links the Trobriand Islanders to a circle of neighboring islands.

langue refers to language and its grammatical rules in contrast to parole which refers to individual speech.

law a system of conflict resolution and criminalization practice.

legal pluralism the coexistence of indigenous and postcolonial systems of law.

legends stories about heroes who overcome obstacles set in familiar historical contexts.

levirate a rule whereby the widow of a deceased man must marry his brother.

lexicon, or dictionary, the complete description of all morphemes and their meanings in a language.

liminal period the in-between stage in a rite-of-passage ceremony when the individual has not yet been reincorporated into society.

lineages unilineal descent groups in which descent is demonstrated.

lineal relative a relative in the direct line of descent.

linguistic imperialism the imposition by a dominant group of its language on minority speakers of other languages.

linguistic relativity a point of view that emphasizes the uniqueness of each language and the need to examine it in its own terms.

linguistics the study of language and the relationship between language and culture.

magic the system based on the belief that the natural world can be compelled to act in the desired way through human intervention.

malanggan a term referring to New Ireland mortuary ritual, as well as the carvings displayed at such a ritual.

mana belief in an impersonal supernatural force or power that is found in all aspects of nature

markedness the process whereby a category (the marked category) is distinguished from a larger, more inclusive category (the unmarked category) by the presence of a single attribute.

masculinities studies exploration of the variation in what constitutes masculinity within as well as between societies.

matrilineal rule of descent a rule stating that a child belongs to his or her mother's group.

maximizing the concept in economic anthropology whereby individuals are seen as interpreting economic rules to their own advantage.

mayu-dama Kachin lineage categories; wife-giving lineages are mayu, and wife-taking lineages are dama.

mediator a third party brought in to resolve conflict between two parties.

mental illness in anthropological terms, posits normal, expected, and acceptable behavior in a culture as a baseline; deviance from this baseline is abnormal behavior or mental illness.

metaphor an analytical concept in which one idea stands for another because of some similarity they seem to share.

metonym the symbolic substitution of one of the constituent parts for the whole.

microfinance a development strategy that provides small business loans to poor individuals and groups of people who otherwise would not have access to credit.

model minority the mythologizing of the skills and abilities of a minority immigrant community.

modernization theory the perspective that underdeveloped states should attain modernization by emulating the industrial strategies of Western countries.

moieties a grouping based upon descent in which the entire society is divided into halves.

monogamy marriage with only one spouse at a time.

morpheme the smallest unit of a language conveying meaning.

multi-sited ethnography an ethnography that draws on information and informants in various locations, often across borders and over different time periods.

myths stories set in the remote past that explain the origin of natural things and cultural practices.

nadleehi transgendered individuals among the Navajo.

nat spirits of the Kachin supernatural world.

nation-state an autonomous state associated with national identity.

nationalism political movement to claim or reformulate shared ideas about identity among citizens within a state's borders.

Native American Graves Protection and Repatriation Act (NAGPRA) federal legislation in the United States requiring return to recognized native groups of human remains and some cultural artifacts.

nativistic movements religious cults that develop in periods of drastic cultural change and synthesize traditional cultural elements with newly introduced ones.

neocolonialism economic interdependency of one-time colonies on former colonial powers despite political independence.

neoliberalism the contemporary revival of classic economic liberalism that stresses the role of private enterprise in all institutions of the state and deregulation of markets and trade.

neolocal residence a rule of postmarital residence in which the newly married couple forms an independent household.

neo-Marxism the contemporary study of power relations in the globalized economy, drawing on Karl Marx's theories of class relations, commodification, production, and consumption.

neo-nationalism the emergence and assertion of newly formed nationalist movement particularly in new states formed from the former Soviet republics.

New Age Movements alternative religious movements.

new immigrants immigrants to the United States in the 1960s resulting from changes in immigration law and policy.

new reproductive technologies (NRTs) manipulation of egg and sperm to create fertilized eggs and viable fetuses through scientific technology; includes the use of surrogate mothers and/or genetic donors.

nibek Wogeo spirits represented by flutes.

nomadic pastoralists societies completely, or almost completely, dependent upon herds of domesticated animals.

nongovernmental organizations (NGOs) development organizations that are structurally independent of state institutions.

nuclear family a family consisting of husband, wife, and their unmarried children.

numaym cognatic descent group of the Kwakiutl.

office a recognized political position.

pantheon the population of gods and deities recognized by a society.

parallel cousins the children of two brothers or of two sisters.

parole see langue.

participant observation the anthropological method of collecting data by living with other people, learning their language, and understanding their culture.

patrilineal rule of descent a rule stating that a child belongs to his or her father's group.

patron-client relationship a hierarchical relationship in which the superior (the patron) acts as an intermediary and protector of the inferior (the client) vis-à-vis the national government.

phonemes the minimal sound units that make up a language.

physical anthropology investigates the physical evolution of the human body.

pidgin a lingua franca that developed when people speaking different languages but no common language needed to communicate with one another.

political economy the interpenetration of politics and economy.

politics the competition for political positions, economic resources, and power.

polyandry marriage in which one woman has several husbands at one time.

polygamy marriage with plural spouses, either husbands or wives.

polygyny marriage in which one man has several wives at one time.

Poro Society secret society associated with the use of masks, found in Liberia and Sierra Leone.

postcolonial studies often interdisciplinary focus on the effects of colonialism on former European colonies.

postmarital residence rule a rule that states where a couple should live after marriage.

postmodernism refers to a contemporary point of view that is opposed to making universalizing generalizations in anthropological thinking.

potlatch a large-scale ceremonial distribution of goods found among the indigenous peoples of the Northwest Coast of North America.

power the ability to command others to do certain things and get compliance from them.

practice individual choices and decision making.

priests full-time religious practitioners who carry out codified and elaborated rituals based on a body of knowledge learned over a lengthy period of time.

primogeniture a rule of succession whereby the eldest child (usually but not always male) inherits the position of power.

private symbols symbols related to an individual's personal life history.

production the process whereby a society uses the tools and energy sources at its disposal and its own people's labor to create the goods necessary for supplying itself.

proto-language ancestral form of a language arrived at by reconstruction

public symbols symbols used and understood by the members of a society.

queer studies theorizes and explores the construction of sexual identities in their cultural contexts.

race a system of classification of groups of people presumed to share biological characteristics.

racism discrimination against an individual or group based on presumed shared characteristics.

reciprocal exchange a type of exchange system in egalitarian societies in which women or material goods of equal value continue to be exchanged over generations.

reflexivity paying attention to one's own cognitive framework as one researches another culture.

religion the cultural means by which humans interact with the supernatural or extra-human domains.

revitalization movements (see nativistic movements).

rites of intensification communal rituals celebrated at various points in the yearly cycle.

rites of passage communal rituals held to mark changes in status as individuals progress through the life cycle.

ritual patterned or repetitive performance that symbolically communicates values and ideas to both participants and observers.

sagali a large-scale ceremonial distribution among the Trobriand Islanders.

salvage anthropology in Boas's time the term applied to the gathering of ethnographic information about disappearing and threatened cultural practices.

scapulimancy predicting the future by interpreting the cracks in animal bones.

science a system of knowledge based on empirically determined connections between aspects of the natural world that will regularly result in predictable outcomes.

segmentary lineage system a descent system, typically patrilineal, in which the largest segments are successively divided into smaller segments, like branches of a tree.

serial monogamy the practice of marrying a series of spouses, one after the other.

sex the physical differentiation between male and female through biological and anatomical composition of genitals and related secondary sexual characteristics.

sexuality refers to erotic desires and the practices associated with them.

shaman part-time ritual specialist who, depending on the cultural context, diagnose and cure illness, cause illness, and divine the future.

shifting cultivation a type of horticulture in which new gardens are made every few years, when the soil is exhausted.

sister exchange a marriage pattern in which two men marry each other's sisters.

social organization behavioral choices that individuals make in connection with the social structure.

social role the behavior associated with a particular social status in a society.

social status the position an individual occupies in a society.

social structure the pattern of social relationships that characterizes a society.

society a social grouping characterizing humans and other social animals, differentiated by age and sex.

sociolinguistics the study of that aspect of language that deals with status and class differences.

sojourners individuals who migrate for economic opportunity with the intention of eventually returning to their homelands.

sorcery the learned practice of evil magic.

sororal polygyny the marriage of a man to several sisters.

sororate the custom whereby a widower marries his deceased wife's sister.

sovereignty the ability of a group to determine their own laws and practices that will be recognized by other groups.

speech community a group of people that interacts and speaks frequently with one another.

spirits the general term for those that populate the supernatural realm.

state a type of political organization organized on a territorial basis encompassing multiple cultural groups.

stem family a two-generation extended family consisting of parents and only one married son and his family.

step immigration process by which a younger generation of immigrants reunites with their parents in their new countries of residence.

stipulated descent a social unit, such as a clan, in which all members consider themselves to be related though they cannot actually trace the genealogical relationship.

structuralism theoretical approach emphasizing relationship between cultural elements.

structure a description of parts or elements of a culture in relationship to one another.

style a characterization of the component elements of art and the way those elements are put together.

subcultural variation cultural differences between communities within a single society.

swidden see shifting cultivation.

symbolic anthropology theoretical approach emphasizing the interpretation of cultural symbols.

syncretism the integration of cultural traits and newly adopted practices.

syntax that part of grammar that deals with the rules of combination of morphemes.

Te the ceremonial distribution of pigs and pork among the Mae Enga of Papua New Guinea.

technology that part of culture by means of which people directly exploit their environment.

terms of address the kinship terms used when talking to a relative.

terms of reference the kinship terms used to refer to a relative when speaking to someone else.

total social phenomena large-scale rituals that integrate all aspects of society—economic, political, kinship, religion, art, etc.

totemic animal (see clan totem).

trance an altered state of consciousness associated with the performance of ritual.

transmigration populations who migrate from their homelands to other parts of the world.

transnationalism migration with strong ties remaining to country of origin.

tribe a unit used by colonial powers to refer to groups with a common language and culture.

tribute presentation of objects by people of lower status to those of higher status.

tschambura among the Abelam, partners who exchange long yams with one another.

ultimogeniture a rule of inheritance of property or office by the last-born child.

unilineal descent group a kin group, such as a clan, in which membership is based on either matrilineal or patrilineal descent.

universal human rights a doctrine that emphasizes inalienable rights of the individual over the cultural norms of the community.

universal symbols certain symbols found in all cultures that convey meaning such as color associations with emotions and hair length as an indication of conformity or resistance. Specific symbolic associations will vary, however, from culture to culture, as in variations in the colors used to indicate mourning.

urban legends stories about contemporary events purporting to be factual that circulate widely and with variation.

urigubu a Trobriand harvest gift given yearly by a man to his sister's husband.

uxorilocal residence a rule of postmarital residence whereby the newly married couple resides with the relatives of the bride.

virilocal residence a rule of postmarital residence whereby the newly married couple resides with the relatives of the groom.

vision quest the search for a protective supernatural spirit through starvation and deprivation.

warabwa large-scale ceremonial distribution in Wogeo.

warlord a militarized big man; he and his followers are structurally similar to a faction.

witchcraft a form of magic practiced by individuals born with this ability.

world systems theory the historic emergence of the economic interrelationship of most of the world in a single economic system.

Photo Credits

xvii: ©Abraham Rosman **xviii:** © Abraham Rosman **xix:** © Maxine Weisgrau **3:** ©Abraham Rosman **4:** ©Abraham Rosman **34:** Library of Congress Prints & Photographs Division, Edward S. Curtis Collection **36:** Courtesy of the American Museum of Natural History **41:** © Bettmann/CORBIS **62:** © Tom McHugh/Photo Researchers **59:** © AP Images/Matt Rourke **67:** © Abraham Rosman **72**: © Jupiter Images **85:** © Maxine Weisgrau **88:** © Abraham Rosman **94:** Courtesy of Newberry Library **104:** ©Abraham Rosman **106:** © Nancy E. Levine **118:** © Julio Etchart **136:** © AP Photo/Sam Morris **144:** © Abraham Rosman **145:** © Maxine Weisgrau **148** © Serena Nanda/imagesofanthropology.com **155:** © Hemis.fr/SuperStock **178:** © Abraham Rosman **181:** © Abraham Rosman **182:** University of Washington Libraries, Special Collections, NA2562 **186:** Malinowski, Bronislaw, Pps, Manuscripts & Archives, Yale University Library **191:** © Paula Rubel **203:** © Abraham Rosman **207:** © Abraham Rosman **223:** AP Photo/Maxim Marmur **231:** © Maxine Weisgrau **244:** Courtesy American Museum of Natural History **246:** © Paula Rubel **252:** © 2008 Ulrike Welsch **261:** *The Island of Menstruating Men: Religion in Wogeo, New Guinea,* by Ian Hogbin. Prospect Hts., Ill: Waveland Press, 1970 (reissued 1996). Reprinted by permission of the publisher and Terry Beavan **266:** public domain image **267:** © Thomas Bucci **273:** © Roger-Viollet/The Image Works **283:** Franz Boas, Primitive Art. New York: Dover Publications, 1955. Reprinted by permission of the publisher **285:** © Abraham Rosman **287:** Wilson Duff, *Images: Stone: B.C.*, 1975, Hancock House Publishers. Reprinted by permission of the publisher **290:** Franz Boas, *The Social Organization and Secret Societies of the Kwakiutl Indians*, 1897 **293:** © Abraham Rosman **301:** © Abraham Rosman **310:** ©AP Photo/Richard Vogel **314:** Library of Congress, Keystone View Company, 1919 **322:** © Maxine Weisgrau **324:** © Paige West **340:** © Robert Mullen – Moon Mullen Photography **346:** © Reuters/CORBIS **352:** © AP Photo/Dexter Cruez **357:** © Jupiter Images **360:** © Jay Mandal/On Assignment

Index

Abelam (New Guinea); Big Men, 202–3; eating symbolism, 86; exchange system, 177–78; horticulture, 167; marriage payments, 104; moieties, 117; organization of work, reciprocal exchange, 177–78; *tshambura*, 177, 202

Abkhazians, 344

abortion, 3

achieved status, 201

adolescence: initiation (*see* initiation rites)

adoption, 134

adultery, 14

aesthetic impulse, 281, 282

affines and affinal links, 121

Afghanistan, 347–50; ethnic groups, 348; and Pakistan, 348; Taliban movement, 255–56, 347; warlords, 348–49

African-American: African language retention, 55, 356; Black Power, 356; cultural creativity, 356–57; folktales, 270; heritage, 356–59; history, 357–58; identity, 333, 334; Kwanzaa, 357, 358; language, 54–56; language and identity, 56; "one-drop rule," 358–59; swept yards, 356

African-American English, 54–56, 356

Agba masks (Igbo), 288

age, categories based on, 153–58

age grades, 154–57

agency, 14, 15

agriculture, 166–70; grain agriculture, 168–69; horticulture, 167; 168–69; irrigation, 168; swidden, 167; in today's world, 169–70

"airport art," 295

Albanians (Kosovo), 130

alliance, 121

allomorphs, 49

allophones, 48

Aluund (Zaire), 93; symbols of the chief, 93; symbols of the state, 203

Amazons, 262, 263

America: colonial period 312; diversity in, 359–60; ethnic groups in, 359–60; European settlement of, 353; immigration, 352–55; land policy, 312

American culture: childbirth, 149; child-rearing, 70; conceptions of masculinity, 152–53; dance, 303–4; ethnic differences, 359–60; ethnic identity, 359–60; ethnic parades, 360; films as legends and myths, 271–72; hyphenated Americans, 359; internal migration, 326; kinship, 126, 127, 128, 138; kinship terminology, 126; legends and folktales in, 269–78; Mafia in 225–26; marriage in, 38–42, 101; masculinity